ALLE ZEIT WACH 1842

T.S. Chua, T.L. Kunii (Eds.)

CG International '90

Computer Graphics Around the World

With 346 Figures, Including 134 in Color

Springer-Verlag
Tokyo Berlin Heidelberg New York
London Paris Hong Kong

Tat-Seng Chua
Senior Lecturer
Institute of Systems Science
National University of Singapore
Kent Ridge
Singapore 0511

Tosiyasu L. Kunii
Professor and Chairman
Department of Information Science
Faculty of Science
University of Tokyo
Tokyo 113, Japan

About the Cover:
The cover picture shows the computer simulation of Japanese martial art *Shorinji Kempo*. The picture is produced by T.L. Kunii and L. Sun of Kunii Laboratory of Computer Science, University of Tokyo.

ISBN-13:978-4-431-68125-0 e-ISBN-13:978-4-431-68123-6
DOI: 10.1007/978-4-431-68123-6

Softcover reprint of the hardcover 1st edition 1990

Preface

This volume presents the proceedings of the 8th International Conference of the Computer Graphics Society, CG International '90, held at the Institute of Systems Science, Singapore, on June 25-29, 1990. This series of annual conferences originated in Japan in 1983 under the name of 'InterGraphics' an then 'Computer Graphics Tokyo'. Since its inception in 1983, the conference series has continued to attract high-quality research papers in all aspects of computer graphics and its applications from around the world. In order to reflect its international status and to encourage even greater international participation and cooperation, the conference was renamed CG International in 1987. The last three CG International conferences were held in Karuizawa, Japan, in 1987, Geneva, Switzerland, in 1988, and Leeds, UK, in 1989. Future conferences are planned for USA in 1991, Japan in 1992, and Canada in 1993.

In recent years, we have witnessed an increasing use of sophisticated graphics in designing and manufacturing complex architectural and engineering systems; in modeling, simulating and visualizing complicated physical processes; in generating highly realistic images and animation and, in most man-machine interfaces. These trends are made possible by the improvement in performance and the lowering in cost of hardware since the mid 1970s, and the continuing advances in many areas of computer graphics. The major advances in computer graphics include: greater sophistication and realism of image generation techniques; improved man-machine interaction techniques; superior geometric modeling techniques for the representation and modeling of complex physical and mathematical objects; sophisticated software systems for animation and modeling incorporating latest AI and software engineering techniques; greater integration of CAD and CAM in CIM, and techniques to represent and visualize complicated physical processes. These advances are reflected in this present volume either as papers dealing with one particular aspect of research, or as multifaceted studies involving several different areas.

This volume contains 29 reviewed papers, 3 invited papers and one keynote paper. The reviewed papers are selected from the large number of papers submitted in response to the Call for Papers for CG International '90 by many researchers from different parts of the world. The papers were selected following rigorous review processes by expert reviewers in their respective fields. Countries represented in this volume include Austria, Belgium, Canada, China, Czechoslovakia, Hong-Kong, Italy, Japan, Netherlands, New Zealand, Singapore, Switzerland, UK and USA. Thus, there is wide international representation.

The papers are grouped into nine chapters. Chapter one contains the keynote paper and the 3 invited papers. These papers cover the recent developments in three of the most exciting fields in computer graphics: computer animation, user interface management systems, and design automation. These papers present leading-edge researches and discuss issues pertinent to the continuing advancement of these fields.

Chapter 2 deals with the modeling of physical and mathematical objects. Recent developments in this field have made it possible to model a wide variety of irregularly shaped objects, ranging from flames, cloths, fractals and even atmospheric conditions. These techniques have produced extremely realistic and artistic images.

Chapter 3 presents the advances in rendering techniques used in a variety of applications including scientific visualization, modeling of physical objects and generation of hard-copy outputs.

The advances in hardware must be matched by similar improvement in the efficiency of algorithms in computing basic graphics primitives such as the generation of arcs, conics etc. These advances are presented in chapter 4 which also presents algorithms for extracting vectors from raster images, an increasingly important process in engineering, and computing paths for NC machines in CAD/CAM applications.

The increasingly important topics of object-oriented graphics and the incorporation of AI techniques in graphics system are discussed in chapter 5. Two systems are described that make use of these technologies to provide better environments for programmers to model and manipulate complex objects and animations.

Chapter 6 deals extensively with the subject of visual language and its applications. A comprehensive survey of the various visual languages are presented. The important topic of visualization of both mathematical and abstract concepts is also included.

The subject of polygon triangulations in computational geometry are dealt with in detail in chapter 7.

Chapter 8 tackles the complex subjects of ray-tracing and radiosity, the best rendering techniques known today. The techniques are introduced through their applications in rendering soft objects and in non-diffuse environments.

Finally, chapter 9 discusses the recent developments in the theoretical, modeling and rendering aspects of curves and surfaces in a variety of applications.

We are grateful to all those who have helped to review the papers and organize and sponsor the conference. Special thanks are due to Ms Vicky Toh, the CGI '90 Secretary, for her help in putting the conference together.

T.S. Chua
T.L. Kunii

Table of Contents

Chapter 1
Invited and Keynote Papers

Dynamic Analysis-Based Human Animation

Tosiyasu L. Kunii and Lining Sun

ABSTRACT

Dynamic analysis-based *human animation* is proposed and implemented. In this approach, the actual human movements are first analyzed to find out the mechanism behind them, then the knowledge obtained by the analysis is used to design new motions desired by animators. Here, the knowledge includes the dynamic parameters such as the forces and torques exerted on the joints, which is obtained through analyzing the actual movements of a human body. In this approach, animation proceeds in three steps: *dynamics*, *constraints* and *inverse dynamics*. In the first step of *dynamics*, each body segment is distinguished and the motion of each segment is derived in the form of dynamics equations. The idea is to reduce the number of degrees of freedom and thus the amount of computations required, and to avoid the complexity of dealing with continuum mechanics. In the second step of *constraints*, the constraints involving both the articulation of the body and the range of the movement of each joint are checked and maintained. A segment which violates its constraints is moved by translations and rotations so that it becomes connected to its super segment or is bent into a natural posture. In the third step of *inverse dynamics*, the forces that produce the motion adjusted according to the two types of constraints are calculated by using dynamics equations, and the results that involve the motions and the forces are then presented to the user. As the result of animation, a walk on the moon, is also presented.

Keywords: computer animation, human body model, dynamics, inverse dynamics.

1. INTRODUCTION

More and more realistic and aesthetic computer animation has been achieved by taking into consideration the physical properties of the objects and the physical principles that govern moving objects (Williams 1979, Isaacs 1978, Forsey 1988, Selbie 1989). Such a technique has another great advantage, that is, it can generate complex behavior with minimal user control. This technique was not invented by computer animators. It came from physics and has been known as *dynamics*.

A simpler means of describing the motions of objects is *kinematics* which differs from dynamics in that kinematics describes the motions only in terms of positions, velocities and accelerations, neglecting the forces and torques responsible (Nigel 1989, Calvert 1989). The main problem with a kinematic technique is that the specification of motions must be controlled explicitly by an animator. However, since the motions of an object are determined by their own nature and their interaction with the environment, the measurements required to generate realistic motions may not be easily available by kinematics animation.

The approach using dynamics avoids the limitations of kinematic motion specification. The dynamical simulation of the movements of simple solids in a frictionless space is straightforward. However, the dynamics of an articulated body with more than 200 degrees of freedom is a hard task. The two main problems with this technique are as follows:

1. The difficulty in estimating the dynamic parameters, such as the moments of inertia, the centers of mass, joint friction and muscle / ligament elasticity. Even more difficult is to obtain the realistic control data for specifying the mechanism of elasticity of muscles / ligaments. Without such control data, dynamic simulation will produce unrealistic motions similar to the case of kinematic animation.

2. The need to solve rather expensive dynamics equations. For an articulated body with 200 degrees of freedom, 600 simultaneous differential equations need to be solved.

Due to the above problems, to the best knowledge of the authors, the complete three dimensional dynamical simulation of a human body is not available in any papers published until now, although there are a number of papers which describe only the methods. The dynamic methods proposed so far are not too well suited for a practical motion specification work, since such a work is often a process by trial and error, and should preferably take place in an interactive and user friendly manner.

In fact, the two problems in dynamics mentioned above are closely related to each other. The lack of the knowledge of the mechanism of human motions is actually the main reason for the complicated computation. In this paper, we propose a new computer animation technique, entitled dynamic analysis-based human animation, which attempts to implement complete dynamical simulation by using the knowledge of the mechanism of human motions that is obtained by analyzing the motions of actual human beings. Our method consists of two stages:

1. Analyzing the basic movements of a human being and finding the dynamic parameters. The dynamic parameters involve the forces and torques exerted on each joint of the body. They are put into a database as the knowledge regarding the basic movements.
2. The user can access the database, find the relevant knowledge and use it after some modifications to interactively design the movements desired. In producing the movements using the dynamic parameters specified by the user, we propose a new technique with computational complexity $O(n)$, so that the user can have feed back in real time and repeat the above processes until the user can obtain satisfactory results.

There are two important differences between our method and existing ones. Firstly, knowledge in our approach has a different meaning from that in existing animation systems. There has been some researches based on AI and expert systems to capture the knowledge and skills of the animator (Zeltzer 1983). Badler used a constraint based approach to constrain his dynamic simulations (Badler 1985), and Drewery and Tsotsos studied a frame-based approach to goal directed animation (Drewery 1986). The knowledge in their researches refers to the basic data on the human being animated (dimensions, moments of inertia, etc) and the constraints that define the range of the movements of individual joints. This knowledge is captured from the intuitive imagination of the animator. The knowledge in our approach refers to the real dynamic parameters which are obtained by analyzing the actual motions of human beings. Hence, the motions produced from the knowledge are more scientific and reliable. This improvement enables the production of more realistic movements.

Secondly, we perform dynamical simulation with the computation complexity $O(n)$, while conventional methods (of perfect dynamics) have complexity $O(n^4)$, where n is the number of the body segments. The forces exerted on each joint of the body serve as the inputs and are supplied by the user. The outputs are the motion caused by these forces as well as forces due to the physical constraints of the body. (The latters are automatically accounted for by the system.) The dynamical simulation proceeds in three steps: *dynamics*, *constraints* and *inverse dynamics*. In the first step of *dynamics*, each body segment is distinguished and the motion of each segment is derived in the form of dynamics equations. The idea is to reduce the number of degrees of freedom and thus the amount of computations required, and to avoid the complexity of dealing with continuum mechanics. In the second step of *constraints*, the constraints involving both the articulation of the body and the range of the movement of each joint are checked and maintained. A segment which violates its constraints is moved by translations and rotations so that it becomes connected to its super segment or is bent into a natural posture. In the third step of *inverse dynamics*, the forces that produce the motion adjusted according to the two types of constraints are calculated by using dynamics equations, and the results that involve the motions and the forces are then presented to the user. The method and the algorithm used in this step constitute the technique which is termed *inverse dynamics*.

Thus, the complete processes for producing human motion involve the following steps (Fig.1):

1. Constructing a human body model;
2. Inputing the actual movements of the human being;
3. Analyzing the movements that have been input (inverse dynamics);
4. Simulating the other movements;
   4.1. Design of the motions;
   4.2. Dynamics;
   4.3. Constraints;
   4.4. Inverse dynamics;

In step 4, a method proposed by Wilhelms is excellent for dynamical simulation (Wilhelms 1985). However, for an actual animation system, the Wilhelms method has not been accepted mostly because of its conceptual complexity and computational expensiveness. Wilhelms uses the Gibbs formula and attempts to solve the dynamics equations exactly. Practical animation work usually requires much trial and error, and hence, real time responses and user friendly interactions are required. Our method has overcome the computational problems that existed in the Wilhelms method, and hence, can provide the user with the real time feedback of the result of constraints in terms of constrained motions and also the result of inverse dynamics in terms of forces. Armstrong proposes also a method which is fast with the computational complexity of only $O(n)$, where n is the numbers of joints. The Armstrong method is based on the hypothetical existence of the relationship between the amount of the acceleration of the joint and the amount of its angular acceleration (Armstrong 1985). His assumption holds

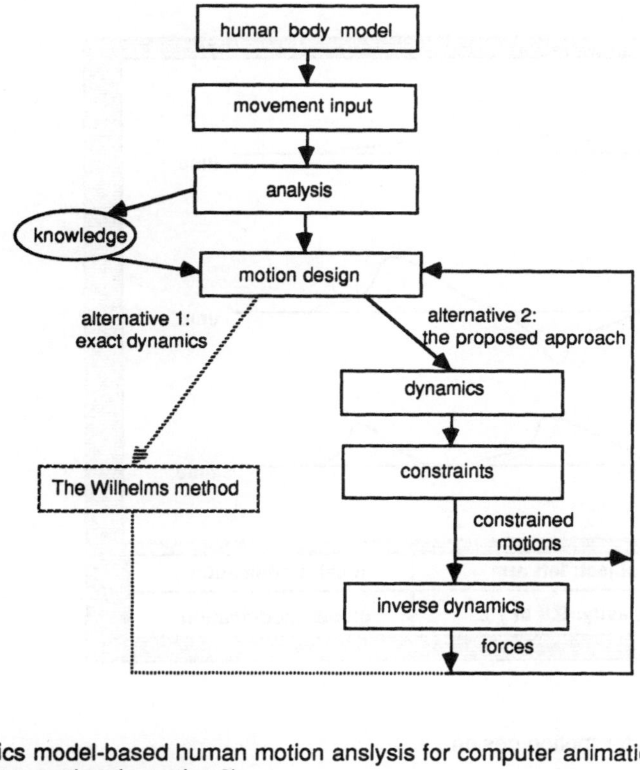

Fig.1. Dynamics model-based human motion anslysis for computer animation (as shown as the alternative 2).

only when a rotation about the principal axes can be neglected. However, this hypothesis is not applicable to our problem, since the rotations about the principal axes cannot be neglected in our case.

The steps 1, 2, 3 were described in our previous paper (Sun 1989). This paper focuses on step 4. The design of dynamics parameters is given in Section 2. The dynamics techniques proposed are described in Section 3 on dynamics, Section 4 on constraints and Section 5 on inverse dynamics. The implementation is presented in Section 6. Section 7 concludes this paper.

2. DESIGN OF DYNAMICS PARAMETERS

Motions are designed at two levels: changing the speed of the motions and the forces causing the motions, and composing a complicated motion from the basic motions.

At first, the user chooses the basic motions from the database. Then the dynamics parameters of the motions chosen are displayed using a two dimensional control graph, where the x-axis represents time and y-axis represents the forces exerted on each joint of the body (Fig.2). Since the two forces exerted on the same joint must be equal in magnitude and opposite in direction, this constraint must be maintained by the system. The user is provided with various facilities to modify these physical parameters using a mouse. To facilitate the modification, two control modes are supported:

1. The global modification: The same changes of the forces are caused to all the human body parts on which the forces are exerted. This modification can involve scaling up or down of the x- or y-axis.

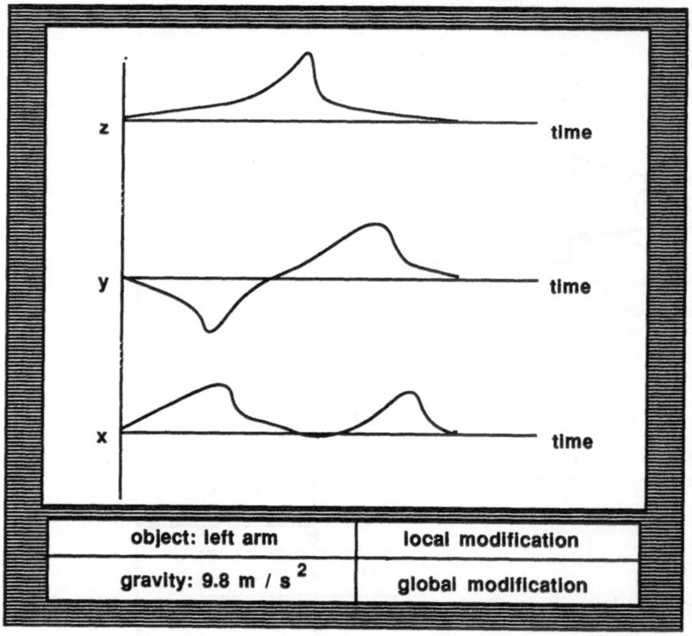

Fig.2. Control graphs for motion design.

2. The local modification: It changes only the force exerted on a specific part of the body.

Another modification other than the motion is the modification of the acceleration due to gravity, which is necessary when simulating the motion outside the earth.

The joint limits restrict the range of the joint movements, because the joints of a real human body cannot rotate arbitrarily in all directions. The limits are the constants of a given human body, which have been put into the database.

A complicated motion is represented by several control graphs, each of which is designed by the user by the same method. For example, the control graphs of somebody standing up from a chair and walking constitute a continuous composite motion. In case of *Shorinji Kempo*, a Japanese martial art, any kind of its motion is based on 12 basic control graphs (Sun 1989).

3. DYNAMICS

Dynamics calculates the path of each body segment independently of the rests, based on the forces specified by the user and the dynamics equations governing the segment movements. In this calculation, each body segment is firstly distinguished (Fig.3), and the articulation of the human body and the constraints regarding the range of the movements of joints are neglected for the present. The idea is to reduce the amount of computation. The results of calculation of the motions of every segment are passed to the next step, where the physical constraints of the body are checked and enforced.

For each segment, we use the Newton-Euler formulation to calculate the motion (Goldstein 1959). Newton's equation is used to derive the linear acceleration of the center of gravity as follows:

$$F_x = m\ddot{\rho}_x$$

$$F_y = m(\ddot{\rho}_y - g)$$

$$F_z = m\ddot{\rho}_z$$

where

F is the force exerted on the segment,

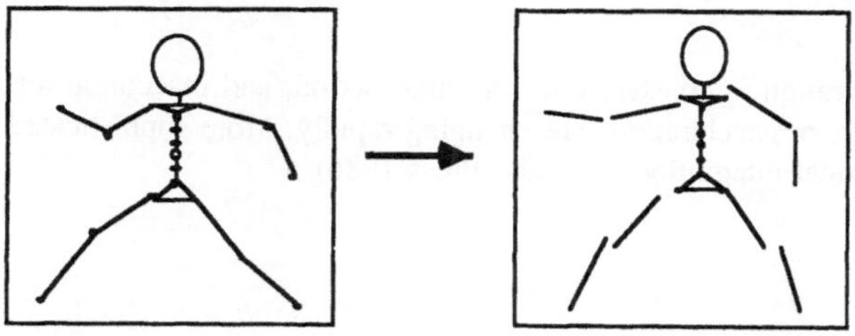

Fig.3. Body segments are identified and each segment is calculated independently.

m is the mass of the segment,

ρ is the position of the center of gravity of the segment, and

g is the acceleration of gravity.

Euler's equations is used to derive the angular acceleration about its center of gravity as follows:

$$N_x = I_x \dot{\omega}_x + (I_y - I_z)\omega_y \omega_z$$

$$N_y = I_y \dot{\omega}_y + (I_z - I_x)\omega_z \omega_x$$

$$N_z = I_z \dot{\omega}_z + (I_x - I_y)\omega_x \omega_z$$

where

x, y, z are the directions of the principal axes,

N is the external torque being applied to the segment,

I is the principal moments of inertia, and

ω is the angular velocity of the segment.

Note that the principal moments of inertia are the diagonal elements when the inertia tensor is diagonalized, which are derived from the eigenvalues of the inertia tensor of the segment. And the corresponding principal axes are obtained from its eigenvector equations. Thus, before solving Euler's equation, the original coordinates must be transformed to the principal axes. The Euler angles can be used to perform the transformations.

Once new linear and angular accelerations are obtained, they must be integrated to find new velocities and integrated again to find new positions. The Euler method is simplest to do this.

$$\mathbf{v}_{t+\delta t} = \mathbf{v}_t + \mathbf{a}_t \delta t$$

$$\mathbf{p}_{t+\delta t} = \mathbf{p}_t + \mathbf{v}_t \delta t + \frac{1}{2}\mathbf{a}_t \delta t^2$$

where

$\mathbf{a}$ is the acceleration,

$\mathbf{v}$ is the velocity,

$\mathbf{p}$ is the position,

t is the time, and

δt is the time period.

This method assumes acceleration is constant over the time period, and inaccurate results are obtained when the time period is large or accelerations are changing rapidly. More sophisticated method may be found in a number of numerical integration methods (Press 1986).

4. CONSTRAINTS

In this step, the two constraints, the articulation of a human body and the range of the movements of body joints, are checked and maintained (Fig.4).

The process starts at the root segment, the position and the orientation of each segment of its subclass are checked and adjusted sequentially. Here, two types of checks are performed:

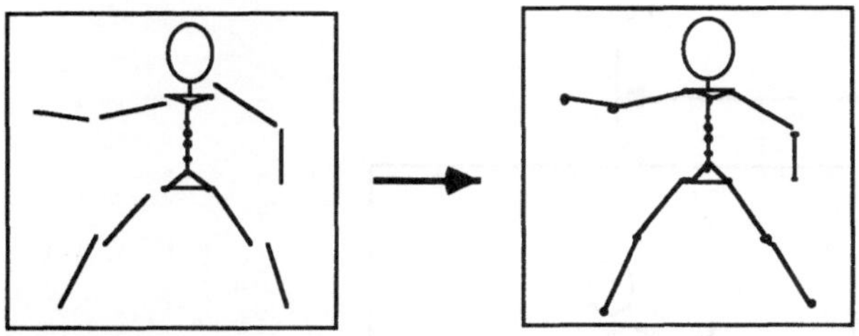

Fig.4. The constraints are checked and enforced. The constraints involve both the articulation of body segments and the range of movements of the body joints.

1. Is a subclass segment connected to its superclass segment? If not so, then the subclass segment is translated in order that it remains to be connected to its superclass segment.
2. Does the movement of each segment joint exceed the range specified? If so, then the movement of the joint is adjusted to its maximal range by rotations.

The algorithm stops at the leaf segment. The new motions adjusted cannot be available from the forces specified by the user. The next step is to calculate the forces that produces the new motions which have been modified due to the constraints.

5. INVERSE DYNAMICS

Inverse dynamics uses Lagrange's equations which describe the relationship between forces and movements to calculate the forces exerted on each joint of the body (Fig.5). In the previous paper (Sun 1989), we have proposed a linear recursive algorithm to perform inverse dynamics, with the computational complexity $O(n)$ where n is the number of the body segments.

Note the fact that inverse dynamics can provide a reasonable and integrated set of forces for dynamics to produce the motions which are adjusted due to the constrains. Without inverse dynamics, it is impossible to expect the user to be able to find out an integrated force specification. In our method, the orientation of each body segment is changed when the related joint limit is exceeded, and the position of each body segment is adjusted to the physical constraints of the body.

Figure 6 shows the real movements of a person while walking on the earth. Figure 7 shows the dynamical simulation of the same person walking on the moon, by using the forces and the mechanisms obtained from Fig.6. The gravity of the moon is about 1 / 6 of that of the earth. Actually, walking on the moon becomes jumping as seen in the US astronauts' pictures on the moon. Our simulation results shown in Fig.6 and Fig.7 successfully demonstrate this. The first step of the walk on the earth is turned into a jump on the moon.

6. IMPLEMENTATION

The analysis and animation system has been implemented on a *Silicon Graphics IRIS 70GT/4D*

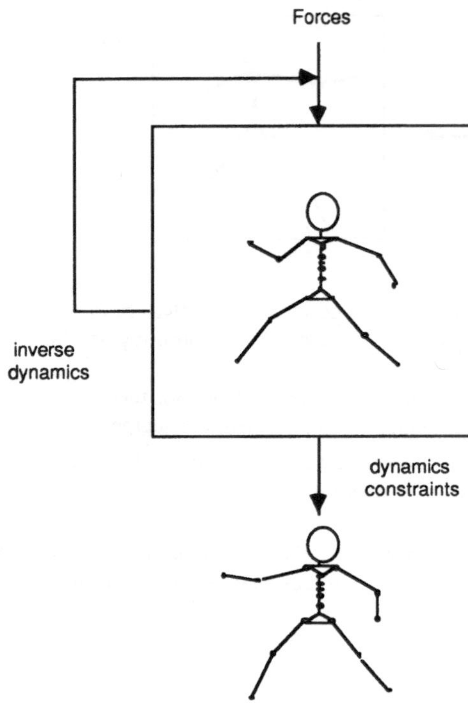

Fig.5. Inverse dynamics calculates the forces which are adjusted due to the physical constraints of the body.

graphics workstation, and is being tested with a Japanese martial art *Shorinji Kempo*. The entire system consists of approximately 10000 lines of C code. The system design and implementation is done to make it portable. The core which is machine dependent is packed into one file and consists of about 500 lines of the C code.

Figures 8, 9 and 10 show some results of the steps 1, 2 and 3 respectively. Figure 8 shows a human body model with smooth shading. Figure 9 shows an interactive specification environment, where a multi-window facility is supported. The user can view the modeled human bodies from various viewpoints on the display screen and translate or rotate the body segments using a mouse interactively. Thus, the user can establish as close a correspondence as possible between the picture and the modeled human body. Figure 10 shows the analytical results obtained in 24 frames where the man in blue is throwing the other man in red. The three mutually perpendicular axes in green indicate the center of gravity, and the arrows in red indicate the forces exerted on the red person by the blue person.

7. CONCLUSIONS

In this paper, we proposed and implemented dynamic analysis-based human motion animation using

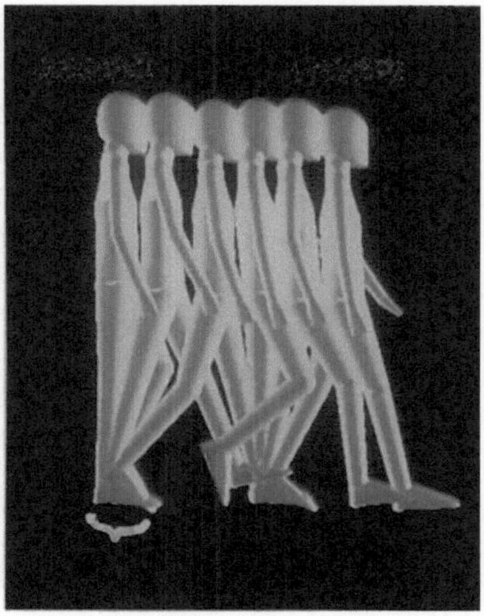

Fig.6. A human being walking on the earth. The portion enclosed by ⌣ indicates the first step.

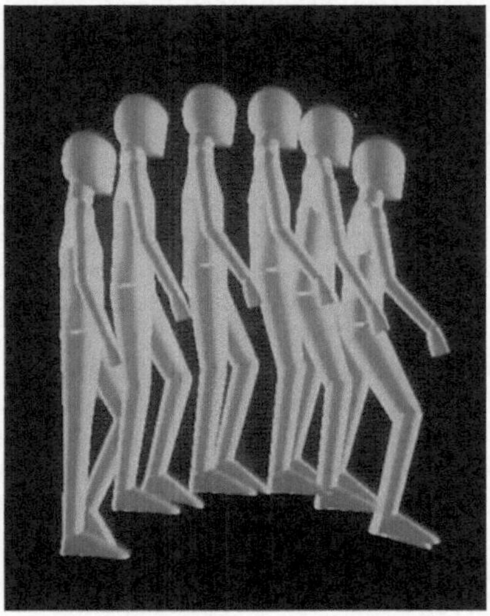

Fig.7. A simulation of the first step of a human being walking on the moon, which actually turns into a jump.

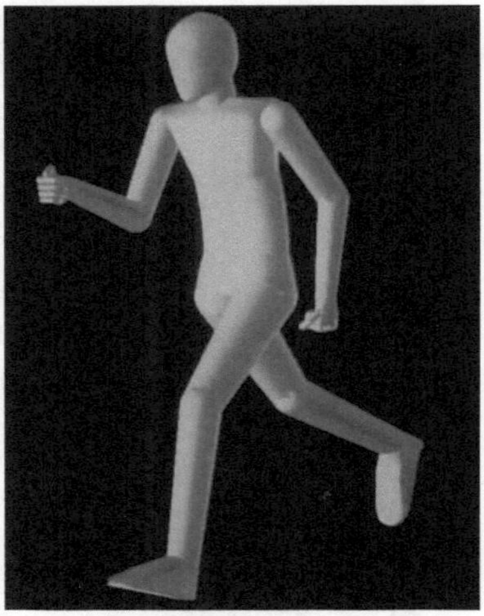

Fig.8. A modeled human body with smooth shading.

an articulated human body model. Our method consisted of two stages: analyzing the basic movements of an actual human being and using the analytical results to produce the new motions dynamically. The processes of dynamical simulation proceeded in three steps: dynamics, constraints and inverse dynamics. The dynamics step distinguished the articulated body into independent 50 rigid segments and the motion of each segment is calculated independently of the motions of other segments by using the Newton-Euler equations. In the constraints step, we checked and maintained the articulation of the body and the range of the movements of body joints. In the inverse dynamics step, we calculated the forces that produced the new motions which had been modified due to the constraints. The total computational complexity was $O(n)$, where n was the number of the body segments. The user interacted with the system by specifying the control forces and getting the motions produced by the dynamics and the constraints, the forces being modified due to the constraints. Our method solved the computational problem that existed in dynamics and enabled dynamics to produce real time feedback so that dynamics were now made well suited for practical computer animation work.

As the future work, we plan to extend the implementation of this animation system by integrating it with a database to store dynamics parameters. We intent to adopt object-oriented paradigm, since this has recently proven to be successful in a number of areas. As a user interface, the object oriented philosophy naturally leads to a direct manipulation paradigm where the screen displayed images correspond to objects which can be addressed and manipulated directly in the object space.

7. ACKNOWLEDGEMENTS

We wish to thank Mr. H. Matsuda and Mr. M. Shirahama of Nippon Shorinji Kempo for their sincere support to provide us with the real data and to serve as the initial users. We also wish to thank Prof. Yasuto Shirai, Ms. Deepa Krishnan and Dr. N. Inamoto and other members of Kunii Laboratory for their help during the course of this work.

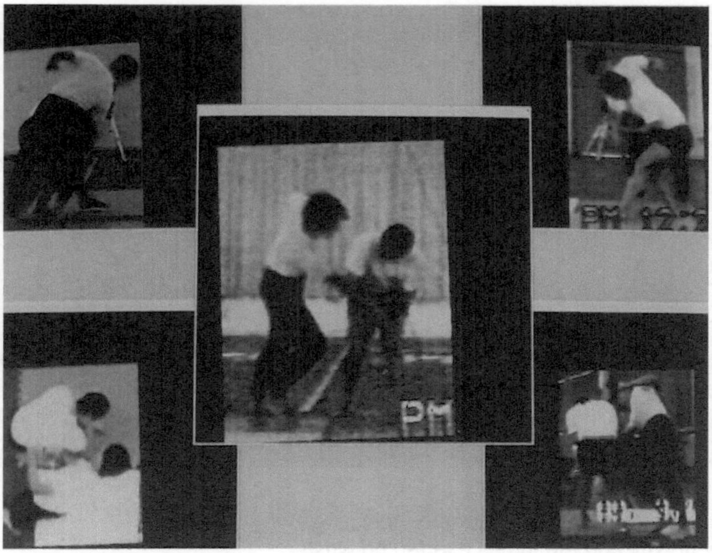

(a)

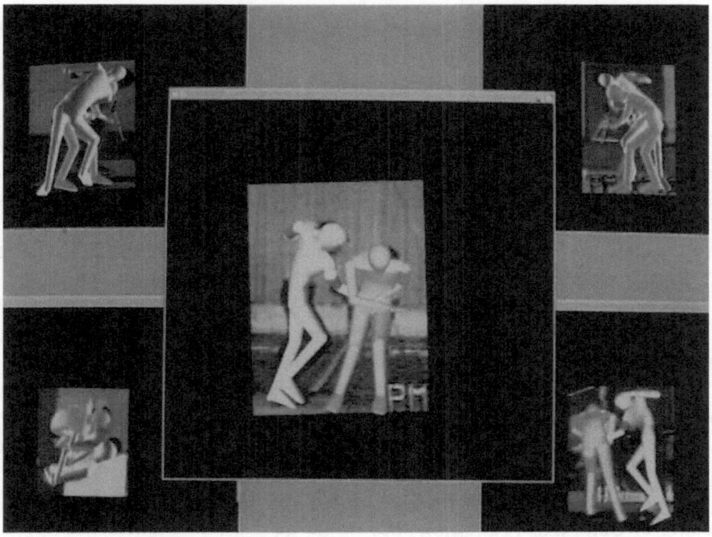

(b)

Fig.9. Multi-windows provide multiple perspective views for interactive specification of the body position. (a) is before human body modeling and (b) is after the modeling.

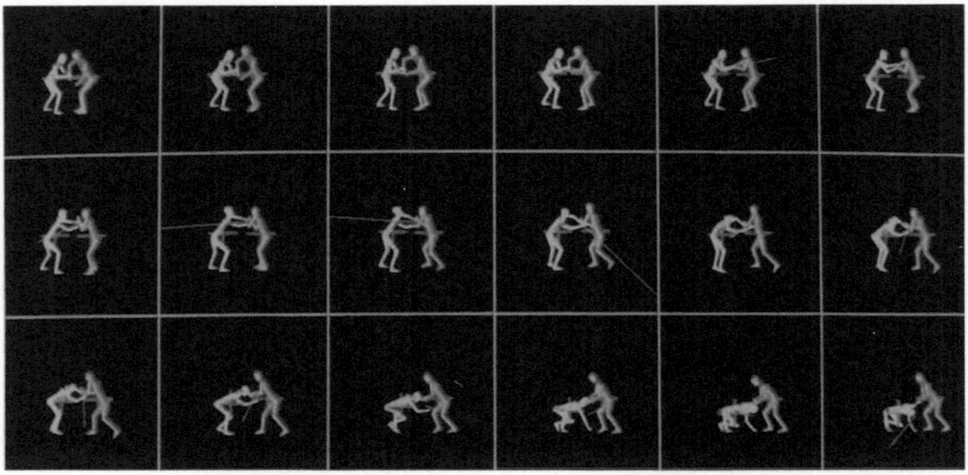

Fig.10. The analytical results of Shorinji Kempo indicating the center of gravity and the forces exerted on wrists.

REFERENCES

Armstrong WW and Green MW (1985) The Dynamics of Articulated Rigid Bodies for Purposes of Animation. *The Visual Computer* 1:231-240

Badler NI et al. (1985) Positioning and Animating Figures in a Task Oriented Environment. *The Visual Computer* 1:212-220

Calvert TW, Welman C, Gaudet S and Lee C (1989) Composition of Multiple Figure Sequences for Dance and Animation. *Proceedings CG International '89* pp 245-254

Drewery K and Tsotsos J (1986) Goal Directed Animation Using English Motion Commands. *Proc. Graphics Interface '86* pp 131-135

Forsey DR (1988) Techniques for Interactive Manipulation of Articulated Bodies Using Dynamic Analysis. *Graphics Interface '88* pp 8-15

Goldstein H (1959) Classical Mechanics. *Addsion-Wesley*

Isaacs PM, Cohen MF (1987) Controlling Dynamic Simulation with Kinematic Constraints, Behavior Function and Inverse Dynamics. *ACM Computer Graphics* 21(4):215-224

Nigel WJ and Philip JW (1989) Some Methods to Choreograph and Implement Motion in Computer Animation. *Proceeding of Computer Animation '89* pp 125-140

Press WH, Flannery BP, Teukolsky SA and Vetterling WT (1986) Numerical Recipes. *Cambridge Univ Press, Cambridge, England*

Selbie S (1989) An Introduction to the Use of Dynamic Simulation for the Animation of Human Movement. *Proceeding of Computer Animation '89* pp 34-44

Sun LN, Shirai L and Kunii TL (1989) An Architecture Design of a Sports Instruction System. *First International Conference and Exhibition on Visual Computing for Defense and Government* (VISUDA'89), Paris, France

Wilhelms J and Barsky B (1985) Using Dynamic Analysis to Animate Articulated Bodies Such as Humans and Robots. *Proceedings, Graphics Interface '85* pp 97-104.

Williams RJ and Seireg A (1979) Interactive Modeling and Analysis of Open or Closed Loop Dynamic Systems with Redundant Actuators. *Journal of Mechanical Design (Transactions of the ASME)* 101:407-416

Zeltzer D (1983) Knowledged Based Animation. *Proc. ACM Siggraph/Isgart Workshop on Motion* pp 187-192

BIOGRAPHICAL SKETCH

Tosiyasu L. Kunii is currently Professor and Chairman of Department of Information Science, the University of Tokyo. At the University of Tokyo, he started his work in raster computer graphics in 1968 which was led to the Tokyo Raster Technology Project. His research interest has been in visual computers which include visual object modeling, computer graphics, database systems, pattern recognition, parallel and distributed computing, and software engineering. He authored and edited more than 30 books in computer science and related areas, and published more than 100 refereed academic/technical papers in computer science and applications.

Dr. Kunii is Former President, Honorary President and Founder of the Computer Graphics Society, Editor-in-Chief of *The Visual Computer: An International Journal of Computer Graphics,* Editor of *Computer Science Workbench Series* of Springer-Verlag and on the Editorial Board of *IEEE Transactions on Knowledge and Data Engineering* and *IEEE Computer Graphics and Applications*. He is a member of IFIP Working Group 2.6 on Database, IFIP Working Group 5.10 on Computer Graphics and IFIP Working Group on Modelling and Simulation. He organized and was chairing the Technical Committee on Software Engineering of the Information Processing Society of Japan from 1976 to 1981. He also organized and was President of the Japan Computer Graphics Association (JCGA) from 1981 to 1983. He served as General Chairman of the 3rd International Conference on Very Large Data Bases (VLDB) in 1977, Program Chairman of InterGraphics '83 in 1983, Organizing Committee Chairman and Program Chairman of Computer Graphics Tokyo in 1984, Program Chairman of Computer Graphics Tokyo in 1985 and 1986, Organizing Committee Chairperson and Program Chairperson of CG International '87, Program Co-Chairman of IEEE COMPSAC 87, and Honorary Committee Chairperson of CG International '88. He served as Organizing Committee Chairperson and Program Chairperson of IFIP TC-2 Working Conference on Visual Database Systems in 1989.

He received the B.Sc., M.Sc., and D.Sc. degrees in chemistry all from the University of Tokyo in 1962, 1964, and 1967, respectively.

Lining Sun received the B.Eng. and M.Eng. degrees in information engineering from Shizuoka University in 1985 and 1987, respectively, and the D.Sc. degree in information science from the University of Tokyo in March 1990. His research interests include computer animation, databases and parallel processing. He is a member of IEEE and the Information Processing Society of Japan.

Authors can be contacted at the following address: Department of Information Science, Faculty of Science, the University of Tokyo, 7-3-1 Hongo, Bunkyo-ku, Tokyo 113 JAPAN.

New Trends in the Direction of Synthetic Actors

Nadia Magnenat-Thalmann

Abstract

This paper surveys the techniques involved in research related to synthetic actors. Research in this area may be arbitrarily split into two levels: 1) the geometric and physical level consisting of the animation and modeling of the human structure itself, and 2) the environment-dependent level consisting of the animation of the actor in his/her environment. These levels are not independent and research in a third level should allow the animator to specify the behaviour in terms of events, goals and constraints. This third level corresponds to task-level and behavioural animation.

Keywords: synthetic actor, task, behaviour, dynamics, collision, obstacle avoidance

1. INTRODUCTION TO SYNTHETIC ACTORS

Three-dimensional animation without three-dimensional characters is becoming less acceptable everyday. Although a few characters have appeared in recent computer-generated films, they are generally based on very traditional techniques like rotoscopy or keyframing. In the future, Computer Animation will have less and less to do with the techniques of traditional animation. The computer director will direct at the video screen synthetic actors (Magnenat-Thalmann and Thalmann 1987), decors, lights and cameras using commands. If it is in real time, it will be like directing a real film but in a synthetic world. We will enter into the era of real computer-generated films, produced in a virtual world and directed by real human directors. A synthetic actor is defined as a human-like autonomous actor completely generated by computer. Applications of synthetic actors are unlimited: in the near future, any human being, dead or alive, may be recreated and placed in any new situation, with no dependence on any live action model. Digital scene simulation will be possible for landscapes with human beings, cinema or theater actors, and spatial vessels with humans; any human behaviour may be simulated in various situations, scientific as well as artistic. From a user point-of-view, TV announcers may be simulated, or people may walk inside their dream house before the house is built. In the biomedical world, applications are also numerous: deformations of the back and the impact of bad postures, simulation of language dysfunctions and visual dysfunctions. Even in sports education, good positions may be shown as well as the effect of acting muscles. Human beings in dangerous situations may be also simulated: car accidents, airplane crashes, fires, explosions, etc.

However, the problems to be solved to achieve this are also numerous and unlimited: computer-generated motions must be as natural as possible. Unfortunately, we know that walking, object grasping, and true personality are very complex to model. Research in this area implies the development of techniques: for improving the physical aspects of the actors: shapes, colors, textures, reflectances, for improving the motion of limbs and their deformation during motion, for improving facial expressions and their animation, for specifying the tasks to be performed, for implementing tools for automatic motion control. Fig.1 shows the interdisciplinary aspects of the research related to synthetic actors and Fig.2 summarizes the most important results.

We consider that research in synthetic actors may be arbitrarily split into two levels:

- the geometric and physical level consisting of the animation and modeling of the human structure itself
- the environment-dependent level consisting of the animation of the actor in his/her environment; this environment includes decors, moving objects and other actors

Both levels are not independent and research in a third level should allow the animator to specify the behaviour in terms of events, goals and constraints. This third level corresponds to task-level and behavioural animation.

This paper will try to survey the researches techniques involved in the development of the three levels described above.

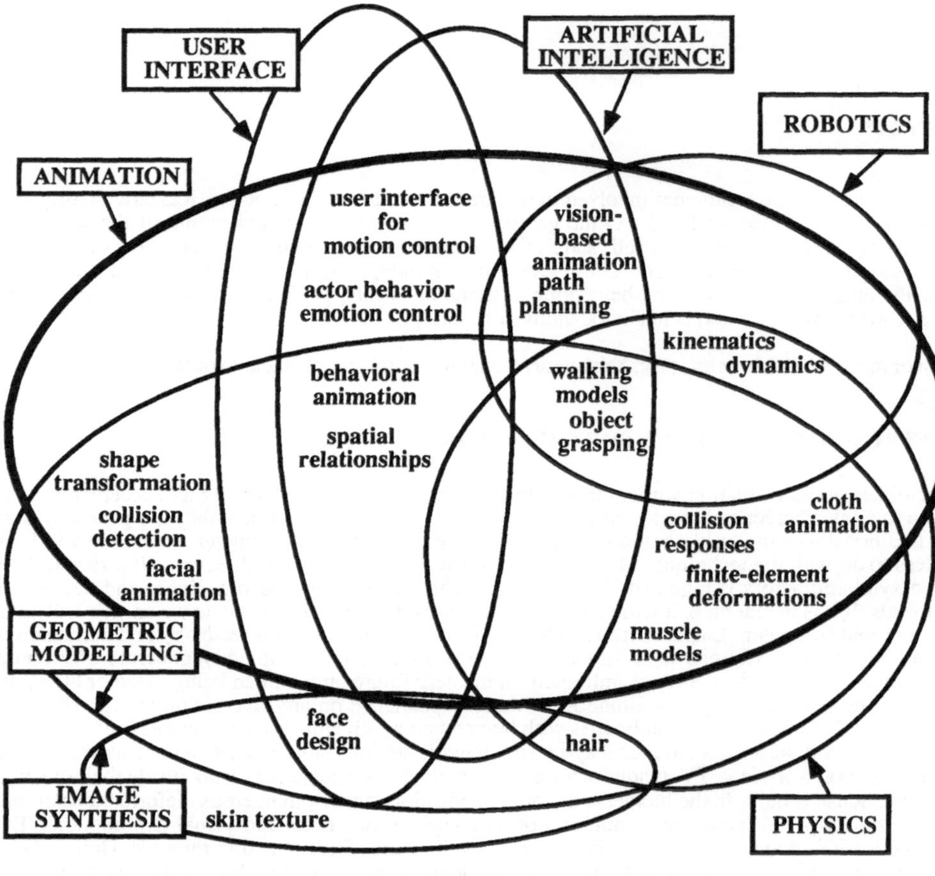

Fig.1 Research in topics related to synthetic actors

2. THE GEOMETRIC AND PHYSICAL LEVEL OF SYNTHETIC ACTORS

2.1. Anatomy and geometry of a synthetic actor

The human body has a complex and irregular surface that is difficult to model using traditional techniques. Three-dimensional digitizing (Blum 1979; Smith 1983) methods are still popular although data acquisition is a tedious and inexact process. Local deformations are probably the best for the modification and even creation of human surfaces. Several authors have proposed methods to perform limited local deformations.

KINEMATICS

Inverse kinematics

- Featherstone 1983, Hollerbach-Sahar 1983, Low-Dubey 1986
- Badler et al. 1985, Girard-Maciejewski 1985, Korein-Badler 1982, Forsey-Wilhelms 1988
- Multiple constraints: Badler et al. 1986

BODY DEFORMATIONS

- JLD operators: Magnenat-Thalmann 1987
- Bézier surface: Komatsu 1988
- Squash and stretch: Chadwick et al. 1989

FACIAL ANIMATION

- FACS: Ekman-Friesen 1978
- Parameterized model: Parke 1974-82
- Underlying structure: Platt -Badler 1981
- Muscle model :Waters 1987
- Abstract muscle procedures Magnenat-Thalmann et al. 1988
- Wrinkler editor: Guenter 1989

PHYSIC-BASED MODELS

- Snakes-Worms: Miller 1988-89
- Repulsive forces: Platt-Barr 1988
- Elasticity: Terzopoulos-Fleischer
- Penetrating impacts: Gourret et al. 1989
- Collision detection: Moore-Wilhelms

TASK-LEVEL ANIMATION

- "Task-level" systems: Zeltzer 1985, Badler et al. 198
- Tasks in natural language Drewery-Tsotsos 1986, Badler 1989

BEHAVIORAL ANIMATION

- Flocks, herds: Reynolds 1987
- Motion of flexible objets: Haumann 1987
- Vision-based model: Renault et al. 1990

HAIR

- fur problem: Csuri et al. 1979, Miller 1988, Kajiya 1989
- Particles systems: Pearce et al. 1986
- Alpha-blending: Leblanc-Thalmann 1990
- Prisms and gravity: Watanabe et al. 1989

DYNAMICS

based on Lagrange's equation:

- Uicker 1965, Kahn 1969, Hollerbach 1980

based on Newton-Euler equation:

- Stepanenko-Vukobratovicz 1976, Orin et al. 1979, Armstrong 1979, Luh et al. 1980
- Armstrong et al. 1987

based on Gibbs-Appel equation

- Wilhelms-Barsky 1985

HAND ANIMATION

- MOP system, Catmull 1972
- B-spline: Badler-Morris 1982
- Magnenat-Thalmann et al. 1988

WALKING MODELS

- Use of dance notation Calvert-Chapman 1978, Smoliar-Badler 1979
- Ballistic model: McMahon 1984
- Dynamic simulation: Bruderlin-Calvert 1989
- Local motor programs: Zeltzer 1982
- Personification: Boulic et al. 1990

CONSTRAINTS

- Geometric constraints: Barzel-Barr 1988
- Dynamic constraints: Isaacs-Cohen 1988
- Spacetime constraints: Witkin-Kass 1988
- Energy constraints: Witkin et al. 1987

OBSTACLE AVOIDANCE

- Visibility graph: Brooks 1979, Lozano-Perez-Wesley 1979
- Visibility graph (BOLLO) Schröder-Zeltzer 1988
- Cost functions: Breen 1989
- Vision-based approach Renault et al. 1990

CLOTH MODELS

- Constraint points: Weil 1986
- Collision detection using force field: Lafleur et al. 1990

▭ robotics methods

Fig.2 Some important results in research related to synthetic actors

Numerous methods based on parametric surfaces are extensively used in CAD and CAE. As these methods deal with control points, they are not very convenient for human modeling when resemblance with existing people is required (Nahas et al. 1987; Komatsu 1988). Field functions (Wyvill and Wyvill 1989) model free-form surfaces and their local deformations, but the application of this for the creation of well-known personalities seems difficult. Barr (1984) defines a locally specified deformation which modifies the tangent space of the solid. Another way of deforming solids is proposed by Sederberg and Parry (1986). The technique is referred to as free-form deformation (FFD). Physically, FFD corresponds to deformations applied to an imaginary parallelepiped of clear, flexible plastic in which are embedded the objects to be deformed. Allan et al. (1989) proposed a general method for manipulating polygonal meshes. They introduced a basic operation "move-vertex", which specifies a new 3D position for a specific vertex called the current vertex. Their basic operation is extended in several ways: definition of a range of influence around the current vertex, decay function over the range of influence, binding and anchoring. Other operations include stretch, grow and randomize.

For the specific case of human faces, Magnenat-Thalmann et al. (1989) introduced three approaches: local deformations, interpolation between two faces and composition of face parts.

2.2. Hair and skin

The task of defining and rendering hair, particularly hair on the head, can be termed as a generalization of the fur problem (Csuri et al. 1979; Miller 1988; Kajiya and Kay 1989) for it must allow longer strands with variable form and orientation. Pearce et al. (1986) used particle systems to generate very elementary forms of hair. Watanabe et al. (1989) modeled the cylindrical shape of each strand of hair as a succession of three sided prisms. The arc of each strand was generated automatically as a function of length and gravity. Aiming above all for fast rendered images, each hair was displayed in Gouraud shading with a common z-buffer algorithm for hidden surface removal. In these two cases, neither proper illumination models nor antialiasing were used. Therefore, the fine and delicate texture of hair could not be achieved.

A new and efficient method for rendering realistic human hair is introduced by Leblanc and Thalmann (1990). Based on alpha-blending concepts, the generated images are completely free of aliasing artifacts and are calculated faster than with previous methods used for rendering fur. A simple but effective anisotropic illumination model is formulated to simulate diffuse backlighting and strong reflected highlights present around each hair. A method is also shown to incorporate the hair among objects generated by other conventional rendering algorithms. Fig.3 shows an example.

Rendering of realistic human skin texture is still an unsolved problem.

2.3. Skeleton animation

Basically a synthetic actor is structured as an articulated body defined by a skeleton. When the animator specifies the animation sequence, he/she defines the motion using this skeleton. A skeleton (Badler and Smoliar 1979) is a connected set of segments, corresponding to limbs, and joints. A joint is the intersection of two segments, which means it is a skeleton point where the limb which is linked to the point may move. The angle between the two segments is called the joint angle. A joint may have at most three kinds of position angles: flexing, pivot and twisting. The **flexing** is a rotation of the limb which is influenced by the joint and cause the motion of all limbs linked to this joint. This flexing is made relatively to the joint point and a flexing axis which has to be defined. The **pivot** makes rotate the flexing axis around the limb which is influenced by the joint. The **twisting** causes a torsion of the limb which is influenced by the joint. The direction of the twisting axis is found similarly to the direction of the pivot.

Skeleton animation consists of animating joint angles. There are two main ways to do that: parametric keyframe animation and procedural animation based on mechanical laws (kinematics and dynamics).

2.3.1. Parametric keyframe animation

Parametric keyframe animation is based on the following principle: an entity (object, camera, light) is characterized by parameters. The animator creates keyframes by specifying the appropriate set of parameter values at given time, parameters are then interpolated and images are finally individually constructed from the interpolated parameters. For example, to bend an arm, it is necessary to enter into the computer the elbow angle at different selected times. Then the software is able to find any angle at any time.

Fig.3 Hair rendering using alpha-blending

Fig.4. A non-human synthetic actor (from the film *Galaxy Sweetheart*)

Lee and Kunii (1989) present a design method for animation systems which includes scene analysis. Analytic forces such as those of gravity, friction, and air resistance are then applied to the objects modeled out of the extracted data. Brotman and Netravali (1988) solve the motion interpolation problems in the context of keyframe animation. They model motion of objects and their environment by differential equations obtained from classical mechanics and use external control to force the motion to satisfy constraints imposed by keyframes.

2.3.2. Direct and inverse kinematics

This direct kinematics problem consists in finding the position of end point positions (e.g. hand, foot) with respect to a fixed-reference coordinate system as a function of time without regard to the forces or the moments that cause the motion. Efficient and numerically well-behaved methods exist for the transformation of position and velocity from joint-space (joint angles) to Cartesian coordinates (end of the limb). Parametric keyframe animation is a primitive application of direct kinematics.

The use of inverse-kinematics (Featherstone 1983; Hollerbach and Sahar 1983; Low and Dubey 1986] permits direct specification of end point positions. Joint angles are automatically determined. This is the key problem, because independent variables in a synthetic actor are joint angles. Unfortunately, the transformation of position from Cartesian to joint coordinates generally does not have a closed-form solution. However, there are a number of special arrangements of the joint axes for which closed-form solutions have been suggested in the context of animation (Badler et al., 1985; Girard and Maciejewski, 1985; Girard, 1987; Korein and Badler, 1982; Forsey and Wilhelms, 1988).

Fig.4 shows an example of kinematics-based actor motion.

2.3.3. Kinematics constraints

A higher level of specification of kinematics motion is based on the use of constraints. The animator impose a limb end to stay at a specified location or to follow a predefined trajectory. Badler et al. (1987) have introduced an iterative algorithm for solving multiple constraints using inverse kinematics. In their system, the user has to specify also the precedence of each constraint in case they cannot all be simultaneously satisfied.

2.3.4. Direct and inverse dynamics

Several factors lead to introduce dynamics in animation control (Arnaldi et al. 1989):

- dynamics frees the animator from the description of the motion due to the physical properties of the solid objects.
- reality of natural phenomena is better rendered.
- bodies can react automatically to internal and external environmental constraints: fields, collisions, forces and torques.

In the case of dynamics, forces and torques are used to control the motion of synthetic actors. Two problems may be considered: the direct-dynamics problem and the inverse-dynamics problem. The direct-dynamics problem consists of finding the trajectories of some point as the end effector with regard to the forces and torques that cause the motion. The inverse-dynamics problem is much more useful and may be stated as follows: determine the forces and torques required to produce a prescribed motion in a system. For a synthetic actor, it is possible to compute the time sequence of joint torques required to achieve the desired time sequence of positions, velocities and accelerations using various methods coming from robotics.

The equations of motion for robots can be derived through the application of the Lagrange's equations of motion for nonconservative systems. Uicker (1965) and Kahn (1969) use the 4x4 rotation/translation matrices introduced by Denavit and Hartenberg. Once the kinetic and potential energy is expressed in terms of these matrices and their derivatives, the Lagrange equation is easily applied and the generalized forces are found. Unfortunately, the equation evaluation is very time consuming, because it is proportional to the fourth power of the number of links. Hollerbach (1980) has proposed a recursive method that significantly reduces the number of operations.

The Newton-Euler formulation is based on the laws governing the dynamics of rigid bodies. The procedure in this formulation is to first write the equations which define the angular and linear velocities and accelerations of each link and then write the equations which relate the forces and torques exerted on successive links while under this motion. The vector force is given by the Newton's second law and the total vector torque by Euler's equation. Newton-Euler's methods were first developed with respect to the fixed, inertial coordinate system (Stepanenko and Vukobratovicz 1976). Then methods were derived with respect to the local coordinate system. Orin et al. (1979) proposed that the forces and the torques be referred to the link's internal coordinate system. Armstrong (1979) and Luh et al. (1980) calculated the angular and linear velocities in link coordinates as well.

The Armstrong method is based on the hypothetical existence of a linear recursive relationship between the motion of and forces applied to one link, and the motion of and forces applied to its neighbors. A set of recursion coefficients is defined for each link and the coefficients for one link may be calculated in terms of those of one its neighbors. The accelerations are then derived from the coefficients. The method is only applicable to spherical joints, but its computational complexity is only O(n), where n is the number of links. To reduce the amount of computer time required, Armstrong et al. (1987) make some simplifying assumptions about the structure of the figure and can produce a near real-time dynamics algorithm. They use frames which move with the links and an inertial frame considered fixed and non-rotating.

Wilhelms and Barsky (1985) have proposed a method based on the Gibbs-Appel formulation, which describes the acceleration energy. Wilhelms (1987) uses this equation to formulate the generalized force for a sliding joint and a revolute joint for animating articulated bodies. This method was used for implementing her animation system Deva; however this formulation does not exploit the recursive nature of the terms, and has a cost of $O(n^4)$. However, it is more general than the Armstrong approach.

2.4. Surface body animation and deformation

Once the motion of the skeleton is designed, the realism of motion needs to be improved not only from the joint point-of-view, but also in relation to the deformations of bodies during animation. For animating rigid bodies like robots, a simple mapping between the surface and the skeleton is needed. For human beings, the surfaces should be transformed according to the wire-frame model ensuring an automatic continuity between the different surfaces and automatic deformations during the animation process.

Magnenat-Thalmann and Thalmann (1987) introduced the concept of Joint-dependent Local Deformation (JLD) operators, which are specific local deformation operators depending on the nature of the joints. These JLD operators control the evolution of surfaces and may be considered as operators on these surfaces. Each JLD operator will be applicable to some uniquely defined part of the surface which may be called the domain of the operator. The value of the operator itself will be determined as a function of the angular values of the specific set of joints defining the operator. The case of the hand is especially complex (Magnenat-Thalmann et al. 1988), as deformations are very important when the fingers are bent, and the shape of the palm is very flexible. Links of fingers are independent and the JLD operators are calculated using a unique link-dependent reference system. For the palm, JLD operators use reference systems of several links to calculate surface mapping. In order to make the fingers realistic, two effects are simulated: joint roundings and muscle inflation. The hand mapping calculations are based on normals to each proximal joint.

The mapping of surfaces onto the skeleton may be based on various techniques. Chadwick et al. (1989) propose an approach which combines recent research advances in robotics, physically-based modeling and geometric modeling. The control points of geometric modeling deformations are constrained by an underlying articulated robotics skeleton. These deformations are tailored by the animator and act as a muscle layer to provide automatic squash and stretch behaviour of the surface geometry.

Komatsu (1988) describes the synthesis and the transformation of a new human skin model using the Bézier surfaces.

2.5. Hand animation

In the MOP system designed by Catmull (1972), hands are decomposed into polygons, but undesired variation of finger thickness may occur. Badler and Morris (1982) propose a model based on B-spline surfaces. The surface is computed based on the skeleton of the hand; spheres are linked to the B-spline surface, which does not itself appear on the image. It is only used for the placement of the spheres.

Magnenat-Thalmann et al. (1988) describe algorithms and methods used to animate a hand for a synthetic actor. The algorithms allow not only to move the hand and grasp objects, but also they compute the deformations of the hands: rounding at joints and muscle inflations. Gourret et al. (1989) propose a finite element method to model the deformations of human flesh due to flexing of members and/or contact with objects.

2.6. Facial animation

Face is a small part of a synthetic actor, but it plays an essential role in the communication. Human people look at faces to find emotional aspects or even read lips. This is a particular challenge to imitate these acutenesses. One of the ultimate objective therefore is to model exactly the human facial anatomy and movements which satisfies both structural and functional aspects of simulation. This however, involves many problems to be solved simultaneously. Some of these are: the geometric representation must be very close to the actual facial structure and shape, modeling of interior facial details such as muscles, bones, tissues, and incorporating the dynamics and movements involved in making expressions etc. each one of these is, in itself, a potential area of research.

This complexity leads to what is commonly called facial expressions. The properties of these facial expressions have been studied for 25 years by Psychologist Ekman, who proposed a parameterization of muscles with their relationships to emotions: the Facial Action Coding System (FACS) (Ekman and Friesen, 1978). FACS describes the set of all possible basic actions performable on a human face. Some of the basic actions are for example inner brow raiser, outer brow raiser etc. Each basic action also called Action Unit (AU) is a minimal action and cannot be broken into smaller actions. Interaction of these AU's cause a facial expression. Each AU is controlled by either a single muscle or a small set of closely related muscles.

Various facial animation approaches have been proposed:. parameterized models, muscle model for facial expressions, abstract muscle action procedures, interactive simulation system for human expressions.

2.6.1. Parameterized models

A set of parameters is defined based on the desired expressions on a given face. In parameterized models, as introduced by Parke (1982), there are two types of parameters considered: parameters for controlling conformation and parameters controlling expressions. Conformation parameters pertain to set of parameters which vary from individual to individual and make each person unique. For example, skin color, neck length and shape, shape of chin, forehead, nose length etc. The development of truly complete set for conformation parameters is very difficult. Since most expressions relate to eyes and mouth for facial expression, primary importance was given to these areas to form a set of expression parameters including pupil dilatation, eyelid opening, eyebrow position, jaw rotation.

Platt and Badler (1981) have presented a model of a human face and developed a notational system to encode actions performable on a face. The notation drives a model of the underlying muscle structure which in turn determines the facial expression. Two separate notations for body and action representation are given: action based notation and structure based notation. Several action based notation system are explored and ultimately FACS is considered for their model. At the level of structure-based notation, the action representations are interpreted and the simulation of action is performed. The representation adopted, simulate points on the skin, muscle, and bone by a set of interconnected 3D network of points using arcs between selected points to signify relations. The skin is the outside level represented by a set of 3D points that define a surface which can be modified. The bones represent an internal level that cannot be moved and is inflexible. The muscles are between the bone and skin layers. Geometrically, a muscle is a group of points with an arc stretching from each fibre point to point on the bone and another stretching from the fibre point to one or more skin points. When a simple fibre contracts, a force is applied to muscle point in the direction of the bone point. This force causes a displacement of the muscle point; the amount of the displacement varies with the elasticity of the flesh at the point. The force is then reflected along all arcs adjacent to the point; these reflected forces are further applied to their corresponding adjacent points. This way a force is propagated out from the initiating point across the face.

2.6.2. Muscle models for facial animation

Waters (1987) proposes a muscle model which is not specified to facial topology and is more general for modifying the primary facial expression. The model is based on a few dynamic parameters that mimic the primary biomechanical characteristics. Muscles can be described with direction and magnitude. The direction is towards a point of attachment on the bone, and the magnitude of the displacement depends upon the muscle spring constant and the tension created by a muscle contraction. The main parameters employed are: the vector contraction, the position of the head and tail of the vector and fall-off radius. Three types of muscles are created using the muscle model: linear/parallel muscle that pull, sphincter muscles that squeeze and sheet muscle that behaves as a series of linear muscles. In linear muscle, the surrounding skin is contracted towards the static node of attachment on the bone until, at a finite distance away the force dissipates to zero. For computing the effect of a muscle vector contraction on the adjacent tissue, it is assumed that there is no displacement at the point of insertion into the skin. The sphincter muscle can be described from a single point around which the surface is drawn together like the tightening of a string bag. It does not require angular displacement and a major and minor axis are employed to describe the elliptical shape of the muscle. The sheet muscle is a broad flat area of muscle fibre stands and does not emanate from a point source. The muscle is a series of almost parallel fibre spread over an area. The limits of a muscle action can be determined by the displacement by the spring constant k which represents the maximum displacement of the muscle. The problem associated with this model is that each muscle action is independent and the actual nodal displacement is determined by a succession of muscle actions.

Magnenat Thalmann et al. (1988b) introduce a way of controlling human face and synchronizing speech based on the concept of abstract muscle action (AMA) procedures. An AMA procedure is a specialized procedure which simulates specific action of a face muscle. These AMA procedures are specific to the simulated action and are not independent i.e. these are order dependent. These procedures work on certain regions of the human face which must be defined when the face is constructed. Each AMA procedure is responsible for a facial parameter corresponding approximately to a muscle., for example, vertical jaw, close upper lip, close lower lip, lip raiser etc. The complex motion is produced by an AMA procedure. AMA procedures are considered as the basic level, there are two more higher levels defined in order to improve the user interface. These are expression level and script level. At the expression level, a facial expression is considered as a group of facial parameter values obtained by the AMA procedures in different ways. Phonemes and emotions are the two types of facial expression considered. Let us have an example: For the phoneme "I" (as in "it"), the teeth are slightly open and the commissures are horizontally pulled towards the outside (risorius muscle); we select 10% of the AMA procedure VERTICAL_JAW, 50% for the AMA procedure LEFT_RISORIUS and 50% for the AMA procedure RIGHT_RISORIUS. At script level, a script in facial animation is a collection of multiple tracks. A track is a chronological sequence of key frames. On each track, a percentage of a facial parameter or the facial expression may be fixed for a given time. For example, "KID" will be pronounced by a character, indicating that the phoneme "K" is used at a given time, the phoneme "I" a short time later, then the phoneme "D". Then the software will progressively transform the facial expression corresponding to the phoneme "K" in order to obtain the facial expression corresponding to the phoneme "I", then to the phoneme "D". Tracks are independent but they may be mixed exactly in the same way as sound is mixed in a sound studio. Fig.5 shows an example of phoneme expressions.

Guenter [1989] proposes an interactive system for attaching muscles and wrinkle lines to arbitrary rectangular face meshes and then for simulating the contractions of those muscles. The system is divided into two modules: the Expression Editor and the Muscle and Wrinkler Editor. The Expression Editor uses the FACS to control facial expression at a very high level, The Muscle and Wrinkler Editor is used to established the correspondence between the high level FACS encoding and low level muscular action of the face. The skin is modeled as linear elastic mesh with zero initial tension and the muscles are modeled as force vectors applied at the vertices of the face mesh.

3. THE ENVIRONMENT-DEPENDENT LEVEL

3.1. Impact of the environment

Synthetic actors are moving in an environment comprising models of physical objects. Their animation is dependent on this environment and the environment may be modified by these actors. Moreover several synthetic actors may interact with each other. Several very complex problems must be solved in order to render three-dimensional animation involving actors in their environment. They may be classified into the following categories:

- contacts and collisions with objects, and deformation of these objects
- reaching or avoiding obstacles
- group behaviour (this problem will be discussed in Section 4).

Fig.5. Phoneme expressions (from the film *Renedez-vous à Montréal*)

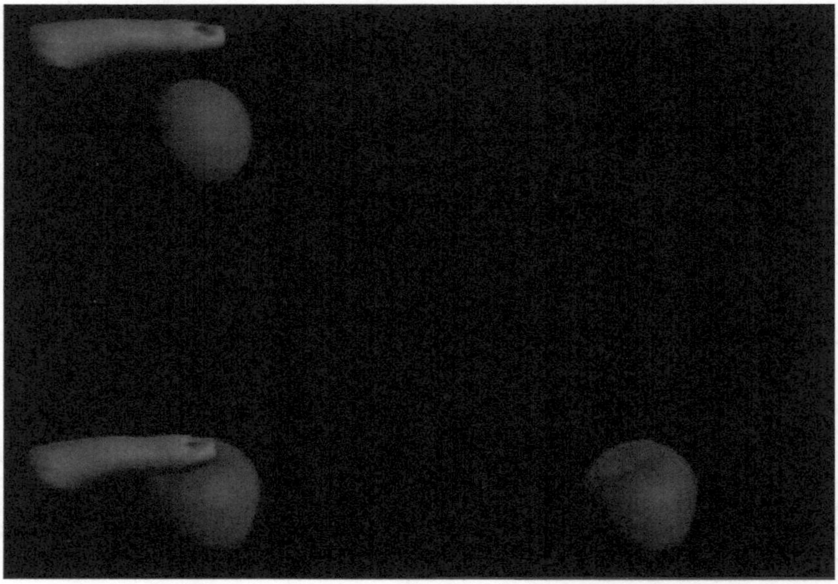

Figure 6 - (a) ball and finger before contact (b) ball and finger after contact (c) deformed ball; this picture presents deformations and fingermarks created by the finger in picture b.

3.2. Contacts and deformations of flexible objects

3.2.1. Deformable and flexible objects

The environment of synthetic actors is made up of physical objects, which should act as if they had a mind. They should react to applied forces such as gravity, pressure and contact. The models recently developed by Terzopoulos et al. [1987] are for example implemented using the Finite Difference Method, and collisions between elastic objects are simulated by creating potential energy around each object, i.e. intersections between deformable bodies are avoided by surrounding the object surfaces with a repulsive collision force. Terzopoulos and Fleischer (1988) developed deformable models capable of perfectly elastic and inelastic behaviour, viscoelasticity, plasticity, and fracture. Miller (1988b) applied dynamic models to the motion of snakes and worms. Platt and Barr [1988] also use repulsive forces and discuss constraint methods in terms of animator tools for physical model control.

3.2.2. Finite-element method

Gourret et al. [1989] propose a finite element method to model the deformations of human flesh due to flexion of members and/or contact with objects. The method is able to deal with penetrating impacts and true contacts. Simulation of impact with penetration can be used to model the grasping of ductile objects, and requires decomposition of objects into small geometrically simple objects. All the advantages of physical modeling of objects can also be transferred to human flesh. For example, the hand grasp of an object is expected to lead to realistic flesh deformation as well as an exchange of information between the object and the hand which will not only be geometrical. This exchange of information using acting and reacting forces is significant for a good and realistic grip and can influence the behaviour of the hand and of the arm skeleton. When a deformable object is grasped, the contact forces that act on it and on the fingertips will lead both to deformation of the object and of the fingertips, giving reacting forces which provide significant information about the object and more generally about the environment of the synthetic human body. Once the various kinds of elements are defined, the modeled object shape is obtained by composition. Each element is linked to other elements at nodal points. In continuum mechanics, the equilibrium of a body presenting the same shape can be expressed by using the principle of stationarity of the total potential or the principle of virtual displacements. The equilibrium relation is applied to each element and the whole body is obtained by composing all elements. Fig.6 shows an example of the use of the finite element method.

3.2.3. Cloth modelling and animation: collision detection

Weil (1986) presents a solution for the following specific problem: a piece of cloth exists in three dimensions and its location is fixed at chosen constraint points. The piece of cloth is to be represented with all its folds as it hangs from these constraint points. The cloth is assumed to be rectangular and is represented by a grid. There are two stages in the method.

. *Approximation to the surface within the convex hull of the constraint points*
  This stage consists of tracing curves from every constraint point to each other constraint point. Weil derived the curve equation from the two end points and the length of the thread hanging between. As constraint points are connected by tracing catenaries between them, the grid points which lie along the lines between the constraint points can be positioned and triangles are created. This series of triangles can then be used for the approximation of the surface. Each triangle is repeatedly subdivided until each grid point in its interior has been positioned.

. *Iterative relaxation process*
  This relaxation of points is iterated over the surface until the maximum displacement of the points during one pass falls below a predetermined tolerance.

Analytical methods for calculating the forces between colliding rigid bodies have been proposed by several authors. Moore and Wilhelms (1988) model simultaneous collisions as a slightly staggered series of single collisions and used non-analytical methods to deal with bodies in resting contact. Hahn (1988) prevented bodies in resting contact from inter-penetrating by modeling their contact as a series of frequently occuring collisions. Baraff (1989) proposes an analytical method for finding forces between contacting polyhedral bodies, based on linear programming techniques. The solution algorithm currently used is heuristic and allows holonomic geometric constraints to be maintained.

Lafleur et al. (1990) combine the Terzopoulos model of flexible objects with a modification of the Moore-Wilhelms method for collision detection. In their method, collision avoidance consists of creating a very thin force field around the obstacle surface to avoid collisions. This force field acts like a shield rejecting the points. This volume is divided into small contiguous non-overlapped cells which completely surround the surface. As soon as a point enters into a cell, a force is applied. The direction and the magnitude of this force are dependent on the velocities, the normals and the distance between the point and the surface. The displacement volume is replaced by a cell built from the points of the triangle and the normals at these points. The velocities are only present in the calculation of the repulsion forces.

3.3. Obstacle avoidance and the reach problem

3.3.1. Obstacle avoidance

An animation system should determine possible trajectories for the actor based on the environment. This obstacle avoidance, may be subdivided into two subproblems:

avoidance of static obstacles (decor) or objects grasped by actors
avoidance of dynamic obstacles

The trajectory planning problem was extensively studied in robotics (Maciejewski and Klein 1985; McGhee and Iswandhi 1979), but also aesthetic criteria are very important in computer animation. For example, given the starting position of a hand and objects on a table, the problem in robotics is to find the trajectory to follow in order to avoid obstacles. For a synthetic actor, the problem is more complex due to the non-rigidity of the actor. For the problem of walking without collision among obstacles, one strategy used is based on the 2D Lozano-Perez algorithm (Lozano-Perez and Wesley, 1979). Obstacles are assumed to be polygonal, while the moving object is convex and its shape is constant. The first step consists of forming a graph. Vertices of this graph are composed of the vertices of the obstacles, the start point **S** and the goal point **G**. Arcs are defined such that a straight line can be drawn joining the vertices without overlapping any obstacle. This graph is called a visibility graph, since connected vertices can see each other. The shortest collision-free path from **S** to **G** is the shortest path in the graph from **S** to **G**. The method may be applied to a 2D motion in computer animation. However, it assumes that the moving object is a point; this restricts the application of the algorithm to camera motions, light motions or motions of very small objects. Lozano-Perez and Wesley (1979) describe a way of extending the method to moving objects which are not points. In the original method, the obstacles may be considered as forbidden regions for the position of the moving point. If the moving object is not a point, obstacles may be replaced by new obstacles, which are forbidden regions for a reference point on the object. In the case of synthetic actors, the result trajectory is then used as input to a positional constraint solver based on inverse kinematics. Schröder and Zeltzer (1988) introduced Lozano-Perez algorithm into their interactive animation package BOLIO.

Brooks (1983) suggests another method called the freeway method. His algorithm finds obstacles that face each other and generates a freeway to passing between them. This path segment is a generalized cylinder. A freeway is an elongated piece of free-space that describes a path between obstacles. This freeway may be described as overlapping generalized cones; it is essentially composed of straight lines with left and right free-space width functions, which could easily be inverted. A generalized cone is obtained by sweeping a two-dimensional cross section along a curve in space, called a spine, and deforming it according to a sweeping rule.

Breen (1989) proposes a technique employing cost functions to avoid obstacles. Cost functions can be used to define goal-oriented motions and actions. A cost function can be defined whose variables are the animated parameters of a scene. The parameters are modified in such a way to minimize the cost function. This cost function technique has been encapsulated in the cost analysis object of The Clockworks, an object-oriented computer animation system (Breen et al. 1987; Breen and Wozny, 1989).

Renault et al. (1990) propose a vision-based approach for avoiding obstacles, the method is further described in Section 4.3.3.

3.3.2. The reach problem

To generate the motion corresponding to the grasping task, a free motion should be synthesized; during this motion the principal goal is to reach the destination without collision, which implies obstacle avoidance. The reach problem (Korein and Badler 1982) is also an important problem to be solved for object grasping. As for manipulators in robotics, we may define a workspace for a synthetic actor. Such a workspace is the volume of space which the end-effector of the actor can reach. In a task environment, the reach problem may only be solved if the specified goal point lies within the workspace.

4. TASK-LEVEL AND BEHAVIOURAL ANIMATION

4.1. Task-level animation

With task level control, the animator can only specify the broad outlines of a particular movement and the animation system fills in the details. A task specification by a sequence of model states using a set of spatial relationships has been described by Popplestone et al. (1980). In this approach, each state is given by the configuration of all the objects in the environment. The specification by a sequence of commands or a natural language interface is the most suitable and popular (Drewery and Tsotsos 1986; Badler 1989).

In task-level animation, the animator specifies what the synthetic actor has to do, for instance, "jump from here to there". Witkin and Kass (1988) propose a new method, called Spacetime Constraints, for creating this animation. The requirements contained in the description, together with Newton's laws, comprise a problem of constrained optimization. The solution to this problem is a physically valid motion satisfying the constraints. More generally, an approach to imposing and solving geometric constraints on parameterized models was introduced by Witkin et al. (1987). Constraints are expressed as energy functions, and the energy gradient followed through the model's parameter space. Using dynamic constraints, Barzel and Barr (1988) build objects by specifying geometric constraints; the models assemble themselves as the elements move to satisfy the constraints. Girard (1989) proposes an algorithm for optimizing limb movement in terms of both kinematics and dynamics-based variables and constraints. The algorithm makes use of dynamic programming to solve for a minimum-cost speed distribution along a parametric splined patch.

4.2. Behavioural animation

Mechanics-based motions are too regular, because they do not take into account the personality of the characters. It is unrealistic to think that only the physical characteristics of two people carrying out the same actions make these characters different for any observer. Behaviour and personality of the human beings are also an essential cause of the observable differences. Several ideas for gracefulness and style in motion control are proposed by Cohen (1989).

Reynolds (1987) studied in details the problem of group trajectories: bird flocks, herds of land animals and fish schools. This kind of animation using a traditional approach (keyframe or procedural laws) is almost impossible. In the Reynolds approach, each bird of the flock decide itself its trajectory without animator intervention. Reynolds introduces a distributed behavioural model to simulate flocks of birds, herds of land animals, and schools of fish. The simulated flock is an elaboration of a particle system with the simulated birds being the particles. A flock is assumed to be the result of the interaction between the behaviours of individual birds. Working independently, the birds try both to stick together and avoid collisions with one another and with other objects in their environment. In a module of behavioural animation, positions, velocities and orientations of the actors are known from the system at any time. The animator may control several global parameters: e.g. weight of the obstacle avoidance component, weight of the convergence to the goal, weight of the centering of the group, weight of the velocity equality, maximum velocity, maximum acceleration, minimum distance between actors. The animator provides data about the leader trajectory and the behaviour of other birds relatively to the leader. A computer-generated film has been produced by symbolic using this distributed behavioural model: *Breaking the ice*.

Haumann and Parent (1988) describe behavioural simulation as a means to obtain global motion by simulating simple rules of behaviour between locally related actors. They developed a test-bed used to create a library of physically behaving actors which can realistically reproduce the motion of flexible objects (Haumann, 1987).

Lethebridge and Ware (1989) propose a simple heuristically-based method for expressive stimulus-response animation. They model stimulus-response relationships using "behaviour functions" which are created from simple mathematical primitives in a largely heuristic manner.

4.3. Walk models

Description of biped gait, and especially human gait, may be easily found in the literature (Inman et al. 1980). In medicine, the problem has been studied for surgery (Murray et al. 1964, Saunders et al. 1953), and prosthetics (Lamoreux 1971). In robotics, much has been written concerning biomechanics for constructing artificial walking systems (Gurfinkel and Fomin 1974, Hemami and Farnsworth 1977, Miura and Shimoyama 1984; McMahon 1984). Several dance notations have been proposed: Benesh notation (Benesh 1956), Eshkol-Wachman notation (Eshkol and Wachman 1958) and Labanotation (Hutchinson 1970) and walking has been described using these notations (Badler and Smoliar 1979; Magnenat-Thalmann and Thalmann 1985). Finally, several authors (Calvert and Chapman 1978; Zeltzer 1982; Magnenat-Thalmann and Thalmann 1987) have developed systems for generating computer-animated walking sequences.

According to Zeltzer (1982), the gait cycle is usually divided into a stance phase, during which the foot is in contact with the ground, and a swing phase, where the leg is brought forward to begin the stance phase again. Each arm swings forward with the opposite leg and swings back while the opposite leg is in its stance phase. For implementing such a cycle walk, Zeltzer describes a walk controller invoking eight local motor programs (LMP): left swing, left stance, right swing, and right stance, which control the actions of the legs, hips, and pelvis; and four other LMPs that control the swinging of the arms. The walk controller and the LMPs are implemented as finite state machines.

One of the most complete descriptions of the motions of the limbs during walking is due to Saunders et al. (1953) reformulated by McMahon (1984). This can be applied to computer-generated walking. In this description, six models were proposed with an increasing complexity relatively to the joints involved. McMahon (1984) proposes a ballistic walking model consisting of three links, one for the stance leg and one for the thigh and shank of the swing leg.

Bruderlin and Calvert (1989) propose a hybrid approach to the human locomotion which combines goal-oriented and dynamic motion control. Knowledge about a locomotion cycle is incorporated into a hierarchical control process. Decomposition of the locomotion determines forces and torques that drive the dynamic model of the legs by numerical approximation techniques. Rather than relying on a general dynamic model, the equations of motion of the legs are tailored to locomotion and analytically constrained to allow for only a specific range of movements.

Isaacs and Cohen (1988) discuss mixed methods for complex constraints in dynamic figure animation. They propose an integration of direct and inverse kinematics specifications within a mixed method of forward and inverse dynamics simulation.

Boulic et al (1990) propose a human walking model built from experimental data based on a wide range of normalized velocities. The model is structured in two levels. At a first level, global spatial and temporal characteristics (normalized length and step duration) are generated. At the second level, a set of parameterized trajectories produce both the position of the body in the space and the internal body configuration in particular the pelvis and the legs. This is performed for a standard structure and an average configuration of the human body. The experimental context corresponding to the model is extended by allowing a continuous variation of global spatial and temporal parameters according to the motion rendition expected by the animator. The model is based on a simple kinematic approach designed to keep the intrinsic dynamic characteristics of the experimental model. Such an approach also allows a personification of the walking action in an interactive real-time context in most cases.

4.3.3. Vision-based animation

Renault et al. (1990) proposes an innovative way of animating synthetic actors based on the concept of synthetic vision. The initial objective was simple and fuzzy: to create an animation involving a synthetic actor automatically moving in a corridor avoiding other synthetic actors. To simulate this behaviour, each synthetic actor uses a synthetic vision as its perception of the world and so as the unique input to its behavioural model. This model is based on the concept of Displacement Local Automata (DLA), which is similar to the concept of a script for natural language processing. A DLA is an algorithm that can deal with a specific environment. Two DLAs are described in detail called *follow-the-corridor* and *avoid-the-obstacle*. Our approach is based on the use of Displacement Local Automata (DLA), which is similar to the concept of script for natural language processing. Vision simulation is the heart of their system. This vision has the advantage to avoid all problems of pattern recognition involved in robotic vision. In input, we have a database containing the description of 3D objects: the environment, the camera characterized by its eye and interest point. In output, the vision is built as a 2D array of pixels. each pixel contains the distance between the eye and the point of the object for which this the projection. It also contains the object identifier. The size of the array should be selected in order to have the maximum of accuracy without implying too CPU time. A definition of 30 x 30 seems convenient. The implementation is based on the IRIS 4D architecture; it extensively uses the Graphics Engine with z-buffer and double frame buffer. The projection which is used is a perspective projection with a view angle of 90°. The front buffer is used to display the projection of objects, which allows the animator to know what the synthetic actor sees. In the backbuffer, for each pixel, the object identifier is stored.

ACKNOWLEDGMENT

This research was sponsored by le Fonds National Suisse pour la Recherche Scientifique. The author would like to thank André Leblanc and Arghyro Paouri for the production of the hair image.

5. REFERENCES

Allan JB, Wyvill B, Witten IA (1989) A Methodology for Direct Manipulation of Polygon Meshes, Proc. Computer Graphics International '89, Leeds, pp.451-469.

Armstrong WW (1979) Recursive Solution to the Equations of Motion of an N-Link Manipulator, Proc. 5th World Congress Theory Mach.Mechanisms, Vol.2, pp.1343-1346

Armstrong WW and Green MW (1985) Dynamics for Animation of Characters with Deformable Surfaces in: N.Magnenat-Thalmann and D.Thalmann (Eds) Computer-generated Images, Springer, pp.209-229.

Armstrong WW, Green M and Lake R (1987) Near real-time Control of Human Figure Models, IEEE Computer Graphics and Applications, Vol.7, No 6, pp.28-38

Arnaldi B., Dumont G., Hégron G., Magnenat-Thalmann N., Thalmann D. (1989) Animation Control with Dynamics in: State-of-the-Art in Computer Animation, Springer, Tokyo, pp.113-124

Badler NI (1989) Artificial Intelligence, Natural Language, and Simulation for Human Animation, in: Magnenat-Thalmann N, Thalmann D (Eds) State-of.the-Art in Computer Animation, Springer, Tokyo, pp. 19-32

Badler NI and Morris MA (1982) Modelling Flexible Articulated Objects, Proc. Computer Graphics '82, Online Conf., pp.305-314.

Badler NI and Smoliar SW (1979) Digital Representation of Human Movement, ACM Computing Surveys, March issue, pp.19-38.Baecker R (1969) Picture-driven Animation, Proc. AFIPS Spring Joint Computer Conf., Vol.34, pp.273-288.

Badler NI et al. (1986) Multi-Dimensional Input Techniques and Articulated Figure Positioning by Multiple Constraints, 1986 Workshop on Interactive 3D Graphics, Chapel Hill, North Carolina

Badler NI, Korein JD, Korein JU, Radack GM and Brotman LS (1985) Positioning and Animating Figures in a Task-oriented Environment, The Visual Computer, Vol.1, No4, pp.212-220.

Baraff D (1989) Analytical methods for Dynamic Simulation of Non-Penetrating Rigid Bodies, Proc. SIGGRAPH '89, Computer Graphics, Vol. 23, No3, pp.223-232

Barr AH (1984) Global and local deformations of solid primitives. Proc. SIGGRAPH '84, Computer Graphics 18(3):21-30

Barzel R, Barr AH (1988) A Modeling System Based on Dynamic Constraints, Proc. SIGGRAPH '88, Computer Graphics, Vol.22, No4, pp.179-188

Benesh R and Benesh J (1956) An Introduction to benesh Dance Notation, A. and C. Black, London

Blum R (1979) Representing Three-dimensional Objects in Your Computer, Byte, May 1979, pp.14-29

Bohm J (1987) A comparison of different contact algorithms with applications, Comp. Structures, Vol 26 No 1-2 pp 207-221

Boulic R, Magnenat-Thalmann N, Thalmann D (1990) Human Free-Walking Model for a Real-time Interactive Design of Gaits, Computer Animation '90, Springer-Verlag, Tokyo

Breen D, Getto P, Apodaca A, Schmidt D, Sarachan B (1987) The Clockworks; An Object-Oriented Computer Animation System, Proc Eurographics '87, North Holland, pp.275-282.

Breen DE (1989) Choreographing Goal-Oriented Motion Using Cost Functions, in: Magnenat-Thalmann N, Thalmann D (Eds) State-of.the-Art in Computer Animation, Springer, Tokyo, pp. 141-152

Breen DE, Wozny MJ (1989) Message-based Choreography for Computer Animation, in: Magnenat-Thalmann N, Thalmann D (Eds) State-of.the-Art in Computer Animation, Springer, Tokyo, pp. 69-82

Brooks RA (1983) Planning Collision-Free Motions for Pick-and-Place Operations, International Journal of Robotics, Vol.2, No4, pp.19-26
Brotman LS, Netravali AN (1988) Motion Interpolation by Optimal Control, Proc. SIGGRAPH '88, Computer Graphics, Vol.22, No4, pp.179-188
Bruderlin A, Calvert TW (1989) Goal Directed, Dynamic Animation of Human Walking, Proc. SIGGRAPH '89, Computer Graphics, Vol. 23, No3
Calvert TW and Chapman J (1978) Notation of Movement with Computer Assistance, Proc. ACM Annual Conf., Vol.2, 1978, pp.731-736
Catmull E (1972) A System for Computed-generated movies, Proc. ACM Annual Conference, pp.422-431.
Chadwick J, Haumann DR, Parent RE (1989) Layered Construction for Deformable Animated Characters, Proc. SIGGRAPH '89, Computer Graphics, Vol. 23, No3, pp.234-243
Cohen MF (1989) Gracefulness and Style in Motion Control, Proc. Mechanics, Control and Animation of Articulated Figures, MIT (to be published in a book by Morgan publ., USA)
Csuri C, Hackathorn R, Parent R, Carlson W and Howard M (1979) Towards an interactive high visual complexity animation system, Computer Graphics, Vol.13, No2, pp. 289-299.
Drewery K, Tsotsos J (1986) Goal Directed Animation using English Motion Commands, Proc. Graphics Interface '86, pp.131-135
Ekman P and Friesen W (1978) Facial Action Coding System, Consulting Psychologists Press, Palo Alto.
Eshkol N and Wachmann A (1958) Movement Notation, Weidenfeld and Nicolson, London
Featherstone R (1983) Position and Velocity Transformations Between Robot End-Effector Coordinates and Joint Angles, Intern. Journal of Robotics Research, Vol.2, No2, pp.35-45.
Forsey D, Wilhelms J (1988) Techniques for Interactive Manipulation of Articulated Bodies Using Dynamics Analysis, Proc. Graphics Interface '88, pp.8-15
Girard M (1987) Interactive Design of 3D Computer-animated Legged Animal Motion, IEEE Computer Graphics and Applications, Vol.7, No 6, pp.39-51
Girard M (1989) Constrained Optimization of Articulated Animal Movement in Computer Animation, Proc. Mechanics, Control and Animation of Articulated Figures, MIT (to be published in a book by Morgan publ., USA)
Girard M and Maciejewski AA (1985) Computational Modeling for Computer Generation of Legged Figures, Proc. SIGGRAPH '85, Computer Graphics, Vol. 19, No3, pp.263-270
Gourret JP, Magnenat-Thalmann N, Thalmann D (1989) Simulation of Object and Human Skin Deformations in a Grasping Task, Proc. SIGGRAPH '89, Computer Graphics, Vol. 23, No 3, pp. 21-30
Guenter B (1989) A System for Simulating Human Facial Expression, in: Magnenat-Thalmann N, Thalmann D (Eds) State-of.the-Art in Computer Animation, Springer, Tokyo, pp. 191-202
Guenter B (1989) A System for Simulating Human Facial Expression, in: Magnenat-Thalmann N, Thalmann D (Eds) State-of.the-Art in Computer Animation, Springer, Tokyo, pp. 191-202
Gurfinkel VS and Fomin SV (1974) Biomechanical Principles of Constructing Artificial walking Systems, in: Theory and Practice of Robots and Manipulators, Vol.1, Springer-Verlag, NY, pp.133-141
Hahn JK (1988) Realistic Animation of Rigid Bodies, Proc. SIGGRAPH '88, Computer Graphics, Vol.22, No 4, pp.299-308
Haumann DR (1987) Modeling the Physical Behavior of Flexible Objects, SIGGRAPH '87 Course Notes on Topics in Physically Based Modeling
Haumann DR, Parent RE (1988) The Behavioral Test-bed: Obtaining Complex Behavior from Simple Rules, The Visual Computer, Vol.4, No 6, pp.332-347.
Hemami H and Farnsworth RL (1977) Postural and Gait Stability of a Planar Five Link Biped by Simulation, IEEE Trans. on Automatic Control, AC-22, No3, pp.452-458.
Hollerbach JM (1980) A Recursive Lagrangian Formulation of Manipulator Dynamics and a Comparative Study of Dynamics Formulation Complexity, IEEE Trans. on Systems, Man, and Cybernetics, Vol. SMC-10, No11, pp.730-736
Hollerbach JM, Sahar G (1983) Wrist-Partitioned, Inverse Kinematic Accelerations and Manipulator Dynamics, Intern. Journal of Robotics Research, Vol.2, No4, pp.61-76.
Hutchinson A (1970) Labanotation, Theatre Books, NY
Inman VT, Ralston HJ and Todd F (1981) Human Walking, Baltimore, Williams and Wilkins
Isaacs PM and Cohen MF (1987) Controlling Dynamic Simulation with Kinematic Constraints, Bahvior Functions and Inverse Dynamics, Proc. SIGGRAPH'87, Computer Graphics, Vol.21, No4, pp.215-224
Isaacs PM, Cohen MF (1988) Mixed Methods for Complex Kinematic Constraints in Dynamic Figure Animation, The Visual Computer, Vol.4, No6, pp.296-305
Kahn ME (1969) The Near-Minimum-Time Control of Open-Loop Articulated Kinematic Chains, Stanford Artificial Intelligence project, AIM-106

Kajiya JT and Kay TL (1989) Rendering Fur with Three Dimensional Textures, Proc. SIGGRAPH '89, Computer Graphics, Vol.23, No3), pp. 271-280.
Komatsu K (1988) Human Skin Model Capable of Natural Shape Variation, The Visual Computer, Vol.3, No5, pp.265-271
Korein J, Badler NI (1982) Techniques for Generating the Goal-directed Motion of Articulated Structures, IEEE Computer Graphics and Applications, Vol.2, No9, pp.71-81
Lafleur B, Magnenat-Thalmann N, Thalmann D (1990) Collision Detection in Cloth Animation, Technical Report, MIRALab, University of Geneva
Lamoreux LW (1971) Kinematic Measurements in the Study of Human Walking, Bulletin of Prosthetics Research, Vol.BPR 10, No15
Leblanc A, Thalmann D (1990) Rendering Antialiased Hair Using an Alpha-Blending Method, Technical Report, Computer Graphics Lab, Swiss Federal Institute of Technology
Lee MW, Kunii TL (1989) Animation Design: A database-Oriented Animation Design Method with a Video Image Analysis Capability, in: Magnenat-Thalmann N, Thalmann D (Eds) State-of.the-Art in Computer Animation, Springer, Tokyo, pp. 97-112
Lethebridge TC and Ware C (1989) A Simple Heuristically-based Method for Expressive Stimulus-response Animation, Computers and Graphics, Vol.13, No3, pp.297-303
Low KH, Dubey RN (1986) A Comparative Study of Generalized Coordinates for Solving the Inverse-Kinematics Problem of 6R Robot Manipulator, Intern. Journal of Robotics Research, Vol.5, No4, pp.69-88.
Lozano-Perez T and Wesley MA (1979) An Algorithm for Planning Collision-Free Paths Among Polyhedral Obstacles, Comm.ACM, Vol.22, No10, pp. 560-570.
Luh JYS, Walker MW and Paul RPC (1980) On-line Computational Scheme for Mechanical Manipulators, Journal of Dynamic Systems, Measurement and Control, Vol.102, pp.103-110.
Maciejewski AA and Klein CA (1985) Obstacle Avoidance for Kinematics Redundant Manipulators in Dynamically Varying Environments, Intern. Journ. of Robotics Research, Fall
Magnenat-Thalmann N, Laperrière R and Thalmann D (1988) Joint-dependent Local Deformations for Hand Animation and Object Grasping, Proc. Graphics Interface '88
Magnenat-Thalmann N, Minh HT, de Angelis M, Thalmann D (1989) Design, Transformation and Animation of Human Faces, The Visual Computer, Vol.5, No3, pp.32-39
Magnenat-Thalmann N, Primeau E, Thalmann D (1988b) Abstract Muscle Action Procedures for Human Face Animation, The Visual Computer, Vol.3, No5
Magnenat-Thalmann N, Thalmann D (1987) The direction of synthetic actors in the film Rendez-vous à Montréal. IEEE Computer Graphics and Applications 7(12), pp.9-19.
McGhee and Iswandhi GI (1979) Adaptive Locomotion of a Multilegged Robot over Rough Terrain, IEEE Trans. Systems, Man and Cybernetics, April, pp.176-182
McMahon T (1984) Mechanics of Locomotion, Intern. Journ. of Robotics Research, Vol.3, No2, pp.4-28.
Miller G (1988b) The Motion Dynamics of Snakes and Worms, Proc. SIGGRAPH '88, Computer Graphics, Vol.22, No4, pp.169-173
Miller GSP (1988) From Wire-Frame to Furry Animals, Proc. Graphics Interface 1988, pp. 138-146.
Miura H and Shimoyama I (1984) Dynymic Walk of a Biped, International Journal of Robotics, Vol.3, No2, pp.60-74.
Moore M and Wilhelms J (1988) Collision Detection and Response for Computer Animation, Proc. SIGGRAPH '88, Computer Graphics, Vol. 22, No 4, pp.289-298.Nahas M, Huitric H, Saintourens M (1987) Animation of a B-spline figure, The Visual Computer, Vol.3, No5,pp.272-276.
Murray MP, Drought AB and Kory RC (1964) Walking Patterns of Normal Men, Journal of Bone Joint Surgery, Vol.46A, No2, pp.335-360
Orin D, McGhee R, Vukobratovic M and Hartoch G (1979) Kinematic and Kinetic Analysis of Open-Chain Linkages Utilizing Newton-Euler methods, Mathematical Biosciences, Vol.31, pp.107-130.
Parke FI (1982) Parameterized Models for Facial Animation, IEEE Computer Graphics and Applications, Vol.2, No 9, pp.61-68
Pearce A, Wyvill B, Wyvill G and Hill D (1986) Speech and expression: a Computer Solution to Face Animation, Proc. Graphics Interface '86, pp.136-140.
Platt JC, Barr AH (1988) Constraint method for flexible models, Proc.SIGGRAPH '88, pp 279-288
Platt S, Badler N (1981) Animating Facial Expressions, Proc. SIGGRAPH '81, pp.245-252.
Popplestone RJ, Ambler AP and Bellos IM (1980) An Interpreter for a Language for Describing Assemblies, Artificial Intelligence, Vol.14, pp.79-107
Renault O, Magnenat-Thalmann N, Thalmann D (1990) A Vision-Based Approach to Behavioural Animation, Visualization and Computer Animation Journal, John Wiley, Vol,1, No1 (July 1990)
Reynolds C (1987) Flocks, Herds, and Schools: A Distributed Behavioral Model, Proc.SIGGRAPH '87, Computer Graphics, Vol.21, No4, pp.25-34 (also published in: Proc. Computer Animation CG 87, Online, pp.71-87)

Reynolds CW (1982) Computer Animation with Scripts and Actors, Proc. SIGGRAPH'82, pp.289-296.
Saunders JB, Inman VT and Eberhart (1953) The Major Determinants in Normal and Pathological Gait, Journal of Bone Joint Surgery, Vol.35A, pp.543-558
Schröder P, Zeltzer D (1988) Pathplanning inside Bolio, in: D.Thalmann (Ed.) Synthetic Actors: The Impact of Artificial Intelligence and Robotics on Animation, Course Notes SIGGRAPH '88, pp.194-207.
Sederberg TW, Parry SR (1986) Free-form deformation of solid geometric models. Proc. SIGGRAPH '86, Computer Graphics, Vol.20, No4, pp.151-160
Smith AR (1983) Digital Filmmaking, Abacus, Vol.1, No1, pp.28-45
Stepanenko Y and Vukobratovic M (1976) Dynamics of Articulated Open Chain Active Mechanisms, Mathematical Biosciences, Vol.28, pp.137-170.
Terzopoulos D, Fleischer K (1988) Deformable Models, The Visual Computer, Vol.4, No6, pp.306-331
Terzopoulos D, Platt J, Barr A, Fleischer K (1987) Elastically Deformable Models, Proc.SIGGRAPH'87, Computer Graphics, Vol 21 No 4, pp 205-214
Uicker JJ (1965) On the Dynamic Analysis of Spatial Linkages Using 4x4 Matrices, Ph.D Dissertation, Northwestern University, Evanston, Illinois
Watanabe Y and Suenaga Y (1989) Drawing Human Hair Using Wisp Model, Proc. Computer Graphics International, Springer, Tokyo, pp. 691-700.
Waters K (1987) A Muscle Model for Animating Three-Dimensional Facial Expression, Proc. SIGGRAPH '87, Vol.21, No4, pp.17-24.
Weil J (1986) The Synthesis of Cloth Objects, Proc. SIGGRAPH '86, Computer Graphics, Vol.20, No.4, pp.49-54
Wilhelms J (1987) Using Dynamic Analysis for Realistic Animation of Articulated Bodies, IEEE Computer Graphics and Applications, Vol.7, No 6, pp.12-27
Wilhelms J and Barsky B (1985) Using Dynamic Analysis to Animate Articulated Bodies such as Humans and Robots, in: N.Magnenat-Thalmann and D.Thalmann (Eds) Computer-generated Images, Springer, pp.209-229.
Witkin A, Fleischer K, Barr A (1987) Energy Constraints on Parameterized Models, Proc. SIGGRAPH'87, Computer Graphics, Vol.21, No4, pp.225-232
Witkin A, Kass M (1988) Spacetime Constraints, Proc. SIGGRAPH '88, Computer Graphics, Vol.22, No4, pp.159-168
Wyvill B, Wyvill G (1989) Field functions for iso-surfaces, The Visual Computer, Vol.5, No3
Zeltzer D (1982) Motor Control Techniques for Figure Animation, IEEE Computer Graphics and Applications, Vol.2, No9, pp.53-59.

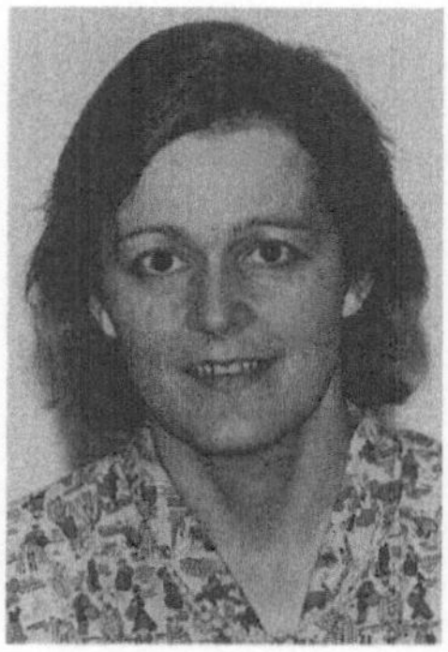

Nadia Magnenat Thalmann is currently full Professor of Computer Science at the University of Geneva, Switzerland. A former member of the Council of Science and Technology of the Government of Quebec and of the Council of Science and Technology of the Canadian Broadcasting Corporation, she also has served on a variety of government advisory boards and program committees. She has received several awards, including the 1985 Communications Award from the Government of Quebec. In May 1987, she was nominated woman of the year in sciences by the Montreal community. Dr. Magnenat Thalmann received a BS in psychology, an MS in biochemistry, and a Ph.D in quantum chemistry and computer graphics from the University of Geneva. Her previous appointments include the University Laval in Quebec, the Graduate Business school of the University of Montreal in Canada. She has written and edited several books and research papers in image synthesis and computer animation and was codirector of the computer-generated films *Dream Flight*, *Eglantine*, *Rendez-vous à Montréal* and *Galaxy Sweetheart*. She served as chairperson of Graphics Interface '85, CGI '88, Computer Animation '89 and Computer Animation '90.

address: MIRALab, CUI
University of Geneva
12 rue du Lac
CH 1207 Geneva, Switzerland
E-mail: thalmann@uni2a.unige.ch

Computer Graphics and Design Automation: Continued Synergy or a Parting of Ways?

Michael J. Wozny

1.0 INTRODUCTION

From its very beginning, computer graphics has had a significant influence on the evolution of engineering design automation. Ivan Sutherland's MIT thesis, "Sketchpad" in 1963 laid the foundation for interactively creating and manipulating line geometry on a computer generated graphical display. This capability lead to the interactive generation of engineering drawings, the first successful commercial venture in computer graphics. From a design point of view, the CAD system simply automated the human process of generating drawings, and only indirectly improved the process of design. Furthermore, the lines drawn on the screen had no associativity, no concept of a surface or volume. In effect, the computer graphics system was just a glorified plotting capability.

Both fields have evolved a long way from this early synergistic relationship. CAD (computer-aided design) geometry has influenced the geometry adopted in graphics systems. On the other hand graphics user interfaces have influenced design procedures.

There are two general views of design automation. One deals with the classical creative process of producing a unique artifact, the cowboy inventor. The other view holds that, since the artifact must ultimately be produced in a timely and cost-effective manner, then the design process must reach out and include input from all involved in the building and supporting processes, i.e., a join ownership.

The first view will continue to maintain a close synergy with computer graphics, but will be influenced more heavily by the cognitive and artificial intelligence research fields. The second view will move toward information modeling of the overall process.

This paper will address only a small portion of this very large area. First it will attempt to identify the general research trends in mechanical design automation. Then the discussion will focus on geometric issues and their effect on the graphics pipeline. Although user interfaces are an important element in design systems, they are not treated here.

2.0 TRENDS IN ENGINEERING DESIGN

Figure 2.1 classifies four key stages in the evolution of mechanical design for discrete batch manufacturing. The stages are drawn on a background curve which depicts the % total cost committed during the design phase. Two trends are apparent from the figure. The first is the trend toward systems which deal with early decision making in the conceptual and preliminary design stages. The second is the horizontal trend toward making available design, manufacturing and support information very early in the design process.

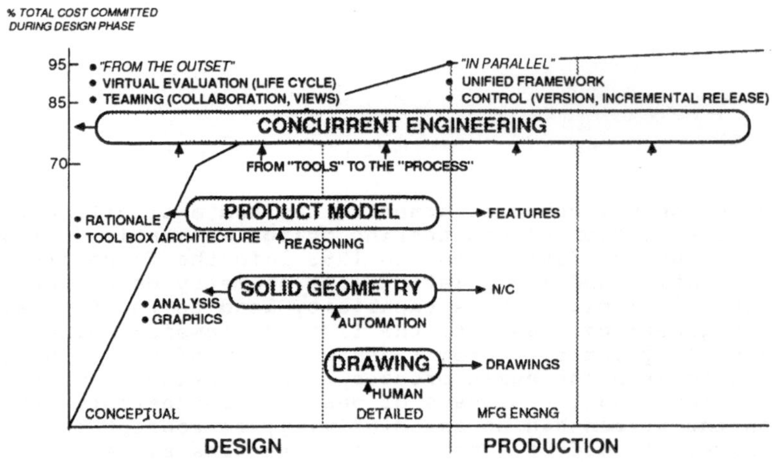

Fig. 2.1 Design Paradigms

2.1 Drawing

The first stage, called "drawing" was outlined above. It represents the human generation and interpretation of engineering drawings. Drawing systems were basically computer graphics systems with specialized software (models) for generating line drawings. As stated above these systems improved the creation of drawings but not necessarily the creation of artifacts.

2.2 Solid Geometric Modeling

The second stage is called "solid geometric modeling", which represented the continuing push toward automation. Since a solid model was a complete and unambiguous computer representation, it facilitated the automatic calculation of mass properties, the automatic generation of finite element meshes for analysis, and the automated planning of cutter paths for numerically controlled milling machines.

Solid modeling also facilitated the direct rendering of color shaded images. Although graphics systems have little need for solid models, per say, both graphics and CAD use free form surfaces extensively. The PHIGS+ (programmers hierarchical interactive graphics standard) standards effort adopted NURBS (non-uniform rational B-spline) surfaces as the standard free form surface representation for highly interactive 3D systems. NURBS surface geometry was extensively researched for the design of aircraft, because they provided a high degree of flexibility yet represented exact curves based on conic sections. Section 7.0 describes the interplay between CAD geometry and computer graphics architectures.

Solid modeling also lead to the concept of a master geometric model, from which projections could be taken to generate drawings. (One needs to be careful here, because drawings, honed to a high degree of conciseness over a hundred years of experience, contain entities which are non-exact projections.)

Unfortunately, a solid model is a very verbose representation. As a result, even simple design problems require large amounts of computer resources and computation time. It seems that the complexity of the design problem grows in proportion to the increase in computer power.

Although great strides have been made in research, the original notion of a fully automated environment is still very illusive and very optimistic. The complexity of the parts and processes preclude it. Thus the "automation" paradigm must be tempered with a "reasoning" paradigm. For example, CAD systems automated the drafting process and provided tools to create sophisticated geometry, but facilitated only indirectly the improved design decision-making necessary to create more cost-effective products. Since it is difficult to separate the process of designing the artifact from the process of manufacturing it, then better design decisions are made when relevant information is taken into account early in the product development cycle.

2.3 Product Model

Geometry is only one aspect of the artifact definition. Knowing how to create geometry does not imply knowing how to create better designs products. This lead to the concept of a complete product model, which includes not only geometry but material properties, tolerance information, features, and any information needed to design and produce the product. The evolving world data transfer standard PDES/STEP (Product Description Exchange Specification) attempts to capture this information.

The term "features" means a "higher level" encapsulation of information about a part that is useful in some sense. Typical form features are pockets, bosses, and ribs. Features facilitate reasoning about the design by allowing the design to be "evaluated" against downstream requirements, like manufacturability or inspectibility. Features also allow design intent to be captured, thus providing a basis for making design changes downstream. In its broadest sense, features not only encapsulate information about geometric form, but also behavior or function. One can see from Fig. 2.1 that at each stage, the communication between design and manufacturing takes place at a higher cognitive level.

2.4 Concurrent Engineering.

The fourth stage attacks head on the global aspect of productivity, only implied in the other stages. Providing high productivity computer tools to a functional unit, like CAD drawing systems to the detailed design unit, increases the productivity of that individual unit, but may result in a marginal overall productivity increase when measured from the perspective of the overall enterprise; individual optimization of the local units does not imply global optimization of the totality of the units.

This realization has focused research attention on understanding and modeling the overall infrastructure, rather than providing more tools for individual units.

The major driver for concurrent engineering is reduced cycle time. It has two major components. The first involves the creation of a framework where requirements of all downstream processes can be focused at design time. This implies the need for improved decision-making tools for conceptual/preliminary design phases, and a balanced requirements definition across all elements of the product life cycle. It also underscores the need for group consensus building (each contributing group to the design has their own view of what is most important in the design) and facilitization of collaboration in critiquing designs, planning and executing modifications, and recording rationale. Computer graphics will certainly play an important role in this arena.

The second component, "designing in parallel" implies the need for a unified framework for representing product and process information, and a means for facilitating concurrency, such as synchronizing several (parallel) versions of the design or sub-design. This control facilitates the designing in "parallel" of both the product and all its related downstream processes (manufacturing and support).

The concept behind this design methodology is the creation of a "virtual" design (i.e., a computer representation) in a framework with hooks for rapid evaluation of performance, cost, quality, manufacturability and supportability, before any physical processes are committed. In effect concurrent engineering supports the broad concept of product realization.

3.0 COMPUTATIONAL MODELS OF THE DESIGN PROCESS

In order to address the infrastructure problem outlined above, one needs a model of the design process. Figure 3.1 illustrates an idealized computational model of the design process [1.].

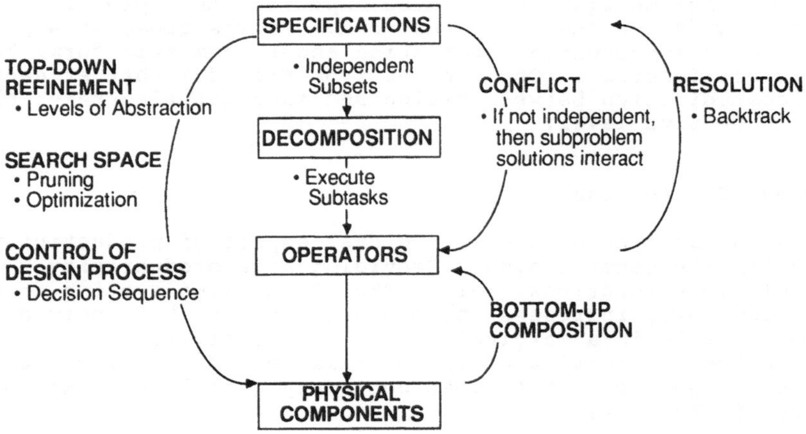

Fig. 3.1 Computational Models of the Design Process

3.1 Idealized Design Process

The objective of the design process is to map a set of specifications into a description of a physically realizable artifact. Given that the specifications represent completely the desired form (or behavior) of the artifact, they are first decomposed into independent (if possible) subsets. (A desired set of specifications is a minimal set that spans an informational space of all possible artifact behavior. See Suh [2].) Then each subproblem, corresponding to a specification subset, is solved generically. The specific design solution is determined by finding a suitable physical component(s) from the set of all possible physical realizations. The final step is to evaluate the interactions between the independent solutions and compose the subsolutions into a suitable, complete artifact. Researchers have studied various ramifications of this general structure.

3.2 Functional Specifications as Objects

Andersson [3] modeled functional specifications as objects in a object-oriented programming environment. Typical physically based functional (behavioral) descriptions include the "transformation", "amplification", and "transmission" of power and energy (human, mechanical linear/rotational, electrical,...), and velocity and displacement (angular, linear) from one constituent form to another. The variables transformed are governed by physical laws which become the constraint equations in the representation.

Using object-oriented and frame-based methodologies, one can, in principle, decompose automatically the functional requirements into a set of independent (if they exist) functional objects, and then find a design solution (an instance from a database of physical elements classified by function) for each functional object in the set. For example, rotational power may be "transmitted" by gears, chains or belts. This is the bottom-up composition. The final design is the collection of these decomposed design solutions. The approach depends on a strongly typed classification of functions, variables, and physical elements. Resolution (e.g., backtracking) methodologies to handle conflicts need to be developed.

3.3 Toolbox Architecture

The toolbox architecture is another emerging computational paradigm for the design process [4]. It provides increased flexibility to the designer by reducing the granularity of the tools. Instead of a single monolithic software system, the user is given a collection of bite-sized tools operating in a framework which allows varied tool sequencing. The designer's requests are posted on the blackboard, and the appropriate tool(s) volunteer to carry out the requested task. A planning function decomposes the tasks and establishes a proper sequence of tool invocations. (It can also resolve sequence conflicts.) The toolbox manager guarantees input/output compatibility of the tools in the sequence.

The advantage of this approach is flexibility, modularity, and extensibility: tools do not necessarily have to follow the same sequence, new tools can be easily added, and the architecture can support a distributed environment where specific tools may exist only on specific machines.

The above planning function can be generalized to a milestone setting goal structure followed by a scheduling/planning structure which generates the detailed sequence (i.e., the design plan) to advance to the next milestone. This approach can handle relatively unstructured design situations [5].

4.0 STATUS OF MECHANICAL CAD

Figure 4.1 depicts the current state of mechanical CAD systems. The shaded region in the figure represents existing, albeit incomplete, capabilities.

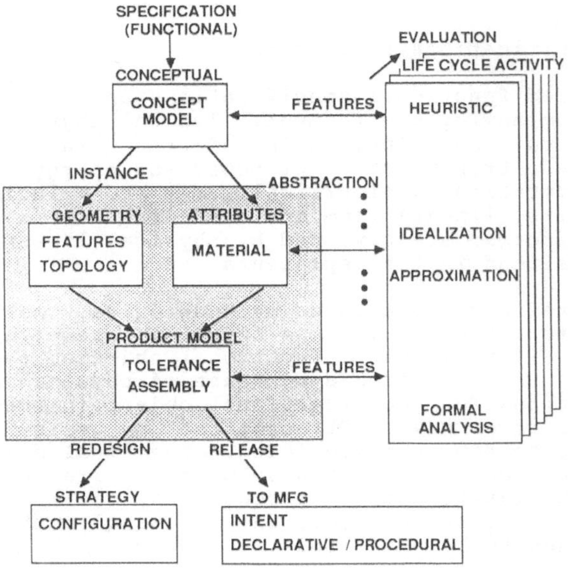

Fig. 4.1 Mechanical CAD

The boxes in white represent future needs involving: (1) the creation of conceptual (or configurational) models of the design which capture design intent, (2) an ability to model specifications, including functional specifications, in a way that they can be used in the design more directly, (3) an ability to evaluate (via features) the life cycle considerations of an evolving design, at all levels of abstraction, (4) an integrated evaluation capability of suitable life cycle (e.g., process) models, (5) an ability to map an instance of the conceptual model directly to the geometry/product model, (6) a redesign strategy that advises the designer on changes at the configuration level, and finally, (7) an ability to release to manufacturing the design intent along with the design.

5.0 EARLY IN THE DESIGN CYCLE

This section focuses on the geometric aspects in conceptual (or configuration) design. The goal is to create a skeleton of a part (configuration model) which captures the design intent, to evaluate that configuration against downstream criteria like manufacturability, and when satisfied, to move to a less abstract description (detailed model) by creating an instance of the skeleton (e.g., add finite volume geometry).

What information about the design should be captured and represented in the computer to satisfy the above requirements? A partial answer is given in the example (due to J. Dixon, University of Mass.) shown in Fig. 5.1.

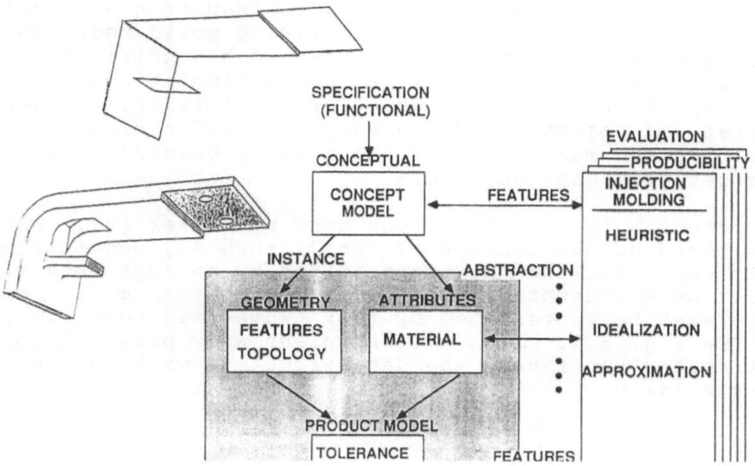

Fig. 5.1 Evaluation via Features

The essence of the part is contained in the walls (represented as planes) connected at joins (edges). The holes are represented by their centers. The tongue is needed to reference the offset portion on the wall. At this level of abstraction, the walls, joins, tongue, offset and holes are the "features" which encapsulate information about the part.

If the decision were made to injection mold this part, the designer would invoke the injection molding evaluation program, which would "evaluate", via heuristic rules, the manufacturability tradeoffs (cost, complexity, throughput,...etc.) of producing this part. The program would inform the designer that a window (change in topology) is needed so that a ram could be inserted when the tongue is molded. The need for the ram complicates the injection molding process and increases the cost. The injection molding evaluation, at this configurational stage of abstraction, is looking for gross topological and geometrical properties such as the amount and orientation of part detail in the direction of die closure. Thus useful manufacturability information can be obtained even at this gross level of geometric description.

6.0 GEOMETRY REQUIREMENTS

Let's look at the geometry requirements for the example in Section 5.0. First of all, the geometric representation must handle finite volume solids as well as zero volume edges and surfaces (e.g., walls). Geometric modelers based on non-manifold topology meet this requirement.

Non-manifold modelers provide a consistent topological base for the associativity of edges and faces in wireframe, surface, and solid representations. They also support the non-manifold conditions of two surfaces touching at a single point or along a curve, or two volumes sharing a face, or a wire edge in space touching a surface at a single point. (These conditions, producible via Boolean or gluing operations on manifold objects, be represented in existing solid modelers.) The non-manifold representation is closed under such conditions, in addition to handling such singularities and manipulations directly. Non-manifold representations have superior flexibility, can represent a larger variety of objects, and can support a wider class of applications than can manifold representations, however, usually at a cost of a larger size data structure.

The initial research in this field was done by Weiler [6]. His data structure is based on the concept of "use", such as, edge-use or face-use. To represent the two faces joined by an edge each side of each face must be represented, since each face may have its own "use". Thus the edge must be represented by four "edge-use" edges in the data structure. See Fig. 6.1. If a cutting plane were passed through the edge separating the two faces, the data structure will maintain correct associativity.

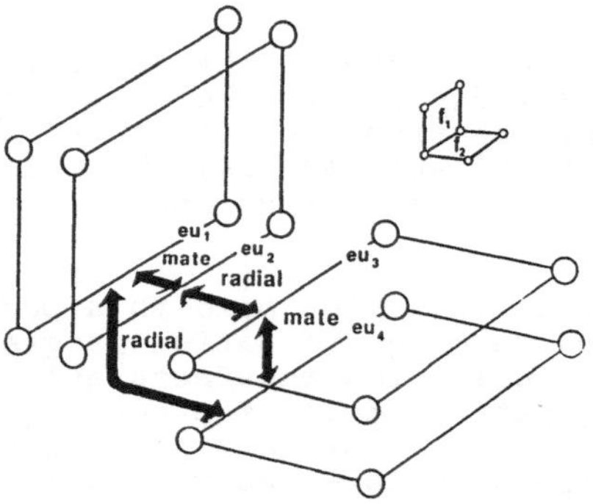

Fig. 6.1 Radial Edge Representation of Two Faces Joined Along a Common Edge

Subsequent research has concentrated on data structures, Boolean operations on non-manifold objects, non-manifold features, and extensions of the Euler-Poincare equations [7]. One prototype non-manifold modeler is NOODLES, developed at the Engineering Design Research Center at Carnegie Mellon University (F. Prinz).

The second geometry requirement is to "flesh out" a geometric instance of the conceptual representation. F. Prinz has developed an interesting approach to represent shape abstractly. Borrowing the notion of medial axis transform from image processing, the essence of the shape of a finite rectangular planar segment, for example, is captured by the locus of centers of circles that fill the plane, where the circles are tangent to at least two edges of the plane, as shown in Fig. 6.2.

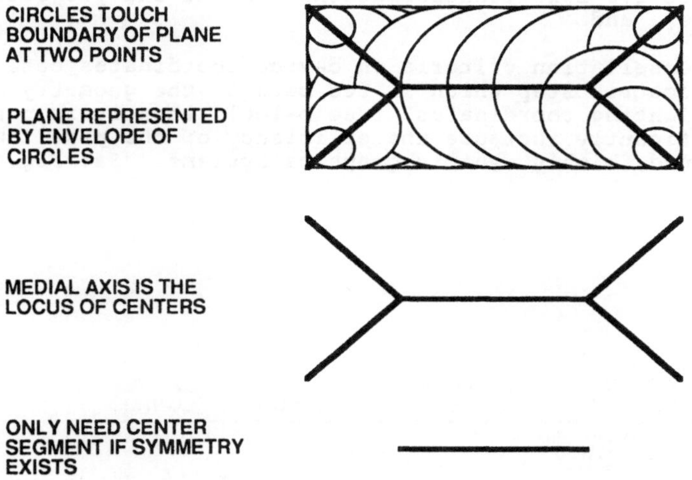
CIRCLES TOUCH BOUNDARY OF PLANE AT TWO POINTS
PLANE REPRESENTED BY ENVELOPE OF CIRCLES
MEDIAL AXIS IS THE LOCUS OF CENTERS
ONLY NEED CENTER SEGMENT IF SYMMETRY EXISTS

Fig. 6.2 Concept of Medial Axis

Symmetry reduces the abstract shape representation of the plane to a straight line segment. Conversely, given a straight line, one can generate the corresponding plane by extracting the envelope of all the circles with centers on the line, taking into account symmetry. In three dimensions the planes become rectangular boxes, the circles become spheres, and the lines (edges) representing shape become planar elements. A non-manifold representation is needed to characterize geometric shape abstractly.

7.0 GRAPHICS PIPELINE IMPLICATIONS

The adoption of non-uniform rational B-spline (NURBS) geometry in PHIGS+ was motivated in part by CAD requirements. NURBS geometry provides a high degree of flexibility in creating free form surfaces; however, existing graphics pipelines, based on polygonal geometry, are not very efficient in handling free form surfaces.

7.1 Lighting Coordinates

The basic problem lies in the need to do the lighting calculations in world coordinates (or in a coordinate system related by a rigid transformation to world coordinates), while the tessellation is done more appropriately in device coordinates (where the tessellation criteria makes more sense and only the control points are transformed and the criteria itself may be specified in device coordinates).

However, existing (polygonal oriented) graphics pipeline architectures require both operations to be done in world coordinates (lighting calculations are done on a tessellated surface). As a result, the 4x4 viewing transformations must handle lots of tessellant coordinates at roughly 28 FLOPS per point.

Recent research at RPI by Abi-Ezzi [8] has shown that if:

(1) the viewing transformation is partitioned into a (a) 3x4 rigid transformation (no angle distortion), and a (b) remaining perspective-like transformation (w-shear and projective divide), and

(2) the tessellation criteria in device coordinates determines an soparametric step which is fed back to the geometry definition in "lighting coordinates" (see below), then it is possible to significantly increase the efficiency of the pipeline for retained, highly dynamic graphics systems. See Fig. 7.1

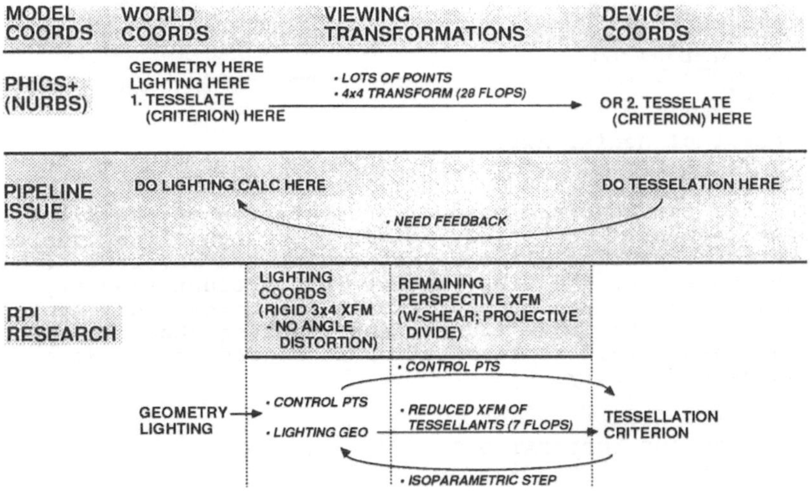

Fig. 7.1 Graphics Pipeline Issues

This partitioning allows the control points of the surface and the lighting calculations to be handled in an intermediate "lighting" coordinate system, i.e., after the 3x4 rigid transformation. The tessellation criterion in device coordinates requires only the control points and feeds back an isoparametric step to the lighting coordinates, where the tessellation can be performed, thus reducing the number of tessellants. At this point the tessellants need to be transformed only by the remaining reduced perspective transformation, namely 7 FLOPS.

7.2 Computing Surface Normals

The lighting calculations for free form surface primitives are very expensive, in part due to the high cost of computing surface normals. Approximation methods for the surface normal function, such as Hermite patches, can reduce the computational cost, but generally produce unacceptable results. See Fig. 7.2

Bohn [9] has developed a means for rapidly computing the unit normal at discrete points across a parametric NURBS surface. The basic concept is to simplify the normal equation and then use only the appropriate portion (in effect, ignore the rational component of the normal).

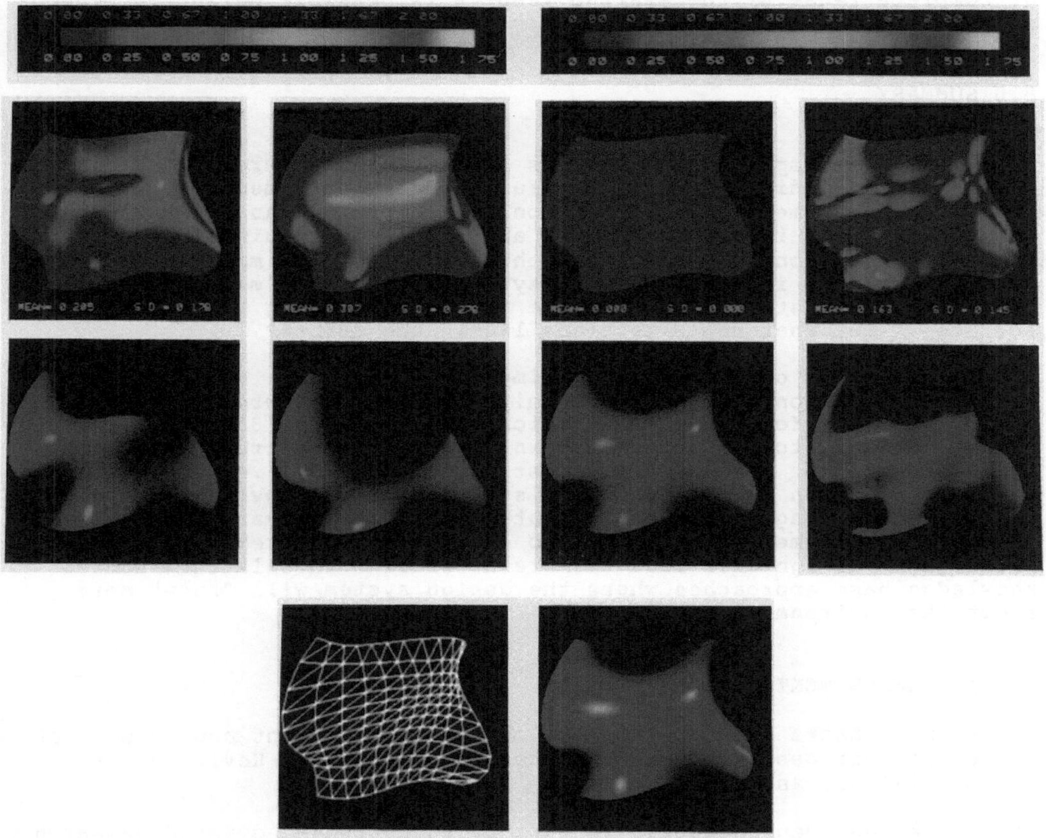

Fig. 7.2 Comparison of normal approximations for a rational bicubic surface: The images in the top row show the resulting color error distribution for the corresponding approximation image below. Second row, from left to right; single biquintic Hermite normal approximation, single bicubic Hermite normal approximation, scaled surface normal, and 4x4 grid of bicubic Hermite normal approximations. The bottom row shows the correct image.

The resulting simplified normal vector is called the "scaled surface normal". The scaled surface normal has the advantage of being a non-rational function that contains the directional information of the surface normal, regardless of whether the surface is rational or non-rational. Given a surface of degree n, the polynomials for the scaled surface normal have degrees 2n-1, and 3n-1 for non-rational and rational surfaces, respectively. The surface normal can now be evaluated across the surface without having to explicitly perform the cross-product, thus speeding up the per point evaluation time.

When combined with a look-up table for normalization, this method for computing the unit normal provides savings of between 30% and 40% (depending on the degree of the polynomial) over current techniques. The savings are even higher (40% to 60%) if the cross-product that defines the normal is precomputed.

This technique works especially well in retained systems where partial or complete reuse of the startup results is possible during subsequent renderings.

8.0 SUMMARY

The growth of computer graphics has always been nurtured by applications. This is certainly true in computer aided design, where the need for geometry representation and rendering was a mutual goal. This was evident in line drawings, and is now continuing in free form surface definition. Each step in this evolution has motivated profound changes in both graphics systems and design methodology. Graphics is now struggling with the issue of handling free form surfaces. But what new directions lie in the future?

An investigation of design trends implies a need for: (1) representing design information at a higher cognitive level, (2) providing an effective means for group interaction and dynamics, (3) allowing design entities to be represented in richer data environments so that the design can be evaluated while still in a fluid (i.e., parameters and configuration not nailed down) state, and (4) providing methods for characterizing configuration rather than define variability only in terms of parameters. It is also clear that the "reasoning" paradigm in design will lead to more artificial intelligence and knowledge base approaches where the design system will "know" more about its environment.

9.0 ACKNOWLEDGMENTS

The author thanks his students and colleagues (present and former) at the Rensselaer Design Research Center in particular, Kevin Weiler, Salim Abi-Ezzi, and Jon Bohn.

This work has been sponsored in part by the Defense Advanced Research Projects Agency (DARPA), under contract No. MDA 972-88-C-0047 for DARPA Initiative in Concurrent Engineering (DICE), the National Science Foundation Grant No. DDM-8914172, and the RDRC Industrial Associates Program.

Any opinions, findings, and conclusions or recommendations expressed in this publication are those of the author and do not necessarily reflect the views of DARPA, the National Science Foundation, or any of the industrial sponsors.

10.0 REFERENCES

1. Nevill, G.E., Jr., "Computational Models of Design Processes," in Design Theory '88, Newsome, Spillers, and Finger, eds., Springer-Verlag, 1989.

2. Suh, N.P., The Principles of Design, Oxford University Press, 1990.

3. Andersson, K., Artificial Intelligence in Computer-Aided Design, TRITA-MAK 1989:1, ISSN 1100-5335, Licentiate Thesis, Department of Mechanical Design, The Royal Institute of Technology, Stockholm, Sweden, 1989.

4. Daniell, J.D., "An Object Oriented Approach to CAD Tool Control," Research Report No. CMUCAD-89-37, Department of Electrical and Computer Engineering, Carnegie-Mellon Univerity, Pittsburgh, April, 1989.

5. Tong, C., "Toward an Engineering Science of Knowledge-Based Design," AI in Engineering, 2, 1987.

6. Weiler, K.J., "Topological Structures for Geometric Modeling," PhD Thesis, Rensselaer Design Reearch Center Report TR-86032, Troy, NY, August, 1986, (also PhD Thesis).

7. Kawabe, S., Shimada, K., and Masuda, H., "A Framework for 3D Modeling: Constraint-Based Description and Non-Manifold Geometric Modeling, presented at 2nd Toyota Conference, Aichi-ken, Japan, October 1988.

8. Abi-Ezzi, S., "The Graphical Processing of NURBS in a Highly Dynamic Environment," Rensselaer Design Research Center Report TR-89001, Troy, NY, May 1989, (also PhD Thesis)

9. Bohn, J.H., "Computing the Unit Normal for Non-Uniform Reational B-Spline Surfaces," Rensselaer Design Research Center Report TR-89061, Troy, NY, December 1989, (also MS Thesis)

Dr. Michael J. Wozny is a professor of two academic departments at Rensselaer Polytechnic Institute (Electrical, Computer and Systems Engineering; and Computer Science), and the director of the Rensselaer Design Research Center (formerly the Center for Interactive Computer Graphics).

The research center, which Dr. Wozny founded in 1977 with support from the National Science Foundation University-Industry Cooperative Research Centers program, maintains an extensive industry sponsored research program in the areas of computer graphics, CAD/CAM, CAE, data engineering and concurrent engineering.

Dr. Wozny was on leave, from 1986 to 1988, from Rensselaer to the National Science Foundation where he was Division Director, for the Design, Manufacturing, and Computer-Integrated Division.

At RPI, Dr. Wozny is Professor of Electrical, Computer and Systems Engineering; Professor of Computer Science; and Director of the Rensselaer Design Research Center, which he founded in 1977. The Center, established as an NSF University-Industry Center, maintains an extensive industry sponsored research program in the areas of graphics, CAD/CAM, and data engineering.

Dr. Wozny received his PhD degree from the University of Arizona in 1965. His previous appointments include Purdue University, Oakland University, GM Research Labs, NASA Electronics Research Center and NSF.

His research interests are in CAD/CAM, engineering design, computer graphics, and dynamics systems.

Dr. Wozny has served on a variety of government advisory boards and review panels, including Office of Technology Assessment, NSF, DoD, and the National Academy of Sciences. He was Chairman of the National Academy panel which prepared a briefing document for the Presidential Science Advisor, "Research Opportunities for Design and Manufacturing" (1983). This report ultimately lead to the establishment of the Engineering Research Centers program at NSF. He has also participated in numerous NSF, NAS/NAE, ASME, IDA/DoD, and IFIP workshops to set research agendas in design, manufacturing, and computer-related areas.

He is on the editorial board of Visual Computer, CAD/CIM Alert, Workstation Alert, and Marquis Who's Who in Computer Graphics.

He was the founding Editor-in-Chief of IEEE Computer Graphics and Applications (1981-85), and on the editorial board of IEEE Proceedings (1985-88).

Dr. Wozny was a member of the IEEE Computer Society Publications Board (1980-84) and a former Director of National Computer Graphics Association (1983). He sits on the board of directors of several companies, as well as on various industrial technical advisory boards.

Dr. Wozny is the recipient of the IEEE Centennial Medal (1984), the IEEE Computer Society Outstanding Contribution Award (1985), and the National Computer Graphics Association Academic Award (1988).

Address: mwozny@rdrc.rpi.edu, Rensselaer Design Research Center, CII7015, Rensselaer Polytechnic Institute, Troy, NY, 12180-3590, USA.

Virtual Reality User Interface: Tools and Techniques

Mark Green

Abstract

Throughout the 1980's user interface design has been dominated by the desk top metaphor. This metaphor has provided a good basis for the design of user interfaces that are based on document processing. There are a wide range of user interfaces that are not covered by this metaphor. One area is sophisticated three dimensional applications, such as scientific visualization and remote manipulation. Recent hardware advances, such as head-mounted displays and the DataGlove, have suggested new approaches to these applications. This approach to user interface design has been called virtual reality, since it places the user in a three dimensional environment that can be directly manipulated. This paper describes a metaphor and a set of software tools that can be used in the design and implementation of virtual reality user interfaces. A logical model of virtual reality systems is presented and used to develop a taxonomy of virtual reality application. This taxonomy provides the requirements for the software tools that will be required to effectively produce virtual reality user interfaces.

Keywords: virtual reality, user interfaces, three dimensional graphics

1. Introduction

Throughout the 1980's user interface design has been dominated by the desk top metaphor. This metaphor views the display screen as the top of a desk, and the windows on the screen as paper documents. A mouse can be used to move the focus of attention from one document (window) to another, but at any point in time the user is interacting with only one document. This metaphor has been combined with direct manipulation to produce a large number of good user interfaces for office and programming tasks. These user interfaces are orders of magnitude better than the command line interfaces that dominated user interface design before the desk top metaphor was popular.

While the desk top metaphor is well suited to certain types of applications, there are a number of applications where its application is not appropriate. In general, the desk top metaphor fits applications that can be viewed as manipulating paper documents. If the application cannot be viewed as document manipulation, then this metaphor usually doesn't work. A good example of such an application area is scientific computing. A large number of scientific computations involve simulating or modeling phenomena that are distributed in time and space. These computations are based on two or three dimensional grids, with values at the grid points computed at discrete points in time. These computations produce large volumes of data, and the challenge facing us (in the graphics and user interface domains) is visualizing this data and interacting with the computations. The effective visualization of this data requires dynamic three dimensional displays.

Other applications that don't fit into the desk top metaphor are described in section 4. All of these applications consist of a three dimensional environment that the user wants to manipulate in some way. These manipulation may be as simple as moving about in the environment, or they could be as complicated as controlling a sophisticated physical computation or an external process (such as a nuclear reactor or a remote manipulator). The production of user interfaces for this type of application has largely been ignored by the graphics and user interface community. There are no well known metaphors or design strategies that can be used to aid the designer of these user interfaces. In addition, the tools that have been developed to assist in the production of user interfaces (such as UIMS's) don't provide adequate support for them.

The desk top metaphor is based on a workstation equipped with a bit-mapped display, a keyboard, and a mouse. The basic ideas behind this metaphor were developed in the 1960's (Engelbart 1968) but it didn't become popular until the appropriate hardware was available at a reasonable cost. Similarly, the development of good metaphors and software tools for sophisticated three dimensional applications will depend upon the availability of appropriate hardware. Over the past few years a number of new devices have become readily available that will form the basis for these user interfaces. These devices include the DataGlove and head mounted displays. The DataGlove consists of two devices, which are a Polhemus digitizer, and a instrumented glove. The Polhemus digitizer determines the position and orientation of the user's hand. The glove is instrumented with fiber-optics that measure the joint angles of the two proximal joints of each finger and the thumb. A head mounted display provides separate images for each of the user's eyes, thus giving him or her a natural stereo view of a three dimensional environment. The combination of these two devices allow us to place the user in a simulated three dimensional environment, which is called a virtual reality.

This paper discusses the design of a particular style of user interface that has been called artificial reality, virtual reality, or cyberspace. The basic idea behind this type of user interface is to place the user in a three dimensional environment that can be directly manipulated by physical gestures. In this paper we call this style of user interface a virtual reality user interface. In this paper we also present a metaphor, called artificial reality, that can be used in the design virtual reality user interfaces. This metaphor is based on designing a micro-world with a consistent set of behavior rules and user manipulations. This metaphor can be used in the design of both two dimensional and three dimensional user interfaces. There is a close relationship between this metaphor and virtual reality user interfaces, therefore, we feel that it is an appropriate metaphor for them. The artificial reality metaphor is described in section two of this paper. The third section of this paper presents a model of virtual reality user interfaces, and the following section presents a taxonomy of virtual reality applications. The model and the taxonomy provide the motivation for the software tools that are described in section 5.

2. The Artificial Reality Metaphor

In order to develop an intuitive understanding of the artificial reality metaphor, consider a fluid dynamics model of a water body, such as a swimming pool or lake. A three dimensional representation must be used to visualize this model. Currently this is done by producing either a wire frame or a smooth shaded perspective image of the flow under study. Unfortunately, this type of image only shows part of the model, and usually leaves significant parts of it hidden. Since fluid flow is a dynamic phenomena, motion must be part of any display technique used for it. This implies that we must be able to quickly generate the images and present the user with an animation of the flow. On top of this the flow is governed by the boundary conditions for the model and any external interactions with the flow. A user of this simulation should be able to change the boundary conditions and instantaneously view the changes in the flow. Similarly, he or she should be able to slap the water and see how the flow changes.

The user wants to interact with a three dimensional phenomena, but we only have two dimensional displays, therefore, hardware is not the solution. With software we can give the illusion of a three dimensional environment by placing the user in the model of the fluid flow. In other words, we explicitly model the user, in the same coordinate space as the model. The image on the screen is from the user's perspective, and he or she is free to move around the model in order to investigate different aspects of it. This feeling of being part of the model can be augmented by using either a head mounted display or video projection. Both of these display technologies fill the user's visual field of view, totally immersing the user in the image (Gibson 1979) In order to interact with the model a DataGlove (Zimmerman 1987) or similar device that senses the position and orientation of the hands can be used. In this way the user can directly use his or her hands to sculpt out the path the fluid follows, apply forces to the flow, or move obstacles into its path. This type of display and manipulation are characteristic of virtual reality user interfaces.

The artificial reality metaphor is based on the user's everyday experience in a three dimensional world. When we want to investigate an object in the real world we normally view the object from different positions either by walking around it, or by picking it up and rotating it in our hands. Similarly, everyday manipulations are normally performed with our hands. When we want to put two things together we pick them up with our hands and push them together (we don't select a combine command from a menu). A user interface based on the artificial reality metaphor tries to conform as closely as possible to the types of manipulations we would perform in an everyday world. The user interface provides a simulation of a micro world (the application), that the user interacts with in a natural way. The term artificial reality implies that we have placed a small part of the real world inside the user interface. This should not be confused with artificial intelligence. The user interface does not need to be intelligent, it only needs to provide a consistent simulation of a particular phenomena.

An artificial reality user interface has three main components, which are: a model, a visualization, and a set of manipulations. The model component represents the microworld corresponding to the application. This includes the geometry of the objects in the application, and their behavior. In the fluid dynamics example, the fluid dynamics computations form the model part of the user interface. This is an extension of the concept of a model in graphical user interfaces, where the model contains only geometrical information. In the artificial reality metaphor the model is active, it can change on its own, or in response to the user's actions. The model in an artificial reality user interface can be divided into two parts. The first part contains the geometry and other information used to produce the images of the phenomena under study. The second part consists of a set of rules or procedures that determine how these objects evolve over time, and how they respond to the user's actions. There are several ways of constructing these models, one approach is described by Sun and Green (Sun 1989).

The visualization component of an artificial reality user interface produces the images that are presented to the user. The visualization component must satisfy the following three conditions. First, the visualization must present all of the relevant information to the user. The user needs certain information to perform his or her tasks, and the visualization must make this information available. Second, the user must be able to manipulate the visualization. He or she must be able to move around the visualization in such a way that it can be viewed from any direction, and any part of it can be seen. The user might also need to change the type of visualization in order to obtain the information that he or she requires. Third, the visualization should attempt to convince the user that he or she is interacting with the real world. The visualization should draw the user into the application. This can be quite difficult, since the factors that contribute to the realism in an image have not been identified. Several studies that have shown that the most photographic image may not be the best for this type of interaction. Experience has shown that placing the user in the model space helps to produce the illusion of artificial reality.

The set of manipulations provides the means by which the user interacts with the application. These manipulations are similar to the interaction techniques that are found in traditional user interfaces. Each action performed by the user is translated into information that is passed on to the application. This information will usually affect the computations performed in the model part of the user interface, or the visualization presented to the user. In addition to providing information to the application, the manipulations must be consistent with the behavior of the model. In other words, the user must not be able to do things that would be considered impossible. The most effective manipulations are based on hand gestures in a three dimensional space, since they correspond to the types of manipulations normally performed in the real world. Ideally, a three dimensional input device, such as a Polhemus or DataGlove should be used for these manipulations.

3. A Model of Virtual Reality Systems

A simple model of virtual reality applications is presented in fig. 1. This model provides a way of classifying the applications of virtual reality and the tools that are required to support these applications. This model divides a virtual reality application into five main components (which are represented by the boxes in the diagram), some of which are optional. All virtual reality applications have viewing and interaction components. The arrows in the diagram represent the flow of information in the applications, and some of these flows are optional. The only required flow is the one between interaction and viewing.

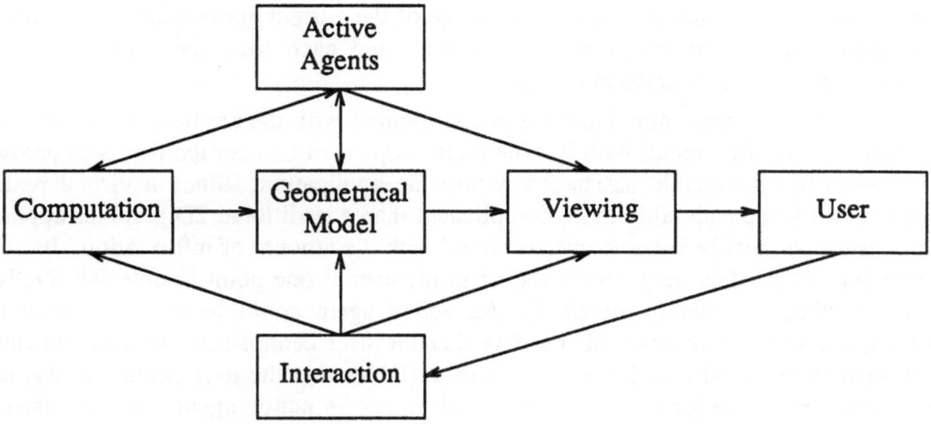

Fig. 1. A model of virtual reality systems

The interaction component is responsible for all the interactions with the user. It is responsible for managing the input and output devices (through interaction with the viewing component) and determining what the user wants to do.

The computation component includes all the non-graphical computations in the application. This component can be divided into application data and a collection of procedures. At each step of the computation, one or more of the application procedures will be executed. The procedures that are executed could be determined by the application itself, or by interaction with the user. At the end of the time step the application data will be in a consistent state, and parts of it can be passed to the geometrical model component, and eventually to the viewing component so the user can view it. We always view the computation as a sequence of time steps. The application data will only be available to the user at the end of the time step, thus the computation is free to do what it wants to its data during a time step. This may seem to be a restricted view of computation, but it has two main advantages. First, a large number of scientific computations and simulations fit into this model, so it is not a major restriction. Second, it provides a clean interface to a large number of existing applications. Most of these applications are organized as a sequence of time steps, and at the end of each time step their data is in a consistent state. By only viewing the data at the end of time steps we minimize the changes we need to make to existing applications.

The geometrical model component contains a high level graphical representation of the data in the computation. This component is responsible for converting the application data in the computation component into graphical data that can be used by the viewing component to produce a visualization of the application data. The mapping from application data to graphical data could be static and thus defined when the application is produced, or it could be dynamic and under the control of the user.

The viewing component produces the views of the application data that the user sees. This is the rendering component of the application. Its input is the graphical data from the geometrical model and viewing parameters (such as eye position) from the interaction component, and it produces an image of the current application data from the current view point. This image must be regenerated each time the application data changes or the viewing parameters change.

The active agents are simulated users that interact with the application in the same way that a user would interact with it. The main purpose of this component is to provide the user with programmable assistance within the application. Since a virtual reality application can be considerably more complicated than a traditional 2D graphics application, the user can quickly become overwhelmed with the amount of information. In a 3D environment, all the data may not be visible to the user at one point in time (all the data displayed behind the user is invisible). An active agent could be used to watch for interesting occurrences in parts of the data that the user cannot see. In a complicated environment there could be a large number of variables that the user could modify, and some of these modifications must occur in real-time. An active agent could be used to control some of these variables while the user concentrates on other parts of the model.

4. A Taxonomy of Virtual Reality Applications

This section presents a taxonomy of possible uses of virtual reality user interfaces. This taxonomy is by no means complete (new applications will appear as the technology becomes widely available), but it covers a wide enough range of applications to give us a good indication of the types of support tools that will be required. The main aim of this exercise is to establish the requirements for a virtual reality tool kit.

4.1. Scientific Visualization and Simulation

One of the obvious applications of virtual reality techniques is in the area of large scale scientific computing. Most scientific computations produce large volumes of output that is hard to interpret. A typical scientific computation models a three dimensional or higher space, and computes a set of values at grid points distributed throughout this space. Each time step of the computation can produce a vast amount of data that must be viewed in the original space in order to maximize the comprehension of the results. This data changes over time as the computation evolves, thus we would like to have a dynamic display of the data. These characteristics of the computation suggest that the results should be viewed in a dynamic 3D environment, such as that provided by a virtual reality user interface.

The scientific applications of virtual reality can be divided into three broad groups. The first group of applications are restricted to the post-processing of the output produced by the computation, which provides the user with a sophisticated mechanism for viewing the results of the computation. For example, the results of a fluid dynamics computation could be stored on a file. The user can then use a head-mounted display to view this data dynamically (essentially playing back the data in the file in the order that it was computed). The user can select the parts of the data to be viewed, the view point, and possibly the type of data (for example, flow velocity or pressure), but he or she cannot affect the computation. For this type of application, the viewing and interaction components are the main parts of the application, with a static geometrical modeling component. Since the data to be displayed is known before run-time, a considerable amount of preprocessing can be done to increase the display rate.

The next group of applications can be characterized as adding a graphical front-end to an existing program. There are a large number of existing programs (mainly written in FORTRAN) that are heavily used in the scientific community. These programs typically read their input from a file (in punched card format) and produce large amounts of printed output. A significant contribution would be adding interactive graphical front-ends to these programs allowing the user to interactively specify the input data and view the results of the computation. Most of these programs could be modified to allow the user to change the course of the computation (by changing variable values) at the end of a time step. This type of application has significant geometrical modeling, viewing and interaction components. The interaction component interacts with the computation, geometrical model and viewing components. These applications have significant computation components, but this part of the application is provided to us and should be left largely unmodified. The main aim is to add a front-end with minimal modifications to the existing program.

The third group of applications is similar to the second group, except the computation component is developed at the same time as the other parts of the application. In other words, we are not adding a front-end to an existing application, but developing the whole application at one time. From the tools point of view, the main difference is that we can influence the design and coding of the computation component, and may want to support its development in the tool kit.

4.2. Data Exploration

This is one of the original applications of virtual reality technology, and a good example of this type of application is the Walk-Through system developed at UNC (Brooks Jr. 1986). The basic idea behind this system is to allow the user to walk through a building before it has been constructed. The same idea could be applied to any multi-dimensional data space. This data space could have a natural 3D interpretation, as in the case of the building, or it could be an abstract data space. One of the applications that has been suggested for the system we are developing is walking through the proof tree of a complicated theorem. In these applications there is a static geometrical model that has been generated by another program, or digitized in some way. The way that the geometrical model is generated is usually is not of interest to the user (this is one difference between this type of system and the scientific visualization system described in the previous section). The data itself is intrinsically interesting, and not the way that it was generated. The main active components of this type of application is viewing and interaction. Again, the geometrical model can be pre-processed to produce an optimal form for viewing.

4.3. Communications and Cooperative Work

Cooperative work is another potential application of virtual reality user interfaces. In particular when there are several users at different locations cooperating on the solution of a particular problem. One possible scenario is a doctor at an isolated location faced with performing a procedure he or she has no experience with. The chance of success could be increased by having the doctor practice the procedure under the guidance of a medical expert. These experts are located at major centers, and cannot travel to remote locations. With a virtual reality system, a computer model of a patient could be shared by the doctor and the expert. The expert could observe the doctor performing the procedure on the computer model, and give directions and make comments on his actions. This applications would require a virtual reality system at both locations and a high speed link between them. While this may seem expensive, moving a patient from a remote location to a major medical center is also very expensive, when the procedure could be performed locally with a small amount of training.

This type of application requires a duplication of the model shown in fig. 1 at each site. The link between the systems could be accomplished in several ways. One obvious way of doing this is to use an active agent for each of the remote users. This active agent would mimic the behavior of the remote user (changing the geometrical model to represent the user operations, and possibly updating the computation or viewing components). This type of application will need multiple computation components that we must design and implement. The geometrical model, viewing and possibly the interaction component must be able to deal with dynamic information that may be coming from more than one source. In many ways this is probably the most ambitious application of virtual reality.

4.4. Control

The control of complex systems is one of the main applications of virtual reality systems (Fisher 1986). In this type of application there are several external processes that are under computer control. Examples of these processes are a chemical plant, a nuclear reactor, or remote manipulators associated with a space station. The user controls these processes through the use of one or more control panels. As the controlled processes become more complicated, the control panels also become more complicated, and the user is faced with a larger control problem. In the case of remote manipulators and the space station, the nature of the controlled process can change over time requiring a redesign of the control panel. Virtual reality introduces the possibility of virtual control panels. The user interacts with an image of a control panel that is generated by the computer, instead of directly interacting with a real control panel. This allows the control panel to be dynamically reconfigured to suit the user or the application.

In this type of application the computation is external to the computer system, it is the process that is under control. Most of the geometrical model is static (for example, the layout of the control panel) and can be pre-computed. The only part of this component that is not static is the status of the process being controlled, and the complexity of this part of the model depends upon the process. The interaction component communicates with the computation, geometrical model and viewing components. Active agents can play a major role in this type of application, since there are a large number of variables to be monitored and controlled. A programmable active agent could be used to monitor part of the process or watch for special situations. It could also be responsible for controlling part of the process when the user's attention is on other operations. In many ways the active agents could be view as sophisticated auto-pilots that can be programmed on the fly for special tasks.

4.5. Computer Aided Design

One potential application of virtual reality is computer aided design, particularly the design of complicated three dimensional structures. A virtual reality user interface would allow the designer to work in the same 3D space that the design object resides in. This will simplify some of the existing problems with 3D design, such as entering 3D positions with 2D devices, and viewing a 3D structure on a 2D screen. It could also be used to actively simulate the behavior of the design. In the case of a mechanical system, the designer could apply forces or torques to the object (using a DataGlove) and observe the mechanism's response. In the case of architectural design, the user will be able to walk through the building during the design process and spot design problems that are hard to detect from 2D diagrams. The designer will have virtual 3D computer based modeling clay, instead of working with a 2D representation of the object.

The main component of this type of application is the geometrical model, which will change over time as the design evolves. The interaction and viewing components will also be important, with a strong tie between the interaction and geometrical modeling components. The computation component will mainly be used to simulate the design. There will be some communications between the interaction and computation components.

4.6. Arts

Virtual reality systems could also be viewed as works of art, they are a combination of media and computer art. The main difference is they are a reactive art as opposed to a static art. This was probably the first application of virtual reality, and Krueger has coined the phrase artificial reality to describe this type of experience (Krueger 1983).

This type of application could involve all the components outlined in our model of virtual reality applications. The interaction and viewing components are quite important. The geometrical model component could vary from static (allowing a considerable amount of pre-computation) to highly dynamic and responsive to the user. The computation component represents the behavior of the art work. If it is a static work that doesn't respond to the viewer, then this component will not be present. For a more responsive environment, this component may be quite significant. Active agents could also play a major role in this type of application. Most artistic environments will probably be multi-media, in contrast to the other types of applications. For example, different parts of the environment may have different music or sounds associated with them, or pre-recorded video could play a major role in parts of the environment.

5. A Virtual Reality Tool Kit

Producing a virtual reality user interface requires a considerable amount of programming. This suggests that a set of software tools should be developed to assist in the development of this type of user interface, in the same way that we have produced software tools for other types of user interfaces (for example see (Green 1985) or (Singh 1989a, Singh 1989b)). We have developed some primitive tools for two of the application areas described in the previous section. For the scientific visualization area we have developed an application skeleton that can be used to add virtual reality front-ends to existing applications. For the data exploration area we have developed an interactive modeler and viewer that can be used in the construction of static environments. Both of these tools are described in this section. In addition we describe the tools that we would like to have in order to produce good virtual reality user interfaces.

Some of the tools described in the following sections are motivated by the current configuration of our virtual reality laboratory. The main output device in our laboratory is the VPL EyePhone, which is a stereo head-mounted display. The images displayed by this device come from two NTSC sources. At the present time we are using two Silicon Graphic Iris workstations (a 3130 and a 2400) with NTSC converters for this purpose. The two workstations are synchronized by packet exchanges over an ethernet. A Polhemus digitizer is used to determine the position and orientation of the user's head. The Polhemus consists of a source that generates an electro-magnetic field and a sensor that detects this field. The source is mounted in a fixed location, while the sensor moves with the user. The main input device in the laboratory is a VPL DataGlove. This devices consists of another Polhemus digitizer to determine the position and orientation of the hand, plus a instrumented glove to determine the finger orientations. The orientation of the fingers is determined by specially treated fiber-optics that are sewn into the glove. We have constructed a navigation box that can be worn on the user's belt. This box consists of three potentiometers and four buttons. This device is used for navigating in the environments.

5.1. Application Skeleton

The application skeleton addresses the problem of adding a virtual reality user interface to an existing application. There are certain aspects of a virtual reality user interface that are essentially the same in all applications. For example, all applications must synchronize the workstations that are generating the images, perform viewing and stereo projections based on the viewer's current position and orientation, and provide navigation through the environment. The application skeleton handles these aspects of the user interface and provides a framework for the application programmer's code. This skeleton can be used with existing applications, or form the basis of new applications.

To use the skeleton the application programmer must provide a procedure that produces an image of his data (the skeleton computes the viewing transformations). A call to this procedure must be placed at the appropriate place in the skeleton (this point in the code is indicated by a comment). After compiling the new version of the skeleton on both workstations, the user can interact with his data. The skeleton provides a default user interface that allows the user to walk around his data and navigate in the environment. Either a mouse or the navigation box can be used to move about the environment. The navigation box is the default device, if it is connected, otherwise the mouse can be used for navigation. If the navigation box is used the three potentiometers on it are used to change the origin of the user's coordinate space. All the user's head motions will now be with respect to this new origin. If button one on the navigation box is pressed, the potentiometers can be used to scale the user's movements. By default, the scale factor is 1.0 in all three dimensions. Thus, if the user moves an inch in his space, he will move an inch in the model space. If the mouse is used, the three mouse buttons are used to move in the x, y and z directions, the scaling option is not available with the mouse.

In many ways the skeleton provides a minimal virtual reality user interface, but it provides a very quick way of getting something running. If the programmer already has a procedure that can draw his data or model, then a virtual reality user interface for that model can be constructed in less than an hour. Thus, the skeleton provides a good prototyping tool, and a convenient mechanism for evaluating different display techniques. The skeleton has been used as the basis for a front-end to an existing fluid dynamics program.

5.2. Interactive Modeler and Viewer

One of the main applications of virtual reality user interfaces is exploring and interacting with three dimensional environments. These environments could represent the design of a new building (Brooks Jr. 1986), the environment that a remote manipulator is operating in (Fisher 1986), or a work of art. In all of these examples the environment consists of a number of objects that the user wants to explore or interact with. These objects are either static or have relatively simple motions (in comparison to fluid dynamics or other physical simulations). The design of this type of application consists of three main activities, designing the geometry of the individual objects, placing these objects in the environment, and designing their behavior. We have designed a simple set of tools for constructing this type of virtual reality user interface. This tool set is not intended to be a production tool, its main purpose is to identify the problems that need to be solved in order to produce more usable tools.

The tool set is divided into three main components. The first component is an interactive modeling program. This program is used to create the objects in the model and place them within the environment. The second component is the interactive viewing program that allows the user to explore the environment. The third component is an environment compiler which converts the output of the modeling program into the format required by the viewing program.

The modeling program is based on two key concepts, which are primitives and masters. A primitive is a template that is used to create an object. The set of primitives in the modeling program can be extended at any time. At the present time a programmer must write a C procedure for each new primitive, but we are in the process of designing a special primitive definition language that will simplify the construction of primitives. Most of the primitives in the modeler are parameterized. When the user creates an instance of the primitive, he specifies parameter values for it using a set of graphical potentiometers. Each of the parameters has a default value that produces a reasonable object. For example, one of the primitives in the model is a floor. The parameters for this object are whether the floor is tiled, and the size of the tiles.

A master is a collection of objects that is treated as a unit. The objects in a master can be either primitives, or instances of other masters. When a object is added to a master the user interactively positions, scales, and orients the object within the master's coordinate system. An environment is produced by creating instances of the masters. When an instance is created, the user can position, scale and orient it in the same way that objects are handled within masters. The transformations used to position the instances within the environments can be interactively edited.

The viewing program is based on BSP trees (Fuchs 1980, Fuchs 1983). A BSP tree is a binary tree that has a polygon at each of its nodes. The left subtree of the current node contains polygons that are behind the polygon at the node, and the right subtree contains polygons that are in front of the polygon at the current node. The normal to the polygon is used to determine its front and back sides. When a BSP tree is displayed, the eye position is compared to the polygon at each node as it is visited. The coordinates of the eye can be inserted into the plane equation for the polygon to determine whether the eye is in front or behind the polygon. If the eye is in front of the polygon, the left subtree is displayed first, then the polygon at the current node followed by the right subtree. Otherwise, the right subtree is displayed first, followed by the polygon at the current node and the left subtree. The BSP tree is independent of the eye position, each time the viewer's eye changes the BSP tree is traversed. Thus, BSP trees are an efficient solution to the hidden surface problem for static environments. For large environments the construction of a good BSP tree can be quite time consuming, therefore, the scene compiler is used to pre-compute the BSP trees.

The viewer has essentially the same user interface as the skeleton application. Each time that the user moves his head, the BSP tree is traversed to give the current view of the environment. The user can use either the mouse or the navigation box to change the origin of the user's coordinate system and to change the scale of his motions. With our current hardware configuration environments with a few hundred polygons give reasonably good response (between 5 and 10 updates per second). The upper limit for this configuration is about 500 polygons. Our experience indicates that most interesting environments will have several thousand polygons, and this should be possible with current workstation technology (one of the workstations we are using in our current configuration is 5 years old).

The scene compiler converts the data structure used by the modeler into a set of BSP trees. Basically, each of the objects in the model is converted into a BSP tree. Using a set of BSP trees instead of one BSP tree for the entire environment solves two problems. First, the size of the BSP tree grows quite quickly as the number of polygons in the environment increases. When each node of the BSP tree is constructed, the remaining polygons in the model must be divided into two disjoint groups depending on whether they are in front of or behind the current polygon. The plane of the current polygon usually cuts several of the polygons in the environment, thus each of these polygons will give rise to two or more polygons in the BSP tree. As the number of polygons in the environment increases, the number of polygons that will be cut also increases (there is a greater probability that any given polygon will be cut). Thus, for large environments it is hard to construct good BSP trees. For a convex polyhedron, none of the polygon planes cut any of the polygons in the polyhedron. Most of the objects that occur in the environments are basically convex, therefore, good BSP trees can easily be built for most of these objects. Thus, building a BSP tree for each object, and then ordering them correctly for each view point, will result in fewer polygons to display, and fewer tree nodes to visit.

The second reason for building a separate tree for each object is to allow for simple motion in the environment. If each object has a separate BSP tree, it can be moved without recomputing all of the BSP trees in the environment. The only thing that will change is the order in which the trees must be displayed. We are currently developing algorithms and heuristics that will accommodate these simple motions.

5.3. Requirements For New Tools

The tools described in the previous sections only address two applications of virtual reality. A complete set of usable tools must be produced before virtual reality becomes a viable user interface style. The following sections outline a number of tools that would be useful in the construction of virtual reality user interfaces. Some of these tools are fairly easy to produce, while others are the subject of major research initiatives.

5.3.1. Work Space Modeling

One of the major technical problems with existing virtual reality software is its dependence on the positioning of devices within the workspace. If a Polhemus source is moved, then the corresponding device will be unusable until all the software has been updated to reflect the new source position. This update may not be trivial, especially if the orientation of a coordinate system changes. Part of this problem can be solved by storing the configuration of the workspace in one place, where it can easily be updated. This solves the problem of updating all the software when a device is moved.

A tool for specifying the geometry of the workspace is also required. This could be a simple 3D CAD system, where the user can interactively position and orient the devices in the workspace. Since there are a small number of devices and a limited amount of interaction between them, this will not be a very sophisticated program. This program could be used to update the stored workspace configuration when a device is moved, or build up a complete new configuration when a new workspace is produced. This type of tool is absolutely necessary for portable virtual reality systems, otherwise setting up at each new location will be a major undertaking.

5.3.2. Calibration

Every user has different physical properties, and a number of the devices used in virtual reality depend upon these properties. Thus, we need to calibrate the system each time that a new user uses it. For example, the conversion from raw joint values to joint angles in the DataGlove depends upon finger geometry. Similarly, producing the correct images for a head-mounted stereo display depends upon the inter ocular distance (the distance between the two eyes). A quick and easy calibration procedure is required to make effective use of these devices. One approach that we have used is to record the calibration values for each user (based on their UNIX user name), and then use this as a first approximation when they get into virtual reality. This works fairly well for the EyePhone, but not quite as well for the DataGlove, since its calibration also depends upon how the glove was put on.

5.3.3. Viewing

The viewing components in the applications that we have built to date have dealt with relatively static environments. For example, the modeler and viewer described in the previous section deal with static environments, in which none of the objects in the environment move. The application skeleton has been used to produce a front-end for a fluid dynamics computation. In this program the surface of the fluid flow is displayed and the user can interact with it through the DataGlove. In this application, there is a continuous surface modeled by a polygonal mesh. This surface is well behaved and we know the general region that each polygon will lie in, therefore, a special purpose hidden surface algorithm can be constructed for this surface. For a more general surface, this approach cannot be used and we will need to rely on slower general purpose algorithms.

We need display algorithms that are fast and can handle arbitrary motion within the environments. It can be argued that hidden surface hardware can be used for this purpose, but this solution only works for relatively small environments. Most hardware hidden surface techniques are based on some version of the z-buffer algorithm. Thus, all of the polygons must be drawn each time the environment is displayed, and the display time is a function of the number of polygons in the environment. For most environments, only a fraction of the polygons need to be drawn, thus a software algorithm could outperform the hardware z-buffer approach. To see how this could happen, consider an environment that consists of a large number of rooms. Each room contains a large number of objects, and thus a large number of polygons, but the contents of a room cannot be seen from any of the other rooms. When the user is in a room, we only need to display the polygons corresponding to the objects in that room, the other polygons can be culled from the model. We need to develop hidden surface algorithms that allow us to perform these culling operations.

5.3.4. Geometrical Design

The modeler described in section 5.2 makes heavy use of masters and primitives. The masters provide a convenient means of producing composite objects, and any modeler for virtual reality systems should have this ability. The concept of a primitive turned out to be far more powerful than we had initially thought. By using primitives, the model builder avoids working with low level details, such as polygons or vertices. Instead he or she works with higher level structures, which are a closer match to the task being performed. The main activity in designing an environment is the positioning of the objects in the environment, and in most cases there is a limited range of objects. These objects correspond to the primitives provided by the modeler. Given a rich set of primitives the model builder could quickly produce interesting environments.

The main problem is, how to design the primitives? From a purely geometrical point of view, all we need is a geometrical modeling program that allows us to enter and edit the geometry and specify the parameters for the primitives. This is a good start, but a primitive is more than geometry, it has other properties that are equally important. For example, how can the user interact with it? If we have a room primitive, how does the user get into the room? The room could have a door, and we need to encode the information that the door can rotate about one of its vertical axes so the user can enter and leave the room. How about windows, can the user open and close them, or possibly go through them? For smaller objects, we need to know things like their weight. Is the user strong enough to pick up the object and move it? If the user throws the object, we need to know its physical properties (such as its moments of inertia) so we can compute its path through space. One of the major challenges is the production of a primitive design system that handles all of the above details, essentially giving us enough information to handle anything the user does.

5.3.5. Behavior

The previous section outlines some of the properties of primitives that are required for them to react to the user. This is just one side of the story, since a primitive could have behavior that is not totally under user control. This behavior could be a reaction to something the user has done, or be totally independent of the user. For example, if the user throws a ball in the environment many things could occur that are not explicitly caused by the user. The path of the ball must be computed, taking into account all of the forces acting on the ball, such as gravity and collisions with other objects. The user is responsible for starting this motion, but has little control over it once the ball leaves his hand. Collisions between the ball and other objects could produce a sequence of events that the user could not predict (or may not want). There could also be autonomous objects in the environment, that the user can interact with. These objects could be the result of a scientific computation (the surface of a fluid flow, or a molecule), or they could be some creature placed in the environment to entertain the user.

We need some way of designing or specifying these behaviors. One of the environments that we have built is a fish tank, with a school of fish swimming in it. The user can interact with the fish through the use of the DataGlove. In this case the behavior of the fish is encoded as a set of rules. This approach seems to work quite well for simple behaviors, but it is not clear how well it will scale. Two of the major problems are handling the conflicts between rules and establishing long term goals.

5.3.6. Active Agents

An active agent assists the user within the environment. It can be responsible for monitoring part of the environment or handling some of the interaction. Active agents will only be useful if they are easy to program and control. The user needs some convenient way of telling the active agent the tasks it has to perform. There are several ways in which the active agent could be programmed. One way is to use a set of rules, such as those outlined in the previous section. The main problem with this is the user will probably need to use some textual notation for specifying the rules, which will make it difficult to program the agent in the environment. Another approach is to use some form of programming by example, essentially showing the agent the tasks it has to perform. This may work for simple tasks, but for more complicated tasks that need to take into account the behavior of the environment this approach may not work. The main advantage of this approach is the agent can be programmed in the environment. A third possibility is to have pre-trained agents that already know how to perform a range of basic tasks. In this case the user only needs to specify the details of the tasks to be performed, and this specification could be done in the environment. The concept of an active agent is quite powerful, but in order to effectively use this technique we need some way of specifying their behavior.

5.3.7. Interaction Techniques

At the present time very few interaction techniques have been developed for virtual reality user interfaces. The two interaction techniques that are well known are gestures (special configurations of joint angles using the DataGlove), and pointing in the direction you want to travel (again using the DataGlove). The form of gesture recognition that has been used with the DataGlove is quite primitive. A gesture consists of a range of angles for each joint in the hand. Gestures can be specified by making the gesture a small number of times and recording the range of angles encountered in these examples. This is essentially gesture by example. There are two problems with this approach. First, the range of angles will in some cases depend upon the user. That is, each user will make the gesture in a slightly different way, and if the ranges are not properly tuned, the gesture may not be recognized, or it could be recognized when the user is making a different gesture. Second, there is no way of stating that certain joints are more important than others in particular gestures. Some of the gestures could depend upon only one or two fingers, the orientation of the other fingers is not important. A gesture could be described as the joint angles in one finger being twice as large as the joint angles in another finger. In other words, an absolute range of joint angles may not describe the gesture, instead some relationship between the joint angles could be the important factor. There needs to be a mechanism for stating these types of constraints.

There are at least three types of tasks that we need interaction techniques for. These tasks are command specification, operand specification and navigation. Gestures have been the main mechanism for command specification, but this need not be the case. Operand specification can be done by grabbing or pointing at objects in the environment. One of the main problems here is feedback. Even with stereo vision it can be hard to tell when the hand is near another object, and when the hand has grabbed it. One approach is to use sound to indicate when an object has been grabbed, or to indicate the distance to the object. Drop shadows are another useful feedback technique. A large amount of work needs to be done in this area.

The user needs to be able to get from one part of the environment to another. The head-mounted display has a usable range of about 5 feet, but most environments are considerably larger than this. Also, the scale of the movements in the environment may not match the scale of the user's physical movements. If the user is exploring a molecule, we don't want a one-to-one mapping between the user's motion and motion in the environment. We need interaction techniques for moving around, or navigating in the environment. One approach is to have virtual vehicles controlled by the user. For example, the user could drive a virtual car through the environment until he or she reaches the place to be explored in detail.

6. Summary

In this paper we have briefly discussed some tools and techniques that can be used in the constructed of sophisticated three dimensional graphical user interfaces. The style of user interface that has been addressed in this paper has been called virtual reality, since it simulates the three dimensional spaces that we live in. A metaphor, called artificial reality, that can be used to guide the design of virtual reality user interfaces has been proposed. This metaphor is based on constructing an artificial world that has a consistent set of behavior rules and user manipulations. A logical model for virtual reality user interfaces has been presented. This model, along with a taxonomy of possible applications, motivated the requirements for a virtual reality tool kit. This tool kit assists with the implementation of virtual reality user interfaces. Hopefully, this paper will motivate other researchers to investigate design methodologies and tools for sophisticated three dimensional user interfaces.

7. Acknowledgments

I would like to thank the graphics group at the University of Alberta for their ideas and input on this paper. In particular, I would like to thank Chris Shaw for reading and commenting on several drafts of this paper.

References

(Brooks Jr.) F. P. Brooks Jr., Walkthrough - A Dynamic Graphics System for Simulating Virtual Buildings, Proceedings 1986 Workshop on Interactive 3D Graphics, 1986, 9-21.

(Englebart 1968) D.C. Engelbart and W.K. English, A Research Center for Augmenting Human Intellect, Fall Joint Computer Conference, 1968, 395-410.

(Fisher 1986) S.S Fisher, M. McGreevy, J. Humphries, and W. Robinett, Virtual Environment Display System, Proceeding of ACM 1986 Workshop on Interactive 3D Graphics, 1986, 77-87.

(Fuchs 1980) H. Fuchs, Z. Kedem, and B. Naylor, On Visible Surface Generation by A Priori Tree Structures, Siggraph'80 Proceedings, 1980, 124-133.

(Fuchs 1983) H. Fuchs, G. Abram, and E. Grant, Near Real-Time Shaded Display of Rigid Objects, Siggraph'83 Proceedings, 1983, 65-69.

(Gibson 1979) J.J. Gibson, The Ecological Approach to Visual Perception, Houghton Mifflin Company, Boston, 1979.

(Green 1985) M. Green, The University of Alberta User Interface Management System, Siggraph'85 Proceedings, 1985, 205-213.

(Krueger 1983) M. W. Krueger, Artificial Reality, ADDISON, 1983.

(Singh 1989a) G. Singh and M. Green, Generating Graphical Interfaces from High-Level Descriptions, Proceeding of Graphics Interface'89, 1989, 70-77.

(Singh 1989b) G. Singh and M. Green, A High-Level User Interface Management System, Proceedings of CHI'89, 1989, 133-138.

(Sun 1989) H. Sun and M. Green, A New Technique for Animating Relation Motion and Character Motion in Natural Scenes, International Conference on CAD & CG, Beijing, China, 1989.

(Zimmerman 1987) T.G. Zimmerman and J. Lanier, A Hand Gesture Interface Device, Proceedings of CHI and Graphics Interface 1987, 1987, 189-192.

Mark Green is an Associate Professor in the Computing Science Department at the University of Alberta. His principal research interests are user interfaces, computer animation, high-performance graphics hardware, scientific computation, and distributed processing. He received his M.Sc. and Ph.D. in computer science from the University of Toronto in 1979 and 1985. He was an Assitant Professor at McMaster University from 1980 to 1983, and moved to University of Alberta in 1984. Dr. Green founded the ACM UIST series of conferences on user interface software and was the general chairman of the first of these conferences held in Banff, Alberta on October 17-19, 1988. Dr. Green is a member of ACM, IEEE, and SIAM.

Dr. Green can be contacted at the Department of Computing Science, University of Alberta, 615 General Services Bldg., Edmonton, Alberta T6G 2H1, Canada.

Chapter 2
Modeling and Realism

A Simple Model of Flames

Masa Inakage

ABSTRACT
This paper presents a simple model for modeling and rendering of flames. The technique is based on physical model of flame processes. This flame model accounts for both laminar and turbulent flames, with premixed and diffusion combustion. The basic geometry of flames relies on the laminar flame model. An anisotropic density field function is used to define the geometry of laminar flames. A stochastic function is added to purturb the basic geometry of flames to simulate the turbulent flames. Luminous flames from carbon particle scattering is added to the model by approximating the Mie scattering function. The color of flames is determined by the combustible fuel and it is also dependent on the flame region inside the flames. A volume rendering technique based on ray tracing is used to render the flames, which we call the volume tracing.

Key Words : atmosphere, combustion, Mie scattering, volume rendering, volume tracing

1. Introduction
Modeling flames is a challenging problem within the realm of modeling natural phenomena in computer graphics. It is important to tackle this problem, despite of its complexity, because flames have been essential to mankind since the discovery of fire. The mechanism of flame and combustion processes is very complicated, requiring knowledge in chemistry and physics. Many aspects of flame and combustion processes are still not well understood today.

Flame and combustion processes are mostly oxidizing reactions, a kind of chemical reactions. Flames are the visual component of these reactions, hence flames do not have distinctly defined surfaces. This leads to the volume representation of flames. The oxidizing reaction necessitates the presence of atmosphere. Consequently, the flame model should account for

- oxidizing reactions
- volume representation
- presence of atmosphere

There have been a few previous research works related to volume representation [1,2,7,10,12,17,19,20] and atmospheric models [6,9,11,13,16] in computer graphics, but no previous attempts have been madeto visualize the oxidizing reactions utilizing the computer graphics to the best of our knowledge.

There are a few previous works to model flames and related area. Reeves[15] modeled fireworks with particle systems. The same technique is used to create the wall-of-fire in the Genesis Demo sequence of the movie Star Trek II: The Wrath of Khan. Perlin[14] presented a technique to visually simulate the corona by turbulence function. More recently, Thalmann[18] has refined both the particle systems and turbulance functions to generate fires. There are other shortcut methods for modeling fire and flames. SABRINA, an image synthesis system developed at the MIRALab, University of Montreal has flame effects as one of the texture functions [18]. Other techniques incorporate transparency to visually simulate the flames.

In this paper, we describe a model of flames which considers the oxidizing reactions. The model is capable of simulating the appearance and behavior of laminar and turbulent flames, and it handles both premixed and diffusion type of flame models. In addition, the luminous flames are also considered as a case of scattering effects due to the presence of carbon particles.

In addition to the criteria mentioned above, the goal of our model includes:

- realistic shape and color synthesis, but not a complete physical simulation
- reasonably efficient
- integration with other modeling and rendering techniques

2. Flames and Combustion Fundamentals

In the field of chemistry and physics,many literatures and experimentation results on flames and combustions [3,4,5,8] are published. Fundamental theories can be found in many books, but we recommend a book by Gaydon, A.G. and Wolfhard, H.G. [4]. For a non-technical reference, a classical book on candle lights by Faraday is highly recommended [3].

Chemical reactions between oxidant and combustible gas are called the oxidation phenomena. Combustion is a special case of an oxidizing reaction, in which luminescence, heat and high temperature are involved. The mixture of fuel and oxidant is called the combustible mixtures. When the temperature of combustible mixtures becomes sufficiently high, the combustible mixtures enter the oxidizing reaction. The luminous state in oxidizing reaction is called the flames. The temperature at the ignition point is called the ignition temperature. The flames propagate heat to the neighboring regions, resulting in wave train of combustion and flames. This phenomena is called the combustion wave, and the flames are called the flame front. The speed of flame propagation is called the flame speed.

The conditions for flames to exist are:

- composition (ratio) of oxidant and fuel
- concentration (density) of oxidant and fuel
- pressure of combustible mixture
- volume of combustible mixture
- temperature of combustible mixture

These elements have both lower and upper limits of inflammability. The flames exist only when these conditions are within the lower and upper limits of inflammability. The region where combustion processes occurs consists of preheat zone and reaction zone. Preheat zone is a region where the temperature of the mixed gas of oxidant and combustible gas rises due to the heat propagation. Reaction zone is a region where the temperature is sufficiently high to react and create flames.

The flames can be classified into premixed flames and diffusion flames. The premixed flames are burning of combustible mixtures which the oxidant and the fuel have been mixed before the combustion process. A typical example of premixed flames is the Bunsen flames. The diffusion flames are burning of combustible mixtures which the oxidant and the fuel are mixed simultaneously as the combustion process occurs. Typical examples of diffusion flames are candle lights and flames of cigarette lighters.

Both premixed and diffusion flames are further classified into laminar and turbulent flames, which depends on the velocity of the flow of combustible mixtures. As the flow velocity increases, the length of the flame becomes longer until it reaches the break point or threshold. As the velocity is further increased, the length of flames becomes shorter and the flame process transits to the turbulent flames beyond this break point (figure 1).

Carbon particles are formed when the combustion process is incomplete due to the lack of oxidant. Carbon particles scatter light, creating bright luminous region called the luminous flames. The Mie theorem explains the mechanism of scattering effect by carbon particles in detail.

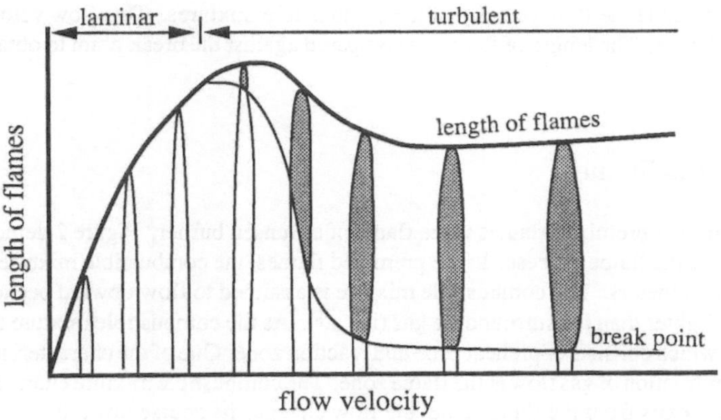

Figure 1 The change of flame length by flow velocity

3. The Basic Model

Our flame model is based on the flame structure described in the previous section. The flame model consists of the basic components common to all types of flames and the extended components to account for the characteristics of different types of flames. Although the flame model is built upon the physical model, it is simplified to synthesize visually realistic flames.

3.1 The Basic Components

The basic components rely on the following parameters:

- type of fuel: ***TYPE***
- ratio of oxidant and fuel: ***RATIO***
- density of the combustible mixtures: ***DENS***
- temperature: ***TEMP***
- flow velocity of fuel: ***VEL_F***
- flow velocity of oxidant: ***VEL_O***

TYPE defines the fuel constituents that determines the flame process conditions: color of the flames and inflammability limits. Flame color is the visual result of the oxidizing reaction. It is easy to observe that different types of fuel react differently in the oxidizing process, hence emitting different colors of light. ***TYPE*** determines the inflammability limits because different types of fuel possess different conditions for combustion. Fireworks show excellent manipulations of oxidizing reactions by different types of chemicals (fuel). Tables regarding the oxidizing reactions of fuel constituents are listed in sources including [4,5,8].

RATIO, ***DENS***, and ***TEMP*** are external factors to determine whether a given volume is flammable. These factors are compared with the pre-defined lower and higher inflammability limit conditions. Only when all of these factors satisfy the flammability conditions are the flames generated.

VEL_C and ***VEL_O*** consitute the flow velocity of the combustible mixtures. This flow velocity is used to calculate the length of flames. The length of flames is compared against the break point to obtain the amount of turbulence.

3.2 Laminar Premixed Flames

A typical example of laminar premixed flames is the flame of a Bunsen burner. Figure 2 depicts the flow of combustible mixtures and the flame process. In the premixed flames, the combustible mixture is predefined by ***TYPE*** and ***RATIO*** parameters. The combustible mixture is assumed to flow upward because the heated combustible mixture is lighter than the surrounding gas (i.e. air). As the combustible mixture flows upward, it enters the flame zone which consists of preheat zone and reaction zone. One of the characteristics of laminar premixed flames is the refraction of gas flow at the flame zone. The combustible mixture enters the flame zone perpendicularly. After it exits from the flame zone, the flow changes its course upward.

The laminar premixed flames constitute two volumes of flames: the inner cone and the outer cone (figure 3). The inner cone is the flame process from the flame zone. In our model, the inner cone is approximated by a cone for ease of calculation. The thickness of the cone is observed to be very thin, typically in the range of 0.1 - 1.0 mm. The radius of the inner cone is equal to the radius of the burner port. The length of flames determines the height of both inner cone and outer cone.

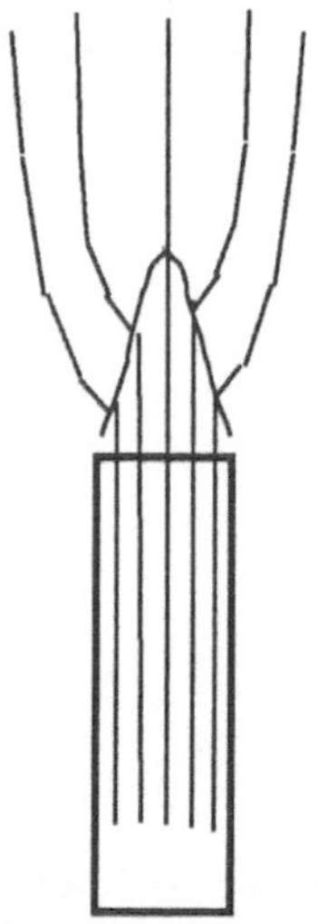

Figure 2 The flow of combustible mixtures, depicting the refraction.

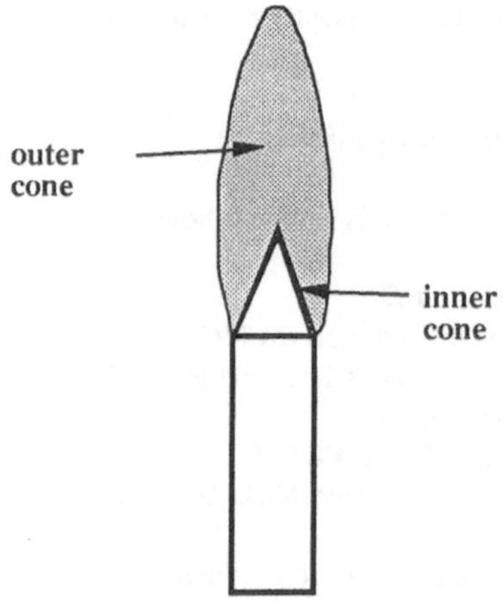

Figure 3 Laminar premixed flames consist of inner cone and outer cone.

Elements in the combustible mixtures that are not reacted in the reaction zone exit the inner cone and continue to flow upward. These elements react to the surrounding air and produce flames that constitute the outer cone. The parabolic geometry of the outer cone is due to the fact that the distribution of initial velocities of the combustible mixtures is parabolic. In other words, the velocity in the center is greater than in the peripheral region. We approximate the parabolic outer cone by an anisotropic density field. The anisotropy of the spherical density field is defined by vectors. The extinction distance of the density field is obtained from the length of flames. (See Appendix for further explanation on anisotropic density field function.)

RATIO controls the balance of inner and outer cones as shown in figure 4. If the amount of the fuel exceeds the amount of the oxidant, only the inner cone is produced. As the amount of fuel exceeds the oxidant, the length of the flame becomes longer and the inner cone becomes weaker.

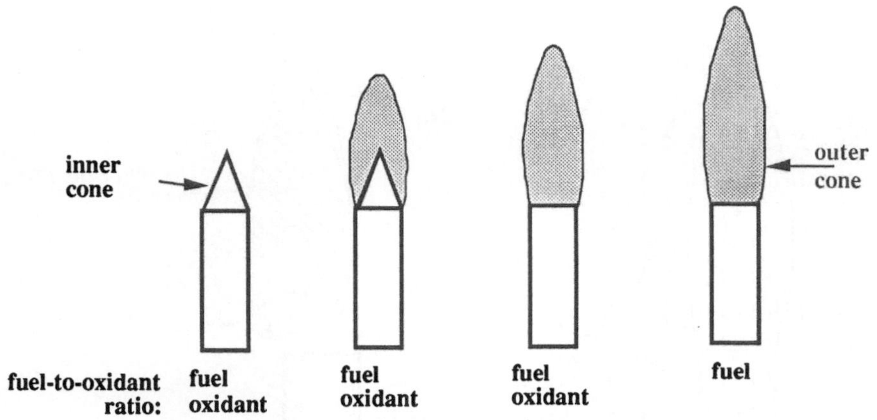

Figure 4 Fuel-to-oxidant ratio controls the formations of inner and outer cones.

3.3 Laminar Diffusion Flames

The diffusion flame process is the oxidizing reaction of separated fuel and oxidant. A combustible mixture is created as both fuel and oxidant are diffused. Only when the ratio of the mixture falls between the lower and upper inflammable limits and other conditions are satisfied will there be a flame process. Thus, the laminar diffusion flame process occur at the boundary region between the fuel and oxidant. Typical examples of laminar diffusion flames are flames of cigarette lighters and candle lights.

Figure 5 illustrates the diffusion flames. The fuel and oxidant flow upward similarly to the premixed flame model, and it creates similar a flame of geometries. However, the flow continues upward without any refraction, due to the lack of distinct flame zone. The luminous region satisfies the conditions for the flame process.

In the case of candle flames (figure 6), the core is surrounded by the non-luminous region. This region is dominated by gasified paraffin (fuel dominance). The gasified paraffin is mixed with the oxidant and creates flames. Different molecules react to different condition, generating different colors of flames. A thin suurounding volume of blue flames is produced by C_2 and CH molecules due to the thermo-decomposition of gassified paraffin. The large region of yellow flames is produced by combustion of paraffin and oxidant mixtures. When the amount of oxidant is insufficient, hot carbon particles and soot are formed because of incomplete combustion and thermo-decomposition of hydrocarbon flames. These carbon particles emit yellowish flames, known as the luminous flames.

In our flame model, the thermo-decomposition phase is neglected. Thus, we model the candle lights by defining multiple fuels of different ***TYPE***. To calculate the luminous flames, Mie scattering may be adopted. Since Mie scattering requires complicated mathematics, we approximate it by an amplification function

$$F(\phi) = K(1 + 9\cos^{16}(\phi/2))$$

where ϕ is the angle between the forward scattering and the direction towards the eye point. K is a constant. This approximation of Mie scattering is taken from Nishita,T., et al. [13].

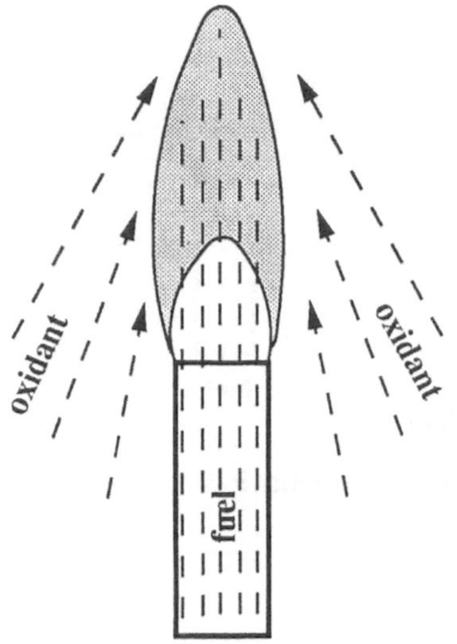

Figure 5 Laminar diffusion flames

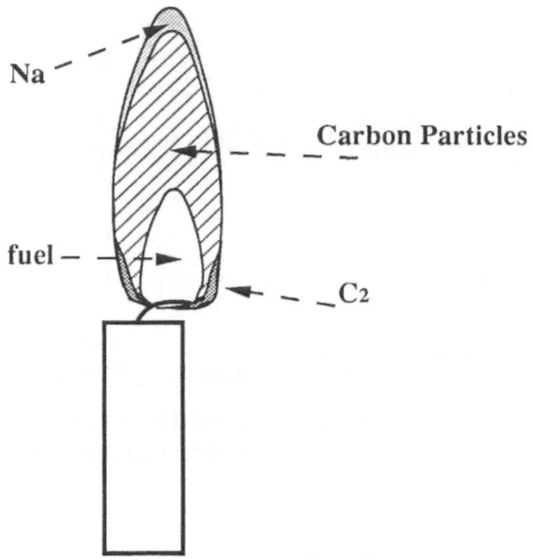

Figure 6 Combustion of candle lights

3.4 Turbulent Flames

Turbulent flames occur when the flow velocity exceeds the break point. The turbulent flame structure involves complex mathematics. Instead of solving complicated formulae, we propose a simplified model of turbulent flames in which the characteristics are extracted.

Damkohler classified turbulent flames into 2 classes by scale of turbulence. For relatively small turbulence, the flames behave similar to the laminar flames. The flame region is wrinkled. This is called the wrinkled laminar flame. For larger turbulent scales, the flames involve eddying motion. The structure and behavior become extremely complex.

Our model of turbulent flames is based on smaller scale turbulence, namely the wrinkled laminar flames. Figure 7 shows the wrinkled flame region. The wrinkle motion is a random motion of distance between the center of flames and the flame front. A stochastic function is added to our anisotropic density field. The length of flames is affected by the stochastic component.

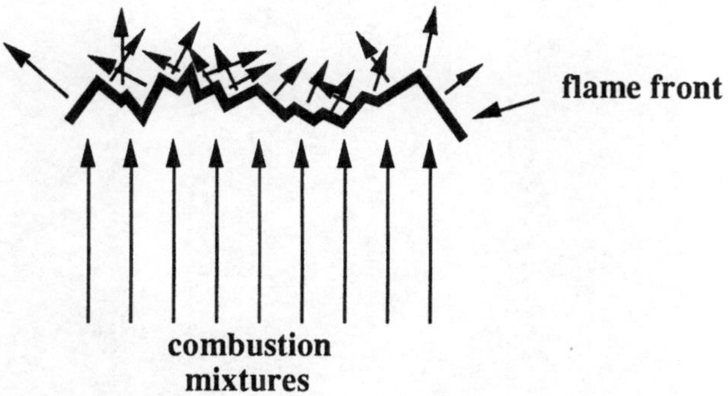

Figure 7 Wrinkled laminar flames refract the flow of combustion mixtures stochastically.

4. Rendering

Our model of flames is described as a volume of density fields. It necessary to adopt a rendering technique that is able to handle volumes. Unlike surface models, the final pixel color on the screen is the total contribution of volumes along the extended path of the eye point and the screen pixel. To implement the model, volume rendering by means of ray tracing is used, which we call the volume tracing [6].

In volume tracing, the screen sampled eye ray is extended incrementally to sample the volume. Each sample point is tested for the flame zone and primitive intersections. The flame zone is a function of an anisotropic density field. If the sample point is inside the flame zone, the flame region is determined. This flame region controls the color and its energy contribution to the final screen pixel. If the sample point is inside the flame region where carbon particles emit yellow flames, the amplification function is used to simulate the Mie scattering effect. The screen sampled eye ray is extended until it is clipped by the maximum distance or it intersects with a primitive of an opaque surface. All the colors of sample points along a given screen sampled eye ray are accumulated to produce the final pixel color.

Figures 8 and 9 show implementation results of the flame model. Figure 8(a) is a laminar premixed flame using a mixture of oxidant and CH_4 as a fuel. The velocity of fuel is increased to create a wrinkled laminar flame in figure 8(b). In figure 9, diffusion flames were rendered, showing the effect of increasing the fuel velocity. Figure 9(a) is an example of a simulated candle, a laminar diffusion flame. As we increase the fuel velocity (figures 9(b)-(d)), the flame is purturbed by a stochastic function. It is visually more realistic because there is constantly an air flow in reality. Multiple types of fuel were defined: C_2, Na and C_2H_4.

Each of the examples was generated in approximately an hour of computation time on a NEC PC-9801 VM2 16-bit computer (8086 CPU with 8087 co-processor), running on MS-DOS operating system. Flames were computed at 100 x 100 x 120 resolution in full color. The ray traced burner ports and candle sticks were composited post-process.

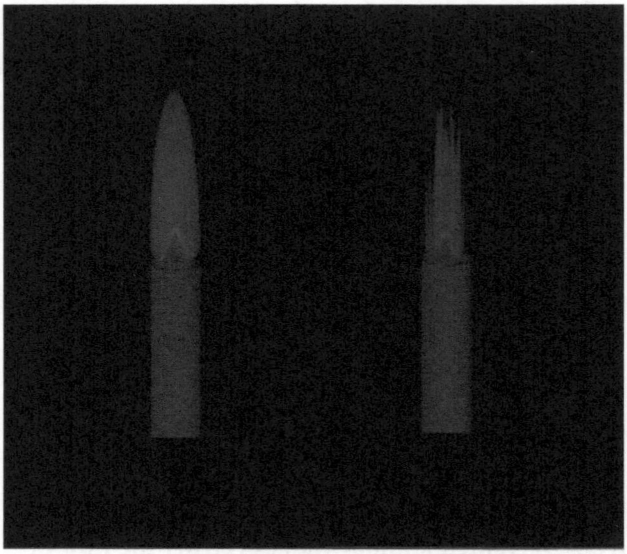

(a) (b)

Figure 8 Volume traced premixed flames (a)laminar, (b)turbulent

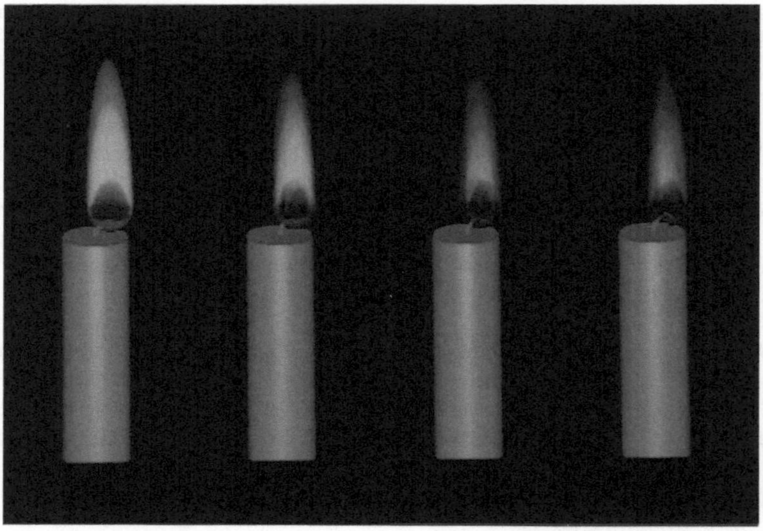

(a) (b) (c) (d)

Figure 9 Volume traced candle lights transition from (a) laminar to (d) turbulent diffusion flames

5. Conclusions

We have described a flame model that accounts for premixed and diffusion flames, in both laminar and turbulent conditions. For laminar premixed and diffusion flames, the flame geometry is defined as an anisotropic density field function. The wrinkle effect of the flame geometry in turbulent flames is achieved by purturbing the density field by a stochastic function. Luminous flames are added to the model as a visual effect using an approximated Mie scattering function.

The rendering of the flame model is done by volume tracing, a ray tracing technique for volume rendering. Volume tracing allows an integration of the flame model to the exisiting ray tracing techniques in the presence of atmosphere.

There are many unresolved problems and refinements required in the current flame model for future research. First, the current model does not account for shadows of flames cast onto other surfaces. Another unresolved problem in our flame model is the consideration of radiation heat transfer of flames. It is an important factor in the flame model when generating the combustion wave. This extension also allows the flame model to interface with the radiosity approach. A refinement is desired for the turbulent flames. We have only considered the wrinkled laminar flames as a case of small scale turbulent flames. A general scheme for turbulent flames is needed to generate wide variety of flames, which accounts for external forces such as wind.

References

[1] Blinn,J.F., "A Generalization of Algebraic Surface Drawing," *ACM Transactions on Graphics, 1,* 3, 1982, p.235-256

[2] Drebin,R.A., Carpenter,L., and Hanrahan,P., "Volume Rendering," *Computer Graphics, 22,* 4, 1988, p.65-74

[3] Faraday,M., The Chemical History of a Candle, Larlin Corp., 1978

[4] Gaydon,A.G. and Wolfhard,H.G., Flames, Their Structure, Radiation, and Temperature, Chapman & Hall, 1979

[5] Hikita,T., The Science of Flames, Corona Pub., 1982 (in Japanese)

[6] Inakage,M., "An Illumination Model for Atmospheric Environments," *to appear in the Proceedings of CG International '89*

[7] Kajiya,J.T. and Von Herzen,B., "Ray Tracing Volume Densities," *Computer Graphics, 18,* 3, 1984, p.165-173

[8] Kinbara,T., Physics of Combustion of Gases, Syokabo Pub., 1985 (in Japanese)

[9] Klassen,R.V., "Modeling the Effect of the Atmosphere on Light," *ACM Transactions on Graphics, 6,* 3, 1987, p.215-237

[10] Lorensen,W. and Cline,H., "Marching Cubes: A High Resolution 3D Surface Construction Algorithm," *Computer Graphics, 21,* 4, 1987, p.163-169

[11] Max,N.L., "Light Diffusion through Clouds and Haze," *Computer Vision, Graphics and Image Processing, 33,* 1986, p.280-292

[12] Nishimura,H., Hirai,M., Kawai,T., Kawata,T., Shirakawa,I., and Omura,K., "Object Modeling by Distribution Function and a Method of Image Generation," *Electronics Communication Conference '85, J68-D,* 4, 1985 (in Japanese)

[13] Nishita,T., Miyawaki,Y., and Nakamae,E., "A Shading Model for Atmospheric Scattering Considering Luminous Intensity Distribution of Light Sources," *Computer Graphics, 21,* 4, 1987, p.303-310

[14] Perlin,K., "An Image Synthesizer," *Computer Graphics, 19,* 3, 1985, p.287-296

[15] Reeves,W.T., "Particle Systems -- A Technique for Modeling a Class of Fuzzy Objects," *Computer Graphics, 19,* 3, 1985, p.279-286

[16] Rushmeier,H.E. and Torrance,K.E., "The Zonal Method for Calculating Light Intensities in the Presence of a Participating Medium," *Computer Graphics, 21*, 4, 1987, p.293-302
[17] Sabella,P., "A Rendering Algorithm for Visualizing 3D Scalar Fields," *Computer Graphics, 22*, 4, 1988, p.51-58
[18] Thalmann,N.M. and Thalmann,D., Image Synthesis, Springer-Verlag, 1987
[19] Upson,C. and Keeler,M., "V-Buffer: Visible Volume Rendering," *Computer Graphics, 22*, 4, 1988, p.59-64
[20] Wyvill,G., McPheeters,C., and Wyvill, B., "Data Structure for Soft Objects," *The Visual Computer, 2*, 4, 1986, p.227-234

APPENDIX. Anisotropic Density Field Function

Geometry

The initial primitive is the ellipsoids. For a given point $P(x,y,z)$, an ellipsoid is expressed as

$$(x - cx)^2 / (radx)^2 + (y - cy)^2 / (rady)^2 + (z - cz)^2 / (radz)^2 - 1 \leq 0$$

where cx, cy, cz are coordinates of the center of ellipsoids C, and $radx, rady, radz$ represent radii for x,y,z axes respectively. The inequality in the equation describes the volume inside an ellipsoid.

Vectors are used to calculate the anisotropy of ellipsoids. Figure 10 illustrates the vector representation of anisotropy. Vector $\vec{F}$ defines the anisotropic direction. For a given point P, its direction is expressed by vector N. The angle ϕ between vectors $\vec{F}$ and $\vec{N}$ sets the anisotropic bias. For ease of calculation, we use $cos(\phi)$ to calculate the bias. The radius for vector $\vec{N}$, $NOWRAD$, is written as

$$NOWRAD = RADIUS + (LENGTH - RADIUS) * cos(\phi)$$

where $RADIUS$ is the radius of the burner port in premixed flames and the radius of the fuel flow in diffusion flames. $LENGTH$ is the length of flames.

We know that the ellipsoid is biased in the direction $\vec{F}$, hence radx, rady, radz in the equation of ellipsoid are written as

$radx = RADIUS$
$rady = NOWRAD$
$radz = RADIUS$

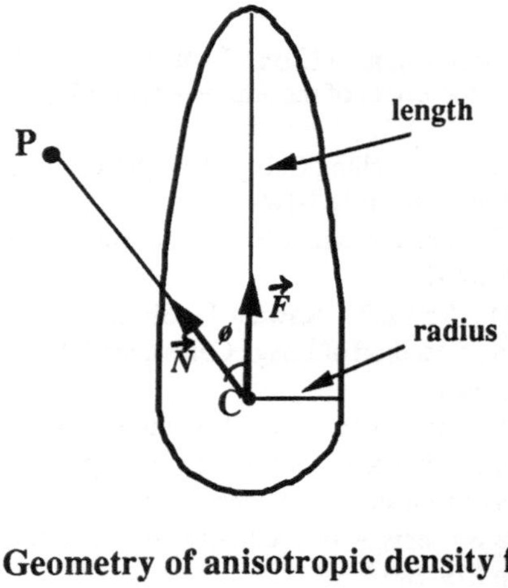

Figure 10 Geometry of anisotropic density field function

Density Field

The first approximation of density at point P is denoted as *NOWDENS*, and it is expressed as

$$NOWDENS = (DISTANCE / EXTINCTION)^2$$

where *EXTINCTION* is the maximum distance of density diffusion, and *DISTANCE* is the distance between points P and C.

The second approximation calculates the paths of combustible mixture flow. The flow differs by type of flames. We approximate the paths as combinations of lines and parabola.

Masa Inakage is a media artist and researcher at the Media Studio, Tokyo, Japan. He obtained his B.A. from Oberlin College, Ohio and M.F.A. from California College of Arts and Crafts. He did research on rendering, animation and user interface issues at the Media Lab., MIT. His current interests include sound and visual integration, various modeling and rendering algorithms, and user interface design.
Address: 3-5-17 Aobadai, #303, Meguro, Tokyo 153, Japan

Optical Models

Geoff Wyvill and Craig McNaughton

Abstract

Artists make pictures that communicate ideas. It is not enough to point a camera and press the shutter. They must show us something individual about the way *they* see the scene they wish to portray. Why, then, has there been so much emphasis in computer graphics on rendering scenes with photographic realism? For most engineering applications, simple diagrams are sufficient.

In this paper we explore the idea of modelling the eye of the artist. We introduce the idea of an *optical model* to describe the way in which what appears in a picture is related to what has been created in a three dimensional scene.

Keywords: geometric modelling, ray tracing, optical models, animation.

Introduction

Every work of art is an act of communication. If you have no idea to communicate then you will not create art. It is not enough to portray the scene before you, you must show us something about it. Photography can be art but it usually isn't. Study a recent holiday snapshot and compare it with a picture from a fashion or travel magazine and you will see the difference between amateur and professional craftsmanship. Compare either with one of the published works of a great photographer like Cartier Bresson and you will appreciate the point without difficulty.

Since the middle ages, and probably before that too, painters have researched and studied techniques to portray the world before them in a manner that we describe as realistic. They have also used these techniques to create, from the imagination, scenes and images that could not possibly be real. The need for technical mastery is exemplified by Renoir's saying: “Painting is first of all a manual job and one must be a good workman.” (Lambourne 1965).

Photography provides a short cut to creating pictures from life but a photograph is only one kind of picture. Although the camera instantly transforms a view into an image, it takes away from the artist the detailed decision as to what appears at each point of the picture plane.

Computer graphics practitioners have worked hard to create pictures with the quality and properties of 'natural' photographic images. This has been described as "the quest for visual realism." (Foley 1982). Bob Parslow calls it "Snapshot realism." (Parslow 1988). This is an apt reminder that we are only establishing a technique. Unless we are masters of image making, our efforts will be more akin to the holiday snapshot than the work of Cartier Bresson.

We applaud the pursuit of realism as we encourage artists to study colour, light and form but the purpose of this realism seems to have been lost. Engineers don't need it and except for a few special applications, artists don't want it.

Our purpose is to extend our techniques and provide the artist with explicit control of the way in which a scene is portrayed by an image. We confine our attention to the business of creating a picture from a three dimensional model. In this context, we have built a tool for modelling the eye of the artist.

To create a picture with a computer, we use a geometric model to describe the shape of objects, a light model to describe the illumination of the scene and the properties of object surfaces, and a colour model to map our ideas of the behaviour of colour to the capabilities of our display. To these, we add an optical model that describes how the three dimensional scene is to be viewed.

The camera model

One of the simplest models is provided by classical ray tracing (Whitted 1980). In effect, our optical model is that of a pinhole camera. A viewing plane is added to the scene and every point on this plane can be used to generate a ray cast into the scene. Each ray explores a single line and determines the colour visible along that path from rules that are approximations to physical laws. In practice, we simplify this geometry as shown in Fig. 1, by putting the viewplane in front of the pinhole or eyepoint. The rays we generate do not correspond simply to pixels in the final image. Extra rays may be cast for antialiasing (Whitted 1980, Fujimoto 1986, Wyvill 1989) or fewer rays may be cast when our knowledge of the scene enables us to deduce the colour of intervening pixels (Roth 1982, Wyvill 1987). For this reason, we do not discuss pixels here, only the relationship between the ideal viewplane and the set of potential rays we may generate.

Cameras in the physical world are not so simple. If we want to model effects such as limited depth of field, then we must include a model of the camera's lens (Cook 1984). For every point in the picture plane, we now require, in principle, a ray directed at every point on the lens, Fig. 1(c). Again, there will be a finite set of rays actually used, but we are interested in the whole set of rays that would be associated, in principle, with a point in the image.

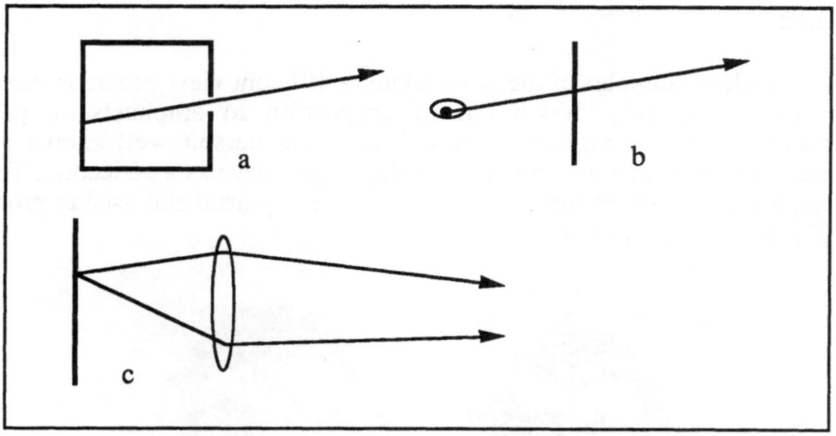

Fig. 1. Simple camera models: (a) Pinhole camera, (b) Eyepoint and viewplane, (c) Simple lens. Each can be regarded as a way to define rays from a point in the viewplane.

The optical model

An optical model defines a set of rays for each point in the image plane. In this paper, we discuss models that handle the *geometry* of the image rather than focus or texture. For this reason, we limit ourselves to optical models that define one ray for each point in the image. From the mathematical point of view, this is a function from points in a plane to rays. A ray can be described by a starting point and a direction. The starting point is represented by three co-ordinates and the direction by two angles. Thus the optical model can be regarded as a mapping from two dimensions to five:

$$\text{Model} = M: \Re^2 \rightarrow \Re^5$$

When we define this mapping we describe a view of a scene. In principle, the definition could be a list of rays for each point on the image plane for which a ray is to be cast. This would be equivalent to painting by hand: defining each point individually. In practice, we use mathematical intuition to construct useful functions.

For example, the simple camera model described by Fig. 1(b) is described thus: Let the eyepoint be represented by a vector **e** and suppose the picture plane is the plane $z = 0$. Then any point $\langle x, y \rangle$ in the picture plane is $\mathbf{p} = \langle x, y, 0 \rangle$ and the ray vector has origin **e** and direction **p** - **e**.

$$M(x, y) = \langle \mathbf{e}, \langle x, y, 0 \rangle - \mathbf{e} \rangle$$

This is the most commonly used model in ordinary ray tracing.

Caricature

One of the simplest examples of the artist taking a different view occurs in caricature. Features are deliberately drawn out of proportion to emphasise a person's characteristics, real or imagined. Figure 2 shows a person well-known at CGI conferences together with a distorted picture that might serve as a caricature. To make this picture, a special camera function was constructed by hand and used to process an original picture captured with a TV camera.

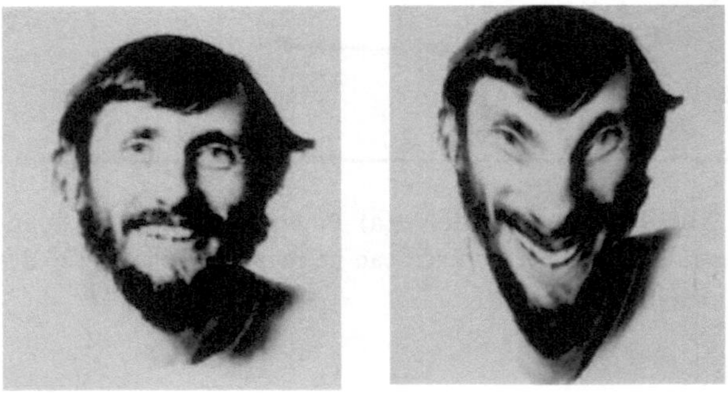

a b

Fig. 2. Photograph and caricature.

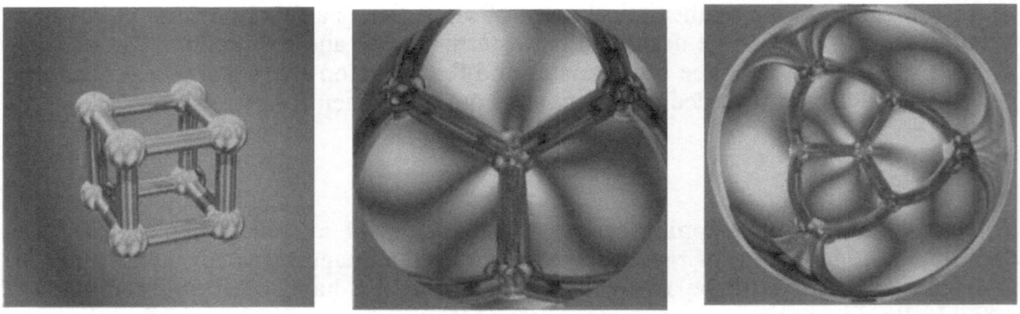

a b c

Fig. 3. (a) Simple object, (b) Fish-eye view, (c) Super fish-eye

Super fish-eye

A fish-eye lens captures 180° of arc. It is the widest angle lens used in ordinary photography and produces a characteristic circular photograph of a complete hemisphere. Using the idea of an optical model, we can view a scene through a lens of any angle, even 360°. Not only that, we can define the function that relates angular position in the scene to radius in the photograph. Figure 4 shows the geometry.

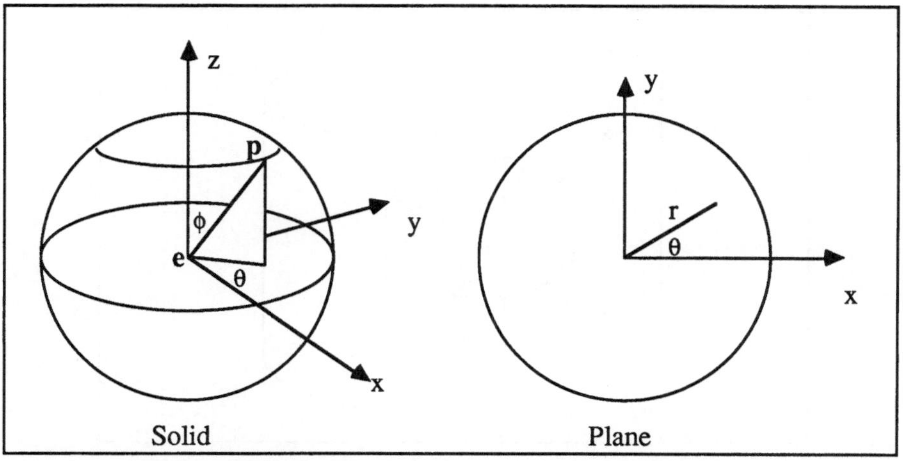

Fig. 4. Super fish-eye geometry. Point <r, θ> in the picture plane is mapped into spherical co-ordinates at **p**. The eyepoint, **e**, is at the centre of the sphere.

For a position <x, y> in the picture plane we find the polar co-ordinates <r, θ>. The ray direction is defined to be <θ, ϕ> where $\phi = \pi r/R$ and R is a constant: the radius of the circular image. Figure 3 shows a simple model viewed through a normal lens, a fish-eye and the super fish-eye 360° lens. The fish-eye cameras are positioned in the centre of the object looking towards one corner. In the case of the super fish-eye, the boundary circle of the image maps to a single ray and the image of the sphere behind the lens stretches around this circle. Of course, instead of $\phi = \pi r/R$, we could use $\phi = f(r)$ where f is any function we choose.

Variable eyepoint

So far, our examples have done no more than provide a flawless conventional camera. But an artist's view is not limited to stretching a conventional image. Picasso, for example, from about 1920 adopted a wholly unconventional use of space. In *Three Musicians,* (1921) a clarinet is viewed simultaneously from the front and from the base. In *La Coiffure,* (1954), a nude is portrayed simultaneously from front and back view. These pictures, and similar examples may be found in Leymarie (1971). As our eye moves over the picture, our point of view shifts. Can we use our notion of optical model to portray this kind of changing viewpoint?

Figure 5 illustrates one simple geometry to achieve this. We wrap the image plane around a cylinder and cast our rays from each point on the image plane to a point, **p**, just behind the object. For each point <x, y> in the image plane, the starting point of the ray is

$$\mathbf{e} = \langle r\cos(x),\ y,\ r\sin(x)\rangle$$

where r is the radius of the cylinder and the direction is given by **p** - **e** .

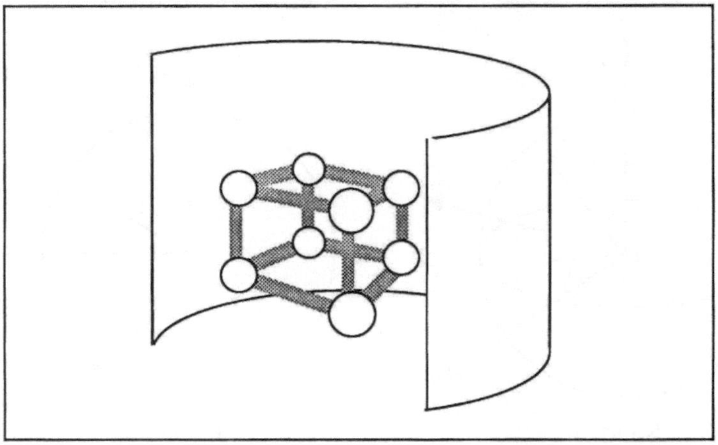

Fig. 5. Geometry for multiple views. The viewing plane is mapped onto a cylinder and rays are cast at a single point.

Figure 6 shows the result of this view. We are now looking at both sides of the object simultaneously.

Fig. 6. View from both sides.

Once we accept that the eyepoint can depend on the image plane position, we are in a position to explore a whole world of image-making tricks. We can map the eyepoints onto the surface of any three dimensional object. The modelling function can wrap the viewplane many times around the same path to create several images of the same object. If for each repeated eyepoint, the viewing direction is different, then the repeated instances of each object each have a different appearance. Figure 7 shows just eight spheres viewed with a convoluted function that maps the eye onto a self-intersecting cycloidal shape. Point **p** is fixed and the equations for **e** are:

$$\theta = 2\pi x / \text{xlimit} - \pi$$
$$\phi = 2\pi y / \text{ylimit} - \pi$$
$$e_x = r\ ((\sin(\theta)+0.4\sin(8\theta))\ (\cos(\phi)+0.4\cos(8\phi))) + s_x$$
$$e_y = r\ ((\cos(\theta)+0.4\cos(8\theta))\ (\cos(\phi)+0.4\cos(8\phi))) + s_y$$
$$e_z = r\ (\sin(\phi)+0.4\sin(8\phi)) + s_z$$

where x, y are screen co-ordinates, xlimit, ylimit are screen bounds and r is the radius of a sphere at point s.

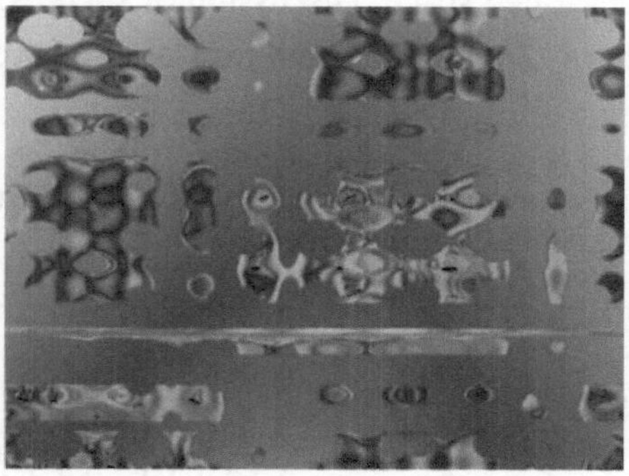

Fig. 7. Multiple views.

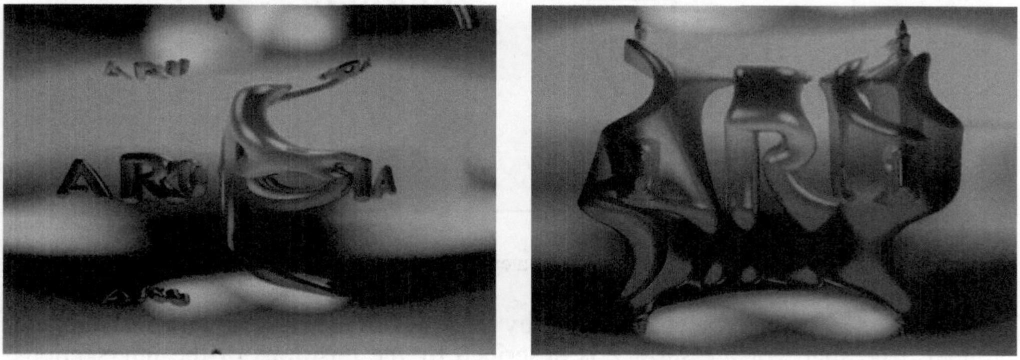

Fig. 8. Frames from the ARU animation.

Animation

Optical models provide a particularly rich set of tools for the animator. It is possible to make the mapping function M(x, y) change with time. For every <x, y> on the image plane, we define the points **e**, **p**. One of the easiest ways to produce an interesting motion is to inbetween from one M to another. In a sequence of n + 1 frames, labelled 0..n we can define $\mathbf{e}_i$, $\mathbf{p}_i$ for the i th frame to be:

$$\mathbf{e}_i = \mathbf{e}_0 + (\mathbf{e}_n - \mathbf{e}_0)\ i / n$$
$$\mathbf{p}_i = \mathbf{p}_0 + (\mathbf{p}_n - \mathbf{p}_0)\ i / n$$

where $\mathbf{e}_0$, $\mathbf{p}_0$ are produced by one mapping, M_0, and $\mathbf{e}_n$, $\mathbf{p}_n$ by another, M_n. Figure 8 shows frames from our Animation Research Unit logo. The only objects in the scene are the golden letters "ARU." The sky is textured with a single, soft stripe to improve the highlights on the letters. The variety of shapes, the sky texture and the motion are created with a single time-dependent optical model.

Deformation

Optical models are not the same as deformation functions. We can define a deformation of a shape by means of a function that maps each point in space to a corresponding point in deformed space. Discussion of such techniques can be found in Barr (1984) and Sederberg (1986). Deformations are functions $\Re^3 \to \Re^3$, whereas our optical models are functions $\Re^2 \to \Re^5$. This difference is very important. If we regarded the optical model as a form of deformation then the image we generate will have the appearance of a deformed object viewed normally. But this interpretation can represent an object not realisable in 3D space.

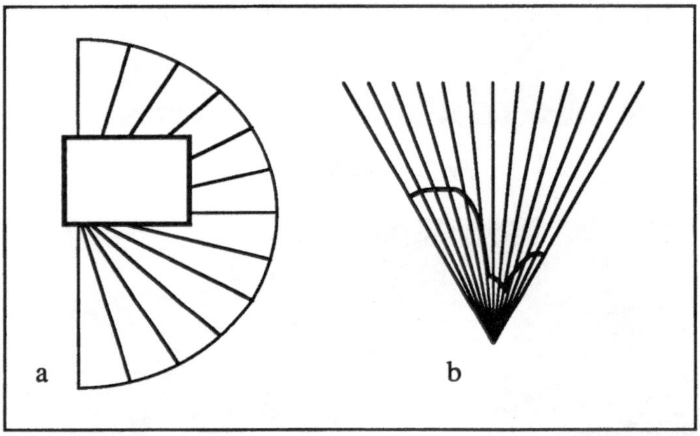

Fig. 9. (a) Projection from a cylinder, (b) Apparent surface

Figure 9(a) shows an object observed by a set of rays pointing inwards from a cylinder. The shape of the surface is described by the positions of the intersections with the rays. Replace each of these rays with a corresponding ray in an ordinary camera projection, Fig. 9(b), and draw a surface that intersects each ray at the appropriate distance and you will construct the surface of the apparent object.

On any smooth surface, we can draw a continuous line and at every point this line is tangential to the surface. Given a starting point, and a definition of the tangent at every point on the line, we can, in principle, determine the position of every point on the line by integrating the tangents along the line. This is true for any line drawn on the surface. In other words, the shape of a surface and its surface normals are closely related. Indeed we all use surface normal directions as deduced from shading to work out what shape a surface is, and it is this feature of our perceptual system that enables bump mapping to work.

When we interpret a picture as representing a three dimensional scene, we use knowledge of the effect of shading as well as depth cues to deduce the shape of objects. Use of an optical model for distortion can produce shading that indicates one shape along with depth cues that indicate another.

If we want to use an optical model as a way to define deformation, we must also take account of the effects of shading. One way would be to reposition the light sources for each ray cast so that when transformed back into the normal camera projection, the image was still consistent. This idea is worthy of further investigation, but there will inevitably be optical models for which it cannot be done because optical models are, in principle, more general than deformation functions.

Conclusion

A new concept, the optical model, provides a way to describe the way in which an object or scene may be viewed. It is easy to implement and has already been used to create a variety of images and animations.

The optical model is flexible because it is described by a mathematical function. Thus it provides a tool by means of which a suitably skilled artist can communicate a non-photographic view of a computer generated scene.

We have done no more than demonstrate the capability of optical models. It remains for the numerate artists to show us their true applications.

Acknowledgements

The computer graphics project at Otago has been jointly funded by Otago University and the University Grants Committee. Our thanks also go to Television New Zealand for loan of equipment and studio time.

References

Barr AH (1984) Global and Local Deformations of Solid Primitives. *Computer Graphics* (Proc. SIGGRAPH 1984) 18 (3) : 21-30

Cook RL, Porter T and Carpenter L (1984) Distributed Ray Tracing. *Computer Graphics* (Proc. SIGGRAPH 1984) 18 (3) : 137-147

Foley JD and Van Dam A (1982) *Fundamentals of Interactive Computer Graphics.* Addison-Wesley, Chapter 14.

Fujimoto A, Tanaka T and Iwata K 1986: ARTS: Accelerated Ray Tracing System. *IEEE CG&A* 6 (4) : 16-26

Lambourne N (1965) *Renoir: paintings, drawings, lithographs and etchings.* The Folio Society, London

Leymarie J (1971) *Métamorphoses et Unité,* Editions D'Art Albert Skira S.A. Geneva (Also *Picasso The Artist of The Century* Viking, New York.)

Parslow Bob 1988: Private communication.

Roth SD (1982) Ray Casting for Modeling Solids. *Computer Graphics and Image Processing* 18 : 109-144

Sederberg TW and Parry SR (1986) Free-Form Deformation of Solid Geometric Models. *Computer Graphics* (Proc. SIGGRAPH 1986) 20 (4) : 151-160

Whitted T (1980) An Improved Illumination Model for Shaded Display. *Comm. ACM* 23 (6) : 343-349

Wyvill G, Ward A and Brown T (1987) Sketches by Ray Tracing. *Computer Graphics 1987* (Proc. CG International '87, Karuizawa) 315-333

Wyvill G and Sharp P (1989) Fast Antialiasing of Ray Traced Images. *New Advances in Computer Graphics* (Proc. CG International '89, Leeds) 579-588

Geoff Wyvill graduated in physics from Jesus College, Oxford, and started working with computers as a research technologist with the British Petroleum Company. He gained MSc and PhD degrees in computer science from the University of Bradford where he lectured in computer science from 1969 until 1978. He is currently senior lecturer in computer science at the University of Otago. He is on the editorial board of The Visual Computer and is a member of SIGGRAPH, ACM, CGS and NZCS.

Address: Department of Computer Science
University of Otago Box 56
Dunedin, New Zealand

Craig McNaughton is a graduate student at Otago University. His research interests include constructive solid geometry and computer animation. He completed his BSc degree in computer science in 1989 and he is a student member of ACM.

Address: Department of Computer Science
University of Otago Box 56
Dunedin, New Zealand

A Wrinkle Propagation Model for Cloth

Masaki Aono

ABSTRACTS

This paper focuses on a physically based non-rigid object model for the behavior of cloth, and its simulation with given forces and boundary conditions. The fundamental model is based on the equilibrium equation in the field of elasticity theory and on D'Alembert's principle. The model is enhanced by taking account of the damping factor, the anisotropic factor, and the modified constitutive equations between strain and stress, specifically viscoelastic factors for both static and dynamic forces. These enhancements greatly increase the flexibility of the model, and result in a capability for expressing very natural "wrinkles" in cloth. Since this model inherently includes differentials with respect to time, animation is easily attained.

KEY WORDS: cloth modeling, elasticity, viscoelasticity, anisotropy, animation

INTRODUCTION

Modeling of cloth objects is a challenging field in computer graphics, being a typical example of non-rigid or soft object modeling. Many efforts have been made to represent cloth objects (Barr 1984; Weil 1986; Terzopoulos 1987, 1988a, 1988b). The approaches can be broadly classified into two categories: one is called *the geometric approach*, which describes the "shape" of cloth entirely by continuous functions, and the other is called *the physical approach*, which describes the "state" of cloth by differential equations. An example of the geometric approach was described by Barr (1984). who employed Jacobians to deform the shapes of solids of various kinds. Another example of the geometric approach was Weil's catenaries (1986). His model was limited to simulating a piece of cloth, but it was suitable for representing cloth objects such as curtains and wrapping cloths. The problems involved in these examples of the geometric approach are that (1) the models have no concept of quantities varying with time, (2) the applicable shapes of cloth objects are limited, and (3) the models are weak in representing physical properties of cloth such as elasticity, anisotropy, and viscoelasticity.

An example of the physical approach was described by Terzopoulos et al. (1987, 1988a, 1988b). They employed deformable models based on the variational principle in a Lagrange form, and applied them to various continua for both elastic and inelastic objects. They incorporated the deformation process in the form of a differential equation based on the energy conservation law. This equation can be regarded as a modification of the "vibration equations" frequently employed in structural analysis. They focused mainly on the controllability of deformed shapes with parameters derived from differential geometric considerations, so they provided strain energy for deformed curves, surfaces, and solids in terms of differential geometry. A flag waving in the wind, as one of their simulations under a viscous force, looked realistic. Their models, however, are not panaceas and they have the following defects:

- Parameters based on their differential geometric considerations were not compatible with those that have been employed in structural analysis, such as Young's modulus, Poisson's ratio, and Lamé's constant. As a result, it is difficult to control the behavior of different cloth objects, each with distinct fiber characteristics.

- Strong anisotropy and inhomogeneity, which are prominently observable properties of cloth, are difficult to incorporate. As a result, the wrinkles in cloth obtained by solving the equation of motion are somewhat unnatural and artificial.

The cloth models described in this paper are basically examples of the physical approach, but they overcome the above-mentioned problems. The fundamental cloth model is based on the equilibrium equation in the field of elasticity theory and D'Alembert's principle (Timoshenko 1982), except that we prohibit displacements along the direction of surface normals of a given cloth, which is a unique constraint introduced here. This equation can be regarded as a kind of "wave equation." A wave equation generally has a dual relationship with a vibration equation, because a wave always entails a vibration, and vice versa. Starting with this basic cloth model, we enhance the model, taking account of the damping factor due to friction and so on (Ishikawa 1962), the anisotropic factor due to fiber characteristics and so on (Ishikawa 1962; Goto 1962), and the modified constitutive equations between stress and strain, specifically the viscoelastic factors for both static and dynamic external forces (Ishikawa 1962; Alfrey 1945). Because our cloth models include parameters popular in material and fiber engineering such as Young's modulus, Poisson's ratio, and Lamé's constant (Griffith 1921; Tobolsky 1943; Halsey 1945; Ripa 1951; Hammerle 1953; Wainwright 1976), they are more intuitive and easily controlled than the former approach mentioned above. Consequently, the behavior of wrinkle propagations can be simulated very realistically. Furthermore, the models are capable of dealing with distinct fiber characteristics such as differences based on the way of weaving on the raw materials of the cloth. Several experiments were carried out to show the validity of the models.

FUNDAMENTAL CLOTH MODEL

Let us assume that there is no wrinkle in a piece of cloth at the beginning and that wrinkles in the cloth are triggered by external forces, and are propagated continuously with the elapse of time. Cloth is thus considered to be a medium that transmits wrinkles. To allow it to play such a role, we must define an appropriate cloth model. The underlying assumptions in our fundamental cloth model are as follows:

1. The cloth is homogeneous, isotropic, and linearly elastic in its initial state.
2. The cloth is in equilibrium at any time under given applied forces, according to d'Alembert's principle.
3. The cloth is a perfectly thin surface, and never expands or contracts along the surface normal.

Assumption 1 is called the 'elastically isotropic assumption.' Homegeneity assures that this assumption applies everywhere in a piece of cloth. It is well-known that within its linearly elastic range, cloth is deformed under Hooke's law. The theory of elasticity (Timoshenko 1982) gives the formula, known as a stress-strain relationship or a constitutive equation, for an isotropic and linearly elastic body. For such a body, the relation between stress (τ_{ij}) and strain (ε_{ij}) is given by the following formula:

$$\begin{pmatrix} \varepsilon_{xx} \\ \varepsilon_{yy} \\ \varepsilon_{zz} \\ \varepsilon_{xy} \\ \varepsilon_{yz} \\ \varepsilon_{zx} \end{pmatrix} = \begin{pmatrix} \frac{1}{E} & -\frac{\nu}{E} & -\frac{\nu}{E} & & & \\ -\frac{\nu}{E} & \frac{1}{E} & -\frac{\nu}{E} & & 0 & \\ -\frac{\nu}{E} & -\frac{\nu}{E} & \frac{1}{E} & & & \\ & & & \frac{1}{2G} & & \\ & 0 & & & \frac{1}{2G} & \\ & & & & & \frac{1}{2G} \end{pmatrix} \begin{pmatrix} \tau_{xx} \\ \tau_{yy} \\ \tau_{zz} \\ \tau_{xy} \\ \tau_{yz} \\ \tau_{zx} \end{pmatrix}, \tag{1}$$

where E is the Young's modulus or the modulus of elasticity in tension, G is the modulus of rigidity or the modulus of elasticity in shear, and ν is the Poisson's ratio. There is a relationship among E, G, and ν for an elastically isotropic continuum: $G = \frac{E}{2(1+\nu)}$. Equation (1) says that the tensile strains ($\varepsilon_{kk}; k=x,y,z$) do not depend upon the shear stresses ($\tau_{ij}; i,j=x,y,z$, and $i\neq j$), and conversely the shear strains ($\varepsilon_{ij}; i,j=x,y,z$, and $i\neq j$) do not depend upon the tensile stresses ($\tau_{kk}; k=x,y,z$).

Assumption 2 is called the 'equilibrium assumption.' In d'Alembert's principle, cloth in motion is considered to be in equilibrium, as it is in a static state, by regarding the inertia force as being in proportion to the product of the density and the acceleration of the displacement. In addition, we assume the existence of a damping factor during motion, in the same way as in a vibration equation (Terzopoulos 1987; Pentland 1989). This damping factor is dependent upon the property of each material, and is proportional to the velocity of the displacement in each direction. Now the equilibrium equation of motion in a Cartesian coordinate system corresponding to assumption 2 becomes

$$\frac{\partial \tau_{ix}}{\partial x} + \frac{\partial \tau_{iy}}{\partial y} + \frac{\partial \tau_{iz}}{\partial z} + f_i = \rho \frac{\partial^2}{\partial t^2} u_i + c_i \frac{\partial}{\partial t} u_i, \tag{2}$$

where f_i is an applied force along the i-axis direction ($i = x,y,z$), c_i is a damping coefficient, u_i (assuming $u = u_x$, $v = u_y$, and $w = u_z$) is a displacement, and ρ is the density of the cloth, which is invariant in every direction. By eliminating τ_{ij} from equation (1),(2), and strain-displacement relations $\varepsilon_{ij} = \frac{1}{2}(\frac{\partial u_j}{\partial x_i} + \frac{\partial u_i}{\partial x_j})$, we obtain

$$G\nabla^2 u_i + (\lambda + G)\frac{\partial}{\partial x_i} e + f_i = \rho \frac{\partial^2}{\partial t^2} u_i + c_i \frac{\partial}{\partial t} u_i, \tag{3}$$

where $\lambda = \frac{E\nu}{(1-2\nu)(1+\nu)}$ is a Lamé's constant. This is a modified version of a famous equation (Timoshenko 1982) for waves propagated within an elastic continuum. Assumption 3 is a local rule specific to this cloth model. Because cloth is supposed to have no thickness along its surface normal, neither tensile nor shear dilatation along the z-axis is allowed. If we denote u,v,w as displacements along the x, y, and z axes, respectively, this assumption is interpreted as:

$$\frac{\partial u}{\partial z} = \frac{\partial v}{\partial z} = \frac{\partial w}{\partial z} = 0. \tag{4}$$

The direction along the z-axis is hereafter called 'the inhibited direction with respect to dilatation.' This assumption differs from both the 'plane stress' ($\tau_{zz} = \tau_{yz} = \tau_{zx} = 0$) and 'plane strain' ($\varepsilon_{zz} = \varepsilon_{yz} = \varepsilon_{zx} = 0$) assumptions, both of which are frequently hypothesized in structural analysis (Timoshenko 1982) to cope with planar objects. This is verified from equation (1): from $\varepsilon_{zz} \equiv \frac{\partial w}{\partial z} = \frac{1}{E}(-\nu\tau_{xx} - \nu\tau_{yy} + \tau_{zz}) = 0$, $\tau_{zz} = \nu(\tau_{xx} + \tau_{yy})(\neq 0)$, and from the definition of the strain-displacement relation, $\varepsilon_{yx} \equiv \frac{1}{2}(\frac{\partial v}{\partial z} + \frac{\partial w}{\partial y}) = \frac{1}{2}\frac{\partial w}{\partial y}(\neq 0)$, and $\varepsilon_{zx} = \frac{1}{2}\frac{\partial w}{\partial x}(\neq 0)$. Figure 1 illustrates the meaning of equation (4). Now, by substituting equation (4) into equation (3), the equation of motion for our fundamental cloth model is obtained:

$$G\nabla^2_{x,y} u_i + (\lambda + G)\frac{\partial}{\partial x_i} e_{x,y} + f_i = \rho \frac{\partial^2}{\partial t^2} u_i + c_i \frac{\partial}{\partial t} u_i, \tag{5}$$

where

$$\nabla^2_{x,y} = \frac{\partial^2}{\partial x^2} + \frac{\partial^2}{\partial y^2},$$

$$e_{x,y} = \frac{\partial u}{\partial x} + \frac{\partial v}{\partial y}.$$

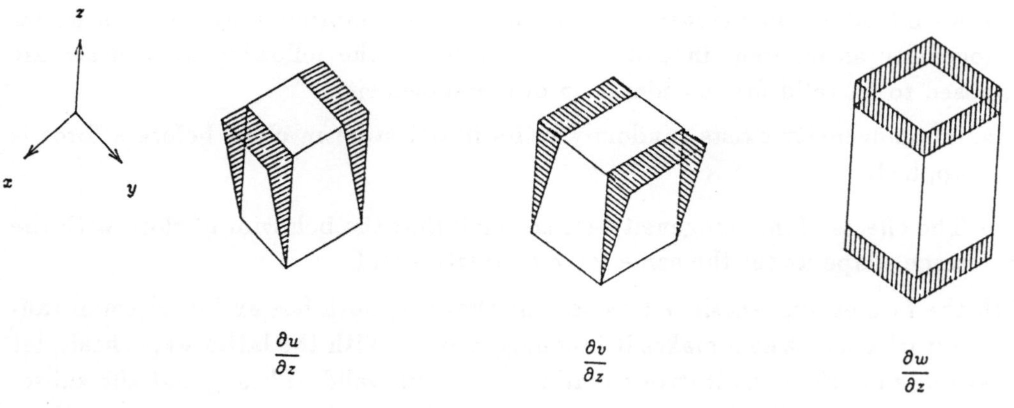

Fig. 1: The z-axis is the inhibited direction with respect to dilatation. The strains along the z-axis shown here are neglected.

It should be noted that assumption 3 can be applied to other coordinate systems. For example, the following equation is equivalent to equation (5), but is expressed in a cylindrical polar coordinate system (r,φ,z). Here the inhibited direction with respect to dilatation is the r-axis.

$$G\nabla^2_{\varphi,z}u_i + (\lambda + G)\frac{\partial}{\partial x_i}e_{\varphi,z} + f_i = \rho\frac{\partial^2}{\partial t^2}u_i + c_i\frac{\partial}{\partial t}u_i,$$

where

$$\nabla^2_{\varphi,z} = \frac{1}{r^2}\frac{\partial^2}{\partial\varphi^2} + \frac{\partial^2}{\partial z^2},$$

$$e_{\varphi,z} = \frac{1}{r}(\cos\varphi\frac{\partial v}{\partial\varphi} - \sin\varphi\frac{\partial u}{\partial\varphi}) + \frac{\partial w}{\partial z}.$$

The same assumption can also be applied to a spherical polar coordinate system (r,θ,φ), taking the r-axis as the inhibited direction with respect to dilatation.

INHOMOGENEITY

In the preceding section, cloth is assumed to be homogeneous in its initial state. This is not true in real life. There are often loosely threaded fibers, frayed and worn-out parts, twisted and distorted parts, and small bumps, all of which make cloth inhomogeneous. Thus, even with an identical force applied to cloth with the same shape, the resulting behavior is similar but not identical.

Here we introduce an extension of the original assumption 1 by considering inhomogeneity as inherent in cloth. For simplicity, the following hypotheses are supposed to be valid for consideration of inhomogeneity:

- Inhomogeneity exists randomly in its initial state in cloth before a force is applied.
- The effects of inhomogeneity are so small that the behavior of cloth with the same shape under the same force is nearly equal.

With the former hypothesis, let us assume that the cloth has an initial small random perturbation, which makes it inhomogeneous. With the latter hypothesis, let us assume that the constitutive equation (1) is still valid. Throughout the subsequent extensions of the fundamental cloth model, the inhomogeneity assumptions described above are supposed to be implicitly included.

ANISOTROPY

In general, fibers have strong anisotropy (Ishikawa 1962), and the ratio between the Young's modulus and the modulus of rigidity is different from that in an isotropic continuum. Here we introduce a second extension of assumption 1 by considering both global and local anisotropy.

Let us first focus on global anisotropy, where anisotropy affects the total shape of a piece of cloth after a force is applied. The constitutive equation (1), which gives a relation between stress and strain, is no longer valid under the assumption of global anisotropy. However, we preserve the assumption of linearity between them. In addition, the assumption that tensile strains have no effects on shear stresses and vice versa is supposed to be still valid here. With these modified assumptions, the constitutive equation for anisotropic continuum is given by the following formula:

$$\begin{pmatrix} \varepsilon_{xx} \\ \varepsilon_{yy} \\ \varepsilon_{zz} \\ \varepsilon_{xy} \\ \varepsilon_{yz} \\ \varepsilon_{zx} \end{pmatrix} = \begin{pmatrix} D_{xx} & D_{xy} & D_{xz} & & & \\ D_{yx} & D_{yy} & D_{yz} & & 0 & \\ D_{zx} & D_{zy} & D_{zz} & & & \\ & & & J_{xy} & & \\ & 0 & & & J_{yz} & \\ & & & & & J_{zx} \end{pmatrix} \begin{pmatrix} \tau_{xx} \\ \tau_{yy} \\ \tau_{zz} \\ \tau_{xy} \\ \tau_{yz} \\ \tau_{zx} \end{pmatrix}, \tag{6}$$

where D_{ij} $(i, j = x, y, z)$ and J_{ij} $(i, j = x, y, z,$ and $i \neq j)$ are independent constants. Normally, there exists the following inverse relation:

$$\begin{pmatrix} \tau_{xx} \\ \tau_{yy} \\ \tau_{zz} \\ \tau_{xy} \\ \tau_{yz} \\ \tau_{zx} \end{pmatrix} = \begin{pmatrix} E_{xx} & E_{xy} & E_{xz} & & & \\ E_{yx} & E_{yy} & E_{yz} & & 0 & \\ E_{zx} & E_{zy} & E_{zz} & & & \\ & & & G_{xy} & & \\ & 0 & & & G_{yz} & \\ & & & & & G_{zx} \end{pmatrix} \begin{pmatrix} \varepsilon_{xx} \\ \varepsilon_{yy} \\ \varepsilon_{zz} \\ \varepsilon_{xy} \\ \varepsilon_{yz} \\ \varepsilon_{zx} \end{pmatrix}. \tag{7}$$

By substituting equation (7) into equation (2), taking account of assumption 3, we obtain the following full set of differential equations for displacements u, v, and w, respectively:

$$E_{xx}\frac{\partial^2 u}{\partial x^2}+\frac{G_{xy}}{2}\frac{\partial^2 u}{\partial y^2}+(E_{xy}+\frac{G_{xy}}{2})\frac{\partial^2 v}{\partial x \partial y}+f_x=\rho\frac{\partial^2 u}{\partial t^2}+c_x\frac{\partial u}{\partial t},$$

$$\frac{G_{xy}}{2}\frac{\partial^2 v}{\partial x^2}+E_{yy}\frac{\partial^2 v}{\partial y^2}+(E_{yx}+\frac{G_{xy}}{2})\frac{\partial^2 u}{\partial x \partial y}+f_y=\rho\frac{\partial^2 v}{\partial t^2}+c_y\frac{\partial v}{\partial t}, \tag{8}$$

$$\frac{G_{zx}}{2}\frac{\partial^2 w}{\partial x^2}+\frac{G_{yz}}{2}\frac{\partial^2 w}{\partial y^2}+f_z=\rho\frac{\partial^2 w}{\partial t^2}+c_z\frac{\partial w}{\partial t}.$$

In a special case, by assigning $G_{xy}=G_{yz}=G_{zx}=2G$, $E_{xy}=E_{yz}=E_{zx}=E_{yx}=E_{zy}=E_{xz}=\lambda$, and $E_{xx}=E_{yy}=E_{zz}=2G+\lambda$, equation (7) or equivalently equation (8) coincides with equation (5) for an isotropic continuum.

Let us turn our attention to local anisotropy, which is mainly due to fiber characteristics. Up to this point, cloth has been considered as a kind of continuous non-rigid surface. However, cloth is usually made up of fibers woven or knitted in various ways. Let us concentrate on the case where cloth is a kind of woven fabric. As is generally recognized, woven fabrics are composed of *warps*, or vertical threads and *wefts*, or horizontal threads. Warps and wefts are normally interleaved in certain ways. As a typical and simple instance, Fig. 2 shows 'plain weaves,' where warps and wefts are interleaved alternately both vertically and horizontally. Intersections of warps and wefts, therefore, appear every other thread, continue for two consecutive grids, and disappear repeatedly. Local anisotropy can be achieved by introducing a variety of methods of wrinkle propagation corresponding to various types of weaving. Let $u_{x,y}$ denote the displacement of a discrete grid whose location is (x, y). Note that displacement $u_{x,y}$ propagates mainly with the diffusion term $\nabla^2_{x,y}u_{x,y}$ in our cloth model, represented by equation (5). The most fundamental and popularly employed interpretation of $\nabla^2_{x,y}u_{x,y}$ is:

$$\nabla^2_{x,y}u_{x,y}\approx u_{x+1,y}+u_{x-1,y}+u_{x,y+1}+u_{x,y-1}-4u_{x,y}.$$

Or, if we take eight neighbors, it will be:

$$\begin{aligned}\nabla^2_{x,y}u_{x,y} \approx\ & u_{x-1,y-1}+u_{x-1,y}+u_{x-1,y+1}+u_{x+1,y-1}+u_{x+1,y}+\\ & u_{x+1,y+1}+u_{x,y+1}+u_{x,y-1}-8u_{x,y}.\end{aligned}$$

In plain weaves, $\nabla^2_{x,y}u_{x,y}$ differs according to whether a warp is in front ($\nabla^2_{x,y}u^{\perp}_{x,y}$) or a weft is in front ($\nabla^2_{x,y}u^{\top}_{x,y}$). For example, if a warp is in front at a particular grid, the effect of the displacement may be bigger on the vertical grids two units apart than on the adjacent horizontal grids. Thus, the following diffusion term is given to the grid where a warp is in front,

$$\nabla^2_{x,y}u^{\perp}_{x,y}\approx 2u_{x,y-2}+2u_{x,y+2}+u_{x-1,y}+u_{x+1,y}+u_{x,y+1}+u_{x,y-1}-8u_{x,y}.$$

In the same way, for the grid where a weft is in front:

$$\nabla^2_{x,y} u^{\mathsf{T}}_{x,y} \approx 2u_{x-2,y} + 2u_{x+2,y} + u_{x-1,y} + u_{x+1,y} + u_{x,y+1} + u_{x,y-1} - 8u_{x,y}.$$

The same arguments can be applied not only to other types of woven fabrics, but to knitted fabrics, lace, and braid.

The difference between global and local anisotropy is summarized as follows: Global anisotropy affects the total shape of cloth after a force is applied in such a way that a wrinkle is produced extensively along the direction of anisotropy. Local anisotropy affects the method of wrinkle propagation by introducing various diffusion terms corresponding to the way of weaving. Local anisotropy may or may not affect the total shape of cloth, because the warp and weft diffusion terms may cancel each other out.

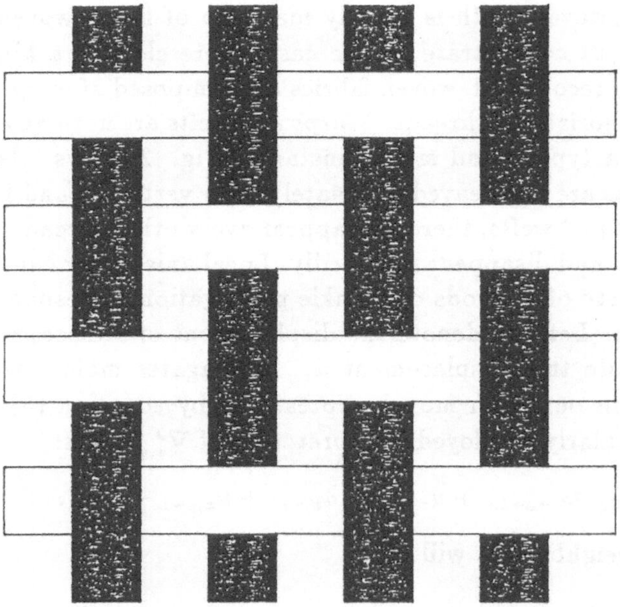

Fig. 2: Plain weaves. Warps and wefts are interleaved alternately both vertically and horizontally. This is a typical example of woven fabrics in which local anisotropy occurs.

VISCOELASTICITY

In addition to the strong anisotropy observed in fiber, another remarkable characteristic is its viscoelasticity, which is a property in-between elasticity and viscosity (Ishikawa 1962; Goto 1962; Ferry 1980). This means that the deformation at one time of cloth made of fibers generally depends on the history of the deformation from the initiation of the applied force. For instance, a continuing static force makes the strain in a fiber increase with time (the creep phenomenon), and conversely a constant strain makes the stress of a fiber decrease with time (the stress relaxation phenomenon). We introduce another extension of assumption 1 by considering viscoelasticity, but the main attention here is paid to the creep phenomena.

Typical well-known viscoelastic models are defined by combining a Hookean spring element and a Newtonian dashpot element. If connected in series, they form a so-called 'Maxwell model,' and if connected in parallel, a 'Voigt model.' Usually a Maxwell model accounts for a simple stress relaxation and a Voigt model for a simple creep. Real creep phenomena in fibers, however, cannot be fully described by this simple Voigt model composed of two elements. The strains in a fiber under static stress can be basically classified into instantaneous elastic strain (ε^e), retarded elastic strain (ε^λ, creep strain of the first degree), and non-recoverable viscous strain (ε^η, creep strain of the second degree). Based on Boltzmann's superposition principle (Ishikawa 1962; Goto 1962), the total strain at time t is represented by the following equation:

$$\varepsilon(t) = \varepsilon^e(t) + \varepsilon^\lambda(t) + \varepsilon^\eta(t). \tag{9}$$

Some kinds of fiber, especially those made from polymers with net-like structure, do not exhibit viscous strain (Ishikawa 1962). Taking account of these phenomenogical aspects, we can employ a generalized Voigt model, as shown in Fig. 3. Actually, it includes a Hookean spring element representing instantaneous elastic strain, multiple Voigt elements in series representing detarded elastic strain, and a Newtonian dashpot element representing static viscous strain. With this model, the above-mentioned strains at time t under a stress function $\tau(t)$ are given as:

$$\varepsilon^e(t) = \frac{1}{G^0}\tau(t), \tag{10}$$

$$\varepsilon^\lambda(t) = \sum_{k=1}^{n} \frac{1}{\eta^k} \int_0^t e^{\frac{G^k}{\eta^k}(\xi - t)} \tau(\xi) d\xi, \tag{11}$$

$$\varepsilon^\eta(t) = \frac{1}{\eta^0} \int_0^t \tau(\xi) d\xi, \tag{12}$$

where G^0 denotes the spring constant for an instantaneous elastic strain, η^0 denotes the viscous coefficient for a static viscous flow, and G^k and η^k denote the spring constant and viscous coefficient in the k-th Voigt element, respectively. It is also

assumed that $\tau(t)=0$ when $t=0$. The number of Voigt elements (k) is usually taken as a small number. For instance, if $k=1$ it becomes a popular four-element model (Terzopoulos 1988; Goto 1962).
In particular, if the stress function $\tau(t) = \tau^0$ (constant), the total strain $\varepsilon(t)$ is as follows:

$$\varepsilon(t) = \tau^0[\frac{1}{G^0} + \sum_{k=1}^{n} \frac{1}{G^k}(1 - e^{-\frac{G^k}{\eta^k}t}) + \frac{1}{\eta^0}t]. \tag{13}$$

This equation represents a creep phenomenon based on a generalized Voigt model. In real life, a cloth wrinkle is often produced by a variety of forces whose intensities are not constant. Some of these phenomena can be treated with the assumption of a periodic stress function. For example, wrinkles in shirts or jackets seem to change periodically with a walking action. Periodic stress functions have been used for measuring the properties of viscoelastic materials in rheology (Ishikawa 1962; Goto 1962; Alfrey 1945). For simplicity, let us assume the following sinuisoidal stress function for the generalized Voigt model:

$$\tau(t) = \tau^0 \sin \omega t.$$

Then, the total strain at time t under the periodic stress $\tau(t)$ is given as follows:

$$\varepsilon(t) = \tau^0[\frac{\sin \omega t}{G^0} + \sum_{k=1}^{n} \frac{\sin(\omega t - \delta)}{G^k\sqrt{(\omega\eta^k/G^k)^2 + 1}} - \frac{\cos \omega t}{\eta^0 \omega}], \tag{14}$$

where $\tan \delta = \omega\eta^k/G^k$.
Although equation (9) is originally defined for shear stresses and shear strains in linear viscoelastic materials, we extend this assumption to the relation between tensile stresses and tensile strains. Again, we assume that tensile strains have no effects on shear stresses and vice versa, and also assume anisotropy as defined in the preceding section. The constitutive equation at time t is then given by the following formula:

$$\begin{pmatrix} \varepsilon_{xx}(t) \\ \varepsilon_{yy}(t) \\ \varepsilon_{zz}(t) \\ \varepsilon_{xy}(t) \\ \varepsilon_{yz}(t) \\ \varepsilon_{zx}(t) \end{pmatrix} = \begin{pmatrix} D_{xx}(t) & D_{xy}(t) & D_{xz}(t) & & & \\ D_{yx}(t) & D_{yy}(t) & D_{yz}(t) & & 0 & \\ D_{zx}(t) & D_{zy}(t) & D_{zz}(t) & & & \\ & & & J_{xy}(t) & & \\ & 0 & & & J_{yz}(t) & \\ & & & & & J_{zx}(t) \end{pmatrix} \begin{pmatrix} \tau^0_{xx} \\ \tau^0_{yy} \\ \tau^0_{zz} \\ \tau^0_{xy} \\ \tau^0_{yz} \\ \tau^0_{zx} \end{pmatrix}, \tag{15}$$

where, for example,

$$D_{ij}(t) = \begin{cases} \frac{1}{G^0_{ij}} + \sum_{k=1}^{n} \frac{1}{G^k_{ij}}(1 - e^{-\frac{G^k_{ij}}{\eta^k_{ij}}t}) + \frac{1}{\eta^0_{ij}}t & \text{if } \tau_{ij}(t) = \tau^0_{ij} \\ \frac{\sin \omega t}{G^0_{ij}} + \sum_{k=1}^{n} \frac{\sin(\omega t - \delta_{ij})}{G^k_{ij}\sqrt{(\omega\eta^k_{ij}/G^k_{ij})^2 + 1}} - \frac{\cos \omega t}{\eta^0_{ij}\omega} & \text{if } \tau_{ij}(t) = \tau^0_{ij} \sin \omega t \end{cases},$$

and $J_{ij}(i, j = x, y, z$, and $i \neq j)$ is similarly defined. D_{ij} (and J_{ij}) is called 'creep compliance' for a static stress, and 'dynamic compliance' for a sinuisoidal stress function. It should be noted that equation (15) does not directly state the relationship between $\varepsilon_{ij}(t)$ and $\tau_{ij}(t)$.

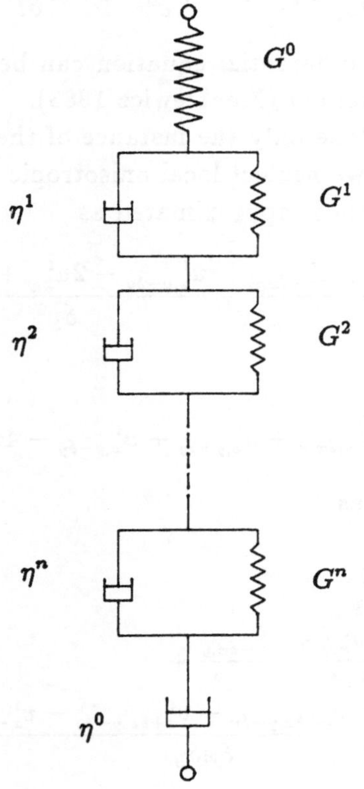

Fig. 3: Generalized Voigt model. This model is suitable for simulating real creep phenomena in fibers.

DISCRETIZATION

Here discretization of the equation

$$G\nabla^2_{x,y}u_i + (\lambda + G)\frac{\partial}{\partial x_i}e_{x,y} + f_i = \rho\frac{\partial^2}{\partial t^2}u_i + c_i\frac{\partial}{\partial t}u_i$$

is described. This type of partial differential equation can be discretized simply by applying the finite difference method (Zienkiewicz 1983).
Without loss of generality, let us take only the instance of the above equation in which $i = 1$ (along the x-axis.) If we neglect local anisotropic effects in our cloth model, the first term of the equation is approximated as

$$\nabla^2_{x,y}u \approx \frac{u^t_{x+\delta x,y} - 2u^t_{x,y} + u^t_{x-\delta x,y}}{\delta x^2} + \frac{u^t_{x,y+\delta y} - 2u^t_{x,y} + u^t_{x,y-\delta y}}{\delta y^2}.$$

Assuming that $\delta x = \delta y = 1$, we get

$$\nabla^2_{x,y}u \approx u^t_{x+\delta x,y} + u^t_{x-\delta x,y} + u^t_{x,y+\delta y} + u^t_{x,y-\delta y} - 4u^t_{x,y}.$$

The second term is approximated as

$$\begin{aligned}\frac{\partial}{\partial x}e_{x,y} &= \frac{\partial^2 u}{\partial x^2} + \frac{\partial^2 v}{\partial x \partial y} \\ &\approx \frac{u^t_{x+\delta x,y} - 2u^t_{x,y} + u^t_{x-\delta x,y}}{\delta x^2} + \\ &\quad \frac{v^t_{x+\delta x,y+\delta y} + v^t_{x-\delta x,y-\delta y} - v^t_{x+\delta x,y-\delta y} - v^t_{x-\delta x,y+\delta y}}{4\delta x \delta y}.\end{aligned}$$

By analogy with the convention of the first term, we obtain

$$\frac{\partial}{\partial x}e_{x,y} \approx u^t_{x+\delta x,y} - 2u^t_{x,y} + u^t_{x-\delta x,y} + (v^t_{x+\delta x,y+\delta y} + v^t_{x-\delta x,y-\delta y} - v^t_{x+\delta x,y-\delta y} - v^t_{x-\delta x,y+\delta y})/4.$$

Meanwhile, the right-hand terms of the equation are approximated respectively as

$$\frac{\partial^2}{\partial t^2}u \approx \frac{u^{t+\delta t}_{x,y} - 2u^t_{x,y} + u^{t-\delta t}_{x,y}}{\delta t^2}$$

and

$$\frac{\partial}{\partial t}u \approx \frac{u^{t+\delta t}_{x,y} - u^{t-\delta t}_{x,y}}{2\delta t}.$$

Now putting these approximated terms back into the equation, we obtain

$$A_x u^{t+\delta t}_{x,y} = B_x \dot{u}^t_{x,y} + C_x u^t_{x,y} + D^t_{x,y}(u, v) + F^t_x,$$

where

$$\begin{aligned}
\dot{u}^t_{x,y} &= (u^t_{x,y} - u^{t-\delta t}_{x,y})/\delta t, \\
A_x &= \rho/\delta t^2 + c_x/2\delta t, \\
B_x &= \rho/\delta t - c_x/2, \\
C_x &= \rho/\delta t^2 + c_x/2\delta t - 2(3G + \lambda), \\
D^t_{x,y}(u,v) &= (\lambda + 2G)(u^t_{x+\delta x,y} + u^t_{x-\delta x,y}) + G(u^t_{x,y+\delta y} + u^t_{x,y-\delta y}) + \\
&\quad (\lambda + G)(v^t_{x+\delta x,y+\delta y} + v^t_{x-\delta x,y-\delta y} - v^t_{x+\delta x,y-\delta y} - v^t_{x-\delta x,y+\delta y})/4, \\
F^t_x &= f^t_x.
\end{aligned}$$

Likewise, the following formulae are obtained:

$$A_y v^{t+\delta t}_{x,y} = B_y \dot{v}^t_{x,y} + C_y v^t_{x,y} + D^t_{x,y}(u,v) + F^t_y,$$

$$A_z w^{t+\delta t}_{x,y} = B_z \dot{w}^t_{x,y} + C_z w^t_{x,y} + D^t_{x,y}(w) + F^t_z.$$

Note that these equations describe deflections u^t, v^t, w^t, and that there is a dependency among them. For example, $D^t_{x,y}(u,v)$ depends both on u and v values.

EXAMPLES

In this section, several examples are described in which the behavior of cloth is simulated under several different circumstances. The focus is on the propagation of wrinkles, or the history of displacements, varying with time.

(1) *A handkerchief with free boundary condition*
As shown in Fig. 4, we assume that a handkerchief is initially located at the $z = 0$ plane, and that one of the corners of the handkerchief is coincident with the origin of the Cartesian coordinate system. Let the x-axis be parallel to one side of the handkerchief, and let the y-axis be parallel to another side of the handkerchief. Two impulse forces, appearing with constant strength only within a certain range of times are given here: F2 in Fig. 4 acts at the origin in a diagonal direction, and F1 acts at the opposite diagonal position toward the origin of the handkerchief. The objective of this example is to compare the ideal behavior of three different cloth models (isotropic, anisotropic, and viscoelastic models), with free boundary condition. This assumption may be thought of as being equivalent to assuming that the handkerchief is located in gravity-free space. The experiments are on three different models: (Case A), an elastically isotropic model; (Case B), an elastically anisotropic model; and (Case C), a viscoelastically anisotropic model. Figures 5a through 5i show the results of behaviors of wrinkle propagation in cloth varying with time for an elastically isotropic cloth model. Here wrinkles are almost regularly propagated in a manner analogous to plane waves. Figures 6a through 6i show the results for an elastically anisotropic model with the same environment as in the preceding case, except that there is strong anisotropy along

the x-axis, which means that the waves propagate fastest along the x-axis. Figures 7a through 7i show the results for a viscoelastically anisotropic model. Because of its viscoelasticity, wrinkles in the cloth will not propagate promptly. However, once they are formed, they tend to keep the deformed shapes for a certain period, instead of disappearing very quickly.

Fig. 4: Coordinate system for a handkerchief. Two forces with opposite directions are applied.

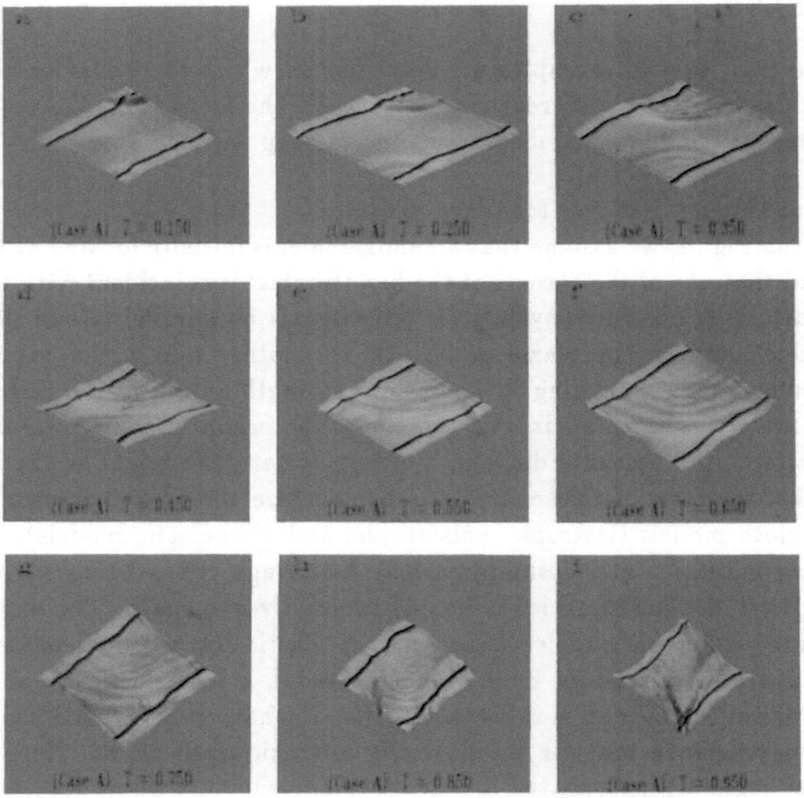

Fig. 5a-5i: Wrinkles propagating in an isotropic and elastic handkerchief

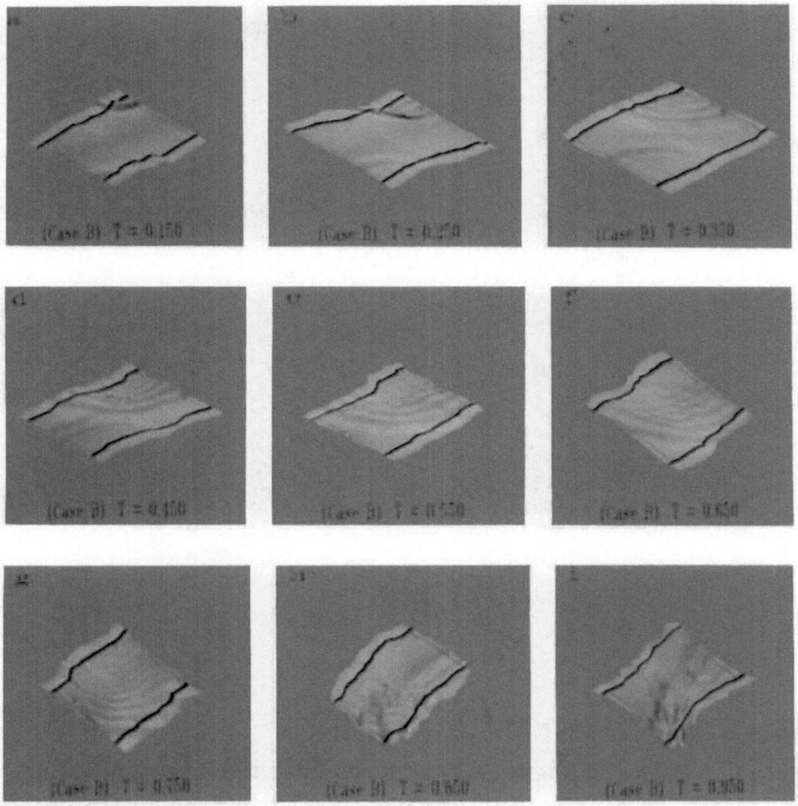

Fig. 6a-6i: Wrinkles propagating in an anisotropic and elastic handkerchief. Strong anisotropy exists here along the x-axis.

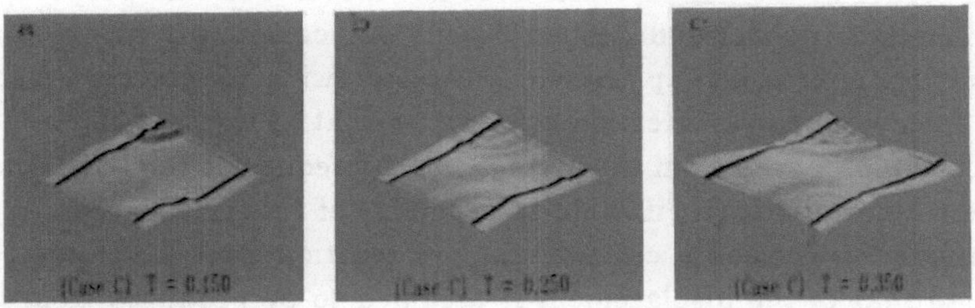

Fig. 7a-7i: Wrinkles propagating in an anisotropic and viscoelastic handkerchief

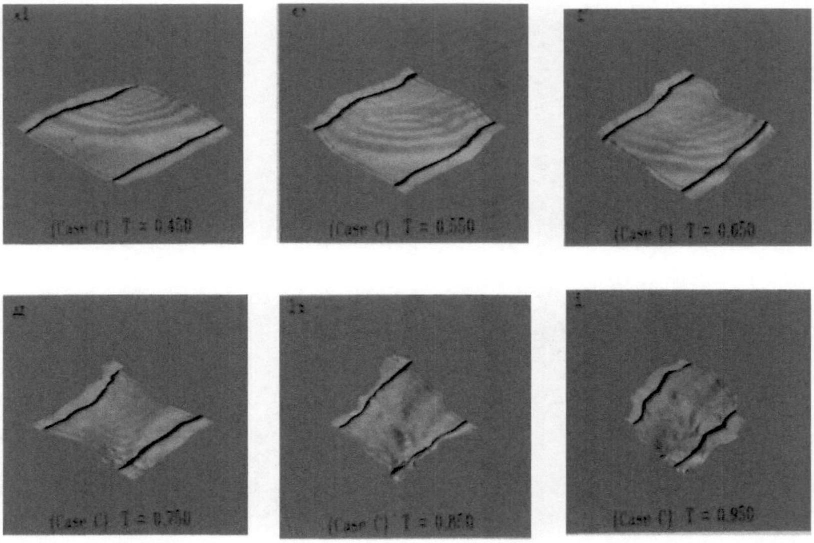

Fig. 7

(2) A handkerchief with fixed boundary conditions

In this example, shown in Figure 8, let us consider the situation in which a handkerchief is located on a plate, and one corner of it is fixed by an immovable pin. The coordinate system is assumed to be the same as in the previous example. The boundary conditions that must be satisfied here are that (**condition A**) the handkerchief does not penetrate the surface of the plate and that (**condition B**) the fixed corner of the handkerchief does not move. For this purpose, a kind of "penalty method" (Platt 1988) is employed: For **condition A**, when a discrete grid point is found to inter penetrate the plate owing to wrinkle propagation, a reaction force vector in a direction opposite to that of the wrinkle propagation is assumed to be produced from the plate at the subsequent discretized time $(t+\delta t.)$ Likewise, for **condition B**, if the displacements of the fixed corner at particular time are found to exceed a certain range, a reaction force vector in a direction opposite to that of the displacement is assumed to be produced from the pin at the subsequent discretized time. Figures 8a and 8b show the results for rather inhomogeneous, but isotropic handkerchieves deformed under the conditions stated above by applying external compressive and tensile forces, respectively. Note that both of these forces are applied only for a short while at the beginning. Each of the figures shows an instant in the process of wrinkle propagation after the corresponding force is released. Because these forces can be regarded as "axial forces," their results demonstrate a kind of "Euler buckling" phenomenon of elastic objects (Timoshenko 1983). Cloth wrinkles of this kind are often observed in daily life.

(3) *A sleeve around a fixed cylinder with a fixed boundary condition*
Here, in contrast to the previous examples, we employ periodical external forces applied at both ends of a cylindrical sleeve. This example is intended to simulate wrinkles in cloth produced by a periodical movement such as "walking." The boundary condition is that a sleeve should not penetrate a cylindrical solid body located just inside the surrounding sleeve. As in the previous example, if a point on the sleeve is found to inter penetrate the cylindrical solid body, a reaction force is assumed to be produced in a direction opposite to the penetrating direction at the subsequent discretized time. Figure 9 demonstrates the result for a sleeve with an isotropic characteristic. We also assume that the periodical external forces initially act in opposite directions at both ends of the sleeve, but have the same amplitude and period.

(4) *A sleeve around a bending cylinder with a fixed boundary condition*
Finally, as an extension of the previous example, we show an example of a sleeve around a "bending" cylinder. We assume that, during the bending, an internal force from the cylinder is generated when a point on the sleeve is found to inter penetrate the cylindrical solid body, and it acts in the same direction with the bending direction. An aggregate of these forces causes wrinkles on the sleeve as a whole, and the wrinkles are especially remarkable around the most curved portion of the cylinder. The boundary condition is almost the same with the previous example except that the forces are internally generated with the bending, instead of being given initially. Figure 10 shows the result.

CONCLUSION

In this paper, physically-based models for cloth were discussed, using a kind of "wave equation" with enhanced features. Because the models include intuitive parameters such as Young's modulus, Poisson's ratio, and Lamé's constant, it is very easy to control the differences among cloth objects with distinct fiber characteristics. In addition, since the models incorporate inhomogeneity, global and local anisotropy, and viscoelasticity of cloth in a unified framework, they can be applied to a great variety of cloth objects, and the resulting wrinkles in cloth are shown to be very natural.

DISCUSSION

The assumption that tensile strains have no effect on shear stresses and shear strains have no effect on tensile stresses, may indeed be a strong imposition on the model. However, the situation becomes extremely complex if we accept general stress-strain relations for cloth, including non-linear ones where tensile strains affect both tensile and shear stresses and vice versa. For practical reasons, it is desirable for the model to have as few parameters as possible, and to give as flexible an output as possible. In view of these considerations, it may be reasonable to postulate the above assumption.

Acknowledgements

The author would like to thank Mr. K. Sugimoto, manager of applied graphics, and Dr. T. Kaneko, manager of the Tokyo Scientific Center, Tokyo Research Laboratory, IBM Japan, for their continuous support and encouragement in this work. Thanks are also due to Dr. A. Koide and Mr. K. Koyamada for their valuable comments concerning physics and the numerical handling of partial differential equations.

REFERENCES

1. Turner Alfrey and Paul Doty (1945) The Methods of Specifying the Properties of Viscoelastic Materials. *Journal of Applied Physics* **16** (November) 700-713
2. Alan H. Barr (1984) Global and Local Deformations of Solid Primitives. *Computer Graphics* **18**(3) 21-29
3. John D. Ferry (1980) *Viscoelastic Properties of Polymers* John Wiley & Sons
4. Renpei Goto et al. (1962) *Rheology and its Applications* Kyoritsu Shuppan Co., Chapter 4 and 5, in Japanese
5. A. A. Griffith (1921) The Phenomena of Rupture and Flow in Solids *Trans. Roy. Soc.* **A221** 163-198
6. George Halsey, Howard J. White, Jr. and Henry Eyring (1945) Mechanical Properties of Textiles. *Textile Research Journal* **15**(9) 295-311
7. W. G. Hammerle and D. J. Montgomery (1953) Mechanical Behavior of Nylon Filaments in Torsion *Textile Research Journal* **23**(9) 595-604
8. K. Ishikawa et al Ed. (1962) *Fiber Physics* Maruzen Co., Tokyo, in Japanese
9. Alex Pentland and John Williams (1989) Good Vibration: Modal Dynamics for Graphics and Animation. *Computer Graphics* **23**(3) 215-222
10. John.C. Platt and Alan H. Barr (1988) Constraint Methods for Flexivle Models. *Computer Graphics* **22**(4) 279-288
11. O. Ripa and J. B. Speakman (1951) The Plasticity of Wool. *Textile Research Journal* **21** 215-221

12. Demetri Terzopoulos (1987) Elastically Deformable Models. *Computer Graphics* **21**(4) 205-214

13. Demetri Terzopoulos and Kurt Fleischer (1988a) Modeling Inelastic Deformation: Viscoelasticity, Plasticity, Fracture. *Computer Graphics* **22**(4) 269-278

14. Demetri Terzopoulos and Kurt Fleischer (1988b) Deformable Models. *The Visual Computer* **4** 306-331

15. Stephen P. Timoshenko and J.N. Goodier (1982) *Theory of Elasticity* McGraw-Hill Book Co.

16. Stephen P. Timoshenko and James M. Gere (1983) *Theory of Elastic Stability* McGraw-Hill Book Co.

17. Arthur Tobolsky and Henry Eyring (1943) Mechanical Properties of Polymetric Materials. *Journal of Chemical Physics* **11** 125-134

18. Jerry Weil (1986) The Synthesis of Cloth Objects. *Computer Graphics* **20**(4) 49-54

19. S. A. Wainwright et al. (1976) *Mechnical Design of Organisms* Princeton University Press

20. O.C. Zienkiewicz and K.Morgan (1983) *Finite Elements and Approximation* John Wiley & Sons

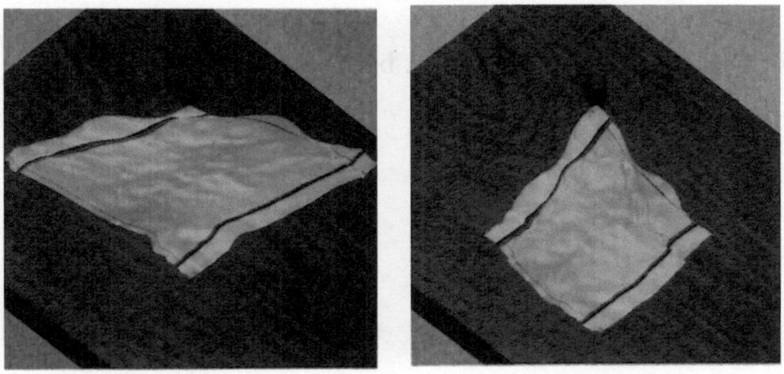

Fig. 8a and 8b: A handkerchief with fixed boundary conditions: a compressive force for Figure 8a and a tensile force for Figure 8b. Both forces are of impulse type, so they are applied only for a short period.

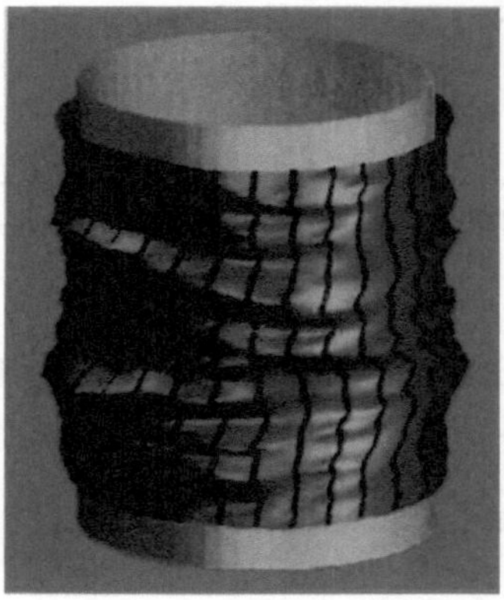

Fig. 9: Wrinkles in a sleeve around a fixed cylindrical impenetrable body

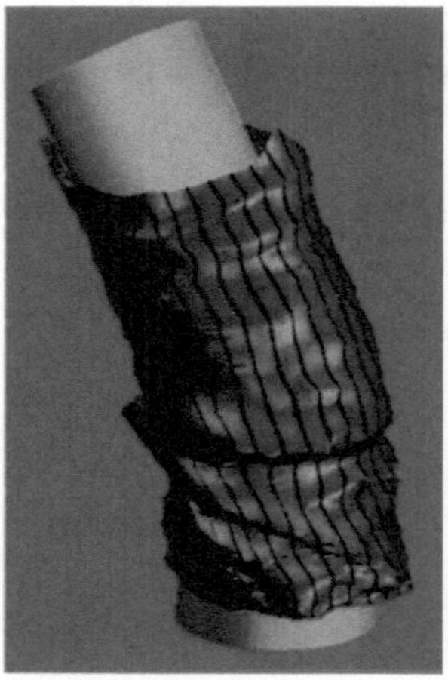

Fig. 10: Wrinkles in a sleeve around a bending cylindrical impenetrable body

Bibliography

Masaki Aono is a researcher in the Applied Graphics Group at the Tokyo Scientific Center in Tokyo Research Laboratory, IBM Japan Ltd. He received BSc and MSc degrees in information science from the University of Tokyo in 1981 and 1984. He is a member of the IEEE Society and the ACM. His research interests include computer graphics, computational geometry, physically and biologically based modeling.

Address: IBM Research, Tokyo Research Laboratory, 5-19 Sanbancho, Chiyoda-ku, Tokyo, 102 Japan.

Highly Realistic Visual Simulation of Outdoor Scenes Under Various Atmospheric Conditions

Kazufumi Kaneda, Takashi Okamoto, Eihachiro Nakamae, and Tomoyuki Nishita

ABSTRACT

A method for creating realistic images is proposed from the view point of displaying simulation results when designing a building in which various weather conditions are taken into account.

So far, in order to create realistic images for interior design, the concept of radiosity as ambient light including spectral distribution has been developed. The method can display not only the brightness but also the hue and saturation of color. In contrast, for designing a building sky light has been treated as ambient light, in which the brightness under various weather conditions could be calculated, but the influences on the hue and saturation of color were ignored.

The proposed method creates realistic images considering the brightness, hue and saturation under various atmospheric conditions by taking into account the spectral distribution of both direct sunlight and sky light. Views of buildings including the influences of the particles in the atmosphere, i.e. clouds, fog, and beams, are useful for design not only of new buildings but also of new city areas.

Key Words: Sky Light, Specular Reflectance, Atmospheric Scattering Model, Visual Environment, Building Design

1 INTRODUCTION

There are two approaches for rendering images: one is displaying realistic images for entertainment and art, and the other is displaying simulation results for environmental assessment and building design. We take the latter approach in this paper.

For designing and pre-evaluating a building, it is particularly desirable to display not only the figures of the completed building but also its images with the surroundings under various atmospheric conditions. A building has its own attributes such as color and reflection. However when it is lit by the sunlight under various atmospheric conditions, the hue of the building changes greatly, as well as its brightness and saturation, caused by various influences such as spectral distribution and intensity of light sources (direct sunlight and sky light in our applications) which are determined by the position of the sun and atmospheric conditions, and the relationship between the position of the building and the various objects obscuring it.

We propose here a method for displaying realistic images of 3-D objects, i.e. buildings, and particles in the atmosphere, i.e. cloud and haze, under various atmospheric conditions taking account of the spectral distribution of direct sunlight and sky light as an ambient light source.

Both direct light and ambient light should be taken into account in order to simulate lighting effect for environmental assessment, and so far the following methods have been developed.

For direct light, in the 1970s, a parallel light source was usually used. In the 1980s, methods for shading and shadowing 3-D objects lit by various artificial light sources such as a point light source [Nishita 85a], a linear light source [Nishita 85a], an area light source [Nishita 83], etc. were developed by the authors. In 1987, Klassen [Klassen 87] proposed a method for displaying the color of the sun and the hue of the sky taking into account both scattering and absorption of the sunlight due to air molecules and aerosols in the atmosphere. Inakage [Inakage 89] improved Klassen's method by approximating geometric optics for large particles such as raindrops, but the method is inadequate to generate realistic images for visual assessment because of not taking into account sky light and specular reflectance.

For ambient light, in the 1970s, the methods of adding either an uniform ambient light to the lighting model or a secondary light source coincident with the viewpoint was employed. In order to calculate exactly ambient light inside a room, Cohen et al. [Cohen 85] and the authors [Nishita 85b] proposed a method considering the inter-reflection of light, so called radiosity. In the former the phenomenon of color bleeding can be rendered, i.e., not only brightness but also hue and saturation of color are taken into account. Furthermore, Immel et al. [Immel 86] and Kajiya [Kajiya 86] developed a method considering specular reflectance, and Rushmeier et al. [Rushmeier 87] generalized the radiosity method for displaying beams of light due to particles in the atmosphere in a room. On the other hand, for ambient light in the open air the authors [Nishita 86] proposed a method for shading and shadowing taking into account of sky light. This method, however, only can display the brightness under various weather conditions, without the influences on the hue and saturation of color caused by spectral distribution of sky light.

Here a method for creating realistic images of outdoor 3-D objects such as buildings and streets considering specular reflection is proposed. In our proposed method, based on Klassen's model, the colors of the sun and sky, calculated by using the atmospheric scattering model and the spectral distribution of sunlight, are employed for direct sunlight and sky light. Ways to display not only shading and shadowing but also beam and fog effects caused by the direct sunlight and sky light with spectral distributions are described. The proposed method can create outdoor images taking account of hue, brightness, and saturation.

Further an improvement to Klassen's model concerning calculation of the color of the sun and sky is described in the next section. Rendering 3-D objects and clouds lit by direct sunlight and sky light are the topics of Section 3 and Section 4, respectively, and beam and fog effects are discussed in Section 5.

2 IMPROVEMENT OF THE ATMOSPHERIC SCATTERING MODEL

It is well known that sunlight is scattered or absorbed by the ozone layer, air molecules, and aerosols, as it passes through the atmosphere. Generally speaking, for visible wavelengths of light, absorption in the ozone layer is negligible compared with absorption by air molecules and aerosols. For particles small compared with the wavelength of the light, i.e. air molecules, Rayleigh scattering predominates. On the other hand, for large particles of a size larger than the wavelength of the light, i.e. aerosols, Mie scattering predominates.

In Klassen's atmospheric scattering model the distribution of Rayleigh particles is divided into two layers with uniform distributed particles in each layer. In fact, the density of air molecules decreases exponentially with altitude. Then, taking into account the density ratio of air molecules to the standard atmosphere (molecular density at sea level,) the light reflected due to Rayleigh scattering is calculated. The molecular density ratio ρ depends on the altitude h and is given by

$$\rho = \exp(-\frac{h}{H_0}), \tag{1}$$

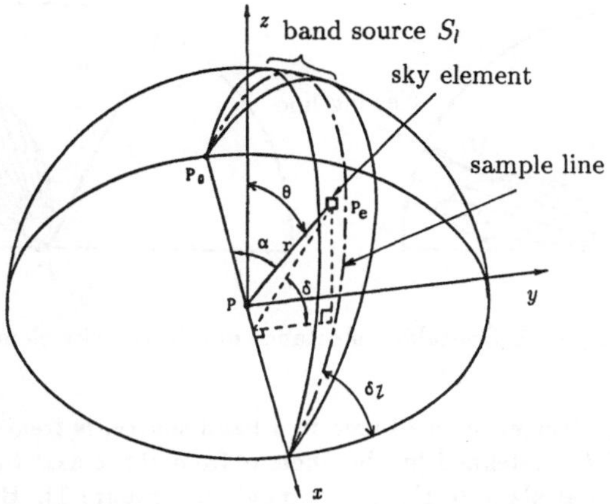

Figure 1: Subdivision of the sky dome into band sources (P : calculation point)

where H_0 is a scale height (H_0 = 7994 [m]), which corresponds to the atmosphere thickness if the density were uniform.

For calculation of the sunlight scattered by aerosols, in Klassen's model the aerosols distribute in a flat layer. When the altitude of the sun is low, i.e. the case of dawn or sunset, the distance between the sunlight and the calculation point, passing through the atmosphere with aerosols, becomes infinite. To deal with this problem, the spherical-shell atmosphere model used for the air molecules mentioned above is used. From the view point of a macro-sized object like the earth, the density of aerosols decreases exponentially with altitude, like the density distribution of air molecules does, even though the rate of decrease is different from that of air molecules. The density can be calculated by setting the scale height, H_0, of Eq. 1 to 1.2 km [Sekine 87]. Displaying fog, in which the density has a different distribution from that mentioned above and is much higher, is described in Section 5.

3 RENDERING 3-D OBJECTS LIT BY SKY LIGHT

The method for rendering 3-D objects lit by sky light calculated by using the improved atmospheric scattering model taking account of its spectral distribution is described here.

The sky is taken as a hemisphere light source with a large radius (called the sky dome). The dome is subdivided into bands in the same way as those of reference [Nishita 86], and in each band the intensity of light varies in the band axis direction and is fixed at a constant value in the width direction (See Figure 1). In the case of the diffuse reflectance described in [Nishita 86], the band width is allowed to be fairly wide and is fixed because of the constant intensity of diffuse reflectance in every direction. On the other hand, it is well known that the intensity of the specular reflectance tends to the specified direction. Therefore, in this case a part of the sky dome may be enough for the calculation of specular reflectance even though the band width is narrow.

3.1 Specular Reflectance due to Sky Light

For calculation of specular reflectance due to sky light, the Cook-Torrance model [Cook 82] is employed, because of its suitability for rendering metallic objects and the fact that it takes into account the spectral distribution.

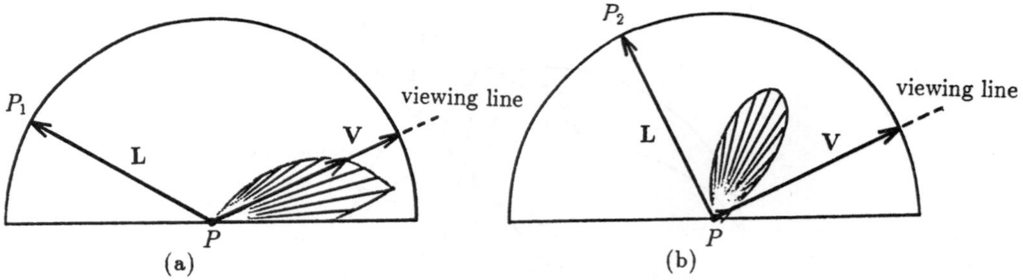

Figure 2: Specular reflectance due to the sky element

Let's assume that a sky element, a small area in a band source, is treated as a point light source, P_e, and the position of P_e is defined by the angle α from the x-axis to the sky element and the angle δ from the horizontal plane to the sky element (See Figure 1). By adding the effect of the specular reflectance to Eq. 1 in [Nishita 86], the intensity of the specular reflectance at P due to the sky element is given by the following equation:

$$dI = R_s(\alpha, \delta, \mathbf{V}) \cdot L(\alpha, \delta) \cdot \sin\alpha \cdot \sin\delta \cdot r^{-2} \cdot dA, \tag{2}$$

where $R_s(\alpha, \delta, \mathbf{V})$ is the coefficient of the specular reflectance, $\mathbf{V}$ is the unit vector from the calculation point P toward the viewpoint, $L(\alpha, \delta)$ is the intensity of the sky element, r is the distance PP_e, and dA is the area of the sky element and is given by

$$dA = (r \cdot d\alpha) \cdot (r \cdot d\delta \cdot \sin\alpha). \tag{3}$$

By integrating Eq. 2, the intensity of the specular reflectance due to the band source S_l is obtained as

$$I_l = \int_0^{\pi} \int_{\delta_l - \Delta_l}^{\delta_l + \Delta_l} R_s(\alpha, \delta, \mathbf{V}) \cdot L(\alpha, \delta) \cdot \sin\delta \cdot \sin^2\alpha \cdot d\delta \cdot d\alpha. \tag{4}$$

In such a narrow band as defined above, $\delta_l - \Delta_l \leq \delta < \delta_l + \Delta_l$ ($2\Delta_l$ is the angular width of a band source), both the intensity of the sky element and the coefficient of the specular reflectance can be held constant. Then $L(\alpha, \delta)$ and $R_s(\alpha, \delta, \mathbf{V})$ are expressed by $L(\alpha, \delta_l)$ and $R_s(\alpha, \delta_l, \mathbf{V})$, respectively. In this paper, the angle δ is sampled as $\cos(\delta_l - \Delta_l) - \cos(\delta_l + \Delta_l) = 1/N$ (constant). Thus, Eq. 4 becomes

$$I_l = \frac{1}{N} \cdot \int_0^{\pi} R_s(\alpha, \delta_l, \mathbf{V}) \cdot L(\alpha, \delta_l) \cdot \sin^2\alpha \cdot d\alpha. \tag{5}$$

Then, the intensity of the specular reflectance due to the sky dome is given by

$$I = \sum_{l=1}^{N} I_l, \tag{6}$$

where N is the number of the band sources.

3.2 Calculation of Specular Reflectance

It is almost impossible to obtain look-up tables like those for the intensity of the diffuse reflectance, because the coefficient of specular reflectance depends on the direction of the viewing line. Using the following property of specular reflectance, however, may save calculation time: if the direction of regular reflection of the sky element P_1 is almost coincident with the direction of viewing line as

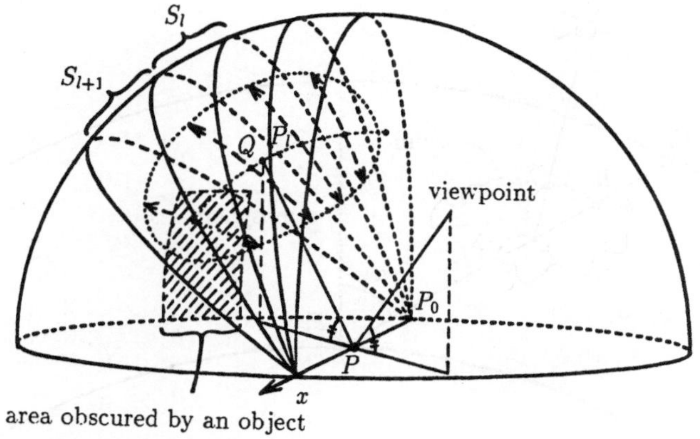

Figure 3: Determination of the integral region for specular reflectance

shown in Figure 2 (a), the intensity of the specular reflectance toward the viewing line is extremely large, and if not as shown in Figure 2 (b), much less intensity of specular reflectance due to the element, P_2, arrives at the viewpoint. These facts suggest that the intensity of specular reflectance due to the sky dome can be calculated without any compensation for preciseness by integrating a part of the sky dome in Eq. 6, that is, with an appropriate integral width and range.

If we define the function to determine the integral range for the sky element P_e as follows:

$$G(\alpha, \delta, \mathbf{V}) = L(\alpha, \delta) \cdot R_s(\alpha, \delta, \mathbf{V}) \cdot \sin\alpha, \tag{7}$$

and set a threshold value ε, then the integral range is limited in the regions where $G(\alpha, \delta, \mathbf{V})$ is greater than ε. The integral area cannot be determined a priori, because the function not only depends on the specular distribution of the lit object but also some objects casting their shadows on it affect the area. The integral starts from a location where the function has a large value and proceeds to a small value area, that is, from the sky element in the direction of the regular reflection to away from the sky element. The details of the integration is as follows (See Figure 3):

(1) Obtain the point, Q, where the direction of the regular reflection for the viewing line intersects with the sky dome. We assume that the point Q is located between two sample lines of the band sources S_l and S_{l+1}, where a sample line is defined by the center line of the band source. Then the tilt angle δ_l of the sample plane which is defined as the plane including the sample line of the band source, S_l, and x-axis is calculated.

(2) Search for the sky element P_l which is closest to the point Q along the sample line of the band source S_l, and calculate the angle α_{l1} between x-axis (PP_0) and PP_l. If $G(\alpha_{l1}, \delta_l, \mathbf{V}) \geq \varepsilon$, then integrate over the band source S_l as follows:

(2.1) Execute trapezoidal integration along the sample line from the sky element $P_l(\alpha_{l1}, \delta_l)$ toward one of the end of the line with a pitch $d\alpha$ corresponding to the width of a segment, until the condition, $G(\alpha_{l1}, \delta_l, \mathbf{V}) < \varepsilon$, is satisfied. When a segment of the sample line is obscured by some objects, the integral of that segment is skipped. The visible segments are obtained by calculating the intersections of the sample plane and those objects.

(2.2) Integrate the sample line from the sky element $P_l(\alpha_{l1}, \delta_l)$ toward the other end of the line in the same way as explained in (2.1).

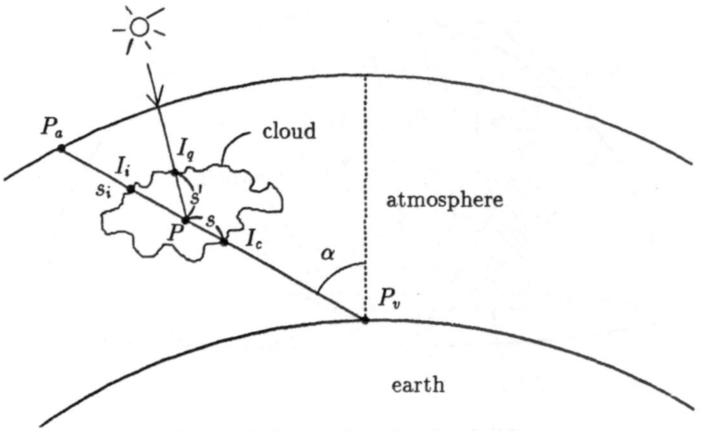

Figure 4: Scattering due to clouds

(3) For an adjacent band source S_{l-1}, the process (2) is employed, when $G(\alpha_{l1}, \delta_l, \mathbf{V}) > \varepsilon$ at the border of S_l.

(4) Continue the above-mentioned process for the band sources S_{l-2}, S_{l-3} and so on. If at the P_i which is the closest sample segment to the point Q on the sample line of the band source S_i $(i = l-1, l-2, \cdots, 1)$ the condition, $G(\alpha_{i1}, \delta_i, \mathbf{V}) < \varepsilon$, is satisfied, then the integral is suspended.

(5) For the other side of the band sources, $S_{l+1}, S_{l+2}, \cdots, S_i, \cdots, S_N$, the processes from (2) to (4) are employed until the condition, $G(\alpha_{i1}, \delta_i, \mathbf{V}) < \varepsilon$, is satisfied.

4 CLOUDS

The size of particles in clouds is larger than that of air molecules or of aerosols mentioned before. Light scattered by large particles such as those in clouds is little influenced by wavelength. However, the spectral distribution of the sunlight onto clouds depends to a fair degree on the position of the sun. Therefore, the light passing through a cloud should be determined by the following three components: i) sky light attenuated by passing through the cloud, ii) light scattered and absorbed by cloud particles illuminated by direct sunlight, and iii) ambient light caused by multiple scattering due to atmospheric particles and cloud particles.

For i), the intensity of sky light, I_i, toward the viewpoint is obtained by using the before-mentioned atmospheric scattering model. For ii), the intensity of direct sunlight, I_q, is assumed to be constant everywhere on the face of a cloud because the cloud thickness is much smaller than that of the atmosphere. Therefore when the distance between the cloud center and the top of the atmosphere is Q, the intensity of direct sunlight on the cloud surface is given by

$$I_q = I_s(\lambda)\exp(-t(Q,\lambda)), \tag{8}$$

where $I_s(\lambda)$ is the solar radiation at the top of the atmosphere, and $t(Q,\lambda)$ is the optical length of the distance Q for the wavelength λ. For iii), ambient light due to atmospheric particles is obtained by using the model mentioned before, and ambient light due to cloud particles is assumed to have uniform intensity for all directions.

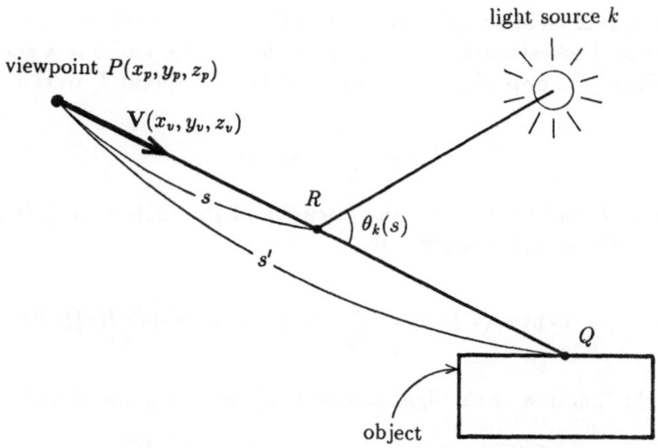

Figure 5: Calculation of the particle density

Finally, the intensity of light just after passing through the cloud, I_c, taking into account the three components mentioned above, is obtained by the following equation (See Figure 4):

$$I_c(\lambda) = I_i(\lambda) \cdot \exp(-t(s_i)) + \int_0^{s_i} (I_q(\lambda) \cdot F(\theta) + I_a) \cdot \exp(-t(s) - t(s')) \cdot \rho_c(s) \cdot ds, \qquad (9)$$

where I_a is the ambient light, and both the phase function F and the density of the cloud, ρ_c, are assumed to be uniform. The shape of the cloud is defined by mapping a thickness function (Fourier series composed of a polynomial of sine waves [Gardner 85]) onto an ellipse.

5 BEAM AND FOG EFFECTS

The space where light passes through atmosphere with vapor and particles brightens, and the intensity of the light weakens before arriving at the viewpoint, because the light is scattered or absorbed by these particles.

Displaying beam and fog effects caused by direct sunlight and sky light calculated by using the atmospheric scattering model is described here.

In Max's model [Max 86], the particles distribute in a flat layer; however, it is well known that the density of particles which cause beam or fog, density of vapor and aerosols, decreases in an exponential or similarway. If the distribution of particles is approximated as an exponential function, and a unit vector from the viewpoint P (x_p, y_p, z_p) to the point Q is expressed by $\mathbf{V}$ (x_v, y_v, z_v), then the particle density at a point R is given by the following equation (See Figure 5):

$$\rho(s) = \rho_0 \cdot \exp(-\frac{z(s)}{h_0}), \qquad (10)$$

where ρ_0 is the particle density at the altitude of zero meters, h_0 is a scale height for the particles, and $z(s) = z_p + z_v \cdot s$, where s is the distance between the points P and R. The attenuation coefficient, the scattering ratio of light during passing through a unit distance in the atmosphere, is proportional to the particle density and is given by

$$\tau(s) = \rho(s) \cdot \tau_0 \cdot (\frac{\lambda}{\lambda_0})^{-b}, \qquad (11)$$

where λ is the wavelength of incident light, λ_0 is a standard wavelength, τ_0 represents the scattering coefficient of the standard wavelength with unit particle density, and b is a coefficient decided by particle size of fog. Then, the optical length, $t(s)$, from the viewpoint P to the point R is obtained by

$$t(s) = \int_0^s \tau(s) \cdot ds. \tag{12}$$

If the distance between P and Q is s' and the intensity of the surface at Q is I_0, the intensity of the ray arriving at the viewpoint P is given by

$$I = I_0 \cdot \exp(-t(s')) + \sum_k \int_0^{s'} \tau(s) \cdot J_k(s) \cdot \exp(-t(s)) \cdot ds, \tag{13}$$

where $J_k(s)$ is the light function of the light source k at the viewpoint P and is given by

$$J_k(s) = I_k(s) \cdot \exp(-t'_k(s)) \cdot F(\theta_k(s)), \tag{14}$$

where $I_k(s)$ represents the intensity of the ray arriving at the point R under the condition of no particles and is calculated by direct sunlight and sky light which are obtained by the atmospheric scattering model, $t'_k(s)$ is an optical distance between the light source k and the point R, and $F(\theta_k(s))$ is a phase function.

For displaying beams taking into account obstacles, the integration is performed only for visible sections of light on the viewing line, where the section is obtained by using shadow volumes [Nishita 87]. Integration in the cases of direct sunlight and sky light is described below.

5.1 Direct Sunlight

$F(\theta_k(s))$ in Eq. 14 has a constant value, because $\theta_k(s)$ is constant as the direct sunlight is a parallel light source. Then, Eq. 13 is able to be calculated analytically (See Appendix).

5.2 Sky Light

Beams often appear when direct sunlight with high intensity is passing through particles in the atmosphere. On the other hand, when the component of sky light is larger than that of direct sunlight, i.e. in a fog or a mist, the whole atmosphere illuminated by the sky light is brightened. In the latter case, Eq. 13 must be calculated by using numerical integration because the analytical integration used for a parallel light source (direct sunlight) cannot be employed. For simplifying the calculation, we assume the conditions of a uniform phase function and no shadow effects of obstacles in this case.

The intensity of sky light, $J_k(s)$, arriving at the point P_i (See Figure 6) is obtained by integrating the sky elements along all band sources which the sky dome is divided into, that is,

$$J_k(s_i) = \sum_{l=1}^{N} W_l \cdot \int_0^{\pi} L(\alpha, \delta) \cdot \sin\alpha \cdot \exp(-t'(s_i)) \cdot d\alpha, \tag{15}$$

where N is the number of the band sources, W_l is the angular width of the band source l, $L(\alpha, \delta)$ is intensity of sky light, and $t'(s_i)$ is a optical distance between the point P_i and each sky element.

By introducing the two assumptions described above, $J_k(s_i)$ can be expressed by only the function of the altitude of P_i; in other words, the relationship with the x and y coordinates of the point P_i

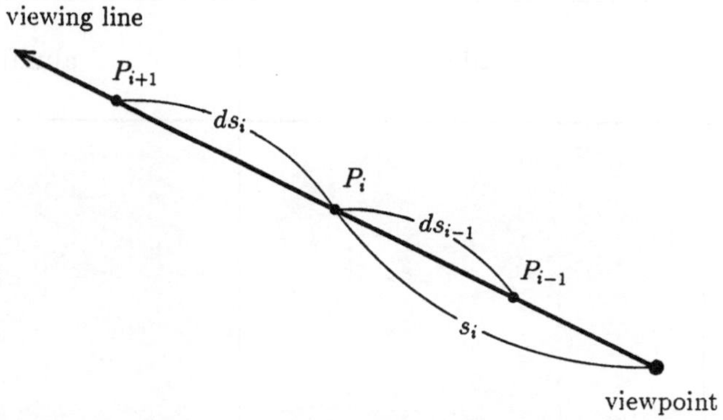

Figure 6: Numerical integral for displaying fog effect caused by sky light

and the directions of viewing line and ray may be neglected. Therefore, look-up tables of $J_k(s_i)$ at every altitude can be created in advance.

Trapezoidal integration is employed for integrating the intensity of the scattered light along the viewing line. That is, the integral starts from the viewpoint with a pitch, ds_i, which is determined by using the following equation (See Figure 6):

$$ds_i = \max(ds_{min}, \min(ds_{max}, \frac{ds_0}{\tau(s_i) \cdot J_k(s_i) \cdot \exp(-t(s_i))})), \tag{16}$$

where ds_{min} and ds_{max} are the minimum and maximum pitches, respectively, and ds_0 is a standard pitch. The integral is continued until the condition, $\tau(s_i) \cdot J_k(s_i) \cdot \exp(-t(s_i)) < \varepsilon$, is satisfied.

6 EXAMPLES

Figure 7 shows an application to building design. The walls of the building in Figures (a) through (c) are made of white tiles (which have mainly diffused reflectance), and the material in Figures (d) through (f) is aluminum (which has almost only specular reflectance). Figures (a) and (d) are the case of early morning (solar altitude is 8 degrees), Figures (b) and (e) are also in the morning (20 degrees), and Figures (c) and (f) are at sunset (3 degrees). These figures demonstrate not only the variation in the hue and brightness of the building but also that of the sky color. Figures (a) through (c) show the variation of the hue of the building due to sun position. Human eyes usually don't perceive such a large differences of the hue on the walls, even though actual color varies as shown in these figures. Because human visual perception takes into account expectations of color and color difference of various objects in the environment rather than their absolute spectral distribution, people do not ordinarily notice this type of color shift.

Figures (b) and (e) show that the color of the highlight on the building is mainly influenced by specular reflectance of the direct sunlight, and Figures (d) through (f) show that except for the highlight region the hue of the building varies according to the sky light. In Figures (a) through (c), the influence of the hue of sky light comes out on the walls whose surface is nearly parallel to the viewing line, because the more parallel the reflection plane is to the viewing line, the greater the effects on the specular reflectance component.

It is assumed that in Figure 8, the position of the sun was behind the building. In this figure, where the sun is in front of the viewpoint, the edges of the clouds are brighter than their central area because of their thickness. When the sun is behind the viewpoint, on the other hand, as in Figure 7, the side of the clouds lit by direct sunlight is brighter than the other side.

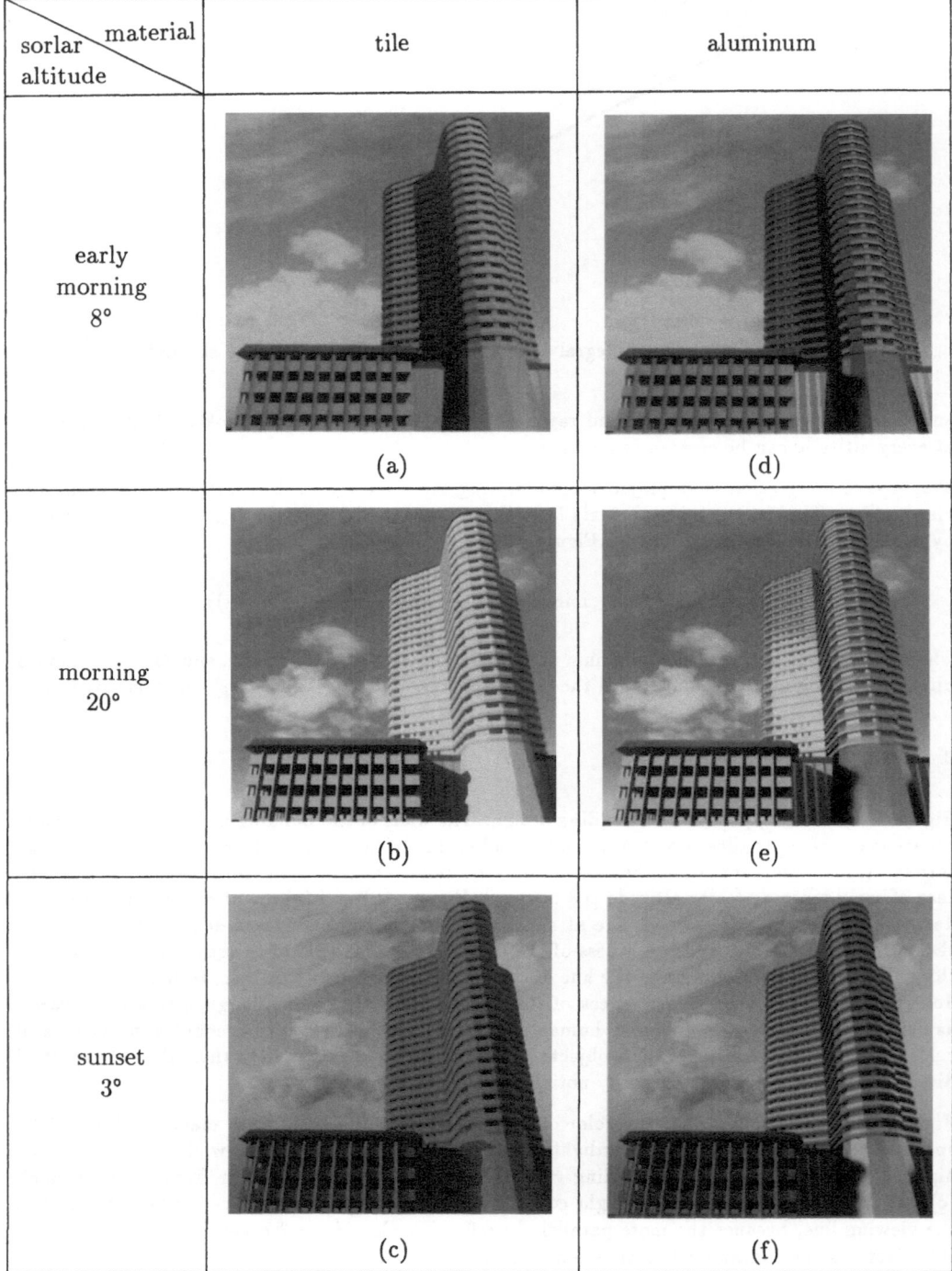

sorlar altitude \ material	tile	aluminum
early morning 8°	 (a)	 (d)
morning 20°	 (b)	 (e)
sunset 3°	 (c)	 (f)

Figure 7: Examples of changing color of the building according to the solar altitude and the material of the walls

Figure 8: Example of the counter-light

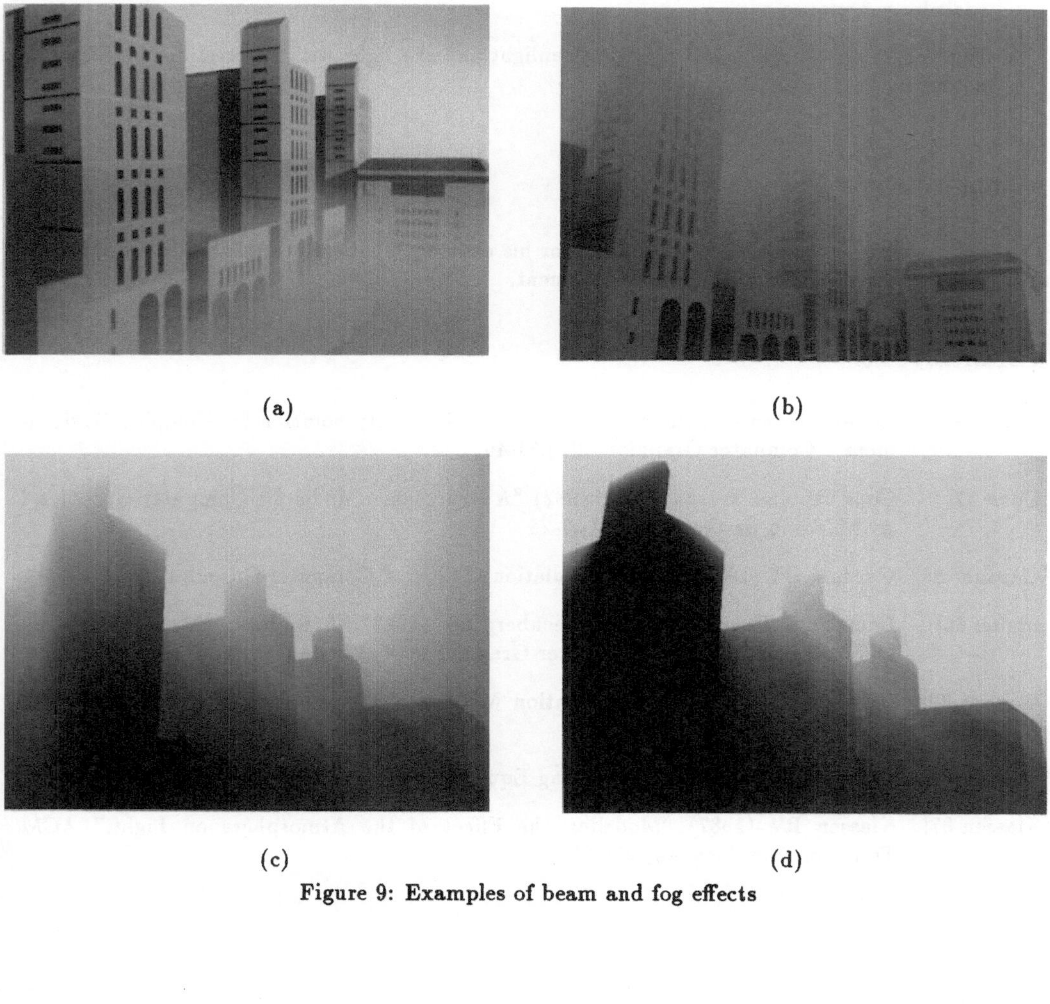

(a) (b) (c) (d)

Figure 9: Examples of beam and fog effects

Figure 9 demonstrates how fog reacts to direct sunlight as well as sky light and shows the variation in the appearance of the buildings. In Figure (a), the parameters ρ_0 and h_0 (in Eq. 10) are set to 0.59 and 10.0, respectively, so the higher the altitude, the lower the density. On the contrary, in Figure (b), the parameters ρ_0 and h_0 are set to 0.037 and -15.0, respectively. Figures (c) and (d) display the silhouette and beam effects. In the former, ρ_0, h_0, and the sun altitude are 0.16, 80.0, and 40 degrees, and in the latter, 0.088, 80.0, and 35 degrees. By using IRIS-4D/70GT, it took about 17 and 20 hours to calculate Figures 8 and 9 (a), respectively.

7 CONCLUSIONS

A method for displaying realistic outdoor images taking into account the spectral distribution of both direct sunlight and sky light is proposed from the view point of displaying the simulation results for designing buildings and performing assessments of their environmental impacts.

The proposal described in this paper has the following advantages:

1. The hue of the sky, clouds, and buildings vary according to both the position of the sun and atmospheric conditions.
2. Buildings lit by both direct sunlight and sky light can be displayed taking into account specular reflectance.
3. Fog and beam effects caused by direct sunlight and sky light with spectral distribution can be displayed.

Acknowledgment

The authors wish to thank Robert T. Myers for his assistance with the English manuscript. The data are courtesy of Osaka Municipal Government.

REFERENCES

[Cohen 85] Cohen MF and Greenberg DP (1985) "A Radiosity Solution for Complex Environment," Computer Graphics 19(3):31-40

[Cook 82] Cook RL and Torrance KE (1982) "A Reflectance Model for Computer Graphics," ACM Trans. on Graphics 1(1):7-24

[Gardner 85] Gardner GY (1985) "Visual Simulation of Cloud," Computer Graphics 19(3):297-303

[Immel 86] Immel DS, Cohen MF, and Greenberg DP (1986) "A Radiosity Method for Non-Diffuse Environments," Computer Graphics 20(4):133-142

[Inakage 89] Inakage M (1989) "An Illumination Model for Atmospheric Environment," Proc. CGI'89 :533-548

[Kajiya 86] Kajiya JT (1986) "The Rendering Equation," Computer Graphics 20(4):143-150

[Klassen 87] Klassen RV (1987) "Modeling the Effect of the Atmosphere on Light," ACM Trans. on Graphics 6(3):215-237

[Max 86] Max NL (1986) "Atmospheric Illumination and Shadows," Computer Graphics 20(4):117-124

[Nishita 83] Nishita T and Nakamae E (1983) "Half-Tone Representation of 3-D Objects Illuminated by Area Sources or Polyhedron Sources," IEEE COMPSAC :237-242

[Nishita 85a] Nishita T, Okamura I, and Nakamae E (1985) "Shading Models for Point and Linear Sources," ACM Trans. on Graphics 4(2):124-146

[Nishita 85b] Nishita T and Nakamae E (1985) "Continuous Tone Representation of Three-Dimensional Objects Taking Account of Shadows and Interreflection," Computer Graphics 19(3):23-30

[Nishita 86] Nishita T and Nakamae E (1986) "Continuous Tone Representation of Three-Dimensional Objects Illuminated by Sky Light," Computer Graphics 20(4):125-132

[Nishita 87] Nishita T, Miyawaki Y, and Nakamae E (1987) "A Shading Model for Atmospheric Scattering Considering Distribution of Light Sources," Computer Graphics 21(4):303-310

[Rushmeier 87] Rushmeier HE, Torrance KE (1987) "The Zonal Method for Calculating Light Intensities in the Presence of a Participating Medium," Computer Graphics 21(4):293-302

[Sekine 87] Sekine S (1987) "Optical Characteristics of Turbid Atmosphere," J. Illum. Engng. Int. Jpn. 71(6):333 (in Japanese)

APPENDIX
INTENSITY OF PARALLEL LIGHT SCATTERED BY FOG

We assume that fog distributes in a flat layer because fog usually distributes in a local area.

The illuminance at the point R and $F(\theta_k(s))$ without fog is given by

$$I_k(s) = I_k, \tag{17}$$

$$F(\theta_k(s)) = F_k, \tag{18}$$

where both I_k and F_k have a constant value because of a parallel light (See Figure 10). By integrating the attenuation coefficient between the point R and the light source (the distance is infinite), its optical distance, $t'(s)$, is given by

$$t'(s) = \rho_0 \cdot \tau_0 \cdot (\frac{\lambda}{\lambda_0})^{-b} \cdot \exp(-\frac{z_p + z_v \cdot s}{h_0}) \cdot \frac{h_0}{z_{Lk}}. \tag{19}$$

Then, the light function, $J_k(s)$, is given by

$$J_k(s) = I_k \cdot F_k \cdot \exp(-t'(s)). \tag{20}$$

Intensity of light scattered by fog between s_1 and s_2 is given by

$$I = \int_{s_1}^{s_2} \tau(s) \cdot J_k(s) \cdot \exp(-t(s)) \cdot ds. \tag{21}$$

To simplify this equation, the following substitution is introduced:

$$\alpha = \rho_0 \cdot \tau_0 \cdot (\frac{\lambda}{\lambda_0})^{-b} \cdot \exp(-\frac{z_p}{h_0}). \tag{22}$$

Then, Eq. 21 is solved by

(1) for $z_v = 0$,

$$I = I_k \cdot F_k \cdot \int_{s_1}^{s_2} \exp(-\alpha \cdot \frac{h_0}{z_{Lk}}) \cdot \alpha \cdot \exp(-\alpha \cdot s) \cdot ds$$

$$= I_k \cdot F_k \cdot \exp(-\alpha \cdot \frac{h_0}{z_{Lk}}) \cdot [\exp(-\alpha \cdot s)]_{s_2}^{s_1}. \quad (23)$$

(2) for $z_v \neq 0$,

$$I = I_k \cdot F_k \cdot \int_{s_1}^{s_2} \alpha \cdot \exp(-\frac{z_v}{h_0} \cdot s) \cdot \exp(-\alpha \cdot \frac{h_0}{z_v}) \cdot \exp(\alpha \cdot h_0 \cdot (\frac{1}{z_v} - \frac{1}{z_{Lk}}) \cdot \exp(-\frac{z_v}{h_0} \cdot s)) \cdot ds. \quad (24)$$

Eq. 24 is solved by the following:

(2.1) for $z_v = z_{Lk}$,

$$I = I_k \cdot F_k \cdot \int_{s_1}^{s_2} \alpha \cdot \exp(-\alpha \cdot \frac{h_0}{z_v}) \cdot \exp(-\frac{z_v}{h_0} \cdot s) \cdot ds$$

$$= I_k \cdot F_k \cdot \alpha \cdot \exp(-\alpha \cdot \frac{h_0}{z_v}) \cdot \frac{h_0}{z_v} \cdot [\exp(-\frac{z_v}{h_0} \cdot s)]_{s_2}^{s_1}. \quad (25)$$

(2.2) for $z_v \neq z_{Lk}$,
We use the following integration by substitution:

$$u = f(s) = \exp(-\frac{z_v}{h_0} \cdot s). \quad (26)$$

Therefore,

$$\frac{du}{ds} = \frac{d}{ds} f(s) = -\frac{z_v}{h_0} \cdot \exp(-\frac{z_v}{h_0} \cdot s). \quad (27)$$

Then, Eq. 24 can be expressed by the following:

$$I = I_k \cdot F_k \cdot \int_{f(s_1)}^{f(s_2)} \alpha \cdot \exp(-\frac{z_v}{h_0} \cdot s) \cdot \exp(-\alpha \cdot \frac{h_0}{z_v}) \cdot \frac{1}{\frac{du}{ds}}$$

$$\cdot \exp(\alpha \cdot h_0 \cdot (\frac{1}{z_v} - \frac{1}{z_{Lk}}) \cdot u) \cdot du$$

$$= I_k \cdot F_k \cdot \frac{\exp(-\alpha \cdot \frac{h_0}{z_v})}{1 - \frac{z_v}{z_{Lk}}} \cdot [\exp(\alpha \cdot h_0 \cdot (\frac{1}{z_v} - \frac{1}{z_{Lk}}) \cdot u)]_{\exp(-\frac{z_v}{h_0} \cdot s_2)}^{\exp(-\frac{z_v}{h_0} \cdot s_1)}. \quad (28)$$

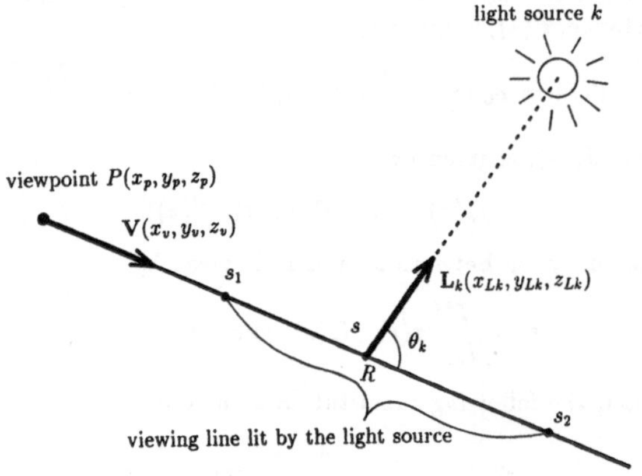

Figure 10: Analytical integral for displaying fog effect caused by direct sunlight

Kazufumi Kaneda is a research associate in Faculty of Engineering at Hiroshima University. He worked at the Chugoku Electric Power Company Ltd., Japan from 1984 to 1986. He joined Hiroshima University in 1986. His research interests include computer graphics and image processing.
Kaneda received the BE and ME in 1982 and 1984, respectively, from Hiroshima University. He is a member of IEE of Japan, IPS of Japan and IEICE of Japan.
Address: Faculty of Engineering, Hiroshima University, Saijo-cho, Higashi-hiroshima, 724 Japan.
E-mail: kin@eml.hiroshima-u.ac.jp

Takashi Okamoto is a graduate student in system engineering at Hiroshima University. His research interests include computer graphics and its application.
Okamoto received the BE degrees in electronics engineering in 1988 from Hiroshima University. He is a member of IPS of Japan.
Address: Faculty of Engineering, Hiroshima University, Saijo-cho, Higashi-hiroshima, 724 Japan.

Eihachiro Nakamae is a professor at Hiroshima University where he was appointed as research associate in 1956 and a professor in 1968. He was an associate researcher at Clarkson College of Technology, Potsdam, N. Y., from 1973 to 1974. His research interests include computer graphics and electric machinery.
Nakamae received the BE, ME, and DE degrees in 1954, 1956, and 1967 from Waseda University. He is a member of IEEE, IEE of Japan, IPS of Japan and IEICE of Japan.
Address: Faculty of Engineering, Hiroshima University, Saijo-cho, Higashi-hiroshima, 724 Japan.
E-mail: naka@eml.hiroshima-u.ac.jp

Tomoyuki Nishita is an associate professor in the department of Electronic and Electrical Engineering at Fukuyama University, Japan. He was on the research staff at Mazda from 1973 to 1979 and worked on design and development of computer-controlled vehicle system. He joined Fukuyama University in 1979. He was an associate researcher in the Engineering Computer Graphics Laboratory at Brigham Young University from 1988 to the end of March, 1989. His research interests involve computer graphics including lighting model, hidden-surface removal, and antialiasing.
Nishita received his BE, ME and Ph. D in Engineering in 1971, 1973, and 1985, respectively, from Hiroshima University. He is a member of ACM, IPS of Japan and IEE of Japan.
Address: Faculty of Engineering, Fukuyama University, Sanzo, Higashimura-cho, Fukuyama, 729-02 Japan.

Julia Sets of $z \leftarrow z^{\infty} + c$

Nagarjuna Vangala, Uday G. Gujar, and Virendra C. Bhavsar

Abstract

The fractal images generated from the generalized transformation function $z \leftarrow z^{\alpha} + c$ in the complex z-plane are analysed. The exponent α can assume any real or integer, either positive or negative, value. When the exponent α is a positive integer number, the fractal image has a lobular structure with number of lobes equal to α. When α is a negative integer number, the generated fractal image has a planetary structure with a central planet and $|\alpha|$ satellite structures around it. When α is varied continuously between two consecutive integer numbers, continuous and predictable changes are observed between the two limiting fractal images. Some conjectures regarding the visual characteristics of the fractal images and the value of α are included.

Keywords : *Algebraic Fractals, lobes, satellites, embryonic structures.*

1 Introduction

Fractals from self-squared function, $z \leftarrow z^2 + c$, have been dealt with extensively in the literature [MAND82,PEIT86]. The images in the c-plane with z_0 as a constant are referred to as the Mandelbrot, or M, set while those in the z-plane with c as a constant are referred to as Julia sets.

Gujar et al. consider a generalized transformation function $z \leftarrow z^{\alpha} + c$ and give a generation process for producing fractal images from this function [GUJA89]. They have also classified the fractal images from this function as :

1. c-plane fractals with $z_0 = K_1$, a constant,

2. c-plane fractals with $z_0 = \phi(x, y)$,

3. z-plane fractals with $c = K_2$, a constant,

4. z-plane fractals with $c = \psi(x, y)$.

The fractals from $z \leftarrow z^\alpha + c$ in the complex c-plane with $z_0 = K_1$, for integer and real values of α, both positive and negative, have been dealt with in [GUJA89].

In this paper, we consider the fractal images from $z \leftarrow z^\alpha + c$ in the complex z-plane with $c = K_2$, a constant. We produce and analyse the images for positive and negative, integer as well as real, values of α and give conjectures about the value of α and the visual characteristics of the fractal image.

Lakhtakia et al. have considered our generalized function for only positive integer values of α and have reported α-fold symmetry; however, they do not consider negative or non-integer values of α [LAKH87]. Pickover has given an image for $\alpha = 5$ without any analysis [PICK88].

The fractal images given in this paper have been generated on IBM 5080 graphics workstation connected to a supercomputer class machine IBM 3090-180VF at the University of New Brunswick. The code for generating fractals has been vectorized to cut down the computation time. The programs are written in VS FORTRAN using graPHIGS [IBM86].

2 Generation of z-plane fractals

Fractal generation is an iterative process: $z_{n+1} \leftarrow f(z_n)$, where z_n and z_{n+1} are the complex quantities after the nth and $(n+1)^{th}$ iteration, respectively. We consider the generalized transformation function, $f(z) = z^\alpha + c$, where z and c are complex quantities and α can take any real or integer, either positive or negative, value.

A fractal image consists of a two-dimensional array of pixels. Each pixel is represented by a pair of (x, y) co-ordinates. For the z-plane fractal images, which are referred to as Julia Sets in the literature [PEIT86,LAKH87], the (x, y) coordinates of each pixel are associated with (z_x, z_y). For each pixel, the value of z is computed iteratively. Two criteria are used to terminate this iterative process:

1. the value of z diverges beyond a certain preset limit L , or

2. the allowable number of iterations, N , is reached.

If the iteration terminates due to condition (1), then that pixel is said to be unstable while if it terminates due to condition (2) then that pixel is stable.

Visually complex and interesting z-plane fractals are generated from the generalized transformation function $z \leftarrow z^{\alpha} + c$, by varying α. The exponent α can be represented as $\alpha = \pm(\eta + \varepsilon)$, where η is a positive integer and ε the fractional part, $0 \leq \varepsilon < 1$.

Two different classes of fractals are generated, one when α is positive and another when α is negative. When the fractional part ε is 0, fractals having similar structures are generated. When $\varepsilon \neq 0$, then a small growth appears and the size of this growth is dependent on the magnitude of ε. As ε increases from 0 to 1 the resulting fractal smoothly changes from the image for $\alpha = \pm\eta$ to that for $\alpha = \pm(\eta + 1)$. The z-plane fractal images can be classified as follows :

1. fractal images for $\alpha = +\eta$,

2. fractal images for $\alpha = +(\eta + \varepsilon)$,

3. fractal images for $\alpha = -\eta$,

4. fractal images for $\alpha = -(\eta + \varepsilon)$.

The z-plane region having a lower left corner of $(-1.5, -1.5)$ and a upper right corner of $(1.5, 1.5)$ is chosen for the pictures given in this paper. The initial complex constant c_0 is $(0.5, 0.5)$. The maximum number of iterations, N, is set to 100 and magnitude of z is tested against a preset value, L $(= 10.0)$, for divergence.

Section 3 presents fractal images for positive integer values of α followed by Section 4 in which fractal images for positive non-integer values of α are described. Fractal images for negative integer values of α are given in Section 5 while Section 6 discusses fractal images for negative non-integer values of α.

3 Fractal images for $\alpha = +\eta$

In this section, several fractal images are given for positive integer values of α. Figure 1 is obtained when $\alpha = 3$. This structure consists of three similar lobes. All the lobes are oriented with angular symmetry around the origin. The stable region, represented in white, is surrounded by unstable region. Figures 2 to 5 are for $\alpha = 4$, $\alpha = 5$, $\alpha = 10$ and $\alpha = 11$ respectively. It can be seen that the number of similar shaped lobes is equal to α. These experiments lead to the first conjecture. To state the conjecture, the following notation is used :

- Λ^z - the total number of major lobes in the z-plane fractal image.
- λ_s^z - a major lobe.
- $\Omega(\lambda_s^z)$ - the angular space spanned by λ_s^z around the origin.

(We use superscript z, such as Λ^z, λ_s^z etc., to differentiate from the notation used for the c-plane fractal images in [GUJA89]).

Conjecture 1 *The fractal image generated from the transformation function $z \leftarrow z^\alpha + c$, in the complex z-plane with c as a constant and $\alpha = \eta$, contains Λ^z major lobes given by $\Lambda^z = \eta\lambda_s^z$, with $\Omega(\lambda_s^z) \cong 2\pi/\eta$.*

4 Fractal images for $\alpha = +(\eta + \varepsilon)$

Fractal images generated from the even and odd values of η, as ε changes from 0 to 1, evolve differently, even though the underlying mathematical formulation is the same. The cases are, therefore, discussed in the following two subsections.

4.1 Odd η

Figure 6 is the fractal image for $\alpha = 3.2$. We can see that there are three major lobes and a small embryonic lobe on the left-hand side, thus creating asymmetry. When α is increased to 3.5, we obtain Fig. 7 where the embryonic lobe has increased in size. It can be seen that this embryonic lobe is always above the real axis on the negative side. There is a clear line demarking the embryonic lobe and the earlier major lobes. In Fig. 8, where $\alpha = 3.8$, the embryonic lobe is almost fully grown. When α equals four, we obtain the fractal image shown in Fig. 2, where the embryonic lobe has grown in a new major lobe.

Several fractal images were generated for other odd values of η as ε changes from 0 to 1. Based on these experiments we propose Conjecture 2 using the following additional notation.

- λ_e^z - an embryonic lobe.
- $\Omega(\lambda_e^z)$ - the angular space spanned by λ_e^z around the origin.

Conjecture 2 *The transformation function $z \leftarrow z^\alpha + c$, for $\alpha = (\eta + \varepsilon)$ and η as an odd integer, with c as a constant, produces a fractal image in the complex z-plane consisting of Λ^z similar lobes, given by $\Lambda^z = \eta\lambda_s^z$, with $\Omega(\lambda_s^z) \cong 2\pi/(\eta + \varepsilon)$ and an embryonic lobe λ_e^z with $\Omega(\lambda_e^z) \cong 2\pi\varepsilon/(\eta + \varepsilon)$. The embryonic lobe is always above and on the negative side of the real axis.*

4.2 Even η

Figure 9 gives the fractal image for $\alpha = 4.2$, where it can be seen that there are four lobes and an embryonic lobe on the left hand side in between the two similar lobes. When the value of α increases to 4.5, this embryonic lobe grows as shown in Fig. 10. The growth of the embryonic lobe is proportional to ε as can be seen in Fig. 11, where $\alpha = 4.8$. This embryonic lobe develops into a major lobe when $\alpha = 5$ (Fig. 3). It can be observed that growth of this embryonic lobe is always below and is on the negative side of the real axis.

Based on these experiments, we state Conjecture 3.

Conjecture 3 *The transformation function $z \leftarrow z^\alpha + c$, for $\alpha = +(\eta + \varepsilon)$ and η as an even integer, with c as a constant, produces a fractal image in the complex z-plane consisting of Λ^z similar lobes, given by $\Lambda^z = \eta\lambda_s^z$, with $\Omega(\lambda_s^z) \cong 2\pi/(\eta + \varepsilon)$ and an embryonic major lobe λ_e^z with $\Omega(\lambda_e^z) \cong 2\pi\varepsilon/(\eta + \varepsilon)$ The embryonic major lobe is always below and on the negative side of the real axis.*

5 Fractal images for $\alpha = -\eta$

We now study the fractal images when α assumes negative integer values. Figure 12 is obtained when α is -4. This fractal image resembles planetary structure with a central planet surrounded by satellite structures. The number of major satellite structures is equal to four. Figures 13 and 14 are for $\alpha = -5$, and $\alpha = -6$, respectively. It can be seen that the number of major satellite structures is always equal to the value of α. The satellite structures are symmetric about the origin. The unstable region is surrounded by the stable region unlike for the positive value of α. Based on these observations, we propose Conjecture 4, using the following additional notation.

- Ξ^z - the total number of major satellite structures.
- ξ_s^z - a major satellite structure.
- $\Omega(\xi_s^z)$ - the angular space spanned by ξ_s^z around the origin.

Conjecture 4 *The transformation function $z \leftarrow z^\alpha + c$, for $\alpha = -\eta$ with c as a constant, produces a fractal image in the complex z-plane consisting of Ξ^z major satellites, given by $\Xi^z = \eta\xi_s^z$, with $\Omega(\xi_s^z) \cong 2\pi/\eta$.*

6 Fractal images for $\alpha = -(\eta + \varepsilon)$

The fractal images generated when α is a negative non-integer number are analysed in this section. The cases of odd and even values of η are discussed separately.

6.1 Odd η

Figure 15 is the fractal image generated for $\alpha = -5.2$. There are five major satellite structures and an embryonic satellite structure has emerged on the left hand side displacing all the major satellite structures proportionally. As the value of α decreases to -5.5, this space, as shown in Fig. 16, increases further and the embryonic satellite grows in that space. This embryonic satellite develops further as α decreases to -5.8 (see Fig. 17), infact the growth of the embryonic satellite structure appears to be almost complete but for the spacing between the major satellite structures. The embryonic satellite structure emerges below the real axis and there is a definite line between the embryonic satellite structure and the major satellites. Based on these observations, we state Conjecture 5, using the following additional notation.

- ξ_e^z - an embryonic satellite structure.
- $\Omega(\xi_e^z)$ - the angular space spanned by ξ_e^z around the origin.

Conjecture 5 *The transformation function $z \leftarrow z^\alpha + c$, for $\alpha = -(\eta + \varepsilon)$ and η as an odd integer, with c as a constant, produces a fractal image in the complex z-plane consisting of Ξ^z major satellite structures, given by $\Xi^z = \eta\xi_s^z$, with $\Omega(\xi_s^z) \cong 2\pi/(\eta+\varepsilon)$, and an embryonic satellite structure ξ_e^z with $\Omega(\xi_e^z) \cong 2\pi\varepsilon/(\eta+\varepsilon)$. The embryonic satellite structure is always below and on the negative side of the real axis.*

6.2 Even η

The fractal images generated when η is even are considered in this section. Figure 18 is the fractal image for $\alpha = -4.2$. There are four major satellite structures and the space between the two left-most major satellites has increased displacing all the satellite structures proportionally. This space increases as α becomes -4.5 (Fig. 19). An embryonic satellite emerges from this space and is clearly seen in Fig. 20 where α is -4.8. The new satellite emerges above and on the negative side of the real axis. When $\alpha = -5$, the number of major satellites increase to 5 (Fig. 13). This shows that the fractal image grows smoothly from $\alpha = -\eta$ to $\alpha = -(\eta + 1)$. Based on these observations we formulate Conjecture 6 as follows.

Conjecture 6 *The transformation function $z \leftarrow z^\alpha + c$, for $\alpha = -(\eta + \varepsilon)$ and η as an even integer, with c as a constant, produces a fractal image in the complex z-plane consisting of Ξ^z major satellite structures, given by $\Xi^z = \eta\xi_s^z$, with $\Omega(\xi_s^z) \cong 2\pi/(\eta + \varepsilon)$, and an embryonic satellite structure ξ_e^z with $\Omega(\xi_e^z) \cong 2\pi\varepsilon/(\eta + \varepsilon)$. The embryonic satellite structure is always above and on the negative side of the real axis.*

7 Conclusion

In this paper we have investigated fractal images generated from the generalized transformation function, $z \leftarrow z^\alpha + c$, in the complex z-plane. When α is a positive integer number, the fractal image has lobular structures whereas when α a negative integer number, we obtain a planetary structure consisting of a central planet surrounded by satellite structures around it. The number of lobes is equal to α while the number of satellite structures is equal to $|\alpha|$. When α is varied continuously between two consecutive integer numbers, continuous and predictable changes occur in the two images which act as limiting images. Six conjectures regarding the visual characteristics of fractal images in the complex z-plane are proposed.

Acknowledgements

This research is partially supported by the National Sciences and Engineering Council of Canada, Grant No. OGP 0089 and a research grant by IBM Canada through the Supercomputing Center, UNB. The encouragement and support provided by Mr Hector Leiserson, IBM Canada, Toronto, and Prof David Macneil, Computing Services, UNB, is gratefully acknowledged.

References

[GUJA89] Gujar U G, Bhavsar V C, *Fractal Images from* $z \leftarrow z^{\alpha} + c$ *in Complex c-plane*, Computers and Graphics, accepted, Sept.1989,(to appear in Vol.14,No.2).

[IBM86] IBM, *Writing Applications with graPHIGS*, SC33-8103,02, IBM Corporation, NY, Sept.1986.

[KALR88] Kalra P K, *Fractals and Their Applications*, Supercomputers and Graphics Group, SG-TR-88-04, M.Sc.(C.S) Thesis, School of Computer Science, University of New Brunswick, Fredericton, Canada, 142 pages, June 1988.

[LAKH87] Lakhtakia A, Varadan V V, Messier R, and Varadan V K, *On the Symmetries of the Julia Sets for the Process* $z \Rightarrow z^p + c$, J. Phy. A:Math. Gen., Vol. 20, pp. 3533-3535, 1987.

[MAND82] Mandelbrot B B, *The Fractal Geometry of Nature*, W H Freeman Company, San Fransisco, CA, 1982.

[PEIT86] Peitgen H O, Richter P, *The Beauty of Fractals*, Springer-Verlag, Berlin, 1986.

[PICK88] Pickover, C A, *Pattern Formation and Chaos in Networks*, Communications of the ACM, Vol. 31, No. 2, pp. 136-151, Feb.1988.

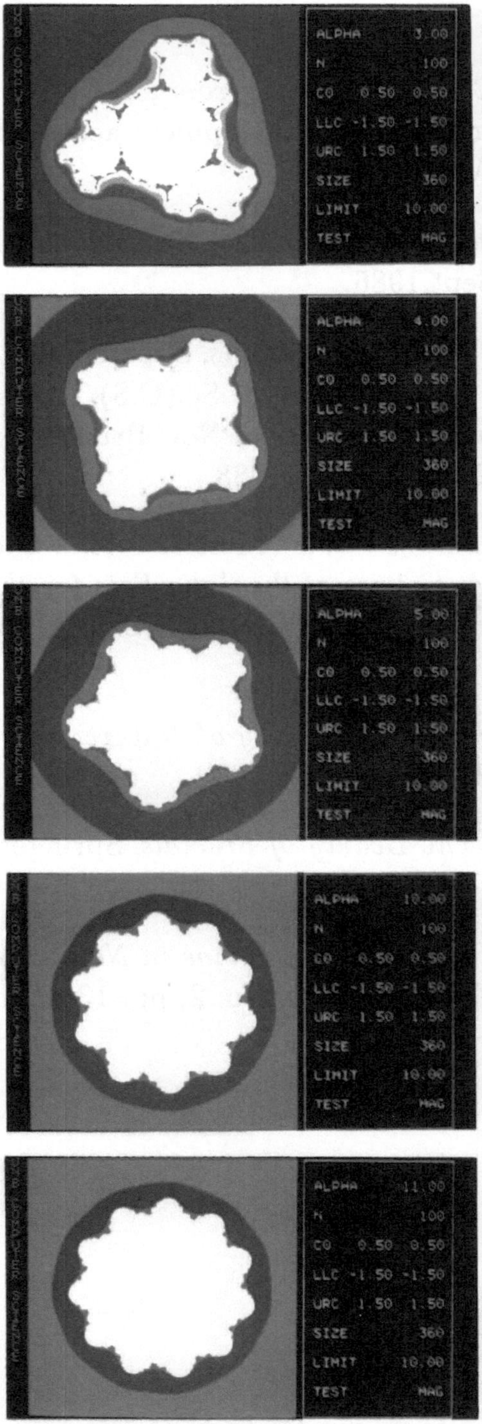

Figures 1 to 5.

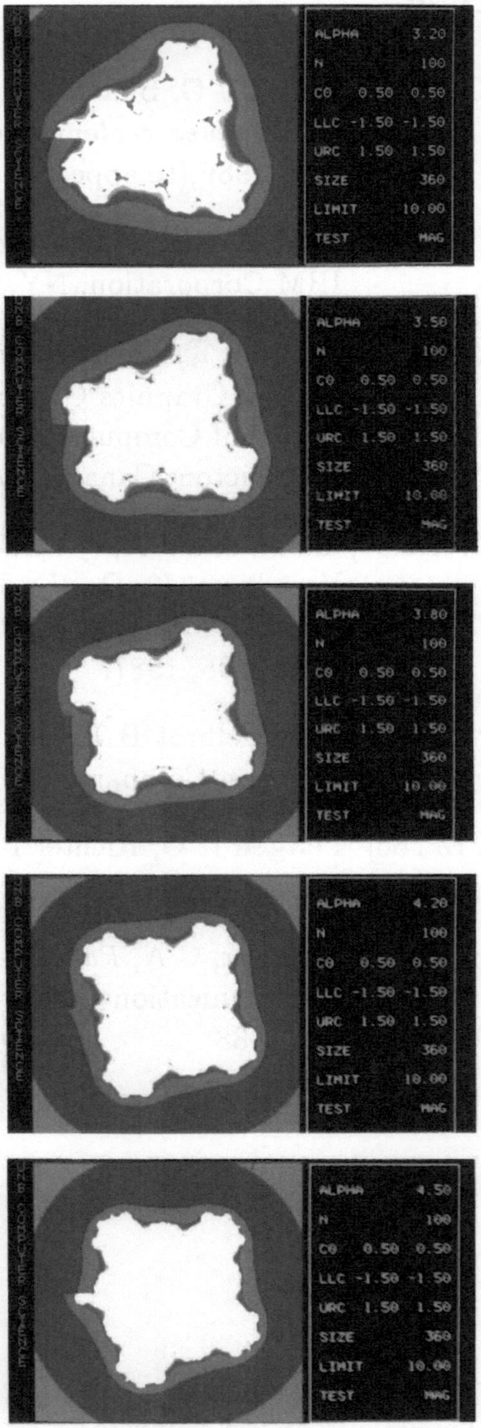

Figures 6 to 10.

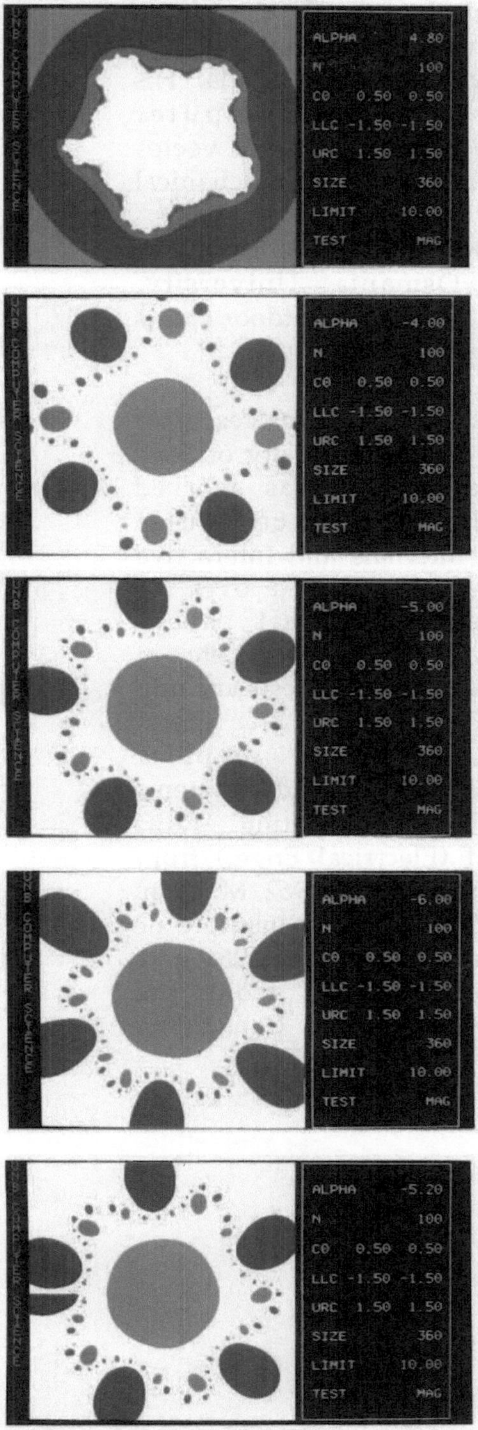

Figures 11 to 15.

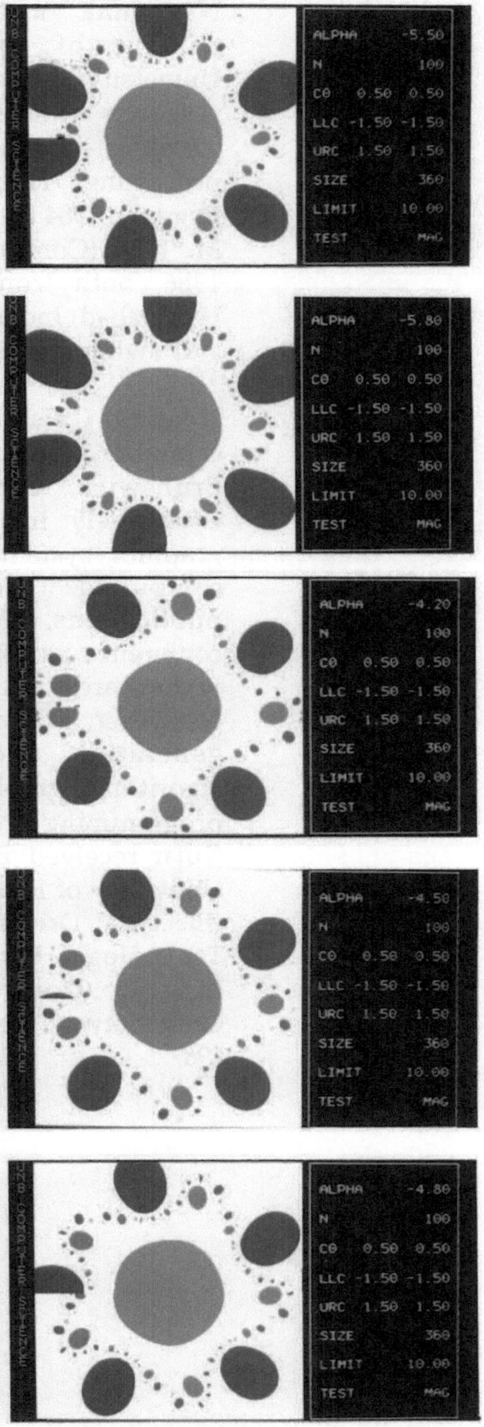

Figures 16 to 20.

Nagarjuna Vangala is currently a graduate student of computer science at the University of New Brunswick, Canada. His research interests include computer graphics, image processing and vector processing. He received B.E. (Mechanical Engg.) in 1984 and
M. Tech (Computer Science and Engg.) in 1986, both from Osmania University, Hyderabad, India. He enjoys outdoor sports and swimming.

Uday G. Gujar is currently a professor of computer science at the University of New Brunswick, Canada. He has worked extensively in the areas of computer graphics, systems internals and interactive computing. He has authored over 75 publications, including journal papers, conference papers, technical reports etc., in various areas. His current interests include computer graphics (fractals, 3-D object generation and rendering, graphics algorithms, graphics systems etc.), systems programming and supercomputing. Prof. Gujar received B.E.(Electrical Engg.) from University of Poona, India, in 1962, M. Tech. (Electrical Drives) from Indian Institute of Technology, Bombay, India, in 1964 and M.Sc.E. (Control Systems) from the University of New Brunswick, Canada, in 1967.

Virendra C. Bhavsar is an Associate Professor of Computer Science at the University of New Brunswick, Canada. At present, he is on sabbatical leave and is a Visiting Professor at the Centre for Development of Advanced Computing, Pune, India. He was on the faculty of the Dept of Computer Science and Engineering, Indian Institute of Technology, Bombay, from 1974-83. He initiated and successfully completed several research projects on parallel processing at I.I.T. Bombay including the development of PLEXUS multi-microprocessor system. His present research interests include supercomputer applications in radiation transport and computer graphics, applications of fractals in modeling natural objects and design and analysis of parallel algorithms. He has authored over 50 research papers in journals and conference proceedings. He is also the President of 'SAI: Super and Intelligent Computer Systems',. Fredericton, New Brunswick, Canada

Bhavsar is a member of IEEE, ACM, SIAM and IMACS. He organized and chaired technical sessions on "Monte Carlo Simulation with Supercomputers" at the 12th IMACS World Congress, Paris, France, July 1988. He was the Program Chairman for the 1989 APICS Computer Science Conference, Fredericton, Canada, Nov, 1989.
Bhavsar received his B. Engg. from University of Poona and M. Tech. and Ph. D. from Indian Institute of Technology, Bombay.

Address: Faculty of Computer Science, University of New Brunswick, Fredericton, New Brunswick, E3B 5A3, Canada.

Chapter 3
Rendering

A New Front to Back Composition Technique for Volume Rendering

Darin Lee Buchanan and Sudhanshu Kumar Semwal

ABSTRACT

Visualization is a powerful tool for better understanding of several scientific phenomenon. In recent years, several techniques have been proposed. We present a new model to render volume data. In this model, each volume element is classified and assigned a shaded color and opacity value. The assignments are applied through either user specified lookup tables or a default mapping. The results are stored in shaded color and opacity volumes via a pipeline approach.

We incorporate a *front-to-back* ray casting model to render the volumes of shaded color and opacity. This model compares favorably to other approaches in terms of image quality, memory use, and efficiency.

Key Words: Medical Imaging, Ray Casting, Scientific Visualization, Voxel.

1 INTRODUCTION

Visualization of scientific data has become one of the most important applications in computer graphics (McCormick 1987). A growing subset of this are the data sets representing three-dimensional volumetric information. Volumetric data are usually a set of scalar or vector values defined on a three-dimensional rectilinear grid. In most cases, the values are point values at the nodes of the grid or voxels representing a constant value for that volume element.

The majority of research in volume rendering has been published in the field of medical imaging. Medical imaging techniques such as computed tomography (CT), magnetic resonance imaging (MRI), and single-photon emission computed tomography (SPECT) use scanners to create volumes by imaging a series of cross sections, resulting in multiple 2D slices of information (Axel 1983). On each slice, there are several rectangular parallelepiped regions (voxels). Every voxel is assigned a value called its density. This density represents some object property (Bates 1983).

2 MOTIVATION

It is difficult to see the three-dimensional structure of the interior of a volume by viewing individual slices. Moreover, with volume data sets being generated in areas other than medical imaging, it is more desirable to create general visualization techniques than algorithms that are specific to one type of data. A general volume rendering software package should have the following features:

1. Be able to image the volume from different viewpoints.
2. Shade the volume in such a manner which brings out surfaces and subtle variations in density.
3. To avoid introducing computational artifacts.
4. To apply operations on the volume that will allow additional viewing options, such as cutting away sections to visualize the interior.
5. To visualize both voxel data and point data.
6. To be able to render the volume without any a priori knowledge of what the values represent. If the user has such knowledge, there should be some way to incorporate it in the model.
7. To be as cost efficient as possible.
8. To allow the user to interactively manipulate features 1-7 described above.

3 BACKGROUND

Visualizing volume data is a relatively new application in computer graphics. Even so, a number of models have been presented. These methods can be classified into two broad categories: thresholding and non-thresholding.

3.1 Thresholding

Thresholding is used to display surfaces within the volume. Values above the threshold are considered to be 1, and are part of the object to be displayed. Values below the threshold are considered to be 0, and are not displayed.

Among the first approaches are algorithms that create surfaces from contours on the adjacent slices of data (Fuchs 1988, Keppel 1975, Richard 1989, Xu 1988). Once the contours have been collected, the reconstruction problem becomes one of constructing a surface between them. Most techniques construct the surface with a mesh of polygons. Once the polygons are extracted, traditional surface shading techniques are applied.

Voxel based models correspond closely to the format in which medical data is collected. The entire object is stored in terms of voxels. Frieder et al. (1985) display the surface by showing voxels in a back-to-front approach. Surfaces can also be constructed from the voxel faces (Chen 1985). A major problem with this approach is surface shading.

Ray casting has also been used to display surfaces. Ray casting is a simpler variation of ray tracing where no secondary rays are produced. A ray stops once it hits a surface. Depth shading algorithms track rays through the volume array until they hit a surface and then assign an intensity inversely proportional to the distance from the eye (Tuy 1984).

Since no surface construction is required, ray casting models are relatively fast. Operations such as rotation, translation, and scaling are easily implemented by changing the viewpoint and recasting the rays.

The major criticism of the ray casting techniques is their use of memory. Most other approaches only need random access to a few adjacent slices of data at one time. With ray casting, the whole data volume must be in RAM for the ray to traverse it efficiently. In Section 5.4, we provide a solution to this problem.

The marching cubes approach given by Lorenson and Cline (1987) is another surface construction model. This model is attractive among thresholding techniques because it works on both point and voxel data. Furthermore, it does not have the ambiguity problems like the contour surface construction models.

3.2 Non-Thresholding Techniques

Non-thresholding models have been proposed to better understand the entire volume data. Surfaces are not constructed, but rather are displayed implicitly. In comparison to the pure thresholding approaches, more continuous images are obtained.

Unlike the thresholding approaches, opacity and color must be considered. Opacity is thought of as the inverse of transparency. Values range from 0 to 1. A value of 1 means the object is solid and cannot be seen through.

There are several models that cast rays into a volume without explicit surfaces. Usually one ray is cast per pixel. In this case, the values encountered along the path of the ray contribute to the pixels final color.

Kajiya and Von Herzen (1984) presented an approach that models the scattering of radiation within the volume. Their model produced pleasing images, but is not useful for scientific evaluation.

Sabella (1988) presented a similar scheme with the use of user controlled density particles that attenuate the intensity at each element the ray encounters. Sabella's model shows the range of values within the volume, but is limited for medical imaging and other applications where surface detection is desired.

Schlusselberg et al (1986) and Levoy (1988) have proposed models that composite the values along the path of the ray in a back-to-front ordering. Each voxel encountered is stored into an array. Once the ray traverses the volume, the final color for the ray is determined from a back-to-front composition of the values in the array.

Upson and Keeler (1988) suggest a front-to back-volume rendering approach. In their model, the color and opacity for the ray is accumulated until the ray traverses the volume or the accumulated opacity reaches a specified value.

Drebin et al (1988), presented a voxel based technique for rendering images of volumes containing mixtures of materials. First a volume of shaded color and opacity is obtained from the volume data. This volume is then displayed by compositing the voxels in back-to-front order. The model has been applied in medical applications on Pixar's powerful imaging system (Fishman 1987, Spitzer 1989). We refer to this model as Pixar's method in the paper. The model resembles a pipeline structure. At each step of the pipeline, a new volume is obtained from one or more existing volumes (See Figure 1). The result is a volume where the values at each voxel are a shaded color and opacity.

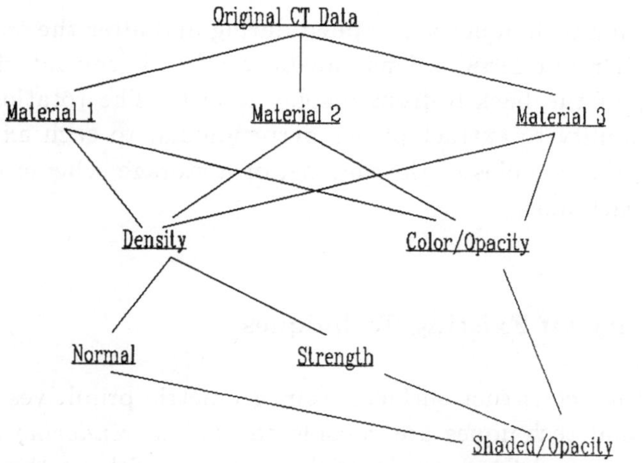

Figure 1: Pixar pipeline to create a volume of shaded color and opacity.

This volume is projected onto the image plane in a back-to- front approach. Each slice is considered an image and is composited on top of every slice behind it. The composition algorithm, explaining how the slices are combined, is discussed in sections 5.1 and 5.2.

In Pixar's method, transformations are performed by creating new volumes. To show perspective, each slice is resized proportional to its distance from the screen and inserted into a new volume. Pixar's method introduces the matte volumes to remove sections or lessen the presence of certain regions or materials. Matte volumes are further discussed in section 6.2.

We feel that Pixar's method is attractive for several reasons. The first is its pipeline structure. By storing intermediate volumes in the pipeline, the cost of generating a new image is reduced. Matte volumes can be applied to any of the volumes in the pipeline to obtain many useful images [Refer section 7.2]. The back-to-front display algorithm is efficient and simple. Finally, at most two slices of data need to be in RAM at one time during the program execution.

On the other hand, this model assumes the user has a priori knowledge of what the data values represent. Moreover, the back-to-front method of displaying the volume only works if the data elements are voxels. There is no apparent simple way in which it can be used on point data.

The Pixar model does not handle rotations effectively. The operation is not simple and artifacts often arise in the process. To reduce the number of artifacts, image processing techniques are applied during and after the construction of the new volume (Drebin 1988). This can be costly. If several views are needed, the efficiency of the back-to-front display is lost. The rotation algorithm also assumes the ability to extract planes perpendicular to each axis. This requires either intermediate copies of the volume, or a storage scheme which allows fast access along each axis.

3.3 Summary Of Existing Techniques

Approaches that construct surfaces from geometric primitives and shade them using traditional techniques are considered *surface rendering* models. *Volume rendering* has been defined as visualizing volumes without the intermediate geometric representation (Levoy 1988). Volume rendering models display surfaces implicitly.

Thresholding algorithms make a binary decision on the data and therefore throw away much of the information in the volume. They can only be used to display surfaces. It has been shown that non-thresholding techniques can produce surfaces while still presenting other information about the volume.

For most voxel based renderers, the voxels must be sufficiently close to produce a continuous image. Point data can be coarse (far apart) and a continuous image, albeit a less accurate one, will still be obtained. This is because point data renderers interpolate intermediate values. Interpolation for voxel data takes place during preprocessing. If the adjacent slices are too far apart, for example, new slices must be interpolated between them. For renderers that work on point data, interpolation takes place during the rendering phase of the algorithm.

Ray casting approaches can render both types of data. For point data, a value along the ray is interpolated from the values of the eight closest points. In the case of voxel data, the ray encounters a constant value for each voxel.

Applications using color, must decide what the color should represent in the final image. Colors can be used to represent specific materials known to be in the volume or properties such as distance from the viewpoint and the value encountered. An arbitrary mapping from values to color can also be used. Different mappings can give totally different images and may not be useful unless the user has some knowledge of what the data values represent.

4 VOLUME DATA CLASSIFICATION

We propose a new front-to-back composition model that renders volumes of shaded color and opacity. Similar to Pixar's model, we use a pipeline to generate these volumes. (Figure 2). However, our model differs from Pixars in the following ways:

- Less volumes are created to save disk space.
- The volumes can be created without any a priori knowledge of what the data values represent. If such information is available, color and opacity lookup tables are used to incorporate it into the volumes.
- The volumes can be point or voxel data. Pixar shades surfaces within voxels. Since surfaces cannot lie inside of points, our model shades points and voxels on surfaces. In other words, the resulting color for a voxel in the Pixar model is a combination of the surface and the material in front of it. In the model presented here, the resulting color of the voxel or point is the color of the surface.
- The shading algorithm is independent of viewpoint. Therefore the voxel or point color is independent of view.
- The normal volume is created by applying a gradient to the original data volume or the opacity volume. Applying the gradient to the opacity volume essentially gives the same results as Pixar's use of a density volume [Refer section 3.2]. They both highlight surfaces between classified materials while displaying a smooth and continuous variation within a material. The variation of values within a material is more visible when the gradient is applied to the original data volume. However, artifacts are more likely to occur.

4.1 Color And Opacity

Each voxel or point in the data volume is assigned a color and opacity. Color and opacity volumes are created to store these values. Lookup tables are formed that map all possible data values in the original volume to color and opacity values. These mappings are specified by the user. Mappings can be created that highlight object features at specified ranges or display isosurfaces at particular thresholds.

In our model Material percentage volumes, as used by Pixar, are not required to incorporate information about material percentages into the final image. The

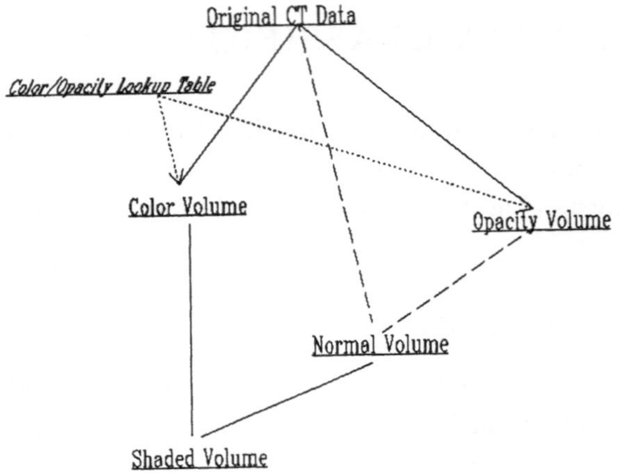

Figure 2: The pipeline to create volumes of shaded color and opacity.

same results can be achieved through the use of color and opacity lookup tables. Each material is assigned a color and opacity. If data value x represents fat and soft tissue, the color and opacity at x is given by

$$Color_x = P_x(fat) \times Color(fat) + P_x(tissue) \times Color(tissue) \quad (1)$$

$$Op_x = P_x(fat) \times Op(fat) + P_x(tissue) \times Op(tissue) \quad (2)$$

where P_x is the percentage of that material at value x. In general

$$Color_x = \sum_{i=1}^{n} P_x(i) \times Color(i) \quad (3)$$

$$Op_x = \sum_{i=1}^{n} P_x(i) \times Op(i) \quad (4)$$

where n is the number of materials in the volume.

If no lookup table exists, or the user does not wish to utilize one, a linear mapping is applied. It shows a smooth variation in color and opacity. The mapping is given by :

$$red = blue = green = opacity = x/MaxRange, \quad (5)$$

where $MaxRange$ = maximum data value − minimum data value.

The result is a gray scale image. In this fashion, our model allows the user to visualize the volume without any a priori knowledge of what the data values represent.

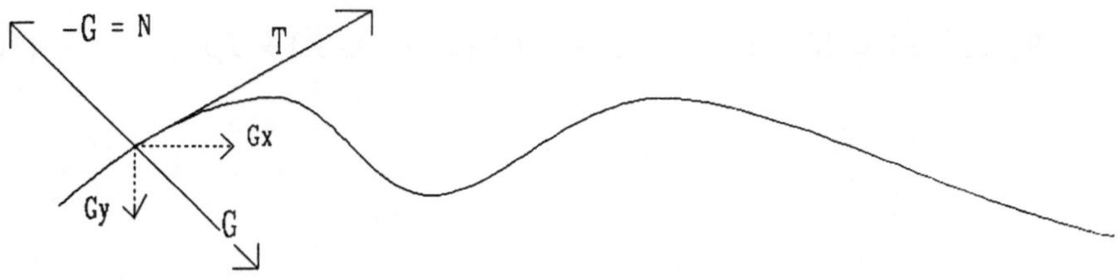

Figure 3: The negative gradient approximates the surface normal.

4.2 Shading

The major purpose of shading is to highlight surfaces within the volume. It also gives a more three-dimensional appearance to the final image. The shading algorithm requires information about the surfaces, specifically their location and normal. A surface is considered to be the boundary between materials of different density. These boundaries are indicated by the difference of adjacent values in the data volume. On a surface of constant density, the gradient (the direction of largest increase in values) is perpendicular to the surface tangential vector and therefore parallel to the normal. Figure 3 shows this on a binary two-dimensional data set.

The gradient vector $\vec{g}(x, y, z)$ can be estimated using central differences along the three coordinate axis (Levoy 1988, Lorenson 1987, Press 1984). The equation is given by

$$\begin{aligned} G_x(i,j,k) &= D(i+1,j,k) - D(i-1,j,k) && (6) \\ G_y(i,j,k) &= D(i,j+1,k) - D(i,j-1,k) && (7) \\ G_z(i,j,k) &= D(i,j,k+1) - D(i,j,k-1) && (8) \end{aligned}$$

where $D(i,j,k)$ is the value at location (i,j,k) of the volume. Then, as shown in Figure 3, the normal $\vec{N}$ is approximated by

$$\vec{N} = -\vec{G}. \tag{9}$$

Once the normal has been calculated, the shading function can be applied. We have chosen a shading model that only considers ambient and diffuse reflection (Foley 1982). The light source is considered to be at infinity, yielding a constant value for every light ray. The equation is :

$$S_\lambda(x,y,z) = Ka_\lambda \times Ia + Kd_\lambda \times (\vec{N}(x,y,z) \cdot \vec{L}) \times Ip \tag{10}$$

where

λ = r,g,b.

$S_\lambda(x,y,z) = \lambda^{th}$ color component at shaded volume location (x,y,z);

Ka_λ = ambient reflection coefficient for the λth color component.

Ia = ambient intensity.

Kd_λ = diffuse reflection coefficient for the λth color component.

$\vec{N}(x,y,z)$ = normal at location (x,y,z) in the normal volume.

$\vec{L}$ = normalized vector in the direction of the light source.

Ip = intensity of the parallel light source.
To simplify further,

$$Kd_\lambda = Ka_\lambda = C_\lambda(x,y,z) \tag{11}$$

where $C_\lambda(x,y,z)$ is the λth color component at location (x,y,z) of the color volume.

The specular term was left out for two reasons. First, it adds only a few visual cues in a volume without distinct surfaces. Secondly, without the specular term, the shading equation is independent of the viewpoint. This allows the user to alter the view without reshading the volume. Distance from the viewpoint was left out for the same reason. Depth cueing can be accomplished during ray casting or through the use of a matte volume [Refer section 7.2].

Originally, our efforts were to apply the gradient to the original data volume. Due to the nature of many data sets, a large range of values can exist within a given material. This produces several non zero values for the gradient. As a result, after the gradient is normalized, surfaces appear within a material in the final image. This helps to visualize the variation of values within a material. However, the surfaces representing the boundaries between materials are difficult to differentiate from the other surfaces.

Often an image is desired that highlights the boundaries between materials and displays a continuous variation within a material. The values in an opacity volume created by a lookup table mapping exhibit this behavior. The change in values between materials or at certain locations is very sharp. Within a material the change of values is smooth and continuous. Therefore, the desired image can be achieved by applying a gradient to the opacity volume instead of the original volume.

5 COMPARISON OF RENDERING APPROACHES

We revisit and compare different approaches that utilize the opacity and shaded color volumes to render the final image. The first method is the back to front voxel display model presented by Pixar. This is compared along with several variations of ray casting. One variation is the approach used by Levoy [Refer section 3.2]. As the ray traverses the entire volume, every value it encounters is stored into an array. These values are then composited on top of one another from back to front to yield a final color for that ray. We apply the same composition theory to ray cast the volumes in a front-to-back approach. In this case, the color and opacity for the ray are accumulated as it traverses the volume. The ray stops when the accumulated opacity is greater than or equal to 1 or the entire volume has been traversed. The accumulated color becomes the final color for the ray.

We apply both of these ray casting approaches to produce orthographic and perspective views. For orthographic projections, the direction of every ray is constant. In the case of perspective projections, the direction of each ray is dependent upon the location of the viewpoint and the pixel the ray intersects. Ray casting is applied to both point and voxel data. For point data, intermediate values encountered along the path of the ray are interpolated. The ray encounters a constant value throughout a voxel when applied to voxel data.

5.1 Composition

Our composition technique is same as used previously by Levoy (1988) and Pixar (1988). The approach chosen is taken from the theory of compositing two-dimensional digital images (Porter 1984).

The equation then becomes

$$C = \alpha_A \times C_A + (1 - \alpha_A) \times \alpha_B \times C_B. \tag{12}$$

Porter refers to this as the **over** operator, and in this case the syntax is $C =$

A **over** B. The front-to-back ray casting model accumulates the opacity for the pixel as the ray traverses the volume. The accumulated opacity α from two points is given by

$$\alpha = \alpha_A + (1 - \alpha_A) \times \alpha_B. \tag{13}$$

5.2 Pixar's Back To Front Voxel Display

The back to front voxel display approach employed by Pixar is used to produce orthographic projections. The model assumes that the projection plane and the volume slices are perpendicular to the viewing axis. Each pixel on the projection plane is mapped to the row of voxels directly in front of it. The projection plane can be located perpendicular to any of the three coordinate axis.

Each slice of the volume, perpendicular to the viewing axis, is overlaid on top of the slices behind it from back to front. If the projection plane is perpendicular to the $-z$ axis, the color of the pixel at (x, y) through the zth slice is

$$C_z(x, y) = V(x, y, z) \textbf{ over } C_{z+1}(x, y) \tag{14}$$

where $C(x, y)$ is the accumulated color for the pixel at (x, y) and $V(x, y, z)$ is the color-opacity of the voxel at (x, y, z). The initial color for the pixel, $C_n(x, y)$, is set to the background and the final color is $C_0(x, y)$. This process is repeated for each pixel on the projection plane.

5.3 Ray Casting For Voxel And Point Data

Ray casting is a popular approach to render an image for non-thresholding models. As with past approaches, the models compared in this paper cast only one ray per pixel. Each ray traverses the shaded color and opacity volumes. Once the point of intersection between a ray and the volume is located, a modified DDA algorithm is used to collect values along the ray as it traverses the volume.

One advantage of ray casting is the ability to render volume data represented by voxels or points. When ray casting a point data volume, a value along the ray is interpolated from the eight points that form the voxel surrounding it (Figure 4). For voxel data, the ray encounters a constant value throughout that volume element.

We utilize a simple three-dimensional interpolation algorithm. Alternative interpolation forms can be found in [19]. To find the scalar value for a unit cube

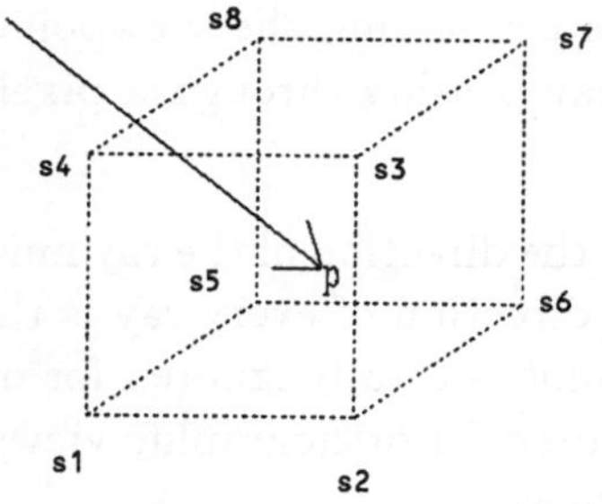

Figure 4: The value at p is interpolated from the neighboring points.

$S(x,y,z)$ where $x1 < x < x2, y1 < y < y2$, and $z1 < z < z2$, the algorithm is as follows:

1. /* get the scalar values at the eight points */
   $s1 = S(x1,y1,z1); s2 = S(x2,y1,z1); s3 = S(x2,y2,z1);$
   s4 = S(x1,y2,z1); s5 = S(x1,y1,z2); s6 = S(x2,y1,z2);
   $s7 = S(x2,y2,z2); s8 = S(x1,y2,z2);$

2. $dx = x - x1; dy = y - y1; dz = z - z1;$

3. $$\begin{aligned} S(x,y,z) = {} & (1-dx)\times(1-dy)\times(1-dz)\times s1+ \\ & dx\times(1-dy)\times(1-dz)\times s2+ \\ & dx\times dy\times(1-dz)\times s3+ \\ & (1-dx)\times dy\times(1-dz)\times s4+ \\ & (1-dx)\times(1-dy)\times dz\times s5+ \\ & dx\times(1-dy)\times dz\times s6+ \\ & dx\times dy\times dz\times s7+ \\ & (1-dx)\times dy\times dz\times s8; \end{aligned}$$

5.3.1 Perspective vs. orthographic projections

The rays can be cast to produce orthographic or perspective images. The differences between the methods of projection is determined by the direction of the rays emanating from each pixel. For perspective projections, the direction of the ray is calculated from the line connecting the viewpoint and the pixel. For orthographic projections, each ray passing through a pixel is perpendicular to the projection plane.

Under perspective ray casting, the direction of the ray must be calculated for every pixel. On the other hand, the direction of every ray is the same for orthographic projection. In fact, the viewpoint is totally ignored for orthographic ray casting. Since less calculations are required for orthographic views, they are usually faster to produce than perspective views.

5.3.2 Back-to-front vs. front-to-back composition

The final comparison in the ray casting models is the composition order of the values accumulated along the ray. By compositing the values from back to front, the ray must traverse the entire volume. As the ray traverses the shaded color and opacity volumes, each encountered color and opacity values are placed into an array. This continues until the ray exits the volume. The resulting color for that ray is given by the following procedure.

1. set I to background color.
2. For $i = n - 1$ *to* 0
   $I = C[i]$ **over** I

Where I is the resulting color for the ray, n is the number of values encountered, and C is the array of color-opacity values.

It is often the case that several values sampled along the path of the ray will not contribute to the final color of that ray. This occurs when a fully opaque object lies in front of several other materials. In addition, the accumulated opacity of several materials may be such that nothing behind them is visible. For this reason, a front-to-back composition approach was developed to make the rendering process more efficient. As the ray traverses the shaded color and opacity volumes, each color-opacity pair is applied to calculate an accumulated color and opacity for that ray. The ray stops when it exits the volumes or the accumulated opacity reaches unity. The procedure is as follows:

1. Get the first color-opacity pair.
   $I =$ color $\times$ opacity
   $\alpha =$opacity

2. while ($\alpha < 1$)
   get the next color-opacity pair along the ray
   $I = I$ **over** color
   $\alpha = \alpha + (1 - \alpha)\times$ opacity
   end while

where I is the resulting color for that ray and α is the accumulated opacity.

Our approach differs from the front-to-back model of Upson and Keeler (1988) in two ways. First, their model integrates through each "computational cell" while ours samples one or more values at each voxel[1]. The second difference is in how the color and opacity values are accumulated. We have chosen the same composition approach as applied in the back-to-front ray casting model and the voxel display model [Refer section 4.2]. This allows us to remain consistent throughout the different approaches compared.

5.4 Front-To-Back Ray Casting And RAM

The major criticism of ray casting approaches is the requirement of random access to the entire volume. This is not necessarily true if a front-to-back, orthographic projection approach is used. One solution is the cell by cell processing approach proposed by Upson and Keeler [Refer section 3.2]. We present another approach in this paper.

For orthographic projections, the coordinate axis along which the rays traverse one voxel at a time is the same for every ray. The "front" slice perpendicular to this axis can then be determined. This is the first slice in which the rays will intersect. The rays are traversed to the plane on which the slice lies. If a point at this location is within the volume, the color and opacity is accumulated for that ray. Otherwise, it is ignored. In this manner, only one slice need be in memory throughout the rendering process by traversing the rays a slice at a time. Figure 5 shows this process graphically.

One obvious problem of our scheme is the storage scheme. Like Upson and Keeler's model and Pixar's rotation approach, quick access along each coordinate axis is required to render the volume efficiently.

[1]In case of coarse point data sets, integration may often produce a more continuous image.

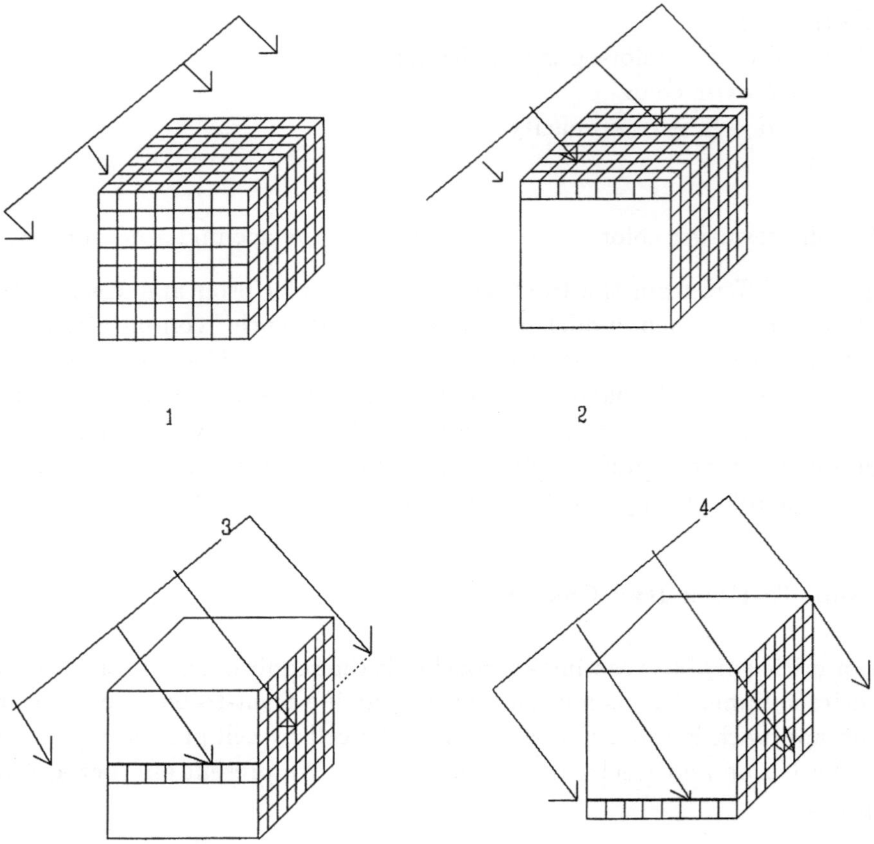

Figure 5: The steps 1-4 to ray cast the volume while reading one slice in memory at a time.

6 Volume Manipulation

6.1 Rotation

Producing an image from different viewpoints is simple in the ray casting model. The viewpoint and the projection plane are oriented as desired and the rays are recast into the volume. However, It is more complicated to produce such views using the Pixar voxel display model. This is due to the requirement that the projection plane and the slices of the volume be perpendicular to the viewing axis.

The approach by Pixar is to rotate the volume and insert it into a new volume such that each slice of the new volume is perpendicular to the viewing axis. The volume is rotated by treating each plane perpendicular to the axis of rotation as an image. Each of these planes is rotated and placed into that particular slice of the new volume.

6.2 Matte Volumes

To do spatial operations on volumes, such as cutting away sections, Drebin et al. introduced matte volumes (Refer section 3.2). A matte is applied by volume element multiplication. For example, if we apply matte M to volume V, the resulting volume R is given by

$$R(x, y, z) = M(x, y, z) \times V(x, y, z) \tag{15}$$

for each element in V and M. Several results can be produced by applying the matte to different volumes in the pipeline. If a matte is applied to both the color and opacity volumes, cutting away sections can be implemented. Depth cueing can be accomplished by applying the matte volume to the opacity volume. In this case, the matte volume contains a smooth decline in values along the viewing axis. Both ray casting and the voxel display approach can be used to render images produced by matte volumes.

7 IMPLEMENTATION AND RESULTS

The volume rendering models were implemented on a DEC 3100 workstation. It is an eight bit machine with eight megabytes of RAM. The workstation is rated at ten MIPS. The Xlib graphics package was used to display points of color on the screen.

The models were applied and compared on four sets of data, one CT data volume and three MR data volumes. Table 1 shows the data sets used their specifications.

The above data sets are represented as voxel data. We did not have access to volumes consisting of point data. In order to test the models on data sets represented by points, we treated the above data sets as such.

Data Sets	Type of Data	Size
1	CT	512 × 376 × 8
2	NMR	256 × 256 × 12
3	NMR	256 × 256 × 38

Table 1: Data sets used

7.1 Image Quality

Figures 8 through 11 show several images produced from the different types of approaches discussed. There is no visible difference between the front-to-back and back-to-front ray casting approaches. If both approaches are utilized to produce orthographic images, there is no visible difference between them and the voxel display model. Moreover, there was no visible difference between the voxel data and point data representations of the same data set.

It is debatable as to what type of projection is more informative; perspective or orthographic. Perspective projections often display invaluable information that cannot be seen from orthographic views. However, they are more prone to produce artifacts. As adjacent rays continue to diverge, several voxels may not be traversed. For orthographic views, the rays remain the same distance apart throughout their traversal. Therefore, the rays are more likely to sample every voxel.

7.2 Memory

In the process of producing a shaded color volume, only three slices need be in RAM at one time. This occurs in the creation of the normal volume, where central differences requires values on three slices. Pixar's voxel display approach only requires one slice in memory at a time. The ray casting models require random access to the entire volume. However, solutions exist for the front to back model [Refer section 7.1]. To fairly compare the models in terms of efficiency, the entire volume was also read in RAM for the voxel display method.

Several memory problems for Pixar's rotation approach were discussed in section 3.2. One problem we did not initially foresee is the extra use of disk space. For example, the CT data set consists of 1540096 elements. If the shaded color of each element is represented as one byte, the resulting shaded color volume is slightly less than 1.5 megabytes. By rotating this volume 45 degrees on the X axis, the new volume becomes approximately 35 megabytes[2]. Obviously, it will also effect the cost of rendering the new volume.

7.3 Efficiency

The process of producing the volumes of shaded color and opacity takes very little time. Table 2 lists the times to create each volume.

Volume	Data Set 1	Data Set 2	Data Set 3
Color	32 sec	15 sec	51 sec
Opacity	11 sec	7 sec	24 sec
Normal	1 min 40 sec	42 sec	2 min 12 sec
Shaded	1 min 20 sec	39 sec	1 min 45 sec

Table 2: Times to Create each Volumes

Table 3 shows the times of the different approaches to render the shaded color volume. All the approaches were applied on voxel data. There are three things that can be seen from this table.

- The Pixar voxel display model is the most efficient approach for displaying voxels.
- The front-to-back approach is the fastest among the two ray casting models. The actual difference between the ray casting models lies in the nature of the data sets [Refer section 5.3.2].

[2] We implemented our interpretation from [6] of the Pixar rotation technique. It is quite possible that this is not the exact method that Drebin et al. use and therefore these problems may not exist with their actual model.

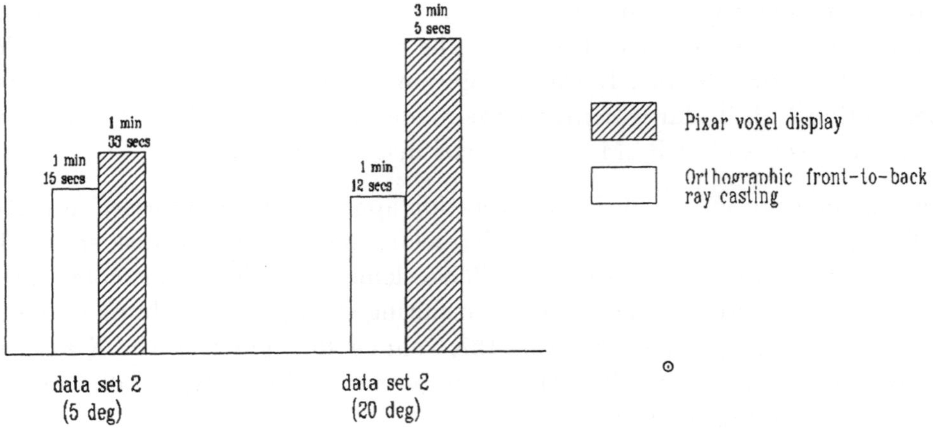

Figure 6: Comparison of ray casting and Pixar model for rendering the volume from different views.

- Orthographic projections are faster than perspective projections for the ray casting approaches. This is because the direction of each ray must be calculated for perspective ray casting. The direction for every ray is constant when producing orthographic views.

Method	Data Set 1	Data Set 2	Data Set 3
Pixar Voxel Display	2 min 45 sec	51 sec	1 min 51 sec
Back to Front Ray Casting (Orthographic Projection)	4 min	1 min 25 sec	3 min 29 sec
Back to Front Ray Casting (Perspective Projection)	10 min 45 sec	2 min 42 sec	3 min 43 sec
Front to Back Ray Casting (Orthographic Projection)	3 min 51 sec	1 min 13 sec	2 min 55 sec
Front to Back Ray Casting (Perspective Projection)	10 min 33 sec	1 min 42 sec	3 min 1 sec

Table 3: Times to Render the Volume

Figure 6 shows the cost of generating images from different views. An orthographic projection of the front-to-back ray casting model is compared with the Pixar voxel display model. Due to the complications of rotation in the Pixar model [Refer sections 3.2 and 7.1], ray casting proves to be more efficient.

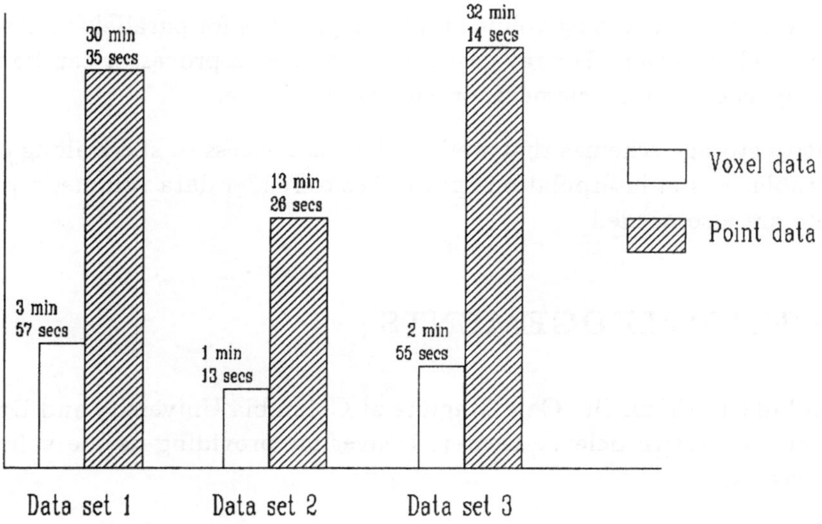

Figure 7: Comparison between ray casting voxel and point data.

Since values must be calculated at each point, it takes a much longer period of time to render volumes represented by point data. The cost of rendering the volumes by both voxel and point data are compared in Figure 7.

8 CONCLUSIONS

A model was presented to create the shaded color and opacity volumes required to render an image. The method was chosen to produce these volumes with no a priori knowledge of what the data values represent. The use of color and opacity lookup tables allows the user to incorporate such knowledge into the final image.

The front-to-back ray casting approach has proven to be the most effective of the rendering models compared. It is more efficient than the back-to-front approach and produces the same images. It is more desirable, in our opinion, than the Pixar voxel display approach for several reasons. First, it produces images from different viewpoints more efficiently. Secondly, ray casting allows the user to produce orthographic and perspective views. They can also render volumes represented by both voxel and point data. Finally, it has been shown that ray casting does not necessarily require random access to an entire volume if a front-to-back, orthographic projection approach is applied.

Several areas can be pointed out for further research. The most obvious is the ability to interactively manipulate the volume in real time. This includes transformations, cutting away sections, and interactive classification of specific materials within the volume. Creating volume rendering models for parallel architectures is the most likely solution. For ray casting approaches, a processor can be assigned to each ray, each volume element, or each volume slice.

Alternative storage schemes that would allow fast access to slices along each axis are desirable. Faster interpolation approaches to render data volumes represented by points are also needed.

9 ACKNOWLEDGEMENTS

We would like to thank Dr. Chip Maguire at Columbia University and Dr. Victor Spitzer at CU Health Science Center, Denver for providing us the volume data for our research.

10 REFERENCES

Axel, L., Arger, P.H., Zimmerman, R.A. (1983) "Applications of Computerized Tomography to Diagnostic Radiology", *Proceedings of the IEEE*, 71(3): 293-297.

Bates, R.H., Garden, K.L., Peters, T.M. (1983) "Overview of Computerized Tomography with Emphasis on Future Developments", *Proceedings of the IEEE*, 71(3): 356-372.

Catmull, E., Smith, A.R. (1980) "3-D Transformations of Images in Scanline Order", *Computer Graphics* 14(3): 279-285.

Chen, L., Herman, G.T., Reynolds, R.A., Udupa, J.K. (1985) "Surface Shading in the Cuberille Environment" , *IEEE CGA*, 5(12): 33-43.

Cook, L., Dwyer, S., Batnitzky, S., Lee, K. (1983) "A Three-Dimensional System for Diagnostic Imaging Applications", em IEEE CGA, 3(5): 137-145.

Drebin, R., Carpenter, L., Hanrahan, P. (1988) "Volume Rendering", *Computer Graphics*, 22(4): 65-74.

Fishman, et al. (1987) "Volumetric Rendering Techniques: Applications for Three-dimensional Imaging of the Hip", *Radiology*, 63(3): 737-738.

Foley, J.D., Van Dam, A. (1974) *Fundamentals of Interactive Computer Graphics*, Addison-Wesley.

Frieder, G., Gordon, D., Reynolds, R.A. (1985) "Back-to-Front Display of Voxel-Based Objects", *IEEE CGA*, 5(1): 52-60.

Fuchs, H., Kedem, Z., Uselton, S. (1977) "Optimal Surface Reconstruction from Planar Contours", *CACM*, 20(10): 693-712.

Fuchs, H., Pizer, S.M., Creasy, J.L., Renner, J.B., Rosenman, J.G. (1988) "Interactive Richly Cued Shaded Display of Multiple 3D Objects in Medical Images" ,Technical Report TR88-015, CS Department UNC.

Hoehne, K.H, Delepaz, R.L, Bernstein, R., Taylor, R.C, "Combined Surface Display and Reformatting for the Three- Dimensional Analysis of Tomographic Data", *Investigative Radiology*, 22(7): 658-664.

Kajiya, J. T., Von Herzen, B.P. (1984) "Ray Tracing Volume Densities", *Computer Graphics*, 18(3): 165-174.

Keppel, E. (1975) "Approximating Complex Surfaces by Triangulation of Contour Lines", *IBM JRD*, 19: 1-21.

Levoy, M. (1988) "Display of Surfaces from Volume Data", *IEEE CGA*: 29-37.

Lorenson, W.E., Cline, H.E. (1987) "Marching Cubes: A High Resolution 3D Surface Reconstruction Algorithm", *Computer Graphics*, 21(4): 163-169.

McCormick, B.H. et al. (ed) (1987) Visualization in Scientific Computing, *Computer Graphics*, 21(6).

Porter, T., Duff, T. (1984) "Compositing Digital Images", *Computer Graphics*, 18(3): 253-260.

Press, W., Flannery, B., Teukolsky, S., Vettering, W. (1986) *Numerical Recipes: The Art of Scientific Computing*, Cambridge University Press.

Richard, M.J., Allard, J., Ghosh, S.K., Bougouss, M. (1989) "Three- Dimensional Reconstruction of Human Limbs from Tomographic Views", *Computers and Biomedical Research*, 22(1).

Sabella, P. (1988) "A Rendering Algorithm for Visualizing 3d Scalar Fields", *Computer Graphics*, 22(4): 51-55.

Schlusselberg, D.S, Smith, W.K, Woodward, D.J (1986) "Three- Dimensional Display of Medical Image Volumes", *Proceedings of NCGA*, 3: 114-123.

Spitzer, V.M., Whitlock, D.G (1989) "A 3-D Database of Human Anatomy", *Advanced Imaging*: pp. 48-49.

Tuy, H.K., Tuy, L.T. (1984) "Direct 2D Display of 3D Objects", *IEEE CGA* 4(10): 29-34.

Upson, C., Keeler, M. (1988) "V-BUFFER: Visible Volume Rendering", *Computer Graphics*, 22(4): 59-64.

Xu, S.B., Lu, W.X. (1988) "Surface Reconstruction of 3D Objects in Computerized Tomography" , *CVGIP*, 44(3): 270-278.

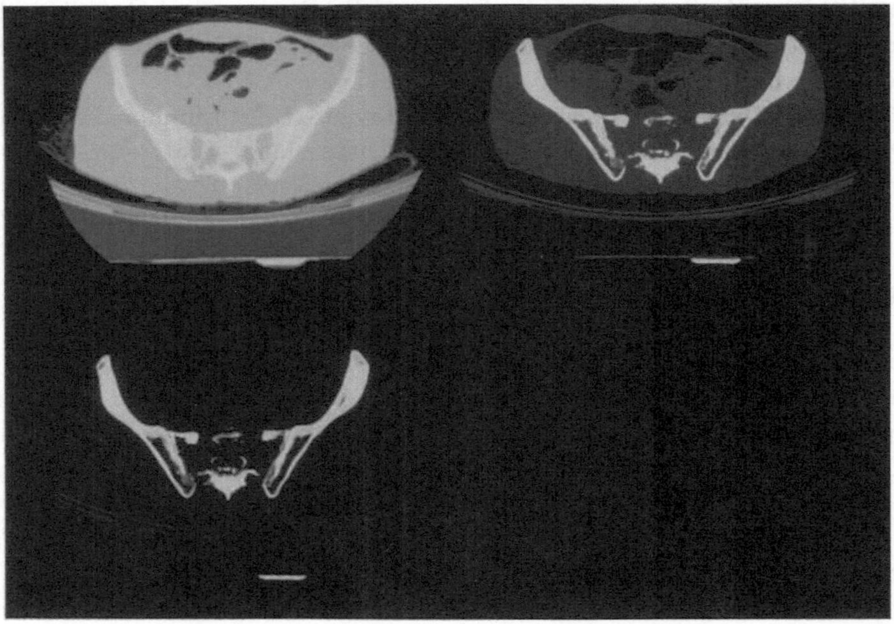

Figure 8: CT data of a hip: original slice (top left), colored volume (top right) and shaded volume.

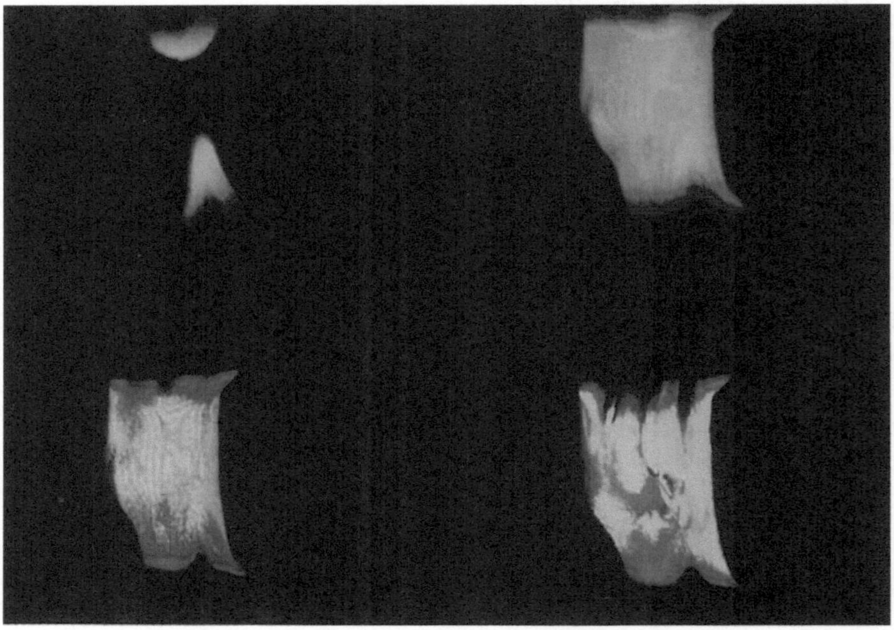

Figure 9: NMR Data of a knee. Original slice (top left), grey scale color volume (top right), shaded volume (bottom left), shaded volume with front cutaway.

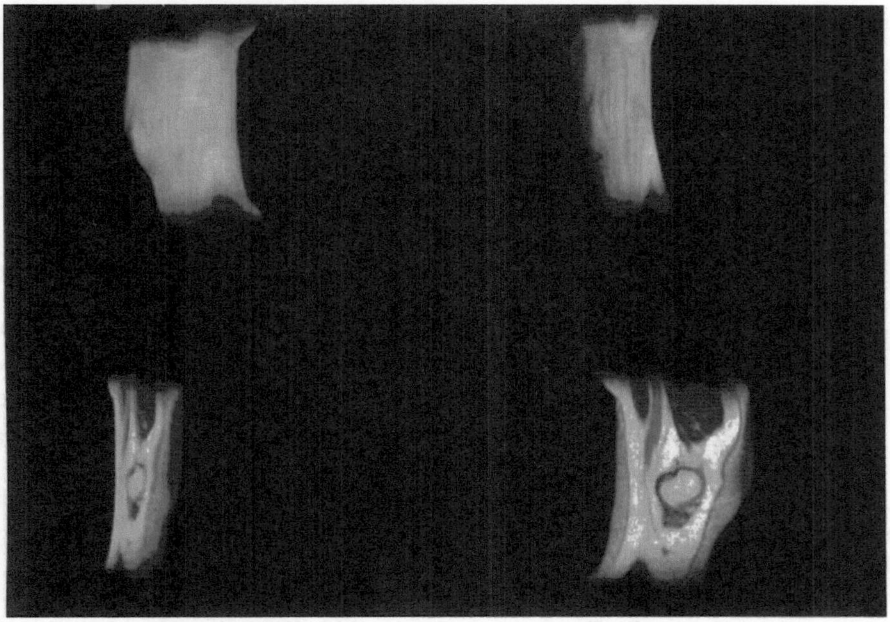

Figure 10: Different grey scale views of the NMR data for the knee.

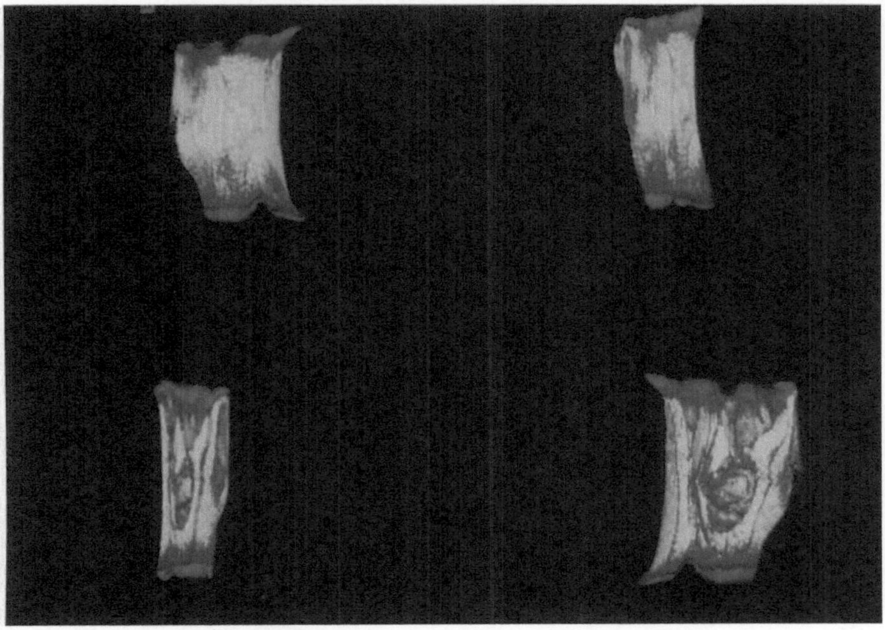

Figure 11: Different shaded views for the NMR data for the knee.

AUTHORS BIOGRAPHIES

Sudhanshu K. Semwal is currently an assistant professor of Computer Science at the University of Colorado at Colorado Springs, Colorado. He joined the faculty in 1987. His research interests include computer graphics (ray tracing; volume rendering; deformations; animation) and parallel processing.

In 1987, Semwal received his Ph. D. from University of Central Florida, Orlando. He worked on ray tracing under the supervision of Dr. J. Michael Moshell. He graduated from University of Alberta, Canada in 1984. His thesis advisor was Dr. Wayne Alto Davis.

Address: Dr. S. K. Semwal, Department of Computer Science, University of Colorado, Colorado Springs, Colorado, U.S.A., 80933-7150.

Darin L. Buchanan obtained his Bachelors degree in Mathematics at Western State College in Gunnison Colorado in 1986. He received his M.S. in Computer Science at the University of Colorado at Colorado Springs in 1989.

Buchanan's graduate research concentrated in the areas of artificial intelligence and computer graphics. His thesis was on volume rendering.

Address: Darin Buchanan, 1202 Pike Dr, Colorado Springs, CO. 80904.

Parameter-Controlled Hair Rendering in Backlight

Y. Watanabe and Y. Suenaga

ABSTRACT

Despite the fact that hair is an essential part of the human body, few reports have been published on hair generation by CG. Especially little attention has been paid to rendering CG hair in backlight. We presented our fundamental idea of hair image generation using a trigonal prism and wisp model at CGI '89. This paper precisely describes the ten hair parameters needed for efficient hair rendering. The relation between the parameters and appearance of hair images is discussed. We show that variation of hair images can be generated quickly by changing only a small number of hair parameters. This paper also presents a new efficient method, called the double z-buffer, to create a realistic backlight effect using standard z-buffer machines. The double z-buffer technique determines for each pixel the closest and farthest hair surface to calculate the hair thickness needed for backlight effect generation. Realistic hair images in backlight have been obtained with reasonable computation time.

Key words: fur image, hair image, trigonal prism, wisp, z-buffer, backlight

1. INTRODUCTION

Recently, fur or hair image generation is becoming an important problem in CG (Yamana 1987; Miller 1988;

Watanabe 1989; Kajiya 1989; Perlin 1989). The appearance of hair or fur is not characterized only by their complex textures alone. Most reports (Yamana 1987; Miller 1988; Kajiya 1989; Perlin 1989), however, treat only the realistic fur or hair texture generation. Our trigonal prism based wisp model (Watanabe 1989) seems to be the first report which clearly handled the hair style (shape) generation. Though the authors presented the rough idea of hair style and hair texture generation with some examples in the previous work (Watanabe 1989), actual parameters needed for realistic hair rendering were not clarified.

The appearance of hairs or furs is strongly affected by the lighting condition. For example, a halo appears around hair when it is placed in front of the light source. In this paper, we call this the "backlight effect," which is important to render more realistic CG hair images. Moreover, we have found no reports on the generation of hair images in backlight. Ray-tracing is a widely used technique to simulate various lighting conditions, but it is too slow, in practice, to calculate all the optical phenomena of many hairs. The main problem of ray-tracing is that its processing time is directly proportional to the number of primitives. Since usual human scalp holds 50,000 to 100,000 hairs, it may take a day to render one head image. Though this time may be reduced by area specific rendering, ray-tracing will be still too slow for hair image rendering. Miller (Miller 1988), Perlin (Perlin 1989) and Kajiya (Kajiya 1989) independently used at least a couple of hours using fast machines for rendering one hair image.

A trigonal prism based wisp model was employed in our hair image generation method (Watanabe 1989) to quickly obtain a hair image on a conventional z-buffer machine. This paper shows ten parameters needed for efficient hair image generation using trigonal prism based wisp model. This paper also presents a new method named "double z-buffer" to reproduce the backlight effect applied to the hair model. The experimental results have shown the feasibility of the "double z-buffer" and the realism of the rendered backlight hair image.

2. PARAMETERS FOR HAIR IMAGE GENERATION

Usually, there are more than 50,000 hairs on a human scalp. To render various hair images efficiently, we devised a hair rendering method using a trigonal prism based wisp model (Watanabe 1989). In this method, each hair is independently modeled as a serial set of trigonal prisms, and a wisp is defined as a bundle of hairs. Consequently, various hair images are easily generated by controlling only ten parameters listed in Table 1.

Table 1. Parameters for hairy image generation

No.	Symbol	Description
1	**t**	Twist angle (of trigonal prisms)
2	**v**	Direction vector (of trigonal prisms)
3	**l**	Length (of trigonal prisms)
4	**d**	Thickness (of trigonal prisms)
5	**N**	Number of trigonal prism(s)
6	**C**	Hair color
7	**M**	Hair density (number of hairs in a wisp)
8	**R**	Direction vector randomness
9	**T**	Total number of wisp(s)
10	**K**	Kind of wisp(s)

Figures 1 and 2 illustrate a trigonal prism model used in our hair rendering. A hair is modeled as a chain of trigonal prisms defined by six parameters: trigonal prism length **l**, twist angle **t**, direction vector **v**, prism thickness **d**, number of trigonal prisms per hair **N**, and hair color **C**. A wisp is composed of a bundle of hairs defined by two parameters: hair density **M** (number of hairs per wisp) and direction vector randomness **R**. The hair style is controlled by total number of wisp **T** and kind of wisp **K**. The role of these parameters are described below using examples.

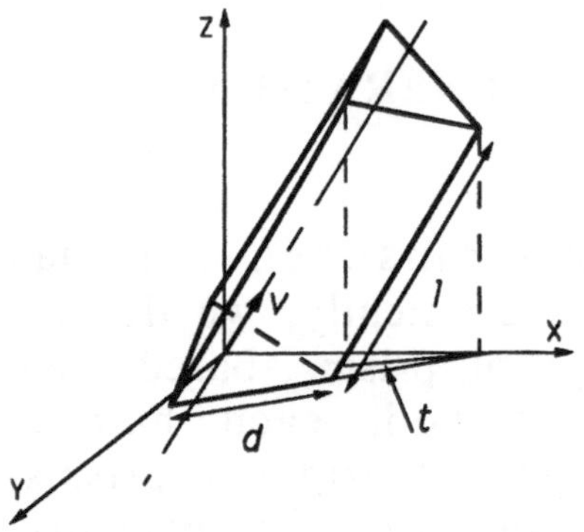

Figure 1. Trigonal Prism

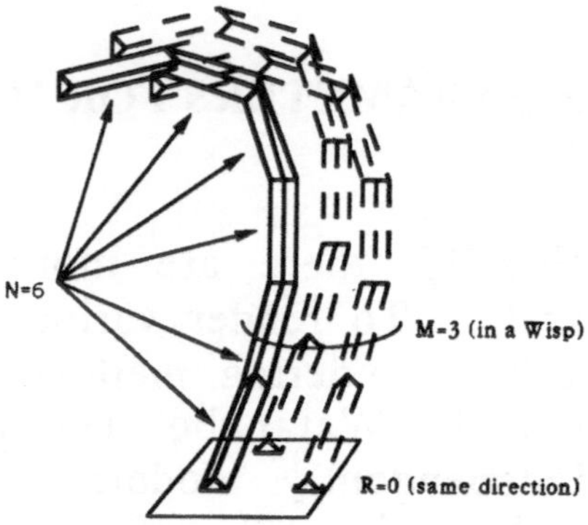

Figure 2. Trigonal Prism based Wisp Model

The hair style is controlled primarily by changing wisp shape. Though a wisp is defined as a set of hairs having various properties, e.g., thickness, stiffness, and straightness, the wisp shape is strongly affected by the external conditions, i.e. gravity, combing, hair oil, permanent wave, etc. The loci of wisps are determined to obtain the desired hair style on specified hair roots. These hair roots are located on the scalp of head model. Both of hair root locations determined by **T** and kind of wisp **K** are indispensable parameters to control the hair style.

Figures 3(a), (b) and (c) show the effect of changing the number of trigonal prisms per hair **N**. Despite the fact that no other parameters are changed, this gives various images having very different hair styles.

Next, hair stiffness control is illustrated based on the image shown in Figure 3(c). Only by changing the direction vector **v**, the images having very hard hair, hard hair, medium hair and soft hair are obtained as shown in Figure 3(c), Figures 4(a), (b) and (c), respectively.

Figures 5(a), (b) and (c) show the change of hair density. Only by changing the hair density **M** (number of hairs per

Rendering time:

(a) N=1 15sec (b) N=6 53sec (c) N=9 77sec

Figure 3. Images rendered for various values of N

Rendering time:

(a) 77sec (b) 77sec (c) 77sec

Figure 4. Images rendered for various values of v

Rendering time:

(a) M=1/2 44sec (b) M=1/4 25sec (c) M=1/8 13sec

Figure 5. Images rendered for various values of M

t, R: Constant, T=5652, K=1
(682 x 682 pixels)

Rendering time:
(a) d=1/2 (b) d=2 (c) d=4
77sec 77sec 77sec

Figure 6. Images rendered for various values of d

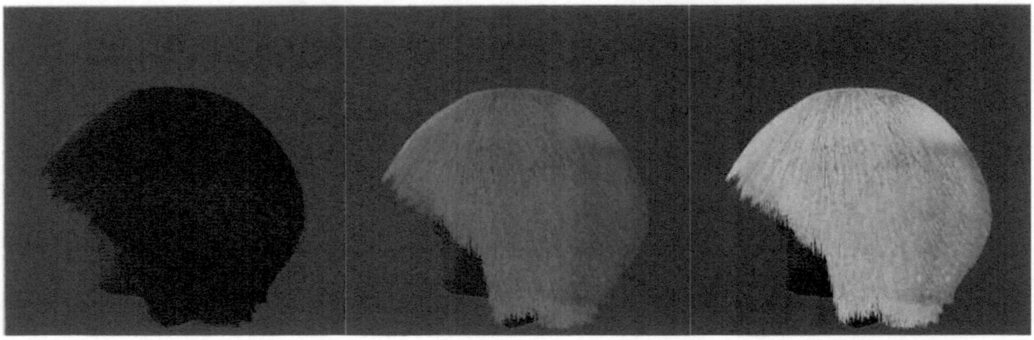

Rendering time:
(a) C:Black (b) C:Red (c) C:Silver
77sec 77sec 77sec

Figure 7. Images rendered for various attributes of C

Rendering time:
(a) (b) (c) (K=2)
80sec 80sec 80sec

Figure 8. Images rendered for various values of l and v

t, R: Constant, T=5652, K=1
(682 x 682 pixels)

wisp) , various images having a lot of hairs, medium number of hairs and few hairs are obtained.

Figures 6(a), (b) and (c) show the change of hair thickness. Only the prism thickness **d** is modified to render various hairs having different textures.

Figures 7(a), (b) and (c) show the change of hair color. Images having black hair, red hair and silver hair are drawn simply by changing the hair color **C**.

The final example shows the change of hair length, consequently the different hair style. This is achieved by simply changing two parameters: trigonal prism length **l** and direction vector **v**, as shown in Figures 8(a), (b) and (c).

The rendering time is proportional to the number of drawing primitives (polygon patches). Therefore, it is proportional to the product of hair density **M** and number of hairs **N**. Comparing the pictures shown in Figures 4(b) and 5(a) for example, picture quality is almost the same, and Figure 5(a) seems to have more hairs than Figure 4(b), while the rendering time is shorter for Figure 5(a). This is mainly due to the difference of hair density **M**. Generally speaking, the rendering time is reduced by making hair thickness **d** larger, and hair density **M** smaller, though the parameters should be properly chosen according to the required picture quality.

3. BACKLIGHT EFFECT

3.1 Backlight hairs

When hair is placed in front of a bright light source, shiny reflection through the hair is observed in the marginal hair area. It looks as if hair becomes partially translucent. This effect is very important to make hair images more realistic. In general, it is not easy to determine in a reasonable time which area should be rendered with backlight effect. No reports seem to have been published on hair image generation in backlight.

The authors reduced the problem to the determination of the hair area which is thin enough to pass the light. In order to specify the area, it is straightforward to measure the thickness of the object (mass of hair) looked from the observation point direction. This is done quite easily by using a usual z-buffer described below.

3.2 Double z-buffer

In order to determine the area having backlight effect during target image generation, we present a new technique named a "double z-buffer," which is illustrated in Figure 9. A z-buffer is generally used to determine the visible surface of a drawing object from a specified observation point. The calculated content of the z-buffer is the depth value of the surface closest to the observation point. For convenience, we call this a front z-buffer. Then we consider another z-buffer to store the depth value of the farthest surface which is referred to as a rear z-buffer. The thickness of drawing object is easily calculated from these two z-buffers. Since usual z-buffer machines do not have two z-buffers, front and rear z-buffers are realized by applying usual z-buffer two times sequentially.

This method is easily implemented on conventional z-buffer machines. The front z-buffer is obtained as a usual z-buffer. The rear z-buffer is obtained by rendering objects from the opposite observation point. Practically, it is convenient to place the observation point far from the object to avoid the annoying problems due to the difference of perspective projections in front and rear sides. When both z-buffers are prepared, the difference between front z-buffer value and rear z-buffer value is calculated for each pixel to define the thickness of drawn objects.

Based on the thickness, the thin areas can be easily identified and halo is created in these areas as isolated hairs. Generally, the appearances of the backlight effect depend on the light sources which are located beyond the hair. These lighting effects are easily obtained by using intensity table which is defined as a pattern of backlight. For simplicity, the authors assumed that the backlight effect is inversely proportional to thickness of hair areas of drawn objects. This simple method turned out to be effective as shown in 3.3, though it is straightforward to employ more strict method to determine the area.

3.3 Experimental results

A hair image rendered from a 3-D head model without the backlight effect is shown in Figure 10. This can be compared with the image with the backlight effect shown in Figure 11. Figure 11 is clearly much more realistic than Figure 10. It took 151 seconds to generate Figure 10, and 345 seconds to generate Figure 11 using IRIS-4D/70GT. The time difference is mostly due to the extra time needed to generate the rear surface.

4. CONCLUSION

This paper described the ten parameters needed for efficient hair rendering using a trigonal prism based wisp model. The paper also presented a new efficient method, a "double z-buffer," for efficient hair image generation in backlight. The double z-buffer method itself can be applied to various purposes and various CG models including our trigonal prism based wisp model. For example, object volume is quite easily calculated by double z-buffer. Experiments using a typical CG workstation proved that the proposed algorithm is very effective for the generation of realistic human hair images in backlight. A notable feature of the proposed method is that it is suited to the conventional z-buffer, the fastest practical rendering tool available today.

It has been clarified that various hair styles are easily generated by controlling a small number of parameters.

Hair texture control, however, is not fully solved yet, together with efficient antialiasing methods for truly photorealistic hair image generation.

ACKNOWLEDGEMENT

The authors thank Mr. Kazuaki Komori, the former Executive Manager, Visual Perception Lab., NTT HI Lab., and Dr. Yukio Kobayashi, the Executive Manager, VPL, for their encouragements and advices, and members of that Lab. for various valuable discussions. The authors also thank Dr. Richard Wallace for his help in improving the manuscript.

REFERENCES

G.S. Miller, (1988) FROM WIRE-FRAMES TO FURRY ANIMALS. Proceedings Graphics Interface '88, pp. 138-145

J.T. Kajiya and T. L. Kay, (1989) RENDERING FUR WITH THREE DIMENSIONAL TEXTURES. Computer Graphics (SIGGRAPH '89 Conference Proceedings), Vol. 23, No. 3, pp. 271-280

Ken Perlin, (1989) Hypertexture. Computer Graphics (SIGGRAPH '89 Conference Proceedings), Vol. 23, No. 3, pp. 253-262

T. Yamana and Y. Suenaga, (1987) A Method of Hair Representation Using Anisotropic Reflection. IECEJ Tech. Report, PRU87-3, pp. 15-20 (in Japanese)

Y. Watanabe and Y. Suenaga, (1989) Drawing Human Hair using Wisp Model. New Advances in Computer Graphics (Proceedings of CG International '89), pp. 691-700

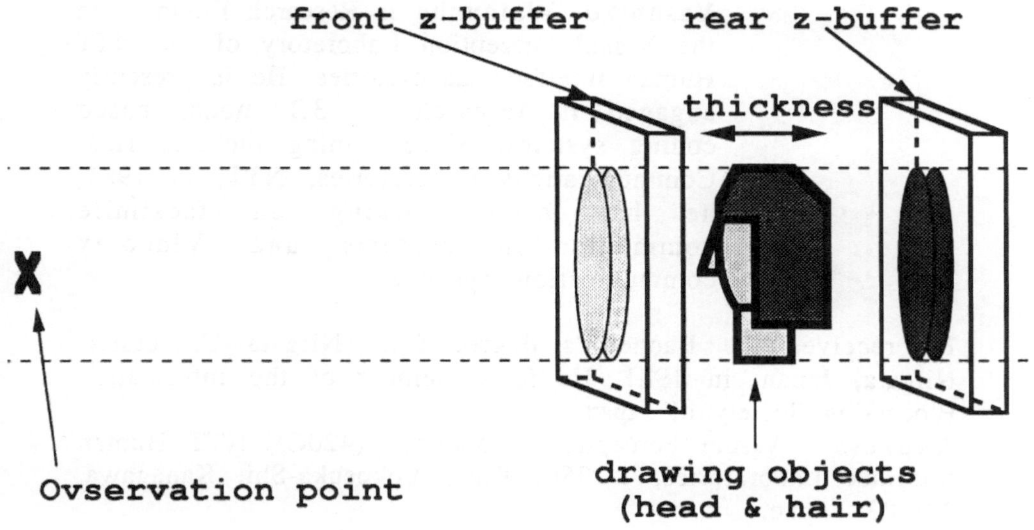

Figure 9. Double z-buffer

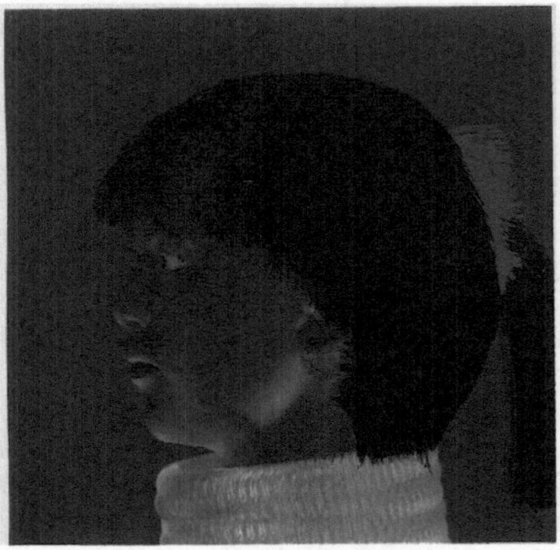

Figure 10. Hair image
Rendering time : 151 sec
(1024 x 1024 pixels)

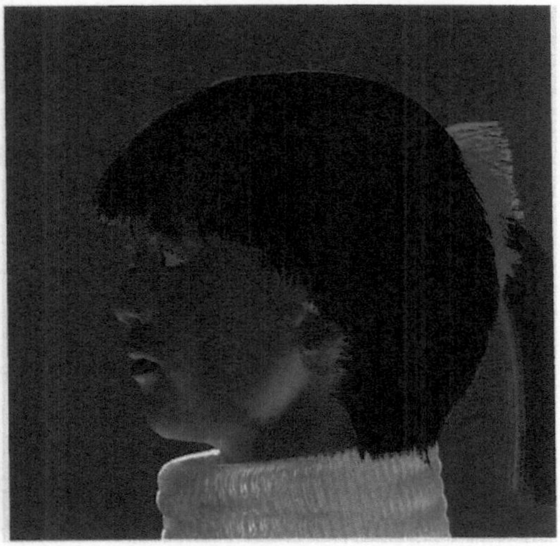

Figure 11. Hair image with Backlight effect
Rendering time : 345 sec
(1024 x 1024 pixels)

Yasuhiko Watanabe is Research Engineer in the Visual Perception Laboratory of the NTT Human Interface Laboratories. He is presently engaged in research on 3D model based coding systems. Since joining the Electrical Communications Laboratories, NTT, in 1981, he has been working on facsimile communication systems and Videotex communication systems.

He received the Bachelor's degree from Niigata University, Niigata, Japan, in 1981. He is a member of the Information Processing Society of Japan.
Address : Visual Perception Laboratory (420C), NTT Human Interface Laboratories, 1-2356, Take, Yokosuka-Shi, Kanagawa, 238-03 Japan.
CS-Net : watanabe%nttcvg.NTT.jp@relay.cs.net

Yasuhito Suenaga is Senior Research Engineer, Supervisor, of Visual Perception Laboratory in NTT Human Interface Laboratories. He leads a research group of computer graphics and vision. Since joining the Electrical Communications Laboratories, NTT, in 1973, he has been engaged in the research of image processing.

He received the B.S., M.S., and Ph.D. degrees in electrical engineering from Nagoya University, Nagoya, Japan, in 1968, 1970 and 1974 respectively. He is a member of the Institute of Electronics and Communication Engineers of Japan, and the Information Processing Society of Japan.
Address : Visual Perception Laboratory (420C), NTT Human Interface Laboratories, 1-2356, Take, Yokosuka-Shi, Kanagawa, 238-03 Japan.
CS-Net : suenaga%nttcvg.NTT.jp@relay.cs.net

A Simple Rendering for Penumbra Caused by Sunlight

Shinichi Takita, Kazufumi Kaneda, Toshio Akinobu, Haruhiko Iriyama,
Eihachiro Nakamae, and Tomoyuki Nishita

ABSTRACT

A simple rendering method for penumbra caused by sunlight is proposed to create more realistic outdoor scenery. To reduce the storage needed for penumbra areas, only four points are used to define a penumbra area. The proposed method can render complex penumbra scenes caused by such objects as curtains. In addition, the calculation method of illumination in the shadows cast by natural objects, such as trees, mapped on a transparent virtual plane are discussed. The photographs of computer generated images with penumbrae are compared to those without penumbra. Those photographs show the usefulness of the proposed method.

key Words: Shadow, Penumbra, Sunlight, Texture Mapping, Transparency Mapping, Photo Realism, Realistic Image, Scan Line Algorithm.

1 INTRODUCTION

Shadowing is an indispensable technique for making photorealistic computer generated images. Shadows consist of umbrae only when a light source is modeled as an ideal point (Appel 1969, Nishita 1974) or parallel light; the edges of shadows cast by obstacles are very sharp. It has been pointed out (Crow 1977) that shadows have penumbrae surrounding umbrae and the intensity of illumination continuously changes from the unshadowed area to the shadowed as every actual light source has a finite size.

The following methods have been proposed for generating penumbrae; 1) simulating a general light source by using many distributed point sources, 2) ray tracing, and 3) calculating penumbra areas. The first method (Brotman 1984) uses many point light sources distributed on a polyhedral surface corresponding to the shape of a light source. Point sources are generated at random or on latticed points, and then a shadow volume is created for each point light source. The intensity of illuminance at a calculation point is proportional to the number of light sources whose shadow volumes do not include that point. The more point light sources, the greater the accuracy of illumination in a penumbra, but the computation cost increases in proportion to the product of the number of point light sources by that of polyhedra to be rendered. In ray tracing, penumbrae can be rendered by "Distributed Ray Tracing" (Cook 1984) and "Ray Tracing with Cones" (Amanatides 1984). In the former the rays emanating from each calculation point to the light sources are distributed. The number of sample points receiving the rays determines the intensity of illumination at that point. In the latter a cone is used instead of rays, and the center line of the cone is defined as the ray in standard ray tracing. The fraction of a cone shadowed by the objects is calculated. Unfortunately both methods are expensive computationally because of the ray tracing involved. In the third method (Nishita 1983, Nishita 1985) penumbra areas on each face are calculated by using shadow volumes prior to removal of hidden surfaces. The penumbra areas for linear and/or area light sources are pre-calculated. The boundary integral for visible parts of the light sources viewed from each processing point in the penumbrae is employed to determine the illumination at the point. The methods mentioned above can be applied to every kind of light source, but a fair amount of calculation is inevitable.

In creating outdoor scenery a parallel light source is usually used. However, the sun has a finite size, and actually we observe penumbrae. Viewed from any point on the earth sunlight is seen as a ray with a definite solid angle. Based on this premise the proposed method approaches the generation of highly realistic shadows caused by the sun's rays using a relatively simple model. The features of this method are as follows:

(a) Fast rendering of shadows with penumbrae for artificial objects constructed with a set of convex polyhedra.

(b) Shadowing for images in scanned-in photographs of natural objects such as trees.

The outline of our algorithm is as follows:

1) Computation of penumbra areas in advance.

2) Calculation of penumbra spans on a scanline and classification of these spans into two types.

3) Efficient calculation of illumination according to the classified spans.

In the following sections, the calculation methods for penumbra area, illumination according to the type of spans, and illumination in the shadows cast by natural objects are discussed.

2 PENUMBRA AREA CAST BY A CONVEX POLYHEDRON

When an obstacle is formed by a convex polyhedron, the shape of shadow on a plane is also convex. To simplify the explanation, a plane casting a shadow on another plane is considered. Fig. 1 illustrates a plane ABCD supposedly obstructing the sun's rays and casting a shadow on a plane F_s. On the earth the sun is observed as a circle with 32′ of angle of view. Hence when the sun's rays pass through an arbitrary point $T_0\,(x_0, y_0, z_0)$ on edge BC, their range is bound within a cone whose center line accords with the direction of the sun's ray and the angle of spread is 32′. Consequently the penumbra area corresponding to point T_0 generally appears to be an ellipse surrounded by the intersection points of the cone and plane F_s. We will call this ellipse "shadowed ellipse". The calculation method of penumbra area is explained in the following three steps: A shadowed ellipse corresponding to an arbitrary point on a contour edge, a penumbra area cast by a contour edge, and penumbra areas cast by more than one polyhedron.

2.1 Shadowed Ellipse Caused by a Point on a Contour Edge

Let $\boldsymbol{L_x}$, $\boldsymbol{L_y}$, and $\boldsymbol{L_z}$ be unit vectors expressing the axes of the system of Cartesian coordinates with an origin referred to as $\boldsymbol{Q}$ in the world coordinates; note that the new system differs from the system of world coordinates. The point (x, y, z) in the new system is expressed by

$$\begin{bmatrix} x_w \\ y_w \\ z_w \end{bmatrix} = \begin{bmatrix} \boldsymbol{L_x} & \boldsymbol{L_y} & \boldsymbol{L_z} \end{bmatrix} \begin{bmatrix} x \\ y \\ z \end{bmatrix} + \boldsymbol{Q}. \tag{1}$$

That is, a point in an arbitrary system of coordinates is easily transformed into the system of world coordinates by using Eq. 1.

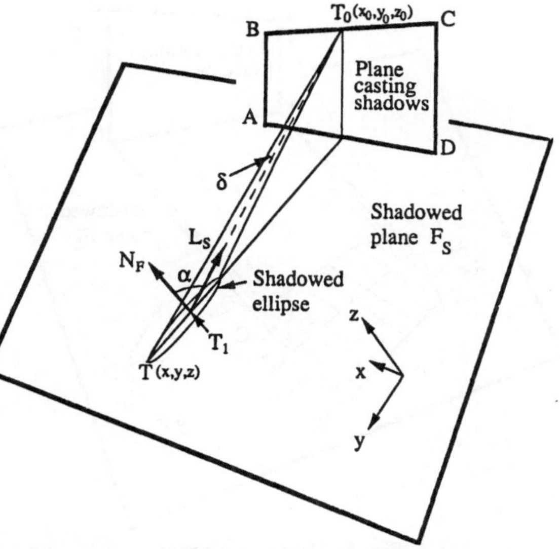

Fig. 1: A shadowed ellipse corresponding to point T_0.

To simplify the expression of equations, the following orthogonal coordinate systems are used; z axis is in the direction of normal $\boldsymbol{N_F}$ ($|\boldsymbol{N_F}| = 1$) of plane F_s, and x axis is in the direction of $\boldsymbol{N_F} \times \boldsymbol{L_s}$, where $\boldsymbol{L_s}$ ($|\boldsymbol{L_s}| = 1$) looks toward the sun. In the system of coordinates mentioned above the major axis of a shadowed ellipse on the xy plane is always parallel to the y axis. Fig. 1 shows the shadowed ellipse corresponding to an arbitrary point $T_0(x_0, y_0, z_0)$ on edge BC in the new system of coordinates. Assumed that T_1 is the intersection between plane F_s and the sun's ray (opposite direction of $\boldsymbol{L_s}$) stretching from the center of the sun through T_0, and that point $T(x, y, z)$ is a point on the cone with a vertex T_0, a center line T_0T_1, and an angle of spread δ, then the following equation is satisfied:

$$\overrightarrow{T_0T_1} \cdot \overrightarrow{T_0T} = \pm |\overrightarrow{T_0T_1}| \cdot |\overrightarrow{T_0T}| \cos\delta. \tag{2}$$

If the angle formed by $\boldsymbol{L_s}$ and $\boldsymbol{N_F}$ is defined as α,

$$\{(y-y_0)\sin\alpha - (z-z_0)\cos\alpha\}^2 = \cos^2\delta\{(x-x_0)^2 + (y-y_0)^2 + (z-z_0)^2\}. \tag{3}$$

If $z = 0$, an ellipse formed by intersection between plane F_s and the cone is expressed by the following:

$$\frac{(x-x_0)^2}{\left(\frac{z_0\sin\delta}{\sqrt{\cos^2\delta - \sin^2\alpha}}\right)^2} + \frac{\left(y - y_0 - \frac{z_0\sin\alpha\cos\alpha}{\cos^2\delta - \sin^2\alpha}\right)^2}{\left(\frac{z_0\sin\delta\cos\delta}{\cos^2\delta - \sin^2\alpha}\right)^2} = 1. \tag{4}$$

Then the center (x_q, y_q) of the shadowed ellipse is represented by

$$\begin{aligned} x_q &= x_0, \\ y_q &= y_0 + \frac{z_0\sin\alpha\cos\alpha}{\cos^2\delta - \sin^2\alpha}. \end{aligned} \tag{5}$$

Major axis r_a, minor axis r_b, and ratio m of these two axes are given by

$$r_a = \frac{z_0\sin\delta\cos\delta}{\cos^2\delta - \sin^2\alpha}, \tag{6}$$

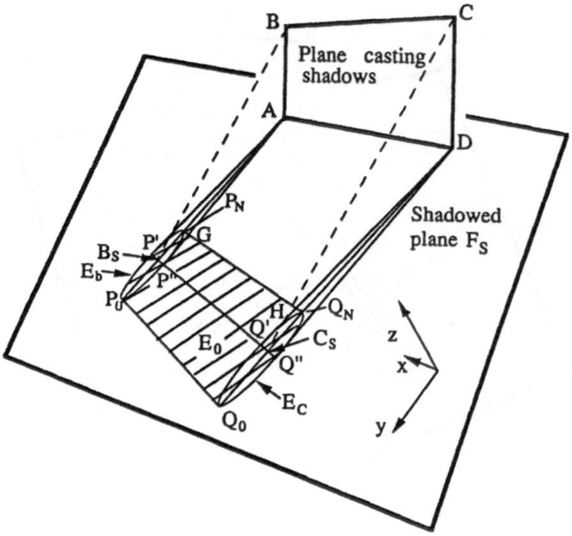

Fig. 2: Penumbra areas.

$$r_b = \frac{z_0 \sin\delta}{\sqrt{\cos^2\delta - \sin^2\alpha}}, \tag{7}$$

$$m = \frac{r_a}{r_b} = \frac{\cos\delta}{\sqrt{\cos^2\delta - \sin^2\alpha}}. \tag{8}$$

As ratio m is a function of only angles α and δ, m has a constant value at any points on one plane.

2.2 Penumbra Area Cast by a Contour Edge

In this section how to calculate penumbra area cast by contour edge BC in Fig. 2 is discussed. The straight lines stretched through points B and C in the opposite direction $\boldsymbol{L}_s$ intersect with plane F_s at points B_s and C_s, respectively. Let the shadowed ellipses corresponding to points B and C be E_b and E_c, respectively. The penumbra area E_0 corresponding to contour edge BC is regarded as the union of shadowed ellipses generated by consecutive points on edge BC. Both line segments P_0Q_0 and P_NQ_N are tangent to the shadowed ellipses E_b and E_c. Thus E_0 is specified as the area surrounded by line segments P_0Q_0, P_NQ_N and arcs of the shadowed ellipses $P_NP'P_0$ and $Q_0Q''Q_N$. The other contour edges AB and BC also produce the penumbra areas $AP'P_0P''G$ and $DHQ'Q_0Q''$, respectively. Thus a penumbra area corresponding to a contour edge consists of two straight lines and parts of ellipses. If the shapes of the ellipses were expressed by a set of points, quite a large memory and computation time would be required. To avoid these inconveniences, a quadrilateral region surrounding the penumbra area called a "penumbra calculation region" is introduced here.

2.3 Penumbra Calculation Region

As mentioned above, the major axes of both shadowed ellipses corresponding to end points of a contour edge are parallel to the y axis. The penumbra corresponding to a contour edge exists in a rectangle surrounding these ellipses and their common external tangents as shown in the hatched region in Fig. 3 (a). Since m (ratio of major to minor axis) in both ellipses is even, both ellipses can

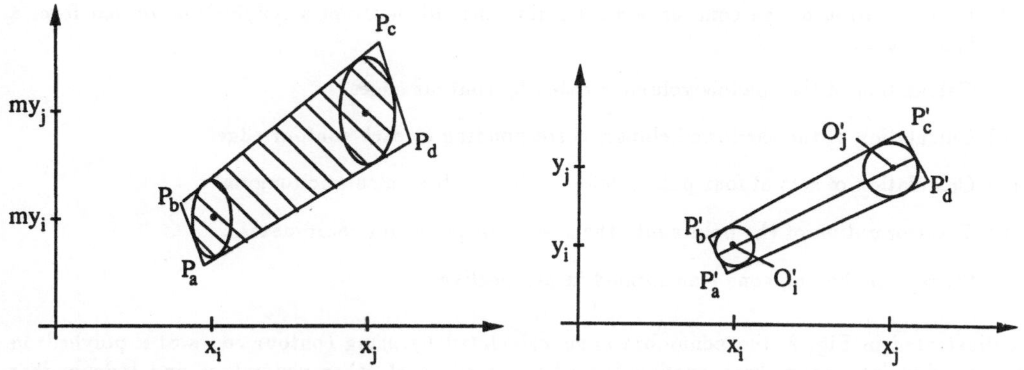

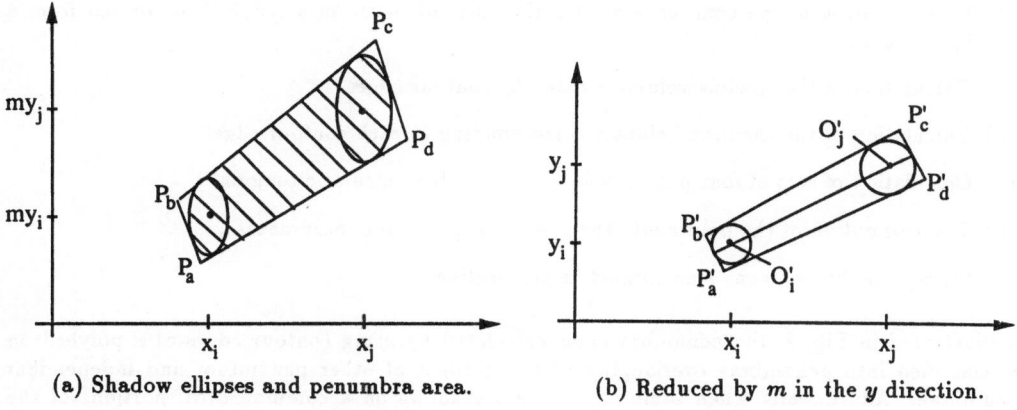

(a) Shadow ellipses and penumbra area. (b) Reduced by m in the y direction.

Fig. 3: Penumbra calculation region.

be expressed as a circle in the new system of coordinates where the y coordinate is divided by m as shown in Fig. 3 (b). In this figure the centers of circle and radii are $O'_i(x_i, y_i)$ and $O'_j(x_j, y_j)$, and r_i and r_j, respectively. A penumbra calculation region is expressed by the rectangle $P'_a(x_a, y_a)$, $P'_b(x_b, y_b)$, $P'_c(x_c, y_c)$, and $P'_d(x_d, y_d)$ defined by Eq. 9. Since 1) lines $P'_aP'_d$ and $P'_bP'_c$ are common external tangents to the two circles, and 2) lines $P'_aP'_b$ and $P'_cP'_d$ are perpendicular to the line passing through both centers of the circles, points P'_a, P'_b, P'_c, and P'_d are defined by

$$
\begin{aligned}
x_k &= x_p + \frac{r(x_j - x_i) + t(y_j - y_i)}{l}, \\
y_k &= y_p + \frac{r(y_j - y_i) + t(x_j - x_i)}{l},
\end{aligned} \tag{9}
$$

where

$$
l = \sqrt{(x_j - x_i)^2 + (y_j - y_i)^2},
$$

$$
\begin{array}{lllll}
\text{if} & k = a; & p = i, & r = -r_i, & \text{and} \quad t = u, \\
\text{if} & k = b; & p = i, & r = -r_i, & \text{and} \quad t = -u, \\
\text{if} & k = c; & p = j, & r = r_j, & \text{and} \quad t = -v, \\
\text{if} & k = d; & p = j, & r = r_j, & \text{and} \quad t = v,
\end{array}
$$

and

$$
\begin{array}{llll}
\text{if} & r_i = r_j; & u = r_i, & v = r_j, \\
\text{if} & r_i < r_j; & u = r_i\sqrt{\frac{l_i - r_i}{l_i + r_i}}, & v = r_j\sqrt{\frac{l_j + r_i}{l_j - r_i}}, \\
 & \text{where} & l_i = \frac{l \cdot r_i}{r_j - r_i}, & l_j = \frac{l \cdot r_j}{r_j - r_i}.
\end{array}
$$

Vertices P_a, P_b, P_c, and P_d in Fig. 3 (a) can be easily calculated by multiplying the y coordinates of P'_a, P'_b, P'_c, and P'_d by m, respectively.

When the shape of a penumbra area is formed by the region $AP'P_0P''G$ as shown in Fig. 2, one of the shadow ellipses might be a point. In this case the radius of circle O_i is equal to 0, so the circle is set to be a small enough value in advance.

2.4 Penumbra Areas Produced by a Polyhedron

The calculation procedure for penumbra areas of a polyhedron is as follows:

(1) Determination of the contour edges forming the silhouette of a polyhedron viewed from a light source.

(2) Calculation of the shadow volume created by contour edges.

(3) Calculation of the shadowed ellipses corresponding to each contour edge.

(4) Calculation of sets of four points defining "penumbra calculation region".

(5) Transformation of the points into the system of the world coordinates.

(6) Storage of the polygons transformed in perspective.

As illustrated in Fig. 2, the penumbra areas calculated by using contour edges of a polyhedron are classified into penumbrae overlapping with the edges of other penumbra, and independent penumbrae. Additionally when some objects cast shadows on a common area, portions of the respective penumbrae also overlap each other.

The penumbra spans with intersections between the penumbra and a scanline are determined for every scanline. Thus there are two types of penumbra spans: independent penumbra spans and overlapping penumbra spans. According to each type of penumbra spans, its intensity of illumination is calculated.

3 ILLUMINATION IN PENUMBRA AREA

Direct illumination I due to diffuse reflection at calculation point P is given by

$$I = (1 - k)I_0 \cos\alpha,$$

where

I_0 : the incident intensity from the sun

α : angle between light direction and surface normal

k : coverage rate

$k = 1$, when P is within umbrae,

$0 < k < 1$, when P is within penumbrae,

$k = 0$, when P is outside shadows.

The calculation method of the coverage rates for both types of penumbra span mentioned in the previous section discussed in the following sections.

3.1 Coverage Rate in Independent Penumbra

Let the faces casting penumbra be F_i. As illustrated in Fig. 4, the line extended from a calculation point P into the direction of the sun's rays intersects with plane F_i at point P_i. Let the point one unit distant from P on line segment PP_i be P_t and set virtual plane F_t including point P_t and orthogonal to line PP_i. Set perspective projection plane of F_i onto F_t be F_i'. Then, circle O_t indicating the sun is set on F_t with center P_t and radius $\tan(\delta)$. Area S which corresponds to the area of F_i covering the sun in ratio is shown as the intersection between circle O_t and plane F_i'. Then the coverage rate is given by

$$S/(\text{area of circle } O_t).$$

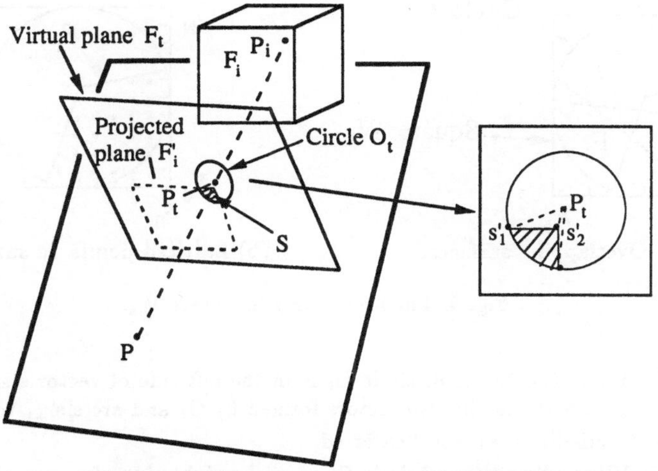

(a) Virtual plane F_t. (b) Magnified circle O_t.

Fig. 4: Virtual plane orthogonal PP_i.

Area S is obtained as follows. Vertices s_1, s_2, $\cdots$, s_m on plane F'_i are perspectively transformed from plane F_i, and these indices are given in a clockwise direction. s_i is labeled "out", if s_i is exterior to circle O_t. Otherwise it is labeled "in". The following in-out test of adjacent points (s_i, s_{i+1}) is carried out for $i = 1, 2, \cdots, m$ (if $i = m$, 1 is used instead of $m + 1$).

a) If s_i is "out" and s_{i+1} is "in", the intersection point between side s_is_{i+1} and circle O_t is labeled "out-in", and stored.

b) If s_i is "in" and s_{i+1} is "out", s_i is labeled "in-in", and stored. Then the intersection point between side s_is_{i+1} and circle O_t is labeled "in-out", and stored.

c) If both s_i and s_{i+1} are "in", s_i is labeled "in-in", and stored.

d) If both s_i and s_{i+1} are "out",

d-1) When side s_is_{i+1} and circle O_t has two intersection points, the intersection point closer to s_i is labeled "out-in", and stored. Another one is labeled "in-out", and stored.

d-2) When side s_is_{i+1} and circle O_t does not have any intersection points, no storing is carried out.

Here the points stored according to the rules mentioned above are defined as being array s'_1, s'_2, $\cdots$, s'_n. The algorithm for calculating area S is as follows:

I. If $n > 0$,

1) Set to $S = 0$.

2) For each of $i = 1, 2, \cdots, n$ (if $i = n$, 1 is used instead of $n + 1$), the following calculations are carried out.

a) If s'_i is "in-out" and s'_{i+1} is "out-in",

a-1) When the center of circle O_t is in the right side of vector $s'_is'_{i+1}$, add the smaller area between the two sectors formed by O_t and arc $s'_is'_{i+1}$ to S.

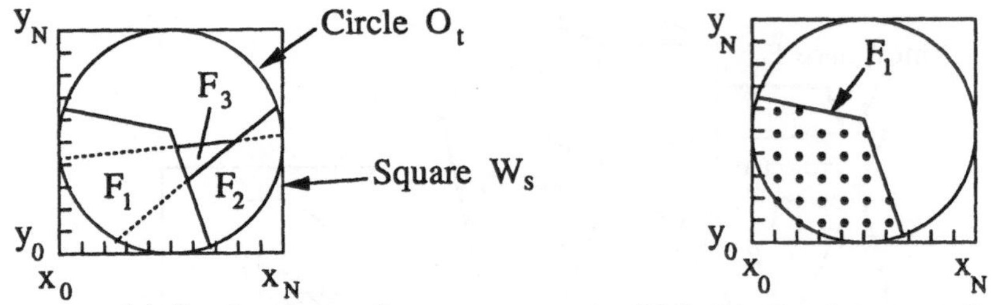

(a) Overlapping surfaces. (b) Latticed points on surface F_1.

Fig. 5: Latticed points in square W_s.

a-2) When the center of circle O_t is in the left side of vector $s'_i s'_{i+1}$, add the larger area between the two sectors formed by O_t and arc $s'_i s'_{i+1}$ to S.

b) If the condition a) is not satisfied,

b-1) When the center of circle O_t is in the right side of vector $s'_i s'_{i+1}$, add the area of triangle $O_t s'_i s'_{i+1}$ to S.

b-2) When the center of circle O_t is in the left side of vector $s'_i s'_{i+1}$, subtract the area of triangle $O_t s'_i s'_{i+1}$ from S.

II. If $n = 0$,
For $j = 1, 2, \cdots, m$ (if $j = m$, 1 is used instead of $m + 1$), the following calculations are carried out.

c) When the center of circle O_t is in the right side of vector $s'_j s'_{j+1}$, S = area of circle O_t because circle O_t is included by convex polygon $s'_1 s'_2 \cdots s'_m$.

d) Otherwise, S = 0 because circle O_t is exterior to the polygon.

3.2 Coverage Rate in Penumbra Area Generated by Complex Objects

Let's assume that the sun is obscured by overlapping surfaces, say $F_j (j = 1, \cdots, K)$, when viewed from a calculation point in a penumbra area. For calculating the union of the overlapping areas generated by each surface of F_j, exterior portions away from the calculation point must be clipped by the nearby surface region (see Fig. 5 (a)). Hence, the computation time increases in proportion to the number of overlapping surfaces. The following simpler approach is used to calculate the approximated coverage rate proposed in this paper. Virtual plane F_t and circle O_t shown in Fig. 4 are used again. Fig. 5 illustrates circle O_t given in Fig. 4 viewed from the calculation point. Consider square W_s bounding circle O_t on plane F_t. Suppose x and y are axes perpendicular to each other as shown in Fig. 5 (a). Divide every side of W_s into N to form latticed points at a resolution of $N \times N$. The maximum values on axis x and y are x_N and y_N, respectively, while the minimum values are x_0 and y_0. Two two dimensional arrays A_m and A_o with $N \times N$ elements are used and each element has one-to-one correspondence to a latticed point on W_s. Let's denote a latticed point where $y = y_i$ and $x = x_i$ cross on W_s as $Z(i, j)$. Every element of A_o is set to 1, if $Z(i, j)$ is inside circle O_t. Otherwise, every element (i, j) of A_o is set to 0. The algorithm for calculating coverage rate using array A_m is explained below.

1) Take the following steps for each value of $j (j = 1, 2, \cdots, K)$.

(1) Set every element of A_m to 0.

(2) Make a perspective projection of F_j onto F_t, and let the projected surface be F'_j.

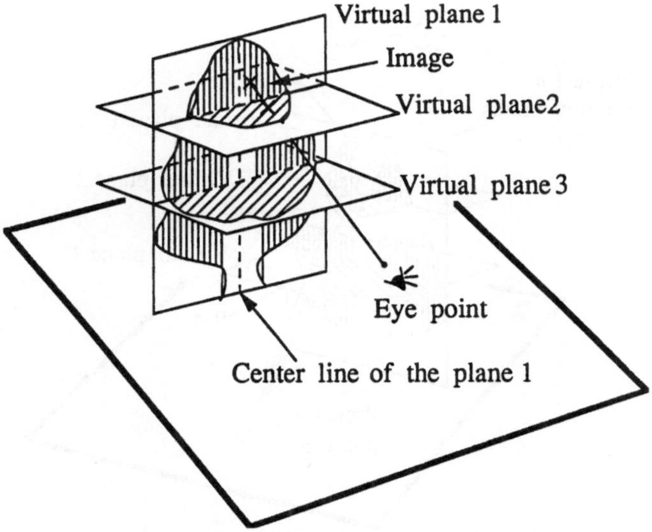

Fig. 6: Transparent virtual planes for image to be mapped on.

(3) Take the following steps for each value of $y_i(i = 0, 1, 2, \cdots, N)$.
   (a) Calculate intersections between line $y = y_i$ and each side of F_j.
   As F'_j is a convex polygon there are two intersections at the most.
   (b) Let the smaller value of intersections be x_a and the other be x_b.
   When there is only one intersection, let $x_a = x_b$.
   If $x_a < x_0, x_a = x_0$.
   If $x_b > x_N, x_b = x_N$.
   (c) Let all elements of A_m corresponding to every latticed point between x_a and x_b be 1.

2) Let the number of elements when both $A_m(i,j)$ and $A_o(i,j)$ are nonzero be m_a, and the number of elements when $A_o(i,j)$ are nonzero be m_o.
Then the approximation of the coverage rate is given by m_a/m_o.

4 SHADOWS OF MAPPED IMAGES ON VIRTUAL TRANSPARENT PLANE

From the point of view of image synthesis natural objects such as trees are made up of numerous complicated objects, thus there is a vast amount of data to be dealt with. We therefore developed the following effective method (Kaneda 1989). Photographs of trees are taken from both vertical and horizontal angles, and their images are scanned in a computer. Then as illustrated in Fig. 6, a vertical transparent plane and a few horizontal ones are set for the images to be mapped on. The set of these transparent planes can be rotated on the center line of the vertical plane. The vertical plane is rotated to face a viewpoint when shading. The color of images on transparent planes where the viewing vector meets is examined and rendered, with the color weighted by the angles between the viewing vector and the normals of the surfaces. For rendering shadows of imaged objects, the calculation method of the illumination in the shadows is described using Fig. 7. The transparent planes are fixed toward the sun's ray. From a computation point P a cone with 32′ of central angle is extended into the direction of the sun's rays which coincide with its center line. Let's define u_{ai} as the number of pixels of images on each transparent plane surrounded by the

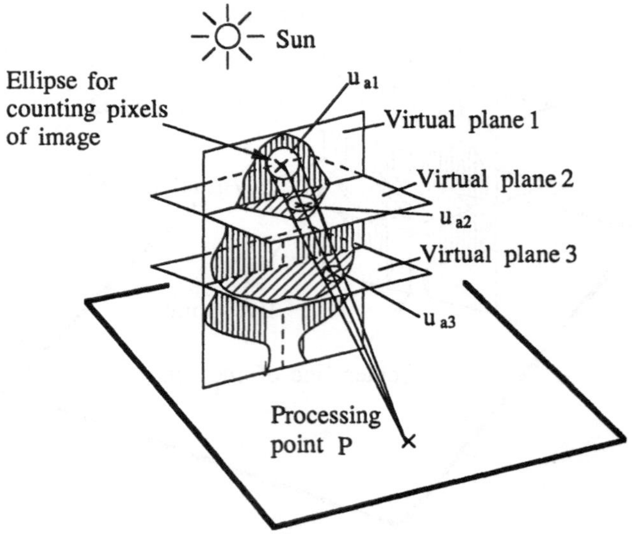

Fig. 7: Calculation of illumination of shadow.

cone. Let the number of colored pixel be $u_{ci}(i = 1,2,3$ in Fig. 6). The values u_{ai} of transparent planes within the cone are compared, and the approximate coverage rate is given by

$$\max_i(u_{ci}/u_{ai}).$$

5 APPLICATIONS

To show the practical benefits of the proposal some pictures with penumbra are compared to those without penumbra. In Fig. 8 a flat ladder shaped plane with three small rectangular holes is illuminated by the sun from the direction of right angle to the plane and at eight degrees elevation. The figures clearly show the proposed method is effective for displaying penumbra caused by the sun. The more distant from the plane, the duller rounder and larger the shapes of the hole's shadows. This is also the case with real shadows generated by sunlight. In Fig. 9 some shadows of images of natural trees mapped onto transparent planes are depicted. Fig. 9 (a) and (b) show the shadows when the angle of elevation of sun light is 35 degrees, and in (c) and (d) 60 degrees where (a) and (c) are without penumbra and (b) and (d) with penumbra.

The following figures show some applications of our proposed method. Fig. 10 shows an example of the interior design. Shadows without penumbra and with penumbra cast by curtains modeled by using groups of long and slender surfaces are shown in Fig. (a) and (b), respectively. Shadow areas in these figures are shown at increased scale in Fig. (c) and (d). Fig. 11 shows an outdoor scene. The scene with penumbra gives a much more photorealistic image. The two proposed types of simple penumbra rendering methods, for polyhedra and for images mapped on virtual transparent plane, are useful for environmental assessment.

6 SUMMARY

The paper has proposed a relatively simple method for rendering penumbra caused by the sun's ray. The usefulness of the proposed method has been illustrated by its applications. The advantages of

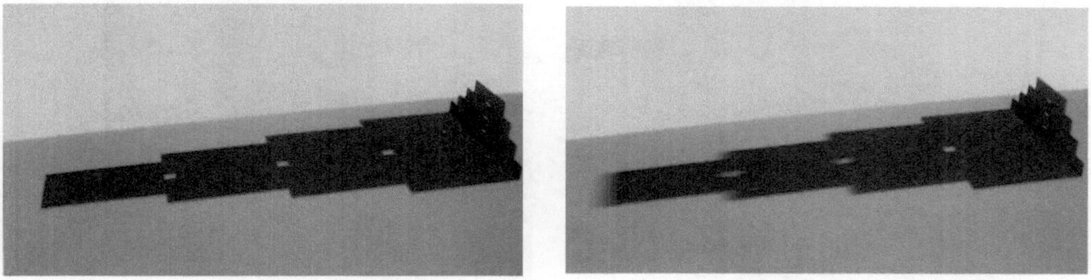

(a) Shadows without penumbra. (b) Shadows with penumbra.

Fig. 8: Shadows cast by a plane.

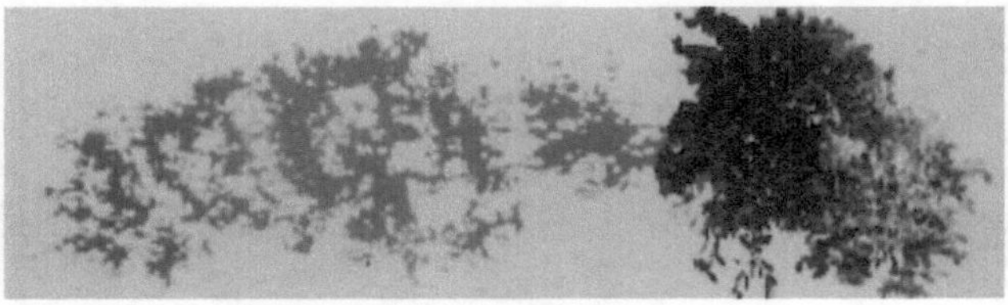

(a) Without penumbra.

(c) Without penumbra.

(b) With penumbra.

(d) With penumbra.

Fig. 9: Shadows of images mapped on virtual transparent planes.

the proposal are as follows:

1) Using an approximated penumbra region expressed by a rectangle reduces required memory for storing penumbra regions and saves calculation time.

2) The illuminance in penumbra areas is easily calculated for objects with complex overlapping penumbra, such as curtains.

3) It is possible to render penumbra not only for objects constructed by convex polyhedra, but also for the images in scanned-in photographs of natural objects such as trees.

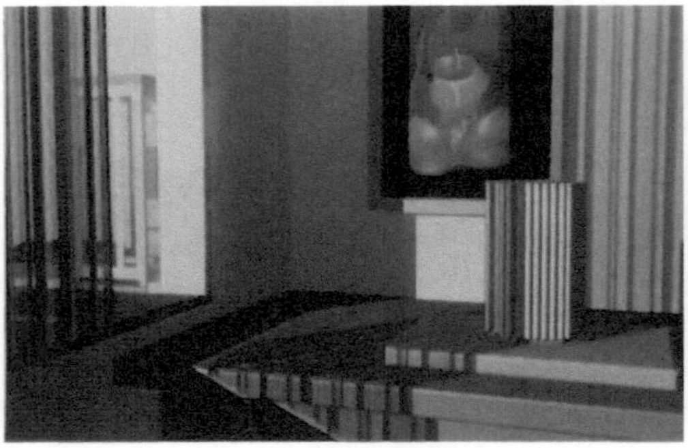

(a) Without penumbra.

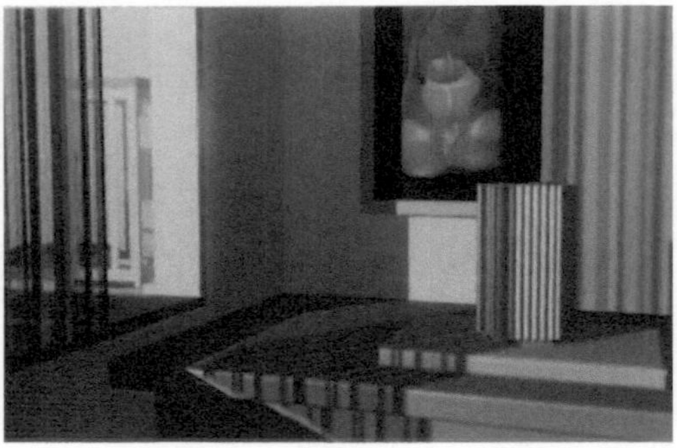

(b) With penumbra.

(c) Without penumbra.

(d) With penumbra.

Fig. 10: Shadows cast by curtains.

(a) Without penumbra.

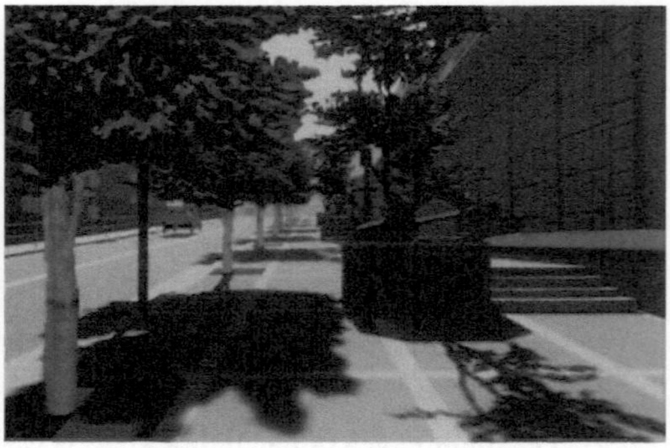

(b) With penumbra.

Fig. 11: Outdoor scenery.

REFERENCES

Amanatides J (1984) ***Ray Tracing with Cones.*** **Computer Graphics 18(3):129-135**

Appel A (1969) ***On Calculating the Illusion of Reality.*** **Hardware :945**

Brotman LS and Balder NI (1984) ***Generating Soft Shadows with Depth Buffer Algorithm.*** **IEEE CG&A 4(10):5-12**

Cook RL (1984) ***Distributed Ray Tracing.*** **Computer Graphics 18(3):138**

Crow FC (1977) ***Shadow Algorithms for Computer Graphics.*** **Computer Graphics 11(3):242-248**

Kaneda K, Akinobu T, and Nakamae E (1989) ***A Display Method of Trees by Using Photo Images.*** **Proc. IPSJ :907-908 (in Japanese)**

Nishita T and Nakamae E (1974) ***An Algorithm for Halftoned Representation of Three Dimensional Objects.*** **Inf. Proc. Japan 14:93-99**

Nishita T and Nakamae E (1983) ***Half-Tone Representation of 3D Objects Illuminated by Area Sources or Polyhedron Sources.*** **IEEE Proc. COMPSAC83 :237-242**

Nishita T and Nakamae E (1985) ***Shading Models for Point and Linear Sources.*** **ACM Transaction on Graphics l4(2):124-126**

Shinichi Takita is a professor in the Department of Education at Kagawa University,Japan. His research interests include computer graphics and CAI. Takita received his BE and ME degrees in electrical engineering form Hiroshima University in 1964 and 1966, respectively. He is a member of the IEE of Japan and the Japan Society of Industrial and Technical Education.
Address: Faculty of Education, Kagawa University, 1-1, Saiwai-cho, Takamatsu, 760 Japan.

Kazufumi Kaneda is a research associate in Faculty of Engineering at Hiroshima University. He worked at the Chugoku Electric Power Company Ltd., Japan from 1984 to 1986. He joined Hiroshima University in 1986. His research interests include computer graphics and image processing.
Kaneda received the BE and ME in 1982 and 1984, respectively, from Hiroshima University. He is a member of IEE of Japan, IPS of Japan and IEICE of Japan.
Address: Faculty of Engineering, Hiroshima University, Saijo-cho, Higashihiroshima, 724 Japan.
E-mail: kin@eml.hiroshima-u.ac.jp

Toshio Akinobu is a graduate student in system engineering at Hiroshima University. His research interests include computer graphics and its application.
Akinobu received the BE degrees in electronics engineering in 1988 from Hiroshima University. He is a member of IPS of Japan.
Address: Faculty of Engineering, Hiroshima University, Saijo-cho, Higashihiroshima, 724 Japan.

Haruhiko Iriyama is a graduate student in system engineering at Hiroshima University. His research interests include computer graphics and its application.
Iriyama received the BE degrees in electronics engineering in 1988 from Hiroshima University. He is a member of IPS of Japan.
Address: Faculty of Engineering, Hiroshima University, Saijo-cho, Higashihiroshima, 724 Japan.

Eihachiro Nakamae is a professor at Hiroshima University where he was appointed as research associate in 1956 and a professor in 1968. He was an associate researcher at Clarkson College of Technology, Potsdam, N. Y., from 1973 to 1974. His research interests include computer graphics and electric machinery.
Nakamae received the BE, ME, and DE degrees in 1954, 1956, and 1967 from Waseda University. He is a member of IEEE, IEE of Japan, IPS of Japan and IEICE of Japan.
Address: Faculty of Engineering, Hiroshima University, Saijo-cho, Higashi-hiroshima, 724 Japan.
E-mail: naka@eml.hiroshima-u.ac.jp

Tomoyuki Nishita is an associate professor in the department of Electronic and Electrical Engineering at Fukuyama University, Japan. He was on the research staff at Mazda from 1973 to 1979 and worked on design and development of computer-controlled vehicle system. He joined Fukuyama University in 1979. He was an associate researcher in the Engineering Computer Graphics Laboratory at Brigham Young University from 1988 to the end of March, 1989. His research interests involve computer graphics including lighting model, hidden-surface removal, and antialiasing.
Nishita received his BE, ME and Ph. D in Engineering in 1971, 1973, and 1985, respectively, from Hiroshima University. He is a member of ACM, IPS of Japan and IEE of Japan.
Address: Faculty of Engineering, Fukuyama University, Sanzo, Higashimura-cho, Fukuyama, 729-02 Japan.

Naive Halftoning

A.J. Cole

ABSTRACT

A method of halftoning rectangular images based on the use of mixed murray polygons is described. This method does not distort the original data by statistical error modification such as dither or dot diffusion and thus does not inherently require edge enhancement methods to restore picture quality. The production of data for high resolution printers is included as part of the method by introducing for each intensity value an extra low level of tiling whose patterns are determined by the intensity value itself along with the previous value of the cumulated sum and the orientation of the low level tile.

KEYWORDS Halftoning, space filling curves, murray polygons, dither free.

BIOGRAPHY

The author retired in 1988 from the Chair in Computational Science in the University of St Andrews which he had held since 1969. His earliest interest in graphics was in the hidden line problem and molecular ball and stick drawings in the early sixties. His current work on the use of murray polygons arose from basic theoretical results first published in 1985. He has published several papers both on the theory of space filling curves in general and the application of murray polygons to problems in raster and bit mapped graphics in particular. Cole received his BSc, M Sc and Ph D in Pure Mathematics from University College London in 1949, 1950 and 1952.

Address: 'Inisheer', Barnyards, Kilconquhar, Fife, KY9 1LB, UK.

INTRODUCTION

The computer graphics problem of representing gray scale images on a bilevel black and white display has been considered by many authors. The technique used traditionally by the printing profession (Ulichney 1987) makes use of a process in which dots on the printed page vary in both size and shape to give the visual illusion of gray scales. Most computer printing devices provide only one size and shape of a single dot so other methods needed to be developed to create a similar illusion of gray scales. In recent years a great deal of work has been done on this problem by various research groups. A survey of methods proposed up until 1976 was given by Jarvis, Judice and Ninke (1976) and at that time the best method seemed to be that of ordered dither as described by Limb (1969) and implemented by various other people (Lippel Kurland 1971; Lippel 1976; Bayer 1973; Jarvis Roberts 1976; Goertzel Gerhard 1987) .

Certain aesthetic problems arise when viewing halftone pictures produced by such methods. These include unpleasant contouring of approximately constant background areas, the introduction of snakelike patterns in some parts of the picture, ghosting, jaggedness of some straight lines caused by aliassing and additional patterning caused by the introduction of standard tiles in order to increase the number of dots for high resolution devices. The following methods attempted to resolve some or all of these problems.

Witten and Neal (1982) proposed the use of polygonal approximations to space filling curves to scan two dimensional space locally rather than linearly. The particular set of polygons that they used were the Hilbert polygons and they reported that, by using a simple technique of accumulating a running sum of intensity values along a Hilbert polygon and outputting a black dot whenever a critical value of that sum was reached, at the same time reducing the running sum by the maximum intensity value, many of the deficiencies of the ordered dither method were eliminated or much reduced. They noted that there was a tendency for dots to fall into small and regular clusters, giving an undesirable graininess to some constantly shaded areas. They suggested that other space filling curves may avoid this problem. Little further work appears to have been done on this approach although Ulichney (1987) recommends experimenting with non-standard raster ordering.

Knuth (1987) discusses ordered dither and notes that although the resulting pictures are ghost free, they tend to be rather blurred. He proposes a method of dot diffusion to alleviate this problem.

Ulichney (1976 1987) describes in detail various dot dither methods concluding with his own "blue noise" method which he claims has the aesthetic advantage that it does not clash with the existing structure of an image by either overlaying its own pattern or by over compensating with too much noise. All of these dither or diffusion methods rely upon introducing statistical error locally so as to break up unwanted patterning but in so doing some picture definition is lost. To compensate for this, edge enhancement techniques are introduced thereby again distorting the original picture to some extent.

Goertzel and Gerhard (1987) discuss halftoning using the IBM 4250 printer which, apart from printing on special paper to simplify photographic platemaking, has round overlapping dots to produce smooth edges on characters and in pictures generally. They use a combination of digital halftone blocks arranged on a 45-degree grid with randomised error propagation in pattern selection and with resolution enhancement in areas of high intensity gradients. The method may be modified to use more conventional printing devices but with some loss of quality in general.

In all of the above methods some additional adjustment has to be made to the raw intensity values to compensate for overall darkening of pictures due to broadening of black pixels in the printing process. This adjustment usually includes a clipping of the tone scale to improve the contrast of the final pictures. Without such an adjustment, all methods of halftoning produce very "sooty" results.

The method to be described in this paper is a continuation of the work of Witten and Neal but uses a different space filling curve. It also applies to a wide range of rectangular picture shapes rather than the usual square space filling curves and in addition suggests a new method of producing a low order tiling to increase the number of dots for high resolution devices.

It should be noted that the method to be described introduces no statistical distortion of the original data either by dither or error diffusion transformations or by edge enhancement algorithms. The pictures produced by this method appear to be quite satisfactory as true representations of the original data but if, for example, edge enhancement was required in some particular application this could be carried out directly either on the raw data or on the generated bitmap. This is in contrast to the use of edge enhancement in some other methods where it is required to compensate for the effects of unwanted statistical distortion (Jarvis Roberts 1976; Knuth 1987). The only preliminary transformation of data required by the method is the usual adjustment of tone scales which never reverses the numeric order of pairs of values.

In the rest of this paper we use a simple quadratic tone scale transformation as shown in figure 1. At the bottom of the scale all values up to 10 are identified with the value 0, that is white, and at the top all values above 240 are identified with 255, or black. In between, the transformation is quadratic and tangential to the raw data axis at intensity value 10. This transformation is arbitrary and has been fixed for all applications in this paper so as not to introduce irrelevant differences in comparative results.

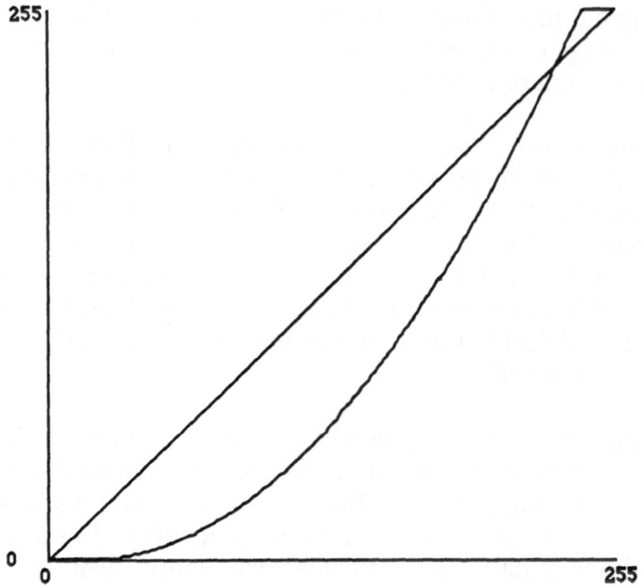

Fig.1 Quadratic tone scale transformation.

SPACE FILLING CURVES AND SEQUENCES OF POLYGONS

The concept of a space filling curve was introduced by Guiseppe Peano (1890). Peano gave an explicit transformation from the unit real line to the unit real square. The following year David Hilbert (1981) gave an alternative geometric definition of a space filling curve based on the limit of a sequence of recursively defined polygons. In a biography of Peano, Hubert C. Kennedy (1980) observes that it was probable that Peano was influenced in the construction of his curve by similar considerations to those of Hilbert since in 1908 Peano referred to an alternative sequence of polygons which have become known as the Peano polygons (Peano 1908). In a paper published in 1900, Moore (1900) also gives a geometric approximation to Peano's curve.

Since Peano was first in the field, all space filling curves and sequences of polygons which converge to a space filling curve have become known generically as Peano curves or polygons which is sometimes confusing when, for example, no distinction is made by authors between Peano and Hilbert polygons.

As mentioned above, the year after Peano's paper appeared, Hilbert (1891) published a definition of a space filling curve based on a sequence of recursively defined polygons. These are usually depicted as shown in figure 2 where the first three polygons H_1, H_2 and H_3 are drawn.

Fig. 2 Hilbert Polygons of order 1, 2 and 3.

In applying Hilbert polygons to problems in graphics it is usual to associate the integer coordinates of a square bit map of dimension 2^n by 2^n with the vertices of the polygon H_n.

The first three of the recursively defined set of polygons known as the Peano polygons, that is, the polygons P_1, P_2, P_3, are shown in figure 3. Again, when applying Peano polygons to problems in graphics it is usual to associate the integer coordinates of a square bit map of dimension 3^n by 3^n with the vertices of the polygon H_n.

Traditionally the standard methods for drawing Peano, Hilbert and other space filling sequences of polygons have utilised iterative, recursive and table driven algorithms. Witten and Wyvill (1983) discussed the value of explicit mappings from the unit line to the unit square but at that time no explicit mappings to generate any of the above polygons were known.

Cole (1985) defined an explicit transformation from an appropriate set of integers to the vertices of the corresponding Peano polygon and in 1986 extended this to a generalisation of these polygons to traverse given rectangles rather than squares. Such polygons are called murray polygons as an abbreviation of multiple radix arithmetic polygons. These will be discussed in more detail below.

Fig. 3 Peano polygons of order 1, 2 and 3.

MURRAY POLYGONS

Murray polygons (Cole 1986) are a generalisation of Peano polygons to any rectangle containing m * n integer coordinate points. The word murray is a mnemonic for multiple radix which has the following relevance.

Instead of a fixed radix as in the Peano polygon algorithm we make use of a number system with a possibly different radix associated with each digit position. The fundamental operations of murray arithmetic are defined in the obvious way by analogy with ordinary arithmetic. In particular, for addition, carry from one digit to the next takes place when the value of the sum digit is greater than or equal to the associated radix value for that digit. This concept is familiar to those who remember computational systems using either yards feet and inches or pounds shillings and pence.

Given a rectangle with m integer coordinate points in the x direction and n integer coordinate points in the y direction, it is, in general, possible to define several polygons to traverse in unit steps all of the points with integer coordinates within the rectangle. In this account we will suppose that both m and n are odd and have several factors. Since we normally use these polygons to scan part or the whole of a bit map this is not a serious restriction (Cole 1986 1988; Cole Buntin 1988).

Now consider any factorisation of m and n into j factors

$$m = m_j * m_{j-1} * \dots m_1$$
$$n = n_j * n_{j-1} * \dots n_1$$

where a factor with value 1 may be included so as to make the number of factors equal in both cases. The factors do not need to be prime numbers or to be in numeric order. The more factors there are, the more choices of alternative murray scans exist. If a number is prime then there is always a number of the same parity within 2 of it which is at least divisible by 3. It is not usually of great importance for a printed picture to have exactly m by n pixels so even if m and/or n are prime a close approximation to the size of the required picture can be found which, as we will see, permits a murray scan with at least one low level of tiling. For example, a picture of size 256 by 256 could usually be reduced to 255 by 255 without serious loss of information and 255 has factors 3 5 and 17.

The algorithm to be described below uses two transformations. The first is a conversion from an ordinary integer, a say, to some fixed base b, to a murray integer, p say, with radix r_i associated with digit d_i. The algorithm is exactly the same as conversion between two numbers with different fixed bases excepting that the divisers used are the successive radices starting with r_1 and the successive remainders are the digits of the corresponding murray integer starting from the right. Similarly for conversion from murray form back to standard form.

The second transformation is the well known Gray coding (Cole 1966). Gray coded integers are such that any two successive integers differ in only one digit position. The algorithm is different for number systems with even parity radices to those with odd oarity radices. We only require odd parity radix systems. For a number system with fixed odd radix r the conversion algorithm replaces digit d_i by $r - 1 - d_i$ if the sum of all its leftmost digits is odd and leaves it unaltered otherwise. The corresponding murray integer gray coding is the same excepting that the fixed radix r is replaced by the variable radix r_i. The de-Gray coding algorithm for odd number bases is exactly the same as the Gray coding algorithm.

The algorithm to transform an integer p ($0 \leq p < mn - 1$) to the corresponding point (x,y) on a murray polygon within a rectangle with sides of length m - 1, n - 1 (Cole 1986 1988) is now as follows.

Basic Murray Algorithm

1. Convert p to murray integer form

$$p = p_n p_{n-1} \cdots p_2 p_1$$

where $n = 2j$ and the radix r_i ($0 \leq i < 2j$) associated with p_i is m_k if

$i = 2k - 1$ and n_k if $i = 2k$.

2. Convert p to the equivalent murray Gray coded integer

$$e = e_n e_{n-1} \cdots e_2 e_1$$

3. Split d into two parts

$$f = e_n e_{n-2} \ldots e_4 e_2$$

and

$$g = e_{n-1} e_{n-3} \ldots e_3 e_1$$

4. De-Gray code f and g to give

$$x = x_j x_{j-1} \ldots x_2 x_1$$

and

$$y = y_j y_{j-1} \ldots y_2 y_1$$

5. The corresponding vertex in murray notation is now (x,y) which may be converted back to normal notation if required.

It should be noted that the same algorithm gives conventional Peano polygons if all radices are set to 3.

The algorithm works for any set of odd positive radix values and may be adapted to include even radix values in special cases (Cole 1988). In particular, some of the radices may take the value 1. The effect of this is to eliminate the step in the direction of that radix. This fact may be used to make the murray polygon be essentially vertical rather than horizontal by introducing an additional first radix with value 1 and then reversing the order of the values of every other pair of radices.

No corresponding algorithm is known for even based number systems. The reason why the above algorithm does not convert immediately to cover even based systems is connected with the fact that for even bases the operations of Gray coding and reduced radix complementation are not commutative (Cole 1985).

It should also be noted that if a scan is made of the original space with the two low order radices set to value 1 and then a second scan is carried out with the pair of low order radices set to the same value a say, then the effect is to replace each vertex in the first scan by an additional tile of dimension a by a but without changing the relative order of scanning of the original vertices. This property will be used in developing high resolution algorithms.

Computationally efficient versions of this relatively inefficient algorithm are known Cole (1988). Examples of essentially horizontal and essentially vertical murray polygons as defined above are shown in figures 4 and 5.

It is also possible to define mixed direction murray polygons in which each tile at any level alternates in essentially horizontal and vertical directions between successive tiles. An example is given in figure 6. Such scans are used later in this paper.

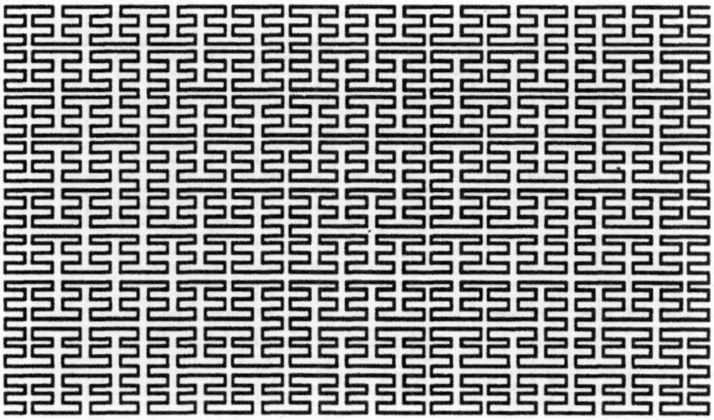

Fig. 4 Horizontal Murray polygon with x radices 3 5 5 and y radices 5 3 3.

Fig. 5 Vertical murray polygon with x radices 5 3 and y radices 3 5

As in the case of simple murray polygons, it is also possible to include an additional level of tiling to a mixed murray scan by introducing an extra pair of radices which are both set to 1 to scan the intensity value matrix and to value a to introduce an additional layer of a^2 bits per initial dot for higher density printing devices.

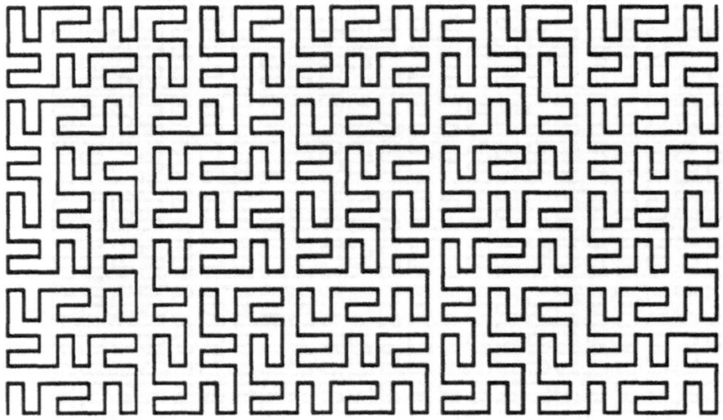

Fig.6 Mixed murray polygon with x radices 3 3 5 and y radices 5 3 3.

It should be noted that any space filling polygon which traverses a given integer coordinate rectangular grid without long jumps between successive vertices is a potential candidate for a vertex ordering for halftoning and other graphics transformations.

BASIC ALGORITHMS

Suppose that m and n are integers and that P(s) -> (x,y) is a mapping from the set of integers between 0 and m * n - 1 inclusive to the integer vertices of a rectangle of sides $0 \leq x < m$, $0 \leq y < n$. The murray algorithm defined above is such a mapping with the implicit assumption that m and n are odd and usually have several factors. Similarly, each Hilbert polygon corresponds to a mapping with $m = n = 2^q$ for some $q > 0$ and each Peano polygon to one with $m = n = 3^q$ with $q > 0$. A straight raster scan with flyback is another example of such a scan although it differs from the others in that not all pairs of points generated from successive integers are adjacent in two dimensional integer space. A serpentine scan (Ulichney 1987) which is a line by line scan without flyback is a special case of a murray scan with only one radix for each coordinate direction.

Suppose now that A is an m by n array of integer intensity values v. These values will be in some finite range $0 \leq v \leq V$ where we will assume that 0 corresponds to white and V corresponds to black. We will also assume that these values have already been scaled by some tone scale transformation such as the quadratic one described above.

Now define a running sum S(t) by

$$S(0) = A(P(0))$$
$$S(t) = S(t-1) + A(P(t)) \text{ if } S(t) < V \text{ div } 2$$

$$S(t) = S(t-1) + A(P(t)) - V \text{ if } S(t) \geq V \text{ div } 2$$

for $0 < t < m * n$.

The algorithm to determine black and white pixels for a halftoned bit map corresponding exactly in size to the image represented by the array of intensities A may now be defined as follows.

Algorithm 1

Let $S(t)$ be as defined above. Then the point with integer coordinates $P(t)$ is white if $S(t)$ was calculated without subtracting V and black otherwise.

This algorithm is almost that used by Witten and Neal (1982) for Hilbert polygon scans, excepting that they did not subtract V until S(t) had reached at least the value V.

Using algorithm 1 one obtains a bit map of the same dimensions as the intensity value array A.

The next algorithm relates implicitly to the scan P being either a murray polygonal scan or a Peano polygonal scan. There will be a similar result if P is a Hilbert scan. Suppose then that $P(t)$ is either a simple or mixed murray scan over an array of intensity values V and let $P_a(t)$ be the corresponding scan with an additional tile level introduced as explained in the section on murray polygons.The scan $P_a(t)$ will be used to generate a bit map B for some printing device which requires a tile of a by a bits for each value in V.

Now define a running sum $S_a(t)$ by

$$S_a(0) = A(P(0))$$
$$S_a(t) = S_a(t-1) + A(P(t \text{ div } a^2)) \text{ if } S_a(t) < V \text{ div } 2$$
$$S_a(t) = S_a(t-1) + A(P(t \text{ div } a^2)) - V \text{ if } S_a(t) \geq V \text{ div } 2$$

for $0 < t < m * n$.

The algorithm to determine black and white pixels for a halftoned bit map with a tile of size a by a corresponding to each value in the image represented by the array of intensities A may now be defined as follows.

Algorithm 2

Let $S_a(t)$ be as defined above. Then the point of the bit map B with integer coordinates $P_a(t)$ is white if $S_a(t)$ was calculated without subtracting V and black otherwise.

The bit map obtained from algorithm 2 has the dimensions of V scaled by a in both directions. Note also that algorithm 1 is a special case of algorithm 2 with a taking the value 1.

The use of algorithm 2 introduces a new idea in the preparation of bit maps for high definition printing devices. Much work has been done in choosing suitable collections of tiles to correspond to different intensity values in building up such bit maps in an attempt to reduce patterning which occurs in nearly uniform intensity areas and this problem gets worse as the scaling factor a gets larger. As can be seen from the algorithm the method generates these tiles on the fly in such a way that patterning will only occur in highly unlikely pathological cases. The reason for this is twofold in the case of Peano and simple murray scans and threefold in the case of mixed murray scans.

Firstly, although the maximum difference in the number of dots assigned to two lower level tiles with the same intensity value is 1, and in practice is frequently 0, the relative positions of those dots varies depending on the value of $S_a(t)$ on entry to the tile.

Secondly, the absolute relative position of these dots in the final bit map also depends on the four possible entry points to the tile.

Thirdly, in the case of mixed murray scans, there are the two possibilities of the scan being essentially horizontal or essentially vertical. Thus, in this case, there are eight possible combinations of entry point and orientation for the patterning of the additional low order tiles.

Together, these facts ensure a thorough mixing of different basic tiles corresponding to different fixed intensity values.

SOME BASIC EXPERIMENTAL RESULTS

In this section we will compare the effect of using different scanning paths in algorithm 1. For most of the paper we will illustrate results by using a printing density of 72 dots to the inch so that the full low level effect of patterning may be seen. In all cases, no transformation other than the simple quadratic tone scale shift will be used. In particular it is not suggested that the results shown for a straight linear scan are necessarily better than can be done after other transformations described in the introduction to this paper have been applied but rather illustrates the relative merits of the placing of halftoning dots on comparable intensity data. Edge enhancement, dither and other techniques could be applied in addition to the basic algorithm whenever this was considered to be necessary.

A common example has been used throughout most of the paper for comparative purposes. This is a fairly noisy portrait with some difficult background areas and some nearly vertical straight edges. The original pictures were captured using a video camera and a frame grabber used in conjunction with an IBM PCAT. Figure 7 is a photograph of the halftone screen and enables comparison to be made with the shadows and shading effects inherent in the original picture.

Figure 8(a) uses a straight raster linear scan with flyback and with the cumulative sum S(t) being reset to zero at the beginning of each new line. Clasical contouring appears not only in the background but also in the outline of the hair and neck. Snaking and other patterning appears in many places and the straight lines of the bookshelves to the right of the picture need enhancement.

Fig. 7 Photograph of original image.

Figure 8(b) uses a serpentine or degenerate murray scan but with the cumulative sum continuing between successive lines, which is reasonable because of the continuity of the scan. This is a considerable improvement on the result of figure 8(a) but the evidence of contouring, snaking, patterning and a need for edge enhancement is still present.

Figure 8(c) uses a Hilbert scan of complexity 7. This is comparable to the method suggested by Witten and Neal (1982). The picture is smaller than the others but this illustrates a problem with the Hilbert polygon scan. The size of picture to be scanned without special modification is always a square of side 2^n. It would also be difficult to increase the resolution by the method described above by anything other than a power of 2.

As reported by Witten and Neal this is a great improvement on either of the earlier results but, as they suggested, there is evidence of graininess in the finished picture.

Figure 8(d) uses a Peano scan of complexity 4. This is a special case of a murray scan but is necessarily square. A scan of complexity 5 would result in a larger picture but with no inherent difference to picture 8(e).

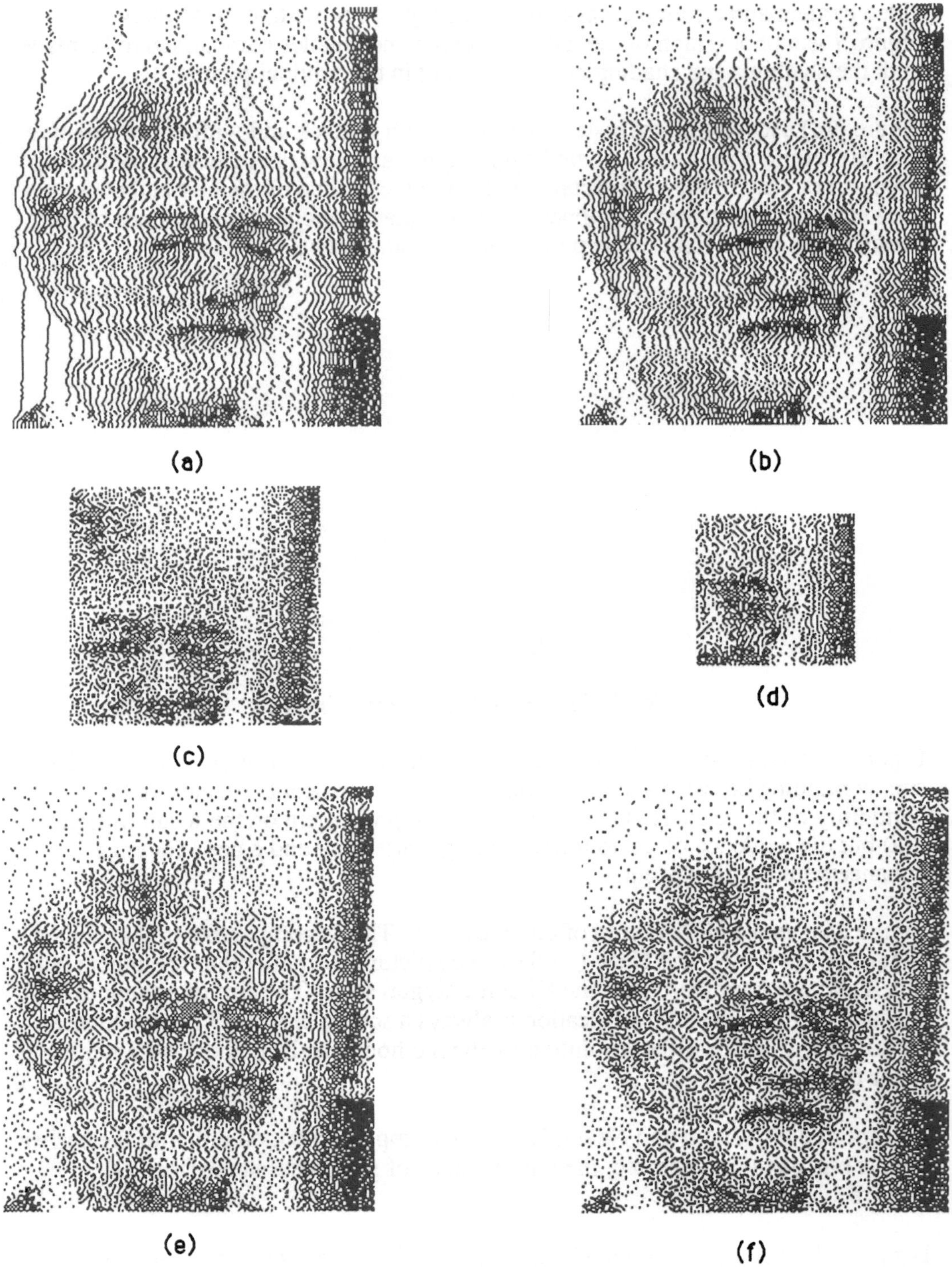

Fig. 8 Naive halftoning using (a) linear scan, (b) serpentine scan, (c) Hilbert scan, (d) Peano scan, (e) simple murray scan and (f) mixed murray scan.

Figure 8(e) uses a straight essentially horizontal murray scan of complexity 3 and with x radices 3 3 9 and y radices 3 5 9. All evidence of contouring has gone from the background and from the hair and there is a lesser tendency to granularity than in 8(c). The edges of the bookcase appear to be straighter than in the earlier pictures. There is some evidence of patterning on the forehead but this is not regular and does not appear distinctly in higher resolution printing.

Figure 8(f) uses a mixed murray scan of complexity 3 and with x radices 3 3 9 and y radices 3 5 9. This is probably marginally better than 8(e) and certainly the patterning on the forehead is reduced.

As with so many problems of this sort the final choice of the best result is very subjective . For the rest of this paper we will restrict our consideration to the mixed murray scan method.

THE EFFECT OF HIGHER RESOLUTION

We now consider the effect of using algorithm 2 to provide higher definition bit maps for higher resolution printing devices. In this part of the paper we will concentrate on mixed murray scans only. In order to continue the comparison at a low level the pictures will still be printed at 72 dots to the inch and will use only part of the pictures shown in figure 8.

Figure 9 uses only the right eye with 9(a) being from the original data with no expansion factor applied. The righthand lens of the spectacles with a dark shadow in the bottom right hand corner and the bridge of the spectacles across the nose are visible. Figure 9(b) expands the resolution threefold in each direction by the addition of a low level 3 by 3 tile. Figure 9(c) uses a 5 by 5 expansion and in each of figures 9(a) to 9(c) the definition remains good, with no noticeable regular patterning introduced and also no obvious rectangular low level tiling all of which contribute to good quality high density printing.

Figure 10(a) uses a 15 by 15 expansion of the middle third of figure 9(a) and shows a serious deterioration of the result with the 15 by 15 tiles clearly visible. This is obviously because at a 15 * 15 tile level the method is equivalent to a serpentine scan with just one intensity value for the whole tile. Figure 10(b) breaks down the 15 by 15 tile into a 5 by 5 tile of 3 by 3 tiles and is a considerable improvement on figure 10(a) even though just one intensity value is still being used for each new block of points. On a high density printer this should give good results.

HIGHER QUALITY PRINTING

All of the above figures have been drawn on an Apple Laserwriter Plus printer at a resolution of 72 dots to the inch. The figures in this section use the original data expanded by a factor of 3 in both directions by an additional layer of 3 by 3 tiles and printed at 300 dots to the inch. As in the previous section no additional processing other than a tone scale adjustment have been made before carrying out the mixed murray scan.

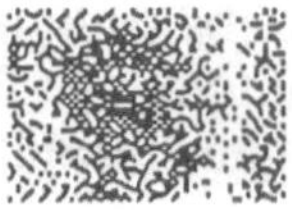

(a)

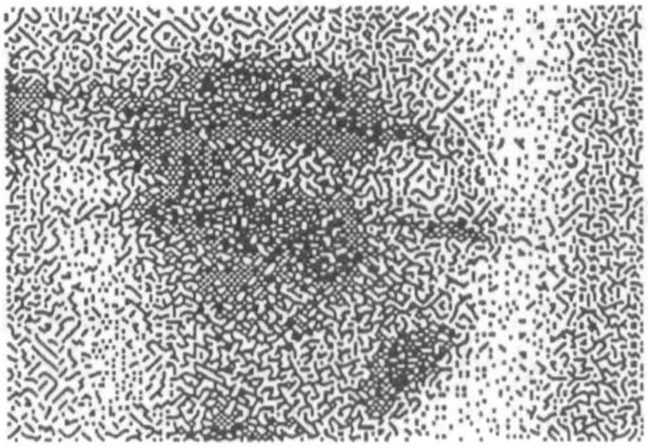

(b)

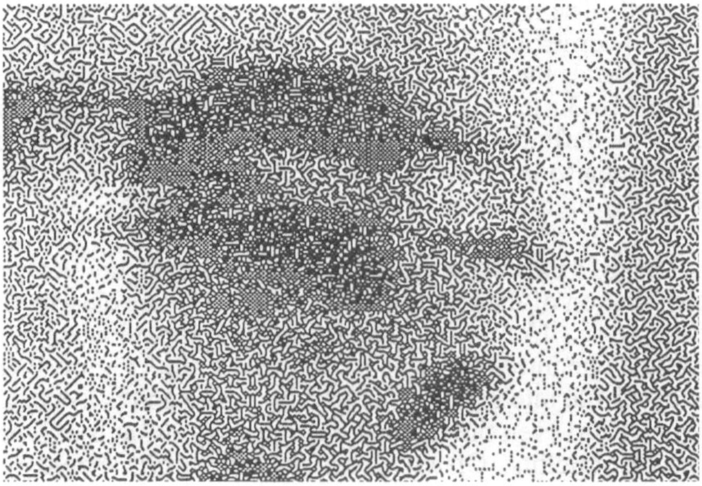

(c)

Fig. 9 Right eye of fig. 8, (a) straight copy, (b) scaled up by 3 and (c) scaled up by 5.

(a)

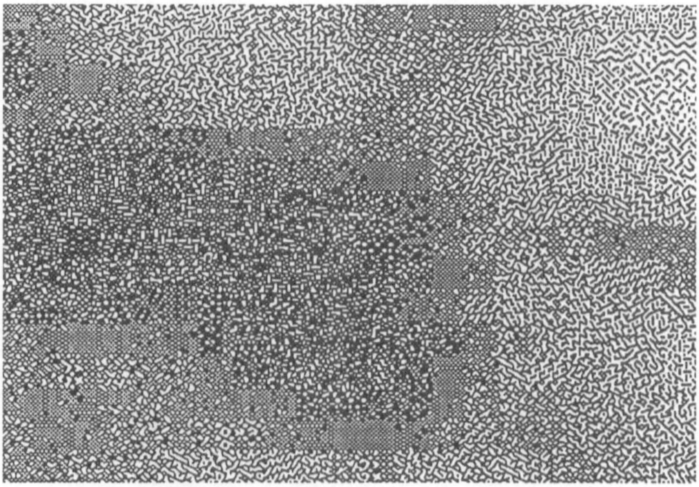

(b)

Fig. 10 Figure 9(a) scaled up by (a) a factor of 15 with one new tile level and (b) a factor of 15 with two new tile levels of size 3 and 5.

Figure 11 is from the image used throughout this paper with an extra level of 3 by 3 tiles and printed at 300 dots to the inch. Considering the noisy initial data the resulting picture shows little patterning and the edges of the bookcase are as good as those in the original picture.

Fig. 11 Head and shoulders corresponding to fig 8(f) scaled up by a factor of 3 and printed at 300 dots to the inch.

Fig. 12 'Fred' scaled up by a factor of 3 and printed at 300 dots to the inch.

Figure 12 is from a much cleaner initial image again scaled by a factor of 3. Both the figure and the detail in the background are of good quality. The variation in tone between the wall and ceiling are pleasing and the straight edges are very satisfactory especially considering that no edge enhancement algorithms have been employed.

Figure 13 shows the head from figure 12 scaled by a factor of 5 rather than 3 and printed again at 300 dots to the inch. The result is still good and the method shows how a denser image may be produced for printing on a higher resolution printer.

Fig. 13 Head of 'Fred' scaled up by a factor of 5 and printed at 300 dots to the inch.

CONCLUSIONS

A method of halftoning based on the use of mixed murray polygons has been described. This method does not distort the original data by statistical error modification and thus does not inherently require edge enhancement methods in order to restore picture quality. The production of data for high resolution, uniform size and intensity dot or laser printers is included as part of the method by the introduction of an extra low level of tiling whose patterns are determined by the actual intensity value at the corresponding point on the original picture as well as the previous value of the cumulated sum and the orientation of the particular corresponding low level tile. The final pictures produced by this method are pleasing to the eye and maintain the detail of the original images. Edge enhancement and other techniques to improve the images from poor quality data may be added if needed but are usually not necessary as part of the basic technique.

No experiments have been carried out to date with colour printing but it is suggested that a similar technique using three cumulative sums may lead to good results in this area.

REFERENCES

Bayer BE (1973) An optimum method for two level rendition of continuous-tone pictures. Proc. IEEE Int. Conf. Communications, Conference Record: (26-11) - (26-15)

Cole AJ (1966) Cyclic progressive number systems. Math. Gazette: 50:122 -131

Cole AJ (1985) A note on Peano polygons and Gray codes. Intern. J. Computer Math: 18: 3-13

Cole AJ (1986) Multiple radix arithmetic and computer graphics. Bull. Inst. of Math. and its Applications: 22(5/6): 71-75

Cole AJ Buntin IM (1988) Some ideas about low speed transmission of moving pictures. Computer Graphics 88: 33-50

Cole AJ (1988) Murray polygons as a tool in raster scan graphics. Proceedings of ICONCG, Nanyang Tech. Inst., Singapore: 195-207

Goertzel G Gerhard RT (1987) Digital halftoning on the IBM 4250 printer: IBM J. Res. and Dev.: 31-1:

Hilbert D (1891) Ueber stetige Abbildung einer linie auf ein Flachenstuck. Math. Ann.: 38: 459-460

Jarvis JF Judice CN Ninke WH (1976) A survey of techniques for the display of continuous-tone pictures on bilevel displays. Computer Graphics and Image Processing: 5: 13 - 40

Jarvis JF Roberts CS (1976) A new technique for displaying continuous tone images on a bilevel display. IEEE Trans. Communications, COM-24: 891-898

Kennedy HC (1980) Peano. The life and works of Giuseppe Peano. D Reidel PC, Dordrecht, Holland

Knuth DE (1987) Digital halftones by dot diffusion. ACM Trans. on Graphics: 6(4): 245-273

Limb JO (1969) Design of dither waveforms for quantized visual signals. Bell Sys.Tech. J: Sep 2555-2582

Lippel B Kurland M (1971) The effect of dither on luminance quantization of pictures. IEEE Trans. Communications COM-19: 6: 879-888

Lippel B (1976) Two and three-dimensional ordered dither in bilevel picture displays. Proc. SID: 17(2): 115-121

Moore EH (1900) On certain crinkly curves. Trans. Amer. Math. Soc.: 1: 72-90

Peano G (1980) Sur une courbe qui remplit toute une aire plaine. Math. Ann.: 36: 157-160

Peano G (1908) Formulario mathematico: vol.5, Torino

Ulichney R (1976) Digital halftoning. Ph.D. thesis, MIT, Cambridge, Mass.

Ulichney R (1987) Digital halftoning. MIT Press, Cambridge Mass.

Witten IH Neal RM (1982) Using Peano curves for bilevel display of continuous-tone images. IEEE CG&A: 47-52

Witten IH and Wyvill B (1983) On the generation and use of space-filling curves. Software-practice and experience: 13: 519-525

Chapter 4
Algorithms

Attribute-Grammar Based Approach to Vector Extraction from a Raster Image

Kyu-Jae Lee, Yasuto Shirai, and Tosiyasu L. Kunii

ABSTRACT

With the advent of many CAD systems, the topic of efficient data exchange between them has attracted much attention in the research community. Data exchange in the CAD environment presents a serious problem of data format conversion. Two most common formats for CAD data storage are the raster format and the vector format, and the conversion between them, particularly from the former to the latter, has for some time been the subject of a challenging research endeavor. A new method is presented for extracting vectors embedded in a raster image file. It is based on the attribute grammar concept, and lends itself to a concise formulation based on that concept. The formulation can be extended by introducing new attributes and rules to the underlying grammar. Moreover, the vector data thus extracted can be easily transferred to a database that stores such vector data.

Keywords: attribute grammar, industrial drawings, vector extraction, chain code, 8-connectivity

1. INTRODUCTION

Today we observe a rapid increase in the number of CAD systems in use. A CAD system represents the design object as a set of data structures which conform to the underlying product model. It maintains the integrity and consistency of this representation through various design phases, performs analysis, and generates manufacturing information using this representation.

Within a single CAD system, the user benefits a great deal from the integrated environment. However, if we are to exchange data between two different systems, we often face a problem of data exchange. Especially in the case of inter-organizational exchange, the problem is inevitable due to the conflicting interests of the organizations concerned. Even within a single organization, integration of existing data from the past into a newly introduced CAD system presents a similar problem.

In many of the engineering fields, exchange of design data is in the form of drawings. In fact, prior to the introduction of integrated CAD systems, drawing was essentially the only means of storing and exchanging design data. Today, producing a drawing using a CAD system takes only one command, such as DRAW, to be issued. Going the other way, however, is not so easy. Inside a computer, a drawing is represented in the vector data format. In order to obtain this machine-readable counterpart of a drawing, all vectors embedded in it must be identified. Here we use the term 'vectors' in a broader sense; curves as well as straight line segments are all considered vectors.

Identifying the objects represented in an image is a problem of image understanding. There are two approaches to image understanding: statistical and syntactic (Fu 1986). In the former, a set of features are extracted from an image, and these features are used to classify patterns. On the other hand, in the syntactic approach a pattern is expressed as a composition of its components, referred to as subpatterns or pattern primitives. In this paper, we introduce the attribute grammar concept to the latter approach, and apply it to the extraction of vectors from the raster image of an industrial drawing.

Section 2 briefly outlines the extraction process. The details of our approach are discussed in

Section 3 along with its formulation. Section 4 discusses the advantage of using the attribute grammar concept. The subject of linking the proposed method with a drawing database is also addressed in this section. Section 5 provides a summary and concluding remarks.

2. OVERVIEW OF RASTER TO VECTOR TRANSFORMATION

In this section, we outline the process of converting the information contained in a drawing into a computer-readable form. To aid our presentation, we use a simple architectural drawing as an example (Fig. 1).

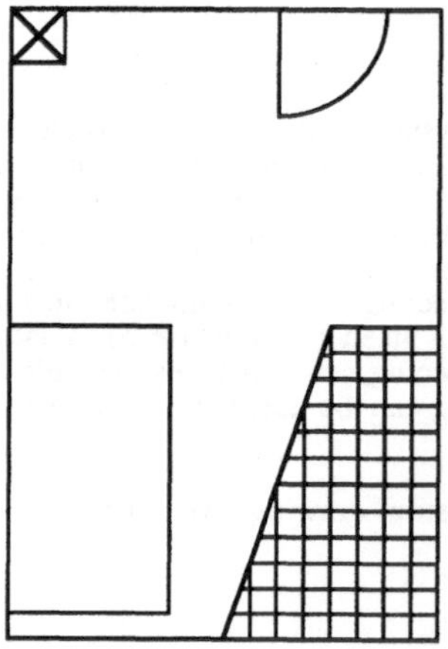

Fig. 1 A sample drawing.

The process consists of the following four steps:

(1) Raster image input
First, the drawing is read in by a scanner, and we obtain a digitized two-tone raster image composed of '1' (black) and '0' (white) pixels.

(2) Thinning
In this digitized two-tone image, lines have the width of more than one pixel. The actual width depends on the resolution of the scanner. For example, if we use a scanner of resolution 200 dpi to read a typical architectural drawing, lines in the digitized image will be three to four pixels wide. Since we are interested in vector data, the width must be reduced to the minimum, i.e., one pixel wide. This is achieved by a thinning algorithm which transforms an object to its medial line of constant width. Several efficient algorithms are known for this purpose (Nakayama et al. 1984, 1986; Stefanelli and Rosenfeld 1971). They preserve the connectivity among the elements in the original picture.

(3) Segmentation
After the thinning operation, we divide the lines in the image at their vertices and intersection points. We refer to each divided unit as a segment. A segment is an array of pixels and constitutes a part of a (longer) straight line or a curve. In Fig. 2, we show the segments thus obtained from the drawing of Fig. 1.

(4) Connecting segments
Finally, the segments are connected to yield longer lines and curves. This process continues until there is no more segment to be connected to/with other segments. After the connecting

operation, the picture of Fig. 2 will look as shown in Fig. 3.

It is in the last two steps, 'Segmentation' and 'Connecting segments,' that we introduce the attribute grammar concept to formulate the process.

3. ATTRIBUTE GRAMMAR

Attribute grammar was first introduced to analyze the semantics of a programming language (Knuth 1968), but has been applied in other areas as well (see for example, Terai 1987; Tsai and Fu 1980). Here we propose a new method for extracting vectors embedded in a raster image. It is based on the attribute grammar concept, and can be concisely formulated using a common notation.

Our method applies to the steps (3) and (4) of the overall process outlined in the previous section. In the following, we focus our attention on these two steps, and formulate the vector extraction process using the common attribute grammar notation. Regarding the input to this process, we assume the followings:

(1) Each line to be extracted has the width of exactly one pixel. (This is achieved by the thinning process.)

(2) 8-connectivity of pixels is preserved. (4-connectivity is not sufficient for our purposes.)

(3) The input image is free of unwanted pixels. (This background noise elimination can be achieved by image modeling, and presents another research subject.)

3.1 Pixel Classification

'1' pixels in a digitized image can be classified into two groups: CONNECT and END. A CONNECT pixel lies on the interior of a pixel sequence; an END pixel marks the end point of such a sequence or their intersections. This classification can be made easily by applying a simple formula to each pixel (Yokoi et al. 1973). Let X_1, X_2, ..., X_8 be the eight pixels surrounding the pixel X_0 (Fig. 4).

Then, the value of the formula

$$N_c^{[8]} = \sum_{i=1,3,5,7} (\overline{X}_i - \overline{X}_i \times \overline{X}_{(i+1) mod 8} \times \overline{X}_{(i+2) mod 8})$$

effectively classifies the pixel X_0. A bar ($\overline{\ }$) indicates the complement of the pixel value. Four patterns of the eight neighboring pixels of X_0 are shown in Fig. 5 along with the value of $N_c^{[8]}$. If $N_c^{[8]}$ is 2, the pixel X_0 is a CONNECT pixel; otherwise, it is an END pixel.

Now, we divide the image into pieces called segments. A segment is an array of pixels satisfying the following two conditions:

(1) all pixels composing a segment, except for the two end points, are CONNECT pixels; and

(2) pixels at the two end points are either END pixels or CORNER pixels.

A CORNER pixel connects two adjacent vectors and marks a vertex of a polyline. In the classification using $N_c^{[8]}$, it is classified as a CONNECT pixel. To extract a segment from a digitized image, we start from an END or CORNER pixel and traverse the adjacent CONNECT pixel until we meet an END or CORNER pixel again.

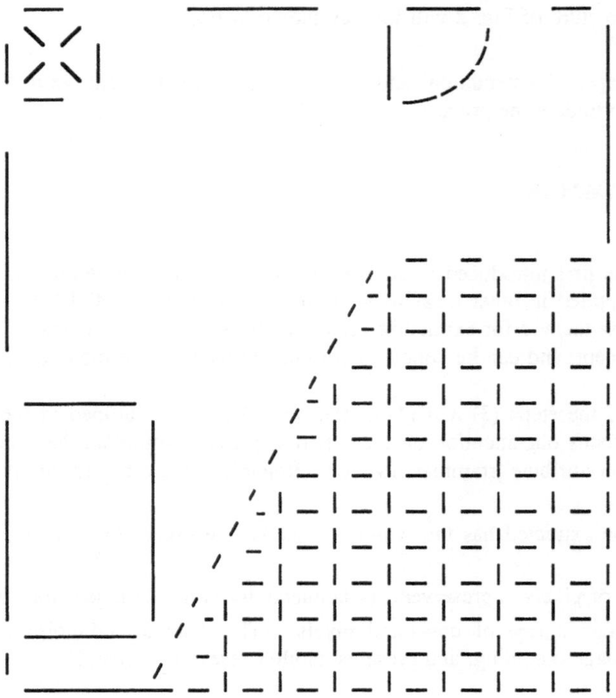

Fig. 2 Figure 1 after segmentation.

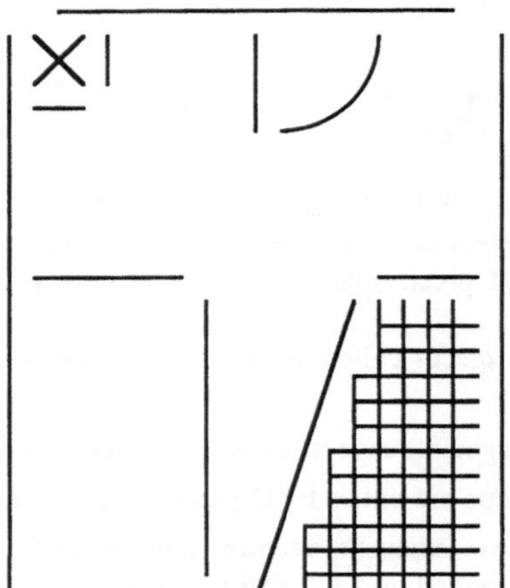

Fig. 3 Segments connected to form longer segments.

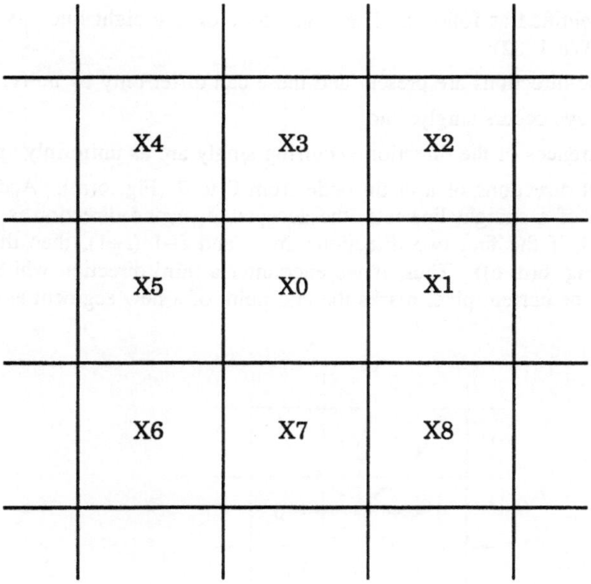

Fig. 4 Eight neighbors of the pixel X0.

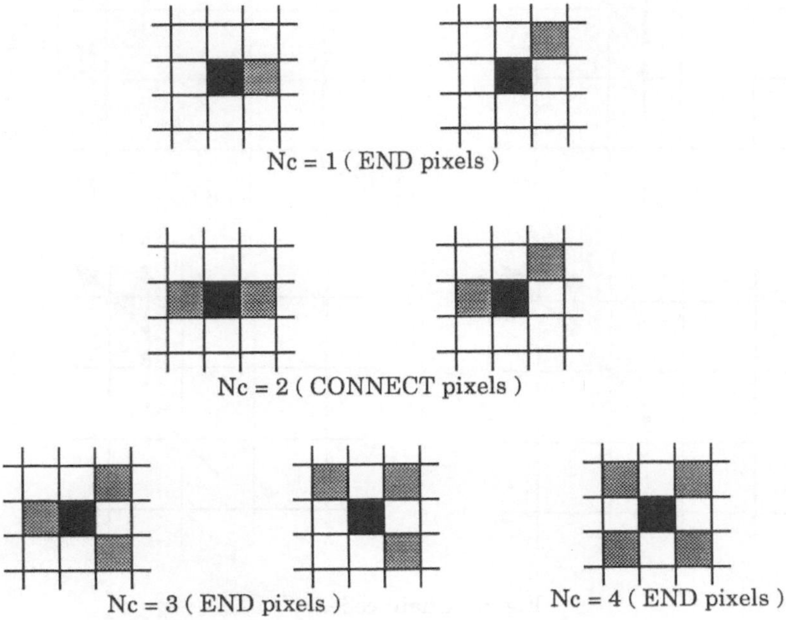

Fig. 5 Four patterns of eight neighbors.

A CORNER pixel is identified as follows. The chain code of a straight line has the following properties (Freeman 1970; Wu 1982):

(1) at most two basic directions are present and these can differ only by unity, modulo eight;

(2) one of these always occurs singly; and

(3) successive occurrences of the direction occurring singly are as uniformly spaced as possible.

Let us number the eight directions of a chain code from 0 to 7 (Fig. 6(a)). According to Property (1), if the first direction of a straight line is i, the acceptable second direction is one of $i-1$, i, and $i+1$ (Fig. 6(b, c)). And, if the first two directions are i and $i-1$ ($i+1$), then the next direction is either i or $i-1$ ($i+1$) (Fig. 6(d, e)). Thus, if we encounter a third direction while connecting pixels to construct a segment, the current pixel marks the end point of a new segment and we conclude it is a CORNER pixel.

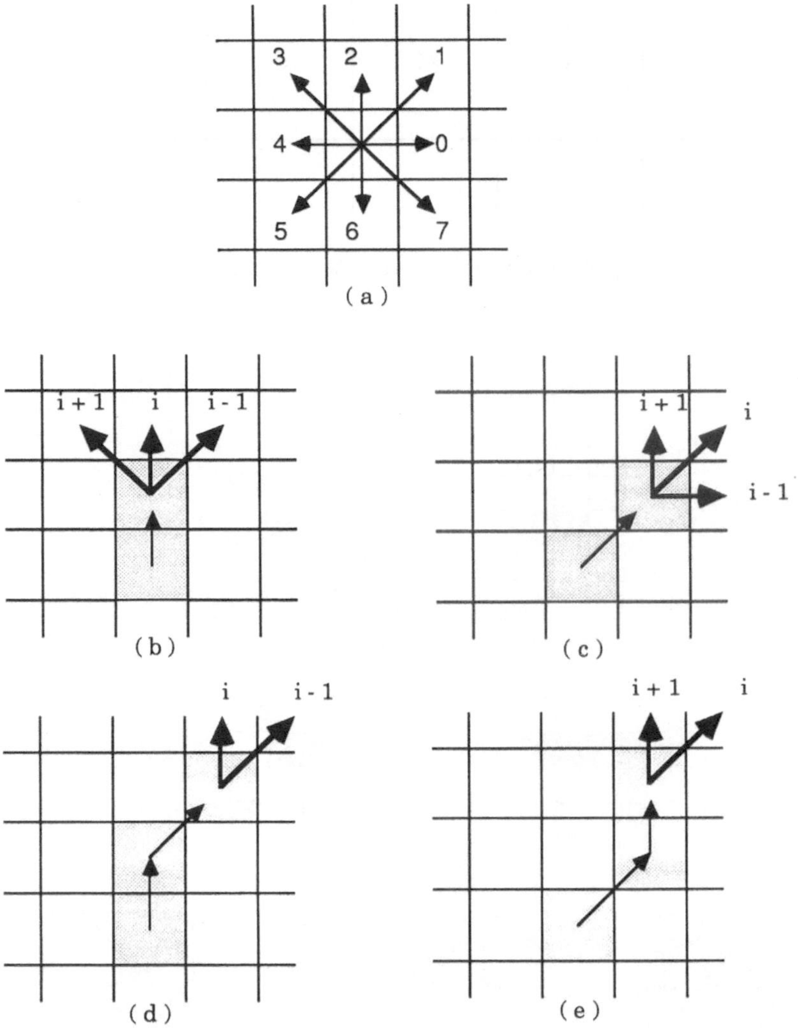

Fig. 6 Chain code.

Therefore, we can identify CORNER pixels as shown in Fig. 7(a) which introduce the third direction while connecting pixels. Some CORNER pixels, however, do not introduce the third direction, and cannot be located in this manner (Fig. 7(b)).

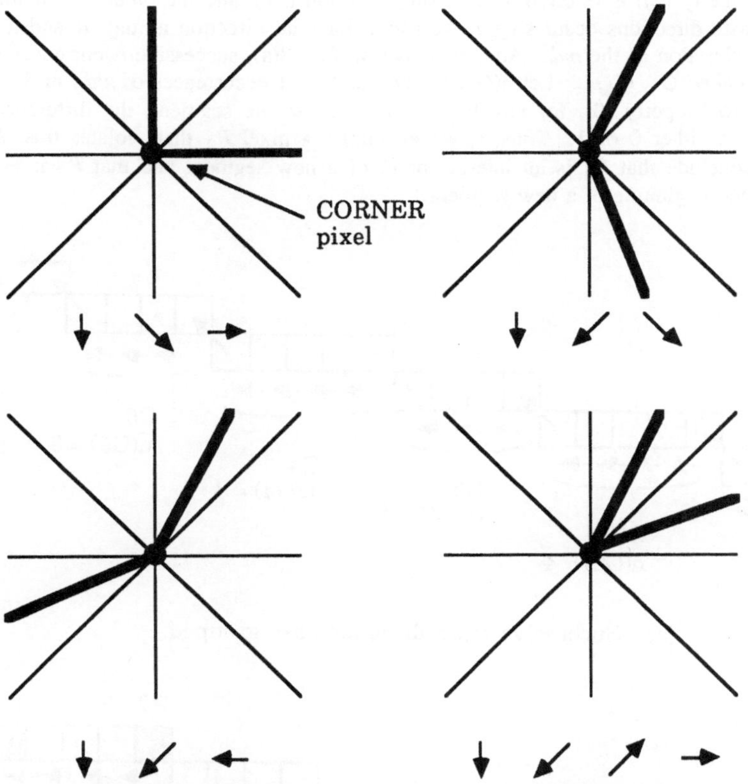

(a) CORNER pixels which introduce the third direction.

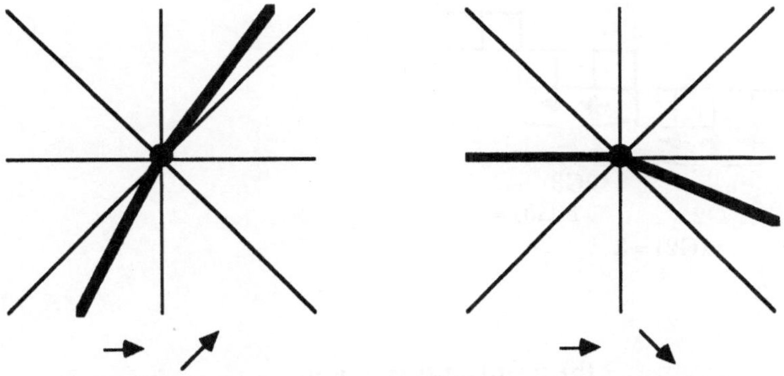

(b) CORNER pixels which do not introduce the third direction.

Fig. 7 CORNER pixels.

In order to identify and locate the latter type of CORNER pixels, we introduce the concept of sub_direction and main_direction in the chain code a straight line segment. First, we note the two basic directions that appear in the chain code of a line segment (Property (1)). The direction which occurs singly (Property (2)) is referred to as a sub_direction (*sd*), and the other as a main_direction (*md*). If both basic directions occur singly, we use a diagonal direction as the *sd* and a horizontal or perpendicular direction as the *md*. And, as shown in Fig. 8(a), successive occurrences of the *md* are grouped and called G_1, G_2, ... Let n(G_i) be the number of occurrences of *md*s in the group G_i. Then, according to Property (3), for any two G_i and G_j in the segment, the difference between n(G_i) and n(G_j) is either 0 or 1. Thus, if we encounter a pixel P_1 that violates this observation (Fig. 8(b)), we conclude that P_1 is an internal point of a new segment and that P_2 is a CORNER pixel and marks the beginning of a new segment.

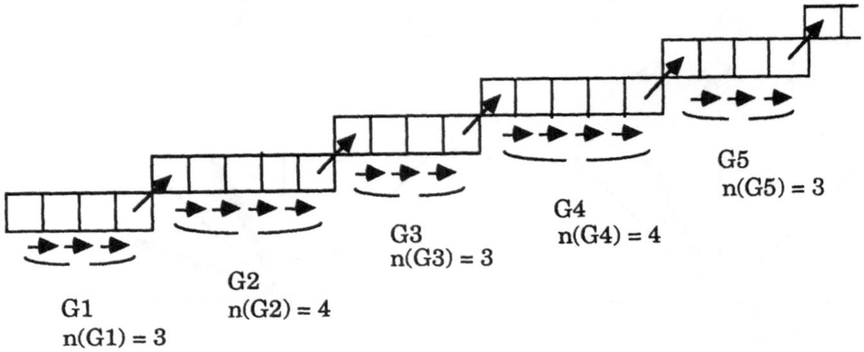

(a) Successive main directions are grouped.

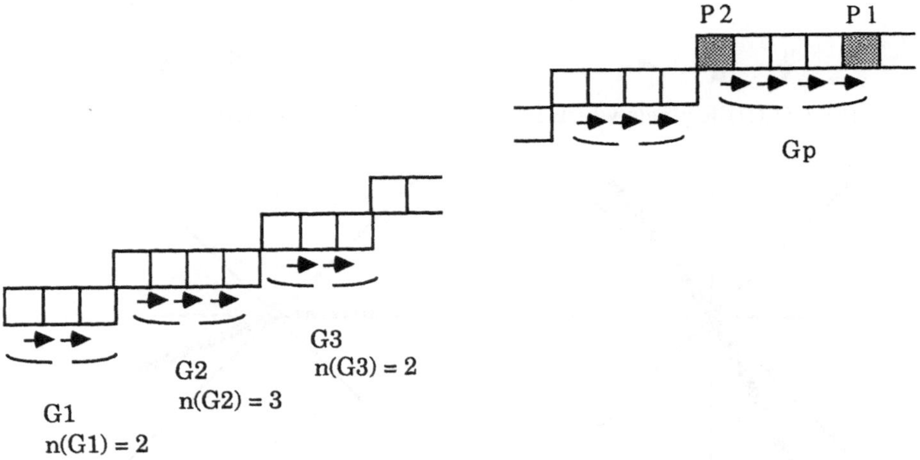

(b) n(Gp) must be 2 or 3.

Fig. 8 Pixel classification..

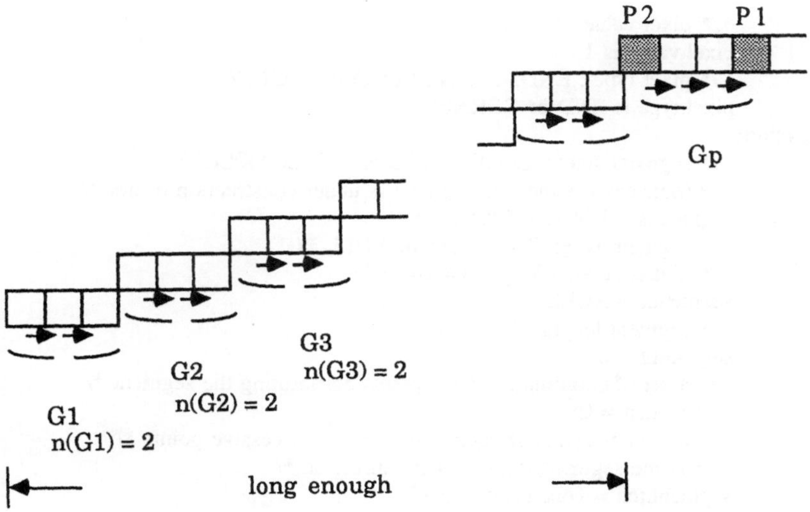

(c) n(Gp) must be 2.

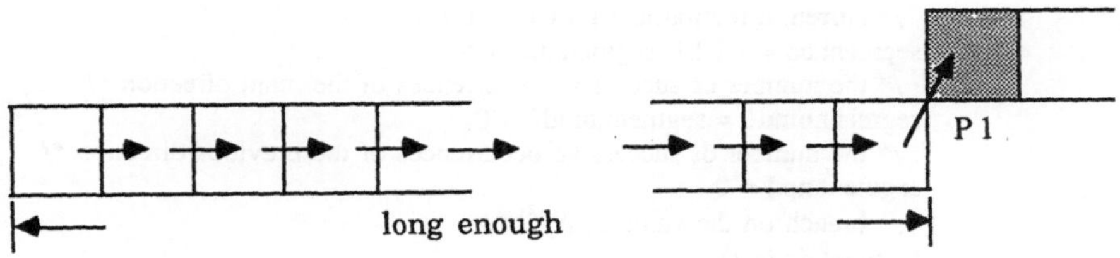

(d) Segment of only one direction.

Fig. 8 (Continued)

There is an unusual case where, even if P_1 causes no violation, we need to conclude that P_2 is a CORNER pixel (Fig. 8(c)). It is when the line segment under construction is long enough, and that, for all i ($i < p$ and G_p contains P_1), n(G_i) has the same value. In this case, even if n(G_p) and n(G_i) ($i < p$) differ by 1, we conclude that P_2 is a CORNER pixel.

Another exceptional case occurs when the chain code consists of only one basic direction (Fig. 8(d)). If we have traversed a long enough sequence of a single direction, we assume that it is a line segment of one basic direction. So, the first pixel that introduces a different direction is a CORNER pixel and again marks the beginning of another segment.

3.2 Segment Construction

The segment construction process is formulated as follows:

<segment> ::= <pixel>
condition:

```
        /* pixel value : 0 or 1 */
       pixel.value is 1
        /* pixel type : END, CORNER or CONNECT */
       pixel.type is END or CORNER
action:
        /* segment status: COMPLETED or UN_COMPLETED
        /* indicates whether the segment is under construction or not */
       segment.s = UN_COMPLETED
        /* segment type: STRAIGHT or NULL */
        /* if it is enough long, STRAIGHT */
       segment.t = NULL
        /* segment length */
       segment.l = 0
        /* a set of coordinates of the points constituting the segment */
       segment.cn = Ø
        /* a temporary set of coordinates of the successive points */
        /* of the segment, causing same direction */
       segment.tcn = {pixel.coordinate}
        /* main direction and sub direction */
        /* in the chain code of the segment */
       segment.md = NULL segment.sd = NULL
        /* current direction and previous direction */
       segment.cd = NULL segment.pd = NULL
        /* the number of successive occurrences of the main direction */
       segment.nmd1 = segment.nmd2 = 0
        /* the number of successive occurrences of the previous direction */
       segment.npd = 0
        /* branch on the value of N_c^[8] */
       if (pixel.nc is 1)
               /* pixel participates on no other segment */
              pixel.value = 0
       else
               /* decrement by 1 */
              pixel.nc = pixel.nc - 1


&lt;segment&gt; ::= &lt;segment&gt;&lt;pixel&gt;
condition:
  pixel.value is 1
  segment.s is UN_COMPLETED
action:
  if (pixel.type is CONNECT) {
    segment.cd = DIRECTION(pixel)
    if (segment.md and segment.sd are NULL) {
      if (segment.pd is NULL or segment.cd is equal to segment.pd)
         CONNECT pixel TO segment.tcn
      else if (segment.cd is different from segment.pd) {
         if (segment.cd and segment.pd differ by 1
              and segment.npd is little than LONG) {
           CONNECT segment.tcn TO segment.cn
           if (segment.npd is equal to 1)
              segment.sd = segment.pd
           else if (segment.npd is greater than 1) {
```

```
        segment.md = segment.pd
        segment.sd = segment.cd
        segment.nmd1 = segment.npd
      }
      CLEAR segment.tcn
      CONNECT pixel TO segment.tcn
    } else {
      CONNECT segment.tcn TO segment.cn
      CLOSE segment
      pixel.type = CORNER
    }
  }
} else if (segment.md is NULL and segment.sd is not NULL) {
  if (segment.cd is equal to segment.pd)
    CONNECT pixel TO segment.tcn
  else if (segment.cd is different from segment.pd) {
    if (segment.cd is equal to segment.sd)
        and segment.npd is little than LONG) {
      CONNECT segment.tcn TO segment.cn
      if (segment.npd is equal to 1) {
        if (segment.cd is diagonal)
          segment.md = segment.pd
        else if (segment.pd is diagonal) {
          segment.md = segment.sd
          segment.sd = segment.pd
        }
      } else if (segment.npd is greater than 1)
        segment.md = segment.pd
      segment.nmd1 = segment.npd
      CLEAR segment.tcn
      CONNECT pixel TO segment.tcn
    } else {
      CONNECT segment.tcn TO segment.cn
      CLOSE segment
      pixel.type = CORNER
    }
  }
} else if (segment.md and segment.sd is not NULL) {
  if (segment.cd is equal to segment.pd) {
   if (segment.cd is equal to segment.md and
      ((segment.nmd2 is equal to 0 and
        segment.npd is not greater than segment.nmd1)
      or (segment.nmd2 is greater than 0 and
        segment.npd is little than segment.nmd1 or segment.nmd2)))
      CONNECT pixel TO segment.tcn
    } else {
      CLOSE segment
      for the first pixel in segment.tcn
        pixel.type = CORNER
    }
  } else if (segment.cd is different from segment.pd) {
   if (segment.cd is equal to segment.md) {
      CONNECT segment.tcn TO segment.cn
```

```
            CLEAR segment.tcn
            CONNECT pixel TO segment.tcn
        } else if (segment.cd is equal to segment.sd and
            ((segment.nmd2 is equal to 0 and
                segment.npd and segment.nmd1 differ by 0 or 1)
              or (segment.nmd2 is greater than 0 and
                segment.npd is equal to segment.nmd1 or segment.nmd2))) {
            CONNECT segment.tcn TO segment.cn
            if (segment.nmd2 is equal to 0 and
                    segment.npd is different from segment.nmd1)
                segment.nmd2 = segment.npd
            else if (segment.nmd2 is equal to 0 and
                    segment.l is greater than LONG and
                    segment.npd is equal to segment.nmd1)
                segment.nmd2 = segment.nmd1
            CLEAR segment.tcn
            CONNECT pixel TO segment.tcn
        } else {
            CLOSE segment
            for the first pixel in segment.tcn
                pixel.type = CORNER
        }
    }
} else if (pixel.type is equal to CORNER or END) {
    if (pixel.type is equal to CORNER
            or (pixel.type is equal to END and pixel.nc is equal to 1)
        CONNECT pixel TO segment.tcn
    else
        pixel.nc = pixel.nc - 1
    CONNECT segment.tcn TO segment.cn
    CLEAR segment.tcn
    CLOSE segment
}
```

The function DIRECTION returns the chain code direction of a pixel relative to the previous pixel. If a constructed segment is enough long, it is treated as a straight line (STRAIGHT); otherwise, its type is left undetermined (assigned the type NULL). The statement "CONNECT pixel TO segment.tcn" adds the coordinate of the current pixel to segment.tcn, sets segment.pd to segment.cd, and increments segment.npd by 1. Also, the statment "CONNECT segment.tcn TO segment.cn" adds the coordinates of the pixels in segment.tcn to segment.cn, and adjusts the length of segment.cn. "CLEAR segment.tcn" sets pixel.value of all pixels in segment.tcn to 0, and clears segment.tcn to an empty set. '0' pixels are considered "processed," and no further processing is performed on them. When a segment being traversed has grown long enough, "CLOSE segment" sets segment.s to COMPLETED, and sets segment.t to STRAIGHT.

3.3 Segment Connection

Finally, these short segments are connected to yield longer segments. Only the adjacent segments are connected. Two segments are connected if their slopes are the same. We introduce a function SLOPE which returns the slope of a line. This process is formulated as follows:

<segment1> ::= <segment1><segment2>

condition:

SLOPE(segment1.cn) == SLOPE(segment2.cn)
segment1 and segment2 coincide at their end points

action:

CONNECT segment2.cn TO segment1.cn
segment1.t = STRAIGHT
REMOVE segment2

These processes will continue until there are no more proper segments to be connected. If there are adjacent NULL segments after all connection processes are completed, they are treated as a part of an arc or a curve. Then, it is checked to see if they constitute a part of an arc. If so, we construct a new segment of type ARC from the segments involved. Otherwise, they are grouped into a longer segment of type CURVE.

4. DISCUSSIONS

4.1 Flexibility and Extensibility

To extract vectors from the raster image of a drawing, the extraction process itself must be equipped with some general knowledge on drawings, such as the type of primitive geometric constructs, and the rules associating them to form larger constructs. In our approach, such knowledge is expressed in the form of attributes assigned to various constructs.

The example presented here is limited to a simple case where a drawing consists of only straight lines and circular arcs, both with uniform line texture. If we are to deal with more complex drawings in which there are more line types, we need only to add those types as the possible values of segment.t. Moreover, a uniform line and a dotted line could be distinguished by introducing a new attribute, such as segment.tex, for the texture of the line and adding a few more rules so that a dotted line may not be connected to a uniform line, and vice versa.

The above observation suggests flexibility and extensibility of our approach. In fact, the use of attribute grammar for combining statistical and syntactic approaches has been proposed in the literature (Tsai and Fu 1980). So it is also possible to integrate the elements of the statistical approach into ours.

4.2 Link with a Database

In an integrated CAD environment, the database mangement facilities will be an indispensable component. Some special requirements are imposed on a database system for CAD applications (Katz 1985). To distinguish from conventional databases, such a system is often called a 'CAD database' or an 'engineering database.' An engineering drawing created by a CAD system can be readily stored in its database, since the data format matches the database organization. But, if an existing drawing is to be stored in a CAD database, the drawing is usually input manually. Involvement of manual tasks impedes the total productivity of the whole system.

The proposed technique is expected to aid this data input step greatly; our method provides a basis for an automatic drawing input subsystem. With the addition of this subsystem at the front end of a CAD system, the amount of human intervention necessary will be kept to the very minimum. Moreover, various attributes introduced in our formulation can also be stored in the database as attribute values of each data item, e.g., segment coordinate and segment type. In this manner, our formulation of vector extraction process could provide a basis for an automatic data acquisition unit of a CAD system.

5. CONCLUDING REMARKS

We have presented a process for extracting vectors from a digitized two-tone raster image. It is to be noted that the whole process can be formulated concisely using the attribute grammar concept.

In this paper, we impose several constraints on the input image, but our approach can be easily extended to more general images by incorporating more rules and attributes.

Two typical problems in a more general image are the followings:

(1) Noise in the scanned image.
There are two types of noise. One is unwanted pixels; they must be eliminated by the pre-processing phase before the thinning operation is applied. The other type can be found at the edges of lines in a scanned image. In a scanned image, a line may not come out as a band of constant width. If a thinning algorithm is applied to such an image, the medial axis is not a single straight line. Some pre-processing is again required to avoid this.

(2) Unsmoothness in a thinned image.
After the thinning operation, the image shown in Fig. 9(a) will be as shown in Fig. 9(b). There is an undesirable dip at the middle of the horizontal line. The segmentation operation yields three segments (Fig. 9(c)), two of which are connected into one segment in the subsequent connection phase (Fig. 9(d)). In the end, we have two lines, horizontal and vertical, but there is a gap between them. Some post-processing is necessary to extend the vertical line so that it touches the horizontal line. To avoid post-processing, a thinning algorithm not based the medial axis may be necessary.

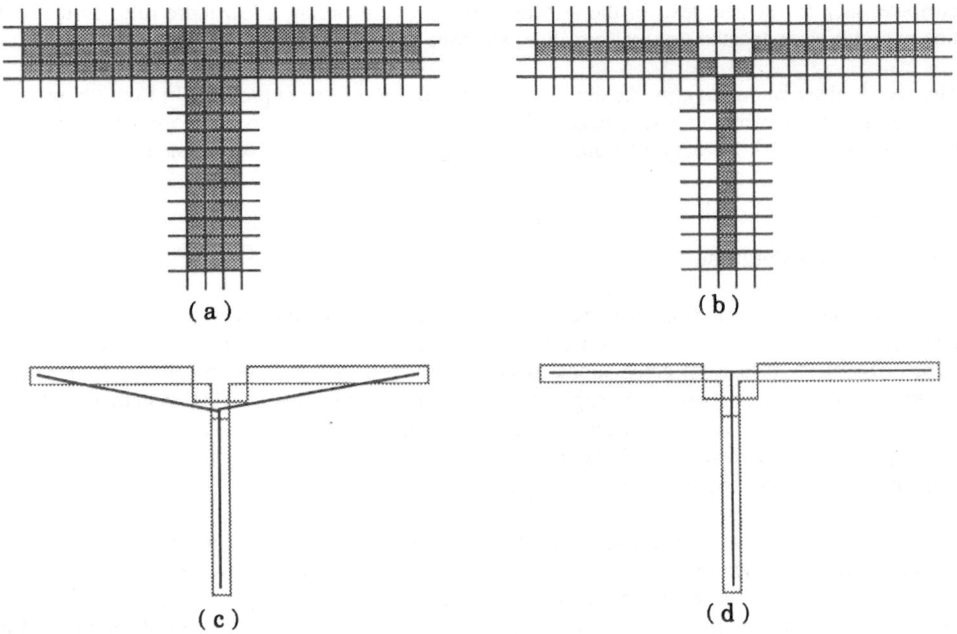

Fig. 9 T - intersection.

We have also argued that our method provides a basis for an automatic data acquisition unit of a CAD database. In order to construct an integrated CAD system, the logical organization of the database must be decided.

REFERENCES

Freeman H (1970) Boundary Encoding and Processing. In: Lipkin BS, Rosenfeld A (ed) Picture Processing and Psychopictorics. New York: Academic, pp 241-266

Fu KS (1986) Syntactic Pattern Recogntion. In: Young TY, Fu KS (ed) Handbook of Pattern Recongnition and Image Processing. Academic Press, pp 55-117

Katz RH (1985) Information Management for Engineering Design. Springer, Berlin Heidelberg New York Tokyo

Knuth DE (1968) Semantics of Contex-Free Languages. Mathematical Systems Theory 2(2):127-146

Nakayama A, Kimura F, Yoshida Y, Fukumura T (1984) An Efficient Thinning Algorithm for Large Scale Images Based upon Pipeline Structure. The Transactions of the Institute of Electronics and Communication Engineers of Japan J67-D(7):761-767 (in Japanese)

Nakayama A, Kimura F, Yoshida Y, Fukumura T (1986) An Efficient Implementation Method of Logical Parallel Algorithms for Large-Scale Images Based upon Pipeline Structure. The Transactions of the Institute of Electronics and Communication Engineers of Japan J69-D(2):259-260 (in Japanese)

Rosenfeld A (1974) Digital Straight Line Segments. IEEE Transactions on Computers C-23:1264-1269

Stefanelli R, Rosenfeld A (1971) Some Parallel Thinning Algorithms for Digital Pictures. J. ACM 18(2):255-264

Terai, K (1987) Computer-Aided Design of Fabrics. Master's Thesis, Department of Information Science, Faculty of Science, the Unviersity of Tokyo

Tsai WH, Fu KS (1980) Attributed Grammar - A Tool for Combining Syntactic and Statistical Approaches to Pattern Recognition. IEEE Transactions on Systems, Man, and Cybernetics SMC-10(12):873-885

Wu LD (1982) On the Chain Code of a Line. IEEE Transactions on Pattern Analysis and Machine Intelligence PAMI-4(3):347-353

Yokoi S, Toriwaki J, Fukumura T (1973) Topological Properties in Digitized Binary Pictures. The Transactions of the Institute of Electronics and Communication Engineers of Japan J56-D(12):662-669 (in Japanese)

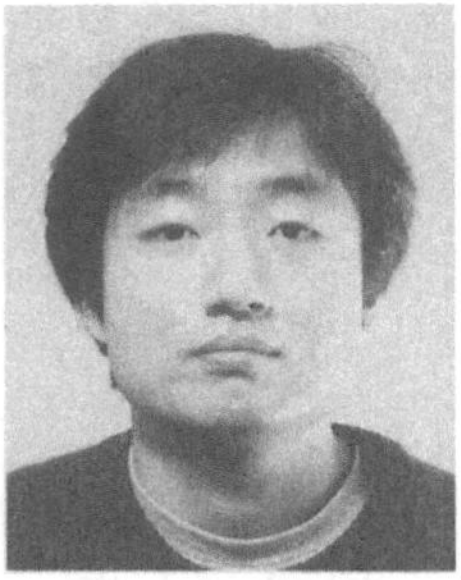

Kyu J. Lee is currently a doctor course graduate student of Information Science at the University of Tokyo. His research interests include CAD/CAM and computer graphics. He received the B.Sc. degree in computer science and statistics in 1985 from Seoul National University, and the M.Sc. degree in information science in 1988 from the University of Tokyo. He is a student member of ACM and IEEE Computer Society.

Yasuto Shirai is Assoicate Professor of Faculty of Education, Shizuoka University, Shizioka, Japan. He received the B.Sc. degree in computer science from the University of Toronto, Canada in 1984, and the M.Sc. degree in information science from the University of Tokyo in 1987. His research interests include computer graphics and its applicatiions, as well as database systems and information systems. He is a member of ACM, IEEE Computer Society and the Information Processing Society of Japan.

Tosiyasu L. Kunii is currently Professor and Chairman of Department of Information Science, the University of Tokyo. At the University of Tokyo, he started his work in raster computer graphics in 1968 which was led to the Tokyo Raster Technology Project. His research interest has been in visual computers which include visual object modeling, computer graphics, database systems, pattern recognition, parallel and distributed computing, and software engineering. He authored and edited more than 30 books in computer science and related areas, and published more than 100 refereed academic/technical papers in computer science and applications.

Dr. Kunii is Former President, Honorary President and Founder of the Computer Graphics Society, Editor-in-Chief of *The Visual Computer: An International Journal of Computer Graphics*, Editor of *Computer Science Workbench Series* of Springer-Verlay and on the Editorial Board of *IEEE Transactions on Knowledge and Data Engineering* and *IEEE Computer Graphics and Applications*. He is a member of IFIP Working Group 2.6 on Database, IFIP Working Group 5.10 on Computer Graphics and IFIP Working Group on Modelling and Simulation. He organized and was chairing the Technical Committee on Software Engineering of the Information Processing Society of Japan from 1976 to 1981. He also organized and was President of the Japan Computer Graphics Association (JCGA) from 1981 to 1983. He served as General Chairman of the 3rd International Conference on Very Large Data Bases (VLDB) in 1977, Program Chairman of InterGraphics '83 in 1983, Organizing Committee Chairman and Program Chairman of Computer Graphics Tokyo in 1984, Program Chairman of Computer Graphics Tokyo in 1985 and 1986, Organizing Committee Chairperson and Program Chairperson of CG International '87, Program Co-Chairman of IEEE COMPSAC 87, and Honorary Committee Chairperson of CG International '88. He served as Organizing Committee Chairperson and Program Chairperson of IFIP TC-2 Working Conference on Visual Database Systems in 1989.
He received the B.Sc., M.Sc., and D.Sc. degrees in chemistry all from the University of Tokyo in 1962, 1964, and 1967, respectively.

Address: Department of Information Science, Faculty of Science, the University of Tokyo, 7-3-1, Hongo, Bunkyo-ku, Tokyo, 113 Japan

Virtual Camera Oversampling: A New Parallel Anti-Aliasing Method for Z-Buffer Algorithms

Frank Van Reeth, Rudi Welter, and Eddy Flerackers

ABSTRACT

In Computer Graphics, aliasing occurs by the reconstruction of a continuous image starting from a set of discrete samples. Most anti-aliasing algorithms give best results in conjunction with a scan-line algorithm. Algorithms for anti-aliasing objects using a Z-buffer were believed to be difficult.
Here we present a new anti-aliasing method for filtering images rendered with the Z-buffer algorithm, using a small virtual camera which provides us locally with a very high sub-pixel rendering resolution. The method lends itself easily for parallelism.

Keywords: Computer graphics, anti-aliasing, virtual camera oversampling, parallel processing systems, z-buffer, transputer

1. INTRODUCTION

Since the advent of image synthesis on bitmapped raster devices, computer graphics research has devoted a considerable amount of attention to the problem of aliasing. Aliasing is a term that originated from the field of signal processing. In digital signal processing, one reconstructs a continuous signal in two major steps: firstly, one samples the signal at discrete steps and subsequently one applies an appropriate filtering technique. When the sampling rate is too low, however, an erroneous signal is reconstructed: it is an alias of the original signal.

In computer graphics, a similar problem occurs: how to reconstruct a continuous object description on the screen, given a limited number of discrete pixel values, without introducing aliases. One way to decrease aliasing is to apply prefiltering methods which integrate sampling values over neighborhoods. This technique, however, requires a lot of mathematical calculations and therefore it is relatively slow. So, a more simple and faster method is asked for. This method can be found in the supersampling approach: render an image at a higher resolution and filter it down to the desired resolution. Such an approach is easy indeed, but it has the disadvantage of having a huge memory requirement. The memory problem becomes even more apparent when Catmull's Z-buffer algorithm (Catmull 1974) is used for hidden surface removal. Moreover, due to the lack of sufficient information about previously processed objects, it is very hard to remove aliasing defects in conjunction with the Z-buffer algorithm.

Taking all this into account, we started to develop an anti-aliasing technique for Z-buffer algorithms, called "Virtual Camera Oversampling", that (1) preserves the advantages of

Taking all this into account, we started to develop an anti-aliasing technique for Z-buffer algorithms, called "Virtual Camera Oversampling", that (1) preserves the advantages of the supersampling approach, (2) doesn't require the memory overhead, (3) has an acceptable performance, and (4) incorporates a parallel implementation. The name encapsulates two major aspects: a Virtual Camera and Oversampling. The last term is called oversampling rather then supersampling because there are some conceptual differences between our method and traditonal supersampling. We will come back to these differences later on in the paper. The most innovative part of our method is the use of the virtual camera. To wit, we represent each pixel to be anti-aliased as the screen of a small virtual camera. This screen will be termed virtual window (or window, for short). Against this window, we clip and render only those polygons that contribute to the pixel's final intensity.

One of the major advantages is the possibility to perform our anti-aliasing algorithm in parallel. In our rendering system, we use a network of transputers (high performance micro-processors which are specifically designed to work in parallel) to run the algorithm. By the use of k transputers, we get an anti-aliasing performance that is about k times better than the mono-processor anti-aliasing performance (i.e., the speed-up is nearly linear in nature).

Section 2 briefly discusses in general terms the problem of aliasing and its solutions. A few references to related work are given also. Section 3 consequently elucidates in more detail the aliasing problem in conjunction with Z-buffer algorithms. In section 4, the virtual camera oversampling technique is explained, whereas section 5 gives an outline of the algorithm in pseudo-code. Section 6 discusses some results. Conclusions and areas for future research can be found in section 7.

2. ALIASING AND ITS SOLUTIONS : RELATED WORK

When we are trying to synthesize an image, adapted to the resolution of the display screen, starting from a model with an infinite resolution in object space, a lot of information is lost. This loss of information introduces aliasing in the generated pictures.

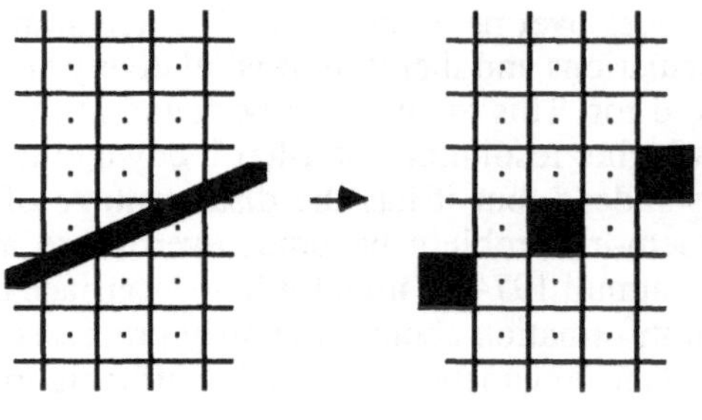

Fig. 1 Disappearing detail, due to aliasing

The most common effects of aliasing are :

- "jaggies" or the staircase effects along lines and edges drawn in contrasting colors;
- disappearing objects when they are small enough to miss the middle of the sample point;
- Moiré patterns in texture mapping.

In computer animation, these effects become even more obvious as :

- crawling jaggies at silhoutte edges and small highlights;
- changing of object shapes;
- stroboscopic effects (such as backward spinning wheels);
- scintillation (small objects blinking on and off according to their position).

The problem of aliasing and its possible solutions are systematically discussed by Crow (1981). He eludicates three classes of anti-aliasing algorithms :

- increase the number of sampling points by simply increasing rendering resolution (this method, however, can only marginally remove aliasing);
- render the image at a higher resolution and filter it down digitally (called supersampling or oversampling). Crow (1981) used this approach with good results;
- filter the image before sampling by convolving picture intensities with appropriate filters to yield proper pixel color values. This method is called prefiltering. It has been applied by Crow (1977), Catmull (1978) and Lobb (1987).

In general, the term aliasing refers to the appearance of a low-frequency signal as an alias of some high-frequency signal during the reconstruction of the latter by discrete sampling.

The Shannon Sampling Theorem states that we can only reconstruct a signal of frequency f correctly if we take samples at a rate r where r satifies the formula :

$$r >= 2 * f$$

The term $r = 2 * f$ is called the Nyquist Limit.

Papers about anti-aliasing methods using scan-line algorithms are plentiful, but papers discussing anti-aliasing in conjunction with a Z-buffer are scarce. (Surely, the Z-buffer is a scan-line method at polygon level. The fact, however, that the polygons arrive in random fashion, without any relation to neighboring or overlapping polygons, clearly makes it necessary to distinguish between anti-aliasing methods for Z-buffer and "true" scan-line methods. Consequently, no direct comparisons are made with true scan-line anti-aliasing methods like, e.g., Lobb (1987)).

Fujimoto (1984) mentions fast anti-aliasing with a Z-buffer. His approach for anti-aliasing polygons is based on blending the shading of polygon edges with the existing background shading. This implies that anti-aliasing is imperfect when obscuring polygons are rendered before obscured polygons (cfr. next section).

The A-buffer method proposed by Carpenter (1984) produces good quality images, but it is rather costly in memory space. He needs two additional memory words for each pixel. Another problem is that the method loses the simplicity of the traditional Z-buffer algorithm.

Duff (1985) produced a method whereby he stores the z-value at each of the four corners of a pixel. Interpolating the z-values, he finds the points where the depths are equal. These points are then used to determine the pixel coverage. Although Duff's algorithm is very simple, it suffers, as most anti-aliasing methods, from losing small objects.

Ghazanfarpour (1989) presented the "gz-buffer" algorithm. Besides a Z-buffer, the algorithm maintains a so-called g-buffer. It stores geometrical information at each pixel for anti-aliasing purposes. On the one hand, the g-buffer has the advantage of simplicity and an acceptable memory overhead. On the other hand, however, the method suffers from disapearing small objects.

3. ALIASING PROBLEMS IN Z-BUFFER ALGORITHMS

The Z-buffer algorithm, presented by E. Catmull (1974), is one of the most simple and elegant hidden surface removal methods for frame buffer displays. A major drawback of this algorithm is the difficulty of performing anti-aliasing. The problems of aliasing are caused by the specific properties of the Z-buffer:

- the image is computed at the resolution of the frame buffer in a random fashion;
- polygons are displayed in no specific order and without depth sorting;
- hidden surface removal and intersections between polygons are done by (partially) overwriting previously displayed polygons. There is no particular preprocessing as in scan-line algorithms.

Ghazanfarpour (1989) enumerates some aliasing problems encountered by the Z-buffer. We will outline them in this subsection, together with a brief statement of how we tackled the problem at issue. A more profound elucidation is given later.

First of all, there is the problem of dealing with small objects. Indeed, when a small object misses the middle of the pixel, it is lost. With our method, we solved this problem by storing all polygons that affect the pixel's intensity in a polygon list. When the actual anti-aliasing is performed later on, all the polygons in the list of the pixel at issue will be taken into account.

The second defect Ghazanfarpour mentions is the change in background color. Let polygon P1 be rendered on a background B. Accordingly, a pixel (x,y) on an edge of P1 is anti-aliased in conjunction with background B. When another polygon P2 afterwards appears behind P1, the color of polygon P2 becomes the background of afterwards appears behind P1, the color of polygon P2 becomes the background of polygon P1. The previously calculated intensity at (x,y) will no longer be correct. In our method, the anti-aliasing at pixel level only takes place *after* all polygons that affect the pixel at issue are rendered. As a result, no intermediate anti-aliasing values are present and the ultimate intensity will always be correct.

A third problem is somewhat similar to the previous one: it concerns adjacent polygons. Suppose polygon P1 is rendered, so all pixels on an edge E are anti-aliased. When subsequently a polygon P2 is rendered that shares the edge E with P1, the pixels on this edge are processed again. Consequently, the color of a pixel on E depends on the color of both polygons and also on the background color, whereas it should only depend on the color of polygons P1 and P2. As mentioned above, in our method the anti-aliasing only starts after all polygons that affect the pixels at issue are processed, so the polygons sharing edges will be treated properly (without any interference of the background color).

The fourth and last problem is that of intersecting polygons. Whenever a polygon P2 intersects a previously rendered polygon P1, a new potentially aliased edge becomes vissible along the intersection line. Detecting whether or not a pixel belongs to an intersecting line can be hard. We solved this issue by firstly rendering the complete (aliased) image and by subsequently applying adaptive anti-aliasing where needed.

4. Virtual Camera Oversampling

For hidden surface removal in polygon rendering, two widely used techniques are available: scan-line algorithms and Z-buffer (or depth buffer) algorithms. When using the scan-line method, anti-aliasing can be performed by incorporating the required calculations in the rendering process. In Z-buffer algorithms, however, this is quite different (cfr. previous section). As mentioned in the introduction, we developed an anti-aliasing technique for Z-buffer algorithms, called "Virtual Camera Oversampling", that (1) preserves the advantages of the supersampling approach, (2) doesn't require a huge memory overhead, (3) has an acceptable performance, and (4) incorporates a parallel implementation. In this section, we'll present the developed method. We begin by explaining the differences between our oversampling approach and traditional supersampling. Consequently, our idea about the virtual camera is explained, and finally the algorithm itself is elucidated.

The core of the method narrows down to a supersampling related technique. We use the term "oversampling" rather than supersampling because there are some distinct differences. A first difference lies in the fact that no averaging takes place across pixel boundaries. I.e., the traditional sharing of sub-pixels in the filtering process from the higher resolution to the required resolution is not present in our method: every pixel is treated here independent of its neighbors. Another important differentiation is that we get high quality anti-aliased images without expensive filtering, due to the high virtual resolution at sub-pixel level (we come back to this in one of the following paragraphs). A last (but not least) distinction manifests itself in the memory requirement. Indeed, in our approach it is not necessary to render the entire image at a higher resolution, so we don't need additional memory for storing depth and color values. On the one hand, this implies a huge saving in memory, especially when sampling at a significant number of times (say, at more than four times) the required resolution. On the other hand, we need additional data structures, and thus memory, for storing polygon information. A major advantage of our memory requirement is, however, that it can be tuned in exchange for performance, depending on the availability of memory. We return to this issue in section 6.

As mentioned before, the most innovative part of our method is the use of the virtual camera. Indeed, at different stages of the algorithm, a virtual camera is the central "tool". More concrete, we utilize three kinds of virtual cameras at three different levels. At the outermost level, the camera is akin to the virtual movie camera (Thalmann et. al. 1986): an entity that transforms and projects 3D object space (or world space) into 2D screen space. It can also perform actions like panning, tilting, tracking, zooming and spinning. In the algorithm, this virtual movie camera provides the raw (aliased) image of which the pixel values are used as selectors for adaptive anti-aliasing.
At a second level, the virtual camera is just procedural software responsible for generating polygon lists. More precisely, we split up the screen of the virtual movie camera into screen regions of mxn pixels (cfr. Fig. 2). Every screen region consequently is looked at as the screen of a virtual sub-camera of the movie camera. This camera will be called "region camera" and the boundary of its screen will be called "region window". In the algorithm, the region camera generates a list (instead of bitmapped pixel values) of all polygons passing through its region window.
At a third level, we introduce the "pixel camera". It is a virtual sub-camera of the region camera (cfr. Fig. 3). In fact, every pixel in the mxn screen region at issue is considered as a pixel camera screen of pxp sub-pixels (cfr. Fig. 4). The boundary of the pixel camera screen will be called "pixel window". In the algorithm, the image generated by the pixel camera at sub-pixel level will be used to perform the actual anti-aliasing.

The anti-aliasing algorithm has a number of consecutive stages.

The first stage consists of rendering the complete scene at the normal screen resolution in order to obtain (aliased) color values in the frame buffer. We utilize the above mentioned virtual movie camera and a traditional Z-buffer algorithm for doing this. The calculated color values will be used in a later stage of the algorithm for checking where anti-aliasing has to be applied. Moreover, the polygon data in the normalized viewing volume will be used later on for speed-up purposes.

In the second stage, we subdivide the screen into regions of mxn pixels (we refer back to Fig. 2). As mentioned above, every screen region is considered to be the screen of a so-called region camera. The region camera is responsible for generating a list of polygons, called "region list", that pass through its viewing pyramid. The region list is utilized to reduce drastically the number of polygons that have to be processed in the third stage of the algorithm. The building up of the region list is done via a modified rendering process. This process doesn't require transforming, 3D clipping and projecting the complete scene all over again, as we start from the data in the normalized viewing volume produced by the virtual movie camera in stage one. The size of the region, i.e. the values of m and n, can be chosen as a function of the (average) number of polygons in the scene. For every region, a third stage in the algorithm is activated.

In this third stage, the actual anti-aliasing by oversampling is performed. Firstly, for all the pixels in the screen region at issue, an extra polygon list, called the "pixel list", is generated (thus giving a total of mxn pixel lists). For building up those pixel lists, every polygon in the region list at issue is (1) clipped against the region window and (2) rendered in such a way that it is put in the pixel list of *every* pixel it passes through. This requires (1) a simple 2D clipping and (2) a simplified polygon scan converter -e.g. no depth comparisons are needed- for filling in the pixel lists instead of generating bitmapped pixel values (we again omit a few details outside the scope of the paper). After the pixel lists have been constructed, adaptive anti-aliasing can begin. For every pixel in the region, we investigate whether or not anti-aliasing should be performed. If it has to be performed, we have recourse to the pixel camera (we mentioned above that it has the corresponding pixel as its screen). In fact, every polygon in the pixel list at issue is rendered at a resolution of pxp sub-pixels with respect to the pixel camera. This signifies that a small-sized (4 <= p <= 24) color bitmap and attending depth buffer have to be generated (we refer back to Fig. 4). The color values in the bitmap are consequently used for filtering out the ultimate color of the pixel at issue. In this filtering process, a plain averaging technique is utilized, rather than an expensive filtering method.

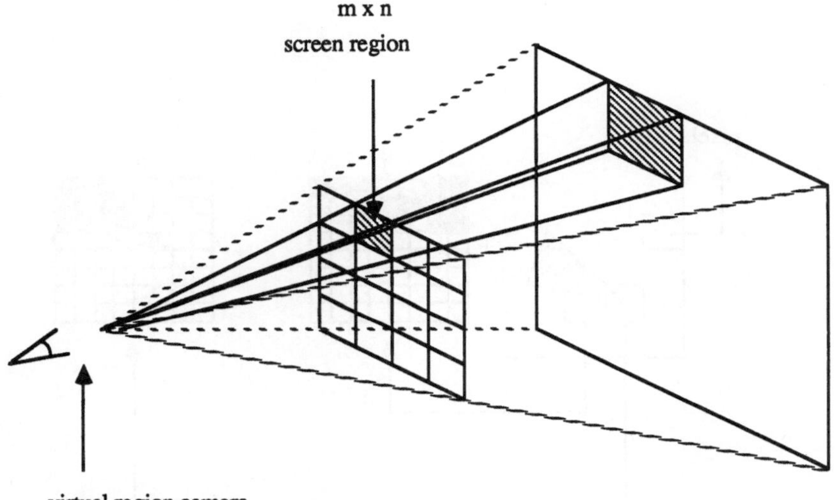

Fig. 2 Viewing pyramid of virtual region camera

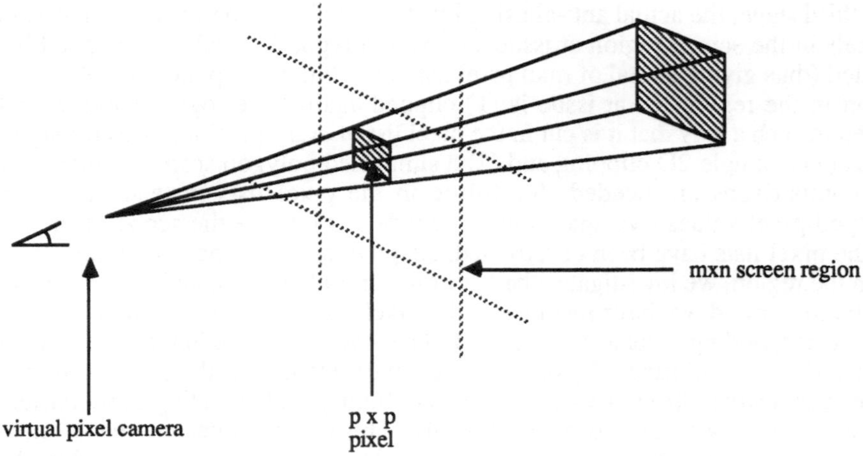

Fig. 3 Viewing pyramid of virtual pixel camera

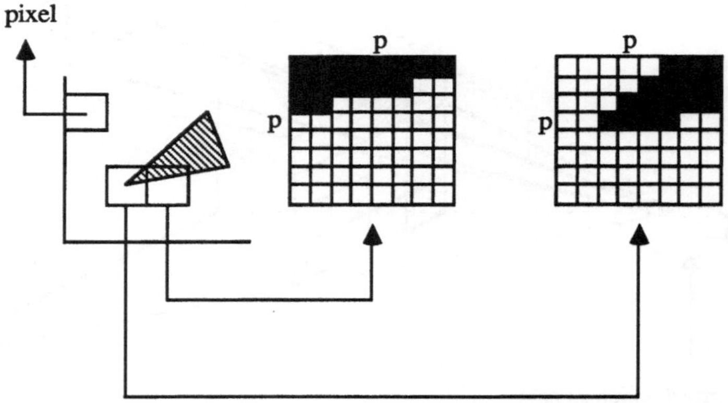

Fig. 4 Local oversampling in pixel windows

5. Outline of the Algorithm

```
BEGIN
   ... preprocessing (e.g. render aliased image)
   y.loop := 0
   WHILE y.loop < resolution.y
      BEGIN
         ... initialization
         x.loop := 0
         WHILE x.loop < resolution.x
            BEGIN
               ... find all polygons passing through mxn screen region
               IF list <> empty THEN
                  BEGIN
                     ... clip each polygon against region window
                     FOR y.for.region = y.loop TO y.loop + n
                        FOR x.for.region = x.loop TO x.loop + m
                           BEGIN
                              ... find each polygon which crosses the pixel at issue
                              IF (list <> empty) AND anti-aliasing-needed THEN
                                 BEGIN
                                    ... clip polygons against pixel window
                                    ... render polygons at sub-pixel level
                                    ... take average intensity
                                 END
                           END
                  END;
               x.loop := x.loop + m
            END;
         ... dump processed lines to screen
         y.loop := y.loop + n
END;
```

6. DISCUSSION AND RESULTS

Three important issues are to be discussed: memory requirement, performance and parallelism.

In the algorithm, two data structures are introduced that occupy a considerable amount of memory: the region list and the set of pixel lists. The size of these data structures is proportional to the size of the regions, in which we subdivided the screen. Let m=128 and n=16 for a mxn screen region. Then we have a total of mxn = 2K pixel lists. Providing a maximum of 50 polygons passing through a pixel, together with the fact that we need 4 byte to identify a polygon, leaves us with a memory requirement of 400K byte. (The provision of a maximum of 50 polygons per pixel doesn't mean the algorithm wouldn't work when this limit should accidently be exceeded, as we have foreseen an ad hoc "overflow list"). It is very important to notice, however, that the requirement of the 400K byte shouldn't pose any problem at all, as we can use the memory of the depth buffer for this purpose (because we don't need it anymore after the first stage in the algorithm). The same reasoning can be followed for the region list data structure. If, for a typical scene, the memory requirement of the pixel list and the region list data structures should exceed the memory requirement of the depth buffer, and if no additional memory should be available, other solutions can be looked for. More precisely, the image can be processed by going through the algorithm in two or more consecutive steps (each time for different parts of the image). In this way, memory requirement can be compensated by a performance penalty.

The performance issue is more difficult to stipulate, as the number of pixels to be anti-aliased is scene dependent. Mainly two parts in stage 3 of the algorithm, namely (1) the clipping of polygons from the pixel list against the pixel window and (2) rendering within the pxp sub-pixel screen, determine the time of anti-aliasing a pixel. Optimizing them can strongly influence the execution time of the algorithm. Given a certain scene to be rendered, the clipping time will be constant, while the total anti-aliasing time can be influenced by determination of the sub-pixel resolution p. Lowering the value of p will lower the anti-aliasing time proportionally (at the cost of somewhat less image quality, but sometimes this could be allowed). The proportionality stagnates at p=6, when clipping time begins to dominate.

As mentioned in the introduction, the algorithm incorporates inherently a parallel implementation. Indeed, the screen regions are treated independently of each other, and so they can be processed in parallel. As the time to distribute the relevant region list across the network of processors can be neglected in comparison with the processing time, we get an almost linear speed up. It has to be said we had maximum of 12 transputers (high performance micro-processors specifically designed to work in parallel with other members of the transputer family) at our disposal.

Figure 5 shows a snapshot of an aliased robot, whereas Fig. 6 holds an anti-aliased one. Both pictures were rendered at a resolution of 512 by 512 pixels. The robot contains about 3000 polygons and was anti-aliased on one processor in 127 seconds (we utilized p=16; p=24 gives 197 seconds; p=12 gives 100 seconds; p=8 gives 82 seconds; p=4 gives 71 seconds).The clipping time, incorporated in the timing values given above, took about 39 seconds (on 1 processor). Figures 7 and 8 give a zoom-in of the bottom side of the robot arm of Fig. 5 and 6 respectively. It doesn't show on Fig. 8, but on the screen a total number of 26 grey values were displayed.

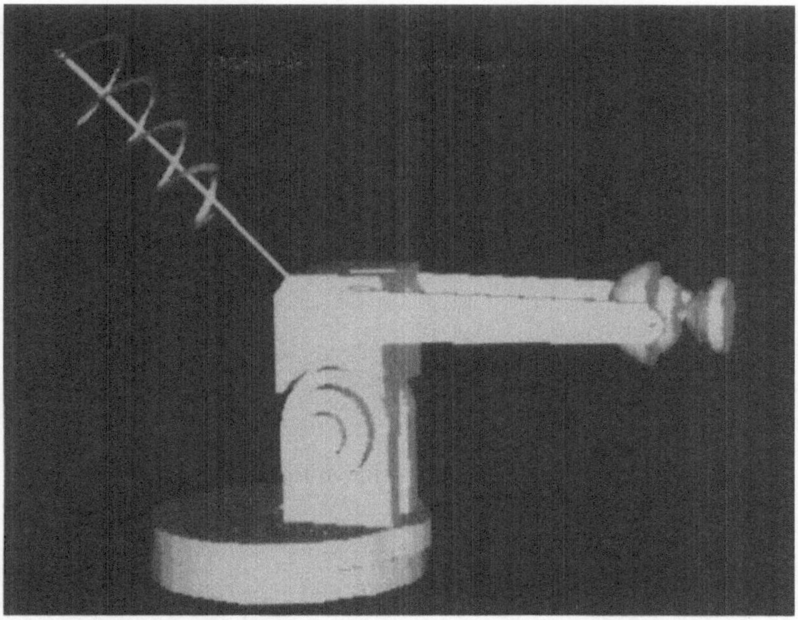

Fig. 5 Aliased robot

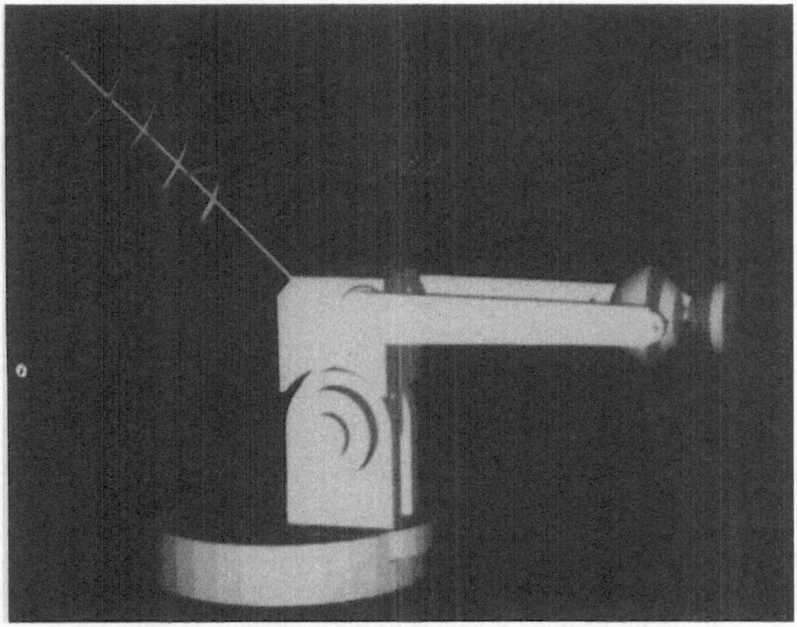

Fig. 6 Anti-aliased robot

Fig. 7 Zoom-in of the bottom side of the aliased robot arm

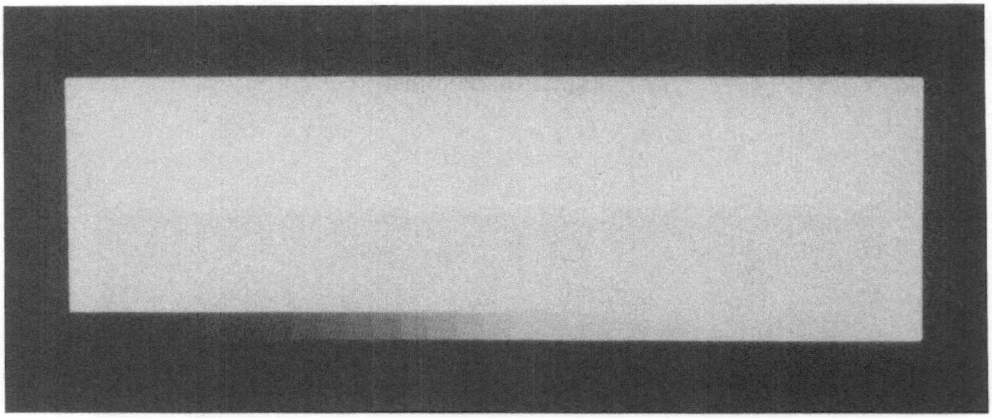

Fig. 8 Zoom-in of the bottom side of the anti-aliased robot arm

7. CONCLUSIONS AND FUTURE WORK

We have presented a new, simple and powerful anti-aliasing algorithm, handling properly the traditional problems encountered when performing anti-aliasing in conjunction with Z-buffers. The Virtual Camera Oversampling method has no memory overhead (as we utilize the memory occupied by the depth buffer) and it can deliver high quality images when needed. It doesn't require complicated filtering and it inherently incorporates a parallel implementation.

Future research around the method could be in a number of fields. First of all, as the algorithm spends most of its time in the clipping of polygons from the pixel list against the pixel window and with scan conversion in the pxp sub-pixel screen, a number of optimizations can be expected there. These optimizations can come from lowering the number of polygons that have to be processed locally and from speeding up the relevant processes themselves. Another issue worth studying is to find out how the algorithm behaves when a low sub-pixel resolution p in combination with a more complex filtering technique should be used. Finally, the "small virtual camera" might have applications in other areas than anti-aliasing. We currently are investigating how to use the small virtual camera in (1) a hybrid ray tracing/Z-buffering algorithm and (2) a (soft)-shadowing method.

REFERENCES

Carpenter L (1984) The A-buffer, an Antialiased Hidden Surface Method. Computer Graphics 18(3) : 103-108

Catmull E (1974) A subdivision algorithm for computer display of curved surfaces, Ph.D. Thesis University of Utah. Salt Lake City

Catmull E (1978) A Hidden Surface Algorithm with Antialiasing. Computer Graphics 12(3) : 6-11

Crow F (1977) The Aliasing Problem in Computer Generated Shaded Images. Comm. ACM : 799 - 805

Crow F (1981) A Comparision of Antialiasing Techniques. IEEE CG&A 1(1) : 40-48

Duff T (1985) Compositing 3D Rendered Images. Computer Graphics 19(3) : 41-43

Fujimoto A (1984) A 3D Graphics Display System with Depth Buffer and Pipeline Processor. IEEE CG&A 4(6) : 11-23

Ghazanfarpour D (1989) Antialaising by Succesive Steps with a Z-buffer. In: Hansmann W, Hopgood FRA, Strasser W (eds) Eurographics 89, pp 235-244

Lobb RJ (1987) Antialiasing of Polygons with a Weighted Filter. In: Kunii TL (ed) Computer Graphics 87. Springer, Tokyo Berlin Heidelberg New York London Paris, pp 107-127

MAGNENAT-THALMANN N, THALMANN D (1986) Special Cinematographic Effects with Virtual Movie Cameras. IEEE CG&A 6(4) : 43-50

Frank Van Reeth is a research assistant at the Limburg University Center and a member of the research staff at the Applied Computer Science Laboratory in the same university. He obtained his Master's Degree in Computer Science in 1987 at the Free University of Brussels, Belgium. His current research interests include 3D rendering, animation, parallel processing and visual programming environments. He is member of CGS.
Address: Applied Computer Science Laboratory, Limburg University Center, B3610 Diepenbeek, Belgium

Rudi Welter is currently a member of the research staff at the Applied Computer Science Laboratory, Limburg University Center, Diepenbeek, Belgium. He obtained his Master's Degree in Computer Science in 1989 at the Free University of Brussels, Belgium. His most recent research has been concerned with computer graphics and parallelism.
Address: Applied Computer Science Laboratory, Limburg University Center, B3610 Diepenbeek, Belgium

Eddy Flerackers is currently full Professor of Computer Science at the Limburg University Center, Belgium. He studied Physics at the University of Louvain, Belgium. He received his PhD in Physics in 1980 at the Free University of Brussels with a thesis on nuclear structure calculations. Since 1987 he is Director of the Applied Computer Science Laboratory at the Limburg University Center. He is also promotor of a Governmental project for the introduction of computers and computer science in education. His research interests include computer graphics, 3D computer animation, scientific visualisation, simulation and programming environments.
Address: Applied Computer Science Laboratory, Limburg University Center, B3610 Diepenbeek, Belgium

Algorithms for Clipping Quadratic Arcs

V. Skala

Abstract

New algorithms for 2D quadratic arcs clipping against convex and non-convex windows are presented. Algorithms do not use parametric equations for the arcs description. Therefore only a square root function is needed. The algorithms require information how edges of the given window are oriented. The design, implementation and verification is the first step toward to the quadratic arcs usage in computer graphics as new basic primitives. The presented algorithms have not been published in a literature known to the author.

Keywords: Clipping, Quadratic Arcs, Algorithms

1. Introduction

Clipping is a very important part of all graphics packages. There are many efficient algorithms as Cyrus (1979), Liang (1984), Nicholl (1987) for clipping lines against convex windows or for clipping lines against a window with holes and with the non - linear boundaries, see van Vyk (1984), Skala (1989). Unfortunately no one known algorithm deals with a problem how to clip circles or ellipses against a window. This problem is a fundamental one if we want to introduce quadratic arcs as a basic primitive for 2D graphics packages. The below described algorithms enable to clip general quadratic curves or arcs against convex or non-convex window.

2. Clipping by a Convex Area

Provided a convex area is given by its vertices in the clockwise order and a oriented circle given by its center $\mathbf{x}_w$ and radius r. We want to find those parts of the given circle which lie inside of the given convex window. For easier understanding the following notation will be used:

$\mathbf{x}_w$ circle center $\qquad$ $\mathbf{x}_i$ polygon vertex

$\mathbf{x}_k$ instead of $\mathbf{x}_{i+1}$; the + is meant as modulo n addition

$\mathbf{s}_i = \mathbf{x}_i - \mathbf{x}_{i-1}$ $\mathbf{s}_k = \mathbf{x}_k - \mathbf{x}_i$

${}^i\mathbf{s}_w = \mathbf{x}_w - \mathbf{x}_i$

$\mathbf{t} = [\, y_w - y \,,\, x - x_w \,]^T$ tangent vector at the point (x,y)

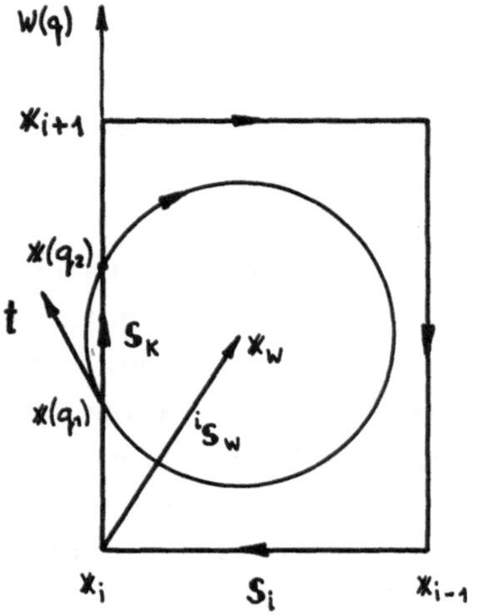

Figure 2.1.

To solve this problem it is necessary to find intersection points of the circle and line w(q) on which the window border lies, i.e. to solve the following equations:

$$\mathbf{x}(q) = \mathbf{x}_i + (\mathbf{x}_{i+1} - \mathbf{x}_i) \cdot q$$

$$(x - x_w)^2 + (y - y_w)^2 - r^2 = 0$$

Solving these equations with regard to the variable q the quadratic equation

$$a\,q^2 + b\,q + c = 0$$

will be obtained, where:

$$a = |\,\mathbf{s}_k\,|^2 \qquad b = -2\,{}^i\mathbf{s}_w^T \cdot \mathbf{s}_k \qquad c = |\,{}^i\mathbf{s}_w|^2 - r^2$$

In the case that the line w(q) intersects or touches the given circle two solutions are generally obtained that are not necessarily different:

$$q_{1,2} = \frac{-b \pm \sqrt{b^2 - 4ac}}{2a}$$

The obtained values q_1, q_2 must be ordered so that $q_1 \leqslant q_2$. For the next processing only points for $q \in \langle 0\,,\,1\,)$ will be considered. Of course some possible situations must be distinguished, see fig. 2.2. For a general case, when $q_1 \neq q_2$, the tangent vector $\mathbf{t}_1$ always points out of the given window while the tangent vector $\mathbf{t}_2$ always points into the given window, see fig. 2.2. cases a and d. Therefore the circular arc $\mathbf{x}(q_1)\ \mathbf{x}(q_2)$ cannot be considered for further processing. The cases b and c from fig. 2.2. are a little bit more complicated because the tangent vectors $\mathbf{t}_1$ and $\mathbf{t}_2$ are equal. It means that it is necessary to introduce some special attributes for the case b while case c must be handled as no intersection points with the given edge have been found. In the case b only one point $\mathbf{x}(q_1)$ will be drawn. But there are still some special cases to be solved, see fig. 2.3.

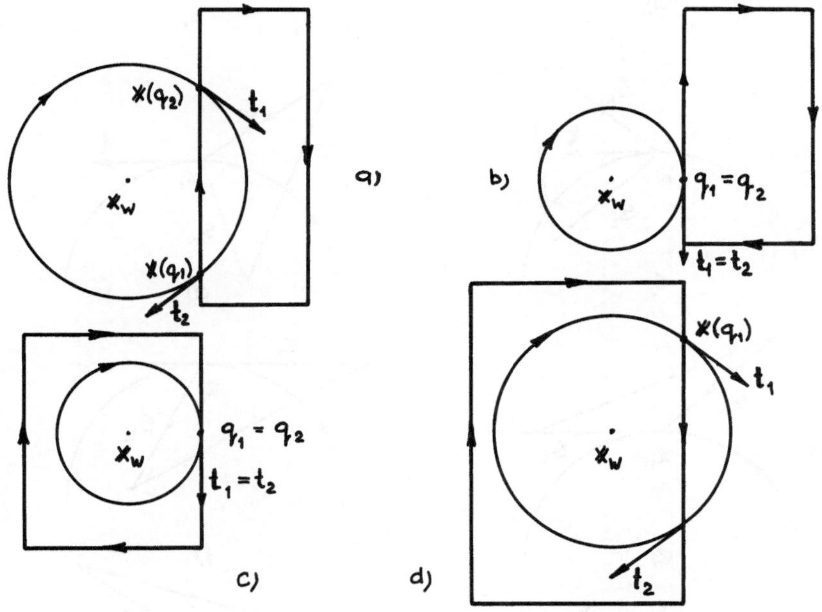

Figure 2.2.

It can be observed that it is necessary to introduce the additional attribute that would determine exactly whether the tangent vector $\mathbf{t}$ points into or out from the clipping window.

First of all it is necessary to distinguish between cases a , b and c , d in fig. 2.3., i.e. to distinguish between "touch" and "pass" types. Now let us examine the result of the cross product of the $\mathbf{s}_i$, $\mathbf{s}_k$ and $\mathbf{t}$ vectors, see fig. 2.3., in order to distinguish some cases, see table 2.1.

It is obvious that in the special cases when both cross products are equal to zero it is necessary to distinguish some very special cases, i.e. cases i and j, if we want to handle them. In case i the "touch" point can be omitted because the whole circle will be processed or drawn, while in case j the double point $\mathbf{x}_i$ with attribute showing that only this point ought to be displayed must be generated. The worst case is shown in fig. 3.3. case k. If the point $\mathbf{x}_a$ is processed then the type "pass" is obtained and similarly for $\mathbf{x}_b$. If $\mathbf{x}_a$ is processed first then the sequence $\mathbf{x}_a\mathbf{x}_b$ is obtained.

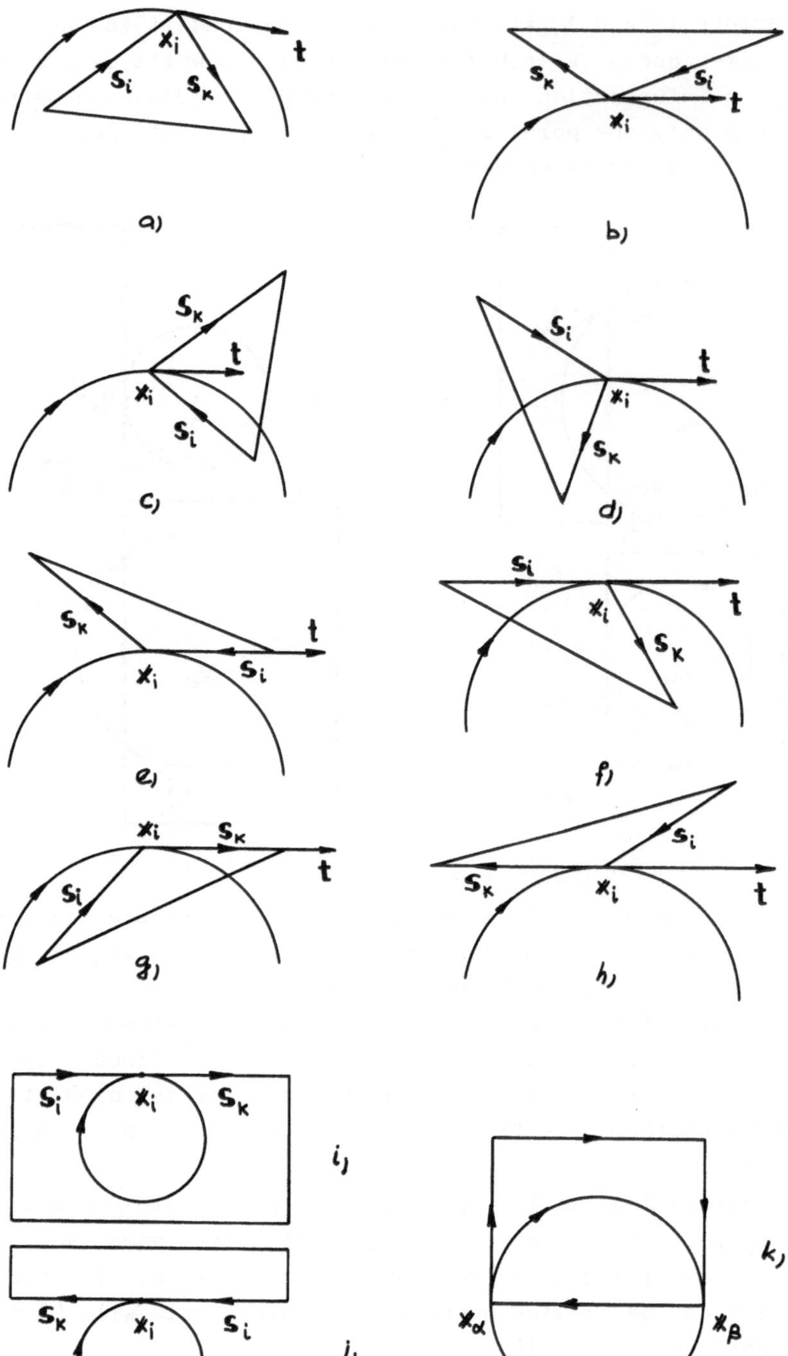

Figure 2.3.

The sequence $x_b x_a$ is obtained if x_b is processed first. It is evident that only the $x_a x_b$ arc should be drawn. It means that an information about the direction for drawing arc is missing. Therefore it is necessary to use the the direction of the tangent vector for determining the attribute.

$[t \times s_i]_z$	$[t \times s_k]_z$	case	type	sequence
> 0	< 0	a	touch	$x_{i_+}\ x_{i_-}$
< 0	> 0	b	touch	$x_{i_+}\ x_{i_-}$
> 0	> 0	c	pass	x_{i_+}
< 0	< 0	d	pass	x_{i_-}
$= 0$	> 0	e	touch	$x_{i_+}\ x_{i_-}$
$= 0$	< 0	f	pass	x_{i_+}
> 0	$= 0$	g	pass	x_{i_-}
< 0	$= 0$	h	touch	$x_{i_+}\ x_{i_-}$
$= 0$	$= 0$	i,j	touch	not allowed

where + - denotes the sign of the cross product z coordinate

Table 2.1.

The whole algorithm can be described by a sequence in PASCAL-type style, see algorithm 2.1.

```
k := 0;  i := n - 1;
flag := true; (*circle is not intersected*)
while k < n do
begin
  s_k := x_k - x_i; (*needed for intersection solution*)
  if COMPUTE VALUES (q_1,q_2)
  then (*intersection points exist and q_1 <= q_2*)
  begin flag:=false;
    if q_1 = 0 then (*pass / touch type*)
    begin
      s_i := x_i - x_{i-1}; t := [ y_w - y_i , x_i - x_w ]^T;
      a := [ t x s_i]_z;
      b := [ t x s_k]_z;
      if ( a > 0 ) or ( b >= 0 ) then GENERATE( x_i ,'+ ');
      if ( a <= 0 ) or ( b < 0 ) then GENERATE( x_i ,'- ');
```

```
      if q2 ∈ ( 0 , 1 ) then
        begin t := [ yw - y(q2) , x(q2) - xw ]T;
              GENERATE ( x(q2) , sign ([ t x sk ]z) )
              (*for circle, ellipse the attribute is always '+' *)
        end
    end
    else
      if q1 ≠ q2 then
      begin
        for j:=1 to 2 do
          if qj ∈ ( 0 , 1 ) then
           begin t := [ yw - y(qj) , x(qj) - xw ]T;
                 GENERATE ( x(qj) , sign ([ t x sk ]z) )
           end
      end
      else
        (*if q1 = q2 then*)
        begin t := [ yw - y(q1) , x(q1) - xw ]T;
          if t . sk < 0 then
          begin
            GENERATE ( x(q1) , '+ ' );
            GENERATE ( x(q1) , '- ' )
          end
        end;
  i := k; k := k + 1
end (*while*);
```

Algorithm 2.1.

As a result of the algorithm 2.1. sequences shown in table 2.1. are obtained. Now it is necessary to draw appropriate arcs that are inside of the given window. This process can be described by the algorithm 2.2.

```
m:= No of intersections;
if m ≠ 0 then
begin i := 2;
  while i < m-1 do
  begin if xi = xi+1 then PLOT ( xi )
        else if attr(xi) = '+ ' then DRAW ARC ( xi , xi+1 , r )
                                 else DRAW ARC ( xi-1 , xi , r );
        i := i + 2
  end
end (*while*)
```

else (*it is necessary to distinguish cases when the*)
    (*circle is totally inside or outside of the given window*)
  if flag **then**
  begin flag:=**true**;
    i := n - 1; k := 0;
    while (k < n) **and** flag **do**
    begin $\mathbf{s}_k := \mathbf{x}_k - \mathbf{x}_i$;
      ${}^{i}\mathbf{s}_w := \mathbf{x}_w - \mathbf{x}_i$;
      if $[\mathbf{s}_k \times {}^{i}\mathbf{s}_w]_z$ 0 **then** flag := **false**;
      i := k; k := k + 1
    end;
    if flag **then** DRAW CIRCLE ($\mathbf{x}_w$, r)
  end

Algorithm 2.2.

The shown algorithm deals with a principal solution and does not particularly care of the arithmetic precision, see Middleditch(1989). In some cases special criteria must be used in order to respect a limited precision.

The presented algorithm is capable to handle all kinds of quadratic arcs. In the general case the quadratic arc must be given as:

$$f(\mathbf{x}) = \mathbf{x}^T \mathbf{A} \mathbf{x} = 0$$

so that

$$f(\mathbf{x}_w) = \mathbf{x}_w^T \mathbf{A} \mathbf{x}_w < 0$$

where $\mathbf{x}_w$ is the center. The tangent vector **t** must be computed as:

$$\mathbf{t} = [\, f_y \, , \, -f_x \,]^T$$

where f_x, f_y are partial derivations of the function f and the matrix **A** represents a general quadratic curve.

3. Non-convex window clipping

So far presented algorithms have solved the quadratic arc clipping by the convex polygon. But some types of applications do require clipping by non-convex window. Of course, it is possible to split the given non-convex polygon into a set of convex polygons, e.g. Roger (1985).

Provided a non-convex polygon is given by its vertices in the clockwise order. It is also assumed that all vertices have different coordinates, that two edges might have only a point as a common point and that no one vertex lies on an edge. Contrary to the previous problem, an arc can intersect the polygon edges in a quite different order than would be previously expected, see fig. 3.1. Therefore some additional operations must be expected. A sequence of points together with their attributes

$$\underset{-}{x}_1 \ , \ \ldots \ , \ \underset{+}{x}_{10}$$

is not the sequence that we need for the further processing, because only the following arcs should be drawn:

$$\underset{+}{x}_4\underset{-}{x}_1 \quad \underset{+}{x}_{10}\underset{-}{x}_9 \quad \underset{+}{x}_8\underset{-}{x}_7 \quad \underset{+}{x}_6\underset{-}{x}_5 \quad \underset{+}{x}_2\underset{-}{x}_3$$

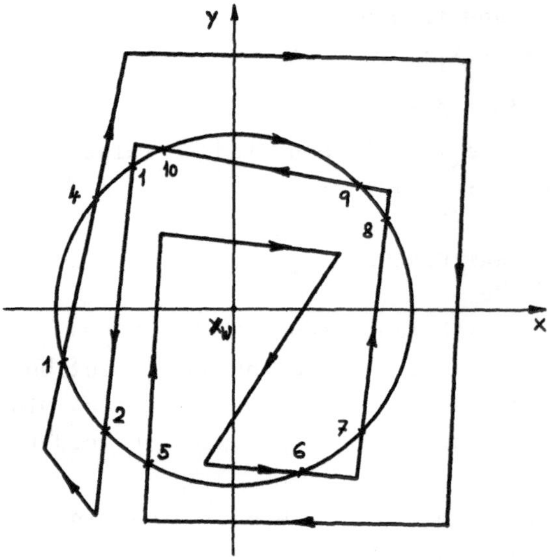

Figure 3.1.

It is obvious that some kind of sort process must be employed in order to get the shown sequence. It is necessary to find a convenient criterion for sorting. The obtained points must be split into two sets according to y value of the given points, i.e.:

$$W_1 = \{ x_j \} \qquad y_j \geq y_w \qquad \text{for all } j$$
$$W_2 = \{ x_j \} \qquad y_j < y_w \qquad \text{for all } j$$

In the case shown in fig. 3.1. two sets W_1 and W_2 are obtained so that:

$$W_1 = \{ \ \underset{-}{x}_1 \ , \ \underset{+}{x}_4 \ , \ \underset{+}{x}_8 \ , \ \underset{-}{x}_9 \ , \ \underset{+}{x}_{10} \ \}$$
$$W_2 = \{ \ \underset{+}{x}_2 \ , \ \underset{-}{x}_3 \ , \ \underset{-}{x}_5 \ , \ \underset{+}{x}_6 \ , \ \underset{-}{x}_7 \ \}$$

Both sets W_1 and W_2 must be sorted according to x value of the given points. The set W_2 must be sorted according to the descending x value of the given points. Then the ordered sets are:

$$W_1 = \{ \ \underset{+}{x}_4 \ , \ \underset{-}{x}_1 \ , \ \underset{+}{x}_{10} \ , \ \underset{-}{x}_9 \ , \ \underset{+}{x}_8 \ \}$$
$$W_2 = \{ \ \underset{-}{x}_7 \ , \ \underset{+}{x}_6 \ , \ \underset{-}{x}_5 \ , \ \underset{+}{x}_2 \ , \ \underset{-}{x}_3 \ \}$$

If a new set W is created as:

$$W = W_1 \ \textbf{cont} \ W_2$$

where **cont** is the concatenation operator, i.e.:

$$W = \{ \ \underset{+}{x}_4 \ , \ \underset{-}{x}_1 \ , \ \underset{+}{x}_{10} \ , \ \underset{-}{x}_9 \ , \ \underset{+}{x}_8 \ , \ \underset{-}{x}_7 \ , \ \underset{+}{x}_6 \ , \ \underset{-}{x}_5 \ , \ \underset{+}{x}_2 \ , \ \underset{-}{x}_3 \ \}$$

then the required parts of the given quadratic curves are obtained.

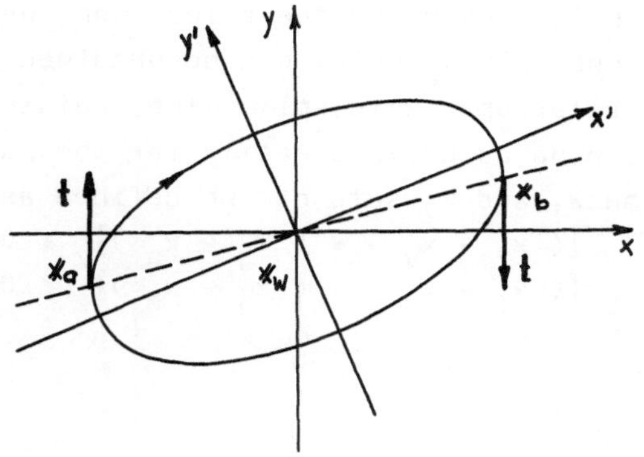

Figure 3.2.

If ellipses are considered the situation is a little bit more complicated. The above shown criterion for splitting the intersection points into two sets W_1 , W_2 is not the right one, see fig.3.2., because the arc for y y_w is not generally a function of x coordinate. It means that two points $\mathbf{x}_a$, $\mathbf{x}_b$ must be found so that the tangent vectors of the given ellipse are collinear with y axis in these points. The points can be found as a solution of the quadratic equations:

$$\mathbf{x}^T \mathbf{A} \ \mathbf{x} = 0 \quad \text{and} \quad \frac{\partial}{\partial y} \mathbf{x}^T \mathbf{A} \ \mathbf{x} = 0$$

Because the $\mathbf{x}_a$, $\mathbf{x}_b$ points are obtained it is possible to split the intersection points of the ellipse and the given window into two sets W_1 and W_2 so that:

$$W_1 = \{ \mathbf{x}_j \} \quad [(\mathbf{x}_b - \mathbf{x}_a) \times (\mathbf{x}_j - \mathbf{x}_a)]_z \geq 0 \quad \text{for all } j$$
$$W_2 = \{ \mathbf{x}_j \} \quad [(\mathbf{x}_b - \mathbf{x}_a) \times (\mathbf{x}_j - \mathbf{x}_a)]_z < 0 \quad \text{for all } j$$

The sets W_1 and W_2 must be sorted again and a new set W must be created in the same way.

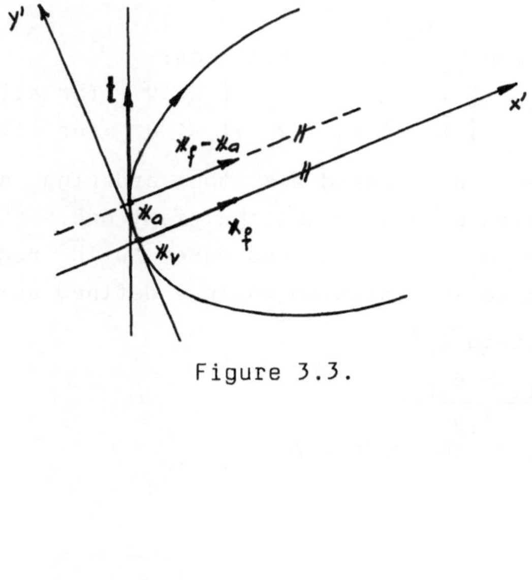

Figure 3.3.

If a parabolic arc is considered the rules can be derived in a similar way. But because only $\mathbf{x}_a$ point can be obtained it is necessary to find a different criterion how to split the obtained points. The points $\mathbf{x}_v$, $\mathbf{x}_f$, $\mathbf{x}_a$ can be determined easily for the parabolic arc, see fig.3.3. Therefore the W_1 and W_2 sets can be defined as follows:

$$W_1 = \{ \mathbf{x}_j \} \quad [(\mathbf{x}_f - \mathbf{x}_v) \times (\mathbf{x}_j - \mathbf{x}_a)]_z \geqslant 0 \quad \text{for all } j$$
$$W_2 = \{ \mathbf{x}_j \} \quad [(\mathbf{x}_f - \mathbf{x}_v) \times (\mathbf{x}_j - \mathbf{x}_a)]_z < 0 \quad \text{for all } j$$

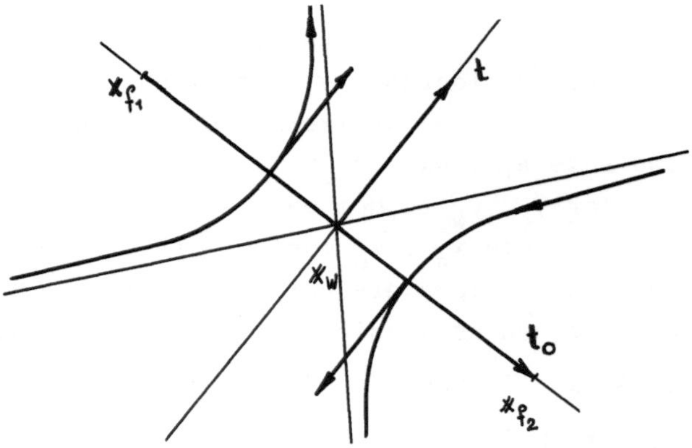

Figure 3.4.

If a hyperbolic arc is considered the main problem is to find a convenient criterion for splitting the intersection points into two sets W_1 and W_2 and the proper criterion for the ordering these sets, see fig. 3.4. In this case it is necessary to find a vector $\mathbf{t}_0$ as:

$$\mathbf{t}_0 = \mathbf{x}_{f_2} - \mathbf{x}_{f_1}$$

and a vector $\mathbf{t}$ orthogonal to the vector $\mathbf{t}_0$ as:

$$\mathbf{t} = [\, t_y \; , \; - t_x \,]^T$$

Now the the sets W_1 and W_2 can be defined as:

$$W_1 = \{ \mathbf{x}_j \} \quad [\, \mathbf{t} \times (\mathbf{x}_j - \mathbf{x}_w)]_z \geqslant 0 \quad \text{for all } j$$
$$W_2 = \{ \mathbf{x}_j \} \quad [\, \mathbf{t} \times (\mathbf{x}_j - \mathbf{x}_w)]_z < 0 \quad \text{for all } j$$

The sets W_1 and W_2 must be ordered and the ordering according to x coordinate of the given points is not the right one.

The sets W_1 and W_2 must be reordered with regard to x or y coordinate according to the rotation angle a defined as:

$$2\alpha = \text{arccotg} \; (\; \xi \;)$$

where $$\xi = \frac{a_{11} - a_{22}}{2 \; a_{12}}$$

and a_{ij} are elements of the matrix $\mathbf{A}$.

It means that if

$\xi \geq 0$ then the y coordinate must be used for sorting

$\xi < 0$ then the x coordinate must be used for sorting

To display the obtained arc segments a similar algorithm to the algorithm 2.2. can be used.

For the non-convex window clipping a special test "point in polygon" must be employed if no intersection point is found in order to distinguish between cases when ellipse or circle lie totally inside or outside of the given window (in the other cases the whole curve must intersect the window boundary if they are inside of the window).

4. Arcs Clipping

The developed algorithms shown above were derived for quadratic arcs clipping, i.e. for clipping the whole circles, ellipsis etc. But for many applications it is necessary to clip only a part of the whole quadratic curve. It means that it is necessary to have an algorithm for computing the **set intersection** of two arcs, if the arcs are given by their end-points and radius. Fig. 4.1. shows the basic possible situations. It is assumed that arcs are clockwise ordered

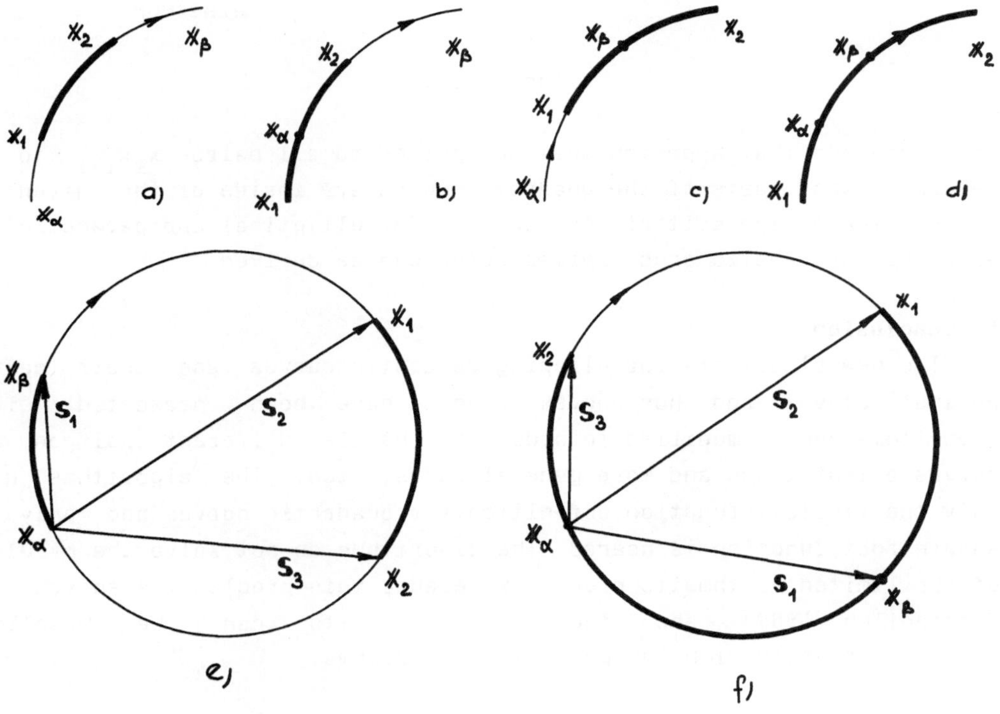

Figure 4.1.

From the previous algorithm the set W is obtained as a set of tuples (start and end points):

$$W = \{ \langle x_i , x_{i+1} \rangle \}$$

For clipping the arcs it is necessary to compute the **set intersection** of the given arc **x x** and computed arc $x_i x_{i+1}$ as

$$x_\alpha x_\beta \cap x_i x_{i+1}$$

The following notation is used to explain criteria for the **set intersection** evaluation (i=1 for simplicity):

$$s_1 = x_\beta - x_\alpha \qquad s_2 = x_1 - x_\alpha \qquad s_3 = x_2 - x_\alpha$$

The results of the **set intersection** of two arcs are given in table 4.1.

$[s_1 \times s_2]_z$	$[s_1 \times s_3]_z$	case	generated sequence
> 0	> 0	a	**if** $[s_2 \times s_3]_z > 0$ **then** $x_\alpha x_2$ & $x_1 x_\beta$
		f	**else** $x_1 x_2$
< 0	> 0	b	$x_\alpha x_2$
> 0	< 0	c	$x_1 x_\beta$
< 0	< 0	d	**if** $[s_2 \times s_3]_z > 0$ **then** $x_\alpha x_\beta$
		e	**else** NOP

Table 4.1.

It is obvious that approach must be applied to all pairs $x_i x_{i+1}$ to determine what parts of the quadratic curve are inside of the given window. The design criteria can be used for elliptical and parabolic arcs. For hyperbolic arcs similar rules can be derived.

5. Conclusion

The new algorithms for clipping quadratic curves and their parts against convex and non-convex window have been presented. The algorithms can be modified in order to handle different polygon or curves orientations and more general cases, too. The algorithms use only the implicit function definition for quadratic curves and only a square root function is needed. The algorithms do not solve the problem of the limited arithmetic precision because this problem was solved by Middleditch (1989) and the shown results can be applied straightforwardly with the presented algorithms.

6. Acknowledgment

The author would like to express his thanks to Mr.K.Karlovec for the help, interest and comments, to the students of Computer Graphics course that stimulated this work, to the members of Computer Graphics and CAD System Group for their invaluable comments, help and understanding, to Teplotechna Comp. (Czechoslovakia) for the support that enabled to finish this work successfully.

7. References

Cyrus,M., Beck,J. (1979) Generalized Two- and Three Dimensional Clipping, Computers Graphics, Vol.3., No.1., pp.23-28

Earnshaw,R.A., Wyvill,B.(Ed.) (1989) New Advances in Computer Graphics, Proceedings Computer Graphics International´89, Leeds, Springer Verlag

Foley,J.D., van Dam A. (1982) Fundamentals of Interactive Computer Graphics, Addison Wesley, Reading, Mass.

Hansmann,W., Hopgood,F.R.A., Strasser,W.(Ed.) (1989) Conference Proceedings EUROGRAPHICS´90, Hamburg 1989, North Holland

Kilgour,A.C. (1987) Unifying Vector and Polygon Algorithms for Scan Conversion and Clipping, Report CSC 87/R7, Computer Sci. Dept., Univ. of Glasgow

Liang,Y.D., Barsky,B.A. (1984) An Analysis and Algorithms for Polygon Clipping, CACM 26, No.11, pp.868-876

Liang, Y.D., Barsky, B.A. (1984) A New Concept and Method for Line Clipping, ACM Trans. on Graphics, Vol.3., No.1., pp.1-22

Middleditch,A.E., Stacay,T.W., Tor,S.B. (1989) Intersection Algorithms for Lines and Circles, ACM Trans. on Graphics, Vol.8.,No.1., pp.25-40

Newman,W.M., Sproull, R.F.(1979) Principles of Interactive Computer Graphics, 2nd ed., McGraw Hill, New York

Nicholl, T.M., Lee, D.T., Nicoll, R.A., (1987) An Efficient New Algorithm for 2D Line Clipping: Its Development and analysis, ACM Computer Graphics, Vol.21.,No.4., pp.253-262

Rodgers,D.F. (1985) Procedural Elements for Computer Graphics, pp.151-152, McGraw Hill

Skala,V. (1989) Algorithms for 2D Line Clipping, inProceedings Computer Graphics International´89 (Ed.Earnshaw), pp.121-128

Skala,V. (1989) Algorithms for 2D Line Clipping, in Conference Proceedings EUROGRAPHICS´90 (Ed. Hansmann), pp.355-366

van Vyk,C.J. (1984) Clipping to the Boundary of a Circular Arcs Polygon, Computer Vision, Graphics and Image Processing, Vol.25., No.3.

Václav Skala is an associate professor of Computer Science at the Institute of Technology. He studied Technical Cybernetics and Computer Science at the Institute of Technology in Plzeň. In 1975 he took a master degree in Computer Science followed by a PhD degree specializing in Database Systems at the Technical University in Prague. From 1975 to 1981 he worked as a researcher. In 1978 he studied Computer Science at MEI in Moscow and in the academic year 1983-84 Computer Graphics at Brunel University in London. In 1981 he took up position as a senior lecturer at the Cybernetics Department teaching Programming Languages, Database Systems and Computer Graphics. He is a member of Czechoslovak Scientific and Technology Society, Society of Cybernetics, chairman of Computer Graphics and CAD Systems Group within Czechoslovak Academy of Sciences. He is a member of EUROGRAPHICS and member of Editorial Board of the Computer Graphics Forum journal.

Address: Václav Skala, Dept. of Informatics and Computer Science,
Institute of Technology, Box 314, 306 14 Plzeň, Czechoslovakia

On the Generation of Points Lying on Origin-Centered Conics

L. R. Neal

ABSTRACT

An earlier paper has presented efficient serial algorithms for generating points on circles based on an extension to an original algorithm attributed to Minsky. This paper summarises that work and generalises the ideas to produce an efficient serial algorithm that generates points that lie on arcs of any ellipse or hyperbola. A general theory for the production of points on these origin-centered conics by both serial and parallel algorithms is provided.

KEY WORDS

serial and parallel algorithms, point generation, ellipses, hyperbolas, origin-centered conics

1 INTRODUCTION

Points on the circumference of a circle can be generated by the following parallel matrix form:

$$\begin{pmatrix} x_{n+1} \\ y_{n+1} \end{pmatrix} = \begin{pmatrix} \cos \phi & -\sin \phi \\ \sin \phi & \cos \phi \end{pmatrix} \begin{pmatrix} x_n \\ y_n \end{pmatrix} \qquad (1)$$

In algorithmic form, the new point x_{n+1}, y_{n+1} can be found using the following code:

$$x_{n+1} := c * x_n - s * y_n$$
$$y_{n+1} := s * x_n + c * y_n \qquad (2)$$

The values for $c = \cos \phi$ and $s = \sin \phi$ can be calculated outside the inner loop. If the value of ϕ needs to vary during the generation, the above form requires a re-computation of a square root for each change. Such a situation arises when a machine tool is taken through acceleration and decelaration phases. Several suggestions have been made to improve the efficiency of the parallel computation [Middleditch 1973 (see form (25) in this paper); Hong Tao 1985]. Alternatively, Blinn (1987) surveys many different approaches to the problem of drawing a circle.

Various suggestions have been made for algorithms of a serial form that approximate to the parallel form of (1). The first, scheme (3), is attributed to Minsky (Sutherland 1963) and produces points on a fat ellipse set at 45° degrees to the major axis. This algorithm uses the parameter $e = 2\sin \phi/2$.

```
x := x - e * y
y := y + e * x
plot point  [x,y]                              (3)
```

A recent approach (Neal and Pitteway 1990) considers an extension of the Minsky algorithm. The serial form (4) produces the points $x_n = r \cos n\phi$ and $y_n = (r/A) \sin n\phi$, starting from (r, 0). Thus points on the ellipse $x^2 + A^2 y^2 = r^2$ are generated where $A = \sqrt{(1 - e^2/4)} = \cos \phi/2$.

```
x := x - e/2 * y
y := y +  e  * x
x := x - e/2 * y
plot  [x,y]                                    (4)
```

The maximum departure from the intended circle is no more than $re^2/8$ (compared with $re/2$ for the Minsky ellipse), exactly matching the error that is inherent in a polygonal approximation of n vectors.

Another form of the extended algorithm produces points that lie exactly on a circle.

```
x := x - t * y
y := y + s * x
x := x - t * y
plot [x,y]                                  (5)
```

where $t = \tan \phi/2$ and $s = \sin \phi = 2t/(1+t^2)$.

This paper generalises algorithms (4) and (5) to the form (6) below, and shows how this form can be used to generate points that lie exactly on any origin-centered conic of the form $x^2 \pm A^2 y^2 = r^2$.

Parameters for the algorithm can be chosen so that the conic can be rotated to any orientation about the coordinate axes. Also a simple transformation of the output will locate the centre of the conic at any finite point.

```
x := x + α * y
y := y + β * x
x := x + γ * y
plot [x,y]                                  (6)
```

The parameters α, β, γ are connected to the length of arc drawn, the eccentricity and the orientation of the conic produced as discussed in section 8.

2 PARALLEL FORMS

In this section we discuss the general theory concerning points generated by the iteration $P_{n+1} = T\ P_n$ where T is a 2 x 2 matrix. For any circle or rectangular hyperbola C, we can generate points P_{n+1} on the circumference by a recurrence relation of the form:

$$P_{n+1} = G\,P_n = G^{n+1}\,P_0 \quad \text{where}$$

$$G = \begin{pmatrix} c & -s \\ s & c \end{pmatrix} \quad (7) \qquad \text{or} \qquad G = \begin{pmatrix} c' & s' \\ s' & c' \end{pmatrix} \quad (8)$$

for a circle — for a rectangular hyperbola

where, in (8), $c' = \text{ch}\,\phi$ and $s' = \text{sh}\,\phi$.

Cohen (1970) discusses the relationship between the generating matrices for a circle, C, and for any conic, E, obtainable from it by a transformation, i.e. E = T C. Let the generating matrix of the conic be H. Then the points S_{n+1} are related to the points P_{n+1} on the rectangular conic by:

$$S_{n+1} = T\,P_{n+1} = T\,G\,P_n = T\,G\,T^{-1}\,S_n = H\,S_n \qquad (9)$$

Thus the matrix H is similar to the matrix G and must have the same value for its determinant of 1.

Let us now consider a conic, $x^2 \pm A^2 y^2 = r^2$, centered at the origin and oriented parallel to the axes. If this conic is rotated through an angle ψ to the coordinate axes then the transformation matrix will be:

$$\begin{pmatrix} \cos\psi & -\sin\psi/A \\ \sin\psi & \cos\psi/A \end{pmatrix} \qquad (10)$$

Using this expression for T in (9), leads to the following generalised forms for the parallel generation of points.

Firstly, for an ellipse

$$S_{n+1} = \begin{pmatrix} c+s[A-1/A]\sin\psi\cos\psi & -s[A\cos^2\psi+\sin^2\psi/A] \\ s[\cos^2\psi/A+A\sin^2\psi] & c-s[A-1/A]\sin\psi\cos\psi \end{pmatrix} S_n \quad (11)$$

And, secondly, for a hyperbola

$$S'_{n+1} = \begin{pmatrix} c'-s'[A+1/A]\sin\psi\cos\psi & s'[A\cos^2\psi-\sin^2\psi/A] \\ s'[\cos^2\psi/A-A\sin^2\psi] & c'+s'[A+1/A]\sin\psi\cos\psi \end{pmatrix} S'_n \quad (12)$$

We can simplify the above by introducing the variables

$A2 = (A - 1/A)/2$ and $A3 = (A + 1/A)/2$

and letting $Q = A2 \sin 2\psi$, $R = A2 \cos 2\psi$

$Q' = A3 \sin 2\psi$, $R' = A3 \cos 2\psi$ (13)

This gives

$$S_{n+1} = \begin{pmatrix} c+sQ & -s[A3 + R] \\ s[A3 - R] & c-sQ \end{pmatrix} S_n \quad (14)$$

$$S'_{n+1} = \begin{pmatrix} c'-s'Q' & s'[R' + A2] \\ s'[R' - A2] & c'+s'Q' \end{pmatrix} S'_n \quad (15)$$

We note that the determinant of both these matrices is one.

3 SERIAL FORMS

Let us now consider the generalised serial form of (6)

$x := x + \alpha * y$

$y := y + \beta * x$

$x := x + \gamma * y$

The corresponding parallel form is:

$$\begin{pmatrix} x_{n+1} \\ y_{n+1} \end{pmatrix} = \begin{pmatrix} 1+\beta\gamma & \alpha+\gamma+\alpha\beta\gamma \\ \beta & 1+\alpha\beta \end{pmatrix} \begin{pmatrix} x_n \\ y_n \end{pmatrix} \quad (16)$$

Again, we note that the determinant here is one.

If we equate coefficients between (14) and (16) for the ellipse and between (15) and (16) for the hyperbola, we arrive at the following expressions for the parameters in terms of ψ and A.

$$\begin{aligned} \beta &= s[A3 - R] & \beta' &= s'[R' - A2] \\ \alpha\beta &= c - 1 - s\,Q & \alpha'\beta' &= c' - 1 + s'\,Q' \\ \beta\gamma &= c - 1 + s\,Q & \beta'\gamma' &= c' - 1 - s'\,Q' \end{aligned} \qquad (17)$$

Letting $P = A3 - R$ and $P' = R' - A2$, and using $t = \tan ø/2$ and $t' = \text{th}\, ø/2$, we have $(c - 1)/s = -t$ and $(c' - 1)/s' = t'$.

Thus for an ellipse we have

$$\beta = s\,P = P*2t/(1+t^2), \quad \alpha = -(t+Q)/P, \quad \gamma = -(t-Q)/P \qquad (18)$$

and for a hyperbola

$$\beta' = s'\,P' = P'*2t'/(1-t'^2), \quad \alpha' = (t'+Q')/P', \quad \gamma' = (t'-Q')/P' \qquad (19)$$

4 THE CONIC ALGORITHM

The following algorithm will generate n points on any arc of the conic $x^2 \pm A^2 y^2 = r^2$ whose axes have been rotated through an angle ψ around the coordinate axes.
The starting point of the arc is (x_0, y_0), and its length is determined by the angle beta that is subtended by radii from the origin to the starting and finishing points of the arc. If the value of A is positive then an ellipse will be drawn; if A is negative a hyperbola.

```
ARCELLIPSE(n, A , x0, y0, beta, ψ )
    t := beta/(2*n);  x  :=  x0;  y  :=  y0;  I := 0
    sa := SGN(A);  A := ABS(A)
    A1 := 1/A;  A2 := (A-A1)/2;  A3 := A1+A2
    d := 2*ψ ; S := sin(d); C := cos(d)
    if  sa = 1  then  P := A3 - A2*C; Q := A2*S
                else  P := A3*C - A2; Q := A3*S
    P1 = 1/P
```

```
        α := -sa*(t+Q)*P1
        γ := -sa*(t-Q)*P1
        β := (2t*P)/(1+sa*t²)
LOOP:       x := x + α * y
            y := y + β * x
            x := x + γ * y
            plot [x,y]

        I := I + 1
        if I=n then stop
        goto LOOP                                    (20)
```

We note that the conic can be centered at the point (x_c, y_c) by outputting points $(x - x_c, y - y_c)$ instead of (x, y).

5 THE GENERAL ELLIPSE WITH NO ROTATION

For no rotation of the ellipse axes with respect to the coordinate axes the angle ψ will be zero and the transformation matrix T will be

$$T = \begin{pmatrix} 1 & 0 \\ 0 & 1/A \end{pmatrix} \tag{21}$$

This gives a general ellipse, $x^2 + A^2 y^2 = r^2$ and the following simplified form for the algorithm where $P = 1/A$, $Q = 0$, and $\alpha = \gamma = -tA$ and $\beta = 2t/[(1+t^2)*A]$.

```
x := x - t A * y
y := y + 2t/[(1 + t²)*A] * x
x := x - t A * y
plot [x,y]                                    (22)
```

6 SPECIAL CASES

Taking $A = 1$ in (22), gives the circle generator (5).

Taking $A = \sqrt{(1 - e^2/4)} = \cos ø/2$, where
$\alpha = \gamma = e/2 = \sin ø/2$ and $\beta = e = 2\sin ø/2$, gives the ellipse (4).

Taking $A = (1 - e^2/4) / (1 - e^2/8)$, where

$\alpha = \gamma = -At = (e/2) /(1 - e^2/8))$

and $\beta = 2t/[(1+t^2)*A] = \sin ø/A = e(1 - e^2/8)$,

gives the following scheme, where $D := (1 - e^2/8)$

```
x := x - (e/2)/D * y
y := y + e*D * x
x := x - (e/2)/D * y
plot [x,y]                                   (23)
```

The parallel form for this is:

$$\begin{pmatrix} x_{n+1} \\ y_{n+1} \end{pmatrix} = \begin{pmatrix} 1-e^2/2 & -e(1-e^2/4)/(1-e^2/8) \\ e(1-e^2/8) & 1-e^2/2 \end{pmatrix} \begin{pmatrix} x_n \\ y_n \end{pmatrix} \qquad (24)$$

An approximation (25) to this form is given in Middleditch and Paul, (1973). The approximation causes the curve to spiral slightly as its determinant no longer has the value one.

$$\begin{pmatrix} x_{n+1} \\ y_{n+1} \end{pmatrix} = \begin{pmatrix} 1-e^2/2 & -e(1-e^2/8) \\ e(1-e^2/8) & 1-e^2/2 \end{pmatrix} \begin{pmatrix} x_n \\ y_n \end{pmatrix} \qquad (25)$$

For the Minsky ellipse, we take the rotation angle to 45° and $A = t + \sqrt{(1 + t^2)}$, gives $\alpha = -2\sin ø/2 = -e$, $\beta = 2\sin ø/2 = e$ and $\gamma = 0$. This produces the original Minsky algorithm (3).

7 THE CONTROL PARAMETERS

The basic parameters for the algorithm are
the number of points (n) to be generated on the arc,
the eccentricity parameter (A) for the required ellipse,
the starting point (x_0, y_0) of the ellipse,
the angle (beta) subtended by the arc,
and the angle of rotation required (ψ).

beta is the angle between the radii of the starting and finishing points of the required arc. Thus nrø = r beta and ø = beta/n, where n is the number of points around the arc. For a large number of points generated, we can take t = beta/(2*n), since ø will be small. To draw a completed curve we take $t = \pi/n$. Also, in this case, the efficiency can be improved by taking s = 2t in the calculation of β.

For no rotation, we have $\psi = 0$ giving Q = 0 in (18) and (19). This means $\alpha = \gamma = tA$ = A * beta/(2*n) and these parameters will be proportional to angle of arc required.

For a rotation we note the symmetric relationships present; α and γ being derived, respectively, by subtracting and adding Q/P to and from the value -t/P.

8 THE PARABOLA

The general conic algorithm presented above generates points around the centre of each conic. This centre may, however, be moved a finite distance to situate the conic anywhere in the plane. As the centre of a parabola is at infinity, the above approach does not lend itself to producing points on that curve.

9 SUMMARY

This paper presents an efficient serial algorithm that can generate points exactly placed on circles, ellipses and hyperbolas. For each curve, the length of the arc drawn can be specified. The algorithm can be used for a curve with general orientation and position.

REFERENCES

Neal LR and Pitteway MLV (1990) The efficient generation of control points on paths of machine tools describing circular arcs. In: Proceedings of 22nd International Symposium on Automotive Technology and Automation, Florence, May 1990.

Hong Tao (1985) A high precision digital differential analyzer for circle generation. From: Earnshaw R (ed) Fundamental algorithms for computer graphics. Springer-Verlag, NATO ASI Series, Vol. F17, 239-256

Blinn JF (1987) How many ways can you draw a circle? From: Computer Graphics and Animation, Aug 1987, 39-45

Middleditch AE and Paul FR (1973) Dynamic performance of a numerical control system for multi-axis contouring machine tools. Presented at the winter annual meeting of The American Society of Mechanical Engineers, 1973

Cohen D (1970) On linear difference curves. In: Parslow R and Elliot Green R (ed) Advanced computer graphics, economics, techniques and applications. Plenum Press, 1143-1177

Sutherland IE (1963) Sketchpad - A man machine graphical communication system. MIT Lincoln Laboratory Technical Report No. 296, Jan 1963.

Dr L.R. Neal has been Director of both Undergraduate and Postgraduate Studies in the Computer Science Department at Brunel University. He published widely in Medical Informatics in the seventies and more recently has taken an interest in fundamental graphics algorithms.
He is a fellow of the British Computer Society and a past member of the Council of the Soceity.

Address: Department of Computer Science, Brunel University, Uxbridge, Middlesex, England UB83PH.

ZigPocket: On the Computational Geometry of Zigzag Pocket Machining

Martin Held

We present a detailed description of a zigzag algorithm for $2\frac{1}{2}D$ pocket machining. The algorithm is capable of computing the zigzag tool path for any multiply-connected planar area ('pocket') bounded by a wide class of curves. Drilled holes and similar cavities can be handled automatically. The underlying geometric principles are simple enough for allowing the algorithm to be included in a CNC.

Keywords: pocketing, tool path generation, zigzag, computational geometry, geometric reasoning, CAD/CAM.

1 INTRODUCTION

1.1 Preface

Numerically controlled machining of mechanical parts requires various working processes such as $2\frac{1}{2}D$ milling of arbitrarily shaped planar areas ('pockets'). Usually, mechanical parts produced from a billet are manufactured by applying a $2\frac{1}{2}D$ roughing process followed by $3D$–$5D$ finishing. Particularly in applications arising at aircraft industries, the resulting $2D$ pockets may have quite complex shapes. Hence, efficiently handling these $2D$ milling tasks constitutes a prerequisite for enabling a profitable production process.

During the last decades, the major goal has been the development of NC programming languages that offer some macros for generating NC code for commonly used milling operations such as pocketing (see Lallande *et al* [L*84] for an example of an advanced APT-like pocketing statement). These pocketing routines are often either limited by severe restrictions concerning the permitted shape of the input area or by poor capabilities of supplying the user with technological data.

Surprisingly, there are only few serious investigations of basic tool path generation for pocketing, although there exist a lot of publications on $3D$–$5D$ machining. The academic research community seems to entirely concentrate on advanced multi-axis NC machining and NC verification. We refer to the following authors whose publications are closely related to our own work on pocketing: Grayer [Gra75], Persson [Per78], Bruckner [Bru82], Preiss and Kaplansky [PK85,Pre89], Wang *et al* [W*87], Hansen and Arbab [HA88], Guyder [Guy89]. Besides, a growing number of researchers concentrates on higher-level path planning by means of solid models, cf. Choi, Barash and Anderson [C*84,CB85], Parkinson [Par86], Yeh and Ying [YY88].

During the last years we have tried to close this gap by building up a workbench of fast algorithms for different pocket machining applications. In the beginning pursuing an 'offset curve milling' strategy[1] – i.e. milling along curves that are equidistant to the contour (cf. Fig. 1) – we have

[1]Sometimes, this strategy is also called 'contour-parallel milling' as opposed to 'zigzag milling', i.e. direction-parallel milling. In [W*87], these strategies are called 'window frame milling' and 'stair case milling', respectively.

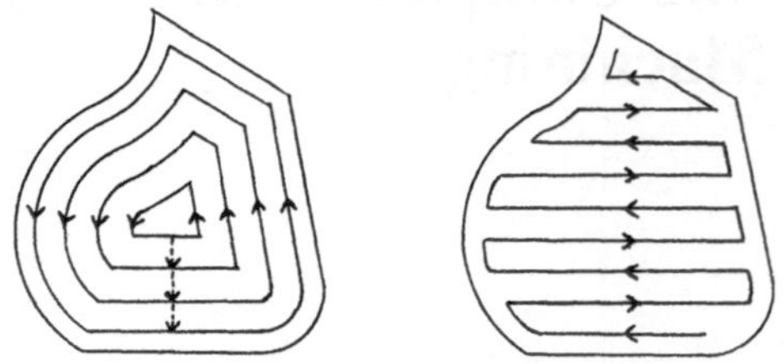

Figure 1: Offset and Zigzag Milling

designed the program package GEOPOCKET for fully automatically computing the tool path. Results have been documented in [Hel88,Hel89]. Here, we present the underlying ideas of our package ZIGPOCKET.

1.2 Informal Problem Specification

In this paper we restrict to techniques for zigzag (and zig[2]) milling. Similar to our previous work, we deal with the following problem, cf. Fig. 2:

Pocket Machining Problem:

Given :

- boundary contours enclosing a multiply-connected planar area ('pocket'),
- boundary contours of drilled holes and similar cavities,
- technological objectives and constraints.

Determine :

- a suitable tool size,
- an optimal inclination of the tool path,
- a correct (and with respect to some criteria hopefully optimal) tool path for machining the pocket according to the technological requirements,
- pre-drill positions for tool plunges.

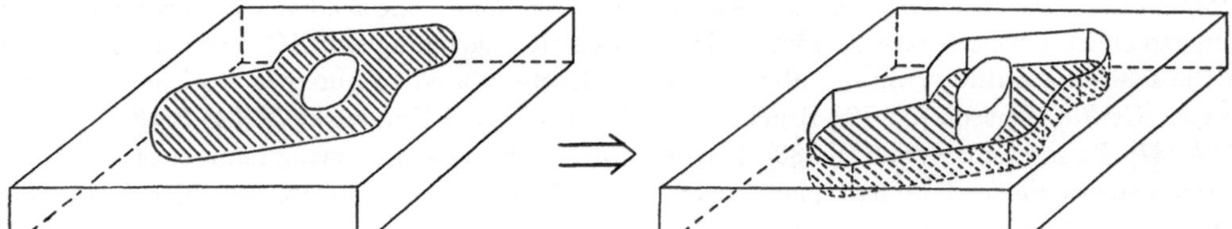

Figure 2: Pocket Machining

Throughout this paper, we will assume that all island contours are contained in the interior of one border contour and that no pairwise intersection of the contours does occur. In order to have

[2]Zig milling is derived from zigzag milling by replacing the sequence of left-to-right and right-to-left movements by a sequence of left-to-right (right-to-left, respectively) and air movements.

well-defined interiors we assume that all contours are oriented and closed curves and do not have coinciding edges or points of self-intersection. In mathematical terms this means that we deal with multiply-connected planar areas bounded by simple contours.

Seen from a theoretical point of view, there is no need to restrict to non-overlapping islands. Indeed, this is only done for the sake of a simplified description of our method and we will point out the slight modifications which would have to be made in order to handle this more general situation. But as the geometric input for ZIGPOCKET will most probably come from a CAD system it should not constitute a big problem to ensure non-intersecting boundary contours.

We do not explicitly restrict our algorithm to specific types of contour elements (such as straight lines and circular arcs). Rather, the presented scheme is powerful enough to deal with a wide class of curves provided that a 'black box' for computing offset curves, intersections with lines, tangents, local extrema, and points of inflection is available. Observe that no restriction is imposed on the number or global shape of the contours. This is of particular importance when dealing with complex-shaped pockets containing a lot of islands.

Actually, for the sake of programming simplicity, up to now our own implementation ZIGPOCKET only supports contours consisting of straight line segments and circular arcs. Besides achieving computational simplicity this is justified by the fact that most of today's NC machines are only capable of executing linear and circular interpolations. But our scheme is completely prepared for handling general input data resulting from $2\frac{1}{2}$D machining of $3D$ objects possibly bounded by sculptured surfaces. Supposed that NC machines become more powerful in the near future ZIGPOCKET can easily be adapted within its framework by simply exchanging or extending the service routines of the above cited 'black box'.

Nevertheless, we would like to remark that offsetting, for instance, becomes a rather difficult task if curves containing elements other than lines and circular arcs are envolved[3]. Hence, a complex mathematical machinery may be required, cf. Klass [Kla83], Tiller and Hanson [TH84], Hoschek [Hos85], Saeed *et al* [S*88], Farouki and Neff [FN89].

2 BASIC ASPECTS

2.1 Geometrical and Technological Problems of Zigzag Pocketing

Intuitively, there is no significant difference between removing material by means of zigzag machining and colouring pixels by means of polygon filling. Hence, one might be attempted to compute and order the intersections of a horizontal line with the boundary. Obviously, every odd interval could be output as a tool path segment. By incrementing the line's y-level (by a value depending on the requested tool overhang) and repeatedly applying this scheme, the pocket should be machined, cf. Bruckner [Bru82], Wang *et al* [W*87].

This simple scheme will work pretty well for convex polygons; but it must not be applied to pockets of more complex shape due to the following reason: in the case that the horizontal line intersects the boundary in more than two points it would be necessary to lift the tool, move it in the air, and plunge it down for continuing the machining process (cf. Fig. 3).

But, in general, it is not possible to plunge down the tool onto the raw material without having a hole drilled previously. Most probably, an additional production step is needed in order to have holes drilled before milling can take place. Clearly, this undesirable production step contributes to the total manufacturing expenses. Hence, tool retractions should be minimized.

[3]This increase in sophistication is due to the fact that intersection routines for handling more general elements such as cubic splines become more difficult and that these elements are not invariant under offsetting. For instance, the offset of a cubic spline is no longer a cubic spline.

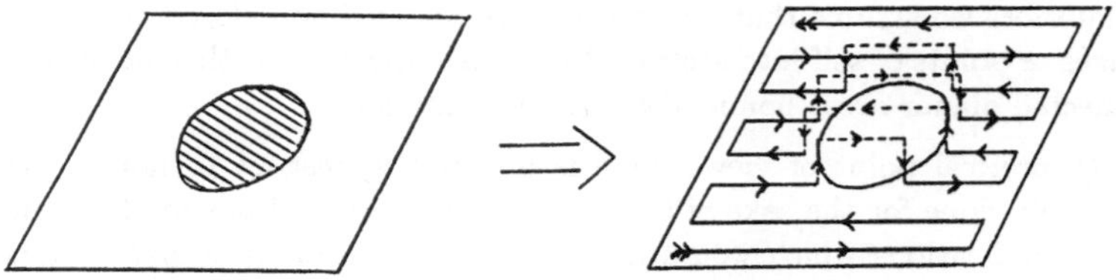

Figure 3: Complex Contours Cause Troubles

Besides locally avoiding to move the tool in the air one should also reflect about some global strategy that would à priori reduce the number of tool retractions. Obviously, the total number of retractions depends on the geometry of the pocket and on the inclination of the zigzag path (and on some additional factors to be investigated). For instance, for the sample contour depicted in Fig. 4, it is reasonable to incline the zigzag path by 90° since this permits to machine the pocket without necessarily moving in the air. In Section 4.1 we will present an algorithm that computes (near) optimum inclinations.

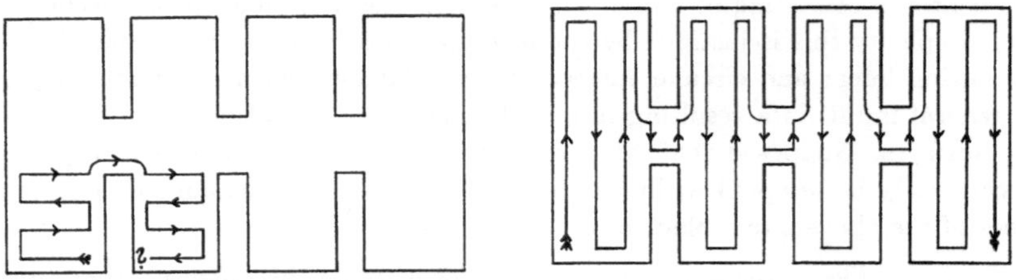

Figure 4: Different Inclinations of the Tool Path

Up to now we have regarded contours as boundaries that must not be crossed by the tool. Indeed, normally a workpiece has to be put to the filings if the border contour or any other avoidance region ('positive' island) has been violated. But there do also exist contours that may (or even should) be crossed. These contours bound so-called 'negative' islands, i.e. regions of the pocket that have a surface lying below the actual machining level (e.g. holes and similar cavities).

As a matter of principle, one can distinguish between two main approaches to handling negative islands:

1. After shrinking the contour of the negative island for some amount (depending on the tool size) one can proceed as in the case of positive islands (i.e. during milling this region is spared).

2. During the computation of the zigzag path the negative islands are not considered but during milling one uses rapid feed for passing over these regions. Of course, using rapid feed will save some amount of machining time (compared to using normal feed during 'machining' these regions).

Since it heavily depends on the geometry of the pocket and on the machining objectives which one of the two strategies is more convenient we have investigated the second approach, too.

The reader should observe that the tool must not cut any material during rapid feed movements. Hence, for carrying out approach 2) it is not sufficient to simply compute the intersections of the zigzag segments with the boundaries of the negative islands and to drive the tool between corresponding intersections thereby using rapid feed. As depicted in Fig. 5, this strategy might cause a lot of regions being damaged.

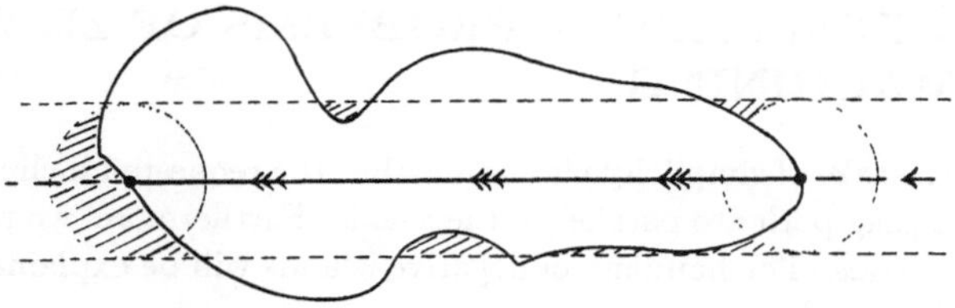

Figure 5: Using Rapid Feed

2.2 Pocketing Features of ZIGPOCKET

Using tools and concepts of Computational Geometry we are able to give efficient solutions to the above stated major geometrical and technological problems of zigzag pocketing. In more detail, we have achieved the following outstanding features which make ZIGPOCKET a versatile tool for the practical machining of complicated mechanical parts:

Advanced Geometrical Features:

- ZIGPOCKET is able to fully automatically compute the tool path for machining any multiply-connected planar area bounded by a wide class of curves. Efficient machining is supported by its capability to use either zigzag or zig[4] machining.
- The powerful geometric concept of our method guarantees that the pocket is 'totally' milled, i.e. that any area which can be cut without violating the boundary will be cut. Furthermore, it is ensured that no contour is damaged no matter how complicated the shape of the pocket is. On the contrary, if requested, it is possible to leave different margins uncut at the border and island contours[5]. Thus, there is no need for a time-consuming and troublesome graphical verification of the tool path.
- ZIGPOCKET executes some additional optimization tasks: As far as possible, retracting the tool is avoided and pocket areas are not machined repeatedly. Due to the first optimization criterion the number of pre-drill positions is minimized.

User Assistance and Advanced Technological Features:

- ZIGPOCKET proposes a (near) optimum inclination of the zigzag path.
- Drilled holes and similar cavities can be automatically handled. By using rapid feed above these regions the cutting time might be considerably reduced. In particular, this is of some importance if moulded workpieces have to be finished.
- Similar to GEOPOCKET, ZIGPOCKET enables a computer-aided tool selection: With respect to a user-specified corner coverage parameter it determines an upper bound for the admissible size of the tool used for contour milling. Furthermore, depending on this selected value and on the minimal width at straits of the pocket contours a suitable size of the tool applied for zigzag milling is suggested. This feature has already been described in [Hel89].

[4]True zigzag machining causes the tool to cut alternately with the spindle direction ('conventional milling'), and against the spindle direction ('climb milling'). Using zig milling it is possible to stick to either conventional or climb milling. This strategy usually ensures a better surface quality.

[5]This excess material is usually cleared away in the finishing step.

3 SOLVING GEOMETRICAL PROBLEMS OF ZIGZAG POCKET MACHINING

For this section, for the sake of simplicity we assume that the requested inclination is zero, i.e. that the segments of the zigzag path are parallel to the x-axis. Furthermore, we restrict to pockets not containing negative islands. The handling of negative islands will be explained in the next section on technological problems of zigzag pocketing.

3.1 Constructing the Mesh

As illustrated in the previous section one has to be careful if the pocket area is not convex. We believe that it is reasonable to build up a data structure providing information on the global shape and connectivity of the pocket. This has been realized by constructing a 'mesh' consisting of the endpoints of the zigzag elements and local extrema of the boundary[6]. As a useful side-effect, performing this preprocessing step separates the computation of the endpoints of the zigzag elements from the actual construction of the tool path. The availability of this mesh will give us the possibility to perform some optimizations of the tool path thereby entirely working on the mesh.

In more detail (cf. Fig. 6), the 'mesh' is a graph-like structure where each node corresponds

- either to an endpoint of a zigzag path element, (i.e. to an intersection of a horizontal (zigzag) line with the outer border contour or with a positive island),
- or to a local minimum (maximum, respectively) of one of these contours with respect to y-coordinates.

Nodes of the first type are called 'original nodes' whereas those of the second type are called 'additional nodes'. Endpoints and extrema form the set of event points.

Define an edge to be 'horizontal' if it interconnects two nodes with equal y-coordinates. Otherwise, call it 'vertical'. Then two nodes of the undirected graph are connected

- by a horizontal edge if both nodes are original nodes, or
- by a vertical edge if their corresponding contour points are located on the same contour and if it is possible to traverse this contour from one point to the second one thereby passing through no other points being nodes of the mesh.

It is easy to realize that each node has at most four outgoing/incoming edges, i.e. the graph is of degree four.

How can we obtain the mesh? This task is efficiently carried out by making use of the plane sweep paradigm[7], cf. Preparata and Shamos' textbook [PS88]. In order to help intuition, imagine that a horizontal line is 'sweeping' across the plane from bottom to top, reporting the sequence of intersection intervals of this line with the boundary, the so-called sweep line status.

It is obvious that no change in the number of intervals will be found without sweeping over a local extremum (with respect to y-coordinates). Hence, only at event points the sweep line status has to be modified. At an event corresponding to a local minimum (maximum, respectively), intervals of the sweep line have to be split up (have to be unified, respectively). In order to draw up the mesh it is sufficient to output the sweep line status at events corresponding to original nodes. Additionally, appropriate vertical edges have to be established.

[6]Obviously, the original boundary has to be offset by an offset equal to or larger than the radius of the tool used for zigzag machining. Otherwise, at the endpoints of the zigzag elements the tool would damage the borders of the pocket.

[7]In the fields of computer graphics this technique is also known as scan-line method.

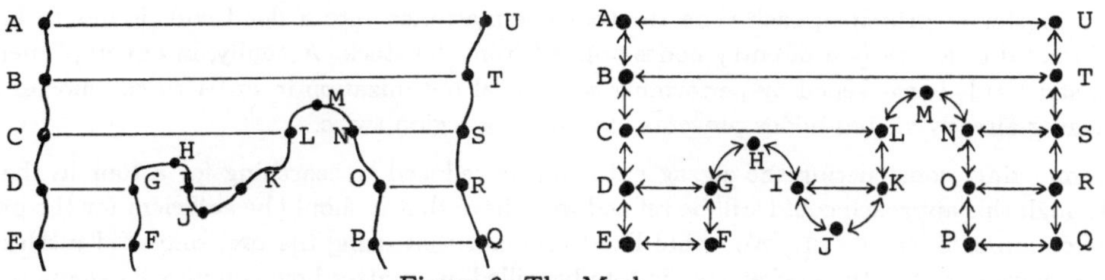

Figure 6: The Mesh

3.2 Computing the Tool Path

Suppose that the mesh is available. Then, constructing the zigzag path corresponds to finding a tour through the graph such that each horizontal edge has been traversed. Jumping between nodes not interconnected by edges (i.e. moving the tool in the air) is permitted but not recommended.

We have not tried to design an algorithm that attempts to solve something like a restricted traveling salesman problem[8] after having assigned a 'weight' or 'cost' to each edge. Instead, we have contented ourselves to guaranteeing that nothing is left uncut that could be cut without violating any contour.

Our goal is realized by stacking areas that cannot immediately be cut, cf. Fig. 7. Assume that the tool has been moved from left to right between two original nodes and is to move upwards. In this case, we proceed as follows in order to get from the actual y-level to the next higher level:

1. If the vertical edge incident at the right node points to an original node then the tool is simply moved upwards along the contour to this new right node.

2. Otherwise, if the vertical edge incident at the right node is pointing to an additional node we keep the tool moving in a right-upwards direction until an original node at the next (higher) level is found.

3. If the vertical edge incident at the left node is pointing to an additional node we search in a left-upwards direction until an original node at the next (higher) level is found. Then the search is continued to the right until the opposite node of the node detected in 1) or 2) is found.

During the search in 2) and 3) intermediate original nodes – representing 'entry' nodes to not yet machined regions – are put on a stack. For the other three directions of movement this algorithm is executed with 'left/right' and 'upwards/downwards' properly exchanged.

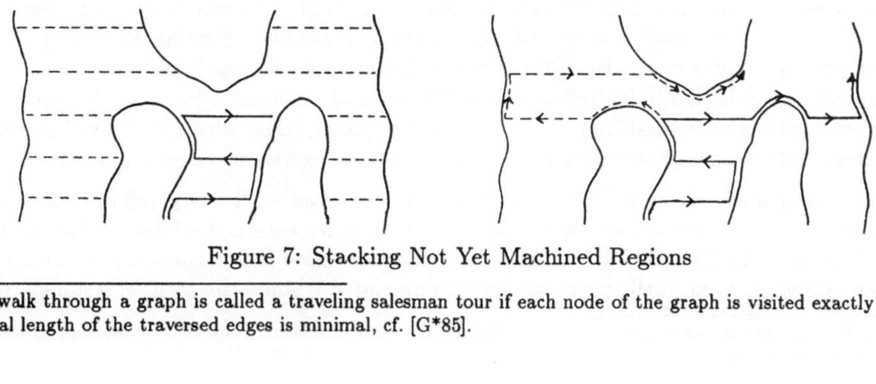

Figure 7: Stacking Not Yet Machined Regions

[8]A walk through a graph is called a traveling salesman tour if each node of the graph is visited exactly once and the total length of the traversed edges is minimal, cf. [G*85].

As a matter of principle, each time the tool has machined into a dead end, it has to be lifted and moved to a new pair of entry nodes popped from the stack. Actually, in our implementation this strict rule is weakened by performing some local optimization in order to get shorter moves. Flagging already visited nodes prevents machining a region twice.

Summarizing, constructing the zigzag path can be reduced to searching for a tour in the mesh. Although this approach could still be refined we believe that it should be sufficient for the practical application of ZIGPOCKET. We would like to remark that using the pre-computed mesh enables us to guarantee that the pocket area is totally milled, no matter how complex its shape is.

4 SOLVING TECHNOLOGICAL PROBLEMS OF ZIGZAG POCKET MACHINING

Up to now we have only been concerned with solving the geometrical problems of zigzag machining. In this section we demonstrate how the important technological features of ZIGPOCKET have been realized.

4.1 Computing a (Near) Optimum Inclination

As it has been motivated by Fig. 4, it is reasonable to compute a suitable inclination of the zigzag path in order to reduce the number of tool retractions. In the following, we explain how ZIGPOCKET determines a (near) optimum inclination.

Recall the plane sweep paradigm used in Section 3.1 for constructing the mesh. Obviously, when sweeping upwards each local minimum splits up the sweep line in two disjoint parts. Similar, when moving downwards the sweep line is splitted by local maxima. Assume that the moving sweep line represents the tool moving on a zigzag path. In this case each extremum corresponds to a region that cannot be milled during the first pass. Hence, minimizing the number of local extrema (by selecting a suitable inclination) means minimizing the number of separated regions, i.e. the number of necessary movements in the air.

Unfortunately, our assumption only holds if 'the size of the tool is significantly smaller than the area to be machined'. This is due to the fact that the tool does not continuously sweep up and down but moves on zigzag lines at discrete y-levels. The smaller the tool is (relative to the size of the pocket), the smaller the distance is between the zigzag lines and the better our assumption of a continous sweep is fulfilled.

How can we compute an inclination such that the number of local extrema is minimized? This task is executed by analyzing 'reflex' chains of contour elements. Before we can carry out our solution we have to make some terms more precise: A point shared by two consecutive contour elements is called a 'vertex'. A vertex is called 'reflex' if the internal angle between its incident elements is $> 180^o$, 'tangential' if the angle equals 180°, and 'convex' otherwise. Similar, assuming that the border contour[9] is counter-clockwise (CCW) oriented and that all island contours are clockwise (CW) oriented, an arc is said to be 'reflex' if it is CW oriented, 'convex' otherwise. A 'reflex' chain of contour elements is generated by picking out a reflex arc or reflex vertex and moving away in both directions (along the contour), until a convex vertex or convex arc is encountered.

Obviously, a particular set of suitable inclinations is associated with every reflex chain. If the chain makes an overall turn $< 180^o$, the recommended angular area is depicted in Fig. 8. If the chain makes a turn equal to 180° this infinite set of recommended inclinations degenerates to one single value. Otherwise, no inclination can be recommended – since one local extremum cannot

[9]Additionally, all contour elements have to be subdivided at points of inflection. Obviously, this task is trivial in the case of lines and circular arcs.

be avoided – but there exists an angular area of forbidden inclinations which would yield two local extrema.

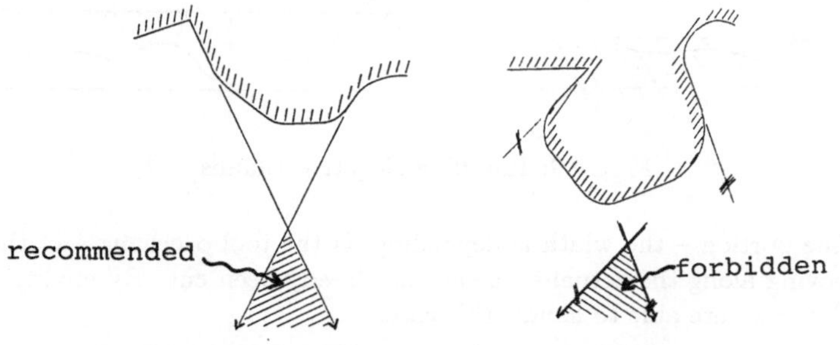

Figure 8: Recommended and Forbidden Inclinations

Applying this method to all reflex chains yields several intervals of recommended and forbidden inclinations. As a matter of principle, it seems to be hard to select a suitable inclination out of this infinite number. This task can be solved by using an algorithm similar to the computation of the measure of a union of intervals, cf. [PS88]. In general, the output of this algorithm will be a number of small intervals of inclinations all yielding the minimal number of local extrema, giving the possibility to impose some further selection criteria.

Unfortunately, in strict mathematical terms this method does not always guarantee to find an inclination actually yielding the minimal number of retractions. Nevertheless, extensive field test have demonstrated that our method works satisfactorily. Results of this heuristic analysis are presented in Section 5.2.

4.2 Handling Negative Islands

Using rapid feed while the tool is cutting raw material may cause a bad surface quality. Even worse, using rapid feed while driving the tool into the raw material most probably results in a tool breakage. Hence, rapid feed may only be used while driving the tool over regions completely lying below the machining level[10]. Consequently, situations as depicted in Fig. 5 have to be avoided.

Assume that the tool is moving with rapid feed within the interior of a negative island. Roughly, avoiding to crash into the raw material can be achieved if care is taken that the center of the tool circle keeps out of a specific region near the contour of the negative island. This region is bounded by offsetting the island contour by an offset $r + \epsilon(r)$, where r denotes the nominal radius of the tool. Usually, it is also requested that the tool should stop some amount $\epsilon(r)$ before the raw material is reached[11].

Hence, a crash can be algorithmically avoided by constructing the offset contour and restricting the usage of rapid feed. But this method still is not optimal. On one hand, it is too weak because the tool circle should have left the raw material at least with its front half before a rapid feed move can be started. Thus, in order to get a satisfying surface quality, each time when leaving the raw material the tool has to be driven for some additional amount of length.

On the other hand, the method is too restrictive if the tool has already been driven along a zigzag segment lying immediately below or above the actual segment. In this case, one has to take into

[10] As a matter of fact, scallop heights tend to be effectively greater than zero, i.e. machined surfaces are not totally smooth. Thus, when moving over already machined regions the tool is usually lifted by a small amount in order to avoid collision.

[11] This security distance depends on the size of the tool. Normally, $\epsilon(r)$ equals about 20% of the tool radius r.

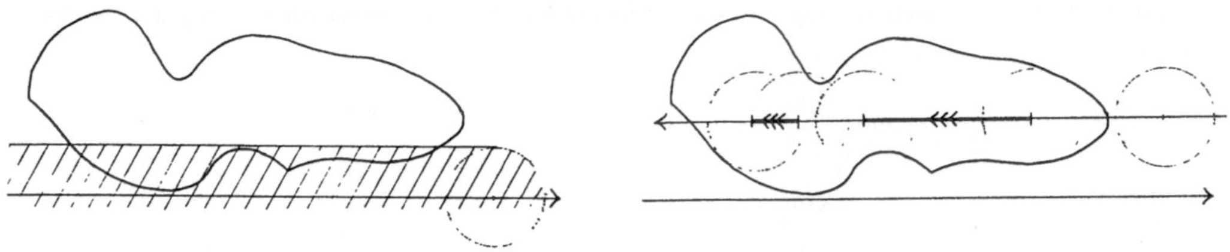

Figure 9: Handling Negative Islands

account that some portion – the width is depending on the tool overhang – of the raw material covered when moving along the actual segment has already been cut. By modifying the method as depicted in Fig. 9 we are able to handle this case.

This general method for handling negative islands has been implemented in ZIGPOCKET. Although the principal idea is rather simple, the algorithm needs a careful implementation in order to ensure correct working even in exceptional cases.

4.3 Avoiding to Drill Unnecessary Holes

By means of selecting a suitable inclination we likely will have achieved a considerable reduction of the number of different areas which have to be milled separately. Nevertheless, as a matter of fact, any minimization of this number is only possible within the limitations imposed by the geometry of the pocket. Hence, in the case of a very complex-shaped pocket one has to expect that it will not be possible to execute zigzag machining in one single pass, without retracting the tool.

In this case holes would have to be pre-drilled. Can this task be avoided? Indeed, this is possible if a small increase of the total path length is acceptable. The key to success is to ensure that any region to be machined is entered from an already machined region. In this case, the tool can be plunged onto this region and moved to the uncut area, cf. Fig. 10. It is easy to understand that by means of our stacking mechanism the unmachined regions are kept in proper order for executing this approach.

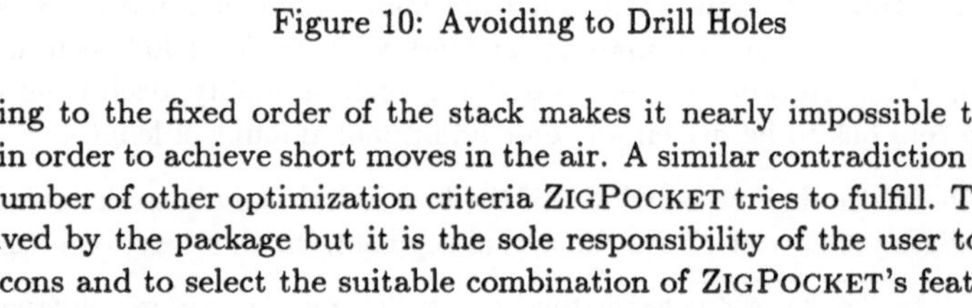

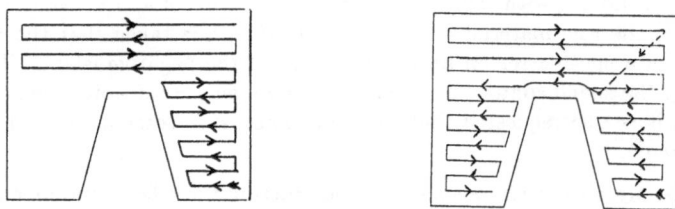

Figure 10: Avoiding to Drill Holes

Clearly, sticking to the fixed order of the stack makes it nearly impossible to perform a global optimization in order to achieve short moves in the air. A similar contradiction may also arise with respect to a number of other optimization criteria ZIGPOCKET tries to fulfill. These contradictions cannot be solved by the package but it is the sole responsibility of the user to carefully consider the pros and cons and to select the suitable combination of ZIGPOCKET's features.

5 PRACTICAL RESULTS AND HEURISTIC ANALYSIS

5.1 The Program Package GEOPOCKET/ZIGPOCKET

Our program package GEOPOCKET/ZIGPOCKET emerged out of diverse work on designing algorithms for pocket machining, starting in the beginning of 1986. The first algorithms have been implemented about one year later. Since this time, we have gradually extended our package up to its current functionality.

GEOPOCKET/ZIGPOCKET have been written in Standard FORTRAN 77 as defind by the ANSI. On one hand, coding the algorithms in FORTRAN ensured the portability of our package and its applicability in industry. On the other hand, it took us a lot of troubles in order to implement recursion and realize advanced data structures. Anyway, the actual implementation of our algorithms provided us with the possibility to carry out a comprehensive heuristic analysis presented in the following paragraphs.

5.2 How Important Is a Suitable Inclination?

Wang *et al* [W*87] have analyzed the relationship between the length of the zigzag path and the selected inclination. Restricting to simple polygons (triangles to heptagons), they have observed that, as a simple rule-of-thumb, the zigzag path should be inclined such that it is parallel to the longest edge of the polygon.

We have designed several programs for producing input data for testing. As a matter of principle, we can confirm the above stated result of [W*87]. In more detail, we can quote our observations as follows:

- For simple polygons (such as triangles, rectangles, pentagons, etc.), there seems to exist a significant correlation between the length and the selected inclination of the zigzag tool path[12].
- This correlation becomes rather apparent for medium-sized[13] tools whereas this effect gradually diminishes with decreasing/increasing size. For large tools it is merely a matter of chance than of any clear rule whether the tool path is long or short for a specific inclination.
- For medium-sized tools, the average variation seems to lie in the range of 4–8 percent. The difference between the best and the worst case is of the order of 10–15 percent of the total length. For small tools, this percentage goes to zero because the total length of the path is increasing much faster than the difference between the longest and shortest path.
- The simple rule-of-thumb does not hold for complex pockets possibly containing some positive islands. Similarly, the correspondence between inclination and path length becomes less significant with increasing number of contour elements, even if the overall shape of the pocket is not varied. For pockets bounded by a lot of arcs it seems to be nearly impossible to predict a reasonable inclination (in order to get minimal tool path length).
- Whereas the impact of the inclination on the resulting length decreases with increasing complexity of the pocket, a strong relationship between the inclination and the number of separate regions (i.e. tool retractions) can be observed. As expected, selecting a suitable inclination becomes the more important, the smaller the tool and the more complex the shape of the pocket is.

[12] In our analysis, a zigzag tool path consists of the actual zigzag path and of the path used for driving the tool along the contour for one time.

[13] We call a tool 'medium-sized' if a NC programmer normally would use a tool of about this size. Clearly, all sizes have to be defined relative to the 'size' of the pocket to be machined.

- Our approach to compute an optimal inclination does not guarantee to achieve a mimimal number of retractions. Nevertheless, for medium-sized (or small-sized) tools a near optimum usually is found, at least. This is of particular importance in the case of complex-shaped pockets where for a human, too, it is difficult to propose a reasonable inclination.

Summarizing, for simple-shaped pockets it is reasonable to select an inclination parallel to one of the longest edges of the input contour. In the case of a more complex shape, our algorithm for selecting an inclination is applicable, producing (near) optimum results.

5.3 Sample Examples of Machined Pockets

Some sample screen simulations of tool paths generated by ZIGPOCKET are depicted in the colour plates of Fig. 11, Fig. 12, and Fig. 13. Throughout the figures, green curves stand for the boundary of a pocket, yellow stands for the boundaries of negative islands, red depicts the tool path, light blue indicates rapid feed moves and dark blue stands for tool moves in the air.

Figure 11 shows different stages of the machining of the RISC-Linz logo. Figure 12 gives a close-up at the handling of a negative island. Figure 13 illustrates the importance of a suitable inclination of the tool path.

6 CONCLUDING REMARKS

6.1 Summary

In the previous sections we have presented an overall description of our pocketing package ZIGPOCKET. Summarizing, we can state its main features as follows: The package is able to handle any multiply-connected pocket area bounded by a wide class of curves. It is possible to deal with positive as well as negative islands. Solving a lot of technological problems, our approach meets most practical requirements of the shop floor.

We have achieved extremely fast computations. For instance, on a VAXstation 2000 running VMS, the CPU-consumption of about 200 tested contour files has always been in the range of 1 to 15 seconds. For most practical applications the CPU-time will be considerably less than 10 seconds.

Furthermore, there is no need for verifying the tool path. Hence, included into a CNC, ZIGPOCKET seems to be a valuable tool for preparing correct geometrical and technological data for the 'total' milling of multiply-connected pockets within reasonably short CPU-time.

6.2 Open Problems

Although ZIGPOCKET is a sophisticated package, it could still be refined. For instance, it would be desirable to handle 'half-open' pockets, i.e. areas that are not bounded by closed contours. Obviously, half-open pockets can easily be simulated by closed pockets. However, this extension is of some importance for practical applications because it enables to carry out some additional possibilities to optimize the tool path.

Furthermore, our work has revealed two issues for theoretical research: Our approach to computing a suitable inclination performs satisfactorily in industrial applications of ZIGPOCKET although it is not guaranteed that an inclination yielding the minimal number of retractions is found. Seen from a theoretical point of view, it would be interesting to design an algorithm that can be proved to solve the requested problem (and not just a very similar one). More generally, it might be interesting to investigate whether an algorithm for computing a traveling salesman tour for our specific mesh can be executed within a polynomial[14] amount of time.

6.3 Acknowledgements

Part of this work has been carried out when the author was with RISC-Linz and has been supported by AIS GmbH (Linz, Austria).

I am grateful to the working group of MTA SZTAKI (Budapest, Hungary) and to H. Persson from SAAB/SCANIA (Linköping, Sweden) for the valuable discussions and exchange of ideas.

When drawing up the final version of this paper I appreciated the helpful comments of H. Mayr from RISC-Linz.

References

[Bru82] L.K. Bruckner. Geometric Algorithms for $2\frac{1}{2}$D Roughing Process of Sculptured Surfaces. In *Proc. Joint Anglo-Hungarian Seminar on Computer-Aided Geometric Design*, Budapest, Hungary, October 1982.

[C*84] B.K. Choi et al. Automatic Recognition of Machined Surfaces from 3*D* Solid Model. *Computer-Aided Design*, 16(2):81–86, March 1984.

[CB85] B.K. Choi and M.M. Barash. STOPP: An Approach to CAD/CAM Integration. *Computer-Aided Design*, 17(4):162–168, May 1985.

[FN89] R.T. Farouki and C.A. Neff. *Some Analytic and Algebraic Properties of Plane Offset Curves.* Technical Report RC-14364, IBM Thomas J. Watson Research Center, Yorktown Heights, NY 10598, USA, January 1989.

[G*85] M Grötschel et al. *Geometric Algorithms and Combinatorial Optimization.* Springer-Verlag, second edition, 1985. (ISBN 3-540-13624-X).

[Gra75] A.R. Grayer. *The Automatic Production of Machined Components Starting from a Stored Geometric Description.* Technical Report 88, CAD Group, Cambridge University, Cambridge CB2 3QX, GB, July 1975.

[Guy89] M.K. Guyder. Automating the Optimization of $2\frac{1}{2}$ Axis Milling. In F. Kimura and A. Rolstadås, editors, *Proc. Computer Applications in Production and Engineering (CAPE'89)*, North Holland, Amsterdam, The Netherlands, Tokyo, Japan, October 1989.

[HA88] A. Hansen and F. Arbab. *An Algorithm for Generating NC Tool Paths for Arbitrarily Shaped Pockets with Islands.* Technical Report CS 88-51, CS Dept., Univ. Southern California, Los Angeles, CA 90089-0782, USA, 1988.

[Hel88] M. Held. Computational Geometry for Pocket Machining. In S.M. Slaby and H. Stachel, editors, *Proc. 3rd Int. Conf. Engineering Graphics & Descriptive Geometry*, pages I:224–231, TU Wien, Austria, July 1988.

[Hel89] M. Held. GeoPocket. A Sophisticated Computational Geometry Solution of Geometrical and Technological Problems Arising from Pocket Machining. In F. Kimura and A. Rolstadås, editors, *Proc. Computer Applications in Production and Engineering (CAPE'89)*,

[14]As a matter of fact, the general decision problem for traveling salesman tours is known to be $\mathcal{NP}$-complete, cf. [G*85].

pages 283–293, North Holland, Amsterdam, The Netherlands, Tokyo, Japan, October 1989.

[Hos85] J. Hoschek. Offset Curves in the Plane. *Computer-Aided Design*, 17(2):77–82, March 1985.

[Kla83] R. Klass. An Offset Spline Approximation for Plane Cubic Splines. *Computer-Aided Design*, 15(5):297–299, 1983.

[L*84] J.B. Lallande et al. Super Pocket. In *Advancing Manufacturing Technologies*, pages 18–29, Long Beach, CA, USA, Numerical Control Society (NCS), March 1984.

[Par86] A. Parkinson. The Use of Solid Models in BUILD as a Database for NC Machining. In J.P. Crestin and J.F. McWaters, editors, *Software for Discrete Manufacturing. Prolamat '85*, pages 175–183, North Holland, Amsterdam, The Netherlands, Paris, France, June 1986.

[Per78] H. Persson. NC Machining of Arbitrarily Shaped Pockets. *Computer-Aided Design*, 10(3):169–174, May 1978.

[PK85] K. Preiss and E. Kaplansky. Automated CNC Milling by Artificial Intelligence Methods. *J. of Manufacturing Systems*, 4(1):51–63, 1985.

[Pre89] K. Preiss. Automated Mill Pocketing Computations. In *Advanced Geometric Modeling for Engineering Applications*, North Holland, Amsterdam, The Netherlands, Berlin, FRG, November 1989.

[PS88] F.P. Preparata and M.I. Shamos. *Computational Geometry - An Introduction. Texts and Monographs in Computer Science*, Springer-Verlag, second edition, October 1988. (ISBN 0-540-96131-3).

[S*88] S.E.O. Saeed et al. *An Efficient 2D Solid Offsetting Algorithm.* Technical Report, Dept. of Mechanical Engineering, University of Leeds, Leeds LS2 9JT, GB, 1988.

[TH84] W. Tiller and E. Hanson. Offsets of Two Dimensional Profiles. *IEEE Computer Graphics & Applications*, 36–46, September 1984.

[W*87] H.-P. Wang et al. On the Efficiency of NC Tool Path Planning for Face Milling Operations. *Trans. of the ASME, J. of Engineering for Industry*, 109(4):370–376, November 1987.

[YY88] Z. Yeh and D.-N. Ying. An Automated Interface Between CAD and CAM. *Computers & Graphics*, 12(3/4):349–357, 1988.

Martin Held studied Technical Mathematics at the University of Linz, Austria, where he received his Dipl.-Ing. degree in 1987. He currently is a staff member and lecturer at the Department of Computer Science, University of Salzburg, Austria. His research interests include geometric modeling, computer-aided (geometric) design, computer graphics, and visualization.
Mr. Held is a member of ACM (and SIGGRAPH), IEEE (and the Computer Society), and the Austrian Computer Graphics Association (ACGA).
Address: University of Salzburg, Dept. of Computer Science, A–5020 Salzburg, Austria.

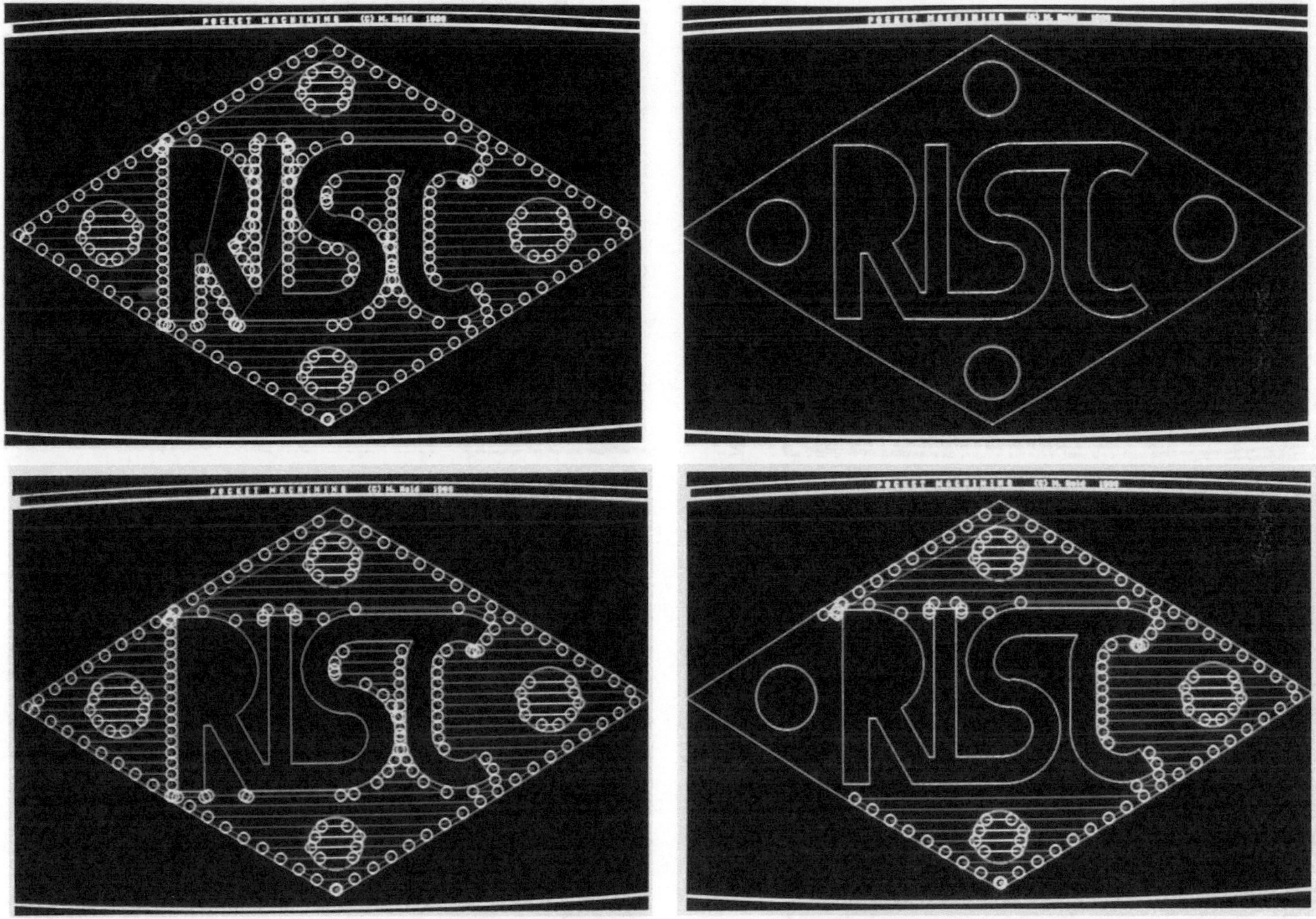

Figure 11: Machining Stages of the RISC Logo

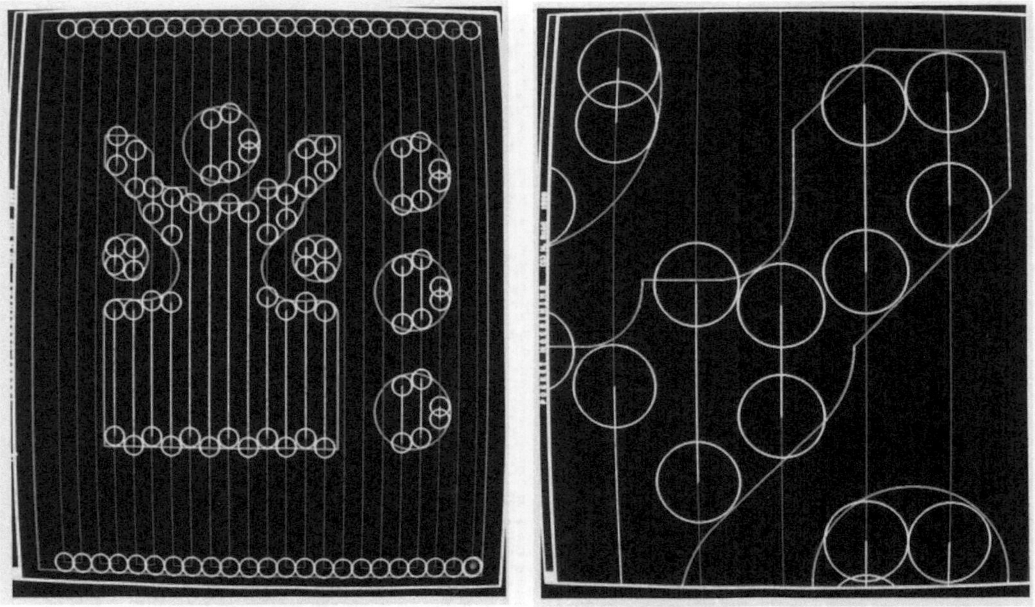

Figure 12: Handling Negative Islands

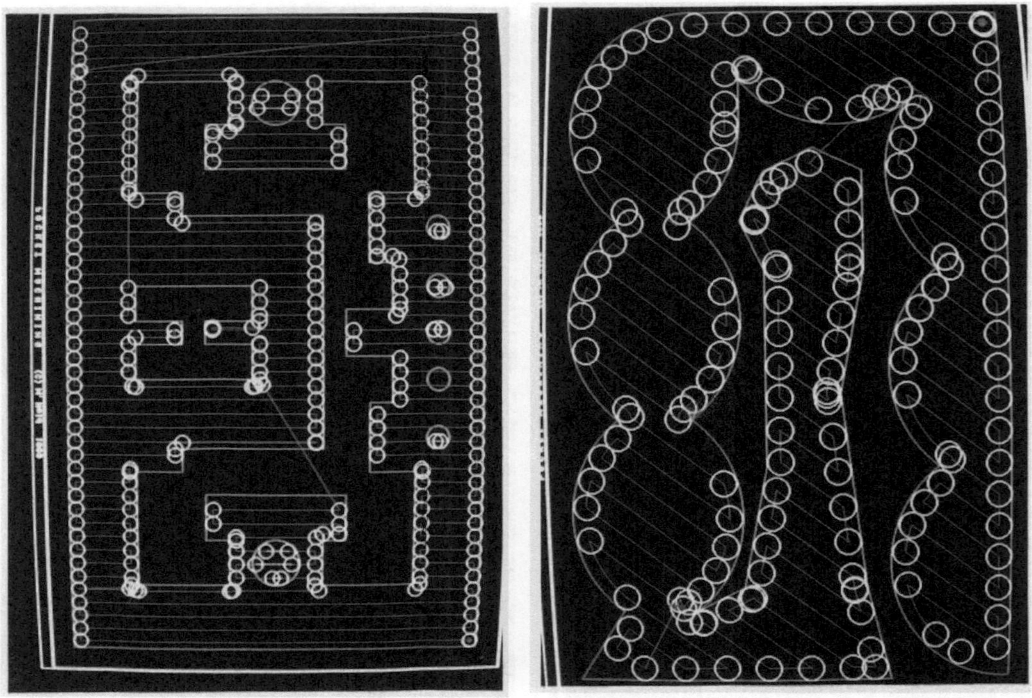

Figure 13: Inclining the Tool Path

Chapter 5
Object-Oriented Graphics

A Frame-Based 3D Graphics System for Kinematic Animation with Constraints

Luis Serra and Tat-Seng Chua

ABSTRACT

This paper describes KICK-3D, a frame-based interactive 3D graphics environment. KICK-3D is aimed at educational and training applications in which users are given the freedom to explore and experiment with 3D structures and even play with their graphics presentation. The frame formalism is used to model the inter-relations (part-of and kinematic with constraints) between the objects, and to use this knowledge to maintain overall consistency of the system. The system is organized around three main classes: a *Solid* class to embody 3D solid objects, a *Camera* class from which to view these objects and a *Utility* class that encompasses the modeling of Lights, Materials and Joints.

Keywords: 3D graphics, frame-based modeling, animation, object-oriented, constraints.

1. INTRODUCTION

While great progress has been made in computer graphics (Earnshaw and Wyvill 1989), and in the development of knowledge-based systems (Fikes and Kehler 1985, Buchanan and Smith 1988), the integration of these two technologies into knowledge-based graphics systems has yet to be fully exploited. Thus, while real-world objects may be realistically modeled, viewed or animated, they are essentially passive, inflexible and require an excessive amount of specifications and controls from the users. There is a need for more powerful techniques, based on common-sense and expert knowledge of graphics to help us model, manipulate and visualize 3D objects. Recent work on 3D graphics systems has pointed towards this direction. Knowledge about computer graphics systems have been used to help creating better images (Thalmann and Thalmann 1986), more realistic animation (Zeltzer 1983), unambiguous presentation (Fiener 1985), and better programming and modeling environments (Sabella and Carlbom 1989, Sheu 1988, Elareef 1986 and Franklin et al. 1986). Other efforts have concentrated towards the use of 3D graphics as a tool to view knowledge-based systems (Richer and Clancey 1985, Fairchild et al. 1988).

This paper describes KICK-3D, a knowledge-based 3D graphics system currently under development at ISS. The emphasis in KICK-3D is towards the use of knowledge to facilitate the viewing, modeling and manipulation of 3D structures. KICK-3D uses the frame formalism (Minsky 1975, Fikes and Kehler 1985) as the basic knowledge representation tool. Our aim is to provide an environment in which users can manipulate 3D solid structures, analyze them and learn about their behaviours. Behaviours can be studied by applying transformations to parts of one structure and observing the effects that they have on other parts of the structure. Such an environment provides a medium for thinking, where users can freely move around the 3D structures and expand their knowledge about the structures. This is in line with the free exploration and association of ideas that hypertext (Halasz 1988) or hypermedia advocates.

The interactivity required for such a learning environment has demanded some sacrifices on the complexity of the modeling. Thus, the initial system presented here only considers kinematic animation with constraints. Realistic or dynamic simulation that takes into account the law of physics (for example Wilhelms 1987, Armstrong and Green 1985, Isaacs and Cohen 1987) will be considered later. This paper deals only with the modeling and maintenance of kinematic constraints during simulation. We will not consider the use of constraint-based modeling approaches for the construction of 3D objects (for example Brüderlin 1986 and Rossignac 1986).

2. BACKGROUND

Reported work on the use knowledge-based technology in a graphics environment has been aimed at facilitating the tasks of modeling and viewing. In terms of viewing, Thalmann and Thalmann (1986) suggest the use of knowledge about computer graphics technology (modeling, lighting, animation) to help creating better images. They describe a Prolog-like extension to their modeling language MIRA to provide a goal-directed approach to specify viewing parameters and animation. Fiener (1985) describes a system where built-in knowledge, encoded in the form of frames, is used to determine the optimal display of a group of objects. Their system will determine not only the list of graphical objects to be displayed, but also their details and positions.

In terms of modeling, Sheu (1986) describes a framework for 3D knowledge based on logic, and discusses how the framework may be used to represent object relationships and constraints consistently. The use of logic in the form of Prolog has also been exploited by Milanese (1988) and Franklin et al. (1986) in an attempt to provide a more flexible and declarative graphics environment for programmers, and by Brudelin to specify geometric constraints. Elareef (1986), on the other hand, introduces the object-oriented flavour system (based on LISP) as a knowledge representation method to facilitate the modeling of complex CAD, where object classes are used to model and manipulate different aspects of solid models and their computations. The use of an object-oriented approach is also described in (Sabella and Carlbom 1989) in reservoir modeling to support multiple representations, rendering, query and computation of reservoir data.

While the above approaches use knowledge representation techniques to provide better modeling environments and presentation, our approach aims at exploiting knowledge about graphics objects not only to facilitate modeling, but also to maintain overall system consistency (Serra 1989). The aspects of modeling considered here are the modeling of hierarchical graphical objects, their inter-relations, and kinematic animation with constraints.

3. A FRAME-BASED APPROACH

A number of systems surveyed have discussed the use of frames (Minsky 1975) as the basic knowledge representation technique. A frame provides a structured representation of an object or a class of objects. Each frame acts as a named collection of information. Each of the items in the collection is known as a slot. Slots have names and contain values. The values can be symbols, lists, names of functions, sets of production rules or links to other frames. Slots may be added, removed or modified dynamically. Inter-object communication is accomplished by sending messages to the frame or to its slots. The slots that contain links (or relations) to other frames allow the creation of networks or hierarchies of frames.

Inherent in the frame formalism is the support for inheritance. Inheritance supplies a frame with an initial set of *implicit* slots and values. These implicit values become default values. Inheritance takes place from class frame to object frame. A class frame provides a prototype description for objects of the same type. Objects thus are said to inherit from the class, becoming *instances* of the class. This idea of definition-by-specialization and default values is a technique that is easy for most domain experts to use.

Another important feature of frames are active values or *demons* which are procedures or collections of production rules attached to slots that are invoked when the slot's value is accessed or stored. Demon mechanism can be used to maintain data integrity by avoiding nonsensical values being added into slots.

Because of our need to model inter-object relationships (such as hierarchies and kinematic constraints), an object-oriented frame-based approach is used. Our decision was based on the way that frames combine explicit declarations with procedural methods attached to these declarations, thus giving a good trade-off between procedural and declarative programming. The frame's inheritance and data encapsulation mechanisms can be used to reduce the complexity of the model, and facilitate the maintenance and extension of the system. The demon mechanism will be used to maintain integrity and consistency of data across the knowledge base. The uniform treatment of data and procedural slots permits the manipulation of knowledge (data slots) and behaviours (procedural slots) about an object in a consistently way. Lastly, production rules may be incorporated with the frame system to support deduction.

4. THE ARCHITECTURE OF KICK-3D

A layered approach is used to develop our frame-based graphics knowledge base environment. The environment is divided into four layers as shown in Figure 1:

1. **Knowledge Representation Layer**: This layer allows a high level description of the frame objects and classes and their inter-dependencies. The descriptions are expressed in a declarative form and are interpreted interactively.

2. **Frame Support Layer**: Below the knowledge representation layer lies the basic frame layer. The frame layer, in the form of a frame language, interprets the knowledge base and channels its requests towards the system resources.

3. **System Support Layer**: This is the system kernel layer, basically handled by the operating system. It consists of the file system and the library of graphics and other system routines which drive the underlying hardware. The graphics package that we used here is the SiliconGraphics Graphics Library (SGGL) - a set of routines that support geometrical as well as graphical transformations, such as projections, I/O interaction, hidden surface removal, lighting and material models (SiliconGraphics 1984).

4. Finally the **Hardware Layer** controls the I/O devices which include the graphics display, mouse and keyboard. Our hardware platform is based on the Silicon 4D/210 GTX workstation. A powerful graphics workstation like this is essential to deliver the real-time interaction and the realism that a learning environment should have. The immediate feed-

back ensures the sustained attention of the user as well as a fast cycle of action-response to his inputs.

This layered approach separates the graphics library or system dependent details from the high-level modeling of solid objects. This has allowed us to develop the same knowledge base on different hardware and libraries, such as the Apollo DN580 (our initial platform) and the SiliconGraphics 4D series, with minor modifications to the knowledge representation layer.

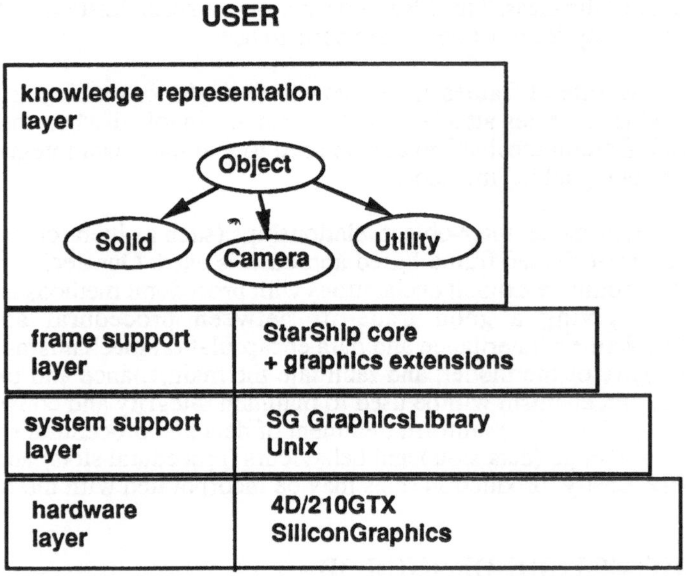

Figure 1: The Architecture of KICK-3D

The philosophy underlying the design of KICK-3D has been the transfer of control from the system layer (the SGGL graphics library) to the knowledge representation layer. This is achieved by: (1) extending the frame language with objects that interface to the system support layer, thus hiding the low level requirements of graphics library from the users. The users can then concentrate on modeling the relations and functionalities of the 3D objects; and, (2) constructing high level object description at the knowledge representation layer. The following sections describe the details of how this is done.

5. THE FRAME SUPPORT LAYER

The frame language we have chosen as the implementation language for the graphics knowledge base is Starship, developed at ISS by Loo (1989). Starship is an interactive and interpretive language. It provides abstractions for the construction and manipulation of complex data structures. Starship is designed to be object-oriented. Data types are organized as objects and objects belong to classes. Objects receive messages and execute methods. In Starship, there is no centralized language parser; each individual object is responsible for interpreting and despatching their own messages. Starship supports the access-oriented paradigm (demon) and implements frames entirely with them. Starship is written in C.

Starship is designed to be a general knowledge representation language such as the SRL language (Tichy 1987). Starship, however, lacks support for 3D graphics and geometric applications. As the purpose of this layer is to hide the idiosyncrasies of the graphics routines from the users, the frame layer must be extended to support graphics applications. This extension also ensures that the graphics and geometric operations are handled in the same way as other knowledge-based operations. The most important new data types are: Geometry, Window, Image, Video, Vector and Matrix.

The object data type *Geometry* deals with the geometries or shape of the 3D structures, stored as planar polygons. This class is necessary to provide an interface to the SGGL routines for the manipulation and display of the polygons. The most important message understood by this class is *display*.

The object data type *Window* represents the physical window on the screen where the solid objects are projected. A Window object has a size and position in the screen, a background colour, window id, etc. Messages understood by a window include setting up the window for display, resize, move, single or double buffer display and picking. The Window data type has been specialized into various subclasses to deal more effectively with different media (3D graphics, images and video).

The object data type *Image* was introduced to deal with 2D images. In addition to the standard image operations (display, zoom, pan, crop) the Image object can also be mapped into the 3D world and display together with other 3D objects. The image object also supports transparency. Video has recently been introduced into the 3D environment as both stand-alone media and synchronized background for 3D animations.

The object data type *Matrix* was included to handle 4x4 matrix transformations, mainly for manipulating positions and rotations. The data type *Vector* was added to deal with x, y, z triads, which can be used to represent positions, sizes of objects or even colour values.

6. THE KNOWLEDGE REPRESENTATION LAYER

Supported by the extended frame language, the knowledge representation layer is used to model the structures and relationships between objects. In our approach, frames are used to model all kinds of objects from solid objects, to lights, material types and joints. Each frame is described in terms of its attributes (slots). Relations can be of different types: class-subclass-instance relation, part-of relation, joint relation between objects etc.

6.1 The Frame Class Hierarchy

A set of frame classes are defined to model the essential graphics processes. The frame classes form a class hierarchy as shown in Figure 2. The root class is the Object. Under the Object class, there are the Solid Class, Camera Class, and Utility Class. The Solid and Camera classes correspond to two of the essential usages of graphics - the modeling of structures and their viewing (Hedelman 1984). The Solid class represents rigid solid objects, and Camera class represents the cameras or eyes with which to view these solid objects. The Utility class groups together a set of sub-classes like Light, Joint, Motion, Material, EquationSolver etc. The objects instanced under these sub-classes are used by the Solid and Camera class objects to define their material, external forces, lights, etc.

These basic classes may be sub-classed to cater for different applications. For example, the Solid class may have sub-classes like Wheel, Engine, Tyre, Cylinder, Piston, etc. Further subdivisions within each subclass are possible, for example, to cater for different types of

Engines (say a car's engine versus an airplane's engine). The sub-class inherits all slots and default values from its parent class with additional slots to cater for its specific needs. The class hierarchy may be traversed to access the meta-knowledge of the class for deduction purposes.

Frame classes only provide the definitions of the objects to be used. Actual instances of a frame class are created by means of the instancing mechanism. The instance created is called a frame object of that class. For example, CarEngine-24 and Piston-2 are instances of the classes CarEngine and Piston, respectively. In a frame system, classes are treated like objects and respond to messages. A frame object cannot have subclasses nor instances.

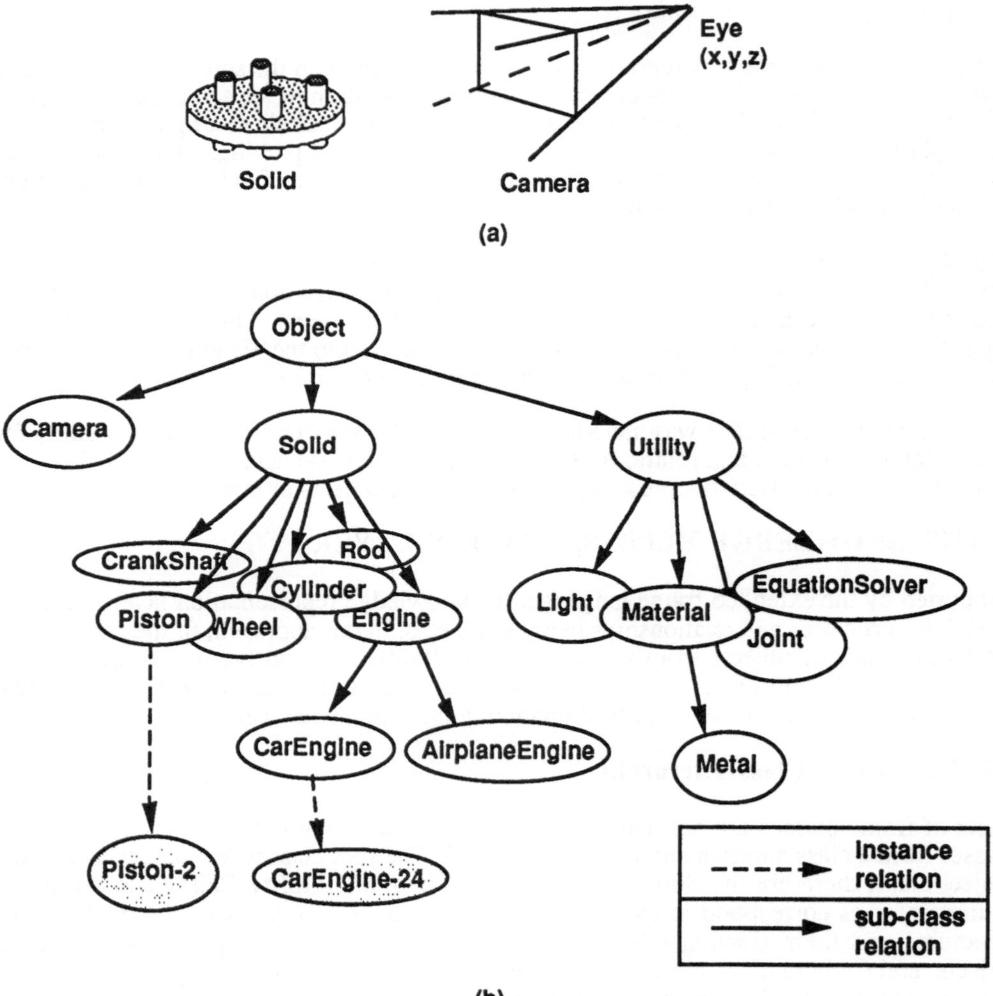

(b)

Figure 2: The Frame Class-Subclass-Instance Hierarchy

6.2 The Solid Class

The Solid class models a solid (rigid body) object. Two types of solids will make the hierarchy of solid objects: solids with a geometry (simple objects) and solids made of other solids (composite objects). Composite objects must eventually be terminated by simple solids as the leaves of the hierarchical tree. The geometries of the simple solids are assumed to be obtained from other solid modelers either through data files or generated algorithmically (we generated our geometries by translational and rotational sweeping). In addition to the geometry, the Solid class also models the positional and display attributes, the composition and the behaviour of solid objects, this last by means of kinematic relations with constraints. To cater for these, the solid class contains slots for geometry shape, position of and rotation around the reference point, material, a list of components (to model composition), a list of joints (to model kinematic relations) and attachments to motion objects (to model external forces). In addition, a set of procedural slots are also defined to operate on the attributes of the solid. In Figure 3, two Frame Solid instances and their relationships are shown: a composite solid (CarEngine-24) and one of its components (Piston-2) shown in some detail. The meaning of some of the slots are further discussed.

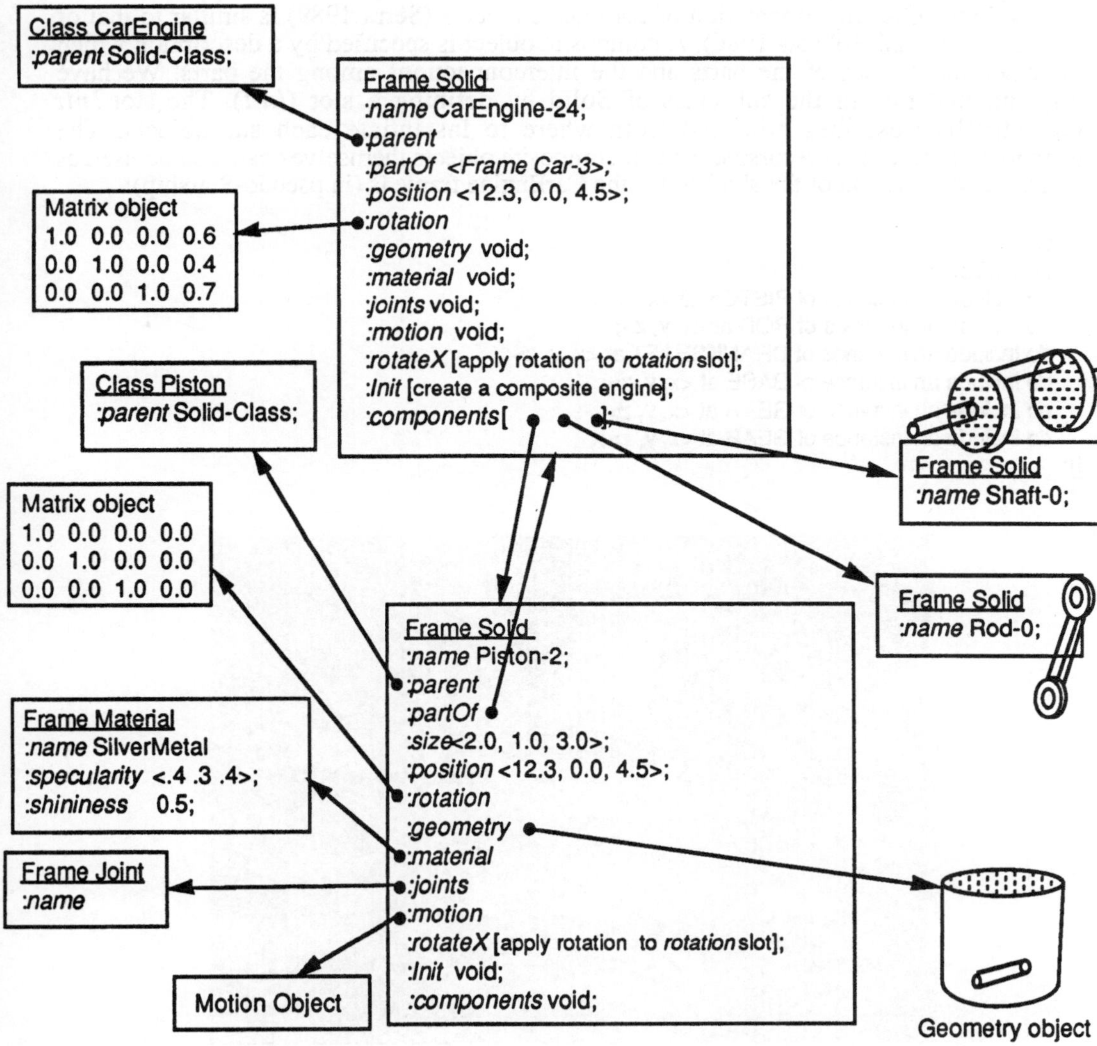

Figure 3: The structure of Frame Class Solid

6.2.1 The Modeling of Composites

Our main concern in describing the static hierarchy of 3D solids was to deal effectively with composite objects. A composite object is a group of interconnected objects that are instantiated together, a recursive extension of the notion of object. Thus, composite objects are objects that contain other objects, which in turn can also be composite objects. One essential relation that deals with the composition of complex object is the part-of relation. The part-of objects are semantically part of their parents and follow all transformations that their parents are subjected to. Figure 4 shows a picture of the crankshaft assembly. The part-of relations between the various components of the crankshaft assembly and the engine are shown in Figure 5. Each of these solid objects can be combined together to form more complex objects.

A composite object can be defined by a template that describes the sub-objects and their connections. Our implementation of composite objects (Serra 1989) is similar to that of Loops (Stefik and Bobrow 1986). A composite object is specified by a description which indicates the classes of the parts and the interconnections among the parts. We have implemented this in the sub-class of Solid by defining a slot (*Init*). The slot *Init* procedurally describes how and from where to instantiate each sub-objects. The instantiation process is recursive, so that composite objects themselves can also be used as parts. The description of the slot Init for the CarEngine frame is (in pseudo-Starship):

```
:Init [{
    do InitObject;
    do include an instance of PISTON at <x, y, z>;
    do include an instance of ROD at <x, y, z>;
    do include an instance of CRANKSHAFT at <x, y, z>;
    do include an instance of BASE at <x, y, z>;
    do include an instance of GEAR at <x, y, z>;
    do include an instance of GEAR at <x, y, z>;
}];
```

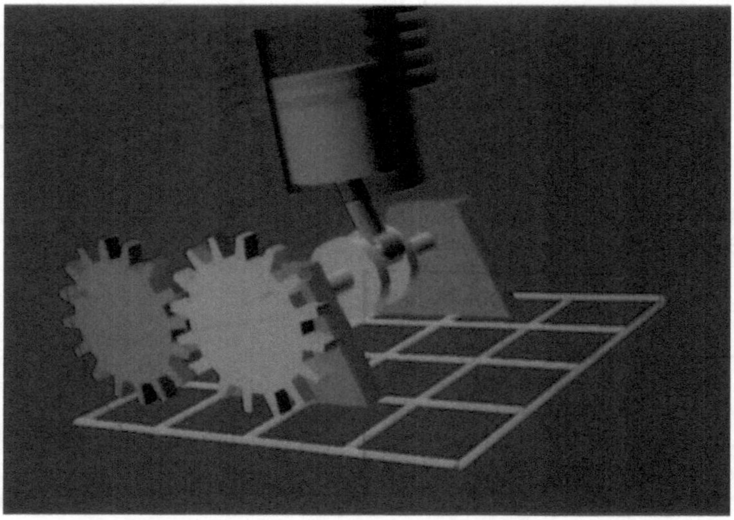

Figure 4: The crankshaft assembly

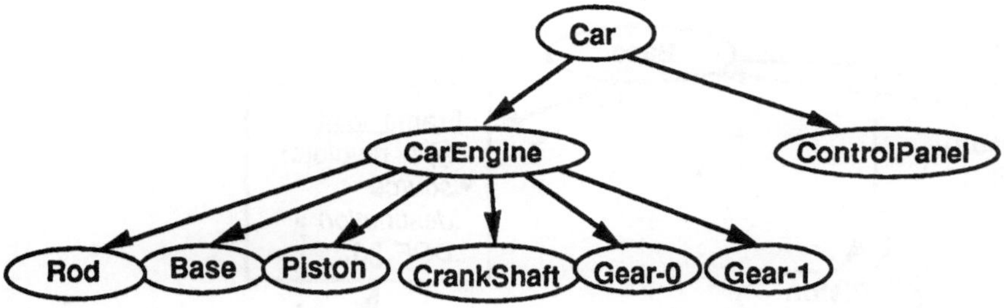

Figure 5: The Relationships between the components of an Engine Assembly

6.2.2 The Modeling of Kinematic Relations

A *part-of* relation expresses the structural composition of a complex object but does not take into account the relative kinematic dependencies of the objects. Therefore, a *joint* relation is needed to express the relative movement of one object with respect to another. A joint thus relates two objects via one to six translational or rotational degrees of freedom. This may impose a constraint between the two objects. For example, in the example of the crankshaft, the end of the rod must be attached to a point on the shaft during motion. Tilove (1983) and Isaacs and Cohen (1987) have studied constraint relations in the form of joints, and Rossignac (1986) and Brüderlin (1986) have proposed visual techniques for specifying constraints. In Tilove's model, a joint constraints exactly two objects. The joints considered are revolute, prismatic, universal, cylindrical, spherical (ball-and-socket), and rigid joints (Isaacs and Cohen 1987). In addition to the standard joints considered in CAD/CAM industries, we also include an angular joint to model the fact that the rotation of one gear is proportional to or constrained by the rotation of another gear. An example of an angular joint is the relationship between the two gears shown in Figure 4.

While Tilove (1983) and Isaacs and Cohen (1987) require a joint to be defined between a parent and a child object, we do not impose any such restriction. A joint may be defined between a sub-object of one composite and a sub-object of another composite. The joint relation provides a way of defining a chain of constraints that must be maintained within the system. In the case where the parts are related together by joints in such a way that the directions of the joints form an open graph, an "open-loop mechanism" results. A "close-loop mechanism" corresponds to a system with a cycle in its graph of joints and parts. Most systems can only handle open-loop mechanism, for example Tilove (1983). Our system attempts also to handle the close-loop mechanism.

To model such kinematic dependency an additional frame class called Joint class has been defined. The joint class relates two solid objects. It contains slots for the source and destination objects, type of joint, the DOFs, and the valid range of values for each DOF. Instances of this class will be used to link together solid object frames at specific points on the object. A diagram showing the joint relations between the components of the crankshaft assembly is given in Figure 6. Semantically, the joint object defines a one way relation (or restriction) from the source object to the destination object (ie the destination object must try to satisfied the constraint at the joint). To define a two way constraints such as between the Rod and the Shaft, two joints must be defined.

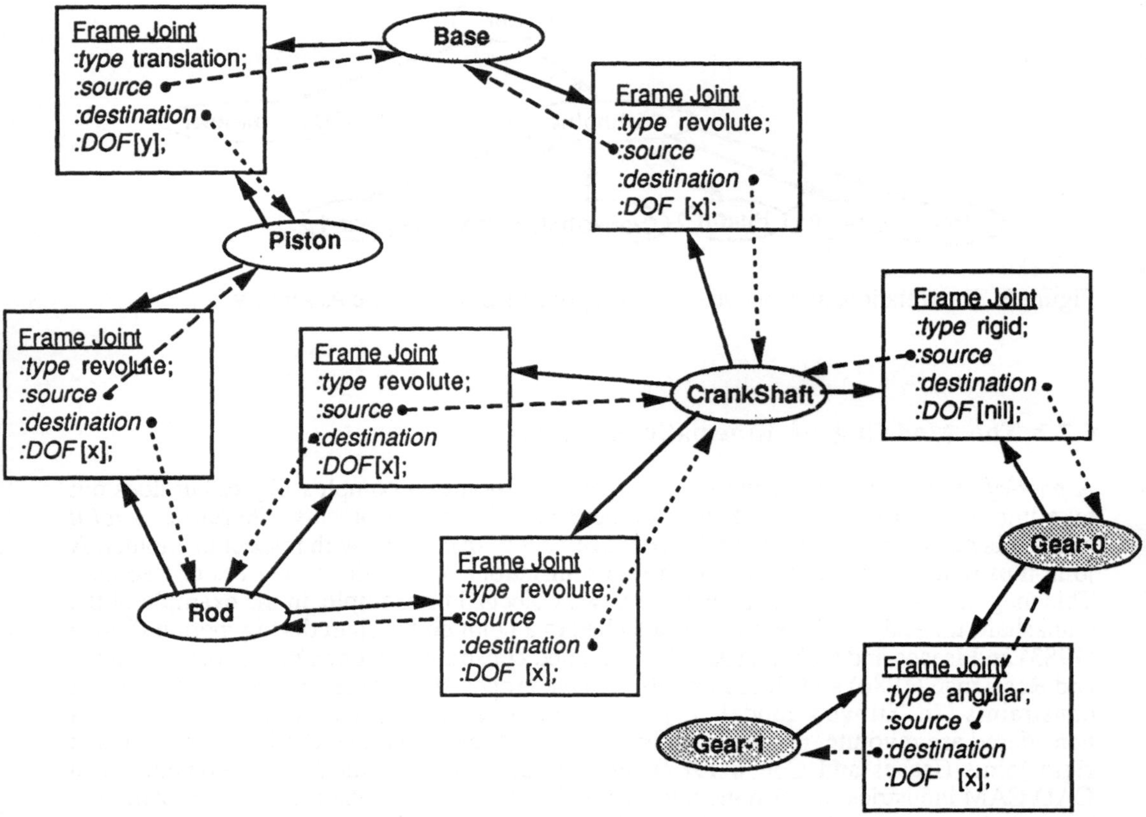

Figure 6: Joint Constraints between Components of a Crankshaft Assembly

In this model, each object knows about its own joints. Constraint maintenance can be handled at each object by inspecting the joint objects that it owns. The description of the maintenance of constraints will be given later.

6.2.3 The Modeling of External Forces

To model the effects of external forces realistically, faithful simulation of the dynamics of the object is necessary. This approach, however, is expensive as a large set of coupled differential equations need to be solved. As our system must be interactive to allow users to experiment and explore, we will not be considering the detailed modeling of physical laws of motions. Motion behaviour which results from the application of an external force, such as friction or gravity will be modeled using Motion Object types (procedural animation approach). When these motion objects are attached to the solid object that is experiencing the force or displaying the behaviour they will produce the desired changes in position. A flexible motion object based on the concept of attribute curve (Chua 1988) is used.

The motion objects compute the new position of the solid object without considering the constraints that the solid object must satisfy. To maintain consistency, these constraints must be considered in computing the new position. A procedural slot *update* for handling this will be discussed later.

6.3 The Camera Class

The class Camera embodies the camera metaphor. A camera has a *subject* to look at (a solid object); a *view-point* or position in 3D space; a viewing direction or *attitude* (defaulted to point to the reference point of the subject); and, a *lens* through which to view and take pictures. In addition, cameras have *lights* attached to them to illuminate their subject. Since cameras have a position in 3D space, the motion objects that animate solid objects can also be attached to them to simulate camera movements. Attaching motion to the camera allows us to inspect the subject from any angle or distance. The definition of frame class camera is given in Figure 7.

The pictures taken by the camera are displayed in a *window* of the screen (an object of the data type Window). Each camera object can have only one window. Multiple cameras can be defined to view the subject in different angles on different windows. The Window object recognizes messages such as resize, move around the screen, iconize, pop-up and down, etc. Displaying in the window is achieved by sending the message *display* to the subject slot (a solid frame) which in turn will propagate the display message to all of its components.

Another functionality that we have implemented with the Camera class object is the *pick* or select facility. The *pick* slot allows the user to select any sub-part of a complex object. Pick also determines what messages the object understands and presents these messages to the user for selection. Upon selection of a part of an object, the user can then decide among other things: (1) to make the selected component the new subject of the window; (2) to move it in 3D space; (3) to change its material characteristics; or (4) to query the class that the selected component belongs to. In this way, the user can navigate through the hierarchy of the objects and change their specifications and attributes.

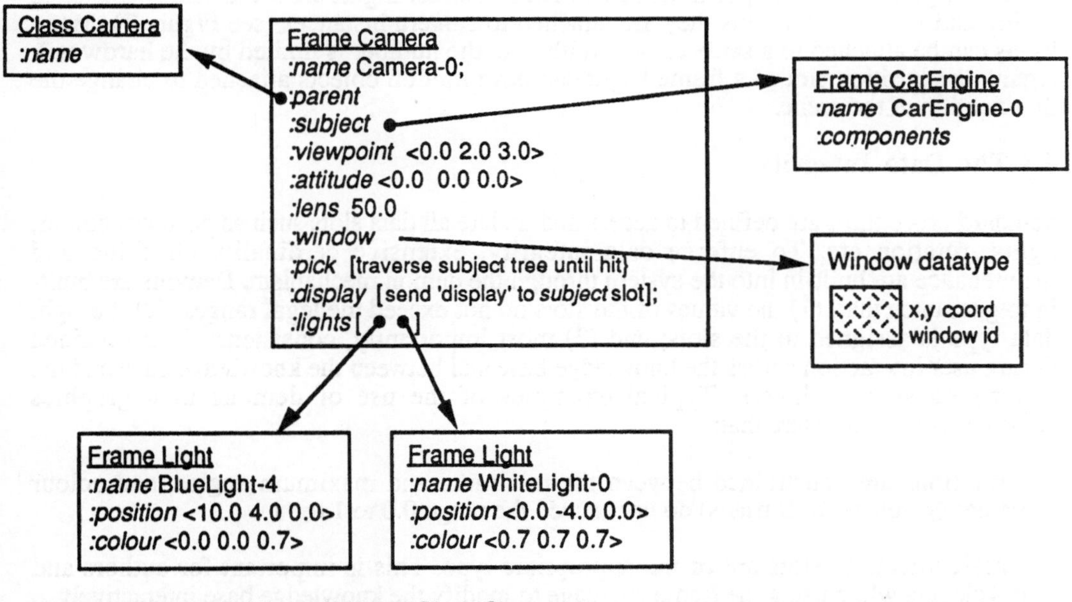

Figure 7: The Definition of Frame Class Camera

6.4 Utility Class - Material and Lighting Class

Solid objects are assumed to be made of a material. This is modeled by associating with each class of solid object a material frame. The material class describes the characteristics of the surface of the object given in terms of a set of RGB triads. The Material Class looks like this:

```
UtilityClass * Material;              % Material is subclass of Utility;
Frame * Material {
      :emission 0.0, 0.0, 0.0;
      :ambient 0.1, 0.1, 0.1;
      :diffuse 0.0, 0.0, 0.0;
      :specular 0.0, 0.0, 0.0;
}
```

More specific types of materials are obtained by modifying the default material properties. For example, Metal class is obtained by enforcing the specularity property; and Plastic class is made by selecting diffuse light properties and no specularity. Only one material can be attached to a solid at a time. Transparency is also supported.

```
MaterialClass * Metal;                % Metal is subclass of Material;
Frame * Metal{
      :transparency 0.5;
      :shininess 0.3;
      :specularity 1.0, 1.0, 1.0;
}
```

Light is also essential in order to visualize any of the solid objects. Basically, lights have a colour and a position in space. Lights are represented within a Light Class with different coloured lights at different positions being their instances. Lights are semantically related to seeing and viewing, and thus they are attached to camera instances (see Figure 7). Many lights can be attached to a same camera (although the number is limited by the hardware). Again, the position slot of a frame Light can have motion objects attached to change the illumination of the scene.

6.5 The Data Integrity

Standard procedures are defined to access and update all data slots such as position, colour, lights, rotation etc. To enforce data integrity, extensive cardinality checking and maintenance are built-in into the system through the demon mechanism. Demons are built-in to guarantee that: (1) the values of the slots do not exceed the legal ranges; (2) the right data type is assigned to the slots; and (3) most importantly, consistency is maintained during user interaction across the knowledge base and between the knowledge base and the underlying support layers. Typical examples of the use of demons in a graphics environment are to ensure that:

- rotations are constrained between the minimum and maximum angles, and colour values (given as RGB triads) do not exceed the range 0.0 to 1.0;

- assignments to slots are of the appropriate type. This is important for authors and developers while using the frame language to modify the knowledge base interactively.

- consistency with the frame support layer is maintained. An example of this is the re-positioning and changing of colour of a light. To accomplish this, the user will have to access the frame describing that particular light, and assign a new value to the slot position of the light, and similarly with the colour. As he changes each value, a demon will be triggered to execute a procedure (in the implementation language) which will change the definition the light in the Graphics Library, and simultaneously check the range of validity of the colour value.

- consistency is maintained across the knowledge base. This means that whenever a slot is accessed or changed, demons will be triggered to update other related slots or compute the value being accessed from related slots. For example, the frame Camera maintains a pointer to its current subject - a frame Solid. A pointer is also maintained at the Solid frame to indicate that it is currently in view at that camera. When the camera's *subject* is changed, a demon is activated that informs its old subject to remove its pointer to the camera as it is no longer in view, and notifies the new subject to include a pointer to the camera.

7. KINEMATIC ANIMATION WITH CONSTRAINT MAINTENANCE

As described earlier, each solid object contains slots to describe the set of external forces and joints that regulate its positioning in space (location and rotation). When a set of objects are constrained together, any external force on one object will affect other objects. Thus, a movement of Piston in Figure 4 will cause a repositioning of the Rod, Shaft and the Gears, so that the joints between all these objects are maintained.

7.1 Description of the Method

One important procedural slot that maintains the object's constraints and consistency is the slot *update*. The slot *update* accesses the attribute slots *motion* and *joints* and determines how much the object should move in order to satisfy all its constraints. To illustrate the function of this slot, consider the example of the crankshaft assembly shown in Figure 4. The joints between the components of the crankshaft assembly are shown in Figure 6, which also indicates the type of joints and the DOFs.

Consider the component Rod, which has a Revolute joint at each end to both the Piston and Shaft. When the Rod receives a message from its parent to update itself, the procedural slot *update* is activated. The slot first accesses its motion slot to determine its pre-defined motion under the external force, if any. It then accesses its *joints* slot and formulates a set of equations based on the definition of each joint. The set of equations derived at the joints of the Rod are given in Figure 8. These equations are sent to the EquationSolver object for solution. To solve for the unknowns at the joints, however, the Rod needs to know the updated positions of Piston and Shaft at those joints. This is achieved by sending messages to the sources of those joints - the Piston and Shaft - to request for this information. If the information is available, the actual values are returned. If, however, the information is not known, as is the case of the Shaft, the Shaft would try to update itself by activating its own *update* slot. The process is repeated until there are sufficient equations for the EquationSolver to solve for the unknowns. The objects involved then update their own attributes and flag themselves as being updated for this time interval. As there is only a finite number of components and joints, the process will terminate. It can also be shown that sufficient equations can always be found to solve for the unknowns.

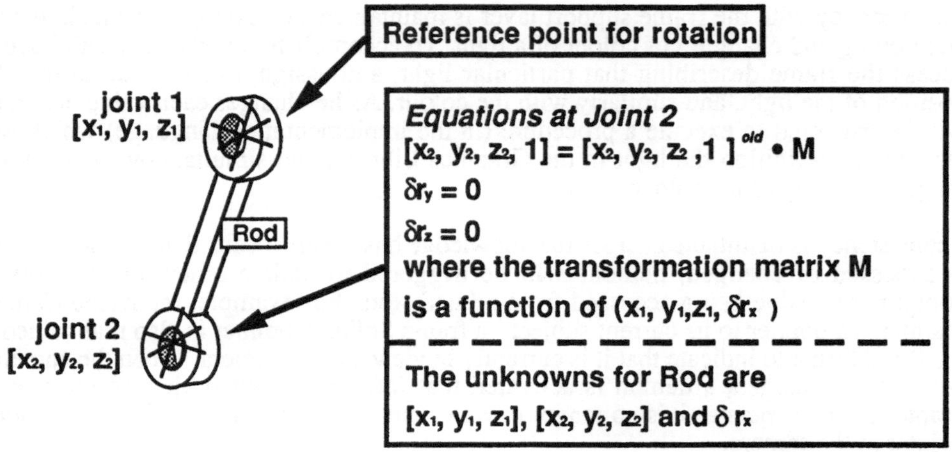

Figure 8: The equations at the joints of the Rod

The above procedures involve the solution of a set of equations, which are solved by an EquationSolver object. The EquationSolver receives the set of equations from the joint objects. It removes redundant equation, and determines whether it has sufficient equations to solve for the unknowns. A Newton-Raphson iterative scheme (Conte and de Boor 1972) is used to solve the set of nonlinear equations.

In addition to the slot *update*, a procedural slot called *extForce* is also defined to simulate the effect of the external force. Based on the external force applied, the slot *extForce* creates and assigns the appropriate motion objects to the desired solid object. For example, the acceleration force on the car engine will result in a message being sent to the *ExtForce* slot of the Piston to define its motions in order to simulate the effects of the acceleration.

7.2 Example

To demonstrate the use of the procedural slots *update* and *extForce* in maintaining system constraints, consider the kinematic simulation of the crankshaft assembly as shown in Figure 4. When the user clicks on the accelerator button on the control panel, a message is sent to the engine to inform it of the current acceleration. The car engine object then sends a message to the *extForce* slot of the Piston. A motion object is set up for the Piston at a rate based on the current acceleration.

At every time step, the Parent object (the Car) sends the *update* message to all its sub-components to update themselves. This message is sent recursively through the object hierarchy to update the individual object's attributes. This is followed by sending the message *display* recursively to all the object components to display themselves. At the end of each update, the system checks for user input events and repeats the above process until the process is terminated.

The action of pressing the car accelerator thus results in an animation of the car engine assembly. Figure 9 shows a typical session.

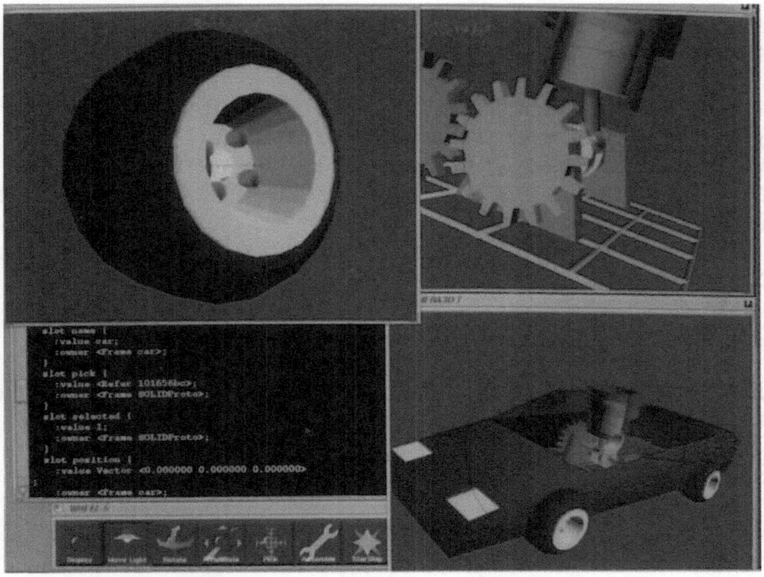

Figure 9: A typical session with KICK.

8. USER INTERFACE

As the idea of the system is to provide an interactive environment for users to learn and study about the behaviour of the 3D structures, an interactive hypermedia-like interface is provided. The user is initially shown a model of the car. The user may select any part of the car to traverse down the hierarchy. The user may click on the menu provided and select any of the components to view its non-geometric information (such as an image of the actual component or a video sequence or a textual description). The user may also view how the engine operates by clicking on the accelerator button to start the engine, or by dragging any of the components, such as the Piston, and observe how other components move in relation to the selected component. The movement of the selected component via dragging is subjected to the constraints that it must satisfy. In addition, user may manipulate the camera interactively to view any components of the car at any angle (as shown in Figure 9).

9. CONCLUSION

KICK-3D, an environment for learning and experimenting with 3D structures has been proposed. The initial implementation in Starship, a frame language, includes a part-of hierarchy of composite objects, and provides kinematic animation by modeling the joint relations between objects. This frame approach has the following advantages: (1) it facilitates the specification of inter-object relations, by means of a descriptive and concise interpretive language; (2) it automatically maintains the consistency of relations and the integrity of data at run-time by means of the demon mechanism; (3) it supports deduction by means of production rules.

KICK-3D is intended for training applications, where users can learn about the structure of a mechanism (by interactively accessing its hierarchy of components), study its operation, and experiment with the effects of externally applied forces (displacements) on other parts of the mechanism.

The work reported here represents the initial stage of our effort towards better educational and training systems. Much work still needs to be done to: (1) test our system on a wider range of problems; (2) implement a full hypermedia-like interface to provide a totally free environment for the users to browse; (3) ensure that the series of joint constraints added are consistent with each other, especially in a close-loop mechanism; (4) study new joint types needed to suit a wider class of problem; and (5) incorporate physical simulation for realistic animation of solid objects.

10. ACKNOWLEDGEMENTS

We would like to thank Wei-Shoong Teh and Joel Loo of the Institute of Systems Science for their contribution to the project.

11. REFERENCES

Armstrong, W.W. and Green, M.W., 1985, "The dynamics of articulated rigid bodies for the purposes of animation", *Proceedings of Graphics Interface '85*, Canadian Information Processing Society, Toronto, Canada, pp 407-415.

Brüderlin, B., 1986, "Constructing three-dimensional geometric objects defined by constraints",*Workshop on Interactive 3D Graphics*, October 1986, ACM, pp 111-129.

Buchanan, B.G., and Smith, R.G., 1988, "Fundamentals of expert systems", *Annual Review of Computer Science,* 3, pp 23-58

Chua, T.S., Wong, W.H. and Chu, K.C., 1988, "Design and implementation of the animation language SOLAR" in "New Trends in Computer Graphics", Magnenat-Thalmann and Thalmann (Eds), *Proceedings of Computer Graphics International 1988*, Springer-Verlag, pp 15-26.

Conte, S.D. and de Boor, C., 1972, "Elementary Numerical Analysis", McGraw-Hill.

Earnshaw, R.A. and Wyvill, B., (Eds.), 1989, "New advances in Computer Graphics", *Proceedings of Computer Graphics International 1989*, Springer-Verlag.

Elareef, T.I., 1986, "Flavor system and message passing as representation of knowledge for solid modeling in CAD expert system", *Computer & Graphics*, 10:4, pp 351-357

Fairchild, K., Poltrock, S.E., and Furnas, G.W., 1988, "SemNet: Three-dimensional graphic representations of large knowledge bases". In *Cognitive science and its applications for human-computer interaction*, edited by Raymonde Guindon, MCC, (New Jersey: LEA publishers), pp 201-233

Fiener, S., 1985, "APEX: an experiment in the automated creation of pictorial explanations", *IEEE Computer Graphics & Applications*, November 1985, pp 29-37.

Fikes, R., and Kehler, T., 1985, "The role of frame-based representation in reasoning", *Communications of ACM*, 28:9, pp 904-920

Franklin, W.R., Wu, Y.F., Samaddar, S., and Nichols, M., 1986, "Prolog and geometry projects", *IEEE Computer Graphics & Applications*, November 1986, pp 46-55

Halasz. F.G., 1988, "Reflections on Notecards: seven issues for the next generation of hypermedia systems", *Communications of ACM*, 31:7, pp 836-852

Hedelman, H., 1984, "A data flow approach to procedural modeling", *IEEE Computer Graphics & Applications*, January 1984, pp 16-26

Isaacs, P.M. and Cohen, M.F., 1987, "Controlling dynamic simulation with kinematic constraints, behaviour functions and inverse dynamics", Computer Graphics, 21:4, July 1987, pp 215-224.

Loo, J.P.L., 1989, *The Starship Manual*, ISS internal report.

Milanese, V., 1988, "A Prolog environment for GKS-based graphics", *Computer Graphics Forum*, 7, pp 9-20

Minsky, M.A., 1975, "A framework for representing knowledge", In *The psychology of computer vision*, edited by P. Winston, (New York: McGraw-Hill)

Richer, M.H., Clancey, W.J., 1985, "GUIDON-WATCH: A graphics interface for viewing a knowledge-based system", *IEEE Computer Graphics & Applications*, November 1985, pp 51-64.

Rossignac, J.R., 1986, "Constraints in Constructive Solid Geometry", *Workshop on Interactive 3D Graphics*, October 1986, ACM, pp 93-110.

Sabella, P. and Carlbom, I., 1989, "An object-oriented approach to the solid modeling of empirical data", *IEEE Computer Graphics & Applications*, September 1989, pp 24-34.

Serra, L., 1989, "A knowledge base for the manipulation of 3D objects", *Second Colloquium on the Application of Intelligent Knowledge-Based Systems for CIM environment*, Nanyang Technological Institute, Singapore, July 1989.

Sheu, P.C.Y., 1988, "Object-oriented graphics knowledge bases", *Computer & Graphics*, 12:1, pp 115-123

Silicon Graphics, Inc., *IRIS User's Guide*, 1984

Stefik, M., and Bobrow, D.G., 1986, "Object-oriented programming: themes and variations", *The AI Magazine*, 6:4, pp 40-62.

Thalmann, D., and Magnenat-Thalmann, N., 1986, "Artificial intelligence in three-dimensional computer animation", *Computer Graphics Forum*, 5, pp 341-348

Tichy, W.F., 1987, "What can software engineers learn from Artificial Intelligence", *IEEE Computer*, November 1987, pp 43-54.

Tilove, R.B., 1983, "Extending solid modeling systems for mechanism design and kinematic simulation", *IEEE Computer Graphics & Applications*, June 1983, pp 9-19.

Wilhelms, J., 1987, "Using dynamic analysis for animation of articulated bodies", *IEEE Computer Graphics & Applications*, June 1987, pp 12-27.

Zeltzer, D., 1983, "Knowledge-based animation", *Proceedings of ACM SIGGRAPH/SIGART Workshop on Motion*, Toronto, Canada.

Luis Serra graduated in Electronics Engineering in 1982 from the Universidad Politécnica de Barcelona, Spain. He then moved to the University of Bradford, UK, where he obtained his MSc (1983) and his PhD in multi-processor systems for real-time 3D image generation (1987). He is currently an Associate, Research Staff at the Institute of Systems Science, National University of Singapore, where he leads a project on interactive 3D graphics and video. His research interests include 3D computer graphics, knowledge representation and video technology. He is a member of the ACM SIGGRAPH.
e-mail: ISSLUIS @ NUSVM.bitnet
Current address: Institute of Systems Science, National University of Singapore, Heng Mui Keng Terrace, Kent Ridge, Singapore 0511

Chua Tat-Seng graduated from the University of Leeds, UK, with a BSc in Civil Engineering and Computer Science in 1979, and a PhD in Computer Science in 1983. His PhD research was concerned with the simulation of British Gas transmission networks. Between 1983 and 1988, he was a lecturer at the Department of Information Systems and Computer Science, where he taught mainly computer graphics-related courses. He was also involved with Institute of Systems Science (ISS) since 1985 in research on computer animation and the design of animation languages. He is now a member of research staff at ISS. He leads ISS research in the areas of hypermedia, 3D graphics and interactive video. His research interests include interactive 3D graphics, hypermedia, information retrieval, and the indexing of multimedia information.
e-mail: CHUATS @ NUSVM.bitnet
Current address: Institute of Systems Science, National University of Singapore, Heng Mui Keng Terrace, Kent Ridge, Singapore 0511

An Object-Oriented Methodology Using Dynamic Variables for Animation and Scientific Visualization

Russel Turner, Enrico Gobbetti, Francis Balaguer, Angelo Mangili, Daniel Thalmann, and Nadia Magnenat-Thalmann

ABSTRACT

An object-oriented design is presented for building dynamic three-dimensional applications. This design takes the form of the Fifth Dimension Toolkit consisting of a set of interrelated classes whose instances may be connected together in a variety of ways to form different applications. Animation is obtained by connecting graphical objects to dynamic variables, which are able to change their values over time by responding to events. The Fifth Dimension Toolkit is the core of the Fifth Dimension Project, a research project for animating synthetic actors in their environment. The design philosophy and methodology of the toolkit are also described, as well as some of the implementation issues for the Silicon Graphics Iris 4D workstation.

Keywords: Object-Oriented, Animation, Scientific Visualization, Dynamic Variables.

1. INTRODUCTION

Complex dynamic three-dimensional graphics systems such as task-level animation systems and scientific visualization systems all involve various activities such as surface modeling, rendering, synchronization and motion control. A major problem in the development of such large systems is that they can become very difficult to maintain and extend.

A potential solution to this problem is to replace the traditional structured programming approach and top-down design strategy, with an object-oriented approach, which supports a bottom-up software design process. We use such an approach in the Fifth Dimension Project, a large research project in three-dimensional animation and visualization. The main objective of the project is the animation of synthetic actors in their environment, which involves a number of related areas of computer animation and scientific visualization. In particular, the following applications are being developed:

- animation of articulated bodies based on mechanical laws
- vision-based behavioral animation (Renault et al. 1990)
- hair rendering and animation
- intelligent object grasping
- facial animation
- personification in walking models (Boulic et al. 1990)
- synchronization in task-level animation
- deformation of flexible and elastic objects
- cloth animation with detection of collision

To coordinate efforts and allow good communication between the various applications, a toolkit of high-level dynamic graphical classes, both two and three dimensional, has been constructed. This toolkit, called the Fifth Dimension Toolkit uses a uniformly object-oriented design for all its data structures, resulting in a high degree of integration between various applications.

In this paper, we discuss the goals of the Fifth Dimension Toolkit and describe its design. We also discuss the toolkit's design philosophy and its motivation, and briefly mention some of the implementation issues for the Silicon Graphics Iris 4D workstations.

2. GOALS OF THE FIFTH DIMENSION TOOLKIT

With the advent of workstations containing three-dimensional graphics engines, it is now easier to display relatively complex three-dimensional images in real-time. However, the accompanying software libraries usually operate at a very low level of drawing polygons. Although there are some commercial software systems available, they are often do not meet the needs of animators and scientific researchers who usually require highly specialized applications. As a result, a large part of their time is spent programming the basic user interfaces and three-dimensional data structures rather than their actual work. The Fifth Dimension Project involves several researchers working on related areas of computer animation and scientific visualization. To facilitate integration between various researchers' software and to allow the reuse of code, a core library of general-purpose, extensible software was required.

2.1 Previous Approaches

Many computer graphics research laboratories have an in-house "system" which includes such features as two and three dimensional modelers, renderers, image displayers and standard image file and model description formats. Some systems also incorporate various modeling and animation languages which can be compiled or interpreted by the system. Examples of such systems are described by Magnenat-Thalmann and Thalmann (1983), Chmilar and Wyvill (1989), Hanrahan and Sturman (1985), Fiume et al. (1987) and Ostby (1989).

Although there are many advantages to using a high-level language, such as the ability to create procedural models, basing a system on a specialized language can make it more difficult to develop interactive tools. Also, it adds another level of translation to the system, requiring interpreters and parsers which have to be maintained and hindering extensibility and reuse of code.

Another design approach is used by ConMan (Haeberli 1987, 1988) in which a number of small two-dimensional and three-dimensional application programs are connected together using inter-process communication. The various applications are "wired" together with the Connection Manager program in different ways to create different tools.

One of the difficulties with such an approach is the necessity of devising a proper inter-process-communication protocol so that all concepts and data structures can be communicated between the applications. A second problem is that, for shear reasons of efficiency, this method tends to force a coarse-grained modularity and the resulting large applications will still need to be built out of smaller software components.

The Pixar's animation system (Reeves et al., 1990) uses both these approaches. This system, which was used to create the animation *Tin Toy*, allows models to be created procedurally using a C-like interpreted language called ML. Interactive tool applications can be used to build models using the language. These tools communicate using a common database with shared memory and an interprocess communication scheme for passing messages between multiple tool processes.

2.2 Toolkit Approach

Another approach to building large graphics systems is the object-oriented toolkit. This is the basis of most current user-interface software packages such as Macintosh's MacApp, the X11 Window's Xt "widgets", Stanford University's InterViews, or NeXT's NextStep. These toolkits allow applications to create two-dimensional interactive "objects" on the screen with very complex behavior. Collections of these objects can be built up to implement user interfaces.

In some cases, user interface objects can be bound to one another so that manipulating one object will have an effect on the other. One of the first commercial object-oriented toolkits to incorporate dynamics into graphical objects was V.I. Corporation's DataViews (Kelly et al., 1988), which uses the concept of "graph" objects bound to dynamic variables to graphically display numerical data changing in real time. NASA's TAE Plus (Szczur, 1989) also uses the concept of "data-driven graphic objects" which display dynamic data on the screen. Both of these systems are essentially two dimensional.

2.3 Why an Object-Oriented Approach ?

All of these toolkits have been successful in part because they have used an object-oriented design philosophy. This is well-suited for the design of two-dimensional user-interface and dynamic graphics toolkits for several reasons. There is a close conceptual analogy between the dynamic object on the screen, which has spatial coherence and an innate behavior, and an instance of a class in memory, with its private variables and methods. Also, the self-contained nature and polymorphism of instances makes them ideal as modular, interconnectable components for building larger components or applications.

As pointed out by Micallef (1989), the kind of reusability which is given by the traditional library of subroutines is limited because the functionality provided by these pieces of software is fixed. A subroutine library can only be reused when exactly the same behavior as that provided by the existing subroutines is needed.

The concept of inheritance through class hierarchy, as described by Goldberg and Robson (1983) provides a mechanism for extensibility of classes and promotes reusability of code. Also, it provides an orderly way of handling special cases without affecting existing code. Finally, as shown by Meyer (1989), object-oriented programming by its nature tends to promote a bottom-up design approach rather than the traditional top-down one promoted by structured languages. This is certainly more appropriate for a research environment, where the final goals may evolve over time.

Object-oriented programming has already been successfully used in the field of computer animation. For example,"The ClockWorks" (Breen et al., 1987, 1989) animation system is implemented using an object-oriented methodology in C and uses message passing as a way to specify a scene's choreography.

All of these arguments strongly suggested to us that a large dynamic graphics system should be constructed using an object-oriented methodology to build a toolkit of classes, taking the object-oriented user-interface toolkit model and extending it to encompass dynamic three-dimensional objects. The toolkit should be developed in a bottom-up fashion, first building a set of reusable, general purpose classes and then going on to construct more powerful classes and complete applications.

2.4 Implementation Methodology

Our hardware consists of a network of Silicon Graphics IRIS 4D workstations. Ideally, the toolkit would be implemented in an object-oriented language, preferably an extension to C which would allow us to take existing C code and "encapsulate" it, turning it into a class. However, the basic concepts of object-oriented programming are not that complicated and it is usually not too difficult to build an object-oriented methodology on top of any standard computer language. So, for portability reasons, a methodology for doing object-oriented programming in C based on the methods described by Cox (1987) was developed.

This technique introduces a new typedef (`id`) which is a pointer to any object. Messages are implemented as functions in which the first parameter is the object that is the receiver of the message. Classes are implemented as external variables which are allocated at compile time.

For example, to send a new message to the Window class, creating a new instance of aWindow, the following statements would be used:

```
id aWindow;
aWindow = new_(Window);
```

By convention, message routines are distinguished with a terminating underscore and class object variables begin with an upper-case letter.

3. FIFTH DIMENSION TOOLKIT DESIGN

The design of the toolkit was based on several principles:

• **Device Independence.** The toolkit should be portable to other windowing systems and other machines with a graphics engine. This requires isolating the windowing system and device specific code to low-level routines and methods.

• **Extensibility.** The toolkit should not become a fixed programming interface, but should be able to be continuously extended through subclassing and the creation of new classes. This requires an open-ended design, with flexibility in the typing of objects.

• **2D and 3D integration.** There should be no conceptual distinction between the two-dimensional and three-dimensional graphical objects, or between the window system and the graphical models. This requires encapsulation of both two-dimensional window objects and three-dimensional models in a uniform way.

• **Inherently Dynamic Objects.** All graphical objects should have the potential to be dynamic in all their visible aspects and this dynamism should be built into the objects, not imposed from the outside. This requires classes specifically related to dynamic change over time, such as dynamic variables, and a mechanism for implementing the dynamics such as events.

3.1 Toolkit Classes and their Relations

The following diagram (Fig.1) shows the basic classes in a typical relationship. This type of diagram, which Rumbaugh (1987) calls an object-relation diagram represents classes as boxes and relationships between them as lines. The cardinality of the relationship is indicated by circles at the end of the lines. A filled circle represents a cardinality of zero to n, an unfilled circle represents a cardinality of zero or one, and no dot represents a cardinality of one. Subclass relationships are represented with triangles.

The classes on the right-hand side of the diagram mostly represent two-dimensional window system and user-interface objects while those on the left represent three-dimensional hierarchical objects, surface properties and lights. The Display class encapsulates the virtual workstation devices and it is the top of the graphical object hierarchy. The graphical link between the two portions of the diagram is the Camera, which represents the projection from the three-dimensional World to the two-dimensional Window.

All of the graphical class instances fit into a rough instance hierarchy going from the Display instance at the top down to the Model3D instances at the bottom. The Node3D instance can have indefinite levels of hierarchy representing three-dimensional hierarchical objects. One thing that all graphical classes have in common is the ability to respond to the `repaint_` message. This message cascades all the way down the instance hierarchy so that a `repaint_` message delivered to the Display instance will result in the whole application being redrawn.

Most of the two-dimensional classes represent standard windowing and user-interface objects found in many user-interface toolkits such as Xt or SunView: windows, panels, sliders, buttons, etc. These objects all fit into a hierarchy so that the display may own multiple windows, windows may own multiple panels, and panels can contain many input or output items. Since all of these classes inherit from the Canvas class, they all have similar behavior and design concepts. For example, they all have foreground and background color, position and dimensions on the screen, and all can be made invisible.

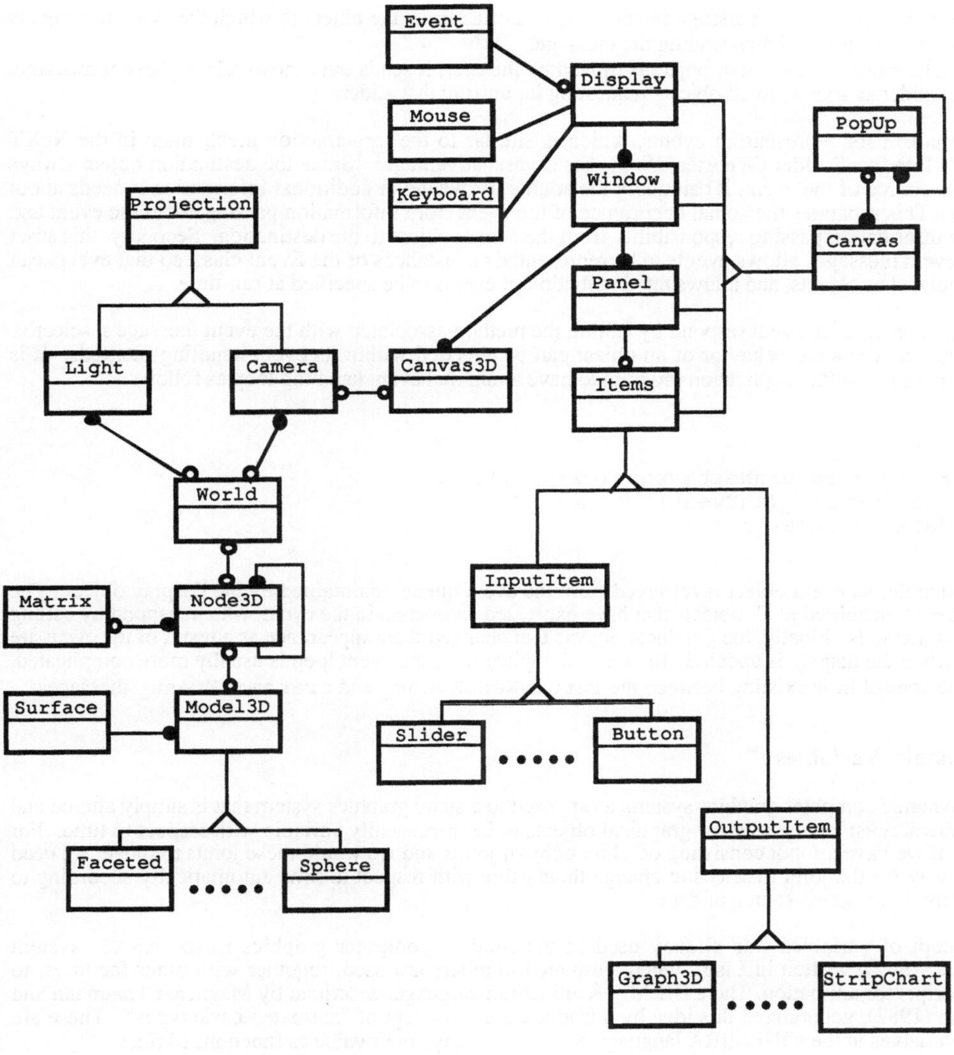

Fig.1 Object-relation diagram of the toolkit

3.2 Event Messages

As in any object-oriented system, object instances in the Fifth Dimension Toolkit communicate with each other by sending messages. In order to respond to user-generated input and to implement the dynamic behavior of objects, we have defined a more formal type of message which we call an event message. This is a message sent by an object during the dynamic or interactive phase of a program's execution to indicate that it has changed state. All event messages have a single parameter which specifies the object that was the source of the event. To send an event message using the toolkit, the following syntax is used:

```
eventName_(destination, source);
```

where `eventName_` is the message selector, `destination` is the object to which the event message is sent, and `source` is the object sending the message.
For example, when a slider input object is moved by the user, it sends out a `newValue_` event message, giving the slider as source, to all objects requesting input from that slider.

This formalism for representing events, which is similar to the target/action mechanism in the NeXT machine's InterfaceBuilder (Webster, 1989), has several advantages. Since the destination object always knows the source of the event, it can query the source for whatever additional information it needs about the event. This separates the actual occurrence of the event from information passing about the event and shifts the information passing responsibility from the source object to the destination. Secondly, this strict form of event messages allows events to be represented as instances of the Event class, so that events can be manipulated as objects, and allows the distribution of events to be specified at run-time.

Objects that receive an event respond by calling the method associated with the event message's selector. In this way, all dynamic behavior of an object can be encoded within its event handling methods. It is therefore possible for the application program to have a minimal event handling loop as follows:

```
for (;;)
     {
     anEvent = returnNextEvent_(display);
     transmitEvent_(anEvent);
     update_(display);
     }
```

In this example, an event object is retrieved from the event queue, maintained by the Display object. The event is then transmitted to all objects that have expressed an interest in the event, which respond by calling their event methods. Finally, the graphical objects that changed their appearance as a result of the event are redrawn when the display is updated. In practical applications, the event loop is usually more complicated, with some control flow existing between the `returnNextEvent_` and `transmitEvent_` messages.

3.3 Dynamic Variables

A truly dynamic computer graphics system, as apposed to a static graphics system that is simply altered and then redrawn, must have a way for graphical objects to be intrinsically variable with respect to time. For example, if we have a robot consisting of a hierarchy of joints and we would these joints to move, we need to find a way for the joint matrices to change their value with respect to time automatically according to some external or internal source of data.

The concept of variables was already used in the field of computer graphics in the ASAS system (Reynolds, 1982), written in Lisp, where animated numbers are used, together with other facilities, to specify scripts for animation. The CINEMIRA animation language, described by Magnenat Thalmann and Thalmann (1982), generalized this idea by introducing the concept of "animated basic types". These are types of variables in the CINEMIRA language which can change their value as functions of time.

Hanrahan and Sturman (1985), introduced in their animation language the idea of parametric models in which a graphical object can be animated by binding its parameters to an animation system or directly to various user input devices. This concept was extended by Pixar (Ostby, 1989) in their Menv system by using “articulated variables”, which can contain other variables in a graph so as to form complicated expressions. A dependency list is maintained and is used to reevaluate only those values that have changed. These variables, like the parameters described by Hanrahan, are manipulated using a high-level interpreted language, called ML.

Rather than using a higher level language such as ML, the Fifth Dimension Toolkit takes the concept of “articulated variables” and implements them as classes. These classes, which we call dynamic variable classes, allow instances to be created that maintain a current mathematical value and can change their value over time. All dynamic variable instances are able to receive and transmit event messages, which change their values, and to respond to the `getValue_` message, which returns the current value of the instance.

Graphical objects can be made dynamic by attaching them to dynamic variables and dynamic variables can be interconnected themselves to form networks that calculate mathematical functions. Consistency is maintained by sending event messages and maintaining a graph of dependencies between the dynamic variables. In particular, every dynamic variable maintains a list of dependants, that is, other objects which depend on its value. Whenever a dynamic variable changes its value, it transmits a `newValue_` event message to all of its dependants. Each dependant object can respond to the event message as it sees fit. If it is another dynamic object, it can alter its own value accordingly and transmit its own `newValue_` message, or if it is a graphical object it can mark itself as out-of-date and redraw itself in response to the next `update_` message. In this way, multiple graphical objects can be bound to the same dynamic variable. For example, two sliders can be bound to a single dynamic float variable so that when one slider moves, the other one moves together with it. Also, InputItems can be bound to OutputItems in various combinations.

Dynamic variables can also be bound to various types of data gathering classes so that their values will be changed in response to events outside the process. In this way, applications can respond dynamically to external data sources in real-time, or display event-driven simulations. It is also possible for dynamic variables to retain history of past values. This can be useful for dynamic objects that need to display some sort of historical process, for example, an OutputItem that emulates a strip-chart recorder.

Certain types of dynamic variables can act as functions. These maintain a list of dynamic variables which are its input parameters. When the function receives a `newValue_` event message from one of its parameters, it recalculates its own value, and sends out a `newValue_` event message to all of its dependants (see Fig. 2).

In general, graphical and dynamic objects can be assembled together into large networks, much like an analog control system or a collection of electronic components. In this way, complicated dynamics with many interrelated graphical objects can be driven by a few input variables.

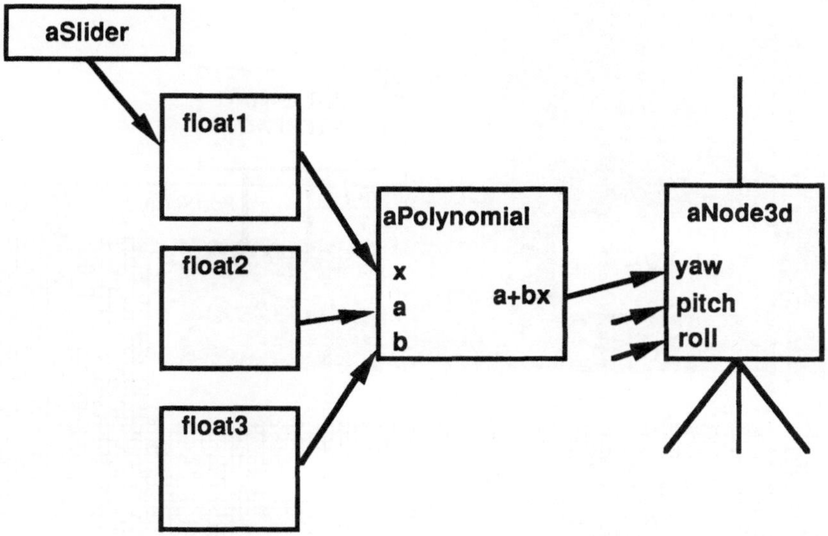

Fig 2. A network used to control the rotation of a three-dimensional graphic node by changing the value of a dynamic float with a slider.

4 Implementation

The Fifth Dimension Toolkit has been implemented on Silicon Graphics Iris 4D workstations. It was designed to support relatively portable applications so that when the toolkit is implemented on other windowing systems or machines with 3D graphics engines, the applications will compile and run properly. This is done by encapsulating all the device-specific graphics calls within a device-independent subroutine layer on top of which the toolkit classes are built. Special classes encapsulate several physical input devices such as Mouse, KeyBoard, SpaceBall and Digitizer.

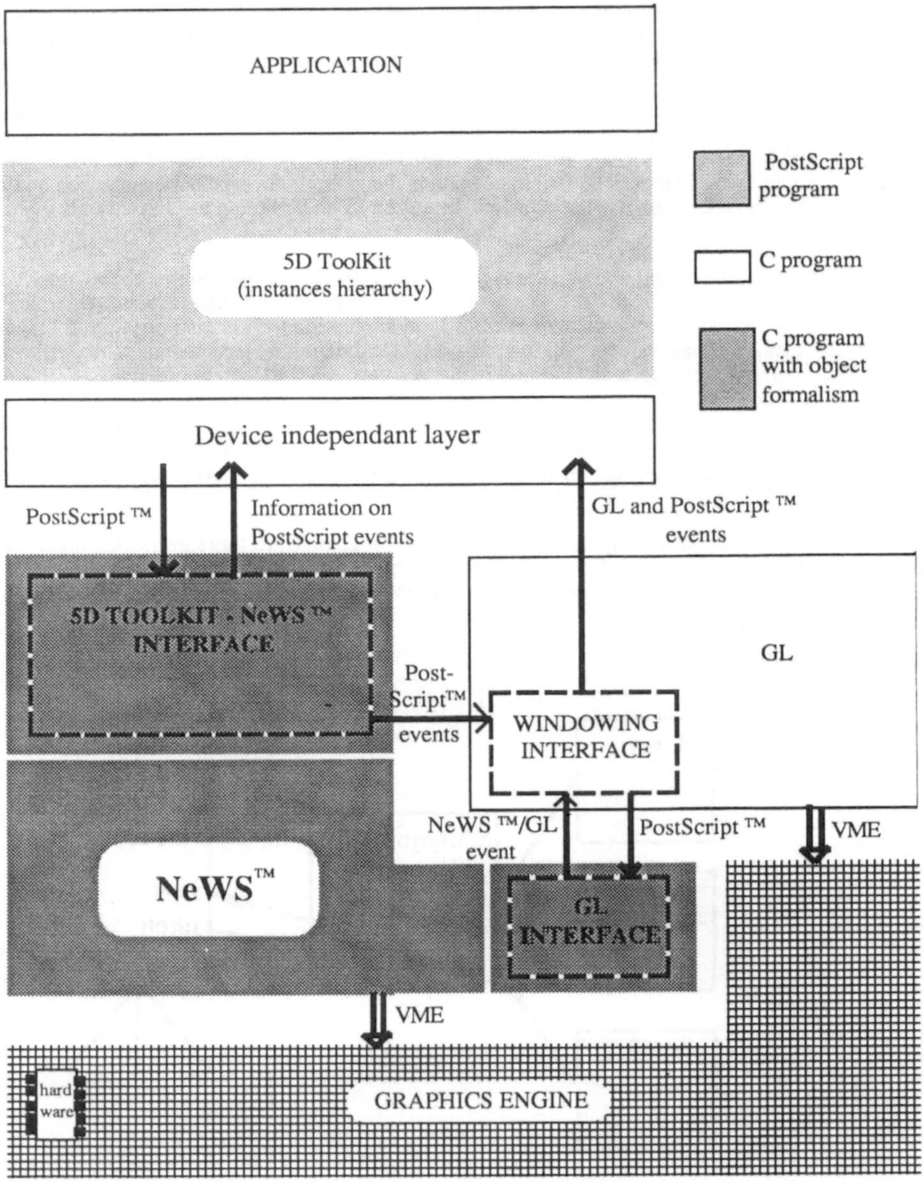

Fig.3 Fifth Dimension System Diagram

As is shown in the diagram (Fig. 3), the underlying graphics engine is accessed by two very different types of software: a C graphics library for accessing the basic three-dimensional functionality of the graphics engine, and a NeWS/PostScript interpreter for implementing the user interaction and window system objects. We have used both software systems in our implementation: PostScript for implementing the two-dimensional InputItems using a set of classes inspired by the LiteItem toolkit (Densmore et al., 1987) and GL (the graphics library distributed by Silicon Graphics) for everything else. However, this division is not apparent to the application programmer using the Fifth Dimension Toolkit. The PostScript portion, for example, could be reimplemented using another language on top of other window systems such as X11 or even on top of the GL library.

One interesting consequence of this implementation is that the "look and feel" of the two-dimensional user-interface portion of the toolkit is implemented entirely in PostScript, and can be altered without having to recompile the C application. This is because PostScript is an interpreted language and all the definitions are downloaded at run-time.

Figure 4 shows an example of an application developed using the Fifth Dimension Toolkit.

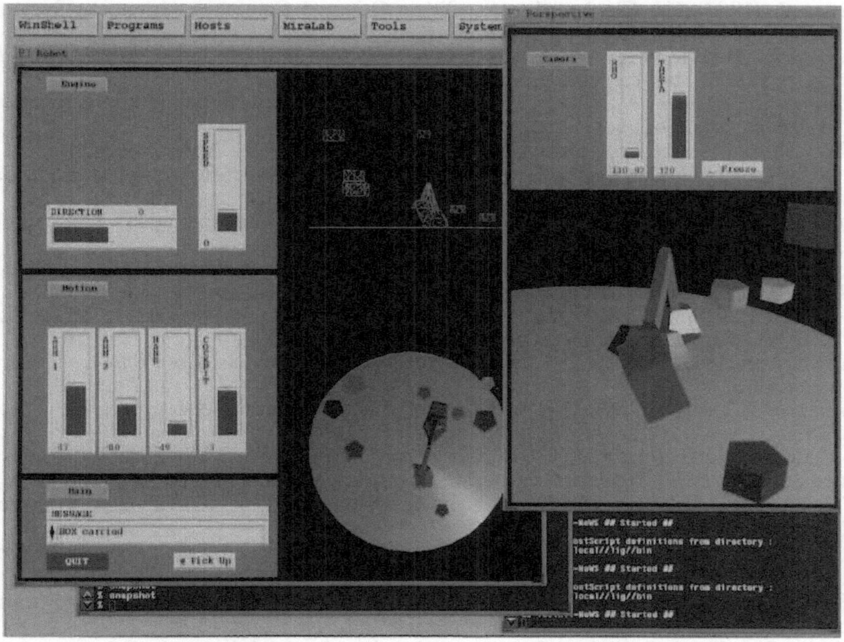

Fig.4 An example of application developed using the Fifth Dimension Toolkit

5. CONCLUSION

While programmers of standard two-dimensional applications have a large choice of user-interface toolkits, user-interface management systems and prototyping systems, the average scientific, engineering or animation software programmer writing software applications for super-computers or the latest "3D workstations" is required to use low-level graphics routines. Since many of the programmers writing three-dimensional dynamic applications are researchers and not professional computer programmers, their time spent coding up applications from scratch is time taken away from their research.

The Fifth Dimension Toolkit provides a working example of how an object-oriented toolkit concept of software building blocks can be applied to the construction of animation and scientific visualization software, resulting in substantial gains in software development productivity and code reuse.

ACKNOWLEDGEMENTS

We are grateful to Olivier Renault for his suggestions and help with the manuscript. The Fifth Dimension Project is partly supported by the Fonds National Suisse pour la Recherche Scientifique.

REFERENCES

Boulic R, Magnenat-Thalmann N, Thalmann D (1990) Human Free-Walking Model for a Real-time Interactive Design of Gaits, *Computer Animation '90*, Springer-Verlag, Tokyo

Breen D.E. et al. (1987) The Clockworks: An Object-Oriented Computer Animation System, *Proc. Eurographics '87*, North Holland, pp.275-282.

Breen D.E. Wozny MJ (1989) Message-Based Choreography for Computer Animation, *State-of-the-art in Computer Animation*, Springer Verlag, pp.69-82.

Chmilar M, Wywill B (1989) A Software Architecture for Integrated Modeling and Animation, *New Advances in Computer Graphics*, Springer Verlag, pp. 275-269.

Cox BJ (1987) *Object Oriented Programming: An Evolutionary Approach*, Addison Wesley.

Densmore OM, Rosenthal DSH (1987) A User-Interface Toolkit in Object-Oriented Postscript, *Computer Graphics Forum*, Vol.6, pp.171-180.

Fiume Eugene et al.: "A Temporal Scripting Language for Object-Oriented Animation". Proc. Eurographics '87, North Holland, pp. 283-294.

Golberg A, Robson S (1983) *Smalltalk-80: The Language and its Implementation*, Addison Wesley.

Haeberli PE (1987) A Data-Flow Manager for Interactive Graphics, *Iris Universe*, fall pp. 3-5..

Haeberli PE (1988) ConMan: A Visual Programming Language for Interactive Graphics, *Proc. SIGGRAPH '88, Computer Graphics*, Vol.22, No4, pp. 103-111.

Hanrahan P, Sturman D (1985) Interactive Animation of Parametric Models, *The Visual Computer*, Vol. 1, No4, pp. 260-266.

Kelly M, Aczel TG, Turner R, Dee D (1988) *DV-Tools User's Guide*, version 6.0, V.I. Corporation, Amherts MA

Magnenat-Thalmann N, Thalmann D (1983) The Use of High-Level 3-D Graphical Types in the Mira Animation System, *IEEE Computer Graphics and Applications* 3(9), pp. 9-16.

Magnenat-Thalmann N, Thalmann D (1983b) Actor and Camera Data Types in Computer Animation, *Proc. Graphics Interface '83*, pp. 203-209.

Meyer B (1989): From Structured Programming to Object-Oriented Design: The Road To Eiffel, *Structured Programming*, Vol. 10, No1, pp.19-39.

Micallef J (1988): Encapsulation, Reusability and Extensibility in Object-Oriented Programming Languages. *Journal of Object-Oriented Programming* Vol. 1 No. 1, pp. 12-35.

Ostby EF(1989) Simplified Control of Complex Animation, *State-of-the-art in Computer Animation*, Springer Verlag, Tokyo, pp. 59-67.

Reeves WT, Ostby EF, Leffler SJ (1990) The Menv Modelling and Animation Environment, *Visualization and Computer Animation Journal*, John Wiley, Vol,1, No1 (July 1990)

Renault O, Magnenat-Thalmann N, Thalmann D (1990) A Vision-Based Approach to Behavioural Animation, *Visualization and Computer Animation Journal*, John Wiley, Vol,1, No1 (July 1990)

Reynolds CW (1982) Computer Animation with Scripts and Actors, *Proc. SIGGRAPH'82, Computer Graphics* Vol.16, No3, pp. 289-296.

Rumbaugh JL (1987): Relations as Semantic Constructs in an Object-Oriented Language, *Proc. OOPSLA '87*, pp. 466-481.

Szczur MR (1989) TAE Plus: Transportable Applications Environment Plus, *Xhibition89*, San Jose, California, June 1989.

Webster BF (1989) The NeXT Book. Addison Wesley.

Russell Turner is a researcher at the Computer Graphics Laboratory of the Swiss Federal Institute of Technology in Lausanne, Switzerland. He received his B.S. in Physics and his M.S. in Computer and Information Science from the University of Massachusetts at Amherst. He has also worked as a software engineer for V.I. Corporation of Amherst, Massachusetts. His research interests include computer animation, user-interfaces and object-oriented programming. He is a member of IEEE and ACM.
E-mail: turner@elma.epfl.CH

Enrico Gobbetti is a researcher at the Computer Graphics Laboratory of the Swiss Federal Institute of Technology in Lausanne, Switzerland. He received his diplôme d'ingénieur informaticien from the same institute. His research interests include visualization, computer animation and object-oriented programming.
E-mail: gobbetti@elma.epfl.CH

Francis Balaguer is a researcher at the Computer Graphics Laboratory of the Swiss Federal Institute of Technology in Lausanne, Switzerland. He received his diplôme d'ingénieur informaticien from the Institut National des Sciences Appliquées (INSA) in Lyon, France. His research interests include computer animation, user-interfaces and object-oriented programming.
E-mail: balaguer@ligsg2.epfl.CH

Angelo Mangili is a researcher at the Computer Graphics Laboratory of the Swiss Federal Institute of Technology in Lausanne, Switzerland. He received his diplôme d'ingénieur informaticien from the same institute. His research interests include computer animation and software engineering.
E-mail: mangili@elma.epfl.CH

Daniel Thalmann is currently full Professor and Director of the Computer Graphics Laboratory at the Swiss Federal Institute of Technology in Lausanne, Switzerland. Since 1977, he was Professor at the University of Montreal and codirector of the MIRALab research laboratory. He received his diploma in nuclear physics and Ph.D in Computer Science from the University of Geneva. He is coeditor-in-chief of the Visualization and Computer Animation Journal, member of the editorial board of the Visual Computer and cochairs the EUROGRAPHICS Working Group on Computer Simulation and Animation. He was director of the Canadian Man-Machine Communications Society and is a member of the Computer Society of the IEEE, ACM, SIGGRAPH, and the Computer Graphics Society. Daniel Thalmann's research interests include 3D computer animation, image synthesis, and scientific visualization. He has published more than 60 papers in this areas and is coauthor of several books including: Computer Animation: Theory and Practice and Image Synthesis: Theory and Practice. He is also codirector of several computer-generated films: *Dream Flight, Eglantine, Rendez-vous à Montréal, Galaxy Sweetheart.*
E-mail: `thalmann@elma.epfl.CH`

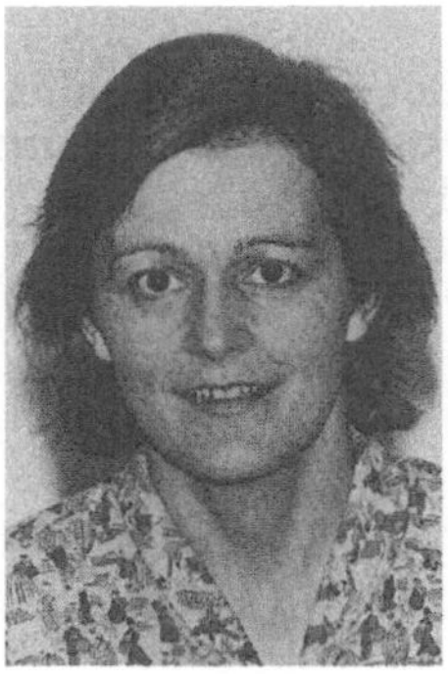

Nadia Magnenat Thalmann is currently full Professor of Computer Science at the University of Geneva, Switzerland. A former member of the Council of Science and Technology of the Government of Quebec and of the Council of Science and Technology of the Canadian Broadcasting Corporation, she also has served on a variety of government advisory boards and program committees. She has received several awards, including the 1985 Communications Award from the Government of Quebec. In May 1987, she was nominated woman of the year in sciences by the Montreal community. Dr. Magnenat Thalmann received a BS in psychology, an MS in biochemistry, and a Ph.D in quantum chemistry and computer graphics from the University of Geneva. Her previous appointments include the University Laval in Quebec, the Graduate Business school of the University of Montreal in Canada. She has written and edited several books and research papers in image synthesis and computer animation and was codirector of the computer-generated films *Dream Flight, Eglantine, Rendez-vous à Montréal* and *Galaxy Sweetheart.* She served as chairperson of Graphics Interface '85, CGI '88, Computer Animation '89 and Computer Animation '90.
E-mail: `thalmann@uni2a.unige.ch`

The authors may be contacted at:

Computer Graphics Lab
Swiss Federal Institute of Technology
CH 1015 Lausanne
Switzerland

MIRALab, CUI
University of Geneva
12 rue du Lac
CH 1207 Geneva
Switzerland

Chapter 6
Visual Languages and Visualization

Graphical Support for Programming: A Survey and Taxonomy

Gurminder Singh

ABSTRACT

Great interest is beginning to arise in using graphics as an aid in programming. Graphics has been applied to program construction and to program debugging and understanding. The systems in the first category are commonly known as "Visual Programming" systems whereas the ones in the second category are called "Program Visualization" systems. This paper presents a taxonomy of these systems. Systems are categorized according to the techniques followed or based on their focus. Example systems from each category are discussed.

Categories and Subject Descriptors: D.2.2 [**Software Engineering**]: Tools and Techniques-Flowcharts; D.2.5 [**Software Engineering**]: Testing and Debugging - Debugging Aids; D.3.2 [**Programming Languages**]: Language Classification; I.3.6 [**Computer Graphics**]: Methodology and Techniques - Languages.

General Terms: Visual Programming, Program Visualization.

Additional Key Words and Phrases: Languages.

1. INTRODUCTION

Great interest is beginning to arise in using graphics as an aid in programming. This interest is a direct result of the great expressive power of graphics and of general dissatisfaction with conventional programming languages. Ever since the inception of computer, researchers have been trying to simplify the task of programming it. The transitions from machine language to assembly language and finally to high level language are steps in this direction. The high level languages have helped in reducing the complexity of programming by making available high level abstractions to the programmer. Although high level languages have been quite successful, there are a number of problems with them. The effort to solve these problems continues even today with the development of higher level programming languages. But these efforts do not seem to be helping very much. Even after years of experience in designing programming languages, the job of programming is still assigned to people specially trained to perform it. Extensive training is usually required before a person becomes fluent in the use of a programming language, and even after gaining fluency in the use of a programming language, considerable time is spent in developing programs and debugging them. Clearly, a radical departure from the conventional programming languages is necessary if a major break through is to be achieved in the ease and efficiency of programming.

Graphics provides exciting opportunities for reducing the complexity of programming and for increasing the productivity of programmers. Graphics provides the ability to add more dimensions to the conventional (linear) style of programming, enabling the programmer to carry concepts directly from his mind over to the computer. These additional dimensions allow the restyling of programming in terms which are more natural for humans to use, automate the mundane portions of the task of programming, and enhance the ability of the programmer to develop correct code and to debug the developed code.

Graphics has been applied quite successfully to program construction and program debugging [Smith 77]. In the case of program construction, the effort is to enable the programmer to program directly using the abstractions he is familiar with, avoiding the translation of these abstractions into cryptic textual specification required by conventional programming languages. In program debugging, graphics is used to visualize the execution of the program or its data, which helps in locating errors in the program. The terms "visual programming" and "program visualization" have been applied to the use of graphics for such purposes.

The aim of this paper is to examine the use of graphics as an aid in programming. A taxonomy of graphical systems for developing and debugging programs is presented. A number of common unsolved problems with these systems are discussed. This paper complements the works of Brad Myers [Myers 86], S.K. Chang [Chang 87], and Nan Shu [Shu 88] .

2. TAXONOMY

Figure 1 shows a possible way of categorizing systems which use graphics to support programming. At the highest level, the systems are divided into two categories: programming and visualization. The programming category consists of systems which support program creation process through visual or graphical techniques. The systems in this category are generally referred to as "Visual Programming" systems. Using a system from this category, the programmer produces a program. In the visualization category, we put all those systems in which graphics is used to illustrate, either directly or information about, program, data, or algorithm. Systems in this category are mainly useful in debugging programs, understanding program behavior, and visualizing data. These systems have been commonly called "Program Visualization" systems, even though some of the systems may be used for visualizing data or algorithm.

The visual programming systems are classified based on the way graphics is used for constructing programs. The first category, called graphical interaction systems, consists of systems in which the user interactions with the system guide or instruct the system to create the program. In such systems, the user actions and the sequence of user actions are extremely important. The second category, called visual language systems, consists of systems in which icons, symbols, charts, or forms are used to specify the program. The arrangement of symbols on the screen, which usually follows some syntactic rules, forms the program. This is similar to conventional programming systems, except that in this case text is replaced by pictures. The main difference between the graphical interaction systems and the visual language systems is that in graphical interaction systems the user interaction with the system is important whereas in visual language systems the arrangement of

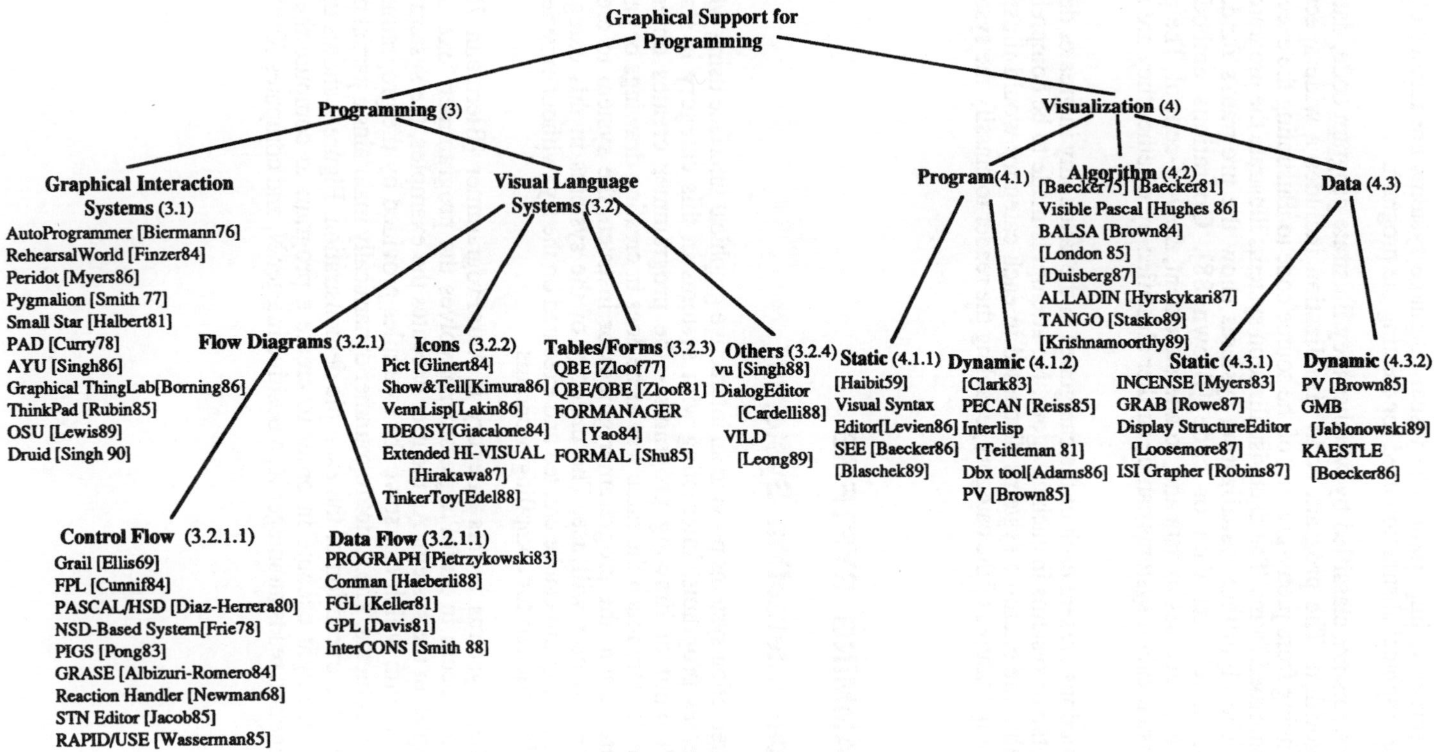

Fig. 1 Classification of Systems
(Small numbers next to the category headings refer to the section in which the category is discussed)

symbols on the screen is important. The visual language systems are further classified depending on the graphical abstraction used for creating the program.

Visualization systems are classified by whether they illustrate program code, data of the program, or algorithm. The program code visualization includes a wide spectrum of visualizations ranging from pretty-printing of the source code to illustrating the execution of the program in animated forms. The data visualization systems illustrate the program data in various forms. The algorithm visualization systems show the program's fundamental operations, not merely its data or code [Brown 88]. Operations embody both transformations and accesses to data and, to a lesser extent, flow-of-control. The program code and data visualization systems can be further classified by whether they are static or dynamic.

The following sections present each of the categories in the taxonomy in greater detail and discuss representative systems in each category. No attempt is made to be comprehensive, but it is hoped that the example systems discussed in each category would illustrate the main distinguishing features of the category, enabling the reader to classify the systems not discussed here.

3. PROGRAMMING SYSTEMS

3.1 Graphical Interaction Systems

The graphical interaction systems provide an interactive graphical interface using which the programmer creates programs. Interacting with systems in this category is similar to interacting with paint or drawing programs - the programmer creates objects and manipulates them in very much the same way as he does in creating drawings or paintings. Through this interaction, the programmer guides or instructs the system to create the program that the end user will use. The majority of the systems in this category are interpretive, i.e. the program can be created and executed on the fly, without experiencing a substantial time lag required for compiling programs.

One of the earliest systems in this category is AutoProgrammer [Biermann 76]. The program creation process in AutoProgrammer involves the programmer "executing" a number of examples in the system. As the user executes the examples, the system tries to infer a general program which can solve the examples provided by the programmer and additional similar problems. The AutoProgrammer dynamically maintains a partial program at all times during the execution of the example demonstration. Figure 2 shows the steps that a programmer might execute in order to create a program to compute the power function. This function reads an integer X, a positive integer N, and computes X**N.

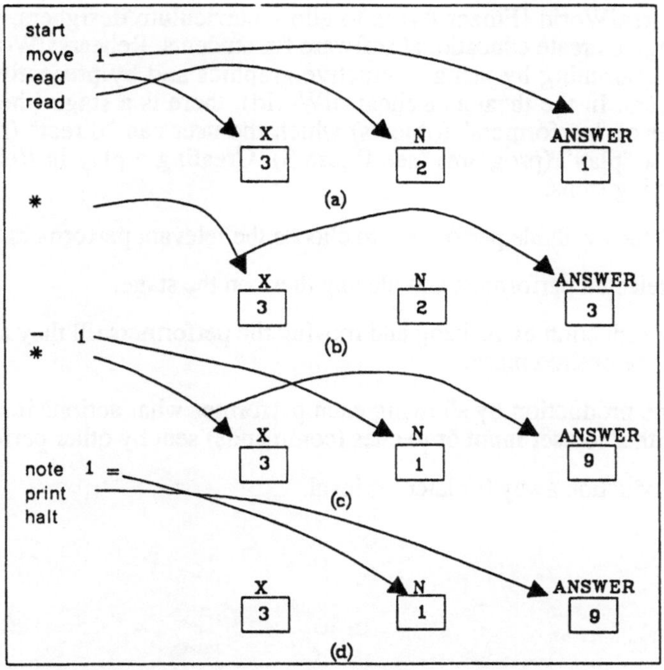

Fig. 2a Demonstrating the Behavior of the Power Function (from [Shu 88])

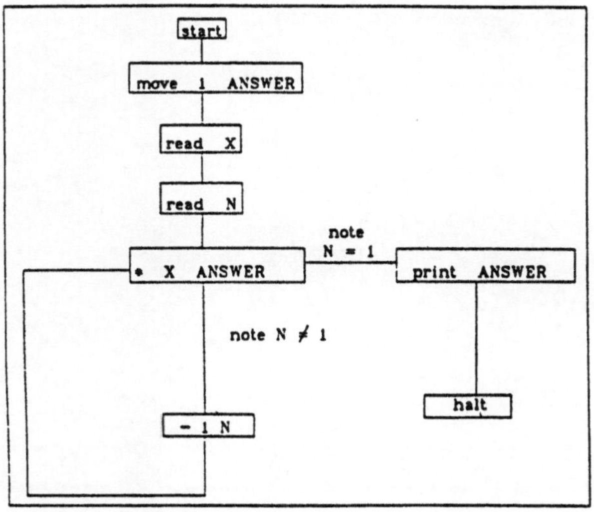

Fig. 2b Automatically Created Power Function (from [Shu 88])

The goal of RehearsalWorld [Finzer 84] is to allow curriculum designers, who may not know programming, to create educational software for students. RehearsalWorld simplifies the process of programming by using interactive graphics and by presenting a "theater" metaphor to its users. In the theater (RehearsalWorld), there is a stage (the screen), and there are a number of "performers" (objects) which the user can "direct" (manipulate or rehears) to create a "play" (program) (see figure 3). Creating a play in RehearsalWorld involves the following steps.

°"Auditioning" the available performers to choose the relevant performers.

°Copying the selected performers and placing them on the stage.

°Blocking the production by resizing and moving the performers till they are the desired size and in the desired place.

°Rehearsing the production by showing each performer what actions it should take in response either to user input or to cues (commands) sent by other performers.

°Storing the production away for later retrieval.

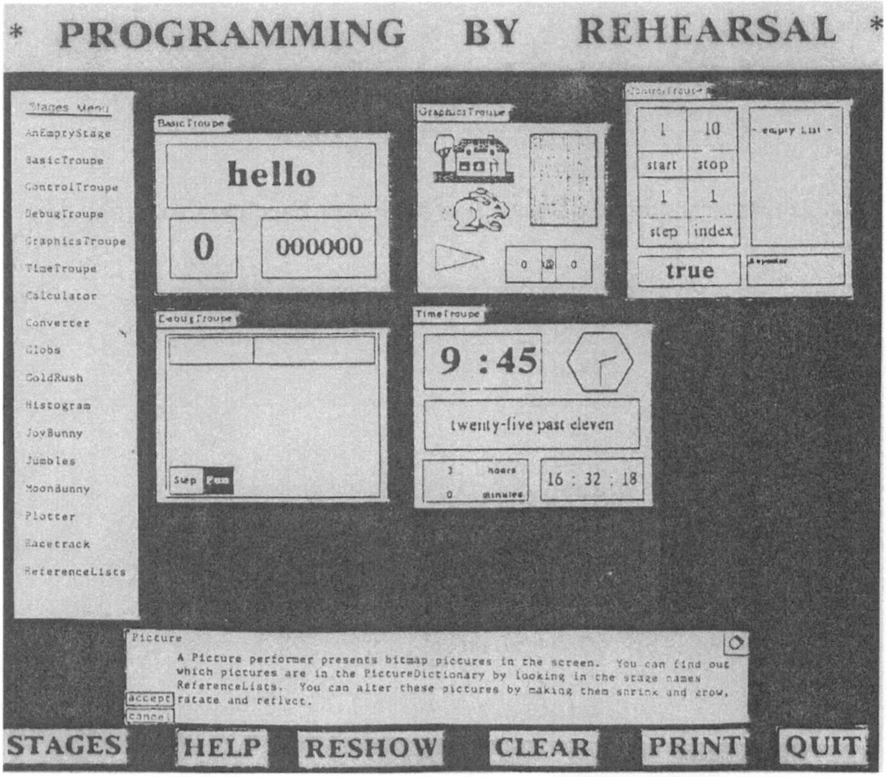

Fig. 3 A Screen from Rehearsal World (from [Finzer 84])

Druid [Singh 90] is a user interface management system which enables interface designers, who are not required to know programming, to create interactive, graphical user interfaces by demonstration. To specify an interface, the designer first creates the layout of the interface by using interactive graphical facilities and then demonstrates to Druid how the end user might interact with the user interface. Druid watches the demonstration given by the designer and implements the demonstrated behavior when the end user interacts with the interface. The results of the specification are immediately visible and executable on the screen. The designer can rehearse partial specifications to "feel" the interface and to find errors in the specification. Figure 4 shows a text editor interface during rehearsal. Druid is similar in a number of ways to Peridot [Myers 86, Myers 88]. The main difference between Druid and Peridot is that while Druid aims at the overall look and feel of the interface, Peridot focuses at low level interaction techniques.

Other systems which can be classified as graphical interaction systems include Pygmalion [Smith 77], Small Star [Halbert 81], PAD [Curry 78], AYU [Singh 86], Graphical ThingLab [Borning 86], ThinkPad [Rubin 85], and OSU [Lewis 89].

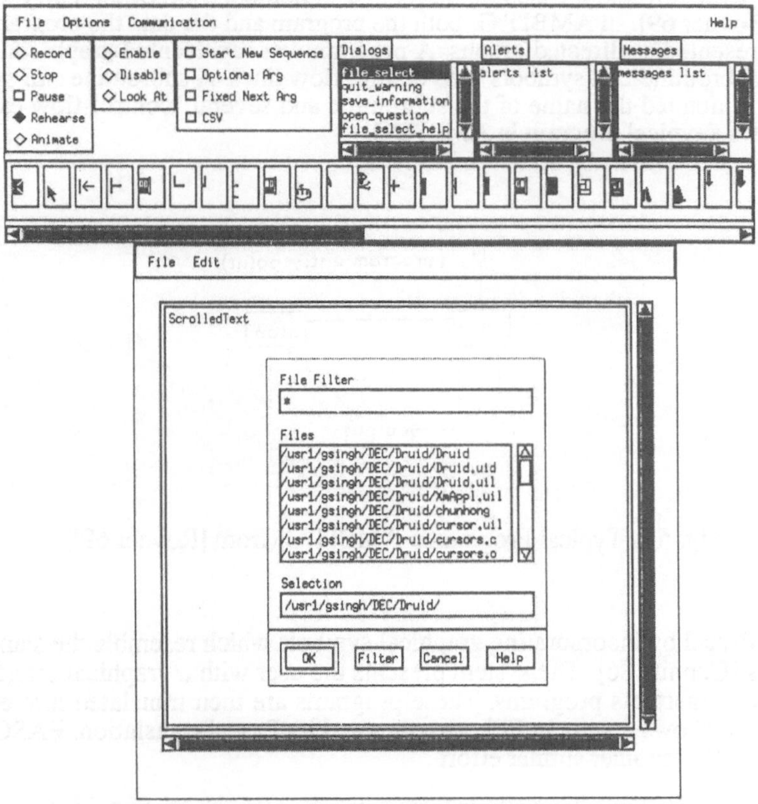

Fig.4 The Druid User Interface Management System during Rehearsal

3.2 Visual Programming Language Systems

3.2.1 Flow Diagrams

Flow diagrams based visual programming systems enable the programmer to construct programs using various types of charts, graphs, and diagrams. The primary use of flow diagrams in these systems is to specify either the flow of control or the flow of data in the program. The graphical specification created by the programmer is either compiled to a conventional programming language or directly interpreted by the system.

3.2.1.1 Control Flow Diagrams

Flow chart is probably the earliest visual representation for programs. Flow charts were originally developed to aid the programmer in organizing large programs and for documentation purposes. The flow charts based visual programming systems use flow charts for a different purpose, to create programs from flow charts automatically.

One of the earliest systems which could compile programs directly from computerized flowcharts appears to be Grail [Ellis 69]. In Grail, the contents of the boxes used in the flow charts were ordinary machine language statements. Another early effort was AMBIT/G [Rovner 69]. In AMBIT/G, both the program and the data the program operated on, were represented as directed graphs. A program was represented graphically as a 2-D network of "subroutine-call symbols" and control flow lines. A subroutine call symbol was a box which contained the name of the subroutine and several "control-flow exit points". Figure 5 shows a typical program in AMBIT/G.

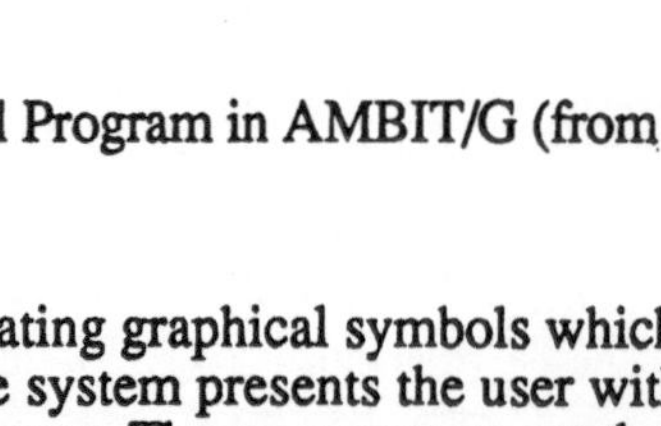

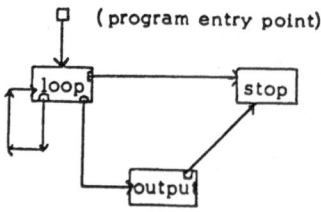

Fig. 5 A Typical Program in AMBIT/G (from [Rovner 69])

FPL extends Pascal by incorporating graphical symbols which resemble the standard flow chart symbols [Cunniff 86]. The system presents the user with a graphical interface using which the user constructs programs. These programs are then translated into executable Pascal. Figure 6 shows a sample FPL program and its Pascal translation. PASCAL/HSD [Diaz-Herrera 80] is another similar effort.

A number of other systems have similar goals but they use Nassi-Shneiderman diagrams [Nassi 73] rather than the standard flow charts. Frei, Weller, and Williams use an extension of Nassi-Shneiderman diagrams to create programs in an interactive graphical environment [Frie 78]. These programs are then compiled into PL/I statements. Figure 7 shows an example of a program constructed using Frei et al's system.

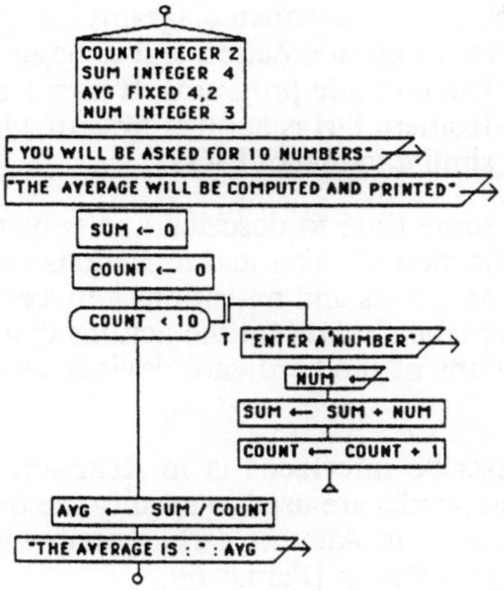
COUNT INTEGER 2
SUM INTEGER 4
AVG FIXED 4,2
NUM INTEGER 3
"YOU WILL BE ASKED FOR 10 NUMBERS"
"THE AVERAGE WILL BE COMPUTED AND PRINTED"
SUM ← 0
COUNT ← 0
COUNT < 10
T
"ENTER A NUMBER"
NUM ←
SUM ← SUM + NUM
COUNT ← COUNT + 1
AVG ← SUM / COUNT
"THE AVERAGE IS : " : AVG

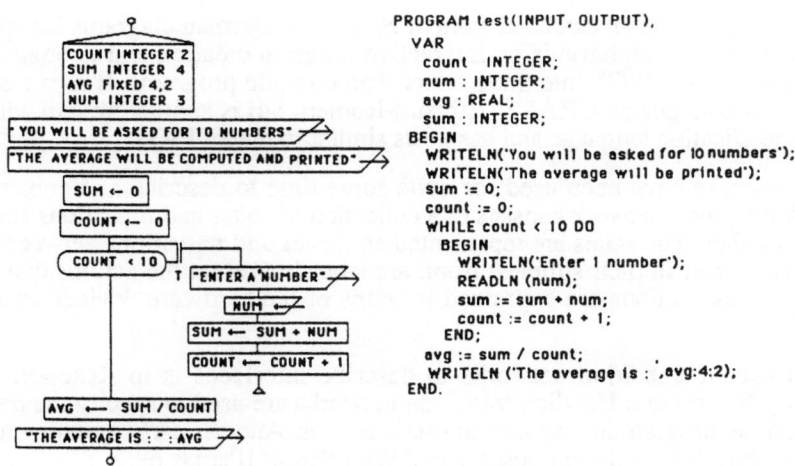

```
PROGRAM test(INPUT, OUTPUT),
  VAR
    count  INTEGER;
    num : INTEGER;
    avg : REAL;
    sum : INTEGER;
  BEGIN
    WRITELN('You will be asked for 10 numbers');
    WRITELN('The average will be printed');
    sum := 0;
    count := 0;
    WHILE count < 10 DO
      BEGIN
        WRITELN('Enter 1 number');
        READLN (num);
        sum := sum + num;
        count := count + 1;
      END;
    avg := sum / count;
    WRITELN ('The average is : ',avg:4:2);
  END.
```

Fig. 6 A Sample FPL Program with Pascal Translation (from [Cunnif 84])

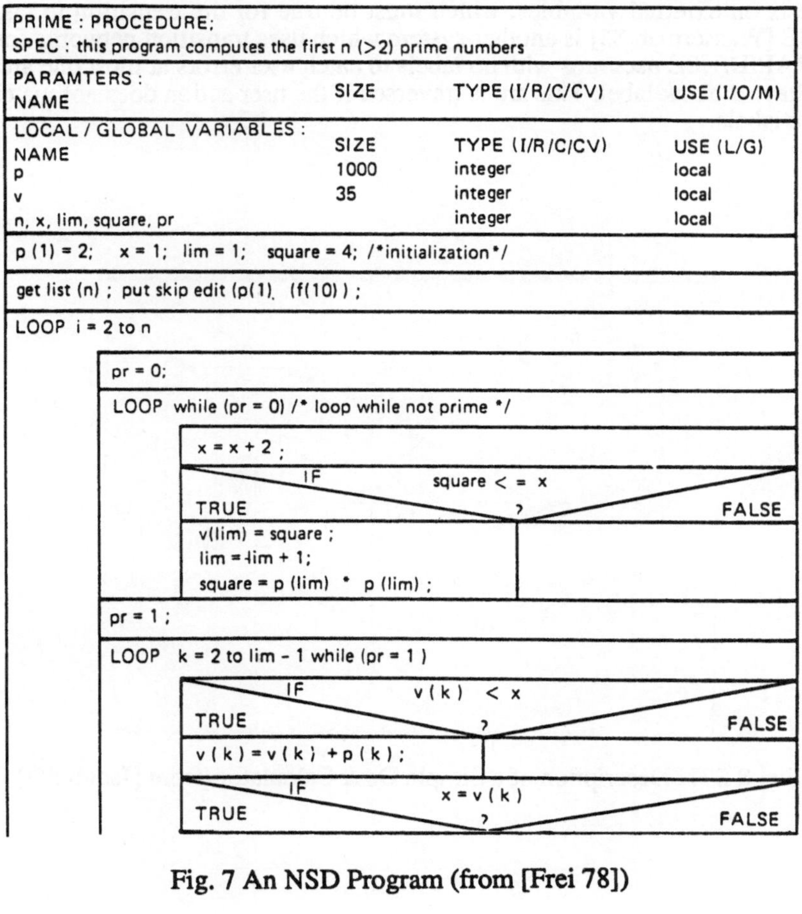
PRIME : PROCEDURE;
SPEC : this program computes the first n (>2) prime numbers
PARAMTERS :
NAME
SIZE
TYPE (I/R/C/CV)
USE (I/O/M)
LOCAL / GLOBAL VARIABLES :
NAME
SIZE
TYPE (I/R/C/CV)
USE (L/G)
p
1000
integer
local
v
35
integer
local
n, x, lim, square, pr
integer
local
p (1) = 2; x = 1; lim = 1; square = 4; /*initialization*/
get list (n) ; put skip edit (p(1), (f(10))) ;
LOOP i = 2 to n
pr = 0;
LOOP while (pr = 0) /* loop while not prime */
x = x + 2 ;
IF
square < = x
TRUE
?
FALSE
v(lim) = square ;
lim = lim + 1;
square = p (lim) * p (lim) ;
pr = 1 ;
LOOP k = 2 to lim - 1 while (pr = 1)
IF
v (k) < x
TRUE
?
FALSE
v (k) = v (k) + p (k) ;
IF
x = v (k)
TRUE
?
FALSE

Fig. 7 An NSD Program (from [Frei 78])

PIGS [Pong 83] also uses an extended from of Nassi Shneiderman diagrams for specifying the program. In PIGS emphasis is on interactive program creation and debugging. As a result of this emphasis, PIGS interprets rather than compile programs. It uses a subset of Pascal as the base language. GRASE [Albizuri-Romero 84] is another system which uses GAL as its specification language and has goals similar to that of PIGS.

Transition networks have been used for quite some time to describe and construct user interfaces. A transition network consists of a collection of states and transitions connecting one state to another. The states are represented as circles and transitions between them as directed labeled arcs. In their simplest from, arc labels represent the actions that the user can perform. These actions are expressed in terms of the hardware devices used by the program.

The earliest use of transition networks to describe interfaces is in Reaction Handler [Newman 68]. In Reaction Handler, transition networks are used to specify the transfer of control within the program in response to user's actions. Another early system which uses transition networks for similar purposes is by David Parnas [Parnas 69].

Many extensions have been proposed to add more power to the basic transition network notation. In Jacob's transition diagram editor [Jacob 85], output tokens are used to display messages and prompt users for input (see figure 8). He also uses conditionals to make arbitrary tests on external variables, which must be true for the transition to take place. RAPID/USE [Wasserman 85] is another system which uses transition networks for similar purposes. RAPID/USE uses arcs with no labels to catch user errors at most one arc leaving a state can have a blank label. This arc is traversed if the user action does not match any of the other arc labels.

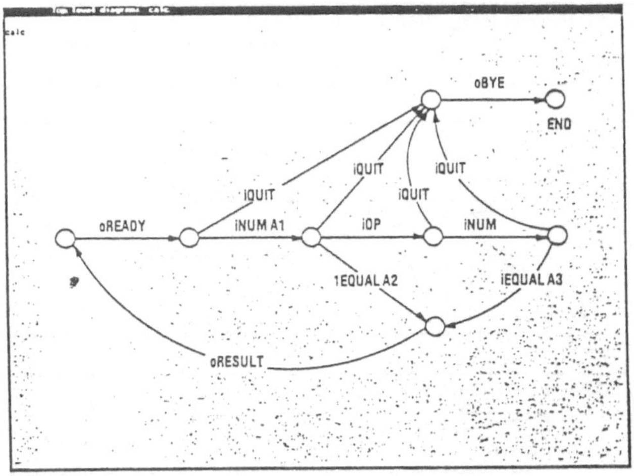

Fig. 8 STN Description of a Simple Desk Calculator (from [Jacob 85])

3.2.1.2 DATA FLOW DIAGRAMS

Data flow diagrams provide a natural representation for programs in data flow languages. Representing data flow programs in diagrams has a number of advantages, including the ease of constructing and understanding the program behavior, especially the concurrent parts of the program [Davis 82].

PROGRAPH [Pietrzykowski 83] is an interactive visual programming system which supports a functional data flow language. In PROGRAPH, programs are created by creating graphs representing the flow of data between operations of a functional language (see figure 9). PROGRAPH also helps in debugging programs by showing a trace of data flow through a selected data path by means of a token moving along wires.

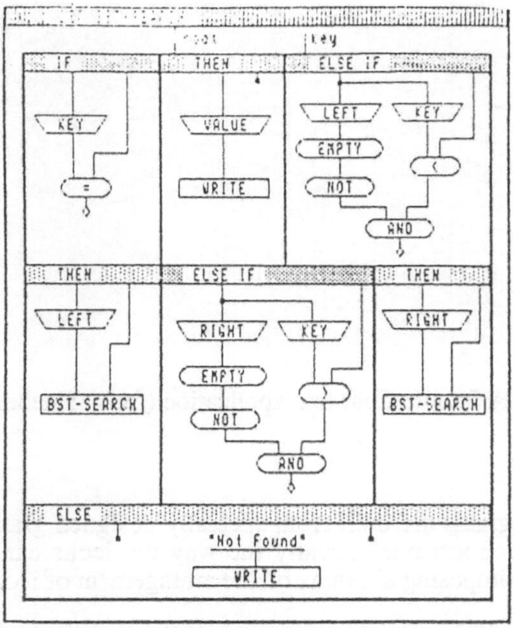

Fig. 9 Prograph for a Binary Search Tree Lookup (from [Pietrzykowski 83])

ConMan [Haeberli 88] is an environment for building graphical applications. To build an application, the user integrates application objects into modular components. By interactively connecting simple components, the user constructs a complete graphical application that matches the needs of a task. A connection manager controls the flow of data between individual components. Figure 10 shows an example of how graphical applications are built in ConMan.

Other Systems which fall in this category of visual programming systems include FGL [Keller 81], GPL [Davis 81], and InterCons [Smith 88].

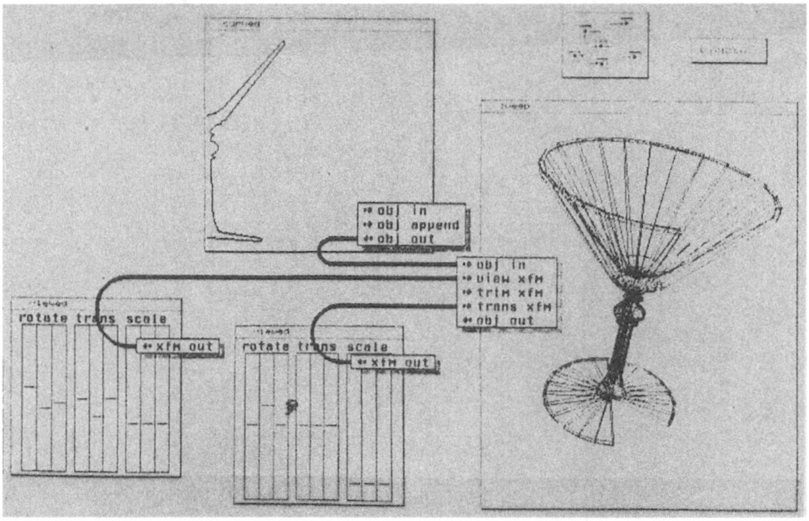

Fig. 10 A Simple ConMan Application (from [Haeberli 88])

3.2.2 Icons

In iconic systems, programs are built from specially designed graphical symbols, called icons, and their interconnections. Usually the way the icons can be interconnected is dictated by the system, imposing a syntax on the arrangement of icons.

Pict [Glinert 84] is an iconic visual programming language system which aims at "initiating novices to the world of computer programming". The Pict system provides the programmer with a number of predefined icons denoting various operations. The programmer constructs programs by selecting the various icons needed to perform the calculations and interconnects them by paths to indicate the desired flow of control (see figure 11). Pict relies heavily on the use of color and pointing in the creation of programs. The user can run his programs, without having to translate them into a coventional programming language, and debug them in the same environment.

Show and Tell [Kimura 86] is another iconic system, similar to Pict, which uses the data flow concepts in the creation of programs. In Show and Tell, programs consists of various types of boxes and arrows which connect boxes to each other depicting the flow of data.

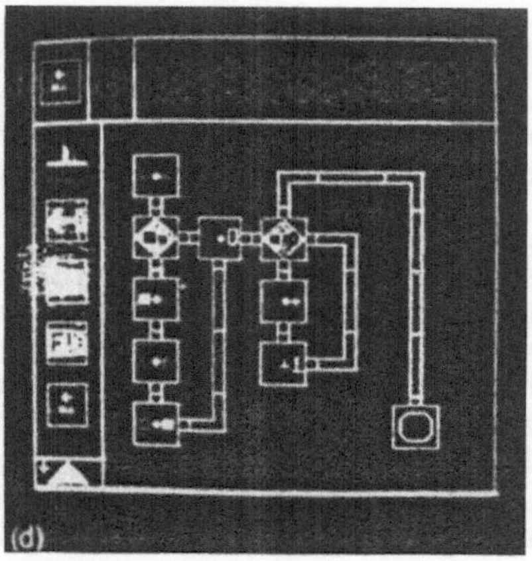

Fig. 11 Multiplication by Repeated Addition in Pict/D (from Glinert 84])

VennLISP [Lakin 86] is different from both, Pict and Show and Tell in that instead of using arrows to depict the flow of data or control, it uses enclosures, much like parentheses in LISP. Figure 12 shows a VennLISP form.

Other systems which may be classified as iconic visual programming language systems include IDEOSY [Giacalone 84], Extended HI-VISUAL [Hirakawa 87], and TinkerToy [Edel 88].

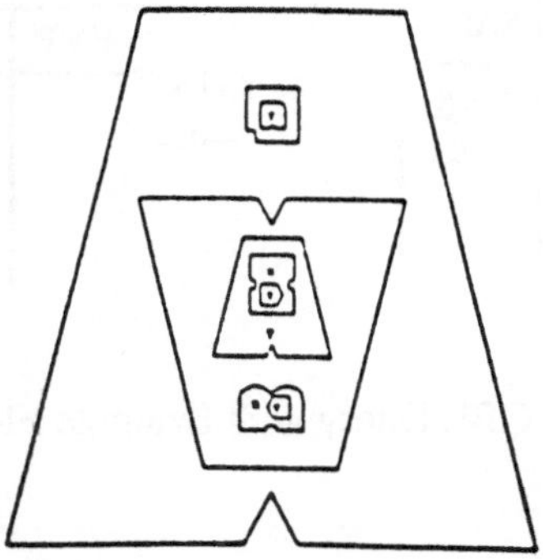

Fig. 12 A VennLisp Form (from [Lakin 86])

3.2.3 Tables/Forms

This category of systems allows the user to construct programs using tables or by filling forms. Form filling and tables have been recognized as easy ways of communicating with the user and are used quite extensively in a number of graphical systems.

QBE (Query By Example) [Zloof 77] allows users to specify queries on a relational database using two-dimensional tables. The user uses QBE to retrieve, insert, delete, or update data by using operators which mimic the manual table operations. QBE enables the users to qualify queries by using constants and example elements. An example element represents an instance of the possible values. Figure 13, shows a query to find names of employees from TOY department whose manager is TOM. Figure 14 shows a query which uses example elements. It shows a query to find the names of employees who earn same as JOHN. QBE/OBE [Zloof 81] extends the concepts of QBE to include office activities such as electronic mail and document processing.

EMP	NAME	SAL	MGR	DEPT
	P.		TOM	TOY

Yields →

EMP	NAME

Fig. 13 An Example QBE Query

EMP	NAME	SAL
	P.	P. = S1
	JOHN	S1

Yields →

EMP	NAME	SAL

Fig. 14 A QBE Query with Example Elements

FORMANAGER [Yao 84] enables users to develop office information systems using forms. A form in FORMANAGER has the appearance of a paper form which contains some text and blank fields which the user fills in. Forms are created by specifying a form schema composed of field definitions, and a form template containing fixed text, graphics, and special non-database fields such as page number. The FORMANAGER translates all user input, which comes from forms, into SQL commands on the underlying database tables.

FORMAL [Shu 85] is a forms-based database language which explicitly represents hierarchical structures. FORMAL emphasizes data manipulation as opposed to QBE and FORMANAGER which emphasize the retrieval, insertion, and deletion of data. FORMAL uses stylized forms to visually represent data structures and data instances, and to create programs. Figure 15 shows an example form in FORMAL. Data processing activity in FORMAL is expressed as a form process (or a series of form processes), where each form process can take one or two forms as input and produce another form as output. Figure 16 shows an example of form process which converts a PRODUCT form into a VENDPROD form.

(PERSON)											
ENO	DNO	NAME	PHONE	JC	(KIDS)		(SCHOOL)			SEX	LOC
					KNAME	AGE	SNAME	(ENROLL)			
								YEARIN	YEAROUT		
105	D1	SMITH	5555	05	JOHN	02	PRINCETON	1966	1970	F	SF
					MARY	04		1972	1976		
105	D1	SMITH	5555	05	JANE	01				F	SF
107	D1	JONES	5555	05	DICK	07	SJS	1960	1965	F	SF
					JANE	04					
							BERKELEY	1965	1969		
111	D1	ENGEL	2568	05			UCLA	1970	1974	F	LA
112	D1	DURAN	7610	05	MARY	08				M	SF
					BOB	10					
					JOHN	12					

Fig. 15 Form Heading and a Few Instances of Person Form (from [Shu 85])

3.2.4 Others

A number of other systems, which use graphics quite extensively in the program creation process, clearly do not fit into any of the above categories of visual programming systems. A number of these systems use a mixture of the techniques discussed above.

Vu [Singh 88] is a visual environment for creating graphical user interfaces. The vu environment provides the designer with a number of standard user interface objects, which the designer can customize to suit the needs of the application. The customization of objects is done in a highly interactive and graphical manner. The vu system uses direct manipulation techniques, such as rubber-banding and dragging, and form filling to handle object customization. The appearance of the forms used in vu depends on the graphical appearance of the objects. Figure 17 shows the vu system in action. Another system which is used for creating user interfaces and uses techniques similar to the ones used in vu is DialogEditor [Cardelli 88].

(PRODUCT)

PROD_NO	PNAME	TYPE	(SUPPLIER) VNAME	(STORAGE) BIN_NO	(STORAGE) LOC	PRICE
110	PIPE	PVC	AQUA CHEMTRON	B1 B2 B3	SJC SJC SFO	0.79
120	PIPE	STEEL	ABC CHEMTRON	B4	SFO	4.10
210	VALVE	STEEL	AQUA ABC CHEMTRON	B5 B6	SJC SFO	0.45
221	VALVE	COPPER	ABC CHEMTRON ROBINSON	B7 B8	SJC SFO	1.25

V

(VENDPROD)

VNAME	(PROD) PROD_NO	(PROD) TYPE	(PROD) PNAME
ABC	120 210 221	STEEL STEEL COPPER	PIPE VALVE VALVE
AQUA	110 210	PVC STEEL	PIPE VALVE
CHEMTRON	110 120 210 221	PVC STEEL STEEL COPPER	PIPE PIPE VALVE VALVE
ROBINSON	221	COPPER	VALVE

Fig. 16 An Example of a Form Process (from [Shu 85])

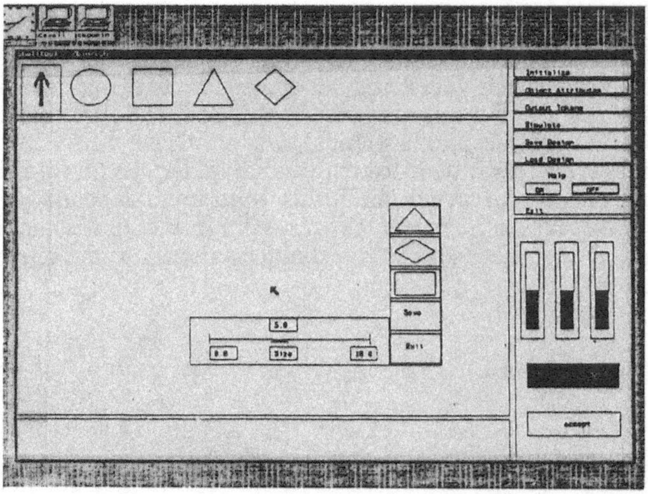

Fig. 17 Modifying Object Attributes in vu (from [Singh 88])

4. VISUALIZATION SYSTEMS

4.1 Program Visualization

4.1.1 Static Program Visualization

The earliest technique for program visualization is based on using flowcharts. [Haibit 59] describes a system which automatically produces flow charts from FORTRAN programs. Another system which produces diagrams from program code is called the "Visual Syntax Editor" [Levien 86]. It depicts LISP programs as pictures, using arrows to depict data flow. Figure 18 shows the Fibonacci function as displayed by the Visual Syntax editor. The equivalent LISP program for figure 18 is shown below. Although we have classified Visual Syntax as a program visualization system, it allows the user to create and edit the programs represented as diagrams.

```
(defun fib (x)
    (if (< x 2) 1)
        (+ (fib (- x 1)) (fib (- x 2)))))
```

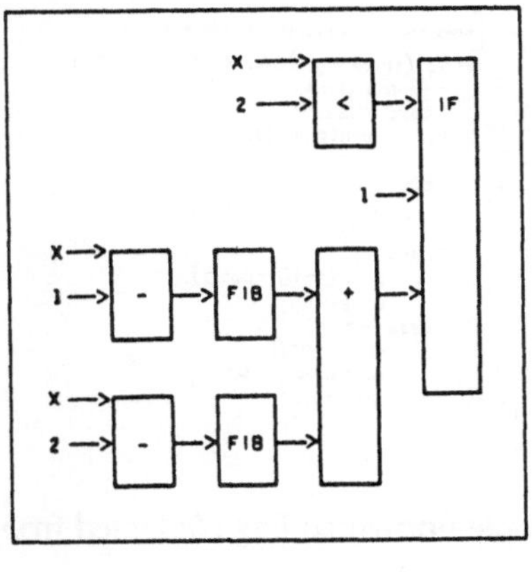

Fig. 18 The fib Function, As Displayed by the Visual Syntax Editor (from [Levien 86])

Another form of static program visualization which does not use pictures is pretty-printing. Most prettyprintng systems use blanks, blank lines, indentation, and comments to enhance the readability of the program. A recent system which pretty-prints Modula-2 and Pascal programs is by Blaschek and Sametinger [Blaschek 89]. This system can adapt to the personal user preferences or to particular project conventions. Blascheks and Sametinger's paper contains references to a number of other pretty-printing systems which follow similar rules.

Baecker and Marcus have developed the SEE visual compiler [Baecker 86] which uses multiple fonts, variable point sizes, proportionate characters, grey scale tints, and other graphics design techniques to pretty-print programs written in the C programming language. Figure 19 shows a sample of a formatted C program.

u2 ron darpa programs	calc1.c	10 Aug 1. 49	Revision 1.2	Printed 30 Aug 85	
Program Visualization Project Human Computing Resources Aaron Marcus and Associates	Calculator	calc1.c	calc()	Page 24	2

Chapter 1 calc1.c

This reverse Polish desk calculator adds, subtracts, multiplies and divides floating point numbers. It also allows the commands '=' to print the value of the top of the stack and 'c' to clear the stack.

```
                                   #include   <stdio.h>
Max size of operand, operator      #define    MAXOP      20
Signal that number found           #define    NUMBER     '0'
Signal that string is too big      #define    TOOBIG     '9'
```

Control Module

calc()

```
Operation type                     int        type;
Buffer containing operator         char       s[MAXOP];
Temporary variable                 double     op2,
Converts strings to floating                  atof(),
point
Pops the stack                                pop(),
Pushes the stack                              push();

Loop while we can get an operation string and type
while ((type = getop(s, MAXOP)) != EOF)
    switch (type)
    case NUMBER:
        push(atof(s));
        break ;
    case '+':
        push(pop() + pop());
        break ;
    case '*':
        push(pop() * pop());
        break ;
    case '-':
        op2 = pop();
        push(pop() - op2);
        break ;
```

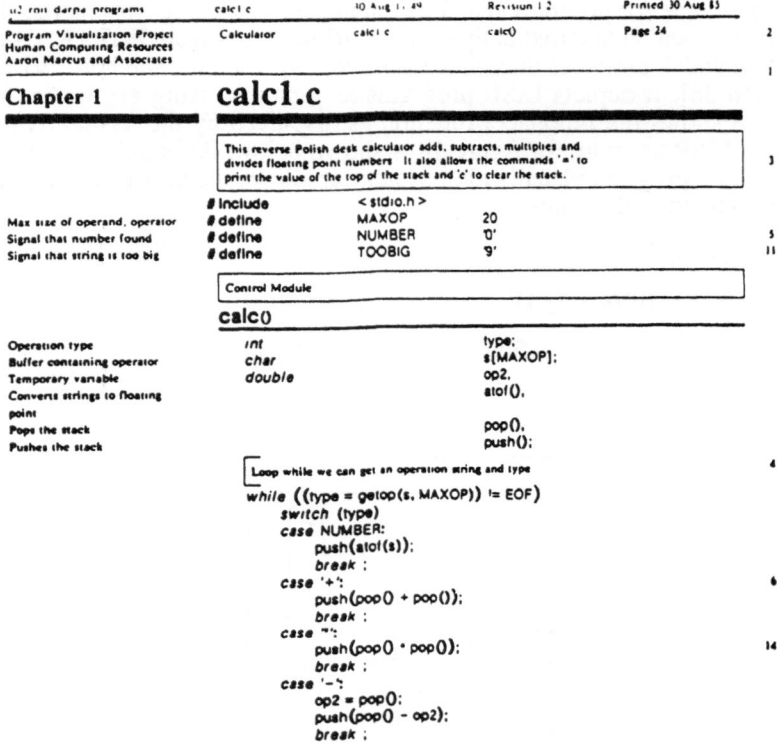

Fig. 19 An Example Formatted Page (adapted from [Baecker 86])

4.1.2 Dynamic Program Visualization

Dynamic program visualization systems show the execution of the program in animated forms, either by animating pictures which correspond to the program or by highlighting the program code. Clark and Robinson [Clark 83] have developed a system which shows Pascal programs in Nassi-Shneiderman chart form [Nassi 73]. At the run-time, the system can mark the currently executing part of the program to show the progress of control through the program.

PECAN [Reiss 85] is a program development system which uses Pascal as its host language. The PECAN system can display multiple views of the program during execution. The currently supported views are control, program, and data (see figure 20). The control view displays textual messages that indicate the current execution state of the program. In the control view, the user can control the speed of execution, reverse the program execution, step through the program one step at a time, and insert break points in the program. The program view displays the program as a flow graph and highlights the parts of the flow graph as they are executed. The data view displays the current state of the execution stack.

Interlisp [Tietleman 81] and some of the program debugging tools, such as Dbxtool [Adams 86] can also be classified as dynamic program visualization as these systems are capable of showing the current state of execution by highlighting the program code. PV [Brown 85] shows dynamic displays of control flow, but places higher priority of dynamic data visualization. As a result of its focus, PV is classified under the dynamic data visualization category, discussed in section 4.2.2.

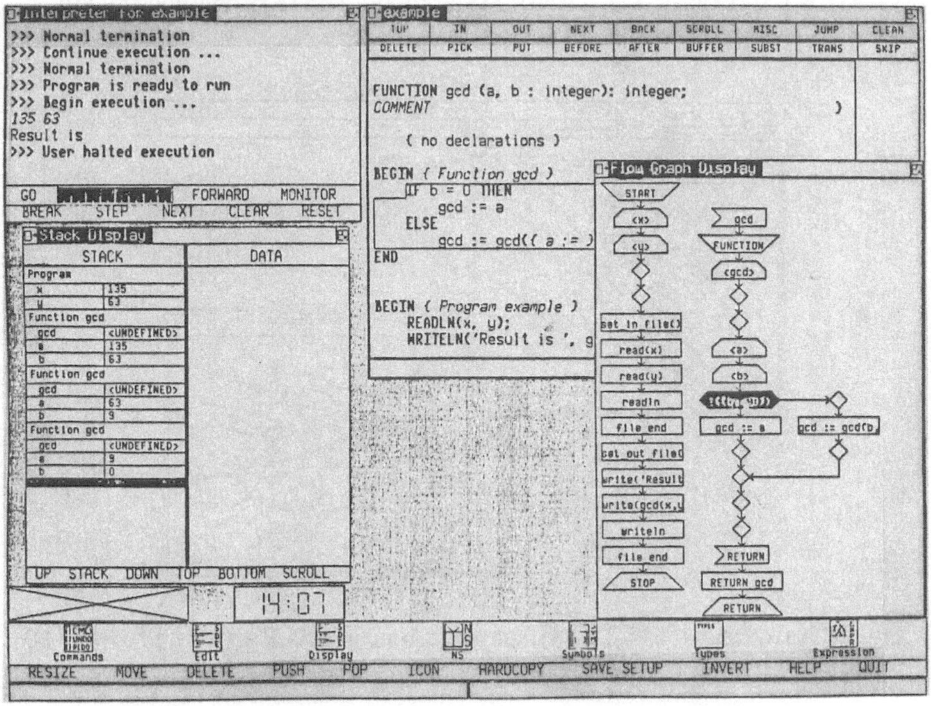

Fig. 20 A PECAN Display Showing Program Execution (from [Reiss 85])

4.2 Algorithm Visualization

Algorithm visualization systems show the program fundamental operations which embody both transformations and accesses to data and flow-of-control. Ron Baecker's system [Baecker 75] is designed to produce animations of algorithms. Instead of producing animation in real time, the system produces sequences of frames which are used to make movies. [Baecker 81] shows an animation of various sorting algorithms produced by using the system.

Visible Pascal [Hughes 86] provides a library of two dimensional graphics animation routines and an interpretive run-time environment for a subset of Pascal. To create an animation, a program must be written in Visible Pascal which, on execution, produces animations in real time.

BALSA [Brown 84] system is designed to aid students in understanding algorithms by showing them interesting events in the algorithm in animated forms. Animations in BALSA are created by inserting "interesting event" procedure calls in the algorithm code. At the run-time, these events trigger graphical views. These views dynamically change in response to interesting events. BALSA has been used in a number of interesting ways, including comparisons among different algorithms by running them on the same data and showing the results in real time (see figure 21).

Duisberg's system [Duisberg 87] aims at creating dynamic algorithm visualizations without programming. In this system, pieces of animation are created by demonstration and calls to these animations are inserted in the program code by pointing with a mouse.

Other systems which may be classified as algorithm visualization systems include [London 85], ALLADIN [Hyrskykari 87], TANGO [Stasko 89], and [Krishnamoorthy 89].

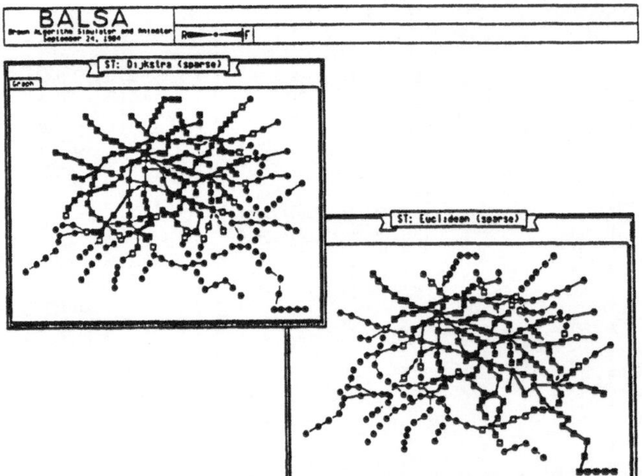

Fig. 21 A Comparison of Two Graph Algoritms in BALSA (from [Brown 84])

4.3 Data Visualization

4.3.1 Static Data Visualization

INCENSE [Myers 80, Myers 83] automatically creates displays of data structures similar to those that the programmer might draw on paper. Figure 22 shows an example of a data structure display created by INCENSE. In addition to providing a library of displays, INCENSE also allows the user to create displays of his choice.

There are a number of systems which are used for visualizing, browsing, and editing various types of data structures such as trees and graphs. Examples of such systems include GRAB [Rowe 87], PS300 Display Strcture Editor [Loosemore 87] and ISI Grapher [Robins 87].

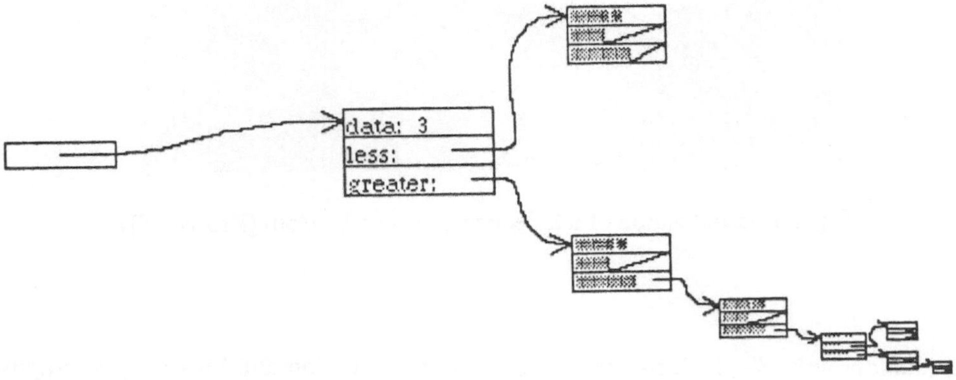

Fig. 22 A Deep Recursive Tree Display in INCENSE (from [Myers 8])

4.3.2 Dynamic Data Visualization

PV [Brown 85] focuses on dynamic visualizations of structured data such data as numeric variables, arrays, linked lists, and trees. It supports a set of graphical capabilities, such as in-place updates of values, indicators that move on vertical and horizontal scales, and the creation, rearrangement and deletion of data cells to reflect altered pointer assignments, that can be used during program execution to track changes in data. The PV system also supports dynamic views of flow of control in programs, but the visualization of data is given a higher priority. Figure 23 shows visualizations of data as well as code for a selection sort program.

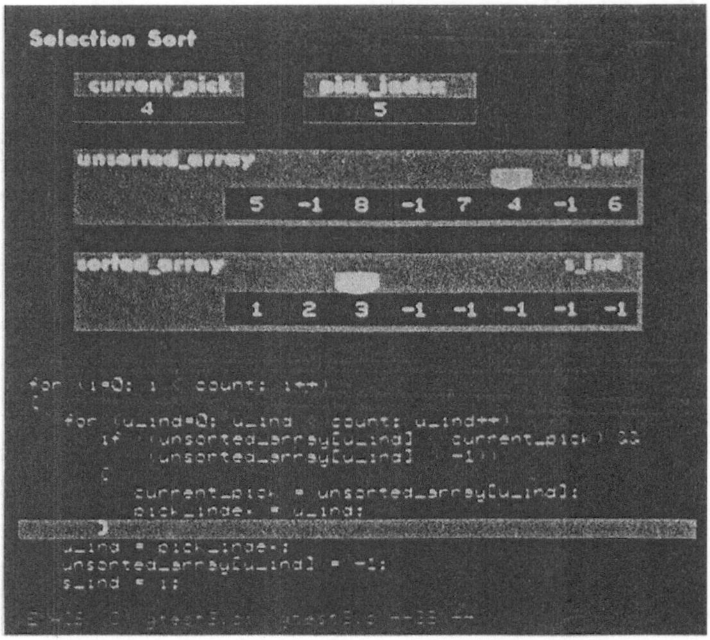

Fig. 23 Visualization of a Selection Sort in PV (from [Brown 85])

GMB [Jablonowski 89] is designed to aid in the construction and browsing of graphs. GMB is functionally similar to ISI Grapher [Robins 87], except that GMB emphasizes animation of graphs. For animation, GMB supports changing colors, shapes of nodes, and visibility. As a result of its animation facilities, GMB is classified as a dynamic data visualization tool.

KAESTLE [Boecker 86] diagrams of Lisp data structures. It uses a layout algorithm to automatically plan the initial display of a structure (see figure 24), but relies on the user to manually rearrange the entire diagram as edits are made. This system also provides hooks for snapshooting dynamic data structures during program execution.

A number of performance meters which dynamically show performance characteristics of operating systems, such as the number of active processes and the cpu load average, can be classified as dynamic data visualization systems.

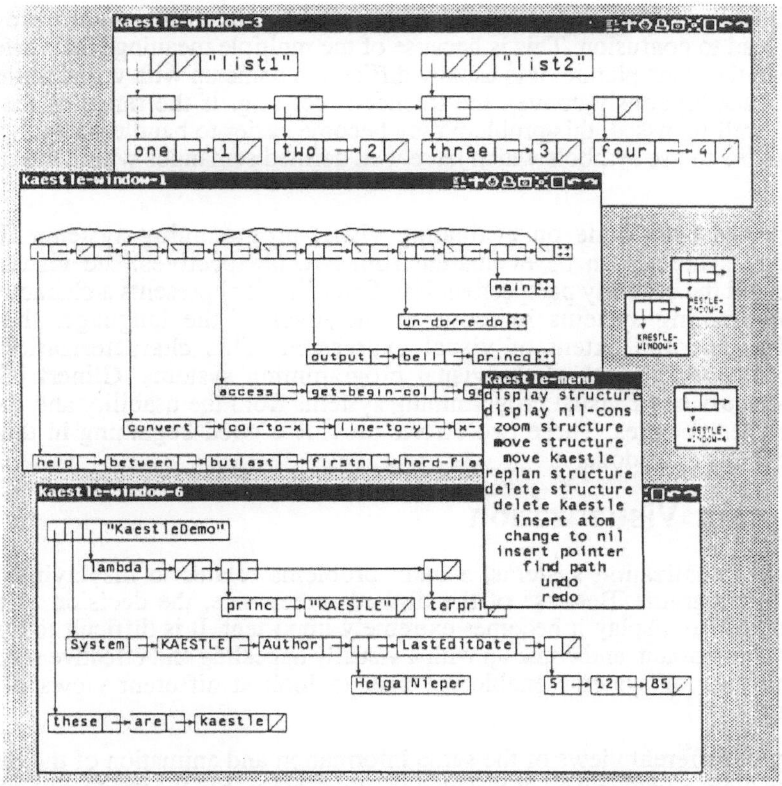

Fig. 24 A KAESTAL Display (from [Boecker 86])

5. FUTURE RESEARCH

Visual programming and program visualization have started getting increasing attention. A number of interesting systems have been built over the last few years and more are being built. Despite these efforts, the full potential of graphics as an aid in programming has still to be realized. This section discusses some of the hard or unsolved problems associated with using graphics in programming.

5.1 Visual Programming

The limited size of the display screen presents a main problem in visual programming systems. In most visual programming systems, the visual representation of the program takes more screen space than its textual representation. This presents a main problem when dealing with large programs; too little fits on the screen. This problems is alleviated to some extent by scrolling and zooming. Another way of solving the limited screen size problem may be to create systems suitable for a small class of applications. It will then be possible to use higher level abstractions relevant to the selected class of application, thus reducing the specification to a smaller size.

The use of pictures, although in general helps in creating and understanding programs, can sometimes lead to confusion. This is because of the multiple meanings that different users may attach to the same picture. It is usually difficult to come up with visual representations which can unambiguously convey the intended meaning. If the range of the system is narrow and well focussed, this problem may become easier to handle. In such a system it may be possible to use symbols which have well defined semantics within the range of the system.

Little work has been done on evaluating visual programming systems. The visual programming systems can be evaluated from two perspectives: the visual language perspective and the usability perspective. Nan Shu [Shu 85a] presents a characterization of visual programming systems in terms of the level of the language, the scope of applicability, and the extent of visual expression. This characterization helps in understanding the "power" of the visual programming systems. Glinert [Glinert 87] presents a discussion of visual programming systems from the usability and the software engineering perspectives. These two efforts provide a good beginning in this area, but more work needs to be done.

5.2 Program Visualization

In program visualization systems, a main problems relates to displaying large data structures or programs. Because of the limited screen size, the decision as to what to display and how to display it becomes extremely important. It is difficult to dynamically select what is important and come up with a visually appealing and effective representation for it. A number of systems enable the user to look at different views of the same information.

The display of different views of the same information and animation of the displays has proven to be quite effective way of visualizing information. But the production of the views and animation requires a great deal of effort and time. It is important to reduce this cost, so that the programmer can create and test different views and animations and select the ones which turn out to be best. Visual programming of the displays and animations used in program visualizations is an interesting research area. Some work in this direction has been done by Duisberg [Duisberg 87].

Another problem with visualization is the binding of graphics routines with the source code. In order to display program code or data, calls to the graphics routines have to be inserted at appropriate places in the program source code. This type of binding hampers the exploration of appropriate displays as the source code must be changed and recompiled. Some systems allow the programmer to create this binding without actually inserting calls to graphics routine in the program source code. Easier ways of creating this binding must be found to facilitate exploration.

6. SUMMARY

In this paper, we have presented a taxonomy of systems which use graphics to aid the programming process. The systems are divided in two broad categories based on the kind of support provided. Systems which use graphics in program construction are called visual programming systems, whereas systems which use graphics to help understand or debug programs are called program visualization systems. These two categories are further divided into smaller categories based on the techniques used or based on the focus of the systems. Example systems from each category are discussed. Finally, areas for future research are discussed.

ACKNOWLEDGEMENTS

Thanks are due to JJ for commenting on a previous version of this paper.

REFERENCES

[Adams 86] Adams, E. and Muchnick, S.S., "Dbxtool: A Window-Based Symbolic Debugger". Software - Practice and Experience, July 1986.

[Albizuri-Romero 84] Albizuri-Romero, M.B., "GRASE: A Graphical Syntax-Direct Editor for Structured Programming". SIGPLAN Notices, vol 19, no 2, 1984, pp 28-37.

[Baecker 75] Baecker, R., "Two Systems which Produce Animated Representations of the Execution of Computer Programs". SIGCSE Bulletin, vol 7, no 1, 1975, pp 158-167.

[Baecker 81] Baecker, R., "Sorting out Sorting". Dynamics Graphics Project, Computer Systems Research Institute, University of Toronto, Toronto, Canada, 1981, 16mm film, 25 minutes.

[Baecker 86] Baecker, R. and Marcus, A., "Design Principles for the Enhanced Presentation of Computer Program Source Text". In Proc. of the ACM CHI 86 Conf. on Human Factors in Computing Systems, ACM, New York, 1986, pp 51-58.

[Baecker 86a] Baecker, R., "An Application Overview of Program Visualization". Computer Graphics, vol 20, no 4, 1986, p 325.

[Biermann 76] Biermann, A.W. and Krishnaswamy, R., "Constructing Programs from Example Computations". IEEE Transactions on Software Engineering, vol SE-2, no 3, 1976, pp 141-153.

[Blaschek 89] Blaschek, G. and Sametinger, J., "User-adaptable Prettyprinting". Software Practice and Experience, vol 19, no 7, 1989, pp 687-702.

[Boecker 86] Boecker, H.D., Fisher, G. and Napier, H., "The Enhancement of Understanding through Visual Representations". In Proc. of the CHI 86 Conf. on Human Factors in Computing Systems, ACM, New York, 1986, pp 44-50.

[Borning 86] Borning, A., "Defining Constraints Graphically". In Proc. of the ACM CHI 86 Conf. on Human Factors in Computing Systems, ACM, New York, 1986.

[Brown 84] Brown, M.H. and Sedgewick, R., "A System for Algorithm Animation". Computer Graphics, vol 18, no 3, 1984, pp 177-186.

[Brown 85] Brown, G.H., Carling, R.T., Herot, C.F., Kramlich, D.A., and Souza P., "Program Visualization: Graphical Support for Software Development". IEEE Computer, vol 18, no 8, 1985, pp 27-35.

[Brown 88] Brown, M.H., "Perspectives on Algorithm Animation". In Proc. of the ACM CHI 88 Conf. on Human Factors in Computing Systems, ACM, New York, 1988, pp 33-38.

[Cardelli 88] Cardelli, L., "Building User Interfaces by Direct Manipulation". In ACM SIGGRAPH Symp. on User Interface Software, ACM, New York, 1988, pp 152-166.

[Chang 87] Chang, S.K., "Visual Languages: A Tutorial and Survey". IEEE Software, vol 29, no 1, 1987, pp 29-39.

[Clark 83] Clark, B.E.J. and Robinson, S.K., "A Graphically Interacting Program Monitor". The Computer Journal, vol 26, no 3, 1983, pp 235-238.

[Cunniff 86] Cunniff, N., Taylor, R.P., and Black, J.B., "Does Programming Language Affect the Type of Conceptual Bugs in Beginners' Programs? A Comparison of FPL and PASCAL". In Proc. of the ACM CHI 86 Conf. on Human Factors in Computing Systems, ACM, New York, 1986, pp 175-182.

[Curry 78] Curry, G.A., "Programming by Abstract Demonstration". Ph.D. Dissertation, Tech Rep 78-03-02, University of Washington, 1978.

[Davis 81] Davis, A.L. and Lowder, S.A., "A Sample Management Application Program in a Graphical Data Driven Programming Language". In Digets of Papers Compcon Spring' 81, 1981, pp 162-167.

[Davis 82] Davis, A.L. and Keller, R.M., "Data Flow Program Graphs". IEEE Computer, vol 15, no 2, 1982, pp 26-41.

[Diaz-Herrera 80] Diaz-Herrera, J.L. and Flude, R.C., "Pascal/HSD: A Graphical Programming System". In Proc. of IEEE Compsac' 80, 1980, pp 723-728.

[Duisberg 87] Duisberg, R.A., "Visual Programming of Program Visualizations". In Proc. of the 1987 Workshop on Visual Languages, 1987, pp. 55-66.

[Edel 88] Edel, M., "The Tinkertoy Graphical Programming Environment". IEEE Transactions on Software Engineering, vol SE-14, no 8, 1988, pp 1110-1115.

[Ellis 69] Ellis, T.O., Heafner, J.F. and Sibley, W.L., "The Grail Project: An Experiment in Man-Machine Communication". RAND Report RM-5999-Arpa, 1969.

[Finzer 84] Finzer, W. and Gould, L., "Programming by Rehearsal". BYTE, vol 9, no 6, 1984, pp 197-210.

[Frei 78] Frei, H.P., Weller, D.L. and Williams, R., "A Graphics-Based Programming Support System", Proc. ACM Siggraph 78, 1978, pp 43-49.

[Giacalone 84] Giacalone, A., Rinard, M.C. and Doeppner, T.W., "IDEOSY: An Ideographic and Interactive Program Description System". ACM SIGPLAN Notices, vol 19, no 5, 1984, pp 15-20.

[Glinert 84] Glinert, E.P. and Tanimoto, S.L., "Pict: An Interactive Graphical Programming Environment". IEEE Computer, vol 17, no 11, 1986, pp 7-25.

[Glinert 87] Glinert, E.P., "Towards Software Metrices for Visual Programming". Tech Rep 87-16, Dept of Computer Science, Rensselaer Polytechnic, 1987.

[Haeberli 88] Haeberli, P.E., "ConMan: A Visual Programming Language for Interactive Graphics". Computer Graphics, vol 22, no 4, 1988, pp 103-111.

[Haibt 59] Haibt, L.M., "A Program to Draw Multi-Level Flow Charts". Proc. of the Western Joint Computer Conference, San Francisco, CA, March 1959, pp 131-137.

[Halbert 81] Halbert, D., "An Example of Programming by Example". M.Sc. Dissertation, Dept. of EE & CS, University of California, Berkley, 1981.

[Hirakawa 87] Hirakawa, M., Iwata, S., Yoshimoto, I., Tanaka, M. and Ichikawa, T., "HI-VISUAL Iconic Programming". In Proc. of the 1987 Workshop on Visual Languages, 1987, pp 305-314.

[Hughes 86] Hughes, C.D. and Moshell, J.M., "Visible Pascal: A Graphics-Based Learning Environment". In Proc. of the Computer Graphics 86 Conf., NCGA, 1986, pp 401-411.

[Hyrskykari 87] Hyrskykari, A. and Raiha, K-J., "Animation of Algorithms without Programming". In Proc. of the 1987 Workshop on Visual Languages, 1987, pp 40-54.

[Jablonowski 89] Jablonowski, D. and Guarana, Jr., V.A., "GMB: A Tool for Manipulating and Animating Graph Data Structures", Software - Practice and Experience, vol 19, no 3, 1989, pp 283-301.

[Jacob 85] Jacob, R.J.K., "A State Transition Diagram Language for Visual Programming". IEEE Computer, vol 8, no 8, 1985, pp 51-59.

[Keller 81] Keller, R.M. and Yen, W-C.J., "A Graphical Approach to Software Development Using Function Graphs". In Digets of Papers Compcon Spring 81, 1981, pp 156-161.

[Kimura 86] Kimura, T.D., Choi, J.W., and Mack, J.M., "A Visual Language for Keyboardless Programming", Technical Report WUCS-86-6, Washington University, St. Louis, Missouri, 1986.

[Krishnamoorthy 89] Krishnamoorthy, M.S. and Swaminathan, R., "Program Tools for Algorithm Animation",. Software Practice and Experience, vol 19, no 6, 1989, pp 505-513.

[Lakin 86] Lakin, F., "Spatial Parsing for Visual Languages". In Visual Languages, Chang, S.K., Ichikawa, T. and Ligomenides, P.A. (eds), Plenum Publishing Corp., 1986.

[Leong 89] Leong, M.K, Sam, S. and Narasimhalu, D., "Towards a Visual Language for an Object-Oriented Multi-Media Database System". In Proc. of the IFIP TC 2/WG 2.6 Working Conference on Visual Database Systems, 1989.

[Levien 86] Levien, R., "Visual Programming". BYTE, Feb. 1986, pp 135-144.

[Lewis 89] Lewis, T.G., Handloser III, F., Bose, S. and Yang, S., "Prototypes from Standard User Interface Management Systems". IEEE Computer, May 1989, pp 51-60.

[London 85] London, R.L. and Duisberg, R.A., "Animating Programs Using Smalltalk". IEEE Computer, vol 18, no 8, 1985, pp 61-71.

[Loosemore 87] Loosemore, S., "A Visual Programming Environment for Hierarchical Data Structures". In Proc. of the 1987 Workshop on Visual Languages, 1987, pp 242-253.

[Myers 83] Myers, B., "INCENSE: A System for Displaying Data Structures". Computer Graphics, vol 17, no 3, 1983, pp 115-125.

[Myers 86] Myers, B., "Visual Programming, Programming by Example, and Program Visualization: A Taxonomy". In Proc. of the ACM CHI 86 Conf. on Human Factors in Computing Systems, ACM, New York, 1986, pp 59-66.

[Myers 86a] Myers, B. and Buxton, W.A.S., "Creating Highly-Interactive and Graphical User Interfaces by Demonstration". Computer Graphics, vol 20, no 4, 1986, pp 249-258.

[Nassi 73] Nassi, I. and Shneiderman, B., "Flowchart Techniques for Structured Programming". SIGPLAN Notices, vol 8 no 8, 1973, pp 12-26.

[Newman 68] Newman, W.M., "A System for Interactive Graphical Programming". In Proc. of the Spring Joint Computer Conf., 1968, pp 47-54.

[Parnas 69] Parnas, D.L., "On the use of Transition Diagrams in the Design of a User Interface for an Interactive Graphics System". In Proc. of the 24th National ACM Conf., 1969, pp 379-385.

[Pietrzykowski 83] Pietrzykowski, T., Matwin, S., and Muldner, T., "The Programming Language PROGRAPH: Yet Another Application of Graphics", In Proc. of the Graphics Interface' 83 Conf., Morgan Kaufmann, CA, 1983, pp 143-145.

[Pong 83] Pong, M.C. and Ng, N., "PIGS - A System for programming with Interactive Graphical Support". Software Practice and Experience, vol 13, Sept 1983, pp 847-855.

[Reiss 85] Reiss, S.P., "PECAN: Program Development Environment that Supports Multiple Views". IEEE Transactions on Software Engineering, vol SE-11, no 3, 1985, pp 276-285.

[Robins 87] Robins, G., "The ISI Grapher: A Portable Tool for Displaying Graphs Pictorially". In Proc. Symbolikka, Aug 1987.

[Rovner 69] Rovner, P.D. and Henderson Jr., D.A., "On the Implementation of AMBIT/G: A Graphical Programming Language". In Proc. IJCAI-69, 1969, pp 9-20.

[Rowe 87] Rowe, L.A., Davis, M., Messinger, E., Meyer, C., Spirakis, C. and Tuan, A., "A Browser for Directed Graphs". Software - Practice and Experience, vol 17, no 1, 1987, pp 61-76.

[Rubin 85] Rubin, R.V., Golin, E.J. and Reiss, S.P., "ThinkPad: A Graphical System for Programming by Demonstration". IEEE Software, March 1985, pp 73-79.

[Shu 85] Shu, N.C., "FORMAL: A Forms-Oriented Visual Directed Application Development System". IEEE Computer, vol 18, no 8, 1985, pp 38-49.

[Shu 85a] Shu, N.C., "Visual Programming Languages: A Dimensional Analysis". In Proc. of the IEEE International Symp. on New Directions in Computing, 1985, pp 326-334.

[Shu 88] Shu, N.C., "Visual Programming". Van Nostrand Reinhold, New York, 1988.

[Singh 86] Singh, G., "Programming by Example for Graphical User Interfaces". In Proc. of the 1986 Canadian Information Processing Society (Edmonton) Annual Conf., 1986, pp 45-50.

[Singh 88] Singh, G. and Green, M., "Designing the Interface Designer's Interface". In Proc. of the ACM SIGGRAPH Symp. on User Interface Software, ACM, New York, 1988, pp 109-116.

[Singh 90] Singh, G., "The Druid User Interface Management System". Institute of Systems Science, National University of Singapore, Singapore, 1990.

[Smith 77] Smith, D.C., "Pygmalion: A Computer Program to Model and Stimulate Creative Thought". Basel, Stuttgart: Birkhauser, 1977.

[Smith 88] Smith, D.N., "Building Interfaces Interactively". In ACM SIGGRAPH Symp. on User Interface Software, ACM, New York, 1988, pp 144-151.

[Stasko 89] Stasko, J.T., "TANGO: A Framework and System for Algorithm Animation". Technical Report CS-89-30 (Ph.D. Dissertation), Dept. of Computer Science, Brown University, Rhode Island, USA, 1989, 257 pages.

[Teitelman 81] Teitelman, W. and Masinter, L., "The Interlisp Programming Environment". IEEE Computer, vol 14, no 4, 1981, pp 25-34.

[Wasserman 85] Wasserman, A.I., "Extending State Transition Diagrams for the Specification of Human-Computer Interaction". IEEE Transactions on Software Engineering, vol SE-11, no 8, 1985, pp 699-713.

[Yao 84] Yao, S.B., Hevner, A.R., Shi, Z. and Luo, D., "FORMANAGER: An Office Forms Management System". ACM Transactions on Office Information Systems, vol 2 no 3, 1984, pp 235-262.

[Zloof 77] Zloof, M.M., "Query-by-Example: A Database Language". IBM Systems Journal, vol 16, no 4, 1977, pp 324-344.

[Zloof 81] Zloof, M.M., "QBE/OBE: A Language for Office and Business Automation", IEEE Computer, vol 14, no 5, 1981, pp 13-22.

Gurminder Singh received his M.Sc. and Ph.D., both in Computing Science, from the University of Alberta, Canada. Singh is currently an Associate, Research Staff at the Institute of Systems Science, National University of Singapore, where he is leading a project on user interface management systems. His current research interests include user interface design, user interface management systems, and visual languages. Singh has served on the conference committee of the ACM SIGGRAPH Symposium on User Interface Software, 1988. He is currently serving as the Panels/Demonstrations chair of the CG International'90 conference and as the conference chair of IT Works'90. Singh is a member of ACM SIGGRAPH.

Current Address: Institute of Systems Science, National University of Singapore, Kent Ridge, Singapore 0511.
Email: ISSGS@ NUSVM.bitnet

A System for Interactive Graphical Modeling with Three-Dimensional Constraints

Maarten J. G. M. van Emmerik

ABSTRACT

This paper presents an interactive graphical system for modeling three-dimensional objects. An object can be specified by a graphical interface or alternatively, by entering a textual description. Both interface styles are integrated in a graphical programming environment. Geometric relations between objects are specified by constraints between local coordinate systems. The user can define constraints graphically and constraints are evaluated real-time. The combination of a direct manipulation interface and a procedural modeling language makes it possible to define and modify parametrized part hierarchies graphically.

1. INTRODUCTION

Complex geometric models are generally built-up from elementary modeling entities (e.g. surfaces or volumes) that are supplied with 3D transformations to specify their position, orientation and dimension in the model. Instead of specifying all individual transformations separately, they can to a large extent be deduced automatically from general shape characteristics as specified by the designer. This approach is generally referred to as constraint-based modeling. A designer specifies local or global constraints (e.g. parallelism, distance, concentricity) between entities, and the system subsequently calculates the individual object transformations that meet the set of constraints.

Constraint-based modeling has advantages in various stages of the design process, including:

- high-level model specification for creating the model
- variational geometry for generating alternatives
- kinematic analysis
- functional information for computer-aided manufacturing (CAM).

In the conceptual design stage, a fast and user-friendly model specification is provided. The user can enter high-level shape characteristics instead of individual object transformations. Once the model is defined, alternative solutions that meet the set of constraints can be generated automatically by modification of shape parameters. If parameters are used to specify a certain state of the model, for instance human figure positioning, constraints can be used to control the kinematic behaviour. Finally, constraints should be embedded explicitly in the geometric model since they represent functional information required for further processing of the designed model. For example, information about parallelism or concentricity of objects is essential for planning an optimal manufacturing strategy.

1.1 Applications of constraint-based modeling

Constraint-based specification is not limited to geometric modeling, but can be applied in various applications such as user interface design, window management, animation, 2D drawing and product modeling. Also, a broad range of techniques for constraint solving have been presented. Borning and Duisberg (1986) use constraints for the construction of interactive graphical user interfaces and apply an object-oriented technique for constraint solving. Cohen et al.(1986) presented a method for creating, destroying and arranging windows on a workstation based on a constraint-based layout system, using a priority algorithm. Other applications of constraint-based modeling have been presented for architectural design (Roth and Hashimshony, 1988), tolerancing (Bernstein and Preiss, 1989) and VLSI design (Roach, 1984).

One of the earliest applications of constraints in geometric modeling was developed by Sutherland (1963). He used a numerical relaxation method for constraint solving in a 2D drawing system. Nelson(1985) used a Newton-Raphson iteration technique for constraint solving in the Juno graphics system. Kim and Lee (1989) proposed a data structure for kinematic analysis of assemblies. The system generates joined coordinate systems between components to solve 'fits' and 'against' constraints. An application of constraints for dimensioning and tolerancing in product modeling has been proposed by Kimura and Suzuki(1986). They use first-order predicate logic in combination with object-oriented techniques to determine the sequence of constraint solving. Although many constraint-based system enhance the modeling functionality, their practical use is often restricted by their non-interactive behaviour and the absence of a good user interface.

Recently, several systems that offer an interactive graphical environment for constraint-based modeling have been presented. Rossignac (1986) proposed an interactive and user-friendly application of constraints in Constructive Solid Geometry (CSG). A graphical interface enables the specification of rigid motions between arbitrary collections of sub-solids in a CSG tree. The rigid motions are stored as constraints which can be evaluated one at a time in a user defined order. An interactive graphical approach towards constraints based modeling for human figure animation is proposed by Badler and Kamran(1987). The system enables the specification of constraints between human limbs and the user can specify goal positions of limbs by a graphics cursor. Cugini et al. (1988) developed a parametric technical drawing system in which topologic relations between geometric entities are defined by 2D constraints. Bier and Stone (1986) presented an interactive 2D drawing system that uses constraints for precise positioning as an alternative for a gravity grid. The constraints are only used as an input mechanism and are not appended to the model description. Fuller and Prusinkiewicz (1988) presented the L.E.G.O. system for describing two- and three-dimensional objects with Euclidian geometry constructions. They specify geometric construction rules by Lisp functions and provide a graphics interface to create the model. Kin et al. (1989) convert constraints to construction operations in the interactive 2D PictureEditor system. The constraint solving algorithm can handle constructions with two degrees of freedom by solving two equations at a time and is quicker and more stable compared to traditional numerical techniques.

The system presented here is focussed on constraint-based modeling in Constructive Solid Geometry (CSG), but can be extended to other geometric representations as well. Constraints are specified graphically and evaluated real-time during manipulation of the model. Section 1.2 gives an overview of the concepts that are incorporated in the system.

1.2 Concepts for 3D constraint-based modeling

The techniques are implemented in an experimental modeling system called GeoNode. GeoNode aims to combine the advantages of a user-friendly interactive graphical interface with the functionality of a procedural modeling language.

The system offers the following features with regard to constraint-based modeling:

- 3D constraints
- interactive graphical specification of constraints
- graphical feedback of constraints
- direct manipulation on a 3D model
- predictable results after constraint evaluation
- mechanism to handle over- and under-dimensioning.
- procedural model description
- part hierarchies

Since CSG is concerned with 3D modeling, the constraints should be applicable in 3D. During the design process, the designer should be able to use a graphical user interface to specify the constraints, rather than having to use an abstract procedural specification. Constraints have to be evaluated immediately after they are specified so that the graphical representation always represents the current state of the model. Also, at any time the designer should be able to have a graphical representation of specified constraints. Direct manipulation (Shneiderman, 1983) implies that the user can modify the model by interaction on a graphical representation of the model instead of entering a sequence of commands. Although many CAD systems enable some kind of direct manipulation, the interaction is in most cases restricted to orthogonal views. The system presented here allows direct manipulation on a perspective or a parallel projection of the model, which is in fact a precondition for extending the direct manipulation paradigm to 3D modeling.

A major requirement for constraint-based modeling is the predictability of the result after constraint evaluation. This is closely related to the interactive evaluation and graphical representation of constraints. Constraints should be evaluated immediately after they are specified, so that the consequences of each individual constraint can be displayed immediately. Also, a mechanism for under- and over-dimensioning of objects by constraints has to be provided. In case of under-dimensioning, the system should generate a suitable solution rather than wait until the designer has specified enough constraints to generate a unique and unambiguous solution. Over-dimensioning can occur in cases where the designer has specified a set of constraints that can not be met simultaneously. The system should either prevent the specification of such conflicting constraints, or provide a mechanism to cope with such cases, for instance by using a constraint-priority mechanism.

The concept of using a procedural (textual) description beside a graphical interface is incorporated in various systems, such as Juno (Nelson, 1985) and L.E.G.O. (Fuller and Prusinkiewicz, 1988). The idea is that all graphical interaction is converted into a list of commands that form the object description. If the user manipulates the model graphically, the corresponding procedural description is automatically updated. An advantage of this method is that two interface styles (command line and graphical) are concurrently available and the user can select the style that is most suitable for a certain task. The last item in the list of concepts concerns part hierarchies. Many constraint-based systems provide a mechanism for specifying relations between geometric primitives, but do not address the problem of complex part hierarchies. For modeling complex objects, it is convenient to split-up the model into a number of predefined sub-assemblies or parts. A predefined part can contain constraints between components of the part and may contain parameters that enable variable dimensioning of an instance of the part. GeoNode provides a graphical parametrization mechanism for instantiation of predefined objects in further designs.

The paper is organized as follows. In section 2 the concept of the geometric tree as a technique for interactive graphical specification of three-dimensional object transformations is presented. Section 3 discusses the kinds of constraints that can be specified and explains how constraints are entered and evaluated. In section 4 we shall discuss how the user can define part hierarchies and how constraints are propagated in the hierarchy. In sections 5 and 6 some implementational issues and conclusions are presented.

2. GEOMETRIC TREE

The concept of the geometric tree has been presented earlier (van Emmerik, 1988). The nodes in the tree are local coordinate systems that are provided with a translation(tx,ty,tz), rotation(rx,ry,rz) and scaling(sx,sy,sz) relative to their parent node. The user can create the tree graphically and nodes can be moved, rotated and scaled by direct manipulation on a 3D representation of the tree (Figure 1). Initially, one root coordinate system is presented to the user. New nodes can be appended to the tree by selecting the option `create-axis` from a menu and selecting the parent node graphically. To modify the position, orientation or scaling of a node, the 2D mouse movements are alternately linked to one of the transformation parameters.

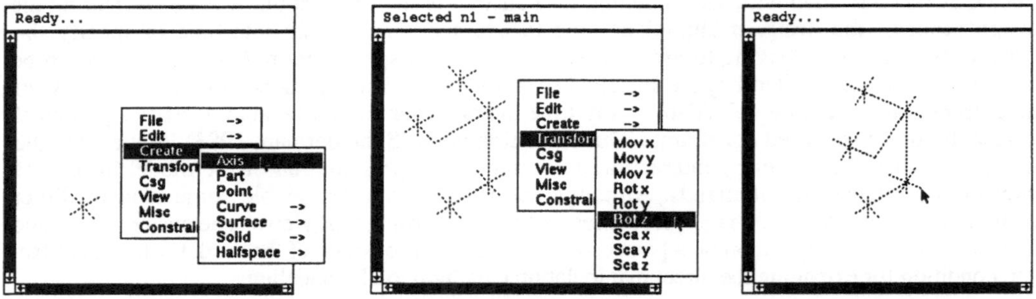

Figure 1. The geometric tree can be created and modified by direct manipulation on a 3D representation.

After the geometric tree is specified, the user can append primitive volumes or instances of predefined parts to the nodes of the tree. Each object is provided with a node that specifies the position and orientation of the object. A second node can be selected to specify the dimensions of an object. The position of the second node is a constraint that specifies the edge-point of an object. Several primitives may be linked to the same nodes, for instance, the dimension of the block and the cylinder in Figure 2 are specified by a common node.

2.1 Procedural representation

Direct manipulation does not directly modify the internal data structure of the model, but is converted into alphanumerical modeling statements which are subsequently processed by an interpreter. The combination of direct manipulation and command line interpretation offers additional facilities with respect to the specification of the model. Since two interface styles are concurrently available, the user can select the one that is most suitable for a certain task. Several standard text-based input facilities such as learn, undo, redo and macro substitution can be used to create and modify the procedural model description. Also, the integration of the modeling system with other text-based application such as editors, filters and database management systems is easy to implement. However, the main reason for the two view approach is the combination of a user-friendly graphical interface with the functionality of a modeling language. A modeling language enables a flexible and powerful model specification by using variables (parametrization), loops (iteration), conditional statements (design rules) and procedures (hierarchy). Applications of such high-level constructs for solid modeling (van Emmerik, 1989a) and feature modeling (van Emmerik and Jansen, 1989b) have been presented earlier.

The graphical interface can be used to create the procedural representation one statement at a time. In order to build a new statement, the user selects an option from a pop-up menu. The system activates a template command statement and the variables in the template statement are filled out by graphics input techniques (picking and dragging). After a new command is generated, it is added to the procedural description and subsequently processed by an interpreter.

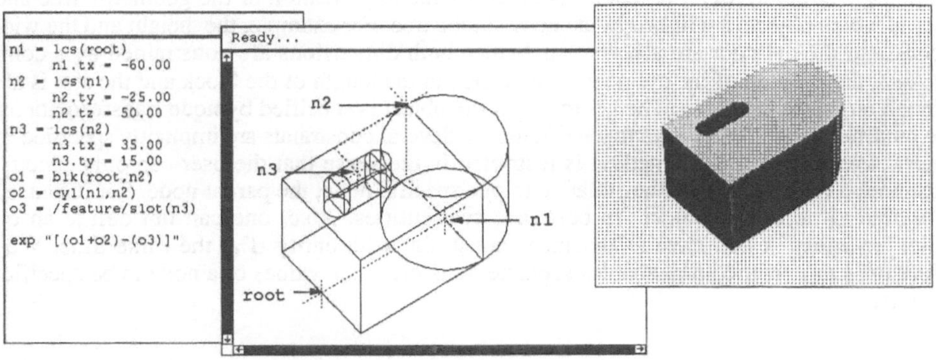

Figure 2. Two primitive volumes and a predefined object are linked to nodes in a geometric tree. The procedural model representation is automatically generated and updated by direct manipulation.

For example, the template commands for the creation of a node and a geometric transformation of a node are as follows:

```
N = lcs(N)      (e.g. "n1 = lcs(root)" )                [2.1]
N.T  = V        (e.g. "n1.tz = 80.05 " )                [2.2]
```

with

```
N = node identifier (name)
T = type of transformation (tx,ty,tz,rx,ry,rz,sx,sy,sz)
V = real value
```

Template [2.1] defines a new coordinate system relative to another coordinate system. The template is filled out as follows. After the user has selected the option `create-axis` from the menu, a default node identifier (e.g. `n1`) is generated by the system and the system request the selection of a parent node (e.g. `root`). The result of the graphical interaction is the command `n1=lcs(root)`. Template [2.2] defines a transformation of a node relative to its parent. The first two fields are filled out by picking at a node in the tree and selecting the required transformation from a menu. The value of the transformation is specified by dragging the mouse. During the drag operation, the node is transformed real-time and the numerical value of the transformation is displayed. Precise specification of transformation values is enabled by a user-definable grid snap option.

Primitives are appended to the tree by selecting the primitive from a menu and picking at the nodes that should be provided as parameters. Predefined objects can be selected graphically from a database. The description in Figure 2 also contains an expression that defines the Boolean combination of volumes. The statement is generated by picking at the block `o1` and the cylinder `o2` and selecting `csg-add` from a pop-up menu. Subsequently, the user picks at the slot `o3` and selects the option `csg-subtract`. Statements are not simply appended to the end of the procedural description. A transformation statement is for instance always inserted after the statement that declares the node. A Boolean expression is always the last line in the description. Also, if a transformation is already defined, the new statement replaces the old statement so that the procedural representation does not contain obsolete information.

2.2 Geometry and topology

The topologic structure of an object is specified by the organization of the geometric tree and the manner in which objects are linked to the nodes in the tree. For example, the height and the width of the block and the cylinder are always equal since both dimensions are constrained by a common node. Also, the position of the cylinder is connected to the length of the block and the slot is always positioned on top of the block. The geometry of the object is specified by node transformations and can be modified by graphical interaction (Figure 3). Several constraints are implicitly specified by the geometric tree. However, the method is restricted in the sense that the user can only specify the transformation only as fixed values relative to one specific node, the parent node. For instance, it is not possible to define an object "in between" two entities. Also, one can not define an object "parallel" to entity A and have a "distance" constraint with entity B at the same time. We will therefore present a method that enables separate transformation values of a node to be specified by constraints.

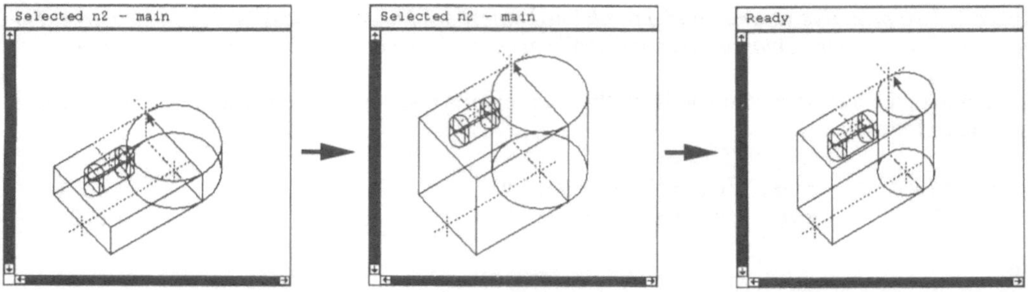

Figure 3. The object can be dimensioned by direct manipulation of the nodes of the geometric tree. Node n2 *(at cursor position) is subsequently dragged in z- and y-direction to modify the height and width of the object.*

3. CONSTRAINTS BETWEEN COORDINATE SYSTEMS

The kinds of constraints that are required for 3D modeling depend on the purpose of the design system. A constraint-based system should therefore be implemented as a modular system which allows the definition of new types of constraints that meet specific modeling requirements. Some examples of constraints that are currently implemented are presented in figure 4.

Basically, any constraint fixes one or more degrees of freedom for positioning(tx,ty,tz) and orienting (rx,ry,rz) an object in 3D space. The number of degrees of freedom that are fixed by a constraint depends on the kind of constraint. For instance, a constraint that specifies an object to be centred in z-direction between two other objects fixes the z-transformation, but leaves the x- and y-transformations unspecified. An xy_parallel constraint fixes the x- and y-rotations, but leaves four other degrees of freedom unspecified. Some constraints do not fix specific degrees of freedom, but specify a constraint between two or more degrees of freedom. These constraints are referred to in this paper as higher-order constraints. An example of such a higher-order constraint is an xy_distance constraint (second order). Evaluation of this constraint does not give a unique solution, since a range of x- and y-positions that satisfy the constraint can be found. A method to process higher-order constraints will be presented later.

constraint	sub-type	description	example	fixes	order	icon
equal	z_equal	z-position of entities in evaluated model equal		tz	1	
linear distance	y_distance	orthogonal y-distance between two entities		ty	1	
ratio	x_ratio	positioning as a ratio between two entities	0.4x x	tx	1	
parallel	yz_parallel	plane through x-axis and y-axis of both entities parallel		ry,rz	1	
pointto	x_pointto	x_axis of entity points to other entity		ry, rz	1	
radial distance	xy_distance	fixed distance between two entities in xy_plane		tx or ty	2	

Figure 4. Example of constraints.

The constraints presented in Figure 4 are not applied between volumes but between local coordinate systems. The reason for this approach is that the technique for constraint solving is much easier and therefore more interactive. Direct specification of constraints between various object types requires a very complex constraint evaluation technique and can even introduce ambiguity. For instance, a distance constraint between two spheres should be evaluated differently from a distance constraint between a cone and a block. Also, a pointto constraint applied between a cylinder and a block would be ambiguous since it is not clear whether the cylinder should point to the centre of the block or to a specific edge. The problem becomes even worse if constraints are not only applied between primitive volumes, but also between complex assemblies.

3.1 Constraint specification

A constraint fixes one or more degrees of freedom of a coordinate system that would otherwise be specified as an absolute transformation by the user. The syntax of a constraint resembles the syntax of a user-defined node transformation (see [2.2] Section 2) and is defined as follows:

```
N.T->N [ =V ] (e.g. "n1.xy_parallel->root" or          [3.1]
                    "n3.xy_distance->n1=0.3")
```

with

```
N = node identifier
T = type of constraint
V = real value
```

The first node identifier *N* specifies the coordinate system that is fixed by the constraint. The second identifier *N* indicates to which node the constraint is applied. The parameter *V* is a real value that is only required for some kinds of constraints (e.g distance). An example of an x_equal constraint is presented in Figure 5 (first picture). The constraint implies that the x-position of node `n2` in the evaluated model should be equal to the x-position of node n1. If the user wants to change the length of the block by moving node n1 along the x-axis, the position of the cylinder is automatically translated by the constraint on node n2. The user can now specify the length, width and height of the object by interaction on a single node n1.

Graphical specification of constraints that do not require a real value is rather straightforward. For example the constraint n2.x_equal->n1 in Figure 5 was generated as follows (template [3.1]): pick at node n2 (*N*), select constraint x_ratio from pop-up menu (*T*) and pick at node n1 (*N*). Suppose the user wants to add two additional constraints for positioning the hole o3; the x-position of the hole should be centred between n1 and root and the hole should also have a distance of 50 from n2. Both constraints can respectively be specified as n3.x_ratio->root=0.5 and n3.xy_distance->n2=50. The values 0.5 and 50, which represent the *V* variable in template [3.1] are deduced from the state of the model at the time the constraints are specified. In general, the user gives an example of a configuration that matches the constraints and the system generates a value for *V* that represents the same configuration after the constraint is specified. For example, constraint n3.x_ratio->root=0.5 is generated as follows: pick at node n3, select constraint x_ratio from the pop-up menu and pick at node root. The current x-translation of n3 relative to its parent n1 is interpreted as a ratio of 0.5 between n1 and root. Figure 5 shows the model before and after the specification of the x_ratio and the xy_distance constraint. The statements that define the fixed node transformations, n3.tx=50 and n3.ty=30, are respectively replaced by the constraints n3.x_ratio->root=0.5 and n3.xy_distance->n2=50.

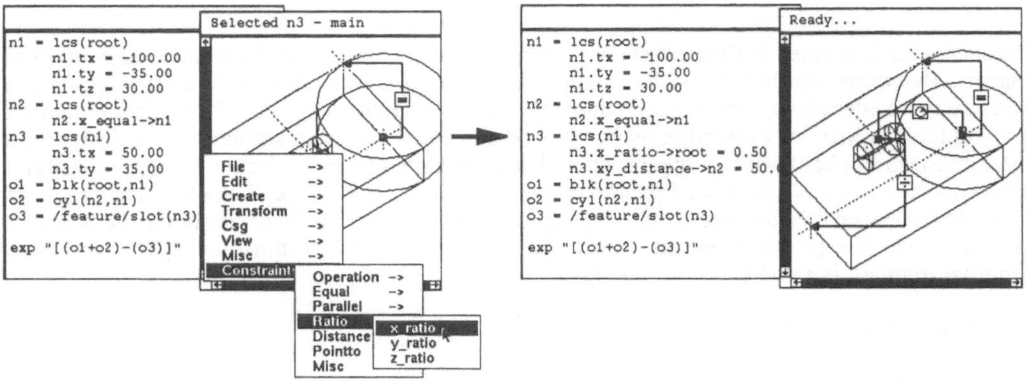

Figure 5. The current current position of node n3 *is interpreted as an x_ratio constraint and an xy_distance constraint.*

The fact that constraints are an alternative for fixed node transformation implies that a model can not be under-dimensioned. If no constraints are specified, the transformation of a node is determined by a default value supplied with the creation of a node, or, alternatively by a user-defined transformation. Over-dimensioning is prevented by deactivation of selections in the constraint pop-up menu. If the user picks at a node, the system checks which degrees of freedom are already fixed by a constraint and deactivates the items in the constraint menu that fix the same degree of freedom. For instance, the x- and y-transformation of node n3 in Figure 5 are fixed by the x_ratio and the xy_distance constraint. After picking at n3, the menu item y_ratio is disabled, since this would also fix the y-transformation. Constraints that fix the z-position or rotation of node n3 are still selectable.

Figure 6 shows what happens if the user moves node n1 in the xy-plane. The first picture represents the state of the model after the constraints have been specified (see Figure 5). The second picture shows the result after dragging node n1 along the x-axis. The hole is centred by the x_ratio constraint and the the y-position of the hole is modified so that the xy_distance constraint is satisfied. If node n1 is dragged in y-direction, the width of the block and the radius of the cylinder are modified but the hole remains at the same position (third picture).

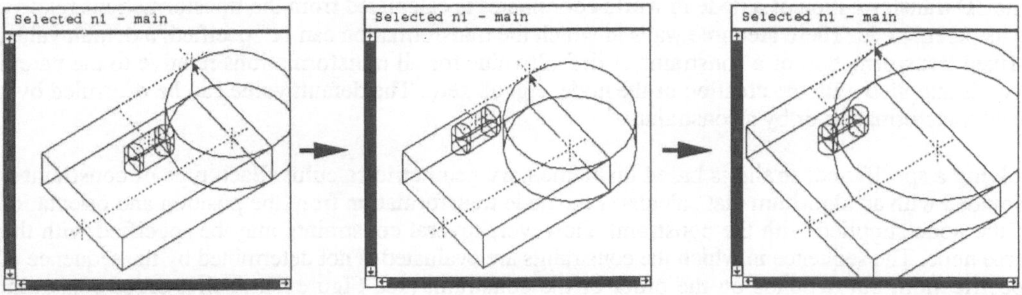

Figure 6. Configuration of the object after dragging node n1 (at cursor position) subsequently along the x-axis and along the y-axis.

3.2 Constraint evaluation

For the discussion of the constraint evaluation technique we have to consider four levels in the model: part, geometric tree, node and object (Figure 7). The part is the complete model description as specified by the user, including nodes, constraints and the CSG expression. In order to obtain the position and orientation of objects in the part, the 3D transformations of nodes in the geometric tree have to be calculated first.

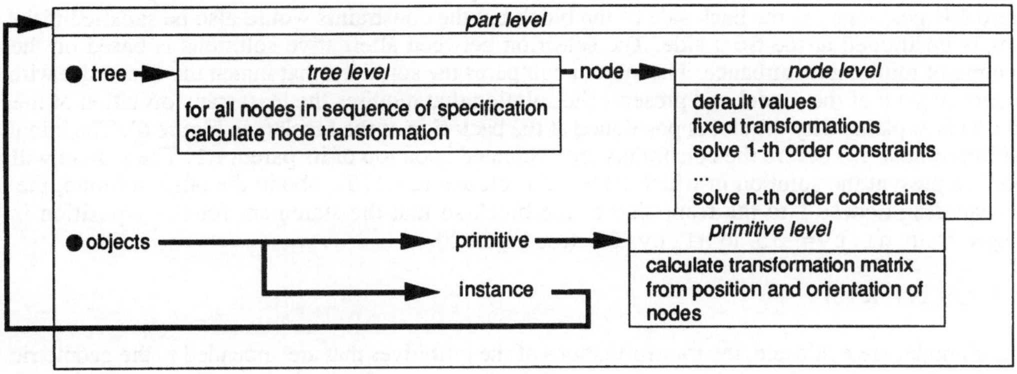

Figure 7. Overview of the various levels in the constraint solving mechanism.

3.2.1 Tree level

Since node transformations are specified relative to their parent, the evaluation is started with the root node and propagated to the leave nodes. A standard tree traversal method, such as breadth-first or depth-first, does not suffice, since constraints can be specified from nodes low in the tree to nodes deep in the tree and vice versa. Instead, the sequence of node evaluation is determined by the sequence in which the nodes are specified. This method guarantees a valid result since the last node or constraint is always appended to an evaluated model.

3.2.2 Node level

The 3D transformation of a node in world coordinates is calculated from the transformations relative to its parent node. There are three ways in which the transformation can be specified: a default value, a fixed transformation or a constraint. A default value for all transformations relative to the parent node is supplied with the creation of the node, e.g. all zero. The default value can be overruled by a fixed transformation or by a constraint.

Solving a specific constraint is based on elementary geometric calculus. Each type of constraint is provided with an algorithm that calculates the node transformation from the position and orientation of the node supplied with the constraint. However, several constraints may be specified with the same node. The sequence in which the constraints are evaluated is not determined by the sequence of specification, but depends on the order of the constraint (see Figure 4). A first-order constraint always gives a unique solution and is evaluated immediately. With higher-order constraints, such as an xy_distance constraint, several solutions that match the constraints can be generated. Instead of waiting until the user has specified additional constraints a mechanism is supplied that generates the most obvious solution by applying two principles:

- delayed evaluation
- minimal disturbance

Delayed evaluation implies that a higher-order constraint is not evaluated before all lower-order constraints are evaluated. For example, if an xy_distance constraint has to be solved, the system first processes the first order constraints in order to check if the x- or y-position is already fixed. If the x-position is fixed, the system modifies the y-position so that the distance constraint is satisfied and vice versa. Even after the delayed evaluation there may be more solutions. For example, the slot in Figure 6 is positioned at the back side of the block but the constraints would also be satisfied if the block is positioned at the front side. The selection between alternative solutions is based on the principle of minimal disturbance. The system compares the solutions that match the constraint with the current state of the model and presents the solution that requires the least transformation of the node. This explains why the slot is positioned at the back side of the block (see Figure 6). The initial position of node `n3` before the constraints are evaluated is on top of its parent `n1`. The system will therefore present the solution in which node `n3` is closest to `n1`. To obtain the other solution, the user can drag node `n1` to the front side of the block so that the statement for the y-position is changed from `n1.ty=-35` to `n1.ty=35` (see Figure 5).

3.2.3 Object level

After all nodes are evaluated, the transformations of the primitives that are appended to the geometric tree are calculated. Each primitive volume is linked to two nodes in the tree. The two nodes are provided as parameters in the statement that creates an instance of the primitive (e.g. "`o1 = cyl(root,n4)`"). The position and orientation of a primitive is determined by the position and orientation of the first node. To obtain the dimension of a primitive, the position of the second node is expressed in the coordinate system of the first node. The x-, y- and z-position of this node relative to the first node specify the parameters for length, width, height or radius of primitives. In fact, the dimension of a primitive is specified as a constraint for an edge point, analogue to the dimensioning of lines, arcs and rectangles in a 2D drawing system.

An overview of the various levels in the constraint solving technique is presented in Figure 7. Note that there are two kinds of objects that can be appended to the tree: primitives and instances of predefined objects. For the evaluation of an instance, the various levels of the constraint evaluation are recursively traversed. Details about instantiation and part hierarchies are discussed in the next section.

4. PART HIERARCHIES

A system that only supports modeling with a fixed set of primitives is generally of little practical use for complex product design. The system should therefore provide a mechanism that enables the definition of predefined objects that can be stored in a database and instantiated in further designs. The description of a predefined object as stored in a database is called the "generic description". An occurrence of a predefined object in the model is called an "instance". If the generic description of an object is modified, all instances of the object are modified automatically.

An example of instantiation is presented earlier in Figure 2 (instance `o3` of generic object `/feature/slot`). The object is selected graphically from a database. Each instance requires at least one node to specify its position and orientation in the model. However, for many modeling purposes it is convenient that dimensions of instances can be specified also. This aspect is referred to as "parametrization". The GeoNode system offers a graphical parametrization mechanism based on so called "external nodes". External nodes are variables in a geometric tree that can be substituted with nodes in another geometric tree. The concept of external nodes can be compared to parameters that are supplied with a procedure call in a conventional programming language.

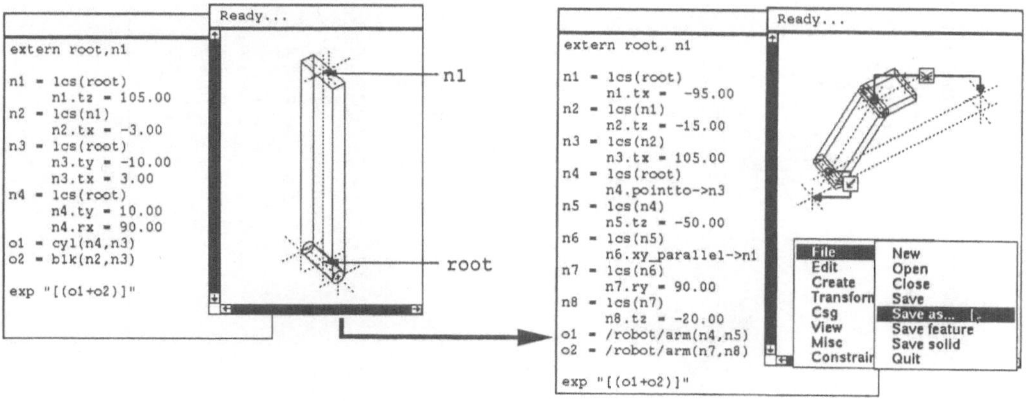

Figure 8. Two instances of the predefined object `/robot/arm` *are used in the assembly* `/robot/grab`*. The length of the instances are parametrized by an external node.*

Figure 8 shows two instances of the predefined object `/robot/arm` appended to an assembly. The length of the arm is controlled by the z-position of node `n1` (left picture). After the user has defined the arm, he picks at node `root` and node `n1` and selects the option external from a menu. The instance is now parametrized by two nodes and can be saved in the database. In the right picture, the user has provided the two instances of the arm with different parameters. The parameters represent the external nodes and can be selected graphically. The values for `root` and `n1` that specify the position, orientation and length of the arm in the generic description are respectively defined by `n4` and `n5` for instance `o1`, and `n7` and `n8` for instance `o2`.

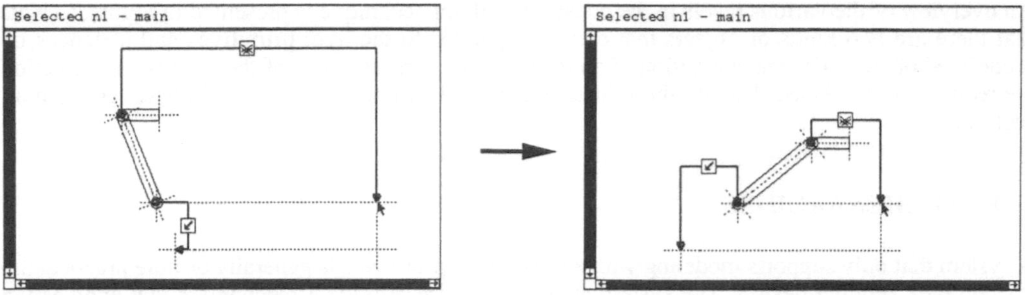

Figure 9. The grab can be opened and closed by direct manipulation on node `n1` *(at cursor position).*

In Figure 8, two constraints are specified. The pointto constraint rotates the node for positioning the first instance `o3` so that the z-axis of the arm points to node `n3`. The xy_parallel constraint applied to node `n6` aligns node `n6` with node `n1` in the xy-plane. An extra node `n7` is required to rotate the second instance of the arm over 90 degrees. After the user has specified the constraint, he can manipulate the assembly by dragging node `n1` along the x-axis, thereby controlling the opening and closing of a grab (Figure 9).

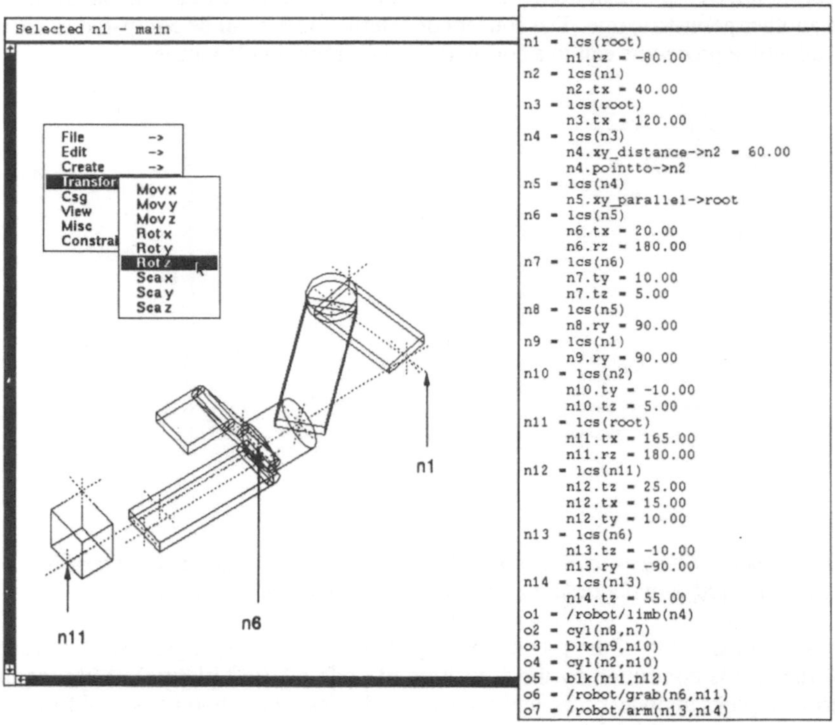

Figure 10. Robot mechanism with an instance of the grab.

Several nodes only serve to define the internal geometry of the assembly and should not be modified afterwards. Only two nodes are important for manipulation of the assembly; node `root` for positioning and orienting the grab and node `n1` for opening and closing the grab. The user can mark these nodes as `extern` and save assembly as `/robot/grab` in the database (Figure 8).

A simple robot mechanism, using an instance of the grab is presented in Figure 10. The user can control the assembly by rotating node `n1` along the z-axis. Several nodes and constraints are used to convert the rotation on node `n1` into a translation of node `n6` along the x-axis. Node `n11` specifies a fixed position for a block, which is not modified by rotation on node `n1`. So, if the user rotates node `n1` along the z-axis, node `n6` will move to or from node `n11`. The instance of the grab is parametrized by nodes `n6` and `n11`. The position of node `n6` and node `n11` is substituted for the external nodes in the grab and the local constraints in the grab are re-evaluated with these parameters. Node `n6` specifies the position of the grab and the distance between node `n6` and node `n11` controls the opening or closing of the grab. If the user rotates node `n1`, the grab will move towards the block and closes automatically (Figure 11).

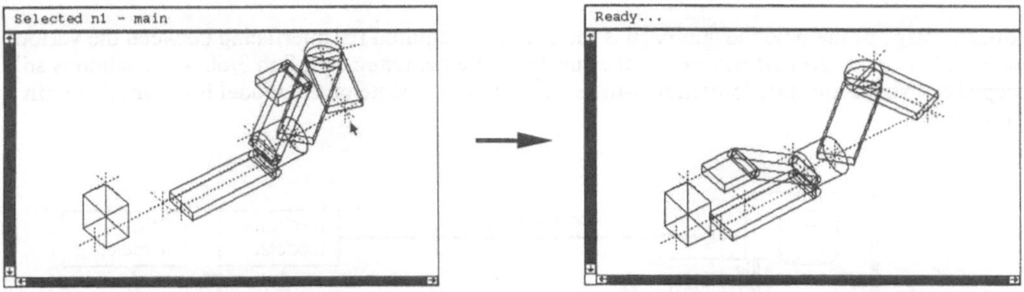

Figure 11. The robot mechanism is controlled by rotating `n1` *along the z-axis.*

The example of the robot demonstrates how part hierarchies are represented and how constraints are propagated by the external node mechanism. Note that there are three levels in the example of the robot; the robot, the instance of the grab and the instance of the arm defined in the grab (Figure 8) The advantage of instantiation is twofold. First, the user can build a model with predefined objects and use several "copies" of the same object in the model. Second, the design of a complex product can be split-up into a number of sub-assemblies which can be tested separately. If the user is satisfied with the dynamic behaviour of individual sub-assemblies, he can define constraints at assembly level.

5. IMPLEMENTATION

The system is built-up from several modules: user interface, database manager, linker, interpreter, tree processor, constraint solver and modeler (Figure 12). At (A), the user can activate a template and supply the parameters for the template by graphics pick and dragging. Basic graphics functionality for event handling and display of the model is implemented with the device independent X11 window system. More advanced user interface features such as pop-up menu's, scroll bars and editor windows are defined with the Xr11 User Interface Toolkit. The result of the graphics interaction is a procedural model that may contain instances of predefined objects.

At (B), the linker loads the generic descriptions of predefined objects from the database and inserts the description into the procedural model. The procedural model is subsequently interpreted (C) and converted into an internal data structure of nodes, constraints and primitives. The interpreter is implemented as a virtual stack machine built with Lex(Kernighan, 1985) for token scanning and Yacc(Kernighan, 1985) for syntax parsing. Frames for processing nested code blocks as required for functions, procedures, iteration statements and conditional statements are supported. The geometric processing of the model, as discussed in Section 3.2, is handled at (D). After the model is processed, a list of primitives with their corresponding 3D transformation matrices is obtained. The evaluated model (E) can be displayed as a wireframe or, alternatively, as a solid CSG model. Algorithms for display, constraint solving and geometric calculations are implemented with the object-oriented language C++.

All modules are implemented as separate applications linked in a Unix pipeline(Kernighan, 1985). Modules can be developed and tested separately and can also be invoked from a command line interface. For instance, the procedural description of the grab in Figure 9 can be displayed as a wireframe by the command:

```
cat /robot/grab | gmlink | gmi | gmgeo | xplot
```

A disadvantage of the pipeline approach is the overhead required for interfacing between the various modules. However, the performance of the current implementation on a Sun 3/60 workstation is still acceptable. Nodes are transformed real-time and a global update of the model is obtained within a few seconds.

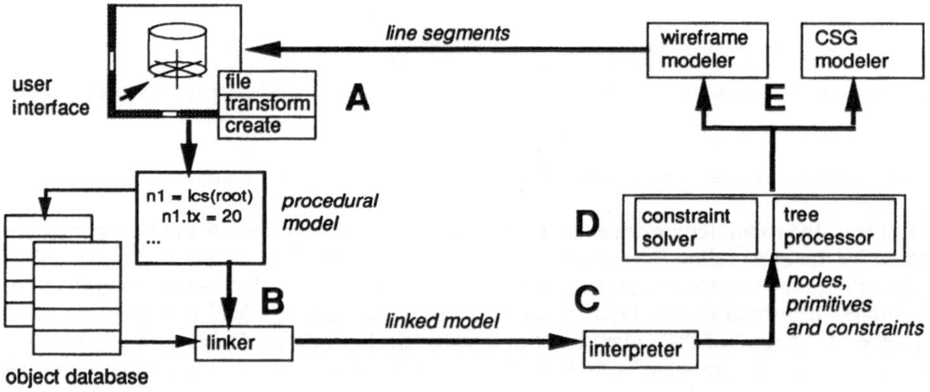

Figure 12. System overview

6. DISCUSSION

GeoNode provides an environment for graphical specification and interactive evaluation of 3D constraints. The combination of direct manipulation and a procedural object description makes it possible to define parametrized part hierarchies graphically. All examples presented in this paper are specified by graphics pick and direct manipulation. Keyboard interaction is only required to name an object for storage in the database.

One of the key concepts in this paper is the fact that constraints are not defined between objects, but between local coordinate systems. This approach simplifies the technique for constraint solving and makes the technique more generally applicable. The system here is presented for CSG, but can also be applied for other representations. Local coordinate systems are basic entities in 3D modeling, regardless of the internal representation used in the system. Nodes can for instance be used as vertices for polygons, transformations for halfspaces or control points for B-spline surfaces.

The current version of the system processes constraints only in one direction. For example, a constraint `n3.xy_parallel->n1` implies that if `n1` is rotated along the y-axis, node `n3` is rotated also. But what should happen when the user tries to rotate `n3`? In the current version nothing happens, the rotation is blocked because the y-rotation is already fixed by a constraint. However, it might be interesting to define constraints between nodes symmetrically. In this case the user could rotate either one of the nodes and the constraint would automatically pass the rotation to the other node. A second modification of the system involves the specification of conditional constraints (e.g. `n2.x_distance->root<40`). A conditional constraint only fixes the node if a certain minimum or maximum value is exceeded. A set of conditional constraints can be used to define an interval in which a node can be positioned or oriented by the user. Conditional constraints can for instance be used to represent tolerance information or to prevent object interference.

Acknowledgments

The concept of integrating a graphical interface with a constraint-based object description and a procedural model representation has originated from various discussions with Erik Jansen. I am also grateful to Wim Bronsvoort en Denis McConalogue for careful review and valuable comments on an earlier version of the paper. The development of the GeoNode system is supported by the product modeling group of Frits Tolman at TNO-IBBC. I would especially like to thank Peter Kuiper for his ideas about the integration of GeoNode with product modeling applications.

References

Badler N.I., Kamran H., "Articulated figure positioning by multiple constraints", *IEEE Computer Graphics & Applications,* June 1987, pp. 28-38

Bernstein N.S., Preiss K., "Representation of tolerance information in solid models", *Proceedings 15th Design Automation Conference,* 1989, pp. 405-411

Bier E.A., Stone M.C., "Snap-Dragging", *Computer Graphics (Proceedings Siggraph'86),* vol. 20 no. 4, 1986, pp.28-38

Borning A., Duisberg R., "Constraint-based tools for building user interfaces", *ACM Transactions on Graphics,* vol. 5 no. 4, 1986, pp. 245-374

Cohen E.S., Smith E.T., Iverson L.A., "Constraint-based tiled windows", *IEEE Computer Graphics & Applications,* May 1986, pp. 35-45

Cugini U., Folini F., Vicini I., "A procedural system for the definition and storage of technical drawings in parametric form", *Proceedings Eurographics'88,* Elsevier Science Publishers, 1988, pp. 183-196

Emmerik M.J.G.M. van, "A system for graphical interaction on parametrized solid models", *Proceedings Eurographics'88,* Elsevier Science Publishers, 1988, pp. 233-242 (Reprinted as "Creation and modification of parametrized solid models by graphical interaction", *Computers & Graphics,* vol. 13 no.1, 1989, pp. 71-75)

Emmerik M.J.G.M. van, "Graphical interaction on procedural object descriptions", *Theory and Practice of Geometric Modelling,* Springer-Verlag, 1989, pp. 469-482

Emmerik M.J.G.M. van, Jansen F.W., "User interface for feature modelling", *Proceedings CAPE'89,* Elsevier Science Publishers, 1989, pp. 625-632

Fuller N., Prusinkiewicz P., "Geometric Modeling with Euclidian Constructions", *Proceedings Computer Graphics International '88,* Springer-Verlag, 1988, pp. 379-391

Kernighan B.W., Pike R., "The UNIX programming environment", *Prentice-Hall software series,* Prentice-Hall, New Jersey, 1985

Kim S.H., Lee K., "An assembly modelling system for dynamic and kinematic analysis", *Computer-Aided Design*, vol. 21 no. 1, 1989, pp. 2-12

Kimura F. Suzuki H., Wingard L., "A uniform approach to dimensioning and tolerancing in product modelling", *Proceedings CAPE'86*, 1986, pp.165-178

Kin N., Noma T., Kunii T.L., "PictureEditor: A 2D picture editing system based on geometric constructions and constraints", *Proceedings Computer Graphics International '89*, Springer-Verlag, 1989, pp.193-206

Nelson G., "Juno, a constraint-based graphics system", *Computer Graphics (Proceedings Siggraph' 85)*, vol. 19 no. 3, 1985, pp. 235-243

Roach J.A., "The rectangle placement language", *Proceedings of the 21th Design Automation Conference*, 1984, pp. 405-411

Roth J., Hashimshony R., "Algoritms in graph theory and their use for solving problems in architectural design", *Computer-Aided Design*, vol. 20 no. 7, 1988, pp. 373-381

Rossignac J.R., "Constraints in Constructive Solid Geometry", *Proceedings Workshop on Interactive 3D Graphics*, ACM Press, 1986, pp. 93-110

Rubin R.V., Golin E.J., Reiss S.P., "Thinkpad: a graphical system for programming by demonstration", *IEEE Software*, March 1985, pp. 73-78

Shneiderman B., "Direct manipulation, a step beyond programming languages", *IEEE Computer*, vol. 16, 1983, pp. 57-69

Sutherland I.E., "SKETCHPAD: a man-machine graphical communication system", *Proceedings Spring Joint Computer Conference*, 1963, pp. 329-346

White R.M., "Applying Direct Manipulation to Geometric Construction Systems", *Proceedings Computer Graphics International '89*, Springer-Verlag, 1989, pp. 446-455

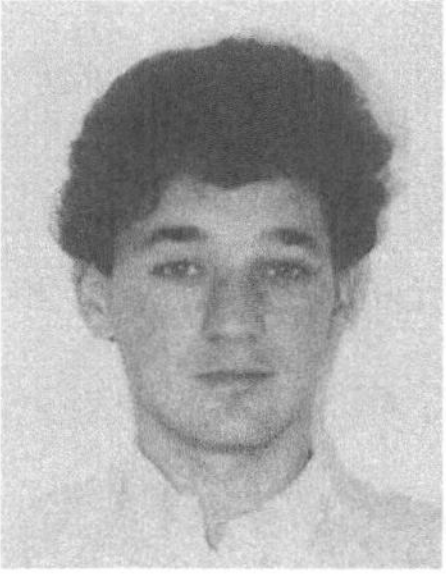

Maarten J.G.M. van Emmerik received a master's degree in Industrial Design Engineering from the Delft University of Technology. He graduated with distinction on the design of a Bitmap Editor in a Desktop Publishing environment. Currently, he is working as a Phd-candidate on the development of interactive graphical techniques for higher-level specification of geometric models. The research is a joint project of the faculties of Industrial Design Engineering and Computer Science at the Delft University of Technology and the Dutch research institute TNO-IBBC. His reseach interest include: solid modeling, constraints, modeling languages, user interface, product modeling and feature modeling.

Address: Faculty of Industrial Design Engineering, Delft University of Technology, Jaffalaan 9, 2628 BX Delft, The Netherlands. Fax: +3115787316. UUCP: {hp4.nl!}dutrun!dutio!mve.

Visualization of Abstract Concepts Using Generalized Path Binding

Ken Nakayama, Satoshi Matsuoka, and Satoru Kawai

Abstract

Our proposed framework for visualization of the domain of abstract concepts A, into the domain of pictures P, defines the visualization function f_v, which maps the abstract objects and relations in A into pictorial objects and constraints in P. Here, we consider one generic and important class — ordering relation between the abstract objects, and how visualization of such relations should occur in general. For this, we propose a new framework, the Generalized Path Binding (**GPB**). **GPB** serves not only as a consistent model for visualizing such relations, but also provides a set of primitives for constructing f_v; this is achieved with a flexible algorithm which binds pictorial objects onto any paths in an arbitrary manner.

Keywords Graphics, Visualization, Constraint-Solving, User Interface.

1 INTRODUCTION

1.1 Framework for Picture Generation from Abstract Concepts

Our research group has been working on formulating a general framework for visualizing abstract concepts(Kamada 1989; Kamada, Kawai to appear; Matsuoka, Kawai 1989). When considering such framework, we think one of the essencial criteria is that it does not generate erroneous pictures that do not convey the intended information of the concepts. Our goal is to provide a visualizaton framework which generates wide variety of pictures while meeting this criterion.

Our overall framework is as follows: we first divide the domain of *abstract concepts*, A, into the domain of *abstract objects*, O_a, and domain of *abstract relations* among the objects, R_a. We express this as $A \equiv (O_a, R_a)$, denoting that concepts are composite of objects and their relations. The elements of R_a have the following property: for all $r_a \in R_a, r_a(\widetilde{o_a^i})$ may or may not hold for some set of objects $\widetilde{o_a^i} \equiv < o_a^1, \ldots, o_a^k >$, where each $o_a^i \in O_a$ for $1 \leq i \leq k$. When r_a holds for some $\widetilde{o_a^i}$, we say that r_a is *satisfied.*

We note here that abstract relations should be well-defined so that its satisfaction should be computable, but that is not our primary concern; rather, for our purpose, we need actual instances of objects that satisfies a given abstract relation. The generation of such objects given a set of relations is a constraint satisfaction problem in

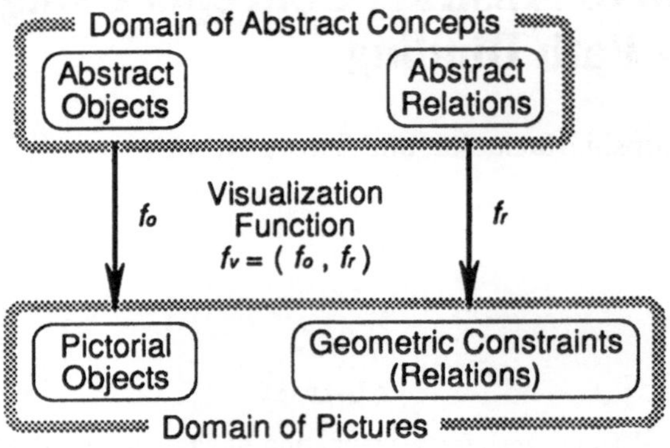

Figure 1: Framework for picture generation

domain A, which can be solved by constraint logic programming or by some other means(Hentenryck 1989).

We next define the domain of *pictures*, P, to be the composite of the domain of *pictorial objects*, O_p, and their *geometric relations* or *constraints*, R_p, i.e., $P \equiv (O_p, R_p)$. Then we define a *visualization function*, $f_v : A \rightarrow P$. For a clean framework, we let $f_v \equiv (f_o, f_r)$; f_o maps the abstract objects to their counterparts in O_p, and f_r maps abstract relations to geometric constraints (Fig. 1). There are requirements that f_v must meet: f_o merely needs to be a total function, i.e., for all $o_a^i \in O_a, \exists 1 o_p^i \in O_p$ such that $o_p^i = f_o(o_a^i)$. There is a slightly more strict requirement that f_r must satisfy: for each $r_a \in R_a$, let $\widetilde{o_a^i}$ be a set of objects that satisfies r_a, and let $o_p^i = f_o(o_a^i)$; then $\exists 1 r_p \in R_p$ such that $r_p = f_r(r_a)$, and $\widetilde{o_p^i}$ satisfies r_p. In other words, when an abstract relation is mapped to a geometric constraint, the constraint must hold for the result of mappings of sets of abstract objects that satisfies the relation.

With the above definitions, pictorial objects and their constraints are generated from the objects and relations in the abstract domain. Then, the constraint solver is invoked to solve the geometric constraints, resulting in the final output. Difficulty arises in under– or overconstrained cases; in practice, overconstrained cases may be handled gracefully by distributing the error using the least square method.

By all means, our framework is not complete in sense that every conceivable pictures of abstract concepts can be generated this way. However, it has proven to be general and robust enough for generation of numerous non-trivial classes of pictures which express abstract concepts. Examples generated by TRIP(Kamada 1989; Kamada, Kawai to appear), which was implemented based on the framework, include visualization of cons cells of LISP, Entity-Relationship diagrams(Chen 1976), and Nassi–Shneiderman diagrams(Nassi, Schneiderman 1973).

1.2 Difficulty in the Well-defined Specification of f_v

The most significant part of our framework is the specification of f_v — in fact, any function which fulfills the above condition is possible. But while this gives the user the utmost degree of freedom, the user must specialize f_v for each particular instance of visualization, a task which reveals to be rather tedious. This is chiefly due to the lack of robust primitives upon which the functions can be constructed; for example, TRIP only provides very simple or somewhat ad-hoc geometric constraint primitives, such as "objects being evenly spaced apart and aligned horizontally"[1]. The error distribution capability in TRIP helps to compensate for this deficiency to some degree; nevertheless, its behavior is unpredictable, and is thus not applicable to all cases.

In our overall research, therefore, we wish to provide high level basis or primitives for our framework that captures and generalizes the essence of numerous instances of visualization in order to aid the construction of f_v. For that purpose, we must analyze what sort of abstract relations are often regarded as being significant in the domain of abstract concepts, and also how that relation will be mapped to the realm of domain of pictures.

In this work, we consider one important basic relation which is common to numerous instances of abstract concepts: some ordering relation exists between the elements of O_a. We then propose the notion of *generalized path binding* (**GPB**). **GPB** serves not only as a consistent model for visualization for such relations, but also as the primitive for constructing f_v, offering flexible mechanism with which the user only needs to specify only few primitives, and the constraint solver takes care of the rest.

2 RELATED WORK

2.1 Visualization of Physical Pictures Using Constraints

There have been a number of researches on visualization of pictures using numerical constraint solving. Such a program was pioneered with Sutherland's SKETCHPAD(1963). This idea was further pursued by Sussman and Steele's CONSTRAINTS (1980) which solves constraints symbolically. Their method offers efficient solving of one-way constraints with the local propagation algorithm.

Van Wyk's IDEAL(1982) is a typesetting system for pictures that acts as a preprocessor for Troff. Its constraint solver can solve limited classes of non-linear equations with Gaussian elimination techniques. Greg Nelson's Juno(1984) attempts to integrate a similar solver which can solve quadratic equations within an interactive picture editor. Pavlidis and Van Wyk's work on picture beautification(1984) does the reverse, inferring desirable constraints which picture elements seem to meet, and then 'beautifying' the picture by solving the constraints whenever possible.

In addition to these and other work, Noma et al. describe an alternative approach to picture generation with constraint solving in their constructive picture description(1988). The pictures are generated from finite set of geometric primitives and

[1] Some of this stems from the fact that solving of some constraints are extremely computationally expensive, often becoming NP-complete.

constructors; the difference is that the constructor may generate new geometric primitives, such as the point of intersection between two circles, which can be used later in the new construction, in defining, for example, a line segment that crosses the midpoint of the line segment which connects the centers of the circles perpendicularly. When a part of a picture is changed, an algorithm similar to one-way constraint propagation is invoked to redraw the affected area.

For work on generating or operating upon pictures along a given path, graphic systems standards such as GKS or PHIGS have provided extremely simple attribute mechanisms which are too low-level for mappings of high-level abstract data. Whitted introduces a system for doing anti-aliased painting along an arbitrary path(1983), with which one can achieve interesting pictorial effects. The scope of the system is totally different from ours in that its imaging model is raster-oriented, and the 'pen' traverses the path in a nearly-continuous manner with no notion of distances. Some professional drawing programs such as Aldus Freehand(1989) allow binding of text to a path. However the functionality for placement is not nearly as robust as in our system, as (1) pictorial objects in this operation is restricted to characters of a text, and (2) the mode of placement is restricted to only a few transformations, and (3) there is no solid framework in which the user may analyze or define his operations. Barr(1984) presents the deformation of geometric shapes along a path. Sederberg et al.(1986) give a similar idea to (Barr 1984) in specifying solids with 3-dimensional deformation operations.

The limitations of all the above systems is that they restrict the domain of data for visualization to the domain of physical pictures. As our framework for visualization and its algorithm will show, one must consider what class of abstract relations they wish to visualize, and create primitives for formulation of f_v. In this process, the scope and the structure of the algorithm for visualization must be strongly tied to the requirements set by the abstract relations. Failure to assess the requirements results in a system which is a collection of ad-hoc functionalities; for example, we see the deficiency in (Aldus 1989), where the binding operation is not generic for all pictorial objects.

2.2 Visualization of Data in User Interfaces

Borning's ThingLab(Borning 1981; Borning, Duisberg 1986), and its successor, ThingLab II(Maloney, Borning, Freeman-Benson 1989) provide tools for building interactive graphical objects in Smalltalk with links to application semantics by using constraints. The difference is that the former can treat circular and some non-linear constraints by employing relaxation techniques, while the latter restricts its scope to one-way constraints which can be solved by value propagation. This is because the former was created for the purpose of simulation of physical systems, while latter is targetted for the creation of interactive graphics in user interfaces, in which the delay of feedback caused by solving complex constraints is highly undesirable. For achieving speed, the latter employs an incremental constraint-solving algorithm called the delta-blue algorithm; when a new constraint is added to the constraint graph, the graph is not re-built from scratch but is updated incrementally. Vander Zanden's CONSTRAINT(1989) further explores the idea of fast incremental solving in one-way constraint systems. It also presents an integration of attribute grammars and constraint-based object system, called *constraint grammars*, that provide a powerful editing model for manipulation of underlying data structures with constraints for interactive graphical user interfaces. Another object-oriented user interface management system GROW(Barth 1986) maintains a one-way constraint system, called the *graphical dependency*.

There are a number of programs that visualize numerical data, such as those that create graphs or charts in business graphics. Systems for scientific visualization can be regarded as much more elaborate versions. There have also been specialized programs for visualizing special classes of abstract concepts, such as computer programs visualized as flowcharts. We will not go into details here, as they are well covered in (Kamada 1989; Kamada, Kawai to appear), and cover systems that visualizes more general classes of relations.

Beach and Stone's work on graphical styles(1983) attempts to separate the abstract content and the physical format of illustration with the use of the *graphical style sheet*. Our work goes beyond this in attempting to visualize the abstract concepts as well.

Friedel's View System(1984) visualizes entity-attribute data in the database by applying a *synthesis operator* to *object frames*, each one consisting of *elements*, *fragments*, and a *region*. The knowledge base maintains the three types of synthesis operators, namely *simile inferences*, *structural couplers*, and *object grids*. Object synthesis proceeds according to the sequential tasks set by the *synthesis agenda*. The system seems to be intended for practical use only, is very complex, and rather lacks organization or formality.

Myer's INCENCE visualizes data structures(1983) in programming languages. Although it is very useful for debugging, it may not be useful for visualization of abstract data, as the data structure is an *implementation* of the abstract data type, so as a result, it does not always convey the true abstract behavior of the data type.

Brown's work in algorithm animation, BALSA(1984) and its successor BALSA II(1987), attempt to animate the abstract behaviors of algorithm. He too points out that it is insufficient to just visualize raw data structures of programs, but is necessary to choose a representation which is more natural to human intuition and understanding. Our visualization framework and its algorithm can be applied to such systems to replace specialized programs for each implementation of views.

2.3 Other Work

Finally, we have to mention the idea of using parallelepipeds as a bounding volume appearing in a work by Kay and Kajiya on tracing(1986). The computation of the geometric constraint satisfaction such as intersection search with our picture approximation approach is much more general, for (1) not only straight lines but also areas bounded by quadratic curves are available as primitive areas, (2) the bounding area can be constructed with arbitrary combinations of set operations among the primitive areas, and (3) the path need not be a straight line as in a light ray, but can be a polynomial curve.

3 The Definition of Generalized Path Binding

3.1 Abstract Notion of Lining Up Objects and its Ambiguity

One important abstract notion that we frequently consider is when a set of objects has some certain total ordering imposed by some relation which covers the entire set. It is our claim and experience from TRIP that the high-level functionality for visualization of total ordering relation is one of the essential basis in construction of robust framework for visualization. Certainly, total ordering relation is only a subset of abstract relations in general. It is, nevertheless, often a part of more general relation; for example, any directed graph can be decomposed into paths so that we can establish total ordering among the nodes in a path.

When such a relation is visualized, the resulting picture would naturally be objects being lined up in some manner. More specifically, objects, which are elements of a totally ordered set, are bound to a certain path in a R^n space with their order preserved. This notion of 'lining up' is rather quite simple. Yet, when we attempt to construct a uniform model which allow flexible, high-level specification of visualization, we find that the task is not at all trivial. This, we believe, is mainly caused by the ambiguity of the term 'lining up'. **GPB** attempts to resolve this by giving a clear definition which generalizes the notion; it is achieved with abstracting out the characteristics common to 'lining up', and leaving the question of *how* to be specifiable depending upon the context. With this framework, we have easy and flexible construction of fv without sacrificing or restricting the expressive power; and most importantly, we avoid generating pictures which cannot be naturally regarded as being 'lined up'.

3.2 Generalized Path Binding Condition

We start with considering the criteria for the notion of "line up along a path". By performing analysis on the characteristics of the pictures in which objects could be regarded as 'lined up', we have abstracted out the following constraint relations to be essential for pictorial objects to be 'path bound'.

(I) **Path binding constraint**
Each pictorial object is *geometrically bound* to a path.

(II) **Path dependent ordering constraint**
There is a *path dependent geometrical ordering* among the pictorial objects.

We define that the satisfaction of these two constraints to be necessary and sufficient conditions for a set of pictorial objects to be *generally bound to a path*, or, in other words, satisfying the **GPB** *condition*.

The path binding constraint is a relation between each pictorial object and a path; i.e., restriction on the relative position of a pictorial object and a path. When a pictorial object is placed in a 2-dimensional Euclidean space, it has total geometric freedom with respect to geometric transformations if there were no imposed constraints. When it is bound to a path, however, the location and direction of the object is constrained by a path in some way (Fig. 2(1)). A pictorial object with a pin guided along a groove

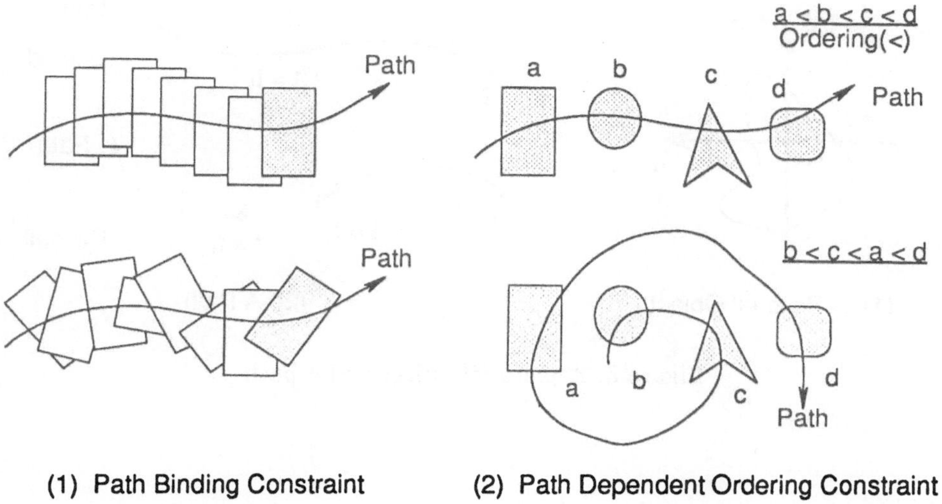

Figure 2: **GPB** constraints

allows us to intuitively envision the 'path bound' situation; the object can only move along the groove and rotate around the pin. The direction of the pictorial object is restricted further if wheels and rails are used instead of a pin and a groove. On the other hand, more lenient binding is possible if there is some measure of elasticity[2] between the pictorial object and the pin.

The path dependent ordering constraint is a geometric ordering among pictorial objects that depends a path. As our purpose is to visualize objects with total ordering relations, the ordering relations among the abstract objects map naturally to the ordering constraint — which is dependent on the path — among the pictorial objects. Note that, even though the objects may be placed in geometrically identical positions, their order may be totally different, as shown in Fig. 2(2).

Now, in order to realize a system based on the above framework, the two constraints presented must be represented in concrete forms; that is, for the construction of f_v, we must be able to formulate a system of concrete solvable constraints from a set of well-defined primitives, and give an efficient algorithm for solving them, in numerical or symbolic way.

4 A GENERALIZED PATH BINDING SYSTEM

Here, we present a set of **GPB** *primitives* with which we can construct parts of f_v that visualizes a variety of 'path bound' pictures, and a **GPB** *algorithm* that solves

[2]Intuitively, a 'rubber band' ties the object and the pin.

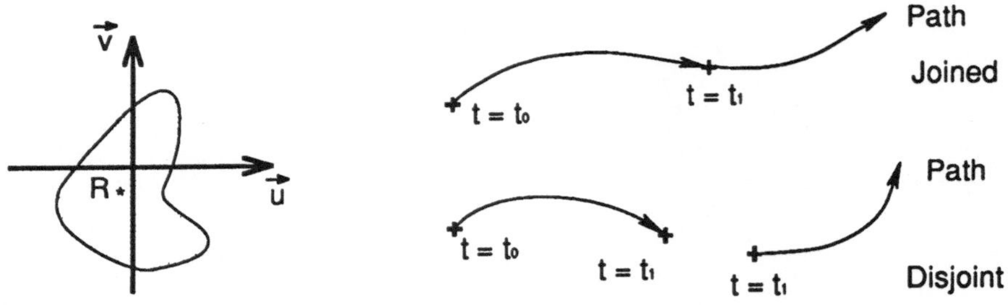

(1) A Pictorial Object (2) A Path

Figure 3: A pictorial object and a path

the system of constraints that arises among these proposed **GPB** primitives. We also introduce *approximated pictorial objects* and *approximated paths* for efficient computation of geometric constraint satisfaction. The strategies for numerical calculation used in the constraint satisfaction will only be covered briefly here; details will be given in section 5.

4.1 The GPB Primitives

The **GPB** primitives constitute the description of "*how* a set of *pictorial objects* should be *bound* to a given *path*." The first two are instances in the geometric domain, namely: (1) pictorial objects and (2) paths. The next two are (3) local geometric transformations of the pictorial object with respect to its own local coordinate system, and (4) transformation of the local coordinate system, parametric to the path direction with respect to the global coordinate system. The next one plays a central role in the visualization process: (5) the function which maps the relative position of a pictorial object and a path to a range of a path[3]. Finally, in order to maintain the path dependent ordering constraint, we define the primitive (6) *generalized distance*, which is a generalization of the distance between two objects on a path.

Let us now describe each **GPB** primitive in more detail.

(i) **Pictorial object**

A pictorial object is composed of three geometric specifications (Fig. 3):

1. its geometrical shape,
2. its *position reference point* R_* — used to designate position of the pictorial object,
3. local coordinate vector $\boldsymbol{u}, \boldsymbol{v}$.

[3]Intuitively, a range on the path represents the path occupied by the pictorial object.

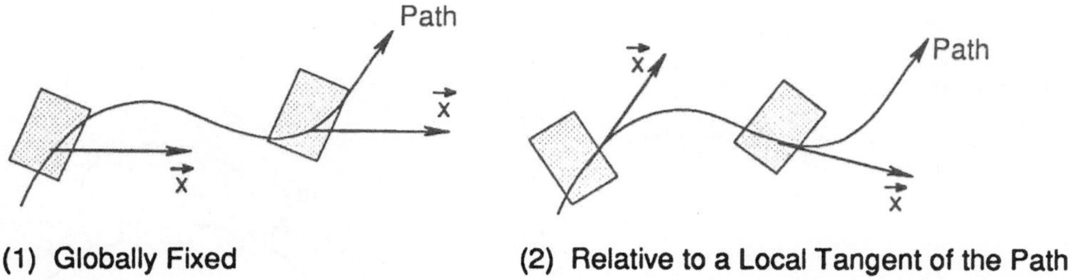

Figure 4: The direction of a pictorial object

Here, in order to make our constraint system efficiently solvable, we adopt a following major restriction: *a position reference point must always be on a path.* The local coordinate system, as a result, has its origin at R_*.

(ii) **Path**
A path is a directed, parametric curve (Fig. 3), denoted $p(t)$. It may have multiple discontinuous points.

(iii) **Local transformation of the object**
Prior to binding an object to a path, arbitrary local transformation can be performed on the object. Our current implementation restricts this to a subset of Affine transformation only, denoted with a transformation matrix M[4]. As indicated earlier, the local transformation cannot translate the position reference point R_*.

(iv) **Path-parametric transformation of the local coordinate system**
The local coordinate system of the object is transformed according to the parameter of the path. This is achieved with applying a transformation to the local coordinate vector u. Our current prototype implementation provides rotation and scaling only. For rotation, there are two types of directional controls for the base unit vector (Fig. 4): (1) globally fixed, (2) relative to a local tangent of the path (e.g., tangential vector of the path). The reason we have two separate stages of transformations is that the latter transformation is parametric to the path, and thus must be restricted in order for the constraint solver to work efficiently. The details will be covered in the later section 5.

Next, we concentrate on the path-dependent ordering constraint. Ordering relations among n objects are broken down into a set of $n-1$ orderings between two neighboring objects. Assume a path, two pictorial objects, and their relative ordering are given; first we map each object into a range on the path (intuitively it represents the range occupied by the pictorial object), and then consider the ordering between these two ranges (Fig. 5 (1)).

[4]This is not based on any fundamental issues, but is rather choice made for the ease of quick

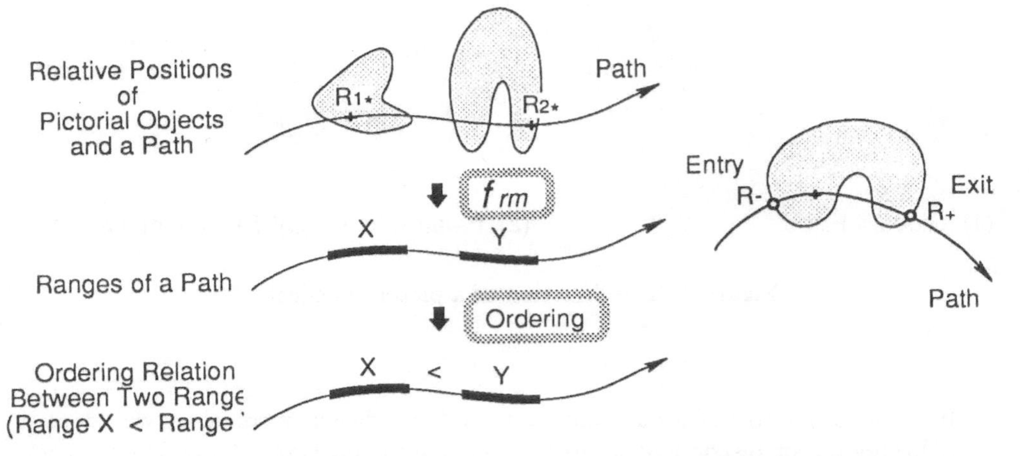

(1) Path Dependent Ordering (2) Alignment reference points

Figure 5: Path dependent ordering

(v) **Range mapping function f_{rm}**

The range mapping function f_{rm} maps an object to a range on a path. A range on the path is defined as a segment of path that is 'occupied by' a pictorial object. We call the two terminal points of a range *alignment reference points* (Fig. 5 (2)); the one at which the path makes an entry into a pictorial object is called the *entry alignment reference point* R_-, and the one at which the path exits is called the *exit alignment reference point* R_+. When the path crosses the boundary of an object several times, the former is the intersection with the smallest parametric value, the latter with the largest, and the range is defined to be the entire segment in-between.

(vi) **Generalized distance between two ranges on a path**

The generalized distance between two ranges of a path represents the ordering relation between the objects. The function $gap(a, b)$ denotes the generalized distance between two neighboring terminal points of the ranges a, b, where $a = f_{rm}(o_a)$, and $b = f_{rm}(o_b)$. Our current prototype provides the following distance functions, but any computable path-dependent function is possible (Fig. 6):

1. Euclidean distance between two points,
2. difference of two path parameters of two points,
3. distance along the path,

---

implementation.

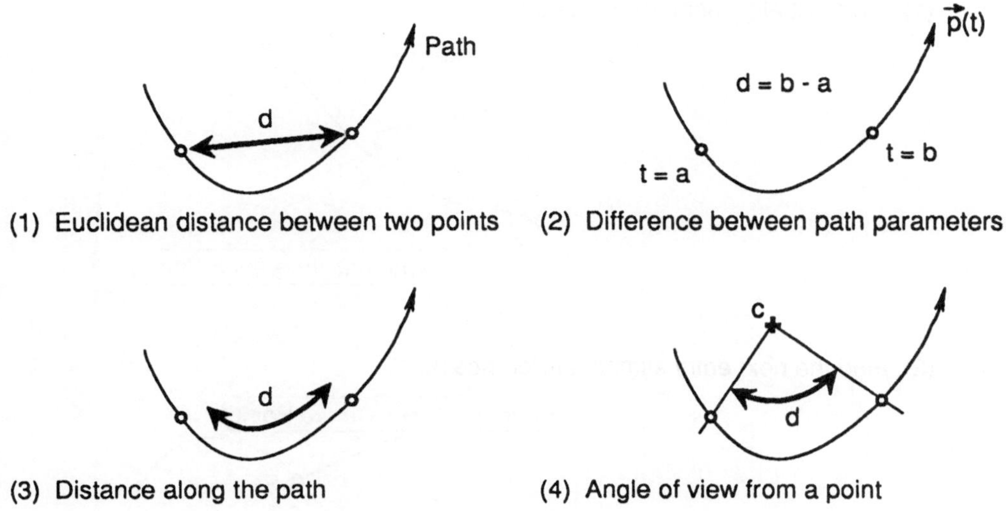

(1) Euclidean distance between two points (2) Difference between path parameters

(3) Distance along the path (4) Angle of view from a point

Figure 6: Generalized distances between two points

4. angle of view from a point.

The ordering relations between neighboring pair of objects are mapped to generalized distances between corresponding n ranges of a path by f_{rm}. When $o_a < o_b$, $gap(a,b)$ is set to some value $d > 0$, which is dependent upon the construction of f_v.

4.2 The GPB Algorithm

We now present the **GPB** algorithm which, given the primitives stated, solves the implicitly formulated constraint system. The constraint-solving is iterative, and conceptually proceeds as follows: map the first pictorial object on a path, find appropriate place for the next pictorial object, and repeat these actions until the sequence of pictorial objects ends[5].

In the following algorithm, $p(t)$ denotes the path in parametric form, and i indexes the pictorial objects in the sequence of their order. The position reference point of the first pictorial object R_{1*} is placed at a given point $p(t_1)$ on the path.

The **GPB** *Algorithm* (Fig. 7)

Preparation

Let $t = t_1$, and $i = 1$.

[5] We assume that the position of the first pictorial object is given.

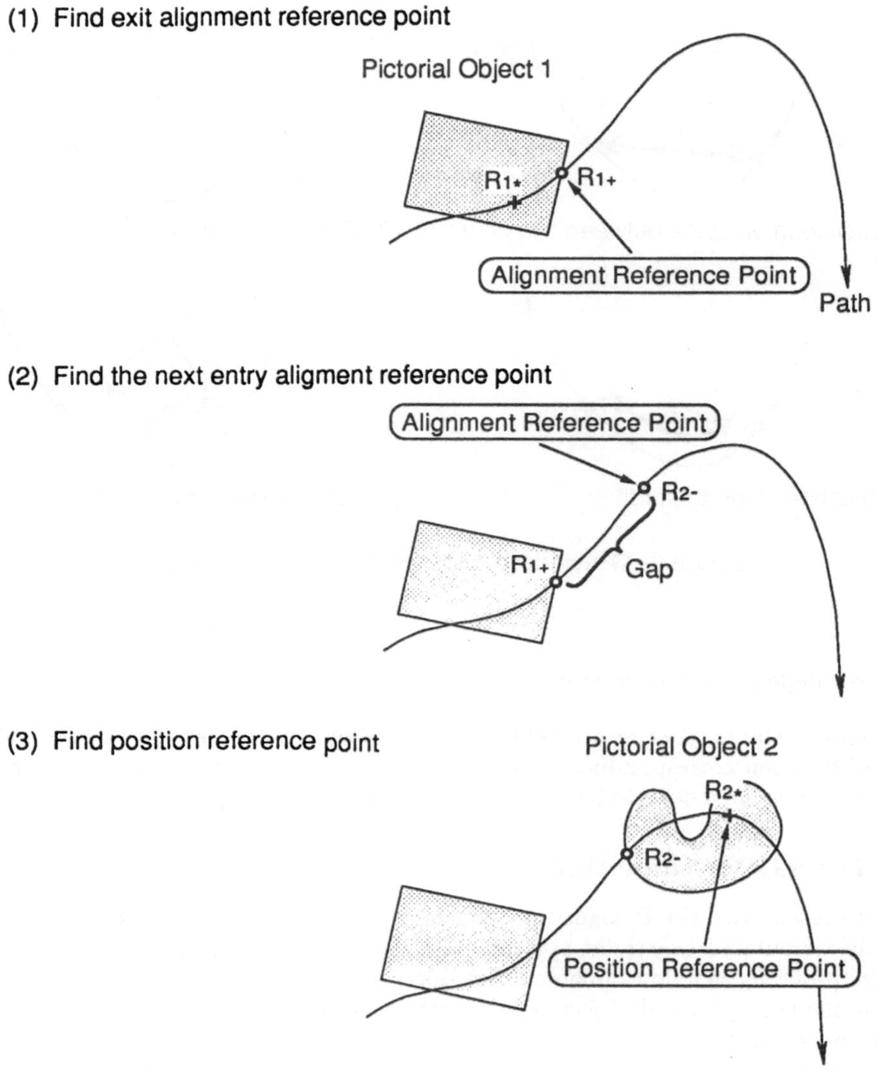
(1) Find exit alignment reference point
Pictorial Object 1
R1*
R1+
Alignment Reference Point
Path
(2) Find the next entry aligment reference point
Alignment Reference Point
R2-
R1+
Gap
(3) Find position reference point
Pictorial Object 2
R2*
R2-
Position Reference Point

Figure 7: **GPB** algorithm

Iteration

Iterate the following steps until the sequence of pictorial objects ends:

1. Map the i-th pictorial object with f_{rm} so that its *position reference point* R_{i*} is at $p(t)$ on the path.
2. Compute the *exit alignment reference point* R_{i+}.
3. Compute the *entry alignment reference point* $R_{(i+1)-}$ for the $i+1$-th object using generalized gap function $gap(R_{i+}, R_{(i+1)-})$.
4. For the $i+1$-th object, compute the *position reference point* $R_{(i+1)*}$ so that the *entry alignment reference point* comes at the point obtained in the previous step.
5. Let $t = t_{i+1}$ such that $p(t_{i+1}) = R_{(i+1)*}$.
6. Increment i for the next iteration.

Step 2 involves solving intersections of the páth and the object boundary, a moderately computationally expensive task if the perimeter of the object is itself an arbitrarily complex path. Step 4 is much more problematic, however, because it must satisfy the constraints simultaneously:

- the boundary of the object must intersect the path at the *entry alignment reference point* $R_{(i+1)-}$,
- the *position reference point* $R_{(i+1)*}$ must be on the path, and
- the local coordinate system of the object must have the direction specified by the path-parametric transformation.

Our first algorithm for solving these constraints involved inefficient iterative satisfaction technique that moves a pictorial object gradually on the path, which converged slowly. This was unacceptable considering that our applications may include real- or near real-time picture generations, especially in an interactive environment. To accomplish this situation, we have devised the *approximated picture* which formulates a constraint system that can be solved efficiently for practical use.

4.3 Approximated Pictorial Objects and Paths

4.3.1 Merits of Approximation

In order to formulate a constraint system which can be solved efficiently, our approach is to approximate the shape of a pictorial object or a path with some kinds of substitutes that have nice geometrical properties for constraint solving. Geometric operations for constraint solving in the GPB algorithm, such as intersection searching, are performed for these approximated pictorial objects and paths in place of the originals. The computation algorithms would be optimized for the approximated pictorial objects and paths, resulting in drastic boost in performance.

There is another merit to this approximation approach besides efficiency of constraint solving — *stabilization* of the alignment reference points for pictorial objects

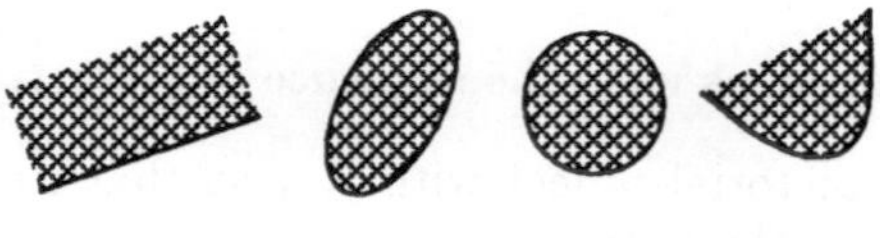

Figure 8: Pictorial object elements

that have irregular, concave shapes. Let us suppose that a path runs through a star-shaped pictorial object. Observe that, even if its relative position to the path might change only slightly, its entry and exit alignment reference points may experience drastic movements. This would result in drastic change in the arrangement of the entire set of objects. Generally, such a instability is undesirable for picture generation, especially in an interactive situation. Approximating this object with more evenly-shaped pictorial elements such as a disk would provide the desired geometrical stability.

The third merit of approximating pictorial objects is that the possibility of overlapping two concave pictorial objects could be reduced if the resulting approximated shape were convex. Some applications, such as road maps, may require that symbols on the road do not overlap. The symbol could have convex approximated shape for satisfying such criteria.

4.3.2 Pictorial Elements and Path Segments

The requirements for approximated pictures in our system are: (1) geometric constraint satisfaction is relatively inexpensive, while (2) arbitrary precision of approximation is attainable. From these considerations, we decided on the following constructive method of approximation. An approximated picture is composed of arbitrary number of basic elements; the more elements are used, the more precise the approximated picture becomes. We call these basic elements for approximated pictorial objects and paths *pictorial elements* and *path segments* respectively.

A pictorial element is an area on a plane which has simple border line(s). Set constructor operations union/intersection/negation can be performed among the pictorial elements to construct more complex approximated pictorial objects as in Fig. 9.

A path segment is a geometrically continuous line which may have finite/infinite length. An approximated path is composed as a sequence of one or more path segments. The function specifying the approximated path must be a total function of path parameter t throughout the entire sequence, but the resulting approximated path need not be necessarily geometrically continuous.

In our current **GPB** prototype system, the following pictorial elements and path segments are available for approximation:

- Pictorial elements are (Fig. 8):

    1. an area bounded by a straight line, or
    2. an area bounded by a quadratic curve.

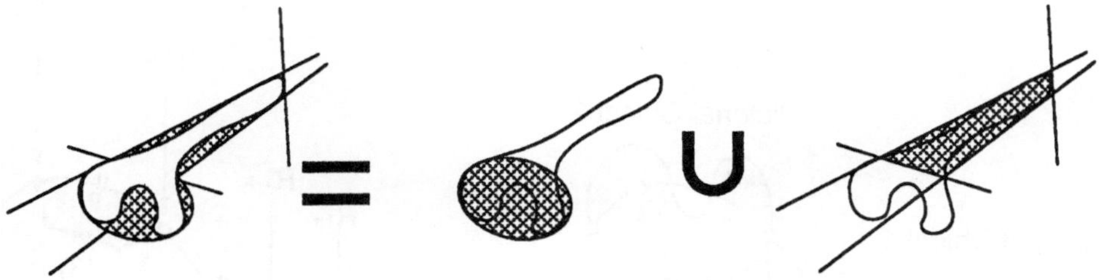

Figure 9: Compound pictorial object elements

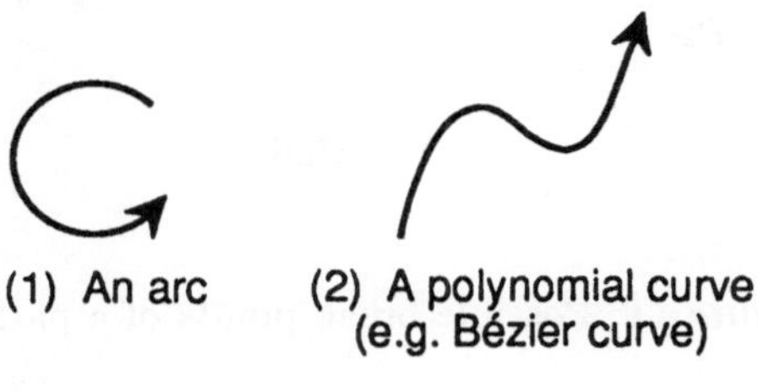

Figure 10: Path elements

Note that each of them may have an infinite extent. In fact, the former is a half-plane, and the latter, too, could have infinite extent if its quadratic border is an 'open' curve such as a parabola or a hyperbola. In practice, intersections are taken with other pictorial elements, forming a pictorial element of finite extent.

- Path segments are (Fig. 10):
  1. an arc, or
  2. a parametric curve in 2-dimensional space, where both $x(t)$ and $y(t)$ are respective polynomials of parameter t, such as a Bézier curve, or a B-spline, etc.

As a note, we comment on the issue on whether it would be desirable to require the approximation of a given pictorial object to be minimally-bounding. Our conclusion is that the requirement is too strong, and it would suffice just to have 'good' approximation in judgement of the user. By all means, it could be said in general that approximation is better in terms of similarity if it had lesser difference between itself and its original. However, it is computationally expensive to determine minimally-bounding areas even in an extremely simple case such as finding a minimal-bounding circle for a given polygon. Furthermore, if some part of the original pictorial object is particularly protrudes from its main body, then the user may not intend to take such part into consideration in the visualization process.

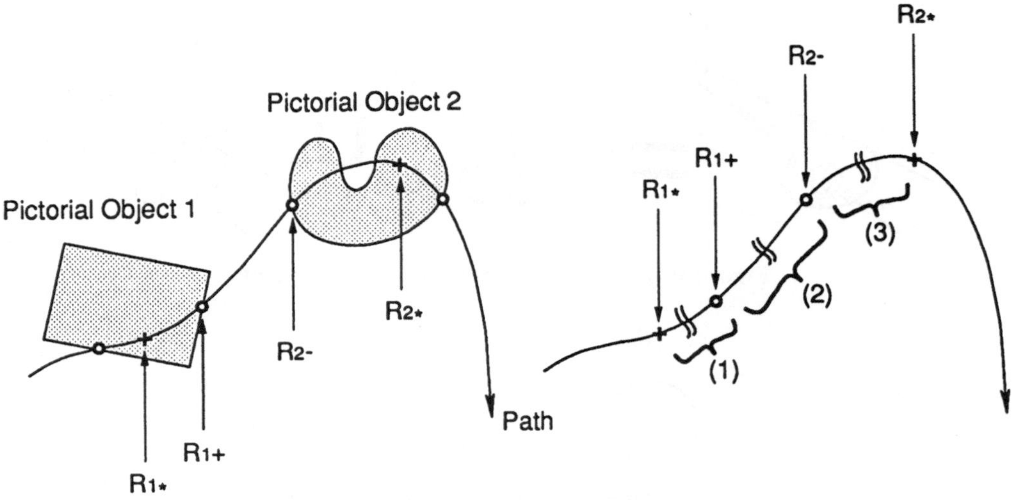

Figure 11: Possible break points of a path

4.4 Extensions for Joining of Path Segments

When a path is composed of a sequence of path segments, the **GPB** algorithm must support advancing from the end of one path segment to the beginning of another. There are two cases, namely: (1) *disjoint* — the endpoint of a path segment is at a different position from the starting point of the following one, and (2) *joined* — they are at the same position, e.g. piecewise continuous polynomial curves. The system must be able to handle both cases so that pictorial objects are lined up 'naturally'. This is especially important for continuous joins, as the user usually cannot immediately see where the segments are actually joined, but rather regards the entire sequence to be a single entity.

Now, the analysis of the algorithm reveals the following three cases when the end of a path segment may be encountered (Fig. 11):

1. when finding an exit alignment reference point from its position reference point (step 2 in the **GPB** algorithm), or
2. when finding an entry alignment reference point from the last exit alignment reference point (step 3), or
3. when finding position reference point from its entry alignment reference point (step 4).

We have found that all three can be sufficiently treated with a single strategy as follows.

Action taken at the end of a path segment:

If any of entry/exit alignment reference points or a position reference point cannot be found on a path segment, continue searching from the next segment in the order of the segment sequence (mainly applicable to joined paths). If there is no appropriate point on all the remaining path segments, place the current/next pictorial object at the beginning of the next path segment (mainly applicable to disjoint paths).

Note that, for the above strategy to work, we can see that it is essential for the constraint solving at step 4 in our **GPB** algorithm to be computable from equations without any iterations that may alter the position reference point. This is another reason we have adopted the approximation of objects; our constraint solver can then meet this requirement, as we describe next.

4.5 Procedure for Finding Alignment and Position Reference Points

Here, we will give a conceptual overview of the calculation procedure; the mathematical details will be given in the section 5.

In solving the geometric constraints, we provide satisfaction methods for two types of directional controls of the base unit vector of the local coordinate system (globally fixed, or relative to a local tangent of the path, i.e. path-parametric). Constraints to be solved are

(1) finding an *exit alignment reference point* given the *position reference point*, and

(2) placing the *position reference point* from the given *entry alignment reference* point.

As pointed out earlier, the latter is more computationally expensive. The candidate solutios are checked to see if each of them can really be a solution. If can not, then the current candidate is discarded, and the next one is tried, and so on.

This process does not involve any iterations which moves the objects back and forth, as the equation solving produces direct parametric values, which are then sorted. Thus, the pictorial object only travels towards the direction of the path in its mapping, avoiding vibration or divergence.

5 GEOMETRIC CONSTRAINT SATISFACTION

In this section, we will give solutions to the *geometric constraint satisfaction* problem in step 4 of our **GPB** algorithm — the problem of finding an appropriate *position reference point* for a given *entry alignment reference point.*

Our general strategy is to transform the geometric constraint equations into a polynomial equation of the path parameter t, then apply numerical methods for obtaining roots of a polynomial equation. As a result, our approach does not involve geometric iterations which change the position of pictorial elements. Thus determination of an optimum iteration step, detection of the divergence, analysis of round-off errors, and such, are avoided. Although numerical methods that solve higher degree polynomial equation involve iterations, they are preferable to iterating over complex geometrical constraints, as the former has been studied by a number of researchers. Currently we use Bairstow's method and Sturm's method as numerical methods for finding zero's of polynomials.

Notice that some of the roots may be false solutions, because some transformations are non-equivalent.[6] Thus, the roots are only *candidates* for the solutions rather than real ones, and therefore each must be checked if it does really satisfy the constraints.

5.1 Definitions

Here we present some definitions of a *boundary function* , an *area* (used as a pictorial element), and basic geometric operations on an area. Each area has its local coordinate system whose origin is the *position reference point* R_* as stated in subsection 4.1 (Fig. 3).

5.1.1 An Area on a Plane

A boundary function. We first define a *boundary function* which divides a plane into (generally) two divisions. We make assumptions on a boundary function $\mathcal{B} : \boldsymbol{R}^2 \rightarrow \boldsymbol{R}$ that (i) $\mathcal{B}$ is defined for all points on a plane $\boldsymbol{x} \in \boldsymbol{R}^2$, and (ii) $\mathcal{B}$ is continuous at any point. For now, only the sign (positive/negative) of $\mathcal{B}(\boldsymbol{x})$ has significance, rather than its exact value; we treat each set of points that have the same sign each other as a *division* of a plane, namely $\{\boldsymbol{x} \in \boldsymbol{R}^2 \mid \mathcal{B}(\boldsymbol{x}) > 0\}$(positive) or $\{\boldsymbol{x} \in \boldsymbol{R}^2 \mid \mathcal{B}(\boldsymbol{x}) < 0\}$(negative), and the set of remaining points as a *boundary* of a boundary function $\mathcal{B}(\boldsymbol{x})$, $\{\boldsymbol{x} \in \boldsymbol{R}^2 \mid \mathcal{B}(\boldsymbol{x}) = 0\}$(boundary). Adopting this definition of a boundary function and divisions on a plane, the determination whether two points $\boldsymbol{x}, \boldsymbol{y} \in \boldsymbol{R}^2$ are in the same division or not will be easier than the use of simple line-style boundary — All we have to do is to compare the signs of $\mathcal{B}(\boldsymbol{x})$ and $\mathcal{B}(\boldsymbol{y})$; they are in the same division if they have the same sign, and they are not otherwise. Strictly speaking, the assumptions on $\mathcal{B}$ are *not* sufficient to exclude 'strange' boundaries, such as $\mathcal{B}(\boldsymbol{x}) = |\boldsymbol{x}|$ where $|\boldsymbol{x}|$ denotes the Euclidean distance between $\boldsymbol{x}$ and the origin of the coordinate. Obviously, its boundary consists of only a point (the origin itself) and all other points on a plane belong to the positive division, and the negative division does not exist. But we are not interested in such an 'unusual' case.

An area. Next, an appropriate way should be provided to designate which division of a boundary function $\mathcal{B}(\boldsymbol{x})$ is of our interest. We prefer choosing a representative point in the division, though direct description of a sign (positive/negative) would also suffice. An *area* $\mathcal{A}$ is specified by a pair $< \mathcal{B}, \boldsymbol{a}_* >$:

$$\mathcal{A}(\mathcal{B}, \boldsymbol{a}_*) \equiv \{\boldsymbol{x} \in \boldsymbol{R}^2 \mid \mathcal{B}(\boldsymbol{x}) \cdot \mathcal{B}(\boldsymbol{a}_*) > 0\}$$

where

$\mathcal{B}(\boldsymbol{x})$	: a boundary function,
$\boldsymbol{a}_* \in \boldsymbol{R}^2$	: an *area representative* point.

[6]For instance, we lose the sign if we square both sides of an equation

The condition $\mathcal{B}(\boldsymbol{x}) \cdot \mathcal{B}(\boldsymbol{a}_*) > 0$ denotes that two points $\boldsymbol{x}$ and $\boldsymbol{a}_*$ are in the same division. The area representative point $\boldsymbol{a}_*$ is assumed not to be on the boundary, i.e., $\mathcal{B}(\boldsymbol{a}_*) \neq 0$.

5.1.2 Translation and Rotation of an Area

Let us proceed with further definitions of two geometric operations that move/rotate an area, and enables us to place an area anywhere in any arbitrary direction. These geometric operations will be necessary for binding an area along a path as described in the following subsection.

Translation of an area. We express a translated area of $\mathcal{A}(\mathcal{B}, \boldsymbol{a}_*)$ by $\boldsymbol{c} \in \boldsymbol{R}^2$ as $\mathcal{A} + \boldsymbol{c}$ (or $\boldsymbol{c} + \mathcal{A}$).

$$\mathcal{A}(\mathcal{B}, \boldsymbol{a}_*) + \boldsymbol{c} \equiv \{\boldsymbol{x} \in \boldsymbol{R}^2 \mid \mathcal{B}(\boldsymbol{x} - \boldsymbol{c}) \cdot \mathcal{B}(\boldsymbol{a}_*) > 0\} \; (= \boldsymbol{c} + \mathcal{A}(\mathcal{B}, \boldsymbol{a}_*))$$

Rotation of an area. To begin with, we will make a preparatory definition for rotation of an area. For a vector $\boldsymbol{s} \in \boldsymbol{R}^2(|\boldsymbol{s}| \neq 0)$, consider a rotation matrix $G(\boldsymbol{s})$ which rotates a point around the origin of its coordinate by the angle θ, an angle taken from the x-axis vector to vector $\boldsymbol{s}$:

$$G(\boldsymbol{s}) \equiv \begin{pmatrix} \cos\theta & -\sin\theta \\ \sin\theta & \cos\theta \end{pmatrix}$$

We are now ready to describe rotation of an area. Rotating an area $\mathcal{A}(\mathcal{B}, \boldsymbol{a}_*)$ so that its u-axis vector of local coordinate comes just on a given vector $\boldsymbol{s} \in \boldsymbol{R}^2(|\boldsymbol{s}| \neq 0)$, we get a rotated area and describe it as $G(\boldsymbol{s})\mathcal{A}$:

$$G(\boldsymbol{s})\, \mathcal{A}(\mathcal{B}, \boldsymbol{a}_*) \equiv \{\boldsymbol{x} \in \boldsymbol{R}^2 \mid \mathcal{B}(G^{-1}(\boldsymbol{s})\boldsymbol{x}) \cdot \mathcal{B}(\boldsymbol{a}_*) > 0\}$$

5.2 Quadratic Boundaries

In our current **GPB** prototype system, a quadratic boundary function (including a linear boundary function) is available. Here we present a description of a quadratic boundary function and a way to find out candidate solutions of the geometric constraint satisfaction.

5.2.1 A Quadratic Boundary Function

A quadratic boundary function $\mathcal{B}(\boldsymbol{x})(\boldsymbol{x} \in \boldsymbol{R}^2)$ is defined as follows:

$$\mathcal{B}(\boldsymbol{x}) \equiv ({}^t\boldsymbol{x} B_{quad} + 2 \cdot {}^t B_{linear})\boldsymbol{x} + b_{const} \tag{1}$$

where B_{quad}, B_{linear} are quadratic and linear coefficients matrices respectively, shown as

$$B_{quad} \equiv \begin{pmatrix} b_{u^2} & b_{uv} \\ b_{uv} & b_{v^2} \end{pmatrix}, \quad B_{linear} \equiv \begin{pmatrix} b_u \\ b_v \end{pmatrix}, \qquad (b_{u^2}, b_{uv}, b_{v^2}, b_u, b_v, b_{const} \in \boldsymbol{R}).$$

Notice that ${}^tX$ indicates transpose operator on a matrix X, and ${}^tB_{quad} = B_{quad}$. If $\boldsymbol{x}$ is written as $\boldsymbol{x} \equiv {}^t(uv), (u, v \in \boldsymbol{R})$, (1) will be

$$\mathcal{B}(\boldsymbol{x}) \equiv (b_{u^2}u^2 + 2b_{uv}uv + b_{v^2}v^2) + 2(b_u u + b_v v) + b_{const}.$$

Using this boundary function $\mathcal{B}(\boldsymbol{x})$, a boundary is defined as $\{\boldsymbol{x} \in \boldsymbol{R}^2 \mid \mathcal{B}(\boldsymbol{x}) = 0\}$. This is a quadratic curve if at least one of $b_{u^2} \neq 0$, $b_{uv} \neq 0$, and $b_{v^2} \neq 0$ hold.

5.2.2 Solutions for Constraint Satisfaction

Case 1: Direction is globally fixed. Placing an area $\mathcal{A}$ so that its local origin R_* comes to a point $\boldsymbol{p}(t)$ on a path, with appropriate rotation such that local u-axis and a given vector $\boldsymbol{s} \in \boldsymbol{R}^2(|\boldsymbol{s}| \neq 0)$ overlap each other, we get $\{G(\boldsymbol{s})\mathcal{A}\} + \boldsymbol{p}(t)$, and its boundary is

$$\{\boldsymbol{x} \in \boldsymbol{R}^2 \mid \mathcal{B}(G^{-1}(\boldsymbol{s})\{\boldsymbol{x} - \boldsymbol{p}(t)\}) = 0\}.$$

As a given entry alignment reference point R_- (position vector $\boldsymbol{r}_-$) is on this boundary, the following equation holds:

$$\mathcal{B}(G^{-1}(\boldsymbol{s})\{\boldsymbol{r}_- - \boldsymbol{p}(t)\}) = 0. \tag{2}$$

Since we assume the path consists of t's polynomials, $\boldsymbol{p}(t)$ can be written as

$$\boldsymbol{p}(t) \equiv \sum_{i=0}^{\nu_p} \boldsymbol{p}_i \cdot t^i \qquad (\nu_p \in \boldsymbol{N}). \tag{3}$$

Here, ν_p is the degree of polynomials $\boldsymbol{p}(t)$. Using this, first we calculate the argument of $\mathcal{B}$ in the equation (2) above and define it as a vector $\boldsymbol{\beta} \equiv {}^t(\beta_x \quad \beta_y)$:

$$\begin{aligned}\boldsymbol{\beta} &\equiv G^{-1}(\boldsymbol{s})\{\boldsymbol{r}_- - \boldsymbol{p}(t)\} \\ &= \begin{pmatrix} \{\cos\theta \cdot r_{-(x)} + \sin\theta \cdot r_{-(y)}\} - \sum\{\cos\theta \cdot p_{i(x)} + \sin\theta \cdot p_{i(y)}\} \cdot t^i \\ \{-\sin\theta \cdot r_{-(x)} + \cos\theta \cdot r_{-(y)}\} - \sum\{-\sin\theta \cdot p_{i(x)} + \cos\theta \cdot p_{i(y)}\} \cdot t^i \end{pmatrix}\end{aligned}$$

Both elements of the vector $\boldsymbol{\beta}$, β_x and β_y, are t's polynomials of (at most) degree ν_p. Applying $\mathcal{B}$ we get

$$\mathcal{B}(G^{-1}(\boldsymbol{s})\{\boldsymbol{r}_- - \boldsymbol{p}(t)\}) = (b_{u^2}\beta_x^2 + 2b_{uv}\beta_x\beta_y + b_{v^2}\beta_y^2) + 2(b_u\beta x + b_v\beta_y) + b_{const}.$$

It becomes clear that $\mathcal{B}(G^{-1}(\boldsymbol{s})\{\boldsymbol{r}_- - \boldsymbol{p}(t)\}) = 0$ is a t's polynomial equation of (at most) degree $2\nu_p$.

Case 2: Direction is relative to a local tangent of the path. A local tangential vector of the path $\boldsymbol{p}(t)$ is given as $d\boldsymbol{p}(t)/dt$. Since we assume the path consists of t's polynomials shown in (3), its tangential vector becomes t's polynomials, too, that are one degree lower than the original; and we name it $\boldsymbol{\tau}$.

$$\boldsymbol{\tau} = \begin{pmatrix} \tau_x \\ \tau_y \end{pmatrix} \equiv \frac{d}{dt}\boldsymbol{p}(t) = \frac{d}{dt}\left(\sum_{i=0}^{\nu_p} \boldsymbol{p}_i \cdot t^i\right) = \sum_{i=1}^{\nu_p}(i \cdot \boldsymbol{p}_i)t^{i-1},$$

which are t's polynomials of (at most) degree $\nu_p - 1$. Placing an area $\mathcal{A}$ so that its local origin R_* comes to a point $p(t)$ on a path, with appropriate rotation such that the local u-axis and a local tangential vector of the path at the point overlap each other, we get $G(\tau)\mathcal{A} + p(t)$, and its boundary becomes

$$\{x \in R^2 | \mathcal{B}(G^{-1}(\tau)\{x - p(t)\}) = 0\}.$$

As a given entry alignment reference point R_- (position vector r_-) is on this boundary, the following equation holds:

$$\mathcal{B}\left(G^{-1}\left(\frac{d}{dt}p(t)\right)\{r_- - p(t)\}\right) = 0. \quad (4)$$

Using tangential vector τ, a matrix which rotates this vector to be the same direction of the u-axis vector, is described as follows:

$$G^{-1}(\tau) = \begin{pmatrix} \cos\theta & \sin\theta \\ -\sin\theta & \cos\theta \end{pmatrix} = \frac{1}{\sqrt{\tau_x^2 + \tau_y^2}} \begin{pmatrix} \tau_x & \tau_y \\ -\tau_y & \tau_x \end{pmatrix}, \quad (5)$$

since

$$\cos\theta = \frac{\tau_x}{|\tau|}, \qquad \sin\theta = \frac{\tau_y}{|\tau|}.$$

Now we introduce one more vactor variable γ for convenience:

$$\gamma = \begin{pmatrix} \gamma_x \\ \gamma_y \end{pmatrix} \equiv \begin{pmatrix} \tau_x & \tau_y \\ -\tau_y & \tau_x \end{pmatrix} \{r_- - p(t)\},$$

γ is (at most) degree of $(\nu_p - 1) + \nu_p = 2\nu_p - 1$. So the LHS of (4) becomes

$$\begin{aligned} &\mathcal{B}(G^{-1}(\tau)\{r_- - p(t)\}) \\ &= \frac{1}{\tau_x^2 + \tau_y^2}(b_{u^2}\gamma_x^2 + 2b_{uv}\gamma_x\gamma_y + b_{v^2}\gamma_y^2) + \frac{2}{\sqrt{\tau_x^2 + \tau_y^2}}(b_u\gamma_x + b_v\gamma_y) + b_{const}, \end{aligned} \quad (6)$$

and multiplying $\tau_x^2 + \tau_y^2$ to both sides of equality sign in an equation (4), and squaring both sides to delete the square root sign, we get

$$4(\tau_x^2 + \tau_y^2)(b_u\gamma_x + b_v\gamma_y)^2 = \{(b_{u^2}\gamma_x^2 + 2b_{uv}\gamma_x\gamma_y + b_{v^2}\gamma_y^2) + b_{const}(\tau_x^2 + \tau_y^2)\}^2. \quad (7)$$

As for t's degree, LHS is degree of (at most) $2(\nu_p - 1) + 2(2\nu_p - 1) = 6\nu_p - 4$, and RHS is degree of (at most) $\{\max(2(2\nu_p - 1), 2(\nu_p - 1))\} \times 2 = \{2(2\nu_p - 1)\} \times 2 = 8\nu_p - 4$; it becomes clear that this equation (7) is (at most) degree $\max(6\nu_p - 4, 8\nu_p - 4) = 8\nu_p - 4$.

Special condition for case 2: When $\mathcal{B}$ is a circle. For a special case, let us consider a circle as $\mathcal{B}$, when $b_{u^2} = b_{v^2}$ and $b_{uv} = 0$. Then the quadratic terms of (6) become

$$\frac{1}{\tau_x^2 + \tau_y^2}(b_{u^2}\gamma_x^2 + 2b_{uv}\gamma_x\gamma_y + b_{v^2}\gamma_y^2) = b_2(\zeta_x^2 + \zeta_y^2),$$

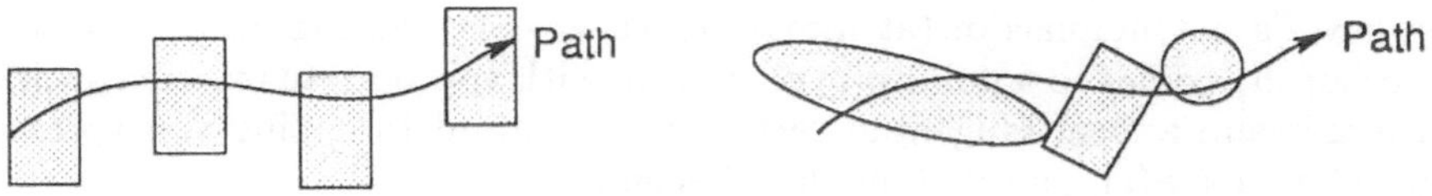

Figure 12: Justification and touching

where $b_2 \equiv b_{u^2} = b_{v^2}$ and $\zeta \equiv r_- - p(t)$. We do not have to multiply $\tau_x^2 + \tau_y^2$ to both sides equation in (4). Instead, $\sqrt{\tau_x^2 + \tau_y^2}$ will be multiplied to get a polynomial equation, and squaring both sides to delete the square root sign, we get

$$b_2^2(\zeta_x^2 + \zeta_y^2)^2(\tau_x^2 + \tau_y^2) = \{2(b_u\gamma_x + b_v\gamma_y) + b_{const}(\tau_x^2 + \tau_y^2)\}^2$$

From the t's degree's point of view, LHS is degree of (at most) $2 \times 2\nu_p + 2(\nu_p - 1) = 6\nu_p - 2$, and RHS is degree of (at most) $\{\max(2\nu_p - 1, 2(\nu_p - 1))\} \times 2 = (2\nu_p - 1) \times 2 = 4\nu_p - 2$; it becomes clear that this equation (7) is (at most) degree $\max(6\nu_p - 2, 4\nu_p - 2) = 6\nu_p - 2$, two degree lower than the general case.

6 CONCLUDING REMARKS

At this time, our prototype implementation of the **GPB** system is nearly complete. We are now able to place pictorial objects that are composed of pictorial elements bounded by quadratic or linear curves, along a joined polynomial path of any degree such as Bézier path. The preliminary benchmark of the constraint solver has shown that the entire constraint system can probably be solved in near real-time for pictures of moderate complexity. Whether it can be scaled to large-scale applications remains to be seen.

We believe that our current framework is robust for constructing f_v for large classes of practical problems. For future work, however, we are aiming to cover classes that have less affinity at present:

- *Justification* is useful in practice but is not supported well within our current system (Fig. 12). One solution is to use the least square method as in TRIP to distribute the error AFTER the position reference points of all the objects have been determined. The problem is that, for the **GPB** conditions to be satisfied, the objects must stay bound to the path; this may cause problems such as undesired overlaps, or unnatural object placement when there are disjoint path segments.
- **GPB** can be extended to cover *partially ordered relations*. Difficulty arises when two paths join — we expect that this can be treated uniformly with justification.
- The path-parametric transformation is currently restricted to scaling and rotation. As indicated earlier, it may be possible to add more complex path-parametric transformation primitives such as deformation of the local coordinate

system according to the path as in (Barr 1984). With this extension, we can visualize classes of pictures that were very difficult to generate with conventional graphics systems, such as a picture of railroad track in Japanese maps.

- The generalized gap between two pictorial objects need not be necessarily restricted to the generalized distance between exit and entry alignment reference points. For example, we could define a gap such that two neighboring pictorial objects touch (Fig. 12). We are now attempting to investigating it with the approximated pictures.

Finally, we are planning to test the effectiveness of this framework as a visual interface tool by integrating it with TRIP and applying it to practical applications.

References

Aldus Corporation (1989) *Aldus FreeHand User's Manual.* Aldus Corporation, Seattle, Washington, 2.0 edition

Barr AH (1984) Global and local deformations of solid primitives. *Computer Graphics*, 18(3):21–30

Barth PS (1986) An object-oriented approach to graphical interfaces. *ACM Transactions on Graphics*, 5(2):142–172

Beach R, Stone M (1983) Graphical style: Towards high quality illustrations. *Computer Graphics*, 17(3):127–135

Borning A (1981) The programming language aspects of thinglab, a constraint-oriented simulation laboratory. *ACM Transactions on Programming Languages and Systems*, 3(4):353–387

Borning A, Duisberg R (1986) Constraint-based tools for building user interfaces. *ACM Transactions on Graphics*, 5(4):345–374

Brown MH (1984) A system for algorithm animation. *Computer Graphics*, 18(3):177–186

Brown MH (1987) *Algorithm Animation.* The MIT Press

Chen PP (1976) The entity-relationship model – towards a unified view of data. *ACM Transactions on Database Systems*, 1(1):9–36

Friedel M (1984) Automatic synthesis of graphical object description. *Computer Graphics*, 18(3):53–62

Hentenryck P Van (1989) *Constraint Satisfaction in Logic Programming.* The MIT Press, Cambridge, MA

Kamada T (1989) *Visualizing Abstract Objects and Relations: A Constraint-Based Approach*. World Scientific, Singapore

Kamada T, Kawai S (to appear) A general framework for visualizing abstract objects and relations. *ACM Transactions on Graphics*

Kay TL, Kajiya JT (1986) Ray tracing complex scenes. *Computer Graphics*, 20(4)

Maloney JH, Borning A, Freeman-Benson BN (1989) Constraint technology for user-interface construction in thinglab ii. In: Mayrowitz N (ed) *OOPSLA'89 Conference Proceedings*. Association for Computing Machinery, ACM Press, pp 381–388

Matsuoka S, Kawai S (1989) On formal treatment of interactive graphics. In *Proceedings of the 39th Annual Convention IPS Japan* (In Japanese)

Myers BA (1983) Incence: A system for displaying data structures. *Computer Graphics*, 17(3):115–125

Nassi I, Schneiderman B (1973) Flowchart techniques for structured programming. *ACM SIGPLAN Notices*, 8(8):12–26

Nelson G (1984) Juno, a constraint-based graphics system. *Computer Graphics*, 19(3):225–234

Noma T, Kunii TL, Kin N, Enomoto H, Aso E, Yamamoto T (1988) Drawing input through geometrical constructions: Specification and applications. In: Magnenat-Thalmann N, Thalmann D (ed) *Proceedings of the CG International '88*. Springer-Verlag, pp 403–415

Pavlidis T, Wyk CJ Van (1984) An automatic beautifier for drawings and illustrations. *Computer Graphics*, 19(3):225–234

Sederberg TW, Parry SR (1986) Free-form deformation of sold geometric models. *Computer Graphics*, 20(3):151–160

Steele GL, Sussman GJ (1980) Constraints – a language for expressing almost-hierarchical descriptions. *Artificial Intelligence*, 14(1):1–39

Sutherland IE (1963) Sketchpad: A man-machine graphical communication system. In: *Proceedings of the SJCC*, pp 329–346

Whitted T (1983) Anti-aliased line drawing using brush extrusion. *Computer Graphics*, 17(3):151–156

Wyk CJ Van (1982) A high-level language for specifying pictures. *ACM Transactions on Graphics*, 1(2):163–182

Zanden BT Vander (1989) *Incremental Constraint Satisfaction and its Application to Graphical Interfaces*. PhD thesis, Dept. of Computer Science, Cornell University

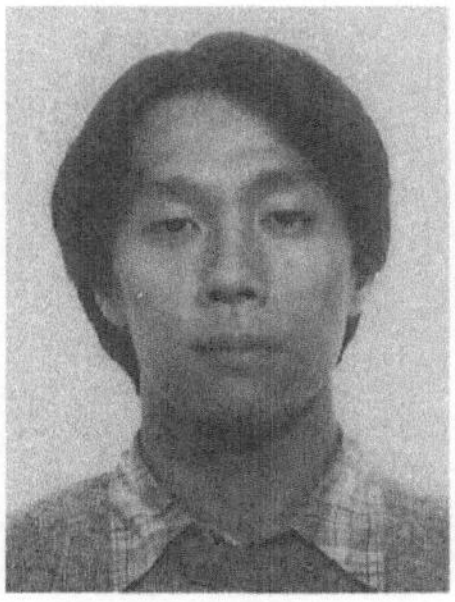

Ken Nakayama received the B.S. degree in information science from the University of Tokyo in 1987, and is currently working towards a M.S. degree in information science at the Department of Information science, the Univ. of Tokyo. His current research interests are visualization in computer graphics, and knowledge representation in artificial intelligence. He is currently a member of the IPSJ.

Satoshi Matsuoka received the B.S. degree and M.S. degree in information science at the University of Tokyo in 1986 and 1988, respectively. After advancing to the doctor of science course at the the University of Tokyo in 1988, he became a research staff at the Department of Information Science, the University of Tokyo in October, 1989. His current research interests are concurrent reflectional object-oriented languages and systems, and formal treatment of interactive graphics in user interfaces. He is a member of the ACM, ACM SIGPLAN, ACM SIGGRAPH, and ACM SIGCHI. He is also a member of two Japanese societies: IPSJ and JSSST.

Satoru Kawai graduated from The University of Tokyo, Japan, in 1967. He joined the Faculty of Science, the University of Tokyo, as a research staff in 1969, and during that time, he was a visiting scholar of University of Cambridge in 1977-1978. After becoming an assistant professor at the Department of Information Science, the University of Tokyo, he became a professor at the Department of Graphic and Computer Science, the College of Arts and Sciences, The University of Tokyo. He is currently the chairman of the department. His research interests include computer graphics, mainly in its theoretical fields, programming language design, and user interface specification and implementation. He is a member of ACM, ACM SIGPLAN,ACM SIGGRAPH, and three Japanese Societies: IPSJ, IEICE, JSSST.

Field Visualization by Interactive Computer Graphics

Y.P. Lee and C.S. Chang

ABSTRACT

An educational software system for the graphical simulation of two-dimensional field problems by the finite element method is described in this paper. The interface is an interactive window-based environment. Boundaries of the field may be closed or open where the exterior stiffness matrix is constructed by the "ballooning" technique. The final system of equations is solved by LDL^T factorization and the graphical display is generated by the convex filling technique. The most characteristic feature of this system is the capability to solve the problem automatically by recursively generating a succession of increasingly finer meshes until the potential difference between each pair of connected nodes is within a specified tolerance.

KEYWORDS

Field, Laplace Equation, Finite Element, Computer Graphics, Visualization

1. INTRODUCTION

Now the computer simulation plays an important role in the study of engineering phenomena for which adequate mathematical models are available. There are many engineering field problems that may be modelled by Laplace equation, and successful simulation of the Laplace equation provides close analogy to reality.

In many engineering phenomena, it is very expensive to set up the experiment in the laboratory. The emergence of interactive computer graphics provides an alternate or sometimes even a better way to conduct engineering experiment through graphical simulation. In a highly interactive environment, students can react with the system by requesting various pieces of information, and or by varying the parameters in order to study their effects on the characteristics of the system. As a result, interactive graphical simulation represents a new tool in the learning of engineering concepts.

Usually, an undergraduate course in field analysis includes the numerical analysis of Laplace equation. By far the most widely used technique is the iteration method in which the potential at a point is found to be the average of the potentials of its surrounding points (Hoburg 1983). An obvious appeal of this finite difference method is its relative ease to understand. However, the main disadvantage of the finite difference method is that it is impractical for complex geometric boundaries problems where equally spaced grid cannot be fitted easily into the irregular regions.

In the past twenty years, the finite element method has been most active in the numerical solution of continuum problems, and is particularly well suited to problem with complex boundary geometries where there is no analytical solution.

Based on the finite element method, a software system for simulating two-dimensional field problems by interactive computer graphics is developed. The system is such flexible that it is capable to handle both open or closed irregular boundaries problems. The most characteristic feature is that the simulation process may be completely automatic or in manual control. In automatic mode, succession of increasingly refined triangular mesh patterns are generated until a specified tolerance is reached (Yokoyama 1985), whereas in manual mode, the user can control the mesh size arbitrary. In the system, the user-interface is a highly interactive window-based environment such that most of the commands are menu-driven. Two additional features are available in this system, the first one is the zooming which allows a particular region of interest to be scaled up and the second is the plotting of the orthogonal set of curves.

2. THE FINITE ELEMENT METHOD

The finite element method to solve Laplace equation for closed and open boundary problems using linear triangular elements is presented in reference (Norrie and Devries 1978) and (Silvester 1977).

2.1 Closed Boundaries

For a field with closed boundaries, the problem domain D is divided up into n finite elements as shown in Fig. 1.

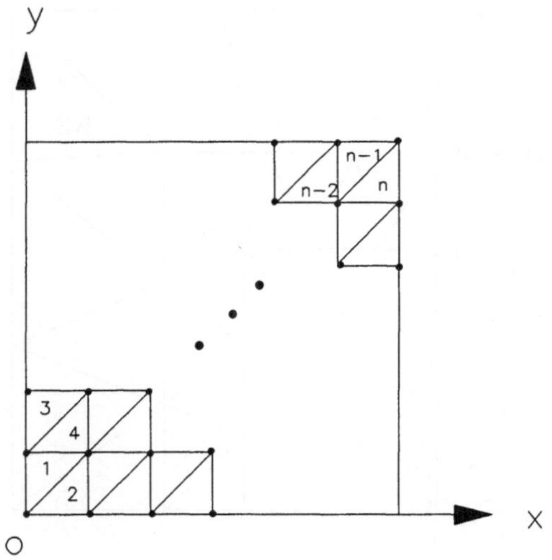

Fig. 1 Domain D divided into n finite elements

Linear triangular elements are used. A system of stiffness matrix equation will be obtained. The solution of the resulting set of simultaneous equations will then produce the values for unknowns at all the nodes by any matrix equation solving technique.

2.2 Open Boundaries

It is the characteristic of many field problems that the boundaries are not closed, or else are so remote that they can be ignored. The customary method of approach is to set an artificial boundary imposed with a boundary condition, usually Neumann or Dirichlet, around the region of interest, which is far away enough to avoid interfering with the solution. However, this may result in an increasing number of nodes where this information is not needed. A much more appealing approach known as "ballooning" (Silvester 1977) is naturally suited to finite element modeling where it does not involve a large surrounding area. To understand the technique, consider Fig. 2, I denotes the picture frame boundary, O denotes a secondary boundary obtained from I by "blowing it up" from the source S by a constant scale factor M, and R_1 denotes the annular region between I and O.

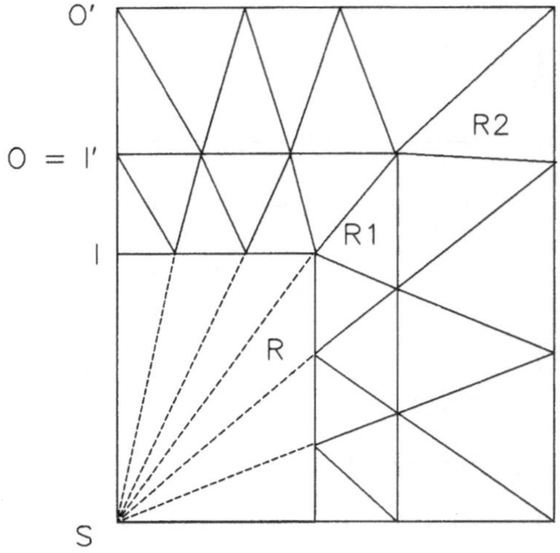

Fig. 2 Finite element grid for the exterior field problem

The outer boundary O may also be considered to be inner boundary I' of the region R_2, which is formed by blowing up I' to O' by the same constant scale factor M. The region R_2 is similar to the region R_1 and will generate the finite element matrix which will be found to be the same as R_1. A stiffness matrix will be formed for the annular region R_1 as well as R_2. By applying "node condensation" process to eliminate the nodes on the common edge O, the union of the two regions, R_1 and R_2, will generate a new stiffness matrix in terms of the interior and exterior nodes on boundaries I and O'.

A new annular region R_3 will be formed by "blowing up" the boundary O' by a constant scale factor M. The same elimination method is then applied at each successive combination of annular regions.

Consequently, each successive step in this recursive process consists of the combination of two stiffness matrices. If the factor M is 1.5 (a value which will commonly give triangular elements of good aspect ratio), the successive scale factors of the sequence of regions will be : M, M^2, M^4, M^8, ... The process converges very quickly to give the contribution of the exterior field to the total field stiffness matrix. As the outermost boundary is far away from the region of interest, the potentials at the outermost nodes can therefore be assumed as zeros.

3. OVERVIEW OF THE SOFTWARE SYSTEM

The software described in this paper is an interactive system which will allow the user to simulate field problem with any given geometrical shape (open or close boundaries) and boundary conditions (Neumann or Dirichlet). The domain of the problem may be further divided into sub-regions when necessary. The flowchart of the system for interactive graphical simulation of two-dimensional field problems by the finite element method is given in Fig. 3. In general, it comprises of five functional components namely: the user-interface, the automatic mesh generation, the local mesh refinement, the assemblage of system matrix with equation solving and the graphics generation. The interface of this system is a window-based environment which is highly interactive and user-friendly in such a way that most of the commands are menu-driven through the use of a mouse. Moreover, the simulation process can be completely automated or in manual control. In automatic mode, mesh size will be made finer until the potential differences between each pair of connected nodes satisfy the specified tolerance, whereas the mesh size is controlled by the user in the manual mode. There are two additional features available in this system. The first one is the plotting of flow line and the second is the zooming.

When the system is invoked, the geometric coordinates and the boundary conditions of the problem domain are acquired through the user-interface. In fact, the problem domain must be made up of straight line segments, finer line segments are used to approximate any body with circular arc. If an automatic mode is requested, uniform mesh generation will be carried out to generate an evenly distributed triangular meshes and nodes across the whole domain. If there are any open boundaries, construction of the exterior finite element matrix is required. After that, construction of the interior system matrix by the finite element method is carried out. When the system matrix has been created, the equations will be solved and the potential difference between any pair of connected nodes of any element is compared with the specified tolerance. If the potential difference between any one pair of the nodes of an element is larger than the allowable tolerance, the process of local mesh refinement will be carried out on that element. As a result, a finer mesh pattern will be generated. The potential difference checking process is applied on those elements again until all connected nodes have satisfied the tolerance and the control will return to the calculation of exterior finite element matrix. Finally, a graphical display of the field is generated.

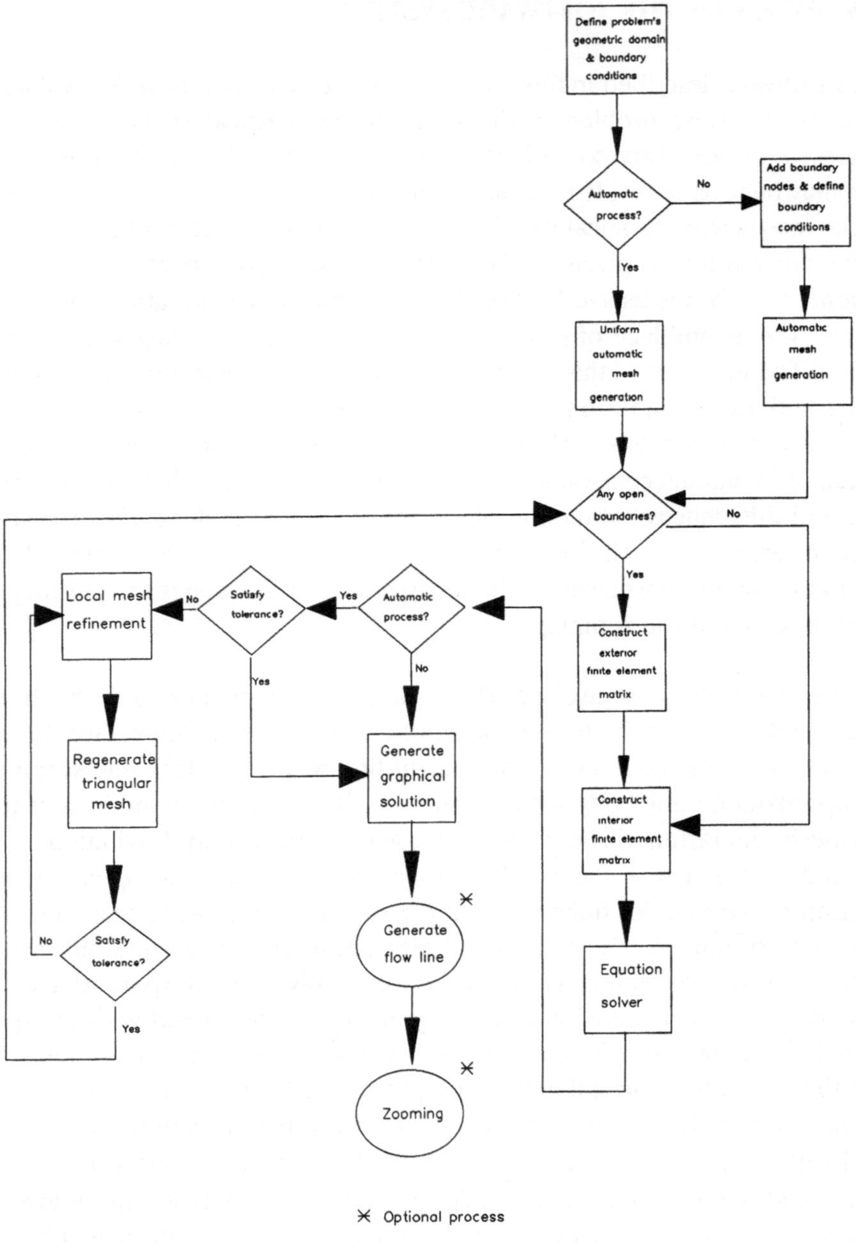

Fig. 3 Flowchart of the complete system

In the manual mode, there will be no uniform mesh generation and no local mesh refinement. Instead, user has to define additional nodes and their boundary conditions on each boundary edge. Then automatic mesh generation will carry out to generate triangular meshes across the domain. Once the numerical solution is obtained by solving the system matrix equations, graphical display of the solution will be generated instantaneously.

4. IMPLEMENTATION DETAILS

The software system for the computer graphics simulation of two-dimensional field problems is implemented on a SUN-3/110 workstation running under the UNIX environment. The major programming language is C language while the automatic mesh generation program is written in Fortran. It consumes approximately seven mega-bytes of memory which is capable to generate 3000 elements and 1500 nodes (i.e. able to solve 1500 equations). On Sun-3/110, it is able to display 256 colors simultaneously, however, only 100 colors are defined by converting the HSV color model to the RGB color model.

As mentioned in the previous section, the system is composed of five main components, the implementation of each component will be explained in details in the following few sections.

4.1 User Interface

The user-interface as shown in Fig. 4 is constructed by SunView where it is a user-interface toolkit to support interactive, graphics-based applications running within windows (SunView 1986). It includes two types of windows: (1) Canvas on which programs can draw and (2) panels containing items such as buttons, choice items and pull-down menu. The interface comprises three canvas and two panels subwindows. SunView also support simple two-dimensional graphics drawing operations and the data are input through a mouse or keyboard on a window.

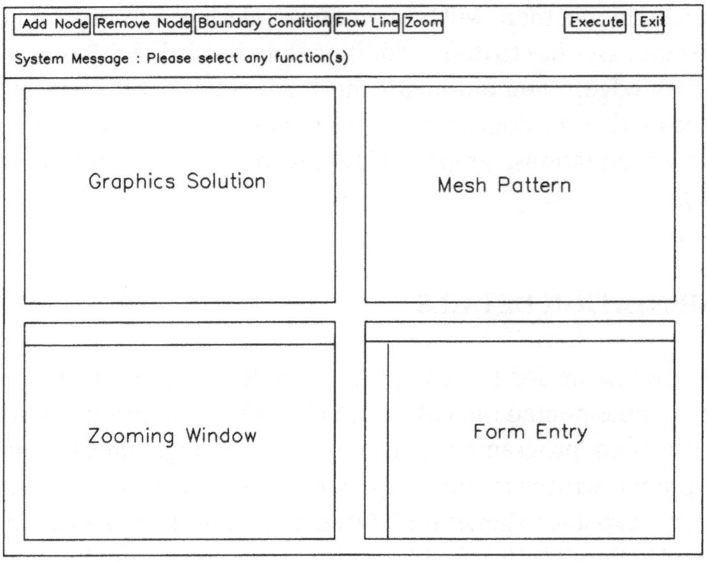

Fig. 4 Layout of the user-interface

The panel area subwindow describes the system message and the items through which the user interacts with the system. The system message tells what action should be taken or gives warning/error message to the user. The graphics solution subwindow is used to display the final solution of the field problem. Besides, the initial geometrical coordinates of the domain is also defined within it. In manual control process, nodes may be added arbitrary on the boundary edge of a domain in order to define the mesh density, the additional nodes are updated and displayed in the mesh pattern subwindow instantly. Moreover, the triangular mesh pattern is also shown in the mesh pattern subwindow after each mesh generation cycle. The zooming subwindow is used to zoom-in a particular part of the domain. Data concern with keyboard input is through the form-entry subwindow. For example, the boundary conditions at each node, the connection information of the domain and the edge number where the boundary nodes are added in the manual control process.

4.2 Automatic Mesh Generation (Lo 1985)

According to the geometric shape of the problem defined, automatic mesh generation will generate triangular meshes across the domain or its sub-regions. Since the size (or density) of the mesh generated will depend on the average nodal spacing of all the boundary segments which make up the region to be triangulated, equally spaced nodes are added along each boundary segments (i.e. uniform mesh generation) in order to have an evenly distributed mesh pattern in the initial stage of the automatic process. However, in manual mode the nodal spacing (i.e. number of nodes on a line segment) is controlled by the user, thus the mesh size can be varied arbitrarily as desired.

Actually, mesh generation is classified into two categories, uniform mesh generation and local mesh refinement which is briefly explained in the following two sections.

4.2.1 Uniform Mesh Generation

For a given number of nodes along each boundary, the generation program first produce additional interior nodes evenly along scan line by scan line according to the average nodal spacing of all the boundary segments as shown in Fig. 5.

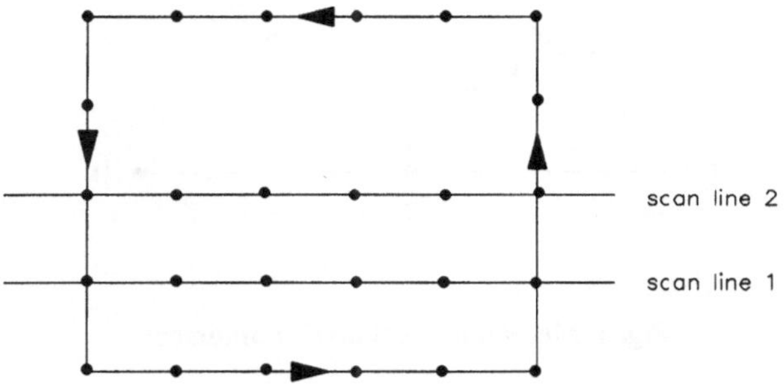

Fig. 5 A domain with nodes generated at the scan line

After the generation of nodes, all the nodes are connected to form triangular elements in such a way that no elements overlap and the entire region is covered. Finally, a smoothing process is carried out to smooth out the element produced as near to equilateral triangles as the system of nodal points permits.

In the initial stage of the automatic process, triangular meshes are evenly distributed in the domain of interest. The nodal solution of each element are first obtained. They are then compared to determine whether local mesh refinement will be required. Since the initial size of the generated triangular mesh is set to be uniform and its size will depend on the average nodal spacing on the boundary, the spacing between nodes on the boundary is initially set to be approximately 20 pixels apart, i.e. the domain is initially formed by a finite number of line segments of which each is approximately 20 pixels in length.

4.2.2 Local Mesh Refinement

It is evident that in the case of large-scale problems, the finer mesh will yield better approximation whereas the trade-off is an increase in time to solve the equations. However, this contradiction can be settled by local mesh division, i.e. by such mesh division that at the region of great potential variation the mesh pattern is made to be finer. To determine what size of the mesh pattern is appropriate, a recursive potential difference checking method and local mesh refinement is adopted.

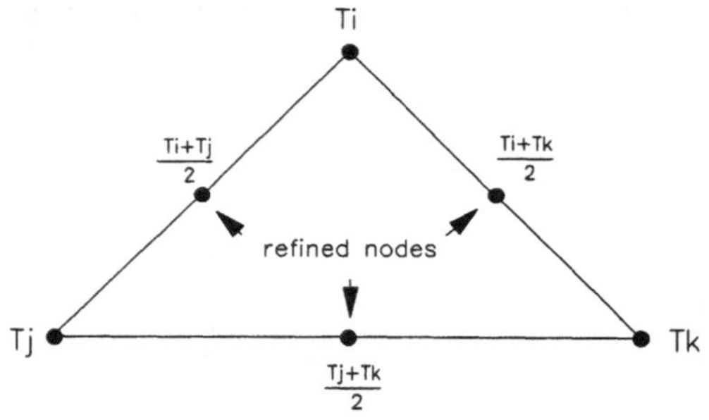

Fig. 6 Method of local mesh refinement

The local mesh refinement is done in such a manner as shown in Fig. 6. With the initial solution obtained in uniform mesh generation, each triangular element will be traversed once where the potential difference between each pair of connected nodes are calculated. If the potential difference between one or more pairs of connected nodes is greater than the specified tolerance, nodes are added to the mid-point of each edge of the concerned element. As a temporary approximation, it is reasonable to assume the potential value at the new node to be the average of two adjacent nodes as shown in Fig. 6.

After the potential difference for all elements have been checked, a set of new nodes are now added. Triangular mesh pattern are then regenerated by connecting all the nodes again. Once again, the potential difference checking process is applied at each element to determine whether the above mentioned refinement process is still required. If potential difference between any pair of the connected nodes within each element satisfies the prescribed tolerance, assemblage of new finite element matrix and the equation solving are invoked hence a more accurate solution at each node will be obtained. However, if in some elements, potential difference between connected nodes may still exceed the tolerance and will require further mesh refinement. As a result, potential difference checking, mesh refinement, mesh regeneration and equation solving are recursively carried on until the potential differences between any pair of connected nodes within each element are within the prescribed tolerance.

4.3 Assemblage of System Matrix and Equation Solving

After the mesh generation is completed, each element is assembled together to form a system matrix. In general, it includes the construction of the interior and also exterior finite element matrices in case of open boundaries. First, the exterior finite element matrix is built-up by the "ballooning" technique. Then the interior matrix is constructed by the classical finite element method. Both of the matrices are assembled together to obtain the final system matrix. Prescribed boundary conditions are then inserted into the system matrix where the final system of simultaneous linear equations are passed to the equation solver to obtain the potentials at all the nodes.

Since the variational finite element method will commonly yield a linear system of symmetric matrix equations. With a symmetric system, the computation and storage of the stiffness matrix can be restricted to either the upper or lower triangular portions of the matrix. With this special properties, the LDL^T factorization technique (Bathe and Wilson 1976) is used to solve the symmetric matrix.

4.4 Graphical Display Technique

Once the system of equations is solved, the solution at each node is obtained and the numerical values within each element can be computed by linear interpolation. A technique must be used to determine every coordinates within an element, and this can be achieved by a technique called convex filling (Berger 1986). Those numerical values are converted into the corresponding colors by a predefined lookup table.

By repeating this process on each element, the whole region is filled up and equipotential contours can be visualized clearly under a high resolution display environment. In fact, the convex filling technique is also used in the zooming process where the triangular elements will be clipped against the zoom window and the size of each clipped triangular element will be scaled up for filling.

4.5 Techniques for Plotting of Flow Lines

In raster graphics display system, pixel values with same level of intensity will exhibit equipotential curves right away. However, a special technique called the maximum gradient method is employed to generate the set of lines which are orthogonal to the equipotential curves. Actually, the method is based on the idea of finding the path of maximum potential gradient flow from source to sink, in theory the line thus drawn will be orthogonal to the equipotentials.

Starting at a source, say, at a pixel (x_i, y_j), the next pixel for the lines orthogonal to the equipotential is determined as follows: With (x_i,y_j) at the center, the potential values at the surrounding eight pixels are known.

Four virtual points are added at equal distances between pixels as shown in Fig. 7. Their potential values can be computed by quadratic interpolation using three consecutive pixels on each side of the square. Furthermore, by assuming that the potential values vary linearly from the center (as a source) to all its surrounding points including virtual points (as sinks), the point with maximum gradient can be found.

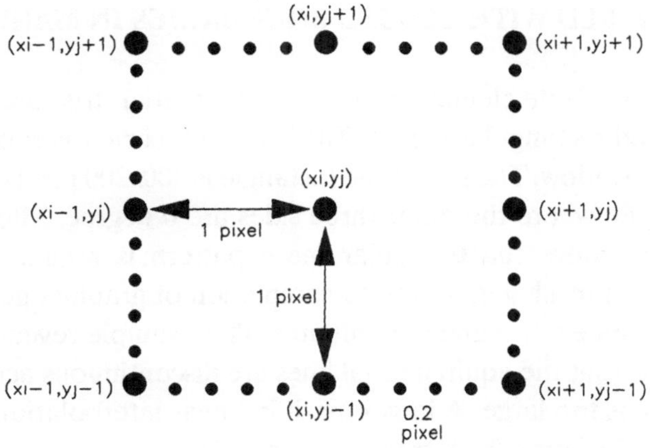

Fig. 7 Refinement between two boundary pixels

As in a raster graphics display system, all points are in integer coordinates (i.e. pixel location). However, the point with maximum gradient may be a virtual point and is in real numbers which cannot be displayed in raster graphics. Thus, x-error and y-error will be accumulated when the real coordinates are rounded up into integer coordinates to activate a pixel. The next relative coordinate value will depends on whether the x- and y-error is greater than 0.5 pixel. If it is the case, one pixel will be increased in the corresponding x- or y-direction. Meanwhile, the corresponding accumulated error will be subtracted by one pixel value. For example, assume the accumulated error is zero initially, if the coordinates of the center is (x_i, y_j) and the coordinates of the selected point are $(x_i+1, y_j+0.4)$, then the accumulated x- and y-error will be 1 and 0.4 respectively. Therefore the actual coordinates of the new pixel is (x_i+1, y_j) where the new accumulated x- and y-error will become 0 and 0.4 respectively.

The new pixel (x_i+1, y_j) will become the source at the next cycle where the above mentioned process is repeated until the boundary of the domain is reached.

5. ILLUSTRATIVE EXAMPLES

To illustrate the usefulness of the software system, some typical examples are described below.

Example 1 THE FIELD WITH CLOSED BOUNDARIES IN MANUAL MODE

Figure 8 shows a finite element grid and equipotential structure for a steady state heat flow in a closed rectangular region. The lower left corner is zoomed up as shown in the zooming subwindow. The size of the rectangle is 300x200 pixels. The left side wall is held at 100 degree where the other three sides are 0 degree. The process is under manual control therefore the triangular mesh pattern is regular and sparse. The execution time (from mesh generation to completion of graphics generation) for this example is approximately two and half minutes. This example reveals the weakness of the manual control, that the equipotential lines are discontinuous across each element since the mesh size is too large. A larger mesh in linear interpolation for this example will induce greater deviation from true potentials.

Example 2 THE FIELD WITH CLOSED BOUNDARIES IN AUTOMATIC MODE

Figure 9 shows a finite element grid and potential distribution which has the same structure as in Example 1. In fact, the simulation process is done automatically by the computer. The tolerance between each node is 10 degrees. The execution time (from uniform mesh generation to completion of graphics generation) for this example is 11 minutes and 11 seconds. Final mesh pattern at the last stage of the simulation process shows that meshes are finer in the region where potential contours are concentrated. Moreover, a set of orthogonal curves is also displayed. This example shows that much more accurate solution will be obtained as compared with manual mode in Example 1.

Although analytical solution exists sometimes for the field with closed irregular boundaries, it may require a great deal of experience on part of the students and will be very time consuming when done manually. Moreover, the set of orthogonal curves are sketched by free-hand with extremely low accuracy. With this system, the problem can be solved easily within a few minutes and the potential distribution can be visualized clearly by different intensity of colors. Moreover, the set of orthogonal curves can be obtained in a fast and accurate manner.

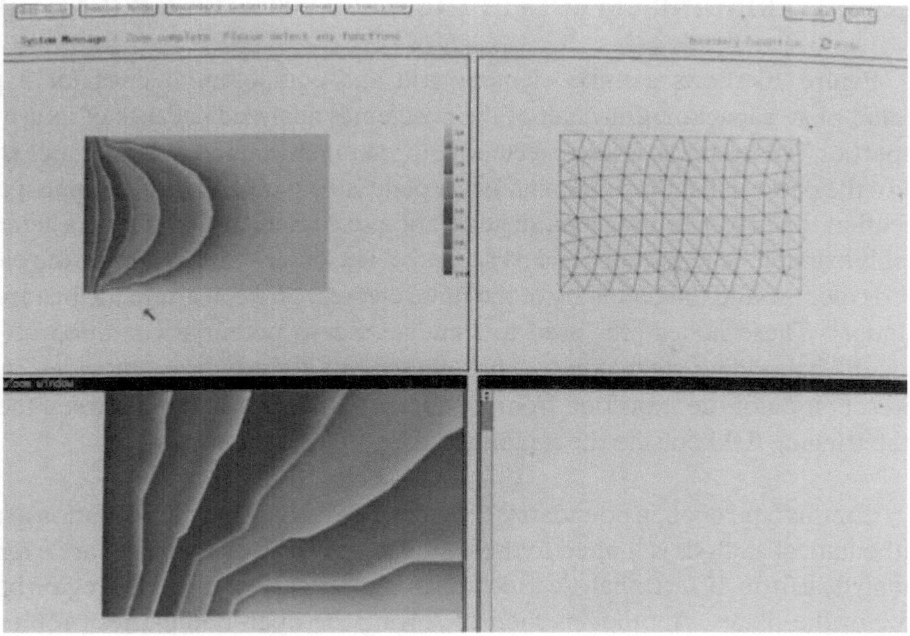

Fig. 8 **Finite element grid and the corresponding equipotential lines in a rectangular region processed by manual mode.**

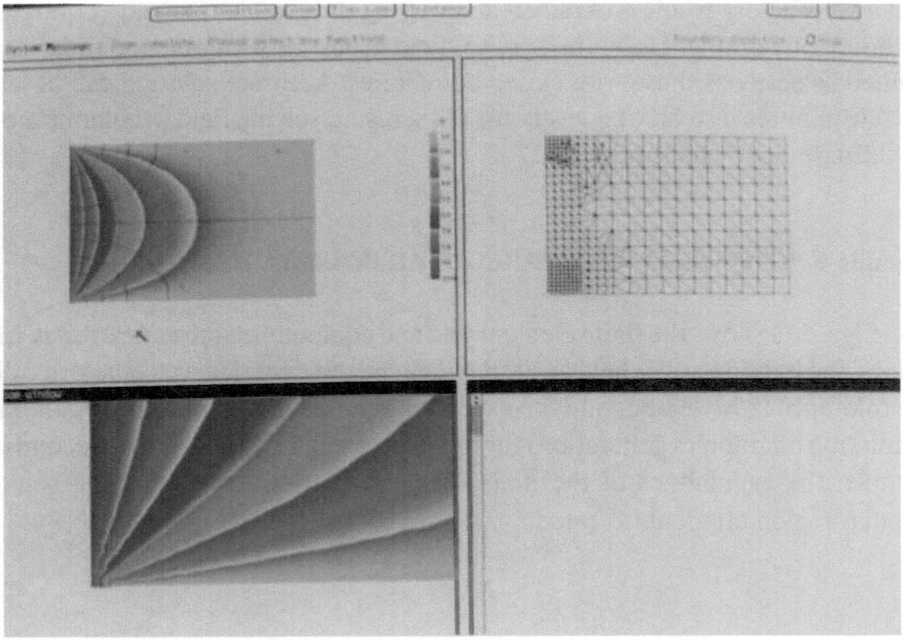

Fig. 9 **Finite element grid and the corresponding equipotential lines in a rectangular region at the last stage of the automatic mode.**

Example 3 FRINGING EFFECTS IN THE FIELD WITH OPEN BOUNDARIES

Figure 10 shows a finite element grid and equipotential lines for a pair of parallel-plate capacitor. Only half of the problem is analyzed because of its symmetric properties. This example is also executed using automatic mode, the tolerance is 10 volt where the potential at the upper and lower plate is 100 volt and 0 volt respectively. The execution time (from uniform mesh generation to completion of graphics generation) for this example is 12 minutes and 31 seconds. The outer most nodes for the elements in red color around the boundary of the finite element grid constitute the picture frame boundary. These nodes are used to simulate a zero potential condition at infinity through ballooning technique. The equipotential structure provides a clear representation of the transition from a uniform field in the region between the plates to the fringing field outside the middle zone.

For this type of open boundaries problem, there is no analytical solution available. Mathematical analysis is limited to those situations where the problem are expressible in analytical form. In fact, analytical technique is applicable to the closed region bounded between the plates. Another method of solving the open boundaries problem is by experimental technique using electrolytic tank or rubber membranes. Unfortunately, those approaches requires the use of equipment that is expensive to purchase and maintain. In most of the problems, it may require a few hours to conduct the experiment until a satisfactory result is obtained and varying the parameters may require another few hours of working. Using this system, field problems with open boundaries can be handled as easily as those with closed boundaries. Accurate solution can be obtained in a few minutes instead of a few hours. As a result, solving field problem is no longer a nightmare but a pleasure!

Example 4 THE FIELD WITH IRREGULAR BOUNDARIES

Figure 11 shows the finite element grid and equipotential structure for an irregular region. The left side wall is held at 100 degrees and the right side wall is held at 0 degrees. The tolerance is 10 degrees and the execution time (from uniform mesh generation to completion of graphics generation) for this example is 1 minutes and 41 seconds. In this example, the capabilities of the finite element method for finding the solution on irregular region are demonstrated.

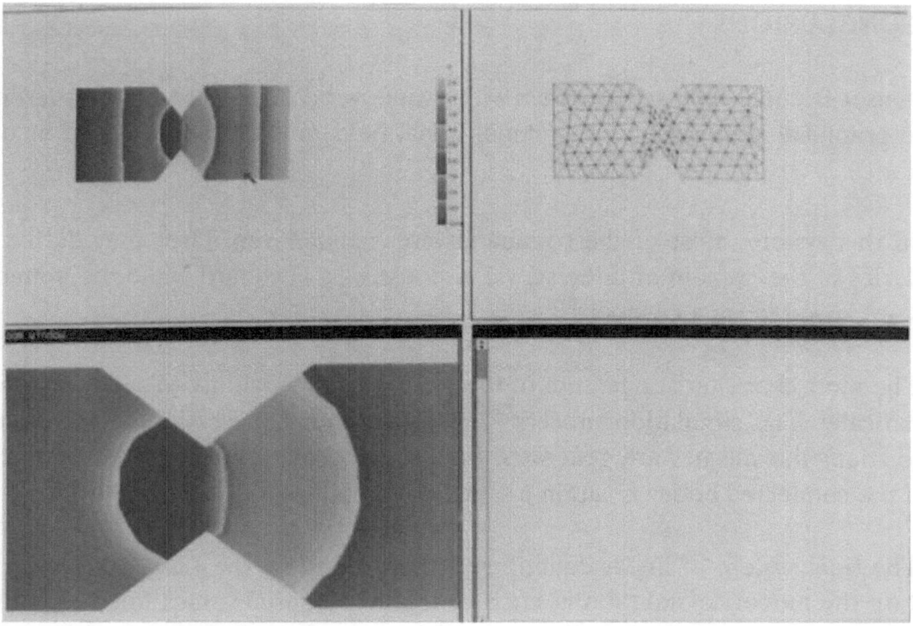

Fig. 10 Finite element grid and the corresponding equipotential lines for half of a parallel plate capacitor at the last stage of the automatic mode.

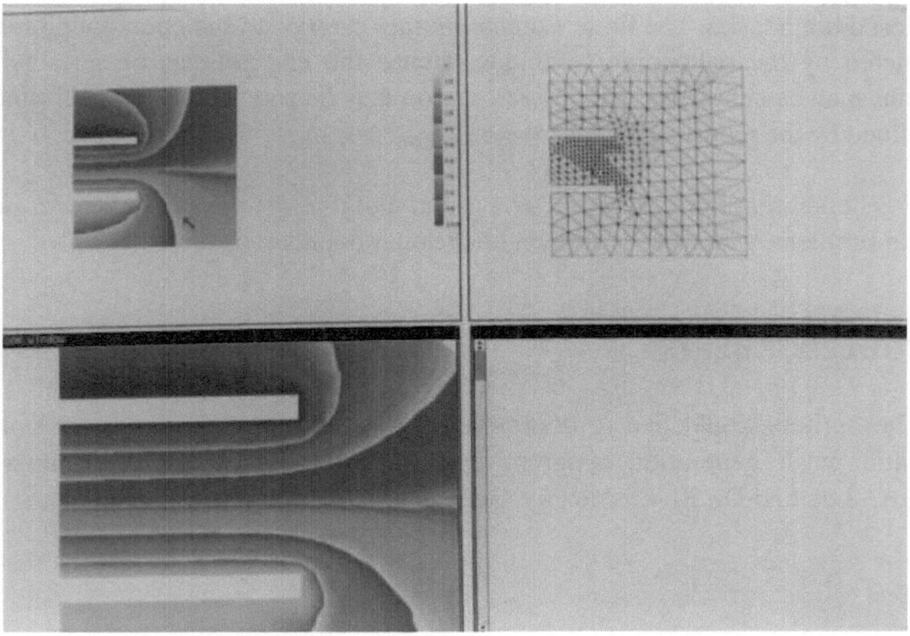

Fig. 11 Finite element grid and the corresponding equipotential lines for an irregular region at the last stage of the automatic mode.

6. CONCLUSIONS

A user-friendly, interactive system with a window-based environment is presented for the graphical simulation of two-dimensional field problems with closed or open boundaries.

In this system, most of the commands are menu-driven. User may define the boundaries of the domain of interests via a mouse or a keyboard while the boundary values are keyed in via a keyboard.

The most characteristic feature of this system is its capability to solve a problem automatically. The simulation process is recursive and a succession of increasingly refined triangular meshes are generated until the potential difference between each pair of the connected nodes is within a specified tolerance.

The final system of linear equations is then solved by the LDL^T factorization. Based on the numerical solution at each node, the potential values for the field are linearly interpolated and displayed by convex-filling technique. Equal potential contours are easily visualized on the screen within a few minutes. The set of orthogonal curves to the equipotential contours are then generated by the maximum gradient method.

Field problems with open boundaries can be simulated with equal ease as those with closed boundaries. The finite element meshes exterior to the open boundaries is constructed by the ballooning technique. Hence the edge effects of certain field problems may be simulated. The interest region may be zoomed after its subwindow are defined by the mouse.

It is hoped that this system will be a useful tool to assist the students to visualize the field problems with closed, or open or irregular boundaries.

ACKNOWLEDGEMENTS

The authors would like to acknowledge gratefully Dr. S. H. Lo's provision of automatic mesh generation program and to express their sincere thanks to Prof. S. C. Loh and Dr. M. F. Yuen for their suggestions and interesting discussion.

REFERENCES

Bathe K. J. and Wilson E. L. (1976), *Numerical Methods in Finite Element Analysis*, Prentice-Hall, Inc.

Berger M. (1986), *Computer Graphics with Pascal*, The Benjamin/Cummings Publishing Company, Inc.

Hoburg J. F. and Davis J. L. (1983), *A Student-Oriented Finite Element Program for Electrostatic Potential Problems*, IEEE Transactions on Education, Vol. E-26, No. 4, pp. 138-142.

Lo S. H. (1985), *A New Mesh Generation Scheme for Arbitrary Planar Domains*, Int. J. Numer. Methods Eng., Vol. 21, pp. 1403-1426.

Norrie D. H. and Devries G. (1978), *An Introduction to Finite Element Analysis*, Academic Press, Inc.

Silvester P.P., Carpenter C. J. and Wyatt E. A. (1977), *Exterior Finite Elements for 2-Dimensional Field Problems with Open Boundaries*, Proc. IEE, Vol. 124, No. 12, pp. 1267-1270.

SunView Reference Menu (1986), Sun Microsystems, Inc.

Yokoyama M. (1985), *Automated Computer Simulation of Two-Dimensional Elastostatic Problems by the Finite Element Method*, Int. J. Numer. Methods Eng., Vol. 21, pp. 2273-2287.

Kenneth Y.P. Lee graduated from Carleton University, Canada, with a Bachelor of Computer Science degree in 1987. He is currently a research student in the Department of Computer Science at the Chinese University of Hong Kong.

Address: Department of Computer Science, The Chinese University of Hong Kong, Shatin, N.T., Hong Kong.

Dr. Chaing-Sing Chang obtained a B.Sc. with First Class Honours in Mechanical Engineering at Leeds University and a Ph.D. at Imperial College of Science and Technology. Dr. Chang worked for C.A. Parsons Co., Newcastle upon Tyne, Queen Mary's College, London, Institute of Mechanics of the Chinese Academy of Sciences, Peking, University of Manitoba, Winnipeg, University of Hong Kong, and is now a senior lecturer in the Department of Computer Science at the Chinese University of Hong Kong.

Address: Department of Computer Science, The Chinese University of Hong Kong, Shatin, Hong Kong. Tel: 6952788, Fax: 6954234.

Chapter 7
Computational Geometry

An Efficient Data Structure for Three-Dimensional Triangulations*

Elisabetta Bruzzone and Leila De Floriani

ABSTRACT

A three-dimensional tesselation can be described by four basic topological elements (vertices, edges, faces, and polyhedral cells) plus their mutual pairwise relations. We present a specific data structure for encoding a three-dimensional tesselation composed of a collection of quasi-disjoint tetrahedra, i.e., a three-dimensional triangulation, and discuss those structure accessing algorithms which retrieve the relations not explicitly stored in the structure. A set of primitive operators for building and manipulating a 3D triangulation are presented. Their use is demonstrated in connection with an algorithm for computing a 3D Delaunay triangulation.

KEYWORDS: Geometric Modeling, Computational Geometry, Cell Decomposition, Tetrahedralization, Algorithms, Data Structures

1. INTRODUCTION

Object representation plays an important role in computer graphics, computer vision, robotics and computer aided design. Object representation schemes can be classified into three major categories: boundary representations, constructive models and decomposition models (Mantyla 1988). Boundary representations describe an object in terms of the surfaces enclosing it, constructive models represent an object as a boolean combination of primitive volumetric component. Decomposition models can be further classified into space-based and object-based schemes. The former decompose the space into elementary volumes (usually, cubes) and describe the object in terms of the volume elements which belong to it. Object-based schemes represent an object D as the combination of pairwise quasi-disjoint primitive 3D cells whose union cover D. Usually, tetrahedra are used as 3D cells. In this case, the model is called a three-dimensional triangulation, or a tetrahedralization. Three-dimensional triangulations are extensively used in the finite element method and in computer vision (see De Floriani 1987, for a survey). They have several important properties, like invariance through rigid transformations, ease of updating, computational efficiency, and suitability for both sparse and dense data (Boissonnat et al. 1988).

Often, the use of a three-dimensional Delaunay triangulation (see, for instance, Boissonnat 1984) is proposed to provide a global geometric structure encoding the neighborhood relations among the points of a given data set. Intuitively, a Delaunay triangulation TG of a set S of points in the k-dimensional Euclidean space is a collection of simplices tesselating the convex hull of S in such a way that the vertices of TG

(*) This work has been entirely supported by the Italian National Research Council.

are the points of S and the circumspheres of such simplices do not contain any point of S inside (Edelsbrunner 1987).

Several data structures for describing a triangulation of a set of points in the plane or any partition of the plane (De Floriani 1987; Preparata and Shamos 1985), or of the boundary of a solid object (Ansaldi et al. 1985; Baumgardt 1972; Weiler 1985; Woo 1985) have been proposed in the literature. Such structures store the basic entities defining a tesselation and their mutual adjacency relations. Ansaldi, De Floriani and Falcidieno (1985), Mantyla (1988), and Weiler (1986) have defined sets of basic operators for building and updating boundary models, called Euler operators. Such operators ensure that the topological validity of the model is maintained at each update.

Considerably less attention has been devoted to the problem of describing and manipulating a 3D tesselation. Dobkin and Laszlo (1989) generalize the quad-edge data structure proposed by Guibas and Stolfi (1985) for describing arbitrary planar subdivisions to the case of volumetric decompositions. They consider the polygon-edge pair as an atom which connects two vertices and two polyhedra. Bruzzone, De Floriani and Puppo (1989) have defined a data structure (together with the structure accessing algorithms assiociated with them) for describing decompositions of an object into polyhedral cells with triangular facets. Such data structure generalizes the concepts underlying the symmetric structure defined by Woo (1985) to polyhedral tesselations with triangular facets.

Here, we define a data structure specific for a 3D triangulation. The space complexity of the data structure and its time complexity referred to the structure accessing algorithms operating on it are evaluated. Operators for manipulating a D triangulation are defined: they ensure that the topological validity of the object represented by the tesselation is satisfied at each updating. The use of such operators is demonstrated in connection with an algorithm for constructing a 3D Delaunay triangulation.

2. PRIMITIVE TOPOLOGICAL ELEMENTS

In this section, we define the basic entities of a 3D triangulation and their mutual adjacency relations.

An m-simplex (or, simply, a simplex in m dimensions) is the convex hull of m+1 points, called the vertices of the simplex. The convex hull of any subset of the vertices of a simplex is called a face. A face that is the convex hull of m vertices is called a facet. Let S denote a set of n distinct points in Em (m>=2, n>=m+1). Assume that S does not lie on a hyperplane. Let C denote the convex hull of S. A triangulation of S is a set of non-degenerate m-simplices {ti} with the following properties:

(i) All the vertices of each simplex are elements of S
(ii) The interiors of the simplices are pairwise disjoint
(iii) Each facet of a simplex is either on the boundary of C or is a common facet of exactly two simplices
(iv) Each simplex contains no point of S other than its vertices
(v) The union of {ti} is C.

In the case m=3, that we consider here, simplices are tetrahedra, while facets are triangles. Triangles are in turn bounded by edges, which join pairs of consecutive vertices belonging to the facets. Hence, tetrahedra, facets (triangles), edges and vertices are the four basic topological elements defining a three-dimensional triangulation of a set of points. The boundary of C defines the boundary of the 3D object described by the set S.

A three-dimensional triangulation, denoted TG, can be expressed as a 4-tuple TG=(T,F,E,V) where T,F,E and V denote the collection of the tetrahedra, facets, edges and vertices of TG, respectively. The number of tetrahedra, facets and edges have been evaluated as a function of the number n of the vertices of TG for the case when TG is a 3D Delaunay triangulation. It has been proven (see Preparata and Shamos 1985) that a 3D Delaunay triangulation of n points contains O(n^2) tetrahedra, O(n^2) facets and O(n^2) edges. Thus, any relational model of a 3D triangulation will have an O(n^2) space complexity in the worst case.

Sixteen pairwise ordered adjacency relations can be defined over the four primitive topological elements. They can be classified into four categories according to the first element of each ordered pair.

1. Tetrahedron-based relations

1.1 Tetrahedron-Vertex (TV) (see figure 1a)
TV(t)={v1,v2,v3,v4}, t in T
{v1,v2,v3,v4}: set of vertices of TG belonging to t.

1.2 Tetrahedron-Edge (TE) (see figure 1a)
TE(t)={e1,e2,e3,e4,e5,e6}, t in T
{e1,e2,e3,e4,e5,e6}: set of edges of TG belonging to t.

1.3 Tetrahedron-Facet (TF) (see figure 1a)
TF(t)={f1,f2,f3,f4}, t in T
{f1,f2,f3,f4}: set of facets of TG belonging to t.

1.4 Tetrahedron-Tetrahedron (TT) (see figure 1b)
TT(t)={t1,t2,t3,t4}, t in T
{t1,t2,t3,t4}: set of tetrahedra of TG sharing a facet with t. A tetrahedron ti, i=1,...,4, is empty if t does not share facet fi with any tetrahedron of TG, i.e., fi is on the boundary of TG.

Note: The four sequences defined above are consistent. For instance, vertices v1, v2, v3 belong to f1, v1, v2, v4 belong to f2, v2, v3, v4 belong to f3 and v3, v1, v4 belong to f4 (see figure 1a).

2. Facet-based relations

2.1 Facet-Vertex (FV) (see figure 2a)
FV(f)=[v1,v2,v3], f in F
[v1,v2,v3]: sequence of vertices of TG bounding f in counterclockwise order (since an orientation is assigned to each face).

2.2 Facet-Edge (FE) (see figure 2a)
FE(f)=[e1,e2,e3], f in F
[e1,e2,e3]: sequence of edges of TG bounding f in counterclockwise order.

2.3 Facet-Facet (FF) (see figure 2b)
FF(f)=[[f11,f21],[f12,f22],[f13,f23]], f in F
[[f11,f21],[f12,f22],[f13,f23]]: sequence of facet pairs sharing an edge with f.
[fi1,fi2]: ordered pair of facets of TG preceding and following f along edge ei and belonging to t1 and t2 respectively, where ei denotes the i-th edge bounding f and t1 and t2 the two tetrahedra sharing f (when t2 is empty, then FF(f)=[f11,f12,f13]). The facet pairs sequence is ordered according to the ccw order of the edges around f.

2.4 Facet-Tetrahedron (FT) (see figure 2b)
FT(f)=[t1,t2], f in F
[t1,t2]: ordered pair of tetrahedra of TG sharing f; t2 is empty if f belong only to one tetrahedron (the order is consistent with the orientation assigned to f).

3. <u>Edge-based relations</u>

3.1 <u>Edge-Vertex</u> (EV) (see figure 3a)
EV(e)=[v1,v2], e in E
[v1,v2]: extreme vertices of edge e (an arbitary direction is assigned to edge e).

3.2 <u>Edge-Edge</u> (EE) (see figure 3a)
EE(e)=[[e1,e2,...,er],[e1',e2',...er']], e in E
[[e1,e2,...,er],[e1',e2',...er']]: ordered pair of sets of edges of TG sharing a vertex with e.
[e1,e2,...,er]: sequence of edges of TG (ordered counterclockwise) sharing vertex v1 with e and bounding the facets sharing e.
[e1',e2',...er']: sequence of edges of TG (ordered counterclockwise) sharing v2 with e and bounding the facets sharing e.

3.3 <u>Edge-Facet</u> (EF) (see figure 3b)
EF(e)=[f1,f2,...,fr], e in E
[f1,f2,...,fr]: sequence of facets of TG sharing edge e in counterclockwise order (by assuming e directed from v1 to v2).

3.4 <u>Edge-Tetrahedron</u> (ET) (see figure 3b)
ET(e)=[t1,t2,...,ts], e in E
[t1,t2,...,ts]: sequence of tetrahedra of TG sharing edge e in counterclockwise order (by assuming e directed from v1 to v2).

4. <u>Vertex-based relations</u>

4.1 <u>Vertex-Vertex</u> (VV) (see figure 4a)
VV(v)={v1,v2,...,vp}, v in V
{v1,v2,...,vp}: set of vertices of TG which are extreme vertices of the edges incident on v.

4.2 <u>Vertex-Edge</u> (VE) (see figure 4a)
VE(v)={e1,e2,...,ep}, v in V
{e1,e2,...,ep}: set of edges of TG incident on vertex v.

4.3 <u>Vertex-Facet</u> (VF) (see figure 4b)
VF(v)={f1,f2,...,fq}, v in V
{f1,f2,...,fq}: set of facets of TG sharing a vertex with v.

4.4 <u>Vertex-Tetrahedron</u> (VT) (see figure 4b)
VT(v)={t1,t2,...,th}, v in V
{t1,t2,...,th}: set of tetrahedra of TG sharing a vertex with v.

The previous sixteen relations can be classified into <u>constant</u> and <u>variable</u> relations depending on the number of elements involved in the second term of the relation. All tetrahedron- and facet-based relations are constant, while the edge- and vertex-based relations, with the exception of the edge-vertex one, are variable.

The topology of a three-dimensional triangulation TG is completely and unambiguously represented by the four primitive topological elements (T,F,E,V) together with a subset R' of the set R of the sixteen adjacency relations. The relations in R' must be <u>sufficient</u> to describe TG unambiguously. In other words, it must be possible to retrieve from (T,F,E,V) and R' all relations in R-R' without any error or ambiguity. Since encoding too many relations increases the storage cost of the resulting data structure (which will have in any case a quadratic space complexity), it is important to identify minimal subsets of relations which are capable of both providing a sufficient topological description of a 3D triangulation and ensuring the efficiency of the basic structure accessing algorithms.

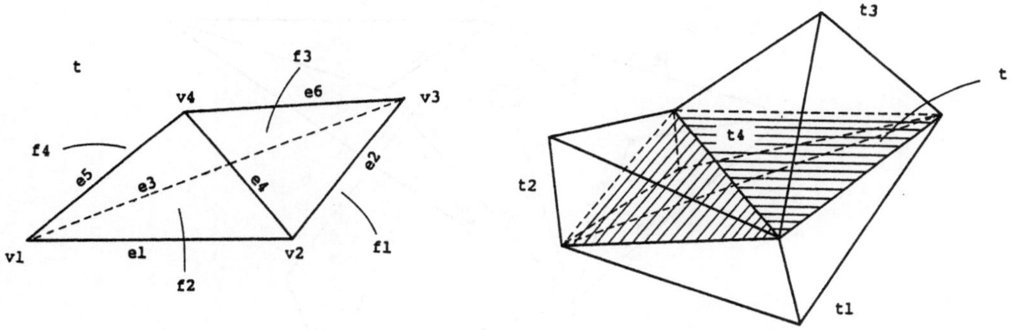

(a) (b)

Figure 1

Illustration of Tetrahedron-Vertex, Tetrahedron-Edge and Tetrahedron-Facet relations (a), Tetrahedron-Tetrahedron relation (b).

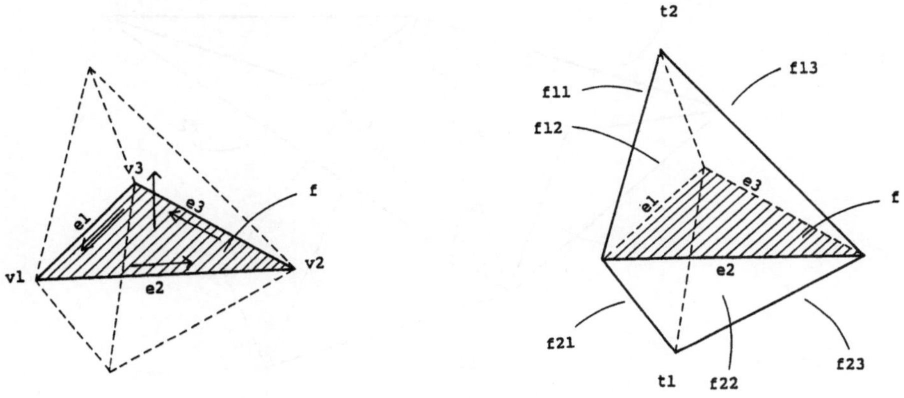

(a) (b)

Figure 2

Illustration of Facet-Vertex and Facet-Edge relations (a), Facet-Facet and Facet-Tetrahedron relations (b).

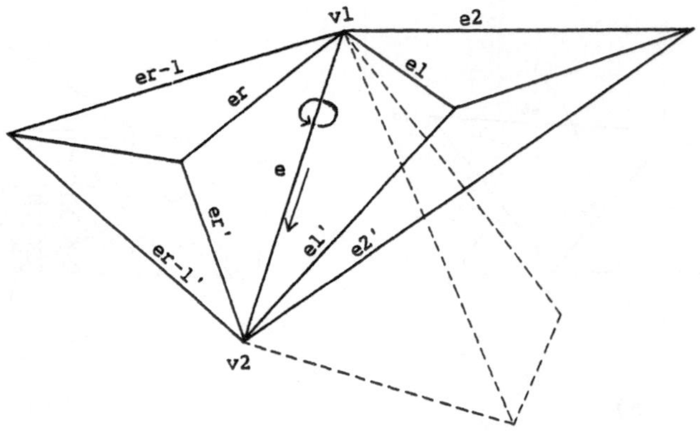

(a)

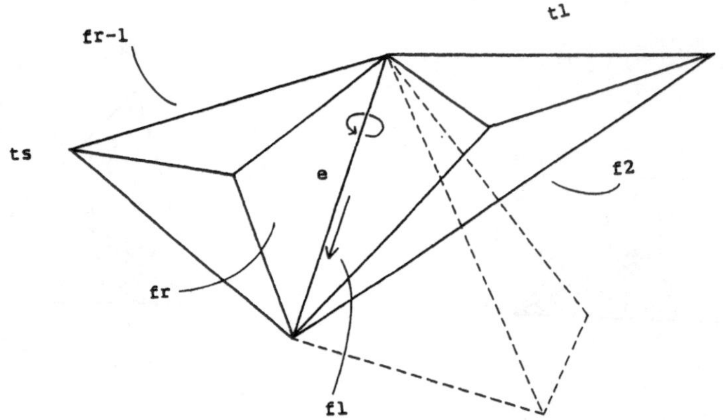

(b)

Figure 3

Illustration of Edge-Vertex and Edge-Edge relations (a), Edge-Facet and Edge-Tetrahedron relations (b).

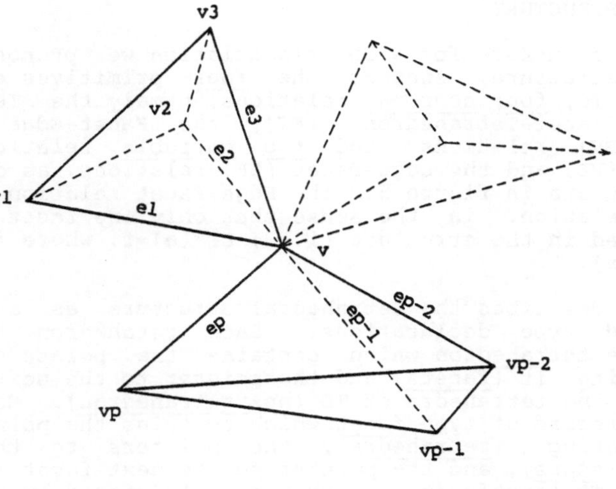

(a)

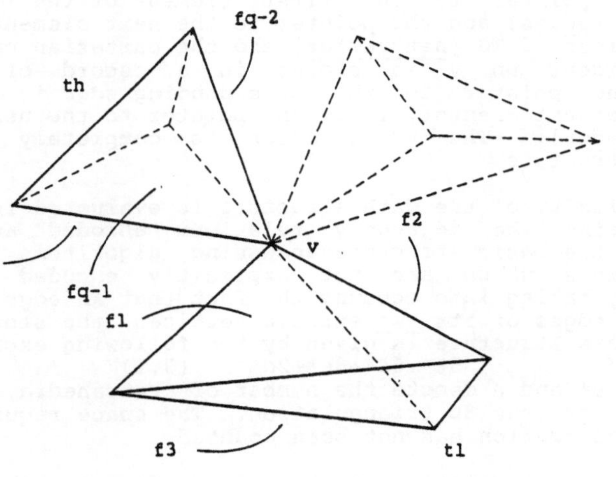

(b)

Figure 4

Illustration of Vertex-Vertex and Vertex-Edge relations (a), Vertex-Facet and Vertex-Tetrahedron relations (b).

3. THE DATA STRUCTURE

The data structure for a 3D triangulation we propose, called the tetrahedral structure, encodes the four primitives elements of a 3D triangulation TG, four constant relations, namely the Tetrahedron-Facet (TF), the Facet-Tetrahedron (FT), the Facet-Edge (FE) and the Edge-Vertex (EV) relations, and two variable relations, i.e., the Vertex-Edge (VE) and the Edge-Facet (EF) relations, as described by the adjacency schemata in figure 5. The Edge-Facet relation is stored as a fractional relation, in the sense that only one facet sharing a given edge is encoded in the structure (i.e., EF*(e)=f, where f is any facet sharing edge e).

Figure 6 describes the tetrahedral structure as a collection of Pascal record type declarations. Each tetahedron t is stored in a record of type tetrahedron which contains the pointers to the four facets bounding it (facets) and the pointer to the next tetrahedron in the list T of the tetrahedra of TG (nexttetrahedron). Each facet f is stored in a record of type facet which contains the pointers to the two tetrahedra sharing f (tetrahedra), the pointers to the three edges bounding f (edges), and the pointer to the next facet in the list F of the facets of TG (nextfacet). Each edge e is stored in a record of type edge, which contains the pointers to the extreme vertices of e (vertices), the pointer to one of the facets sharing edge e (facet) and the pointer to the next edge in the list E of the edges of TG (nextedge). Each vertex v is stored in a record of type vertex, which contains the pointer to the first element of the list of the edges incident on v (edges) and the pointer to the next element in the list V of the vertices of TG (nextvertex) and the cartesian coordinates of v. Each edge incident on v is stored in a record of type edgelist containing the pointer to the corresponding edge in E (edge) and the pointer to the next element, i.e., the pointer to the next edge incident on v (nextedge). The VE relation is completely stored in the tetrahedral structure.

The complexity of the data structure is evaluated in terms of the cost of storing the adjacency relations encoded and of the time complexity of the basic structure accessing algorithms which retrieve those relations which are not explicitly encoded into the data structure. By taking into account the fact that an edge belongs to the list of the edges of its two extreme vertices, the storage cost of the tetrahedral data structure is given by the following expression

$$5t^*+6f^*+8e^*+2n \qquad (3.1)$$

where t*, f*, e* and n denote the number of tetrahedra, facets, edges and vertices of the 3D triangulation. The space required for storing geometrical information has not been counted.

The complete EF relation can be retrieved from the structure by combining of the EF*, FT, TF and FE ones (i.e., EF=EF*+FT+TF+FE) as described by procedure Edge_Facet presented below. Such a procedure makes use of standard primitives of sorted list manipulation (see Aho, Hopcroft and Ullman 1983).

```
Procedure  Edge_Facet(e,Lf);
(* e:  edge of TG;
   Lf: sorted list of the facets of the 3D triangulation TG sharing
       edge e, i.e., sorted list of the elements of EF(e) *)
begin
     CREATE_EMPTY_LIST(Lf);
     f:=EF*(e);
     INSERT_LIST(Lf,f);
     [t1,t2]:=FT(f);
     if CCW(t1,t2,e) then t=t2 else t=t1;
     (*CCW(t1,t2,e) returns the value true if t2 follows t1
```

```
    around e in ccw order, the value false otherwise*)
    {f,f1,f2,f3}:=TF(t);
    let f1 the facet bounding t and sharing edge e with f;
    while f1<>FIRST_ELEMENT(Lf) do begin
        INSERT_LIST(Lf,f1);
        [t1*,t2*]=FT(f1);
        if t=t1* then t*:=t2* else t*:=t1*;
        {f1,f1*,f2*,f3*}:=TF(t*);
        let f1* the facet bounding t* and sharing edge e with f1;
        f1:=f1*;
        t=t*;
    end
end.  (*Edge_Facet*)
```

Algorithm Edge_Facet is asymptotically optimal, since it is linear in the number of facets sharing a given edge e.

The remaining ten adjacency relations not stored into the tetrahedral structure can be expressed as the combination of the five relations stored and of the complete EF relation as described in table 1 (such relations are classified according to their first term).

<u>Tetrahedron-based</u> relations
TT=TF+FT
TE=TF+FE
TV=TF+FE+EV

<u>Face-based</u> relations
FF=FT+TF+(FE)
FV=FE+EV

<u>Edge-based</u> relations
ET=EF+FT
EE=EF+FE+(EV)

<u>Vertex-based</u> relations
VT=VE+EF+FT
VF=VE+EF
VV=VE+EV

Table 1

The tetrahedron- and facet-based relations are combinations of constant relations, while the remaining relations are variable. Because of the definition of the FF and EE relations, we need the FE relation for retrieving the FF one and the EV relation for retrieving the EE one. Extracting relations which are not stored in the tetrahedral structure requires a constant number of operations for any constant relation and a number of operations which is linear in the size of the output for any variable relation. Thus, no relation requires a number of operations which is linear in the <u>total</u> number of tetrahedra, facets, edges or vertices in TG. In this sense, the time complexity of the data structure can be considered optimal since no structure accessing algorithm requires searching the entire data structure.

In the 3D symmetric data structure described by Bruzzone, De Floriani and Puppo (1989), the "complete" Edge-Facet relation is stored. Some structure accessing algorithms are simpler, but they have the same time complexity. The storage cost of the resulting structure is, on the other hand, equal to

$$5t^*+18f^*+8e^*+2n \qquad (3.2)$$

which is higher compared with that of the tetrahedral structure (the difference is equal to $6f^*$). In order to optimize the storage cost of

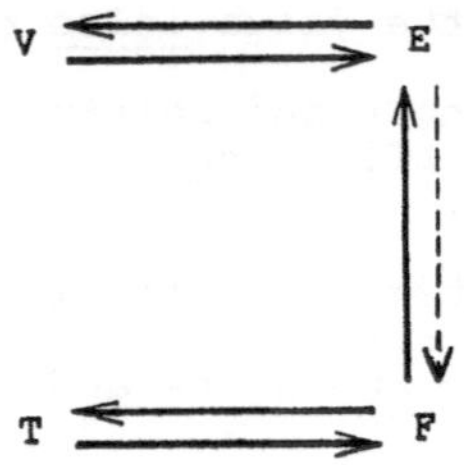

Figure 5

Adjacency schemata describing the tetrahedral structure (heavy arrows denote constant relations, dashed arrows fractional relations).

```
type

     tetrahedron = record
                     nexttetrahedron: ^tetrahedron;
                     (*Tetrahedron-Facet relation*)
                     facets: array [0..3] of ^facet
                   end;

     facet = record
               nextfacet: ^facet;
               (*Facet-Tetrahedron relation*)
               tetrahedra: array [0..1] of ^tetrahedron;
               (*Facet-Edge relation*)
               edges: array [0..2] of ^edge;
             end;

     edge = record
              nextedge: ^edge;
              (*Edge-Vertex relation*)
              vertices: array [0..1] of ^vertex;
              (*Edge-Facet fractional relation*)
              facet: ^facet
            end;

     vertex = record
                nextvertex: ^vertex;
                x,y,z: real;
                (*Vertex-Edge relation*)
                edges: ^edgelist
              end;

     edgelist = record
                  nextedge: ^edgelist;
                  edge: ^edge
                end;
```

Figure 6
Pascal record type description of the tetrahedral structure.

the structure, we have considered the alternative of storing all variable relations as fractional. The resulting data structure is similar to the tetrahedral structure except for the fact that the VE would be stored as fractional. The storage cost of such a structure is equal to

$$5t^*+6f^*+4e^*+2n \qquad (3.3)$$

which is lower than the cost of the tetrahedral structure (see (3.1)). Unfortunately, the time complexity would increase, since retrieving the Vertex-Facet relation from the fractional VE requires a number of operations proportional to the product of the number of edges and the number of facets incident on a given vertex. Hence, the tetrahedral structure is optimal with respect to both space and time complexity.

4. BUILDING AND UPDATING A 3D TRIANGULATION

In this section, we define a complete set of primitive operators to build and modify a three-dimensional triangulation. Such operators, that we call Euler operators, ensure that both the topological validity condition expressed by Euler-Poincare' formula in the form given below (see Greenberg, 1967) is satisfied and a tetrahedrization is produced at each step of the updating process.

For convenience, we consider the case in which a 3D triangulation consists of several connected components. Each of such components, that we call a volume, is a maximal connected set of tetrahedra. If we denote by v* the number of volumes in a 3D triangulation TG of a set of n points, Euler-Poincare' formula becomes

$$n-e^*+f^*-t^*=v^* \qquad (4.1)$$

where e*, f* and t* denote respectively the number of edges, facets and tetrahedra of TG. The topological validity of a general tesselation (not necesserely composed by tetrahedra) can be checked by applying formula (4.1). To avoid performing a validity check of a 3D triangulation after each updating, it is convenient to decompose each modification of the triangulation into a sequence of simple atomic steps provided by Euler operators. Suitable sequences of Euler operators can be used to build or destroy a valid 3D triangulation consisting of one or more volumes with no holes.

The Euler operators we have defined are listed below with an informal description of both their effect on a 3D triangulation and the transformations in the parameters in the Euler-Poincare' formula. Only modifications of topological entities are described regardless of geometric constraints.

Constructive Euler Operators

1. INITIALIZE_TRIANGULATION(TG,t,v1,v2,v3,v4)
   It creates a 3D triangulation TG consisting of a single tetrahedron t defined by the four (no-coplanar) vertices v1, v2, v3 and v4.
   Transformation
   (,,,,)--->(4,6,4,1,1)

2. MTFEV(TG,f,t',t,f1,f2,f3,e1,e2,e3,v)
   (Make_Tetrahedron_Facets_Edges_and_Vertex)
   It creates a new tetrahedron t by joining the vertices bounding facet f (which is a facet of a tetrahedron t' of TG) to a new vertex v (v must belong to the half-space defined by f and not containing t'). Three new facets (f1, f2 and f3) and edges (e1, e2 and e3) are created as well (see figure 7a).
   Transformation
   (n,e*,f*,t*,v*)--->(n+1,e*+3,f*+3,t*+1,v*)

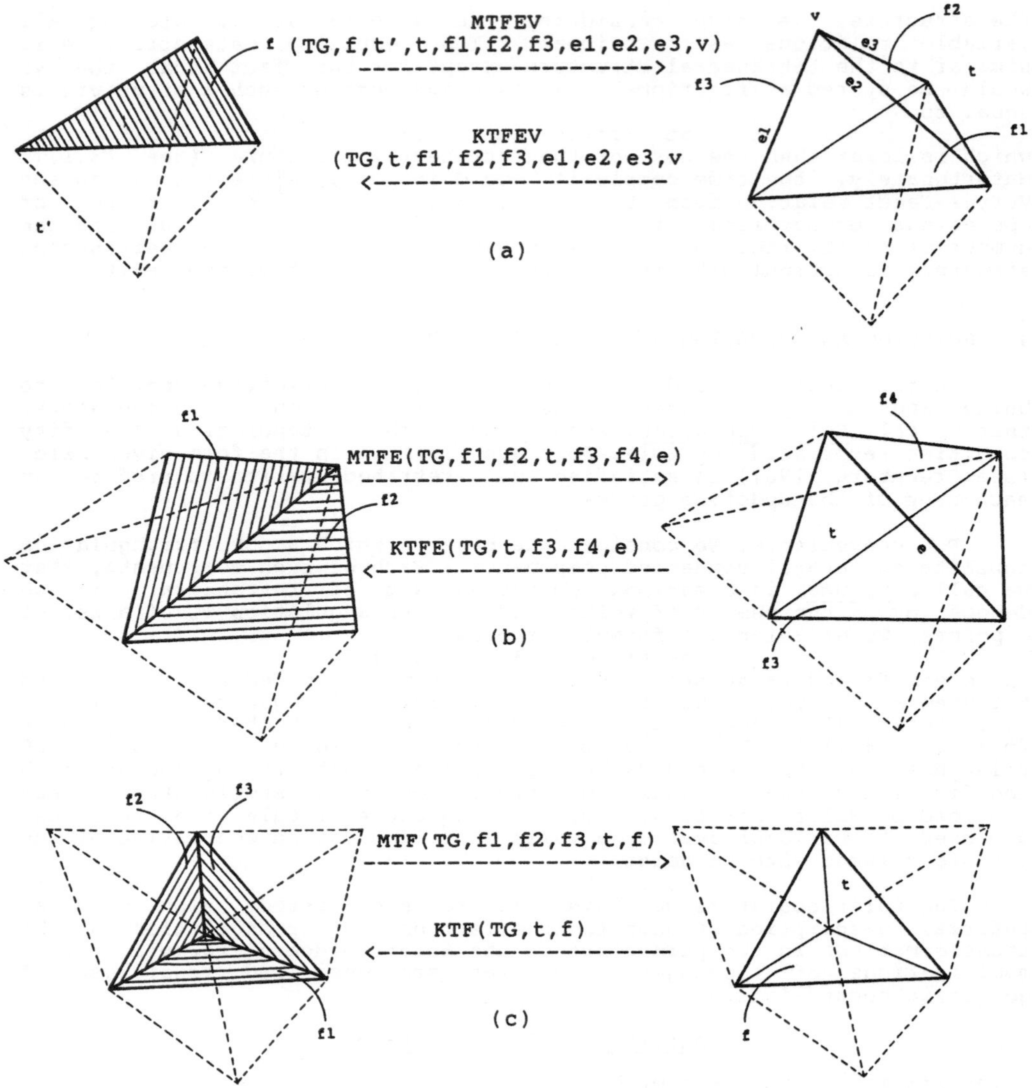

Figure 7

Illustration of the effect of the three constructive Euler operators MTFEV (7a), MTFE (7b) and MTF (7c) and their inverse ones.

3. MTFE(TG,f1,f2,t,f3,f4,e)
   (Make_Tetrahedron_Facets_and_Edge)
   It creates a new tetrahedron t formed by completing two adjacent facets f1 and f2 belonging to the boundary of TG with two new facets f3 and f4. Edge e is the edge shared by facets f3 and f4 (see figure 7b).
   Transformation
   (n,e*,f*,t*,v*)--->(n,e*+1,f*+2,t*+1,v*)

4. MTF(TG,f1,f2,f3,t,f)
   (Make_Tetrahedron_and_Facet)
   It creates a new tetrahedron t by adding a new facet f to three adjacent facets f1, f2 and f3 sharing a common vertex and belonging to the boundary of TG (see figure 7c).
   Transformation
   (n,e*,f*,t*,v*)--->(n,e*,f*+1,t*+1,v*)

These latter three operators cover the three cases when a tetrahedron is added on the boundary of TG. If we want to create tetrahedra inside TG we can only split an existing tetrahedron t of TG into four tetrahedra by adding an internal vertex v as performed by SPLIT_TETRAHEDRON.

5. SPLIT_TETRAHEDRON(TG,t,v,t1,t2,t3,t4)
   It splits tetrahedron t into four tetrahedra (ti, i=1,...,4) by joining the new vertex v to the four vertices bounding t (see figure 8).
   Transformation
   (n,e*,f*,t*,v*)--->(n+1,e*+4,f*+6,t*+3,v*)

<u>Inverse Euler Operators</u>

1. DELETE_TRIANGULATION(TG,t)
   It deletes a 3D triangulation consisting of a single tetrahedron t.
   Transformation
   (4,6,4,1,1)--->(,,,,)

2. KTFEV(TG,t,f1,f2,f3,e1,e2,e3,v)
   (Kill_Tetrahedron_Facets_Edges_and_Vertex)
   It deletes a vertex v, three edges e1, e2 and e3 incident on v, three facets f1, f2 and f3 sharing vertex v and the tetrahedron t bounded by facets f1, f2 and f3 from the 3D triangulation TG. Facets f1, f2 and f3 must be the only facets of t on the boundary of TG (see figure 7a).
   Transformation
   (n,e*,f*,t*,v*)--->(n-1,e*-3,f*-3,t*-1,v*)

3. KTFE(TG,t,f1,f2,e)
   (Kill_Tetrahedron_Facets_and_Edge)
   It deletes edge e, the facets f1 and f2 sharing edge e and the tetrahedron t bounded by f1 and f2 from TG. Facets f1 and f2 must be the only facets of t on the boundary of TG (see figure 7b).
   Transformation
   (n,e*,f*,t*,v*)--->(n,e*-1,f*-2,t*-1,v*)

4. KTF(TG,t,f)
   (Kill_Tetrahedron_and_Facet)
   It deletes a facet f and a tetrahedron t bounded by f from TG. Facet f must be the only facet of t on the boundary of TG (see figure 7c).
   Transformation
   (n,e*,f*,t*,v*)--->(n,e*,f*-1,t*-1,v*)

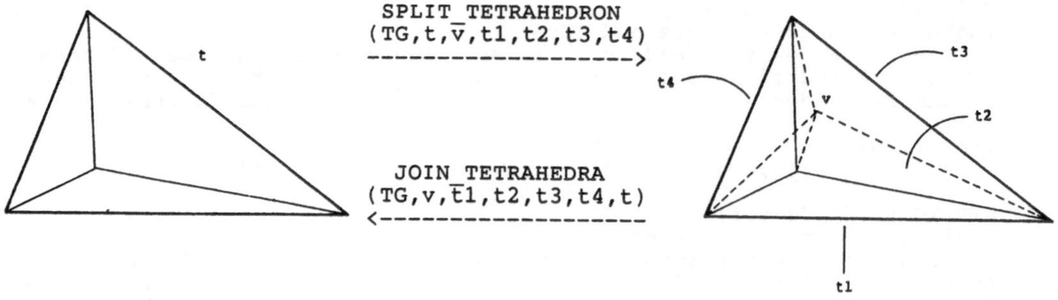

Figure 8

Illustration of the effect of SPLIT_TETRAHEDRON and JOIN_TETRAHEDRA.

5. JOIN_TETRAHEDRA(TG,v,t1,t2,t3,t4,t)
   It creates a new tetrahedron t by deleting a vertex v and the four tetrahedra ti, i=1,...,4, sharing vertex v from TG. The constraint is that the union of the four ti's forms a tetrahedron (see figure 8).
   <u>Transformation</u>
   (n,e*,f*,t*,v*)--->(n-1,e*-4,f*-6,t*-3,v*)

5. AN APPLICATION OF EULER OPERATORS

The 3D Delaunay triangulation is a special triangulation defined as the geometrical dual of the Voronoi diagram of the set S of 3D points. If S={v1,v2,...,vn}, the Voronoi diagram of S is a collection (V1,V2,...,Vn) of polyhedra covering E3, where Vi is formed by all the points of E3 which have vi as the nearest point in S. The Delaunay triangulation is obtained by connecting the points of S that are neighbors in the Voronoi diagram. In a 3D Delaunay triangulation, the circumspheres of each tetrahedron do not contain any point of S inside. Algorithms for computing a 3D Delaunay triangulation and, in general, an n-dimensional tesselation of a set of points are discussed by Avis and Bhattacharya (1983), Bowyer (1981) and Watson (1981). We present here a description, based on the constructive operators defined in section 4, of the algorithm by Avis and Bhattacharya, which builds a 3D Delaunay triangulation of a set of points. A characteristic of this algorithm is that it forms tetrahedral cells at each step.

Let S be a set of n points in the 3D space. The 3D Delaunay triangulation TG of S is built by starting with an initial tetrahedron and iteratively adding tetrahedra until a 3D triangulation of S covering the convex hull of S is obtained. The initial tetrahedron t is built by considering a facet f on the boundary of the convex hull of S and a vertex v in S (different from the vertices of f) which defines with f a sphere of minimum radius. The other tetrahedra are generated by finding, for each facet f' of the boundary B of the current triangulation TG which does not belong to the boundary of the convex hull of S, a vertex v′ belonging to the half-space opposite to the one containing the tetrahedron to which f′ belongs and defining a minimum-radius sphere with the vertices of f′. The process stops when all the facets of B belong to the boundary of the convex hull of S.

```
Algorithm Delaunay_Triangulation(S,TG);
(* S: set of n (n>=4) points;
  TG=(T,F,E,V): Delaunay triangulation of S *)
begin
   compute the boundary BC of the convex hull C of S;
   let f1 be a facet on BC;
   [v1,v2,v3]:=FV(f1);
   let v the vertex of S (<>v1,v2,v3) defining a minimum-radius
   sphere with v1, v2 and v3;
   INITIALIZE_TRIANGULATION(TG,t,v1,v2,v3,v);
   {f1,f2,f3,f4}:=TF(t);
   CREATE_EMPTY_LIST(F*);
   for i:=2 to 4 do
       if fi is not on BC then INSERT_LIST(F*,fi);
   while not IS_EMPTY_LIST(F*) do begin
          f*:=FIRST_ELEMENT(F*);
          [t1,t2]:=TF(f*);  (*t2 is an empty tetrahedron*)
          t*:=t1;
          [v1,v2,v3]:=FV(f*);
          FIND_NEAREST_VERTEX(S,v1,v2,v3,v,t*);
          (*It identifies the vertex v of S which lies in the
          half-space not containing t* and defining a
          minimum-radius sphere with v1, v2 and v3*)
          i:=CURRENT(TG,v,v1,v2,v3);
          (*CURRENT(TG,v,v1,v2,v3) returns:
          1 if there not exists any other facet on the boundary
            of TG (<>f*) bounded by vertices v ,v1 v2 or v3;
          2 if there exists only one facet on the boundary
            of TG (<>f*) bounded by vertices v, v1, v2 or v3;
          3 if there exists two facets on the boundary
            of TG (<>f*) bounded by vertices v, v1, v2 or v3.
          CURRENT(TG,v,v1,v2,v3) is implemented by using the
          Vertex-Vertex relation*)
          case i of
               1: begin
                        MTFEV(TG,f*,t*,newt,f1,f2,f3,e1,e2,e3,v);
                        for j:=1 to 3 do
                           if fj is not on BC then INSERT_LIST(F*,fj)
                  end;
               2: begin
                        let f1 the facet of TG (<>f) bounded
                        by vertices v, v1, v2 or v3;
                        MTFE(TG,f*,f1,newt,f2,f3,e);
                        for j:=2 to 3 do
                           if fj is not on BC then INSERT_LIST(F*,fj);
                        DELETE_LIST(F*,f1)
                  end;
               3: begin
                        let f1 and f2 the two facets of TG (<>f)
                        bounded by vertices v, v1, v2 or v3;
                        MTF(TG,f*,f1,f2,newt,f3);
                        if f3 is not on BC then INSERT_LIST(F*,f3);
                        for j:=1 to 2 do DELETE_LIST(F*,fj)
                  end
          end;    (*case*)
          DELETE_LIST(F*,f*)
   end    (*while*)
end.   (*Delaunay_Triangulation*)
```

6. Summary

The problem of defining a data structure for storing a three-dimensional triangulation has been considered. A data structure which stores the four basic topology elements of a 3D triangulation and six mutual adjacency relations, has been defined and which is specific for a 3D triangulation. Extracting the ten relations which are not explicitly stored in the structure requires a constant number of operations for any constant relation (namely tetrahedron- and facet-based relations and the Edge-Vetrex relation), or a number of operations which is linear in the output size for any variable relation. We have presented an algorithm which explicitly extracts the complete Edge-Facet relation from the fractional EF relation stored.

A set of primitive operators for building and manipulating a 3D triangulation has been defined. Such operators ensure the topological integrity of the resulting triangulation, i.e., that the Euler-Poincare' formula is verified at each update and that a tetrahedralization is formed at each step. Operators MTFEV, MTFE and MTF together with their inverse (KTFEV, KTFE and KTF) form a minimally complete set, as it can be proven by algebraic considerations. These operators have been used to express the 3D Delaunay triangulation algorithm of Avis and Bhattacharya.

REFERENCES

Aho, A.F., Hopcroft, J.E., Ullman, J.D. (1983) Data Structures and Algorithms. Addison Wesley Publ.,Reading, Ma.

Avis, D., Bhattacharya, B.K. (1983) Algorithms for Computing d-Dimensional Voronoi Diagrams and Their Duals. Advances in Computing Research, 1, Preparata, ed., JAI Press, Greenwich, CT.

Ansaldi, S., De Floriani, L., Falcidieno, B. (1985) Geometric Modeling of Solid Object by Using a Face Adjacency Graph Representation. Computer Graphics 19: 131-139.

Baumgardt, M.G. (1972) Winged-Edge Polyhedron Representation. Tech. Rep. CS-320, Stanford University.

Boissonnat, J.D. (1984) Geometric Structures for Three-Dimensional Stage Representation. ACM Trans. on Graphics 3:266-286.

Boissonnat, J.D., Faugeras, O.D., Le Bras-Mehlman, E. (1988) Representing Stereo Data with Delaunay Triangulation. Proceeding IEEE Robotics and Automation, Philadelphia, April 1988.

Bowyer, A. (1981) Computing Dirichlet Tesselations. The Computer Journal 27:165-171.

Bruzzone, E., De Floriani, L., Puppo, E. (1989) Manipulating Three-Dimensional Triangulations. Proceedings FODO, Paris, June 1989.

De Floriani, L. (1987) Surface Representations Based on Triangular Grids. The Visual Computer, 3:27-50.

Dobkin, D.P., Laszlo, M.J. (1989) Primitives for the Manipulation of Three-Dimensional Subdivisions. Algorithmica 4:3-32.

Edelsbrunner, H. (1987) Algorithms in Combinatorial Geometry. Springer-Verlag.

Guibas, L., Stolfi, J. (1985) Primitives for the Manipulation of General Subdivisions and the Computation of Voronoi Diagrams. ACM Trans. Graphics, 4:75-123.

Greenberg, M.J. (1967) Lectures on Algebraic Topology. W.A. Benjamin, Inc., New York.

Mantyla, M. (1988) An Introduction to Solid Modeling. Computer Science Press.

Preparata, F.P., Shamos, M.I. (1985) Computational Geometry: an Introduction. Springer-Verlag.

Watson, D.F. (1981) Computing the n-dimensional Delaunay Tesselation with Applications to Voronoi Polytopes. The Computer Journal 24:167-171.

Weiler, K. (1985) Edge-based Data Structures for Solid Modeling in Curved-surface Environments. IEEE Computer Graphics and Applications 5:21-40.

Weiler, K. (1986) Topological Structures for Geometric Modeling. Ph.D. Thesis, Rensselaer Polytecnic Institute, Troy (NY).

Woo, T.C. (1985) A Combinatorial Analysis of Boundary Data Structure Schemata. IEEE Computer Graphics and Applications 5:19-27.

Elisabetta Bruzzone got an advanced degree in Mathematics from the University of Genova in 1987 From July 1987 to April 1989 she was a Research Associate at the Institute of Applied Mathematics of the Italian National Research Council (CNR). From May to October 1989 she has been a visiting scholar at the Rensselaer Polytechnic Institute, Troy (USA). She is currently a member of the research staff of Elettronica San Giorgio in Genova, Italy. Her research interests include geometric modeling, computer vision and computational geometry.

Address: Elettronica San Giorgio - Elsag S.p.A., Via Puccini, 2, 16154 Genova, Italy.

Leila De Floriani is a Senior Scientist at the Institute of Applied Mathematics of the Italian National Research Council, Genova, Italy, and an Adjunct Professor at the Department of Computer Science of the University of Genova. From 1977 to 1981 she was a Research Associate at the Institute of Applied Mathematics, and from 1981 to 1982 an Assistant Professor at the Department of Mathematics of the University of Genova Her research interests include computational geometry, geometric modeling, computer graphics, and data structures. Leila De Floriani received an advanced degree in Mathematics from the University of Genova in 1977. She is a member of ACM, IEEE Computer Society, and IAPR.

Address: Istituto per la Matematica Applicata, Consiglio Nazionale delle Ricerche, Via L.B. Alberti, 4, 16132 Genova, Italy.

An Output-Complexity-Sensitive Polygon Triangulation Algorithm

Godfried Toussaint

This paper describes a new algorithm for triangulating a simple n-sided polygon. The algorithm runs in time $O(n(1+t_0))$, with $t_0 < n$. The quantity t_0 measures the *shape-complexity* of the *triangulation* delivered by the algorithm. More precisely t_0 is the number of triangles contained in the triangulation obtained that share zero edges with the input polygon and is, furthermore, related to the shape-complexity of the *input* polygon. Although the worst-case complexity of the algorithm is $O(n^2)$, for several classes of polygons it runs in linear time. The practical advantages of the algorithm are that it is simple and does not require sorting or the use of balanced tree structures. On the theoretical side it is of interest because it is the first polygon triangulation algorithm the *computational* complexity of which is a function of the *output* complexity. As a side benefit we introduce a new measure of the complexity of a polygon triangulation that should find application in other contexts as well.

1. Introduction

We are concerned with triangulating a very special type of polygon in the Euclidean plane E^2 referred to as a *simple* (also *Jordan*) polygon. For any integer $n \geq 3$, we define a *polygon* or *n-gon* in the Euclidean plane E^2 as the figure $P = [x_1,x_2,...,x_n]$ formed by n points $x_1,x_2,...,x_n$ in E^2 and n line segments $[x_i,x_{i+1}]$, i=1,2,...,n-1, and $[x_n,x_1]$. The points x_i are called the *vertices* of the *polygon* and the line segments are termed its *edges*. A polygon P is called a *simple* polygon provided that no point of the plane belongs to more than two edges of P and the only points of the plane that belong to precisely two edges are the vertices of P. A simple polygon has a well defined interior and exterior. We will follow the convention of including the interior of a polygon when referring to P.

Our problem is that of constructing a *triangulation* of P, i.e., decomposing P into a set of non-overlapping triangles (their interiors do not intersect) without adding new vertices. Mathematicians have been interested in constructive proofs (algorithms) of the existence of triangulations for simple polygons as early as 1911 [Le]. The "algorithm" of Lennes [Le] works by recursively inserting diagonals between pairs of vertices of P and runs in $O(n^2)$ time. Since then this type of "algorithm" has reappeared in a score of papers and text books during the past seventy years very often and surprisingly containing fundamental errors. See the paper by Chung-Wu Ho [Ho] for a series of counter-examples to published triangulation "proofs." A rather different inductive proof was offered more recently by Meisters [Me]. He proposed a method based on searching for "ears" and "cutting" them off. We call a vertex x_i of polygon P a *principal* vertex provided that no vertex of P lies in the interior of the triangle $[x_{i-1},x_i,x_{i+1}]$ or in the interior of the diagonal $[x_{i-1},x_{i+1}]$. A *principal* vertex x_i of a simple polygon P is called an *ear* if the diagonal $[x_{i-1},x_{i+1}]$ that bridges x_i lies entirely in P. We say that two ears x_i and x_j are *non-overlapping* if $int[x_{i-1},x_i,x_{i+1}] \cap int[x_{j-1},x_j,x_{j+1}] = \emptyset$. The following *Two-Ears* Theorem was proved by Meisters [Me].

Theorem: (the *Two-Ears* Theorem, Meisters [Me]) Except for triangles every simple polygon P has at least two *non-overlapping ears*.

A straightforward implementation of this idea leads to a complexity of $O(n^3)$. However, it was recently discovered that a prune-and-search technique will actually find an ear in linear time thus yielding an $O(n^2)$ implementation of Meisters' algorithm [EET].

The first algorithm to break the $O(n^2)$ upper bound was that of Garey, Johnson, Preparata & Tarjan [GJPT]. Their algorithm runs in time O(n log n) which is the time required by the first step to decompose the polygon into monotone sub-polygons. Then they apply an algorithm for triangulating monotone polygons in linear time. Note that a simpler linear-time algorithm for the latter problem is now available [To1]. An alternate decomposition method with the same complexity appears in [FM]. An entirely different *divide-and-conquer* approach by Chazelle [Ch] also achieves an O(n log n) upper bound. Finally this upper bound was reduced even further by Tarjan & Van Wyk [TV]. With very complicated and sophisticated data structures they are able to triangulate a simple polygon in O(n log log n) time. However, recently the same complexity was demonstrated using simple data structures [KKT].

It remains one of the most outstanding open problems in computational geometry to determine if a simple polygon can be triangulated in O(n) time. As an alternative some researchers are looking for large classes of polygons that can be triangulated in linear time. Such classes include *monotone* polygons [GJPT],[To1], *star-shaped* polygons [SV],[WS], *edge-visible* polygons [TA], *spiral* polygons [FP],[T3], *L-convex* polygons [EAT], *intersection-free* polygons [LC], *weakly-externally-visible* polygons [EI], *palm-shaped* polygons [ET], and *anthropomorphic* polygons [To2]. In yet another approach to the problem researchers are looking for adaptive algorithms that will run fast in many situations. Hertel & Mehlhorn [HM] have described a sweep-line based algorithm that performs better the fewer reflex vertices it has. The running time of their method is O(n + r log r) where r denotes the number of reflex vertices of P. Hertel & Mehlhorn's algorithm takes the first step towards obtaining an adaptive algorithm sensitive to the *shape* of the polygon. Unfortunately r is not a truly relevant measure of the shape complexity. To see this it is sufficient to realize that given any polygon of no matter what shape it is a trivial matter to insert n vertices (one between every original pair) and pull them an infinitesimal amount towards the interior of the polygon. Such a transformation will make r proportional to n without changing the basic shape of the polygon.

Chazelle and Incerpi [CI] took a further step to achieve a time complexity that more faithfully reflects the *shape complexity* of the polygon. They describe a triangulation algorithm that runs in time O(n log s) with $s < n$. The quantity s measures the *sinuosity* of the polygon, i.e., the number of times the polygon's boundary alternates between complete spirals of opposite orientation. Unlike r, s has the advantage that in many practical situations it is very small or a constant even for very winding polygons. Consider the motion of a straight line $L[x_i,x_{i+1}]$ passing through edge $[x_i,x_{i+1}]$ as i goes from 1 to n-1. Every time $L[x_i,x_{i+1}]$ reaches the vertical position in a clockwise (respectively counter-clockwise) manner we increment (respectively decrement) a *winding-counter* by one. $L[x_i,x_{i+1}]$ is said to be *spiraling* (respectively *anti-spiraling*) if the winding counter is never decremented (respectively incremented) twice in succession. In this way the polygon may be decomposed easily in O(n) time into spiraling and anti-spiraling polygonal chains. An example of a polygon with a sinuosity of five is shown in Fig. 1. Note that a new polygonal chain is restarted only when the previous chain ceases to be spiraling or anti-spiraling. The *sinuosity* s of P is defined as the number of polygonal chains thus obtained.

The Chazelle-Incerpi algorithm is much more interesting theoretically than the algorithm of Hertel & Mehlhorn because of the implications it has on the complexity of triangulating different known classes of polygons. Since r, the number of reflex vertices, is independent of whether a polygon is *monotonic, star-shaped, edge-visible* or whatever, Hertel & Mehlhorn's algorithm can run in O(n log n) time for these classes of polygons for which linear time algorithms are known. On the other hand *star-shaped* polygons have a sinuosity of one and thus the Chazelle-Incerpi algorithm runs in linear time for these polygons. Furthermore the algorithm makes no use of the *kernel* of P. In [SV] and [WS] a point in the *kernel* is required and this implies a non-trivial (although linear time) effort. For a completely different and extremely simple algorithm for triangulating a *star-shaped* polygon without making use of the *kernel* of P see [ET1] or [ET2]. However, the sinuosity is not completely satisfactory as a measure of the shape complexity. It has the disconcerting property that it can vary by an order of magnitude depending on the orientation of the input polygon. Consider the *edge-visible* polygon illustrated in Fig. 2. Recall that a polygon P is edge visible if there exists an edge [u,v] of P such that for each point x in P there exists a point y in [u,v] such that the line segment [x,y] lies in P. The sinuosity for the polygon in Fig. 2 is O(n) and thus the Chazelle-Incerpi algorithm runs in O(n log n) time on this polygon whereas a linear-time algorithm exists [TA]. Furthermore by rotating the polygon through an angle of 90 degrees the sinuosity reduces to O(1). This represents an order of magnitude change in the *sinuosity* of P for no change in the *shape* of P (naturally we assume shape is invariant under translation and rotation).

In this paper we describe a new algorithm for triangulating a simple n-sided polygon. The algorithm runs in time $O(n(1+t_0))$, with $t_0 < n$. The quantity t_0 measures the complexity of the triangulation delivered by the algorithm. More precisely t_0 is the number of triangles in the output triangulation obtained that share zero edges with the input polygon and is related to the *shape-complexity* of the

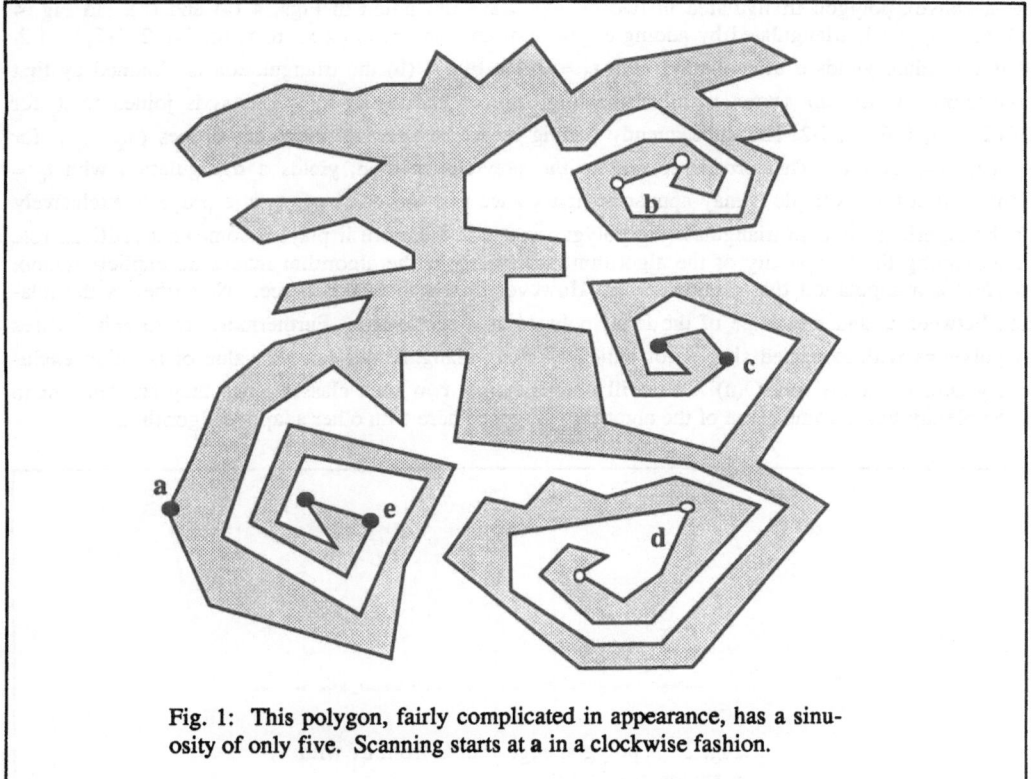

Fig. 1: This polygon, fairly complicated in appearance, has a sinuosity of only five. Scanning starts at a in a clockwise fashion.

polygon. Although the worst-case complexity of the algorithm is $O(n^2)$, for several classes of polygons it runs in linear time. The practical advantages of the algorithm are that it is extremely simple and does not require sorting or the use of balanced tree structures. On the theoretical side it is of interest because it is the first polygon triangulation algorithm whose *computational* complexity is a function of the *output* complexity. Section 2 discusses a new measure that we propose as the complexity of a triangulation of a polygon. The algorithm is presented in Sections 3 & 4 and some concluding remarks are offered in Section 5.

2. A Measure of the Complexity of a Triangulation

The graph theoretical dual of every polygon triangulation is a tree (see Fig. 3). The nature of a tree suggests a rather natural measure of its shape complexity, namely, its fragmentation, arborescence or "branchiness." Is a tree like a *palm* tree or more like an *oak* ? Is it locally very different and smoother than it is globally or is it self-similar in the way *fractals* [Ma] are? There are a variety of methods of quantitatively measuring such fragmentation. The *degree* of a node in a tree is an integer that indicates the number of edges emanating from that node. In a tree that is the dual of a polygon triangulation the nodes are all of degree one, two, or three. For our purposes a good measure of the amount of branching in a tree is its number of nodes of degree three. Let t_i denote the number of triangles in a triangulated polygon T(P) that share i edges with P. It is clear that t_0, which we also refer to as the number of "free" triangles in T(P), corresponds to the number of nodes of degree three in the dual tree of T(P). Thus t_0 is a very natural measure of the complexity of a triangulation. This is not to say that it is necessarily a good measure of the *shape-complexity* of P. Consider for example a convex polygon triangulated in two distinct ways illustrated in Figs. 4 (a) and (b). In Fig. 4 (a) the polygon is triangulated by adding edges from an *anchor* vertex x_i to x_j for j=i+2, i+3, ..., i-2. This procedure yields a triangulation with $t_0 = 0$. In Fig. 4 (b) the triangulation is obtained by first connecting the *anchor* vertex to all alternating vertices starting at x_{i+2}, i.e., x_i is joined to x_j for j=i+2, i+4, i+6, ..., i-2, and subsequently adding edges between *all pairs of vertices* (x_k, x_{k+2}) *for* k=i+2, i+4, ..., i-4. This procedure, unlike the previous method, yields a triangulation with t_0 = O(n). From this example it may appear at first glance that the value of t_0 is a property exclusively of the algorithm used to triangulate the polygon and that therefore it plays a somewhat artificial role in measuring the complexity of the algorithm particularly if the algorithm makes no explicit attempt to yield a triangulation that minimizes t_0. However this is in fact not true. Nevertheless the relation between t_0 and the shape of the input polygon is a subtle one. Furthermore, there exist classes of polygons with restricted shapes for which all their triangulations have a value of t_0 either exclusively zero or exclusively O(n). We will now illustrate two such classes since they are relevant to a complexity-based comparison of the algorithm proposed here with other adaptive algorithms.

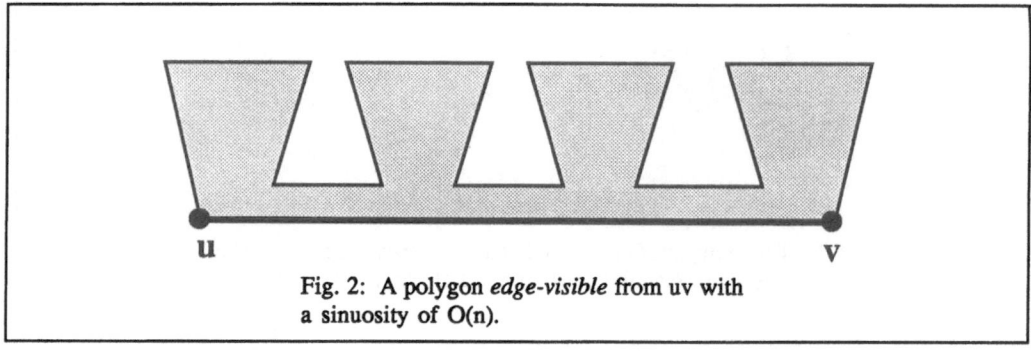

Fig. 2: A polygon *edge-visible* from uv with a sinuosity of O(n).

Consider the *anthropomorphic* polygon illustrated in Fig. 4 (c). A simple polygon P is called *anthropomorphic* provided it contains precisely two ears and one *mouth* [To2]. A *principal* vertex x_i of a simple polygon P is called a *mouth* if the diagonal $[x_{i-1},x_{i+1}]$ is an *external* diagonal, i.e., the interior of $[x_{i-1},x_{i+1}]$ lies in the exterior of P. Surprisingly, although anthropomorphic polygons are quite structured in some ways, they are quite general in other ways. Fig. 4 (c) illustrates an uncomplicated anthropomorphic polygon. Shermer [Sh2] has considered the problem of generating more complex anthropomorphic polygons. The crucial aspect for our purpose here is that for an *anthropomorphic* polygon $t_0 = 0$ for all its triangulations. This is so because the *dual-tree* of every triangulation of a two-ear polygon is a *chain*, i.e., a tree in which all its nodes are of degree either one or two. This suggests that the extreme values of t_0 over all triangulations of a given polygon may be more appropriate measures of the shape of a polygon in certain applications. In this case, for example, since the minimum value of t_0 for any convex polygon is zero, both polygons in Figs. 4 (a) and (b) would have the same shape complexity.

It is also possible that a polygon will admit only a single triangulation and that its value of t_0 = O(n). Such a family is illustrated in Fig. 4 (d). Let the vertices x_{i-1}, x_i, x_{i+1} have coordinates (0,1), (0,-1), and (1,0), respectively and insert edges $[x_{i-1},x_i]$ and $[x_i,x_{i+1}]$. Place two thirds of the remaining n-3 vertices on *C*, the smaller of the two arcs of a unit circle centered at (1,1). Starting with the first of these vertices, connect with an edge each adjacent alternating pair and call these vertices "red." Finally, place the remaining vertices, called "blue," sufficiently far from this circular arc *C* such that each of them is connected to a pair of adjacent red vertices on *C* not yet connected to each other such that no blue vertex is visible from x_i. Recall that two points x,y in P are visible from each other if the line segment [x,y] lies in P.

Consider now triangulating P. A blue vertex x_k is not visible from any vertex of P non-adjacent to x_k. Therefore all blue vertices are ears of P. Therefore all triangulations of P must contain the blue vertices as ears of T(P). It remains to triangulate $P^* = [x_i,x_{i+1},x_{i+3},x_{i+4},x_{i+6},x_{i+7},\ldots,x_{i-4},x_{i-3},x_{i-1}]$. However, all the vertices of this polygon other than x_i form a concave chain and thus the only way to

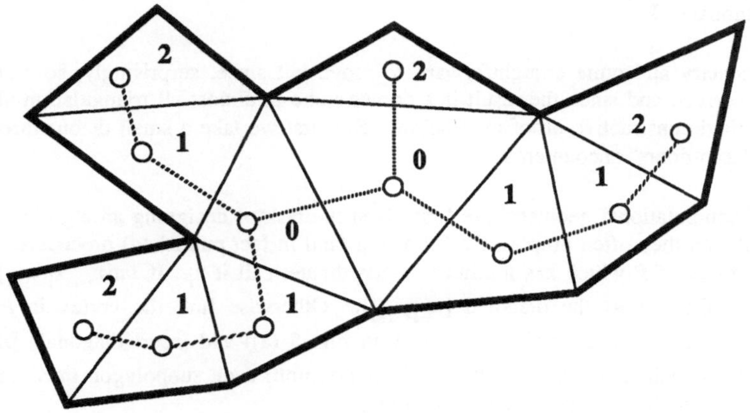

Fig. 3 A triangulation (solid lines) of a simple polygon P, its *dual tree* (dotted lines), and the integer value t_i associated with each triangle.

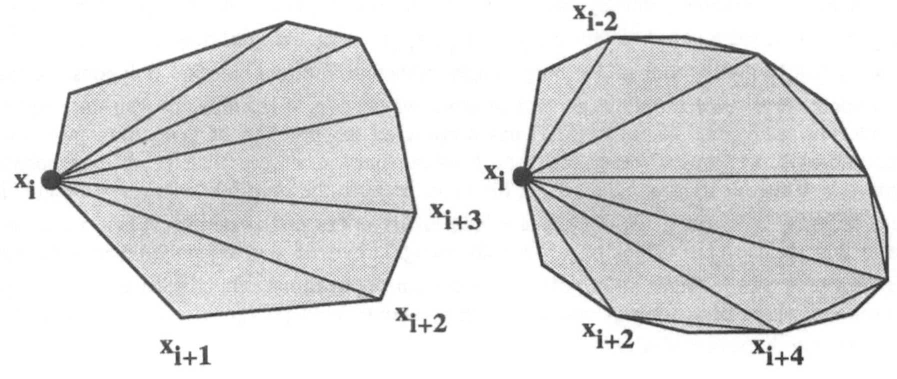

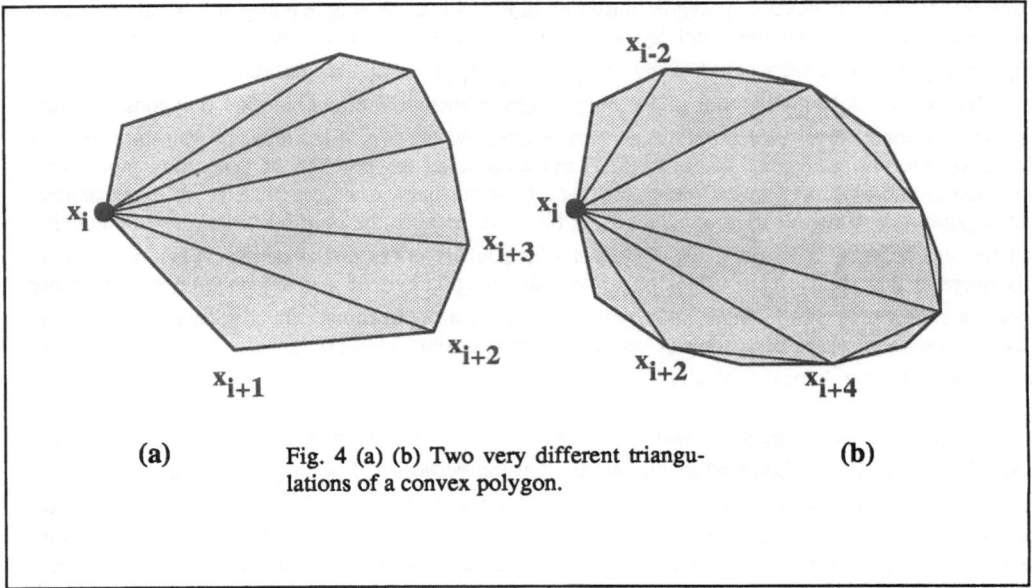

Fig. 4 (a) (b) Two very different triangulations of a convex polygon.

triangulate P* is to join x_i to all the vertices on this chain other than x_{i-1} and x_{i+1}. This results in the only possible triangulation with a value of $t_0 = O(n)$.

3. Finding a Diagonal in a Simple Polygon

A fundamental lemma that is often used to prove by induction that a polygon triangulation always exists (which surprisingly is not true in three dimensions [RS]) and which forms the backbone of most triangulation algorithms concerns the existence of diagonals.

Lemma 1: Every simple n-gon P with $n \geq 4$ can be partitioned into two sub-polygons in O(n) time by inserting some diagonal of P.

Lemma 1 is elementary and quite straightforward to prove but since, surprisingly, so many published proofs of it are incorrect, and since the result is a corner stone in almost all triangulation algorithms we will include a detailed constructive proof of it below. But first we take a small detour through some of the most frequent "trap-doors" encountered.

When students of computational geometry are first given the task of designing an algorithm for triangulating a simple polygon they often propose the following (and in fact published) procedure. (refer to Fig. 5 (a)) Find the vertex of P which has minimum x-coordinate; call it x_i. If $int[x_{i-1},x_i,x_{i+1}]$ contains no other vertices of P then insert the diagonal $[x_{i-1},x_{i+1}]$. Otherwise find the vertex in $int[x_{i-1},x_i,x_{i+1}]$ whose Euclidean distance to x_i is smallest (vertex v in Fig. 5 (a)) and insert diagonal $[x_i,v]$. Recursively continue this procedure on each resulting subpolygon until each subpolygon thus created is a triangle. A counter-example to this algorithm is given in Fig. 5 (b).

A proof of lemma 1 appears in Knopp's *Funktionentheorie* [Kn1]. During translation F. Bagemihl discovered that the original proof was incorrect and inserted a proof of his own, also incorrect as it turns out. Bagemihl chose the vertex p in $int[x_{i-1},x_i,x_{i+1}]$ such that the $\angle x_{i-1}x_i\, p$ is smallest (vertex u in

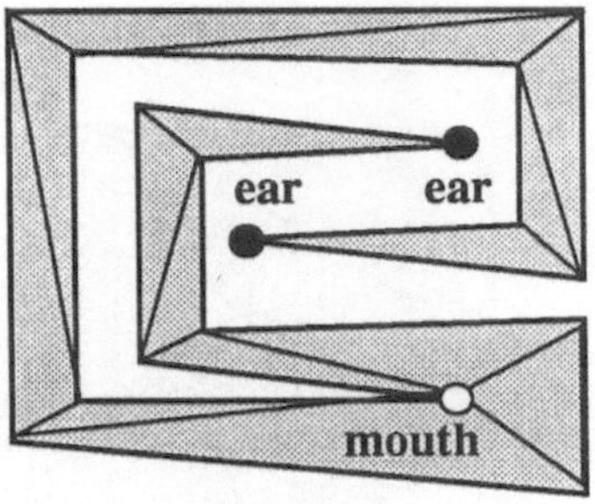

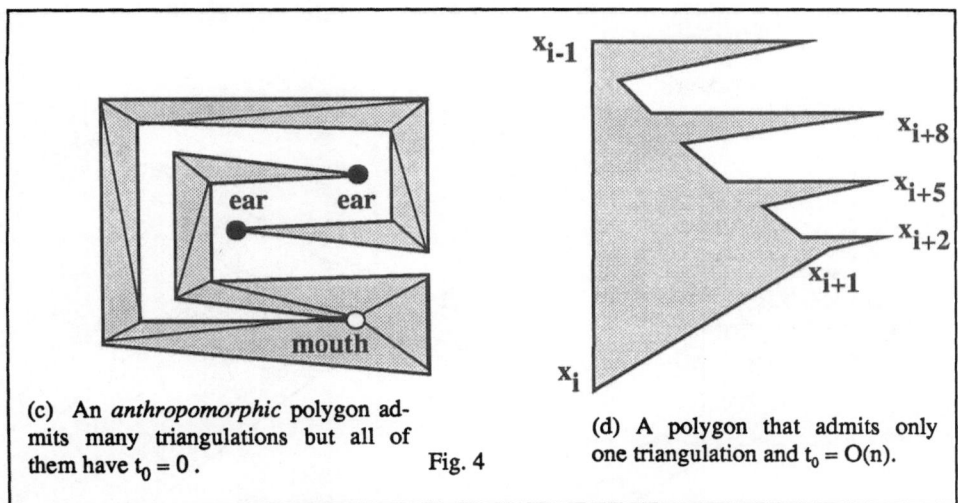

(c) An *anthropomorphic* polygon admits many triangulations but all of them have $t_0 = 0$.

Fig. 4

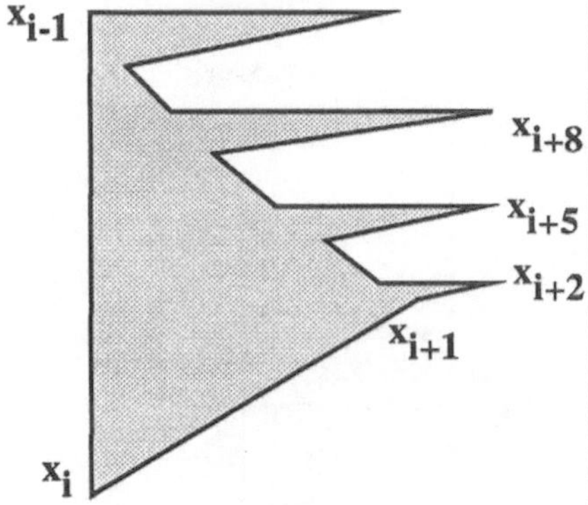

(d) A polygon that admits only one triangulation and $t_0 = O(n)$.

Fig. 5 (a)). A counterexample to this proof is given in Fig. 5 (c). We note here that the new German edition of ***Funktionentheorie*** has a new proof [Kn2]. Several other incorrect proofs have also appeared. See for example Forder [Fo] and Cairns [Ca]. Cairns chose the vertex p in $int[x_{i-1},x_i,x_{i+1}]$ such that p has the second least abscissa after x_i (vertex w in Fig. 5 (a)). A counterexample to this situation is given in Fig. 5 (d). For a discussion on several correct and incorrect proofs the reader is referred to the paper by Chung-Wu Ho [Ho]. Our proof given below is a constructive version of Levy's proof [Le1] and will also establish that such a diagonal can be found in O(n) time. We present it in the form of an algorithm called *PROCEDURE* DIAGONAL (refer to Fig. 6).

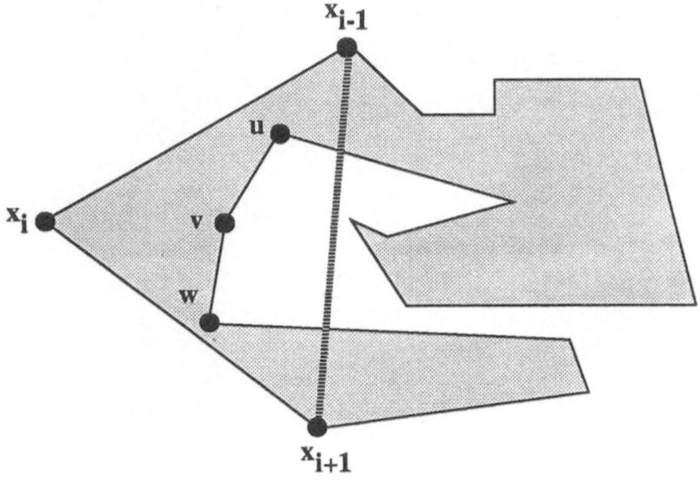

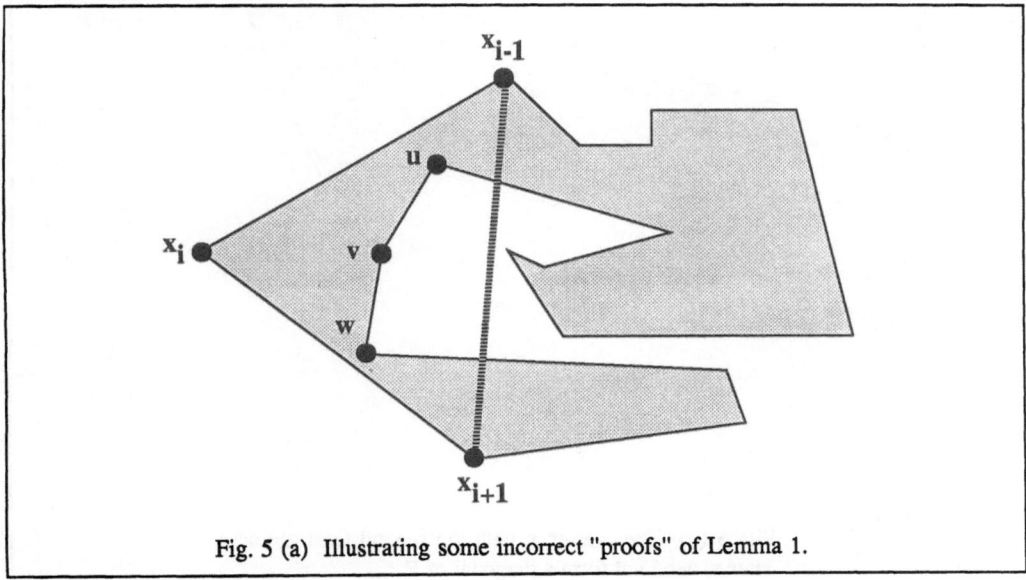

Fig. 5 (a) Illustrating some incorrect "proofs" of Lemma 1.

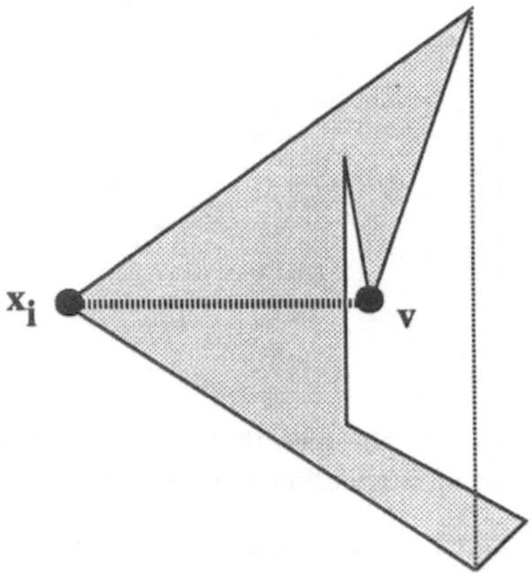

Fig. 5 (b) The closest vertex v to x_i need not form a diagonal of P.

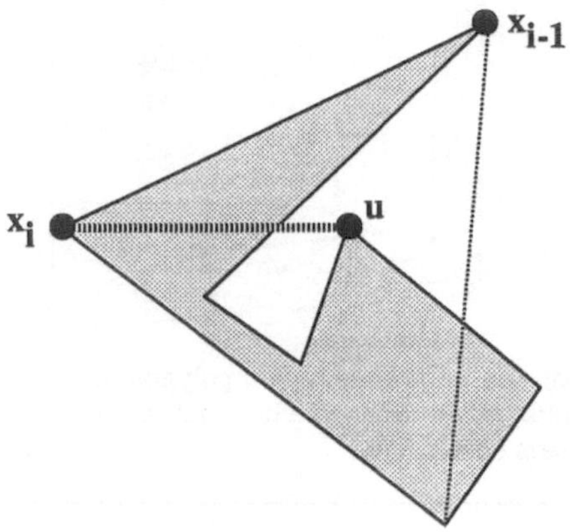

Fig. 5 (c) The vertex u that has smallest $\angle x_{i-1}x_iu$ need not form a diagonal.

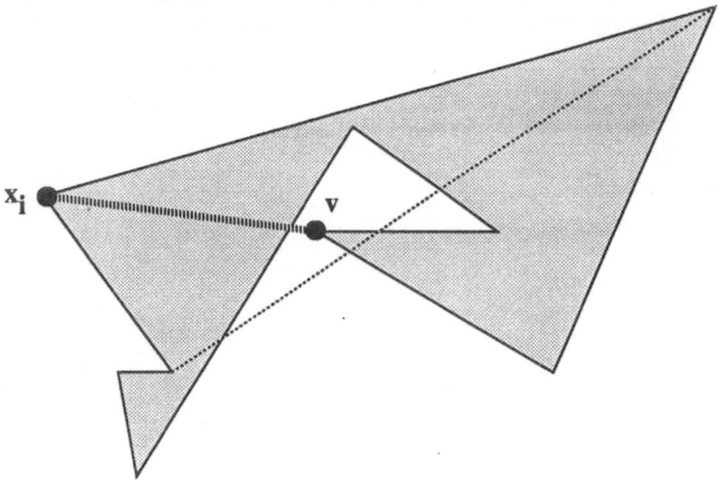

Fig. 5 (d) The vertex v with the second least abscissa after x_i need not form a diagonal of P.

==

PROCEDURE DIAGONAL

Input: A simple polygon P oriented in a counterclockwise direction.
Output: Polygon P with a *diagonal* inserted in P.

Begin

Step 1: Find a convex vertex x_i of P.

Step 2: Construct a ray at x_i, *ray*(x_i), that bisects the interior of $\angle x_{i-1}x_ix_{i+1}$.

Step 3: Find the first intersection point of *ray*(x_i) with *bd*(P) . Let y be the intersection point on edge $[x_j,x_{j+1}]$; **If** y is a vertex of P, **Exit** with $[x_i,y]$ as the *diagonal.*

Step 4: Construct the triangle $[x_i,y,x_{j+1}]$.

Step 5: For all $j+1 < k < i$ if x_k lies in triangle $[x_i,y,x_{j+1}]$ label x_k as x^*_k.
If there are no labeled vertices, **Exit** with $[x_i,x_{j+1}]$ as the *diagonal.*

Step 6: For all labeled vertices compute $\angle yx_ix^*_k$ and select that vertex (call it z) that minimizes this angle. **If** $z \neq x_{i-1}$, **Exit** with $[x_i,z]$ as the *diagonal.*

Step 7: Construct the triangle $[x_j,y,x_i]$.

Step 8: For all $j > k > i$ if x_k lies in triangle $[x_j,y,x_i]$ label x_k as x^*_k.
If there are no labeled vertices, **Exit** with $[x_i,x_j]$ as the *diagonal.*

Step 9: For all labeled vertices compute $\angle yx_ix^*_k$ and select that vertex (call it w) that minimizes this angle. **If** $w \neq x_{i+1}$, **Exit** with $[x_i,w]$ as the *diagonal.*

Step 10: **Exit** with $[x_{i-1},x_{i+1}]$ as the *diagonal.*

End

==

Proof of Lemma 1: *Procedure* DIAGONAL establishes that a diagonal can always be found. Therefore let us consider its complexity. A convex vertex can always be found in O(n) time since any extreme vertex of P is convex. Thus it suffices to pick the vertex with maximum y coordinate for example. Steps 2,4,7 and 10 are constant time operations. The first intersection point y in step 3 can be found in O(n) time by simply scanning all the edges of P in the order in which they occur and testing each for intersection with *ray*(x_i). The complexity of step 5 is clearly O(n). Its correctness follows from the Jordan Curve Theorem and the fact that $[x_i,y]$ is a chord of P. The complexity of step 6 is clearly also linear and its correctness follows from the fact that by construction *int*$[x_i,y,z']$ $\cap$ *bd*(P) = $\emptyset$, where z' is the intersection of the line colinear with $[x_i,z]$ that intersects $[x_j,x_{j+1}]$. Steps 8 and 9 are similar to 5 and 6. Q.E.D.

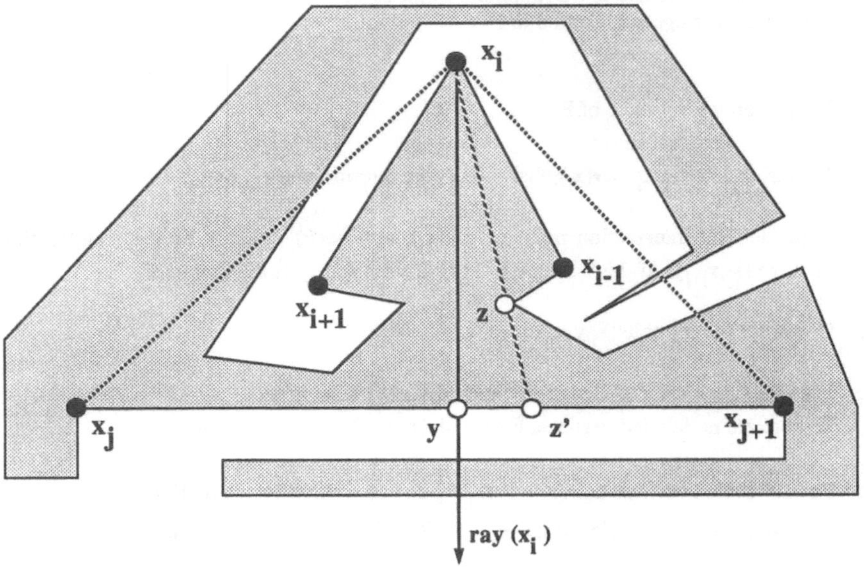

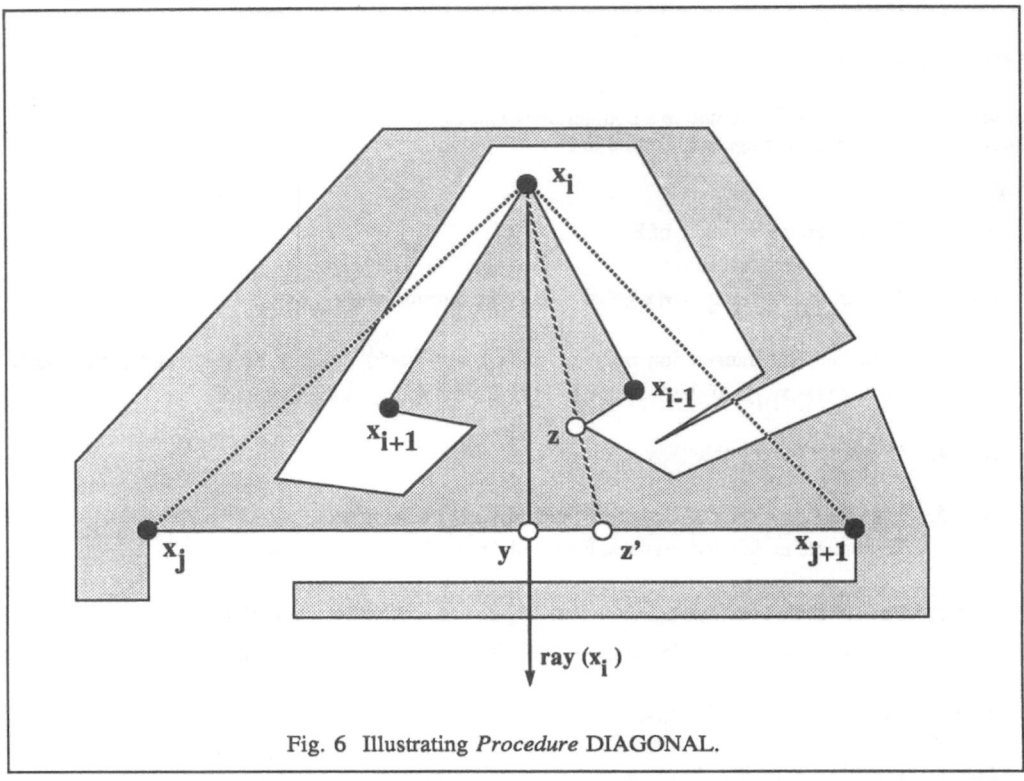

Fig. 6 Illustrating *Procedure* DIAGONAL.

4. The New Triangulation Algorithm

A triangulated polygon can be viewed as the "gluing" together of a set of *sleeves.* A *sleeve* is a triangulated polygon whose dual-tree is a chain. The new algorithm proposed here in effect performs a "blind" search for sleeves. Initially the algorithm finds a diagonal **d** and proceeds to attempt to triangulate the polygon in both directions starting from the initial diagonal assuming that the polygon is in fact a sleeve as "viewed" from **d.** If it detects at some point in time that the assumed sleeve it is triangulating is no longer a sleeve the algorithm backtracks undoing the triangulation until the triangulated portion is a *bona-fide* sleeve. At this stage two new diagonals are inserted (identifying a triangle corresponding to a node of degree three in the dual tree of the triangulation completed thus far) and the algorithm begins again recursively from these two new diagonals which themselves will appear in the final triangulation. Before we describe the algorithm in more detail we present a series of lemmas we will need to establish the correctness and complexity of the algorithm.

It is well known and clear from *Step 10* of *Procedure* DIAGONAL that a *convex* vertex of a simple polygon P does not always admit a diagonal in T(P). Much less well known is the result that every *concave* vertex on the other hand does admit a diagonal as the following lemma establishes. In fact we prove a stronger property. In the following we denote by $H(x_i,x_{i+1})$ the open half-plane to the left of the directed line $L[x_i,x_{i+1}]$. Here $L[x_i,x_{i+1}]$ denotes the line colinear with x_i and x_{i+1} and the direction is determined by orienting from x_i to x_{i+1}.

Lemma 2: Let x_i be a *concave* vertex of a polygon P. Then P admits a diagonal $[x_i,x_j]$ such that x_j lies in $H(x_{i-1},x_i)$ and furthermore, such a diagonal can be identified in O(n) time.

Proof: Let x_i be a *concave* vertex of P and refer to Fig. 7 for illustration. As in Lemma 1 we construct a ray $r(x_i)$ that bisects the internal angle at x_i and find the intersection point y of this ray with *bd*(P). By construction x_i and y are visible and $y \in H(x_{i-1},x_i)$. Actually in this case it is also true that $y \in H(x_i,x_{i+1})$. Therefore if y is a vertex of P we are done. Therefore assume y lies in the interior of some edge [A,B] of P and consider the triangle $\Delta\ yBx_i$. We proceed in a manner similar to that described in the proof of Lemma 1 to look for a vertex in $CH[B,...,x_{i-1}]$ other than x_{i-1} that is visible from x_i with the added requirement that such a vertex x_j not only lie in *int*($\Delta\ yBx_i$) but also in $H(x_{i-1},x_i)$. If such a vertex is found we are done. Therefore assume that no such vertex exists for $CH[B,...,x_{i-1}]$ and consider $\Delta\ Ayx_i$. We determine whether a vertex of $CH[x_i,...,A]$ lies in *int*($\Delta\ Ayx_i$). If not then A is visible from x_i. Furthermore, since $L[x_i,x_{i-1}]$ intersects *int*[A,B] it follows that *int*($\Delta\ Ayx_i$) $\in H(x_{i-1},x_i)$. Therefore $A=x_j$ and we have our desired diagonal. On the other hand, if vertices of $CH[x_i,...,A]$ do lie in $\Delta\ Ayx_i$ then we proceed as in the proof of Lemma 1 to find a vertex x_j visible to x_i and exit with this diagonal. It is straightforward to verify that all the steps can be performed in O(n) time. Q.E.D.

Lemma 3: Let x_i and x_{i-1} be two adjacent *concave* vertices in a simple polygon P. Then there exists a vertex x_k, $k \neq i,i-1$ such that $[x_i,x_k,x_{i-1}]$ forms a triangle in a triangulation of P and furthermore, x_k can be identified in O(n) time.

Proof: Lemma 2 implies that x_i admits a diagonal of P, $[x_i,x_k]$ such that $x_k \in H(x_{i-1},x_i)$ and such that x_k can be found in O(n) time. If x_{i-1} is visible from x_k we are done. If not we scan $CH[x_k,...,x_{i-1}]$ to determine which of its vertices lie in $\Delta\ x_kx_{i-1}x_i$ and of these we select the vertex x_{k*} that minimizes the angle $\angle\ x_{k*}x_{i-1}x_i$ which lies in $\angle\ x_kx_{i-1}x_i$. This can be done in O(n) time. Since x_{i-1} is a concave vertex it follows that x_{i-2} cannot lie in $H(x_{i-1},x_i)$ and cannot be a candidate for either x_k or x_{k*} , thus ensuring that $[x_i,x_{k*}]$ is not an edge of P. Therefore in either case we are guaranteed that x_k or x_{k*} are visible from both x_i and x_{i-1} and together they form a *free* triangle in some triangulation of P. Q.E.D.

Any diagonal **d** of P partitions P into two sub-polygons P_1 and P_2. The triangulation algorithm we will describe begins by finding a diagonal **d** using *Procedure* DIAGONAL given in section 3 and subsequently, starting at **d** triangulates one of the sub-polygons in a single pass. A second pass starting at **d** in the opposite direction triangulates the second sub-polygon. We will refer to the step used to find **d** as the *initialization* phase and the subsequent steps as the *triangulation* phase.

Consider for the moment that at some stage in the execution of the triangulation phase of the algorithm, diagonal $\mathbf{d}_{ij}$ has been inserted between vertices x_i and x_j and refer to Fig. 8. Let $CH[x_i,..., x_j]$ denote the portion of the polygonal boundary of $P = [x_1,x_2,...,x_n]$ from x_i to x_j in a counterclockwise orientation. Assume that the diagonal **d** added connects vertices x_u and x_v. Therefore the polygon $[x_v,...,x_i,x_j,...,x_u]$ has already been triangulated. Note however that all of this triangulation may not be possible in P and a portion of it may have to be undone at some later stage in the execution of the

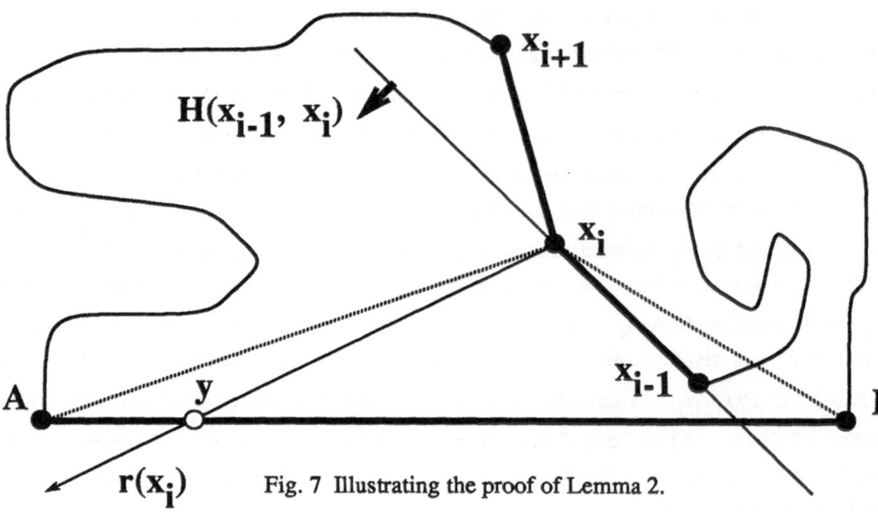

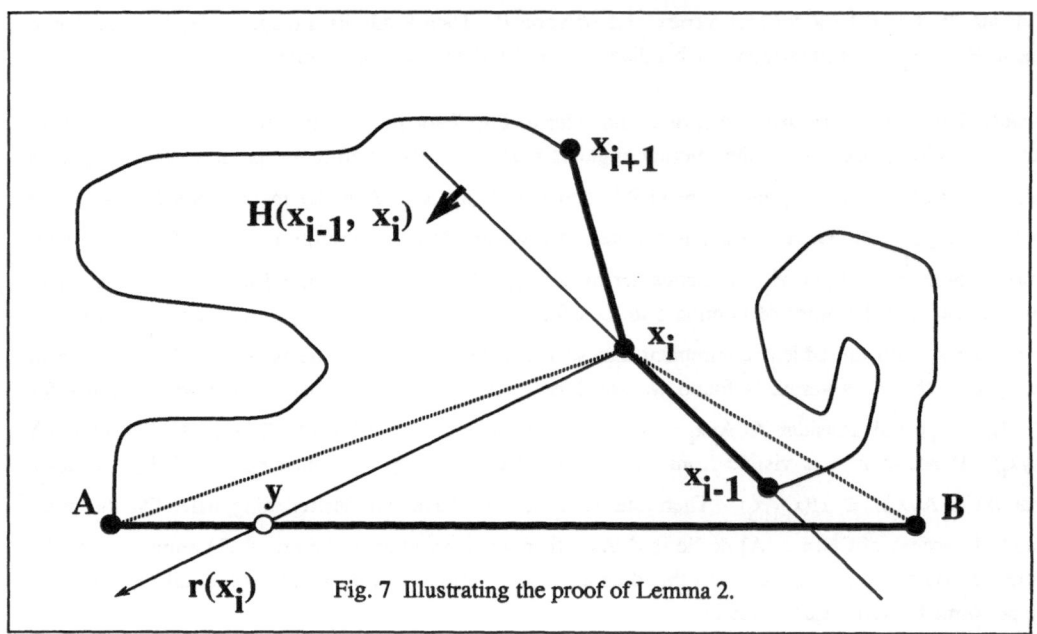

Fig. 7 Illustrating the proof of Lemma 2.

algorithm. Let Wedge[$x_i x_j x_{i-1}$] denote the region of the plane swept out by a ray anchored at x_i as it sweeps in a clockwise manner starting from a position colinear with x_j and ending in a position colinear with x_{i-1} and refer to Fig. 9. In order to add a new diagonal we test to determine if [x_i,x_{i+1}] lies in Wedge[$x_i x_j x_{i-1}$], (we refer to this as condition A), or [x_j,x_{j-1}] lies in Wedge[$x_j x_{j+1} x_i$], (we refer to this as condition B). We then have the following lemmas.

Lemma 4: Let $\mathbf{d}_{ij}$ be a line segment joining x_i to x_j in P. If either condition A *or* condition B

(A) $[x_i, x_{i+1}] \in$ Wedge[$x_i x_j x_{i-1}$],

(B) $[x_j, x_{j-1}] \in$ Wedge[$x_j x_{j+1} x_i$],

does *not* hold then $\mathbf{d}_{ij}$ cannot be a diagonal of any triangulation of P.

Proof: If both conditions (A) and (B) are violated then by the Jordan Curve Theorem it follows that $\mathbf{d}_{ij}$ is an *external* diagonal of P or CH[x_i,...,x_j] intersects $\mathbf{d}_{ij}$ at least twice. If only one of conditions (A) or (B) is exclusively true then CH[x_i,...,x_j] intersects $\mathbf{d}_{ij}$ at least once. In all three cases $\mathbf{d}_{ij}$ is invalidated as a candidate for a diagonal of T(P). Q.E.D.

As we mentioned earlier, at some steps in the execution of the triangulation phase of the algorithm it may be required to undo a portion of the triangulation constructed thus far. Such an action involves the possibility of doing a linear amount of work and therefore, in all such situations, we must be sure that a *free* triangle will be added in T(P). Lemma 5 below together with lemma 3 will ensure the desired outcome. Assume for the moment that the chain CH[x_j,...,x_i] of P has been triangulated as a sleeve

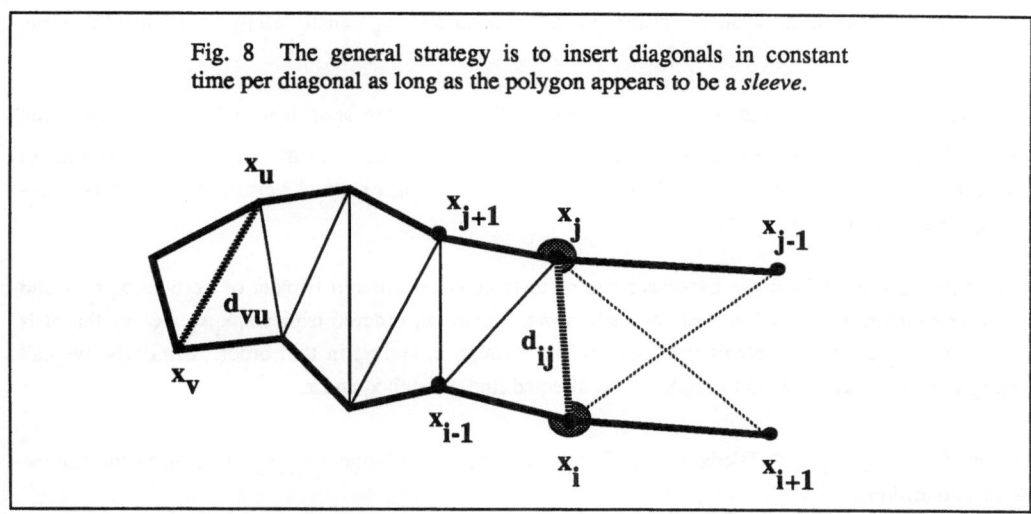

Fig. 8 The general strategy is to insert diagonals in constant time per diagonal as long as the polygon appears to be a *sleeve.*

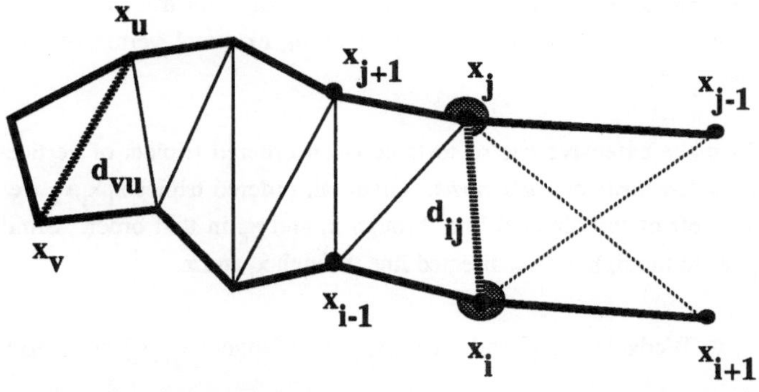

(denoted by $T(CH_{ij})$) using O(1) time per diagonal insertion and that it is discovered at the next step that either condition A ($[x_i,x_{i+1}] \in$ Wedge$[x_ix_jx_{i-1}]$) or condition B ($[x_j,x_{j-1}] \in$ Wedge$[x_jx_{j+1}x_i]$) is violated and refer to Fig. 9. This implies that $CH[x_i,...,x_j]$ either intersects $\mathbf{d}_{ij}$ and possibly at least one other diagonal of $T(CH_{ij})$, does not intersect $\mathbf{d}_{ij}$ but possibly at least one other diagonal of $T(CH_{ij})$ or it does not intersect any diagonal of $T(CH_{ij})$ in which case it lies completely in the triangle of $T(CH_{ij})$ determined by $\mathbf{d}_{ij}$. In either of the three cases it follows that $\mathbf{d}_{ij}$ cannot be a diagonal of T(P) and some diagonals (at least $\mathbf{d}_{ij}$) must be removed from $T(CH_{ij})$. Since $T(CH_{ij})$ is a sleeve the diagonals, as well as the triangles they flank, are ordered. Furthermore, since the dual of $T(CH_{ij})$ is a chain it follows that all but the last triangle in $T(CH_{ij})$ must have precisely one of its edges as an edge of P. Let $\Delta\, x_rx_sx_t$ denote the "deepest" triangle (furthest from $\mathbf{d}_{ij}$ in $T(CH_{ij})$) the interior of which is intersected by $CH[x_i,...,x_j]$. Without loss of generality assume that $[x_s,x_t]$ is the edge of $\Delta\, x_rx_sx_t$ that is also an edge of P and that $[x_{i-1},x_i]$ is the edge of $\Delta\, x_{i-1}x_ix_j$ that is also an edge of P. Therefore $CH[x_i,...,x_j]$ properly intersects $[x_r,x_t]$ but does not intersect $[x_r,x_s]$. Furthermore, assume that $x_{j-1} \notin$ *int* $\Delta\, x_ix_jx_{i-1}$. We now show that among the vertices of $CH[x_i,...,x_j]$ that lie in the interior of $\Delta\, x_rx_sx_t$ there is at least one vertex x_k that is visible from both x_r and x_s and is not adjacent to either of them in P thus affording the insertion of two permanent diagonals $[x_r,x_k]$ and $[x_k,x_s]$ and forming a *free* triangle $\Delta\, x_rx_sx_k$. Furthermore, all this can be done in O(n) time.

Lemma 5: Let V_{rs} denote the set of vertices of P that lie in the interior of $\Delta\, x_rx_sx_t$ and let $x_k \in V_{rs}$ be the vertex that minimizes the angle $\angle\, x_kx_rx_s$. Then x_k is visible from both x_r and x_s, is not adjacent to either of them in P, and can be identified in O(n) time.

Proof: Let the ray emanating from x_r in the direction of x_k intersect $[x_s, x_t]$ at z_k. Then, by the definition of x_k, it follows that $\Delta\, x_rx_sz_k$ is empty. Therefore x_k is visible from both x_r and x_s. Since x_k must be different from x_t by definition, and different from x_{j-1} by assumption, it follows that x_k cannot be adjacent to either x_r or x_s in P. Using point inclusion tests x_k can be easily found in O(n) time. Q.E.D.

We should note here that the selection of x_r rather than x_s as the apex from which to measure the angles $\angle x_k x_r x_s$ for selecting x_k is crucial. The reader can easily construct an example similar to that of Fig. 5 (c) to show that with x_s as an apex the resulting extremal vertex selected is not necessarily visible from either x_r or x_s.

In the following we will make extensive use of tests between ordered triplets of vertices x_i,x_j,x_k and will refer to them as either *left turns* or *right turns*. Given an ordered triplet x_i,x_j,x_k we say that it is a *left turn* if x_i lies to the left of the directed line through x_j and x_k in that order. Similarly, we call x_i,x_j,x_k a *right turn* if x_i lies to the right of the directed line through x_j and x.

Lemma 6: Let $[x_i,x_{i+1}] \in$ Wedge$[x_i x_j x_{i-1}]$ and let $[x_j,x_{j-1}] \in$ Wedge$[x_j x_{j+1} x_i]$ and define the following two conditions:

(a) $x_{j-1} \in int\,\Delta\, x_j x_i x_{i+1}$,

(b) $x_{i+1} \in int\,\Delta\, x_j x_i x_{j-1}$.

If x_{j-1},x_j,x_i is a *left turn* and x_{i+1},x_i,x_j is *right turn* then it is impossible for conditions (a) and (b) to be satisfied simultaneously.

Proof: Assume $x_{j-1} \in int\,\Delta\, x_j x_i x_{i+1}$. By convexity $\Delta\, x_j x_i x_{i+1}$ must contain $[x_i x_{j-1}]$. It follows that $int\,\Delta\, x_j x_i x_{j-1} \in int\,\Delta\, x_j x_i x_{i+1}$. Therefore $x_{i+1} \notin int\,\Delta\, x_j x_i x_{j-1}$. A similar argument applies in the case we assume $x_{i+1} \in int\,\Delta\, x_j x_i x_{j-1}$. Q.E.D.

Lemma 7: Let $[x_i,x_{i+1}] \in$ Wedge$[x_i x_j x_{i-1}]$ and let $[x_j,x_{j-1}] \in$ Wedge$[x_j x_{j+1} x_i]$. If x_{j-1},x_j,x_i is a *left turn* or x_{i+1},x_i,x_j is *right turn* then at least one of the vertices from the set $\{x_{i+1},x_{j-1}\}$ forms a triangle with $\mathbf{d}_{ij}$ as base in the triangulation of the sleeve considered so far. Furthermore, such a vertex can be identified in O(1) time.

Proof: *Case 1:* If x_{j-1},x_j,x_i is a *left turn* and x_{i+1},x_i,x_j is a *left turn* then it follows that $x_{i+1} \notin int\,\Delta\, x_j x_i x_{j-1}$. Therefore x_{j-1} forms a valid triangle with $\mathbf{d}_{ij}$. *Case 2:* If x_{j-1},x_j,x_i is a *right turn* and x_{i+1},x_i,x_j is a *right turn* then it follows that $x_{j-1} \notin int\,\Delta\, x_j x_i x_{i+1}$. Therefore x_{i+1} forms a valid triangle with $\mathbf{d}_{ij}$. *Case 3:* If x_{j-1},x_j,x_i is a *left turn* and x_{i+1},x_i,x_j is a *right turn* then by Lemma 6 we have only three subcases to consider. *Sub-Case 3.1:* If $x_{i+1} \in int\,\Delta\, x_j x_i x_{j-1}$ then x_{i+1} is the desired vertex. *Sub-Case 3.2:* If $x_{j-1} \in int\,\Delta\, x_j x_i x_{i+1}$ then x_{j-1} is the desired vertex. *Sub-Case 3.3:* If $x_{i+1} \notin int\,\Delta\, x_j x_i x_{j-1}$ and $x_{j-1} \notin int\,\Delta\, x_j x_i x_{i+1}$ then either x_{i+1} or x_{j-1} can be chosen to form the triangle with $\mathbf{d}_{ij}$. Clearly we have only a constant number of operations in the case analysis and therefore a diagonal can be found in O(1) time. Q.E.D.

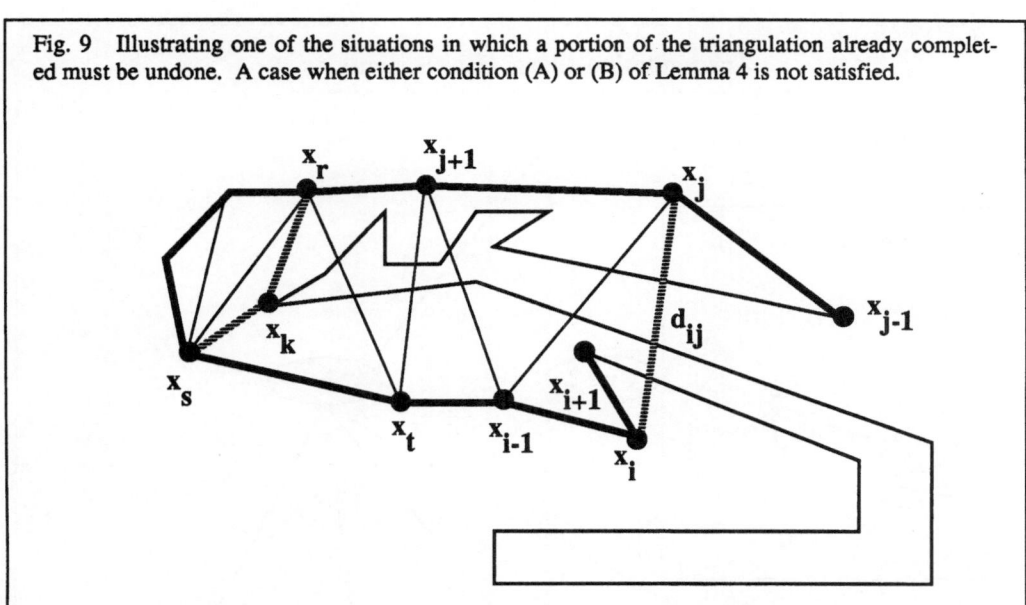

Fig. 9 Illustrating one of the situations in which a portion of the triangulation already completed must be undone. A case when either condition (A) or (B) of Lemma 4 is not satisfied.

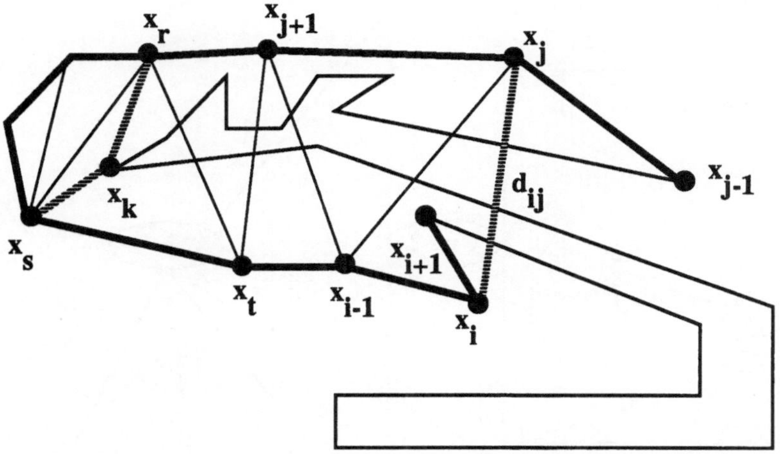

We will now describe the triangulation algorithm in simple outline form . A decision tree illustrating the case analysis considered by the triangulation phase of the algorithm is shown in Fig. 10. In the following TS[$\mathbf{d}_{ab}$,$\mathbf{d}_{cd}$], where a<b<c<d, denotes the triangulated sleeve starting at $\mathbf{d}_{ab}$=[x_a,x_b] and ending at $\mathbf{d}_{cd}$=[x_c,x_d]. }

==

ALGORITHM TRIANGULATION

Input: A simple polygon P of n sides oriented in a counterclockwise direction.

Output: Polygon P with n-3 *diagonals* inserted in P, i.e., T(P).

Begin

Step 1: Find a diagonal [x_i,x_j] of P using *PROCEDURE* DIAGONAL.

Step 2: Triangulate CH[x_i,...,x_j] using *PROCEDURE* TRIANGULATION.

Step 3: Triangulate CH[x_j,...,x_i] using *PROCEDURE* TRIANGULATION.

End

==

Triangulation-Phase Case Structure

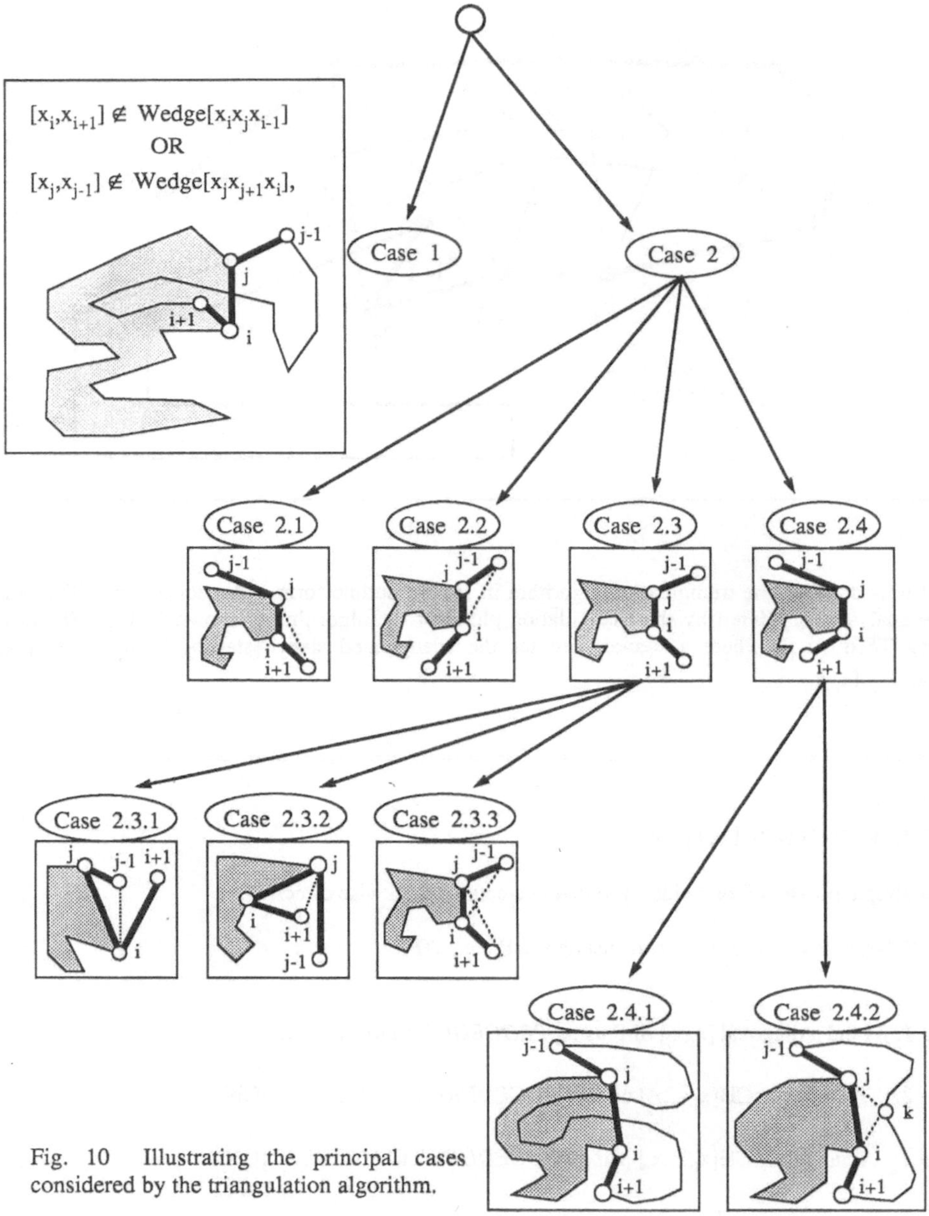

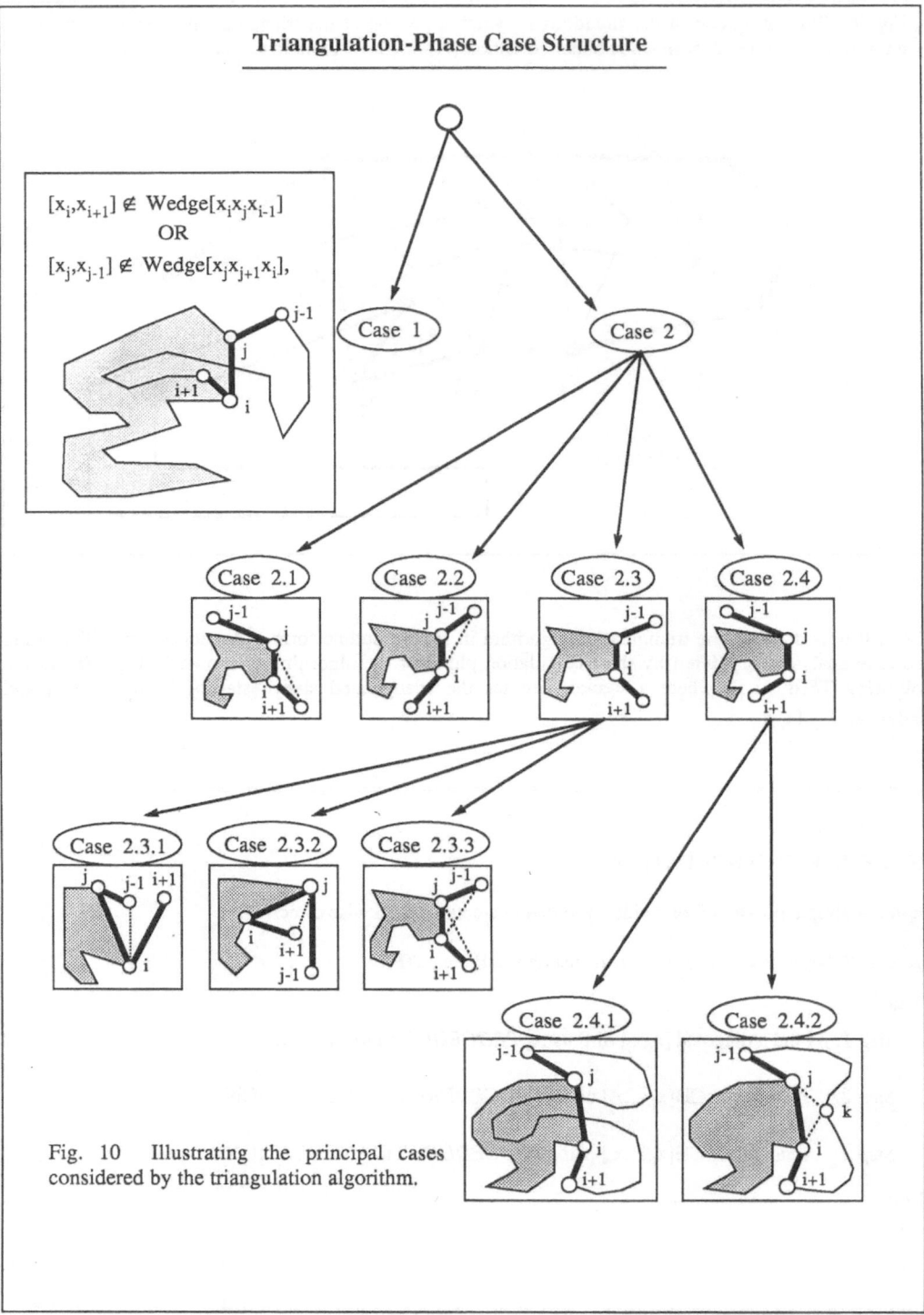

Fig. 10 Illustrating the principal cases considered by the triangulation algorithm.

PROCEDURE TRIANGULATION

==

Input: A simple polygon P of n sides oriented in a counterclockwise direction along with a diagonal $\mathbf{d}_{ab}=[x_a,x_b]$ inserted in P.

Output: Polygon P with $CH[x_a,...,x_b]$ triangulated.

Comment: {*D* is a list of diagonals on which the algorithm iterates and is initially empty. T(P) initially consists of P and at the end of execution also contains a triangulation of $CH[x_a,...,x_b]$}

Begin

Initialization Step: $D \leftarrow \mathbf{d}_{ab}$

While *D* is not empty **Do:**

1. Pick a diagonal $\mathbf{d}_{ab}=[x_a,x_b]$ from *D* and delete it from the list.

2. $i \leftarrow a$; $j \leftarrow b$.

While $i \neq j$ **Do:** {triangulating a sleeve rooted at $\mathbf{d}_{ab}$}

1.1 Test whether $[x_i,x_{i+1}] \in$ Wedge$[x_ix_jx_{i-1}]$ or $[x_j,x_{j-1}] \in$ Wedge$[x_jx_{j+1}x_i]$.

1.2 **If** either test is violated (Case 1 in Fig. 10) (a) **then** determine the deepest triangle $\Delta\, x_rx_sx_t$ in TS$[\mathbf{d}_{ab},\mathbf{d}_{ij}]$ (see Fig. 9) that contains vertices of $CH[x_{i+1},...,x_{j-1}]$; (b) determine which vertex x_k of $CH[x_{i+1},...,x_{j-1}]$ is visible to both x_r and x_s ; (c) insert diagonals $\mathbf{d}_{sk}=[x_s,x_k]$ and $\mathbf{d}_{kr}=[x_k,x_r]$ into T(P) and *D*; (d) delete all the diagonals in TS$[\mathbf{d}_{ab},\mathbf{d}_{ij}]$ starting from and including $\mathbf{d}_{ij}$ and ending with and including $\mathbf{d}_{tr}$, insert all the diagonals remaining in TS$[\mathbf{d}_{ab},\mathbf{d}_{ij}]$ into T(P) and **Exit.**

1.3. **Else** (Case 2 in Fig. 10) **If** x_{j-1},x_j,x_i is a *right turn* and x_{i+1},x_i,x_j is *right turn* (Case 2.1 in Fig. 10) **then** append $[x_{i+1},x_j]$ into TS$[\mathbf{d}_{ab},\mathbf{d}_{ij}]$ to create TS$[\mathbf{d}_{ab},\mathbf{d}_{i+1,j}]$; $i \leftarrow i+1$ and **go to** *1.1.*

1.4 **If** x_{j-1},x_j,x_i is a *left turn* and x_{i+1},x_i,x_j is a *left turn* (Case 2.2 in Fig. 10) **then** apend $[x_{j-1},x_i]$ into TS$[\mathbf{d}_{ab},\mathbf{d}_{ij}]$ to create TS$[\mathbf{d}_{ab},\mathbf{d}_{i,j-1}]$; $j \leftarrow j-1$ and **go to** *1.1.*

1.5 **If** x_{j-1},x_j,x_i is a *left turn* and x_{i+1},x_i,x_j is a *right turn* (Case 2.3 in Fig. 10) **then:**

1.6 **If** $x_{j-1} \in int\, \Delta\, x_{i+1}x_ix_j$ (Case 2.3.1 in Fig. 10) **then** apend $[x_{j-1},x_i]$ into TS$[\mathbf{d}_{ab},\mathbf{d}_{ij}]$ to create TS$[\mathbf{d}_{ab},\mathbf{d}_{i,j-1}]$; $j \leftarrow j-1$ and **go to** *1.1.*

1.7 **If** $x_{i+1} \in int\, \Delta\, x_ix_jx_{j-1}$ (Case 2.3.2 in Fig. 10) **then** apend $[x_j,x_{i+1}]$ into TS$[\mathbf{d}_{ab},\mathbf{d}_{ij}]$ to create TS$[\mathbf{d}_{ab},\mathbf{d}_{i+1,j}]$; $i \leftarrow i+1$ and **go to** *1.1.*

1.8 **If** $x_{i+1} \notin$ *int* $\Delta\ x_i x_j x_{j-1}$ **and** $x_{j-1} \notin$ *int* $\Delta\ x_{i+1} x_i x_j$ (Case 2.3.3 in Fig. 10) **then** arbitrarily select for appending either (a) $[x_j, x_{i+1}]$ or (b) $[x_{j-1}, x_i]$ into TS[$\mathbf{d}_{ab}$,$\mathbf{d}_{ij}$] . **If** (a) is chosen **then** i ← i+1; **If** (b) is chosen **then** j ← j-1. **Go to** *1.1.*

1.9 **If** x_{j-1}, x_j, x_i is a *right turn* and x_{i+1}, x_i, x_j is a *left turn* (Case 2.4 in Fig. 10) **then:**

1.10 **If** CH[$x_{i+1}, \ldots, x_{j-1}$] intersects $\mathbf{d}_{ij}$ (Case 2.4.1 in Fig. 10) (a) **then** determine the deepest triangle $\Delta\ x_r x_s x_t$ in TS[$\mathbf{d}_{ab}$,$\mathbf{d}_{ij}$] (see Fig. 11) that contains vertices of CH[$x_{i+1}, \ldots, x_{j-1}$]; (b) determine which vertex x_k of CH[$x_{i+1}, \ldots, x_{j-1}$] is visible to both x_r and x_s ; (c) insert diagonals $\mathbf{d}_{sk}=[x_s, x_k]$ and $\mathbf{d}_{kr}=[x_k, x_r]$ into T(P) and ***D***; (d) delete all the diagonals in TS[$\mathbf{d}_{ab}$,$\mathbf{d}_{ij}$] starting from and including $\mathbf{d}_{ij}$ and ending with and including $\mathbf{d}_{tr}$, insert all the diagonals remaining in TS[$\mathbf{d}_{ab}$,$\mathbf{d}_{ij}$] into T(P) and **Exit.**

1.11 **Else** (Case 2.4.2 in Fig. 10) (a) find a vertex x_k of CH[$x_{i+1}, \ldots, x_{j-1}$] that is visible from x_i and that lies to the right of the directed line through x_i and x_j (see Fig. 12). (b) **If** x_k is also visible from x_j **then** insert diagonals $\mathbf{d}_{ik}=[x_i, x_k]$ and $\mathbf{d}_{kj}=[x_k, x_j]$ into T(P) and ***D*** and **Exit. Else** (c) find the vertex $x_{k*} \in$ CH[$x_k, \ldots, x_j$] that lies in the interior of $\Delta\ x_i x_k x_j$ and that minimizes the angle $\angle\ x_{k*} x_j x_i$; insert diagonals $\mathbf{d}_{ik*} = [x_i, x_{k*}]$ and $\mathbf{d}_{k*j} = [x_{k*}, x_j]$ into T(P) and ***D***.

End While

End While

End

==

Theorem: *ALGORITHM* TRIANGULATION triangulates a simple polygon P of n vertices in $O(n(1+t_0))$ time.

Proof: Since the correctness and linear time complexity of Step 1 of *ALGORITHM* TRIANGULATION follows from *PROCEDURE* DIAGONAL and Lemma 1 we need only concern ourselves with *PROCEDURE* TRIANGULATION. Steps 1, 2 and 1.1 can be done in constant time. The correctness of Step 1.2 (a) follows from Lemma 4 and can be implemented by scanning simultaneously the chain CH[$x_{i+1}, \ldots, x_{j-1}$] and the triangulated sleeve TS[$\mathbf{d}_{ab}$,$\mathbf{d}_{ij}$]. Since the diagonals in TS[$\mathbf{d}_{ab}$,$\mathbf{d}_{ij}$] are ordered, so are the triangles penetrated by CH[$x_{i+1}, \ldots, x_{j-1}$]. Thus if we keep pointers between adjacent triangles as TS[$\mathbf{d}_{ab}$,$\mathbf{d}_{ij}$] is formed we can easily search for the deepest triangle whenever we have to by advancing either an edge along CH[$x_{i+1}, \ldots, x_{j-1}$] if the previous edge does not intersect the following diagonal in TS[$\mathbf{d}_{ab}$, $\mathbf{d}_{ij}$] or advancing a diagonal in TS[$\mathbf{d}_{ab}$,$\mathbf{d}_{ij}$] as long as it is intersected by the same edge of CH[$x_{i+1}, \ldots, x_{j-1}$]. The complexity of this procedure is proportional to the sum of the cardinalities of CH[$x_{i+1}, \ldots, x_{j-1}$] and TS[$\mathbf{d}_{ab}$,$\mathbf{d}_{ij}$] and in the worst case is O(n).

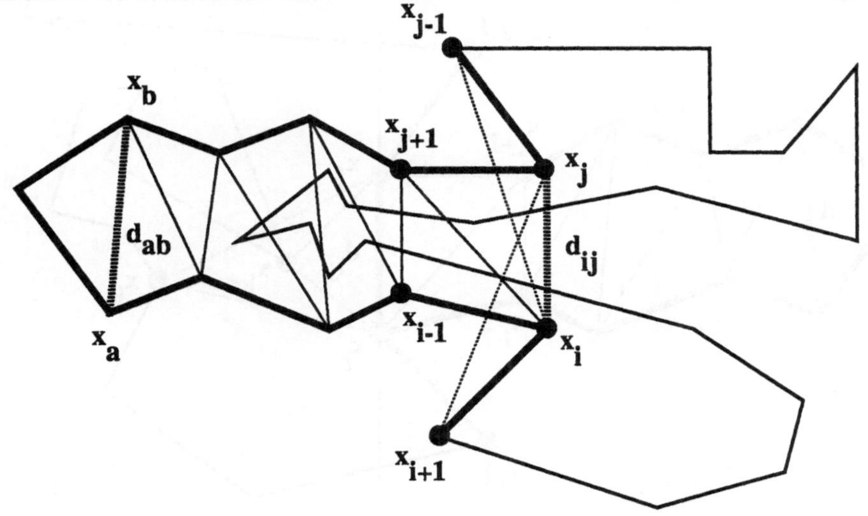

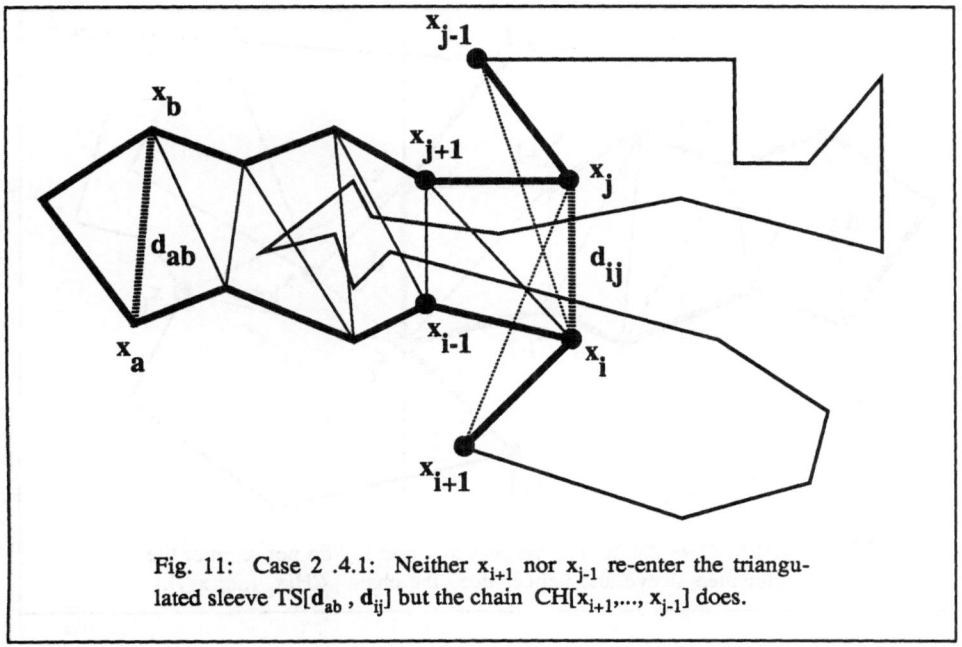

Fig. 11: Case 2 .4.1: Neither x_{i+1} nor x_{j-1} re-enter the triangulated sleeve TS[$\mathbf{d}_{ab}$, $\mathbf{d}_{ij}$] but the chain CH[x_{i+1},..., x_{j-1}] does.

Consider Step 1.2 (c) and refer to the discussion preceding Lemma 5. We can assume that $x_{j-1} \notin$ *int* $\Delta\ x_i x_j x_{i-1}$ whenever this step is executed because initially $\mathbf{d}_{ij}$ is a diagonal of T(P) and subsequently if this condition were not true it would imply that at the previous diagonal insertion of $\mathbf{d}_{i-1,j}$, $x_{j-1} \in$ *int* $\Delta\ x_j x_{i-1} x_i$ contradicting the choice of diagonal $[x_{i-1}, x_{j-1}]$ that Step 1.6 would have made. It follows that Lemma 5 implies that Step 1.2 (c) is correct and can be implemented in O(n) time.

The correctness of Steps 1.3 - 1.8 follow straightforwardly from Lemmas 6 and 7 and can each be performed in O(1) time. The arguments for the correctness and complexity of Steps 1.9 and 1.10 are similar to those for Steps 1.1 and 1.2. Finally, Lemmas 2 and 3 ensure the correctness and linear time complexity of Step 1.11.

Every time a diagonal is selected from ***D*** in the outer **While** loop it is possible to do a linear amount of work, in the worst case, only in Steps 1.2, 1.10, and 1.11. All other steps require no more than a O(1) time per step. Furthermore, every time a linear amount of work is done in Steps 1.2, 1.10, and 1.11 a *free* triangle is inserted in T(P) and two diagonals are inserted in ***D***. Since the only time a pair of diagonals is inserted in ***D*** is precisely when a free triangle is inserted in T(P) the outer **While** loop is executed only t_0 times, where t_0 denotes the number of *free* triangles in the triangulation delivered by the algorithm. It follows that the overall complexity of the algorithm is O(n) + O(nt_0). Q.E.D.

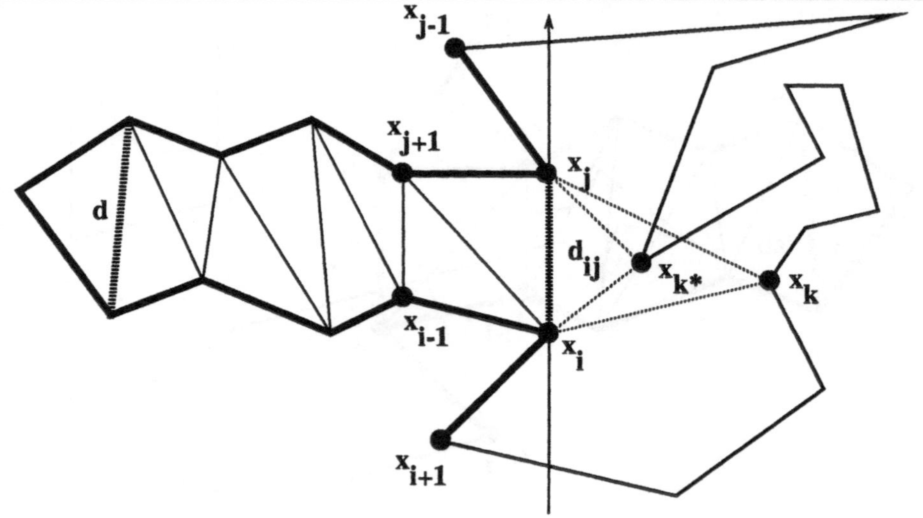

Fig. 12: Case 2.4.2: The vertices x_{i+1} and x_{j-1} do not re-enter the triangulated sleeve and neither does the chain $CH[x_{i+1},..., x_{j-1}]$.

5. Concluding Remarks

On the practical side we remark that the algorithm proposed here has already been implemented by researchers at NTT in Japan for graphics applications and the reader is referred to [YTT] for experimental results. We also add that a more elegant and perhaps faster implementation of the algorithm is possible with the recent result of ElGindy, Everett & Toussaint [EET]. In the algorithm presented in the present paper a diagonal is first found which decomposes P into two subpolygons. *PROCEDURE* TRIANGULATION is subsequently called twice and applied to each of the two subpolygons. In [EET] it is shown that an *ear* of P can be found in linear time by a quick prune and search procedure. Thus using the ear-finding procedure of [EET] in Step 1 of *ALGORITHM* TRIANGULATION affords only one call to *PROCEDURE* TRIANGULATION. It remains to be determined experimentally which approach is more viable.

On the theoretical side it is interesting to compare the new "sleeve-searching" algorithm proposed here with the only other known adaptive algorithm that is sensitive to the input shape, i.e., the "sinuosity" algorithm of Chazelle & Incerpi [CI]. In particular it is of interest to compare these two algorithms from the point of view of worst-case complexity for certain known classes of simple polygons. Table 1 summarizes the worst-case complexities of both algorithms for *convex, anthropomorphic* and *edge-visible* polygons. Note that although t_0 can be as large as O(n) for convex polygons as illustrated in Fig. 4 (a) the algorithm described here will always obtain a value of $t_0=0$, and hence the complexity on convex polygons is O(n) thus matching the complexity of the sinuosity algorithm. For anthropomorphic polygons "sleeve-searching" is better than "sinuosity" because $t_0=0$ whereas $s=O(n)$. For edge-visible polygons on the other hand the latter is better although a linear-time algorithm exists [TA].

Type of Polygon	Sleeve Searching Algorithm $O(n(1+t_0))$	Sinuosity Algorithm $O(n \log s)$
Convex	$O(n)$	$O(n)$
Anthropomorphic & Two-Ear polygons	$O(n)$	$O(n \log n)$
Edge-visible	$O(n^2)$ †	$O(n \log n)$

Table 1: A comparison of the sleeve-searching algorithm with the sinuosity algorithm of Chazelle & Incerpi in terms of worst-case complexity for some classes of polygons.
† Edge-visible polygons can be triangulated in O(n) time with the algorithm in [TA].

Measures of the shape of a polygon are of great interest in pattern recognition and computational morphology [To4]. While t_0 may vary too much as a function of the triangulation of a polygon rather than the polygon's shape in order to be a faithful measure of shape, we can remove its dependence on the triangulation by taking the extreme values of t_0 over all triangulations of the given polygon. Accordingly we define two new measures of the shape of a polygon: $T_{max} = \max\{t_0\}$ and $T_{min} = \min\{t_0\}$, where maximization and minimization is carried out over all triangulations. Thomas Shermer [Sh1] has shown that for a given polygon P, T_{max} and a triangulation exhibiting T_{max} can be computed in O(T(n)) time where T(n) is the time taken to obtain any triangulation of P. He has also shown that T_{min} can be computed in $O(n^3)$ time and $O(n^2)$ space. It would be interesting to determine how useful both measures are in pattern recognition applications and other areas of computational morphology [To4] as well as to determine if a sub-cubic time or sub-quadratic space algorithm exists for computing T_{min}.

6. Acknowledgments

The author would like to thank Hossam ElGindy, Tom Shermer, and Rafe Wenger for stimulating and helpful discussions on this topic as well as Tokiichiro Takahashi of NTT, Japan for pointing out some ambiguities in an earlier draft of this paper as well as his comments on the implementation of the algorithm.

7. References

[Ca] Cairns, S. S., "An elementary proof of the Jordan-Schoenflies theorem, *Proc. Amer. Math. Soc.*, vol. 2, 1951, pp.860-867.

[Ch] Chazelle, B., "A theorem on polygon cutting with applications," *Proc. 23rd IEEE Symposium on Foundations of Computer Science, Chicago*, November 1982.

[CI] Chazelle, B. and Incerpi, J., "Triangulation and shape complexity," *ACM Transactions on Graphics*, vol. 3, 1984, pp.135-152.

[El] ElGindy, H. A., "A linear algorithm for triangulating weakly externally visible polygons," Tech. Report MS-CIS-86-75, University of Pennsylvania, September 1985.

[ET1] ElGindy, H. and Toussaint, G. T., "On triangulating palm polygons in linear time," *Proc. Computer Graphics International '88*, Geneva, May 24-27, 1988.

[ET2] ElGindy, H. and Toussaint, G. T., "On geodesic properties of polygons relevant to linear-time triangulation," *The Visual Computer*, vol. 5, no. 1/2, March 1989, pp. 68-74.

[EAT] ElGindy, H., Avis, D. and Toussaint, G. T., "Applications of a two-dimensional hidden-line algorithm to other geometric problems," *Computing*, vol. 31, 1983, pp.191-202.

[EET] ElGindy, H., Everett, H. and Toussaint, G. T., "Slicing an ear in linear time," internal memorandum, School of Computer Science, McGill University.

[FM] Fournier, A. and Montuno, D. Y., "Triangulating simple polygons and equivalent problems," *ACM Transactions on Graphics*, vol. 3, April 1984, pp.153-174.

[FP] Feng, H-Y. F. and Pavlidis, T., "Decomposition of polygons into simpler components: feature generation for syntactic pattern recognition," *IEEE Transactions on Computers*, vol. C-24, June 1975, pp.636-650.

[Fo] Forder, H. G., *The Foundations of Euclidean Geometry*, Cambridge University Press, 1927.

[GJPT] Garey, M. R., Johnson, D. S., Preparata, F. P. and Tarjan, R. E., "Triangulating a simple polygon," *Information Processing Letters*, vol. 7, 1978, pp.175-179.

[HM] Hertel, S. and Mehlhorn, K., "Fast triangulation of simple polygons," *Proc. FCT, LNCS* 158, 1983, pp.207-215.

[Ho] Ho, W.-C., "Decomposition of a polygon into triangles," *The Mathematical Gazette*, vol. 59, 1975, pp.132-134.

[KKT] Kirkpatrick, D. G., Klawe, M. M., & Tarjan, R. E., "O(n log log n) polygon triangulation with simple data structures," *Sixth Annual Symposium on Computational Geometry*, Berkeley, California, June 6-8, 1990.

[Kn1] Knopp, K., *Theory of Functions*, Part I, translated by F. Bagemihl from the fifth German Edition, Dover.

[Kn2] Knopp, K., *Funktionentheorie* I., Sammlung Göschen Band 668, Walter de Gruyter, 1970.

[LC] Lee, S. H. and Chwa, K. Y., "A new triangulation linear class of simple polygons," *International Journal of Computer Mathematics*, vol. 22, 1987, pp.135-147.

[Le] Lennes, N. J., "Theorems on the simple finite polygon and polyhedron," *American Journal of Mathematics*, vol. 33, 1911, pp.37-62.

[Le1] Levy, L. S., *Geometry: Modern Mathematics via the Euclidean Plane*, Prindle, Weber & Schmidt, Inc., Boston, Mass., 1970.]

[Ma] Mandelbrot, B. B., *Fractals: Form, Chance, and Dimension*, W. H. Freeman & Co., 1977.

[Me] Meisters, G. H., "Polygons have ears," *American Mathematical Monthly*, June/July 1975, pp.648-651.

[RS] Rupert, J. and Seidel, R., "On the difficulty of tetrahedralizing 3-dimensional non-convex polyhedra," *ACM Symposium on Computational Geometry*, June 5-7 1989, Saarbrucken, West Germany, pp. 380-392.

[SV] Schoone, A. A. and van Leeuwen, J., "Triangulating a star-shaped polygon," Tech. Report, RUV-CS-80-3, University of Utrecht, April 1980.

[Sh1] Shermer, T., "Computing bushy and thin triangulations," in *Snapshots of Computational and Discrete Geometry*, G. T. Toussaint, Ed., Tech. Rept. SOCS-88.11, June 1988, pp. 119-133.

[Sh2] Shermer, T., "Generating anthropomorphic k-spirals," in *Snapshots of Computational and Discrete Geometry*, G. T. Toussaint, Ed., Tech. Rept. SOCS-88.11, June 1988, pp. 233-244.

[TA] Toussaint, G. T. and Avis, D., "On a convex hull algorithm for polygons and its application to triangulation problems," *Pattern Recognition*, vol. 15, No. 1, 1982, pp.23-29.

[To1] Toussaint, G. T., "A new linear algorithm for triangulating monotone polygons," *Pattern Recognition Letters*, vol. 2, March 1984, pp.

[To2] Toussaint, G. T., "Polygons are anthropomorphic," Memorandum, School of Computer Science, McGill University, March, 1988.

[To3] Toussaint, G. T., "New results in computational geometry relevant to pattern recognition in practice," in *Pattern Recognition in Practice II*, E. S. Gelsema and L. N. Kanal, Editors, North-Holland, 1986, pp.135-146.

[To4] Toussaint, G. T., Editor, *Computational Morphology*, North-Holland, 1988.

[TV] Tarjan, R. E. and Van Wyk, C. J., "An O(n log log n)-time algorithm for triangulating simple polygons," *SIAM Journal on Computing*, 1988.

[WS] Woo, T. C. and Shin, S. Y., "A linear time algorithm for triangulating a point-visible polygon," *ACM Transactions on Graphics*, vol. 4, January 1985, pp.60-70.

Godfried T. Toussaint received the B.Sc. degree from the University of Tulsa, Tulsa, OK., and the M.A.Sc. and Ph.D. degrees from the University of British Columbia, Vancouver, B.C., Canada in 1968, 1970, and 1972, respectively, all in Electrical Engineering.
Since 1972 he has been with the School of Computer Science at McGill University teaching and doing research in the areas of information theory, pattern recognition, and computational geometry. During the summers of 1975 and 1977 he was a Visiting Scholar at the Information Systems Laboratory, Stanford University. The sabbatical year 1980-81 he spent as a Visiting Scientist at the Applied Mathematics Research Center of the University of Montreal. During the spring of 1986 he was a Visiting Scholar at the Courant Institute of Mathematical Sciences, NYU. During the fall of 1988 he was a British Columbia Advanced Systems Institute Fellow at Simon Fraser University. In the spring of 1989 he was a visiting professor in the Mathematics Department at the University of West Indies, Cave Hill, Barbados, and during the summer of 1989 he was a Visiting Scientist in the Department of Mathematics and Computer Science at the University of Amsterdam.
Dr. Toussaint is past council-member of the North American Branch of the *Classification Society*, and past Associate Editor of the *IEEE Transactions on Information Theory*. Presently, he is Associate Editor of the *Plenum Press Series on Advanced Applications in Pattern Recognition*, Associate Editor of *Pattern Recognition*, Associate Editor of the *IEEE Transactions on Pattern Analysis and Machine Intelligence*, and Associate Editor of *The Visual Computer*. He is also on the editorial boards of the journals *Discrete & Computational Geometry* and *Science on Form*. He is a member of several learned societies including the *IEEE*, the *Pattern Recognition Society* and the *New York Academy of Sciences*. He recently edited two books published by North Holland, *Computational Geometry* in 1985 and *Computational Morphology* in 1988 as well as a special issue of *The Visual Computer* (May 1988) on computational geometry. In 1978 he was the recipient of the Pattern Recognition Society's Best Paper of the Year Award and in 1985 he was awarded a *Killam Senior Research Fellowship* by the Canada Council to carry out a two-year research project on movable separability of sets.
Address: Computational Geometry Laboratory, School of Computer Science, McGill University, 3480 University Street, Montreal, Quebec, CANADA H3A 2A7, electronic-mail:godfried@opus.cs.mcgill.ca.

Chapter 8
Ray Tracing and Radiosity

Ray-Tracing Soft Objects

Geoff Wyvill and Andrew Trotman

Abstract

Soft objects, also known as metaballs or implicit surfaces, are deformable free-form shapes represented as a surface of constant value in a scalar field.

We present a simple, robust method for ray tracing soft objects defined by polynomial field functions. The method is guaranteed to find all the intersections of a ray with a soft object. Thus it is suitable for use in CSG systems where all intersections may be required.

Keywords: geometric modelling, ray tracing, soft objects, animation.

Introduction

Soft objects are solids described by scalar fields. A scalar field is a function that has a real value defined for every point of space. The surface of the soft object is a set of points that have the same field value. For this reason, they are sometimes called iso-surfaces. Soft objects have been described by Blinn (1982), Nishimura (1985), Wyvill (1986b) and others. Both Blinn and Nishimura used a form of ray casting to render their surfaces but both algorithms are of an ad hoc nature and have not been proven to find the intersection of any given ray with the surface. Our earlier papers on soft objects all used polygonal approximations for rendering (Wyvill 1986a, 1986b, 1987a, 1989). Kalra (1989) has described a provable algorithm for ray tracing, but it is more complicated, and (we believe) slower than the one presented here. Also, Kalra's algorithm, as described, finds only the nearest intersection of a ray with a soft object. In constructive solid geometry, a shape is built by adding and subtracting volumes. It often happens that an intersection point of one primitive object has disappeared in the final model because something has been subtracted from that region of space. In cases like this, we must find all the intersections and eliminate the ones that we don't need. It often happens that the correct intersection is not the nearest to the eye.

Kalra's algorithm appears to be more general than ours. They establish a criterion to determine whether a Newton's iteration will converge in a given region of space. If it does not, they divide the region until it will and apply Newton's method in each region. We have restricted our field functions to a polynomial type for which we can guarantee solvability without resorting to space division. Thus we believe our method, while less general, is more practical in most cases.

The field function

The purpose of using soft objects is to model free-form surfaces. These surfaces are usually edited by hand and it is important that we can exercise local control of their shape. Sometimes we need hundreds of data points, and it is important that we can calculate the field value at a point without having to refer to all of them. For this reason, we use a field function that is guaranteed to have only a local effect. Our basic field function is calculated from a set of *key points* as follows:

Key points form a kind of skeleton around which the soft object is drawn. We regard each key point as a source of energy, a hot spot around which the temperature drops off as a function of distance. The field value due to two or more key points is the sum of the values due to the individual key points. To achieve local control, the field produced by each key point has to conform to certain rules. In particular, the field function, f(r), and its derivative: $\frac{df}{dr}$ must drop to zero at some special distance, R from the key point. R is called the 'radius of influence' of a key point: the distance at which the field contribution falls to zero. In earlier work (Wyvill 1986a, 1986b, 1987a) we described a suitable function as a cubic in r^2:

$$C(r) = \begin{cases} -0.4444 \frac{r^6}{R^6} + 1.8888 \frac{r^4}{R^4} - 2.4444 \frac{r^2}{R^2} + 1.0 \ , & r \leq R \\ 0 \ , & r > R \end{cases} \qquad (1)$$

where the coefficients were chosen so that the volumes of the soft objects behaved reasonably when key points were combined. The surface of our soft object lies by definition everywhere where C(r) = *magic*. The value of *magic* is chosen by evil art but in most cases, if we are using equation (1), *magic* = 0.5 works well.

In this paper, we demonstrate that this field function can be ray traced with a provable algorithm for any number of key points. The method can also be extended to non-spherical keys. That is key points for which the effective 'radius' is not simply the geometric distance from the key point, but may depend on direction too.

The algorithm

Because our field function is a polynomial in r, the ray intersection calculation for a single key is done by solving a simple polynomial. The geometry is shown in Fig. 1. For a ray from eyepoint **e** in a direction **v** the line is given by the parametric equation:

$$\mathbf{p} = \mathbf{e} + \mathbf{v}\,t \qquad (2)$$

For a key point at **k**, the distance from **k** to **p** is $r = |\mathbf{p} - \mathbf{k}|$ and the field value is:

$$f = C(|\mathbf{e} + \mathbf{v}\,t - \mathbf{k}|) \qquad (3)$$

where C(r) is given by equation (1), provided we are within the radius of influence of **k**. The significant point here is that f is a polynomial of degree six in t, and all the coefficients are calculated from the geometry. If there are more key points, then the field is given by the sum of the effects of the individual keys:

$$f = \sum_i C(|e + v\,t - k_i|) \tag{4}$$

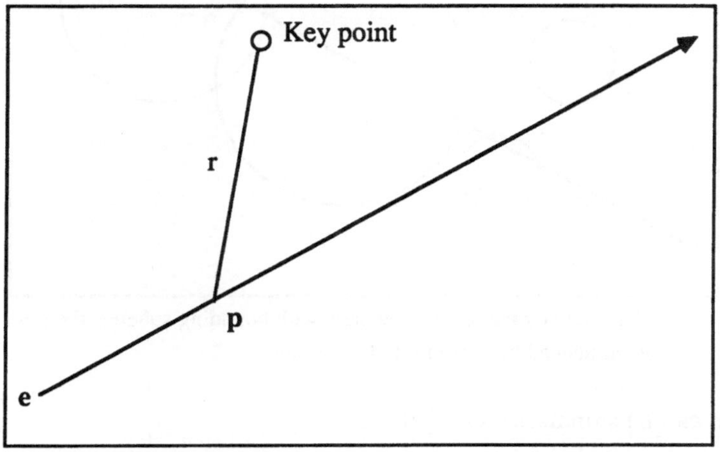

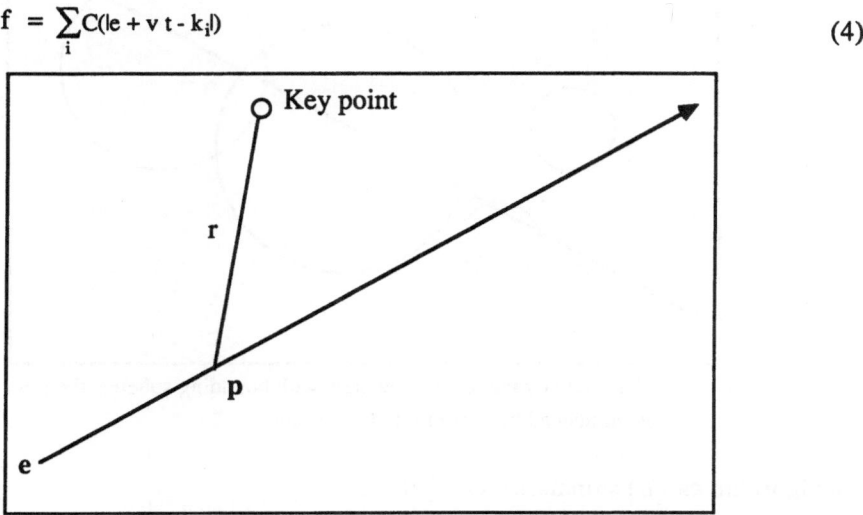

Fig. 1. Ray geometry.

Since this is still a polynomial of degree six, we can solve it for f = *magic* by standard methods. We use Laguerre's method which is guaranteed to find all the roots and, in the case of single roots, has third order convergence. Details of this method can be found in standard texts on numerical analysis; see, for example, Ralston (1965). Substituting the value of t back into (2) gives the point **p**, the intersection of the ray with the surface.

The function defined in (2), of course, is polynomial only within the radius of influence, R. So the simple polynomial solution works only in regions where we remain within the radius of influence of all the key points being considered.

In the general case, the ray will pass into and out of the radius of influence of key points. Each radius of influence defines a sphere around a keypoint and we find the points of intersection of the ray with all of the bounding spheres. Of course, in many cases, most of these spheres will be well away from the ray and it will not be necessary to check them for intersection. Spatial sorting (Wyvill 1986a) can eliminate most of these tests and this will improve the efficiency. Here we are mostly concerned with provability.

The intersection points are sorted according to distance from the eyepoint, **e**. Between any pair of points, the ray neither enters nor leaves a radius of influence so we can check for intersections in that interval using the simple polynomial solution. Each of these intervals is defined by an upper and lower limit of the parameter, t, of equation (2) and the solutions of the polynomials are also values of t. If any solution is outside these limits, then this is not an intersection in that interval and it can be discarded.

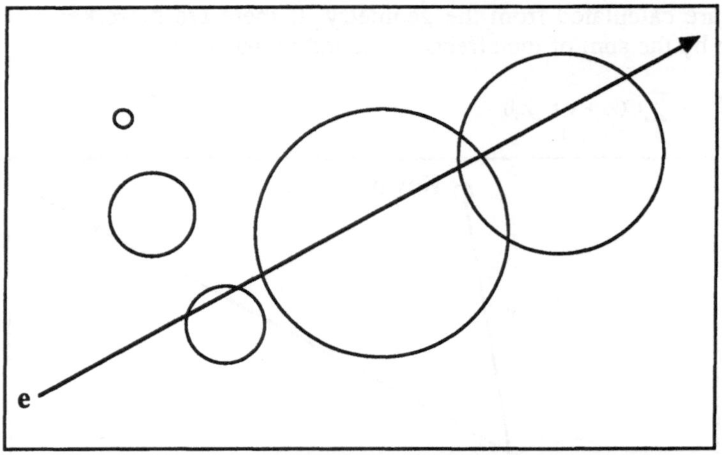

Fig. 2. Between any pair of intersections with bounding spheres, the field is influenced by a fixed set of key points.

The algorithm can be summarised as follows.

1 Find the intersections with all bounding spheres and order them along the ray.

2 Solve the polynomial equation (4) for f = *magic* in each interval.

3 Return those intersection points that fall within each interval.

Quadric surfaces

The basic algorithm can be adapted easily to handle primitives that are not spherical. We represent a point in space by a vector

$$\mathbf{u} = \begin{pmatrix} x \\ y \\ z \\ 1 \end{pmatrix}$$ and we write its transpose, (x, y, z, 1) as $\mathbf{u}'$.

The general quadratic form:

$$Q = \mathbf{u}' \, M \, \mathbf{u} \tag{5}$$

is a scalar value, a function of x, y and z, where the coefficients of each term are defined by the elements of M. It is convenient to regard Q as analogous to r^2 in the equation of a sphere and we can use the same cubic in Q to manufacture a soft object field of general quadric shape. The surface $Q = R^2$ gives us a bound and our algorithm can be extended to ray trace soft objects made by combining these shapes.

The quadric surfaces include ellipsoids, cylinders and cones and provide a convenient extension of the shapes we can make using only a few primitives. This extension was used by Blinn (1982) and it is important to note that our algorithm is not limited to spheres.

Negative key points

Blinn (1982) also introduced negative weights for some key points enabling holes and concavities to appear in the soft shapes. Use of such points can create rather complicated and sharply curving shapes. It is worth pointing out that these negative key points are handled equally well by our algorithm.

CSG operations

The soft object ray tracer has been incorporated into our *Katachi* solid modelling system at the University of Otago. *Katachi* supports set operations on volumes described by combining many primitive types (Roth 1982, Wyvill 1987b, 1988). Because we find all the intersections of a ray with the soft object, we are able to incorporate it into the solid modelling scheme. We can add and subtract the soft objects to and from any of the other primitives of *Katachi*.

Figures 3 and 4 illustrate all these things. A teapot has been built from five quadric key points, one of them negative. In Fig. 3, it has been coloured with a symmetrical synthetic marble texture. In Fig. 4, the teapot is given a metallic appearance and is shown with half of a mould from which it could have been cast. The mould was created in the CSG system by subtracting the teapot from a block.

Conclusion

We have developed and tested a robust and simple method for ray tracing soft objects that is guaranteed to find all the intersections of a ray with an implicit polynomial surface defined by key points.

The method has been tested in a CSG environment and works well.

Acknowledgements

The computer graphics project at Otago has been jointly funded by Otago University and the University Grants Committee. Our thanks also go to Television New Zealand for loan of equipment and studio time.

Fig. 3. Textured teapot.

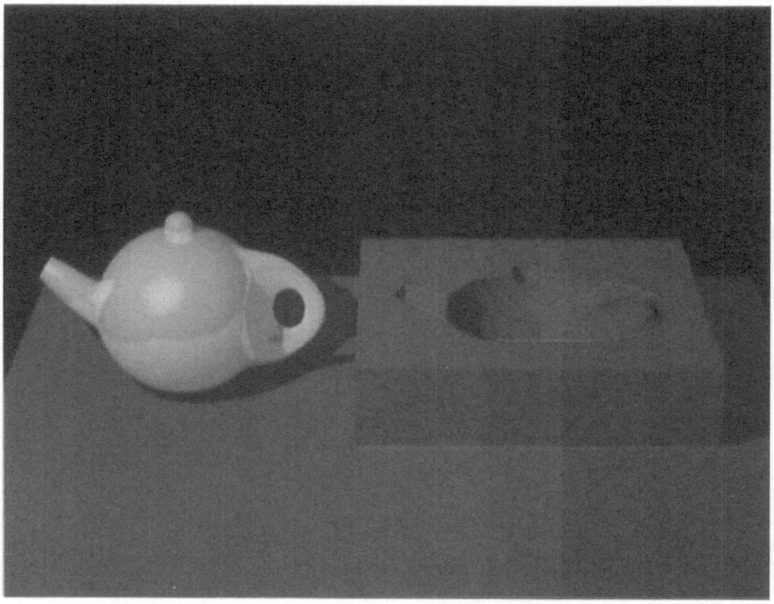

Fig. 4. CSG operations on soft objects.

References

Blinn J (1982) A Generalization of Algebraic Surface Drawing. *ACM Transactions on Graphics* 1 : 235 - 256

Kalra D and Bar AH (1989) Guaranteed Ray Intersections with Implicit Surfaces. *Computer Graphics* (Proc. SIGGRAPH 1989) 23 (3) : 297-306

Nishimura H, Hirai M, Kawai T, Kawata T, Shirakawa I and Omura K (1985) Object Modeling by Distribution Function and a Method of Image Generation. *Journal of papers given at the Electronics Communication Conference '85* J68-D (4) (in Japanese)

Ralston A (1965) *A First Course in Numerical Analysis.* McGraw Hill 368-371

Roth SD (1982) Ray Casting for Modeling Solids. *Computer Graphics and Image Processing* 18 : 109-144

Wyvill BLM, McPheeters C and Wyvill G (1986a) Animating Soft Objects. *The Visual Computer* 2 (4) : 235-242

Wyvill G, McPheeters C and Wyvill BLM (1986b) Data Structure for Soft Objects. *The Visual Computer* 2 (4) : 227-234

Wyvill G, Wyvill B and McPheeters C (1987a) Solid Texturing of Soft Objects. *IEEE CG&A* 7 (12) : 20-26

Wyvill G, Ward A and Brown T (1987b) Sketches by Ray Tracing. *Computer Graphics 1987* (Proc. CG International '87, Karuizawa) 315-333

Wyvill G and Sharp P (1988) Volume and Surface Properties in CSG. *New Trends in Computer Graphics* (Proc. CG International '88, Geneva) 257-266

Wyvill BLM and Wyvill G (1989) Using Soft Objects in Computer Generated Character Animation. In: *Computers in Art Design and Animation,* Springer Verlag 283-297

Geoff Wyvill graduated in physics from Jesus College, Oxford, and started working with computers as a research technologist with the British Petroleum Company. He gained MSc and PhD degrees in computer science from the University of Bradford where he lectured in computer science from 1969 until 1978. He is currently senior lecturer in computer science at the University of Otago. He is on the editorial board of The Visual Computer and is a member of SIGGRAPH, ACM, CGS and NZCS.

Address: Department of Computer Science
University of Otago Box 56
Dunedin, New Zealand

Andrew Trotman is a graduate student at Otago University. His research interests include constructive solid geometry and computer animation. He completed a BA degree in computer science in 1988 and he is a student member of ACM and SIGGRAPH.

Address: Department of Computer Science
University of Otago Box 56
Dunedin, New Zealand

An Adapted Solution of Progressive Radiosity and Ray-Tracing Methods for Non-Diffuse Environments

Hong Chen and En-Hua Wu

ABSTRACT

The rendering technique of progressive refinement radiosity method newly appeared has reduced the computation and storage cost dramatically in comparison with the standard radiosity approaches, though the method is still constrained to perfect diffuse environments. In this paper, an adapted two-pass approach with a combination of progressive refinement radiosity and ray tracing methods is presented. The method proposed has inherited the merits and practical value of the progressive refinement radiosity solutioin, and at the same time capable of dealing with non-diffuse environment by an improved calculation of specular reflections and a step of postprocess of ray tracing. Besides, treatment has also been provided in a postprocess for improving shadow effect caused by point-like light sources within a non-diffuse environment.

KEY WORDS:

radiosity, ray tracing, specular reflection, progressive refinement, shadow detection

1. INTRODUCTION

The radiosity method, based on the principle of heat transfer(Sparrow,1978), was introduced by Goral, Torrance and Greenberg (1984). Because it is well suited to calculating diffuse interreflection, much progress has been made since its inception.

Cohen and Greenberg (1985, 1986) and Nishita et al. (1986) extended the simple radiosity to complex diffuse environments with occluded surfaces. By their methods, the energy transfer within an environment is calculated by constructing and solving a set of simultaneous equations, and the form-factors between patches are determined by a well established hemi-cube algorithm. To maintain accuracy at the place where illuminance changes rapidly, patches can be adaptively subdivided into elements (Cohen 1986). A further approach was introduced by Immel et al. (1986) to cover non-diffuse environments. Unfortunately, its computation cost is too expensive to make the approach practical. In 1987, Wallace, Cohen and Greenberg (Wallace 1987) proposed a two-pass solution by which a combination of ray tracing and radiosity technique was adopted. It successfully simulates both the diffuse and specular reflection within a non-diffuse environment. P. P. Shao et al. (1988) designed a new algorithm to evaluate the specular form-factors in terms of hemi-cube. During the same period, M. Z. Shao et al. (1988) developed a new radiosity method for non-diffuse environments by procedural refinement with the delta form-factors progressively approximated by procedural iteration so that the cost for simulating specular reflection is reduced in comparison with the previous methods.

However, for all the solutions mentioned, there is a serious shortcoming that all the form-factors, including mirror or specular form-factors in some methods, are pre-evaluated for the whole environment before the solution begins. As a result, no usable results can be provided until the solution is complete. The prohibitive computation and storage requirement of $O(N^2)$ also degrades the potential practical value of the methods, where N is the number of discrete surface patches in the whole environment.

In 1988, Cohen, Chen, Wallace and Greenberg (Cohen 1988) proposed a reformulated radiosity algorithm based on an idea of progressive refinement. In their method, a simple approximation of global diffuse illumination is taken as an initial solution for further refinement. The illumination of all surfaces in the environment is updated at each iterative step, and the image produced is improved progressively. The selection of shooting patch in a sorted order at each step makes the correct solution to be approached very fast in the process. Efficiency is particularly obtained by the hemi-cube processing since only one hemi-cube of the shooting patch need to be established at each iterative step, so that the storage requiement for form-factors is only $O(N)$. In fact, the progressive radiosity has been a breakthrough to the tranditional methods and makes it possible for radiosity to be used for image synthesis in an interactive way, and in comprehensive environments covering a large amount of objects.

However, the progressive radiosity is still constrained to perfect diffuse environments and is view-independent. In this paper, we will extend the method to deal with view-dependent effects such as highlights and specular reflection. The contribution of radiant energy from a non-diffuse shooting patch will be derived by a delta specular irradiation formula introduced. Besides, an optional treatment is also available as a postprocess for improving shadow effect caused by small area light sources.

2. PROGRESSIVE REFINEMENT RADIOSITY METHOD FOR PERFECT DIFFUSE ENVIRONMENTS

The radiosity of a patch i is related to the radiosities of all the other patches in an environment by

$$B_i = E_i + \rho_i \sum_{j=1}^{N} B_j F_{ji} A_j / A_i \qquad \text{<1>}$$

where
B_i is radiosity of patch i $(watts/m^2)$,
E_i is emission of patch i $(watts/m^2)$,
ρ_i is reflectance of patch i,
A_i is area of patch i (m^2),
F_{ji} is form-factor which represents the fraction of energy leaving patch j and landing on patch i,
N is number of discrete patches in the environment.

Equation <1> may be explained in two ways. The first consideration is that the radiosity of patch i is due to the contribution of other patches in the environment plus the emission emitted itself. Because the diffuse form-factors between patches i and j have a reciprocity relationship $F_{ij}A_i = F_{ji}A_j$, the radiosity equation for a diffuse environment in general is

$$B_i = E_i + \rho_i \sum_{j=1}^{N} B_j F_{ij} \qquad \text{<2>}$$

By solving the set of simultaneous equations above, the standard radiosity method is then established in this so called "gathering" way. It is possible to reverse this process by determining the contribution made by a patch, say j, to the radiosity of all other patches i:

$$\Delta B_i = \rho_i \Delta B_j F_{ji} A_j \; / \; A_i \qquad \text{<3>}$$

Consideration in this way led to another so called "shooting" method. "Gathering" allows the radiosity of one patch to be updated each time, while the "shooting" alllows the whole environment's radiosity values to be updated simultaneously.

Based on the idea of radiosity shooting, Cohen et al. (1988) developed the progressive radiosity method. In their method, each step of the progressive solution consists of selecting a patch with greatest unshot energy as shooting patch, performing a single hemi-cube over the shooting patch to determine the diffuse form-factor to all other patches and then adding its contribution to the radiosities of all other patches. Every intermediate step simultaneously improves the solution for many patches, providing intermediate results which can be displayed before the solution converges within a desired tolerance.

3. PROGRESSIVE REFINEMENT RADIOSITY METHOD FOR NON-DIFFUSE ENVIRONMENTS

The progressive radiosity provided by Cohen et al. (1988) is for diffuse environment. Taking this method as a starting point, a two-pass solution is designed here for non-diffuse environments.

Within a non-diffuse environment, surfaces are no longer perfectly diffuse reflectors and emitters, therefore, all interreflections of light between diffuse and non-diffuse surfaces should be taken into consideration. For a non-diffuse surface, the bidirectional reflectance function is approximated as a sum of a diffuse portion ρ_d and a specular portion ρ_s (Immel 1986; Wallace 1987; P.Shao 1988):

$$\rho''(\theta_{out}, \theta_{in}) = k_s \rho_s(\theta_{out}, \theta_{in}) + k_d \rho_d \qquad \text{<4>}$$

where k_s, k_d are specular and diffuse reflectance of the surface respectively. $k_s + k_d \leq 1$.

The diffuse part of interreflection is still determined by the diffuse information on patches. The relationship between the radiosity of one patch and that of all other patches in the environment is given by P. P. Shao (1988):

$$B_i = E_i + k_{di}\rho_{di}\pi \sum_{j=1}^{N} \frac{B_j F'_{ji} A_j}{A_i} \qquad \text{<5>}$$

where

F'_{ji} is the form-factor between two patches within a general environment:

$$F'_{ji} = F_{ji} + \sum_{k=1}^{n} F_{jk} F_{jki} k_{sk} + \sum_{k=1}^{n}\sum_{l=1}^{n} F_{jk} F_{jkl} F_{kli} k_{sk} k_{sl} + \cdots \qquad \text{<6>}$$

here F_{ji} is the standard form-factor;

F_{jkl} represents the fraction of energy shooting out from patch j to patch k and finally landing on patch l via specular reflection of non-diffuse patch k;

k_{sk}, k_{sl} are specular reflectance of patch k, l respectively.

Thus, $A_j B_j F_{jk} F_{jki} k_{sk}$ is the energy emitted by patch j which lands on patch i via specular reflection of patch k.

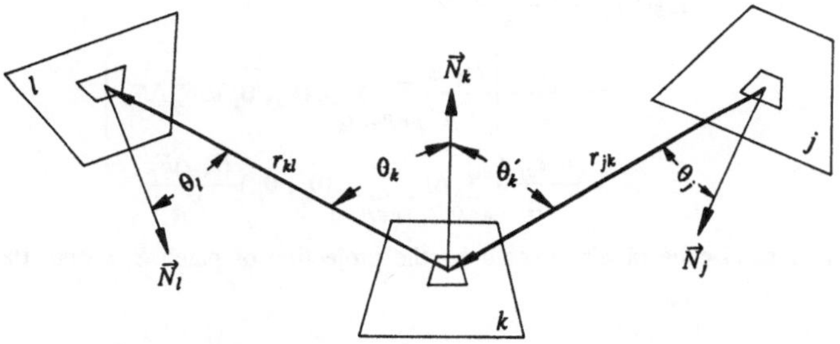

Fig. 1 Specular Form-factor Geometry

P. P. Shao defined the specular form-factor as (Fig. 1)

$$F'_{jkl} = \frac{1}{\pi}\int_{A_l}\int_{A_j} \rho_s(\theta_{out}, \theta_{in}) \frac{\cos\theta_j \cos\theta'_k}{r_{jk}^2} \frac{\cos\theta_k \cos\theta_l}{r_{kl}^2} dA_j dA_l$$

and

$$F_{jkl} = \frac{F'_{jkl}}{F_{kj}}$$

F_{jkl} is evaluated from hemi-cube by

$$F_{jkl} = \frac{\pi}{F_{kj}} (\sum_{p \in P} \sum_{q \in Q} \rho_s(\theta_q, \theta_p) \Delta F_q \Delta F_p) \quad \text{<7>}$$

where P, Q are the set of hemi-cube pixels covered by projection of patch j, l onto the hemicube; ΔF_p and ΔF_q are delta form-factors related to pixel p and q respectively.

The equation above can also be utilized in two ways. When considering in a "gathering" way, the energy which is emitted by a patch j and lands on patch i can be considered as a sum of the direct emission from patch j and the reflection reflected via other specular patches. Based on this thinking, P. Shao (1988) proposed an improved two-pass solution for non-diffuse environments, with a preprocess obtaining the diffuse radiosity but also covering specular effect among patches by solving a set of linear equations derived from <5>, and the result of preprocess is finally utilized as a basis for a postprocess of ray tracing for specular patches.

We notice that it is also possible to reverse the "gathering" process in the preprocess previously mentioned by shooting out the emission and reflection of a patch to the radiostiy or irradiation of all other patches, so that the calculation of form-factors may be considerablly reduced and at the same time the effect of specular reflection may be incorporated into the progressive refinement process.

In order to realize such a progressive solution, we reformulate equation <5> in the following form:

$$B_i = E_i + k_{di} \rho_{di} \pi \sum_{j=1}^{N} H_{ji} \quad \text{<8>}$$

here H_{ji} is the irradiation incident on patch i due to the radiation of patch j. For a non-diffuse patch j, H_{ji} consists of a diffuse term, H_{ji}^d, and a specular term, H_{ji}^s, reflected onto patch i via patch j, or:

$$H_{ji} = H_{ji}^d + H_{ji}^s \quad \text{<9>}$$

$$H_{ji}^d = A_j B_j F_{ji} / A_i \quad \text{<10>}$$

$$H_{ji}^s = \sum_{k=1}^{N} A_j H_{kj} F_{kji} k_{sj} / A_i \quad \text{<11>}$$

Denote $H_{ji}^s(k) = A_j H_{kj} F_{kji} k_{sj} / A_i$, we get

$$H_{ji}^s(k) = \frac{A_j H_{kj} F_{kji} k_{sj}}{A_i}$$

$$= \frac{A_j k_{sj}}{A_i} \left[\frac{H_{kj} \pi}{F_{jk}} \sum_{p \in P} \sum_{q \in Q} \rho_s(\theta_q, \theta_p) \Delta F_q \Delta F_p \right]$$

$$= \frac{A_j k_{sj} \pi}{A_i} \sum_{q \in Q} \Delta F_q \sum_{p \in P} \rho_s(\theta_q, \theta_p) \frac{H_{kj} \Delta F_p}{F_{jk}}$$

where P, Q is the set of hemi-cube pixels covered by the projection of patch k, i onto the hemicube over patch j.

Let $H_p = \frac{H_{kj} \Delta F_p}{F_{jk}}$, is the *delta irradiation* related to pixel p covered by the projection of patch k onto hemi-cube and the hemicube can be used to evaluate H_p. Therefore, we have

$$H_{ji}^s = \frac{A_j k_{sj} \pi}{A_i} \sum_{k=1}^{N} \sum_{q \in Q} \Delta F_q \sum_{p \in P} \rho_s(\theta_q, \theta_p) H_p \quad \text{<12>}$$

Because the non-diffuse patch j satisfies the phong-like bidirectional reflectance (Cohen 1986; Wallace 1987; P.Shao 1988), the specular reflective energy leaving patch j through hemi-cube pixel q is approximated by the weighted summation of energy which reaches the patch j through the area $P(q)$ on the hemi-cube (Fig. 2). Therefore,

$$H_{ji}^s = \frac{A_j k_{sj} \pi}{A_i} \sum_{q \in Q} \Delta F_q \sum_{p \in P(q)} \rho_s(\theta_q, \theta_p) H_p \quad \text{<13>}$$

$\rho_s(\theta_q, \theta_p)$ is employed as a weighted factor and presented by an array of weights during implementation.

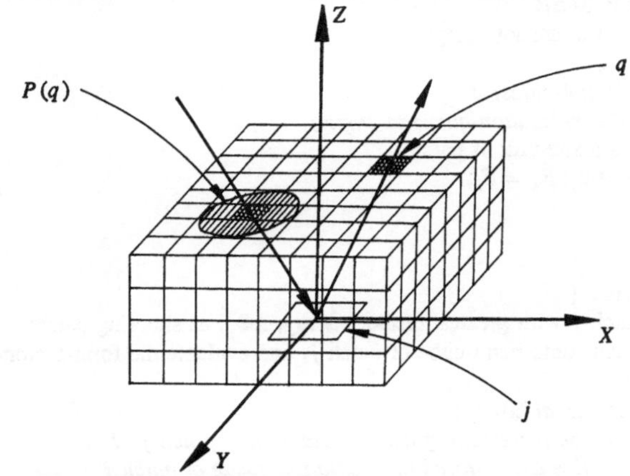

Fig. 2 Relationship Between Outgoing and Incoming Energy Distribution

4. IMPLEMETATION

The shooting light of a non-diffuse patch will cause the whole environment's irradiation and radiosity values to be updated simultaneously. The linear equations <10>,<13> are reformulated in a way of pregressive refinement as

$$\Delta H_{ji}^d = \frac{\Delta B_j^d A_j F_{ji}^d}{A_i} \tag{14}$$

$$\Delta H_p = \Delta H_{kj} \frac{\Delta F_{j(p)}^d}{F_{jk}^d} \tag{15}$$

$$\Delta H_{ji}^s = \frac{A_j k_{sj} \pi}{A_i} \sum_{q \in Q} \Delta F_{j(q)}^d \sum_{p \in P(q)} \rho_{sj}(\theta_q, \theta_p) \Delta H_p \tag{16}$$

and

$$\Delta H_{ji} = \Delta H_{ji}^d + \Delta H_{ji}^s \tag{17}$$

$$\Delta B_i^d = k_{di} \pi \rho_{di} \Delta H_{ji} \tag{18}$$

Based on the equations above , a two-pass progressive solution for non-diffuse environments is established, with a progressive preprocess iteratively refining the distribution of radiosities including specular reflections, followed by a postprocess of ray tracing for adding view-dependent effects such as highlight and specular reflection. Instead of directly using the specular form-factors like in Shaos' methods (M.Shao 1988; P.Shao 1988), in our method, the hemi-cube constructed on a non-diffuse shooting patch is utilized to evaluate the standard form-factors and delta irradiations. For each non-diffuse patch, a queue, for instance, ΔH_{kj} for a non-diffuse patch j, is set up to register increment in irradiation. Each time while a patch selected is shooting, the irradiation increment is queued onto all the receiving non-diffuse patches, preparing for the calculation of specular reflections next time when they are selected as shooting patches.

If a selected patch is a light source, its radiosity and radiosity increment are initialised to the emission value, otherwise both are zeros. For all non-diffuse patches, the queues of irradiation are initialized to empty.

With a similar method of adaptive patch subdivision (Cohen 1988) adopted, the preprocess of progressive radiosity can be described in pseudocode as follows.

```
/* initialization */
```

```
for each patch i {
    ΔB_i = E_i; B_i = E_i;
 /* determine initial unshot energy */
    ΔΦ_i = ΔB_i A_i;
   if ( patch i is non-diffuse )
      initialize the irradiation-queue to empty;
 /* element e is a sub-unit of patch i */
   for each element : B_e = E_i;
}

/* preprocess */
 Until convergence {
   select the patch j with greatest unshot energy, ΔΦ_j, as shooting patch;
   project elements onto hemi-cube of patch j, and evaluate the form-factors from patch j to
   element e, F_je;
   if ( patch j is non-diffuse ) {
     /* determine the increment of delta irradiation of patch j */
      for each value ΔH_kj stored in irradiation queue of patch j
         determine hemi-cube pixels p covered by projection of patch k onto hemicube;
         for each pixel p : ΔH_p = ΔH_kj ΔF_p / F_jk ;
      }
   for each element e in environment {
     /* determine diffuse irradiation increment of element e */
        ΔH = ΔB_j A_j F_je / A_e;
      if ( element e is non-diffuse ) {
         /* initialize specular irradiation increment*/
            ΔH^s = 0;
         /* determine specular irradiation increment of element e */
            for each pixel q covered by projection of element e   {
               determine the area P(q) on the hemi-cube;
               for each pixel p in P(q) : ΔH^s += w_j(q, p)ΔH_p;     /* w_j is array of weights */
              ΔH^s *= A_j k_sj π/A_e;
            }
              ΔH += ΔH^s;
      }
        derive ΔB_e from ΔH;
        B_e += ΔB_e;
        ΔB_i += ΔB_e A_e / A_i;   /* element e is a sub-unit of patch i */
        derive ΔΦ_i from ΔH;
      if ( patch i is non-diffuse ) ΔH_ji += ΔHA_e / A_i;   /* ΔH_ji is set in the irradiation queue
                                                                  of patch i */
   }
   interpolate vertex radioaities from neibouring elements;
   if ( area exists of high radiosity gradient )
      subdivide elements in this area and reshoot patch j to these smaller elements;
     ΔB_j = 0;
     ΔΦ_j = 0;
   remove the irradiation queue of patch j;
   display intermediate image;
 }
```

Because the specular reflection is directional. For a non-diffuse shooting patch, it may cause significant illumination change with a relatively small unshot energy. So in the sorting operation, the unshot energy of non-diffuse patch is multiplied by a promotion coefficient bigger than unit to promote the shooting priority of non-diffuse patch.

As the process proceeds, the solution for many patches are improved simultaneously at each iterative step and the intermediate result can be displayed. The intermediate display will be more graceful if an "ambient term" (Cohen 1988) is utilized, and it is straitforward to embody the ambient term to the algorithm above. The final result of the preprocess is the discretized diffuse radiosities at the center of patches. The radiosity values are then transferred from patches' center to vertices of patches, and at any point on a patch the diffuse radiosity is evaluated from bilinear interpolation of the values at vertices of the patch. As a result of the preprocess, the view-independent diffuse intereflection within the environment is obtained, and finally the ray tracing process is invoked as a postprocess to account for view-dependent effects and thereby completes the solution.

Figure 3 and 4 show a test environment which contains three light sources composed of ten emission patches. A very bright light source faces to the left wall on which a nearly perfect mirror ($k_d = 0.07$, $k_s = 0.93$) is hanging. In Fig. 3, only diffuse patches are involved with shooting so that merely diffuse-to-diffuse transfer has been taken into consideration in the procedure of progressive radiosity iteration (Cohen 1988). But in Fig. 4, non-diffuse patches are included in the sorting procedure and some of them have been selected as shooting patches, so the light spots which are caused by specular to diffuse transfer clearly appeared on the table, ceil and floor. Experience shows that the specular reflectional illumination is significant during the first ten iterations. Figure 5 shows an image in a similar environment with 200 hemi-cube calculations.

The hemi-cube resolution is 100 by 100 for the images produced above. On an average, the iteration time of each shooting for diffuse patches is about 5.2 seconds, and non-diffuse patches, about 6.1 seconds. The image on the mirror and the fuzzy image on the non-diffuse sphere ($k_d = 0.25$, $k_s = 0.75$) are produced in the ray tracing postprocess. The color textures are generated by color texture mapping technique (Cohen 1986).

In progressive radiosity, the elements are projected onto the hemi-cube over the shooting patch. Therefore, the cost of hemi-cube operation is affected by the level of recursive subdivision. On the other hand, only a few shooting patches will cause high gradients over some surface. So we set a maximum subdivision depth for surfaces to limit the subdivision times to maitain the efficiency. Of course, the scheme may cause aliasing sometimes on some surfaces, especially on the surfaces which is very close to shooting patches (Fig. 3 and 4). The other reasons for aliasing are that hemi-cube algorithm computes form-factors by point-sampling technique and the rendering is in a pixel-by-pixel way.

5. SHADOW POSTPROCESS FOR SMALL AREA LIGHT SOURCES

In the progressive radiosity method areas in an environment which exhibit high radiosity gradations such as those around shadow boundaries are subject to further subdivision. An initial guess for patch and element subdivision must be performed to form an initial mesh providing a base for further subdivision. However, shadow cast by a very thin object may still be missed, especially in progressive radiosity method. A light source which is relatively small compared to the environment may creat very sharp shadows even for a very thin object just as a point light source does. Lacking such shadows will make images artificial as shadows can provide effective information for the observer to accurately comprehend complex spatial environments. In general radiosity methods, the only way to simulate such case is to build finer initial mesh and higher resolution hemi-cube, as a result, the computation cost will be considerably increased.

In this section, we will suggest a shadow postprocess for small area light sources to produce realistic sharp shadows based on the progressive radiosity solution started from a coarse initial mesh. Though the standard ray tracing method (Whitted 1980) can produce very graceful shadow effects accounting for point light sources and many shadow algorithms (Crow 1977; Atherton 1979; Brotman 1984; Nishita 1985; Haines 1986) for point light sources have been developed, they are still unable to be utilized in an environment of (diffuse) interreflection. Our method to be proposed is based on the result of progressive radiosity so that both interreflection and sharp shadow effects can be simulated gracefully. Though some advanced ray tracing methods (Kajiya 1986; Ward 1988) may solve the problem, our solution which is cooperated with the progressive radiosity is more efficicent in terms of time expense.

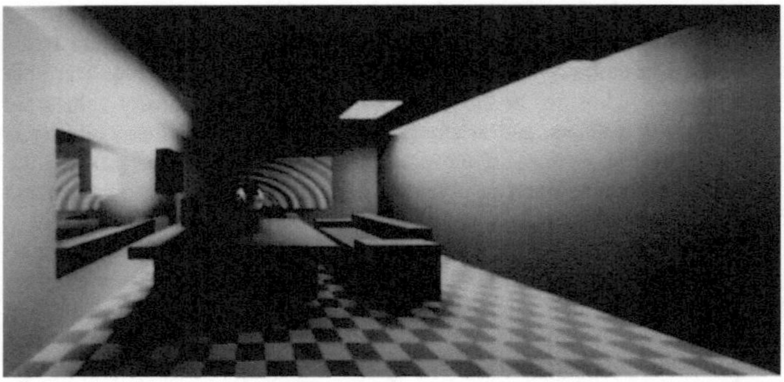

number of iterations	time of iteration (minutes)	time of rendering (minutes)
10	0.9	3.4

Fig. 3 Progressive Radiosity only Shot by Diffuse Patches

number of iterations	time of each iteration (seconds)		time of iteration (minutes)	time of rendering (minutes)
	specular shooting	diffuse shooting		
10	5.2	6.1	1.0	3.4

Fig. 4 Adapted Progressive Radiosity Accounting for both Diffuse And Specular Shooting Patches

Fig. 5 Progressive Radiosity Method for Non-diffuse Environment

5.1 Detection of Shadowed Areas

If an emiting patch is very small but its emission is very strong, it can be treated as a point light source. As already mentioned, the radiosity of a visible point on a patch is derived from bilinear interpolation of the radiosities at vertices of the patch. If the visible point is within a shadow area created by a point light source, the contribution of the point light source's emission must be excluded so that the sharp shadow can be simulated. By re-shooting the point light source, its contribution to environment's radiosity is derived. The attenuated radioisty of a visible point is obtained by bilinear interpolation just as the conventional radiosity method does. Of course, there are some other ways to register the radiosity contribution of point light sources.

Assume the ray from source to a visible point P outgoes through hemi-cube pixel q(Fig. 6). If the visible patch index stored at pixel q is different from the index of patch on which the point P is, P is within the shadow cast by some other patch and its radiosity must be attenuated.

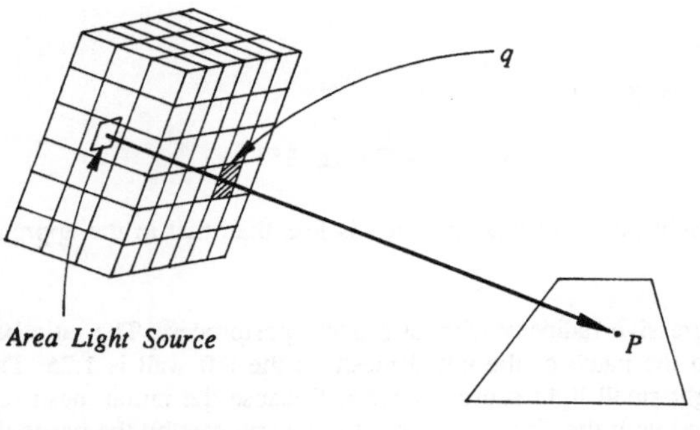

Fig. 6 Detection of Shadowed Areas

5.2 Attenuated Factor

Because a small light source is not a perfect point light source, it creates both umbrae and peumbrae. A precise way to calculate the attenuated radiosities is to treat a small light source as a set of sample point light sources, and build a high resolution *light hemi–cube* for each of these sample points. The attenuated radiostiy of point P is then

$$B_{att} = \frac{m}{n} B^e \qquad \text{<19>}$$

where B^e is the contribution of the small light source to the radiosity of point P,
m is the number of occluded sample point light source,
n is the number of sample point light source,
$\frac{m}{n}$ acts as an *attenuated factor*.

This method is similar to Brotman and Norman's method (1984), but its time/space requirement is relatively expensive if the number of small area sources is large. When occluding objects are relatively far from the small light source, we suggest an approximate method as follows.

Because the shadows of big objects can be detected by adaptive subdivision effectively, the purpose of shadow postprocess is to simulate the small shadow cast by a nearby thin object due to the radiation of a very small area light source. As shown in Fig. 7, a ray leaves light source O, intersects a thin occluding object at point Q and extended to point P on an occluded object. The attenuated radiosity of point P decreases as the distance between point M and P increases due to the effect of penumbra effect. Therefore, we propose an approximated formula for attenuated radiosity of point P :

$$B_{att} = f(\alpha)B^e \qquad \text{<20>}$$

where $f(\alpha)$ is attenuated factor, an increase function of α, $\alpha = \dfrac{|\vec{OQ}|}{|\vec{OP}|}$.

If $f(\alpha)$ is smaller than a constant minimum approximation coefficient β, let $f(\alpha) = \beta$.

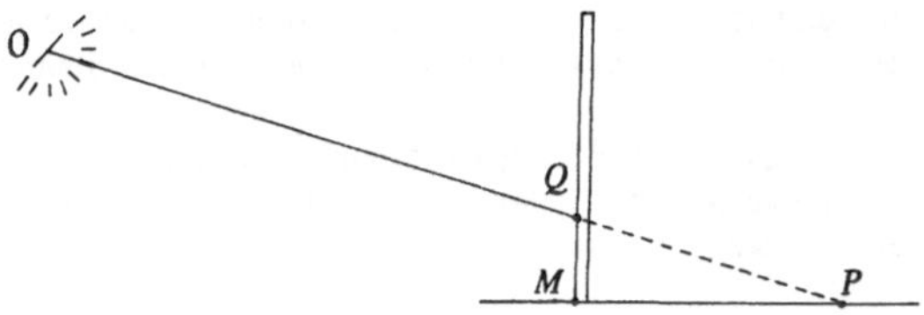

Fig. 7 Approximate Attenuated Factor

Combine formula <19> <20>, we get

$$B_{att} = \frac{1}{n}\sum_{i=1}^{n} f(\alpha_i)B^e \qquad \text{<21>}$$

Here, the number of sample light points in this approach is less than that in the approach using formula <19> alone.

Figure 8a is the result of progressive radiosity without shadow postprocess. The ratio between the width of the thin bar near the left wall and the patch of the initial mesh on the left wall is 1:25. The ratio of the width of the bar to the size of the bright small light source is 1:2.5. Because the initial mesh for patch division on the left wall is too coarse compared with the size of the bar, the shadow cast by the bar is therefore missed. Figure 8b, c and d show the same test evironment for which the shadow of the bar is produced by the shadow post-process. As compared with Fig. 8a, the improvement is obvious. In Fig. 8b, the small area source is taken as a single point light source, so the boundary of the shadow is very sharp. The area source is treated as a set of six point light sources using formula <19> in Fig. 8c. The number of sample light points is two and the approximate formula <21> is used. Since all the shadow-generating are relatively far from light source ($\alpha > 0.5$), Fig. 8d is very similar to Fig. 8c.

The hemi-cube resolution for preprocess and re-shooting is 80 by 80, and the light hemicube resolution for shadow postprocess is 180 by 180.

Figure 9 contains an image produced by progressive radiosity preprocess with 250 iterations, followed by ray tracing postprocess and shadow postprocess. The small area light source which is surrounded by a lampshade (Fig. 10) is sampled as eight point sources. The ratio between the width of the thin bar near the right wall and the patch of the initial mesh on the left wall is 1:40. The mirror is a nearly perfect specular reflector ($k_s = 0.999$, $k_d = 0.001$). The hemi-cube resolutions for preprocess and shadow postprocess are 100 by 100 and 200 by 200 respectively. The total time of processing is about 33 minutes.

By carefully looking into the Fig. 9, we notice that visual banding effects are produced within the shadow of the lampshade on the right wall. It is becausethe sampled light sources are evenly spaced over the small area source and the light source is too close to the occluding lampshade so that it is hardly to be looked as a small one compared with the lampshade. In fact, this aliasing may be eliminated or made trivial by random generation of sampling. Another simple method to solve the problem is to impose supersampling on the source patch. In our experience, a sampling of ten points will make the aliasing in Fig. 9 hardly noticable.

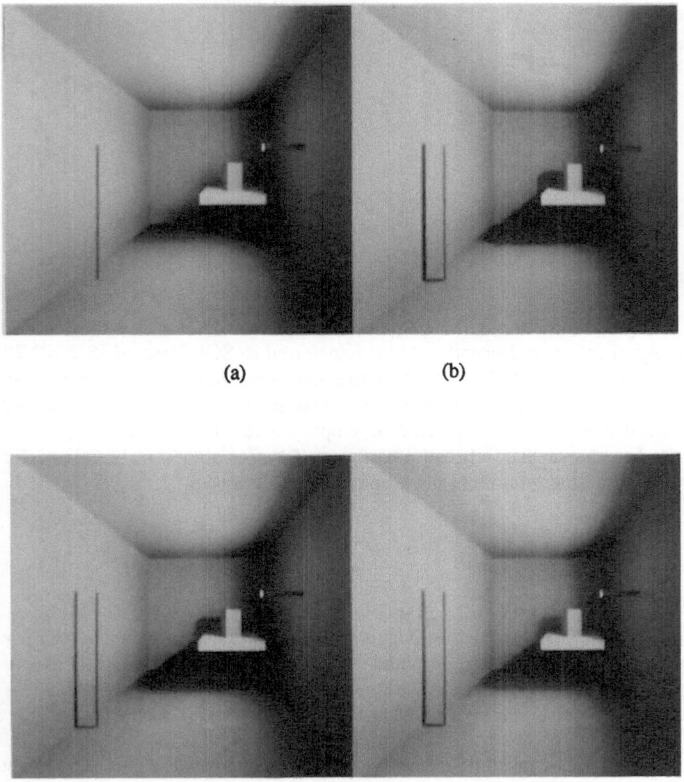

(a) (b)

(c) (d)

Fig. 8 Shadow Postprocess for Small Area Source

progressive radiosity	shadow postprocess	time of rendering
(minutes)	(minutes)	(minutes)
25.4	2.1	5.2

Fig. 9 A Room with Mirror and Small Area Light Source

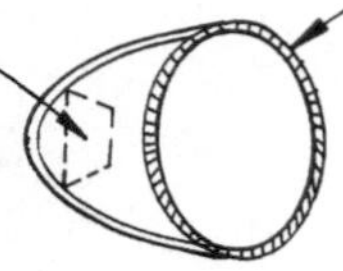

Fig. 10 Geometry of Lamp and Lampshade

The method described in the paper was programmed in C language and implemented on a Apollo DN-580, with the algorithms implemented entirely in software. Recently, it was transferred to SGI Personal IRIS 4D/20 workstation. The figures reported were measured on 4D/20, with the entire software originally implemented on DN-580 unchanged or without taking any advantages of hardware and software facilities of 4D/20. As a matter of fact, the performance will be improved if the hardware pipeline is employed for the hemi-cube operation and the rendering (Chen 1990). Result has shown that, when the hardware Z-buffer algorithm is utilized for the hemi-cube calculation, around 70% of computation time in the preprocess can be saved.

6. CONCLUSION

To sum up, an adapted two-pass solution has been proposed, in which a new progressive refinement radiosity method is combined with ray tracing within a non-diffuse environment. Consequently, interreflection in a non-diffuse environment can be simulated in a fairly efficient way. Besides, an optional shadow postprocess has been introduced as a complement method to adaptive patch subdivision for improving image realism.

At present, the radiosity method can simulate the physical phenomena such as shading, shadow, color bleeding and the interreflection of light between neighbouring surfaces, and make use of color texture mapping technique. However, no successful work so far on the incorporation of radiosity and bump texture generation has been reported. We have done some preliminary work on this topic and the results are presented in another paper (Chen 1990).

It is imaginable that the efficient radiosity which can simulate rich visual effects will be utilized in applications in the near future.

ACKNOWLEDGEMENTS

We are grateful to Liang You-Dong and Peng Qun-Sheng of Zhejiang University for their generous help in providing related theses for references long before their papers appeared at conferences. Thanks are also given to Dong Yun-Mei for providing related hardware facilities required.

The work has been supported by the National Natural Science Foundation (Grant no. 68973017).

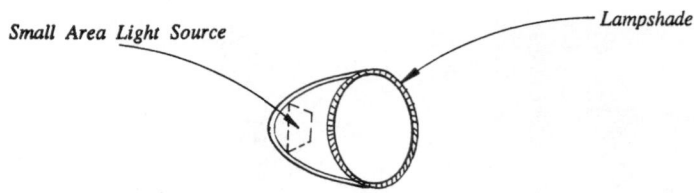

REFERENCES

Atherton P, Weiler K, Greenberg DP (1979)
Polygon Shadow Generation. Computer Graphics 12(3)

Brotman LS, Norman NI (1984)
Generation Soft Shadows with a Depth Buffer Algorithm. IEEE CG&A 4(10)

Chen H, Wu EH (1990)
An Efficient Radiosity Solution for Bump Texture Generation. to appear

Cohen MF, Chen SE, Wallace JK, Greenberg DP (1988)
A Progressive Refinement Approach to Fast Radiosity Image Generation. Computer Graphics 22(4):75-84

Cohen MF, Greenberg DP (1985)
The Hemi-cube: A Radiosity Solution for Complex Environment. Computer Graphics 19(3):31-40

Cohen MF, Greenberg DP, Immel DS, Brack PJ (1986)
An Efficient Radiosity Approach for Realistic Image Synthesis. IEEE CG&A 6(2):26-35

Crow FC (1977)
Shadow Algorithms for Computer Graphics. Computer Graphics 11(2)

Goral CM, Torrance KE, Greenberg DP (1984)
Modelling the Interaction of Light between Diffuse Surfaces. Computer Graphics 18(3):213-222

Haines EA, Greenberg DP (1986)
The Light Buffer : A Shadow-Testing Accelerator. IEEE CG&A 6(9)

Immel DS, Cohen MF, Greenberg DP (1986)
A Radiosity Method for Non-diffuse Environment. Computer Graphics 20(4):133-142

Kajiya JT (1986)
The Rendering Equations. Computer Graphics 20(4):143-150

Meyer GW, Rushmeier HE, Cohen MF, Greenberg DP, Torrance KE (1986)
An Experimental Evaluation of Computer Graphics Imagery. ACM Transaction on Graphics 5(1)

Nishita T, Nakamae E (1985)
Continuous Tone Representation of Three-dimensional Objects Taking Account of Shadows and Interreflection. Computer Graphics 19(3):22-30

Nishita T, Okamura I, Nakamae E (1985)
Shading Models for Point and Linear Source. ACM Trans. on Graphics 4(2)

Shao MZ, Peng QS, Liang YD (1988)
A New Radiosity Approach By Procedural Refinements for Realistic Image Synthesis. Computer Graphics 22(4):93-101

Shao PP, Peng QS, Liang YD (1988)
Form-factors for General Environments. Proc. Eurographics'88:499-510

Sparrow EM, Cess RD (1978)
Radiation Heat Transfer. McGraw-Hill, New York

Wallace JR, Cohen MF, Greenberg DP (1987)
A Two-pass Solution to the Rendering Equation: A Synthesis of Ray Tracing and Radiosity Methods. Computer Graphics 21(4):311-320

Ward GJ, Rubinstein FM, Clear RD (1988)
A Ray Tracing Solution for Diffuse Interreflection. Computer Graphics 22(4):85-92

Whitted T (1980)
An Improved Illumination Model for Shaded Display. Comm. ACM 23(6):343-349

Chen, Hong finished his undergraduate study in 1986 at Dept. of Computer Science, Nanjing University. Since then he registered as a postgraduate student at Institute of Software of Academia Sinica, and received his Master degree in Sept., 1989. His main interests are Computer Graphics, CAD/CAM.
Address: 6th Division, Institute of Software, Academia Sinica, P. O. Box 8718, Beijing 100080, P. R. China.

Wu, En-Hua is currently an associate professor and director of Software Tools & Computer Graphics (6th) division of Institute of Software, Academia Sinica. He undergraduated from Dept. of Mathematics and Mechanics of Tsinghua(Qinghua) University, Beijing in 1970, and since then he had been lecturing at Dept. of Computer Science and Technology of Tsinghua University until 1978. After a short period of postgraduate study in Academia Sinica, he had registered as a research postgraduate student from 1980 at Dept. of Computer Science, University of Manchester, U. K., and received his Ph.D degree there in 1984. He is a member of Eurographics Association and standing council member of Beijing Software Industry Association.

His main interests are Computer Graphics, CAD/CAM, System Software, Numerical Analysis and Application Software.
Address: Institute of Software, Academia Sinica, P. O. Box 8718, Beijing 100080, P. R. China.

Chapter 9
Curves and Surfaces

High-Quality Rendering of Parametric Surfaces by Using a Robust Scanline Algorithm

Tomoyuki Nishita, Kazufumi Kaneda, and Eihachiro Nakamae

ABSTRACT

Displaying objects with high accuracy is seriously required not only for CAGD (Computer Aided Geometric Design) but also for the synthesis of photo-realistic images. Traditionally, polygonal approximation methods have been employed to display curved surfaces. They bring on low accuracy of display not only in shape but also in intensity of objects. In this paper a scanline algorithm to directly display surface patches, expressed by Bezier surfaces, without polygonal approximation is proposed. In our proposal, curved surfaces are subdivided into subpatches with curved edges intersecting with a scanline, and the intersections of every subpatch and the scanline are calculated. This method is extremely robust for calculation of the intersections, which can be obtained with only a few iterations. Furthermore, the greater the number of patches, the more effective the method is regarding required memory and calculation time. Anti-aliased images with shadows and texture mapping are given to show the effectiveness of the method proposed.

Key Words: Bezier Surfaces, Scanline algorithm, Robustness, High-quality rendering, Surface trimming, Silhouette detection, Shadowing

1 Introduction

Raytracing algorithms are a useful tool for rendering realistic images, but require extensive calculation time, while scanline algorithms can save calculation time. Traditionally, polygonal approximation methods have been employed to display curved surfaces. They can save calculation time and be easily implemented, but the displayed shape is not so accurate to a defined curved surface. To solve these problems some scanline algorithms rendering bicubic surfaces directly from parametric description have been proposed.

Blinn [Blinn 78] and Whitted [Whitted 78] employed the Newton-Raphson method to calculate the intersections of a scanline and curved surfaces. This method needs an initial guess and is not robust, and moreover a weakness in Whitted's approach is the lack of generality in finding silhouettes. To find silhouettes robustly, Schweitzer and Cobb [Schweitzer 82] proposed a method of dividing curved surfaces into polygons consisting of the boundary curves which are monotonic in y. In this method extraction of silhouettes is fairly complicated because several points on a silhouette need to be calculated by using normals of a curved surface approximated to cubic surfaces.

Lane, Carpenter [Lane 80] and Clark [Clark 79] rendered curved surfaces after subdividing them into small polygons. That is, curved surfaces are subdivided into subpatches until flat enough, then the subpatches are reckoned as polygons, and finally a polygon-oriented scanline algorithm is employed. In Clark's method curved surfaces are subdivided into subpatches before scan-conversion, while in Lane-Carpenter's method curved surfaces are dynamically subdivided for every scanline. Lane-Carpenter's method has the disadvantage that gaps arise between approximated polygons because of the difference between the approximated polygons and the original surface patches. This problem is caused by straight lines consisting of the approximated polygons. In the subdivision methods taking into account surface flatness, only when the tolerance of surface flatness is within one pixel size, the silhouettes become smooth.

Griffiths [Griffiths 84] dealt with curved surfaces in the parametric plane. In this method, a curved surface is decomposed into grid cells, and some of them intersecting with a scanline are further divided. Then, linear interpolation is employed to get their depths and intensities. In this method silhouettes are extracted by using normal vectors stored in the grid cells. Pueyo and Brunet [Pueyo 87] improved upon Griffiths' method; they proposed that curved surfaces are decomposed into grid cells beforehand, and intersections of the restricted scanline and curved surfaces are calculated without interpolation (making use of the y-coordinates stored in the grid cells), and interpolation in parametric space is employed to intersections of the other scanlines. Silhouettes are detected by using the z-components of normal vectors stored in the grid points. One of the disadvantages of the previous two methods is missing those silhouettes formed by a smaller loop than the grid span.

Important elements for rendering curved surfaces are robustness (in the detection of silhouettes), accuracy, required memory, image quality (i. e., anti-aliasing and shadows), and calculation time. In all the above-mentioned methods, there are some problems, such as lack of robustness, inaccuracy caused by the approximations, large memory caused by beforehand subdivision. Our proposal overcomes all these problems.

The proposed method has the following advantages, although it is partially based on Lane-Carpenter's method. (a) Subpatches on a scanline are effectively obtained, and no gaps arise between the subpatches. (b) Proposed root finder using curve clipping is accurate and robust for calculation of intersections of the scanline and subpatches. (c) This method is especially effective for displaying scenes with a number of patches because only the curved surfaces intersecting with the active scanline are subdivided. (d) Anti-aliased images with shadows can be rendered.

2 Outline of the Algorithm

Bezier surfaces are used in this paper, because almost all surfaces, such as B-splines and NURBS, can be converted into Bezier surfaces. In this paper, curved surfaces are subdivided into subpatches on a scanline. These subpatches are processed as polygons with curved edges, and intersections of every subpatch and the scanline are calculated. Finally, traditional polygon-oriented scanline algorithms represented by Watkins's algorithm [Watkins 70] are employed to display images.

Outline of the proposed algorithm is as follows:

Step 1: Calculate a bounding box for each surface patch after the perspective transformation of every control point of each surface patch.

Step 2: Find surface patches intersecting with the scanline, and subdivide them into subpatches on the scanline.

Step 3: Calculate every span (called a scan segment) where subpatches intersect with the scanline.

Step 4: Find visible parts on each scan segment.

Step 5: Calculate shadow sections on each visible part.

Step 6: Display intensity of each pixel by using Phong's smooth shading algorithm.

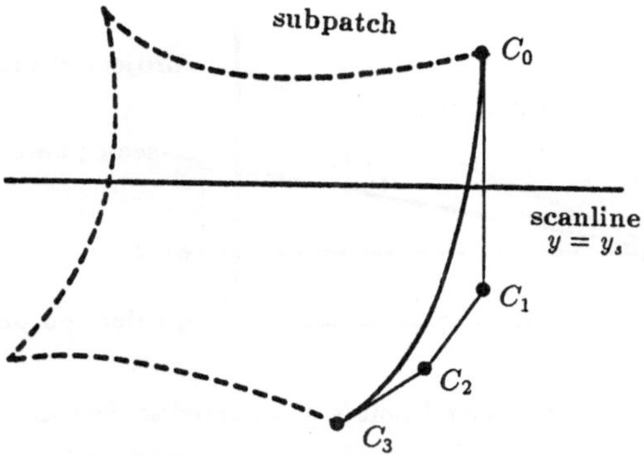

Figure 1: Intersection test of a boundary curve and a scanline.

In **step 1**, a convex hull property of each Bezier surface is useful to determine its bounding box. That is, the bounding box is determined by using the minimum and maximum values of the coordinates (x, y) of control points. In **step 2**, each subpatch is recursively subdivided until a desired degree of surface flatness is achieved. In **step 3**, the spans of scan segments are calculated by using intersections of a curved boundary of each subpatch and the scanline.

The proposed method basically belongs to polygon-oriented scanline algorithms, but **steps 2, 3,** and **5** are different from them. In the following sections, these steps are discussed.

3 Intersections of Curves and a Scanline

In the proposed method, after subdivision of curved surfaces into subpatches on each scanline, subpatches are scan-converted into scan segments. For the convenience of explanation of this method, first the calculation method of the intersections between curves and the scanline in **step 3** is described, although it follows **step 2**.

Let's assume that a curved surface is defined by Bezier surface of degree n, and the boundary curves of the surface, $P(u, v)$, are expressed by $P(u, 0)$, $P(u, 1)$, $P(0, v)$, and $P(1, v)$. These curves are also expressed by Bezier curves of degree n. Then, each boundary curve, $C(t)$, in a space, is defined by the following.

$$C(t) = \sum_{i=0}^{n} C_i B_i^n(t), \tag{1}$$

where $C_i(X_i, Y_i, Z_i)$ $(i = 0, 1, \cdots, n)$ are control points and B is the Bernstein basis polynomial:

$$B_i^n(t) = \binom{n}{i} (1-t)^{n-i} t^i.$$

The calculation on the intersections of a projected curve $C(t)$ and a scanline, $y = y_s$ (see Fig. 1) is discussed in the following. Assumed that as shown in Fig.2 control points, C_i, are defined by the eye coordinate systems whose origin is set to the viewpoint and the z axis is perpendicular to the projection plane of which distance is R from the viewpoint, the points, (x, y, R), on a curve projected onto the projection plane can be defined by the following rational Bezier function.

$$\begin{aligned} x(t) &= \textstyle\sum_{i=0}^{n} X_i B_i^n(t)/z(t) \\ y(t) &= \textstyle\sum_{i=0}^{n} Y_i B_i^n(t)/z(t) \\ z(t) &= \textstyle\sum_{i=0}^{n} Z_i B_i^n(t)/R. \end{aligned} \tag{2}$$

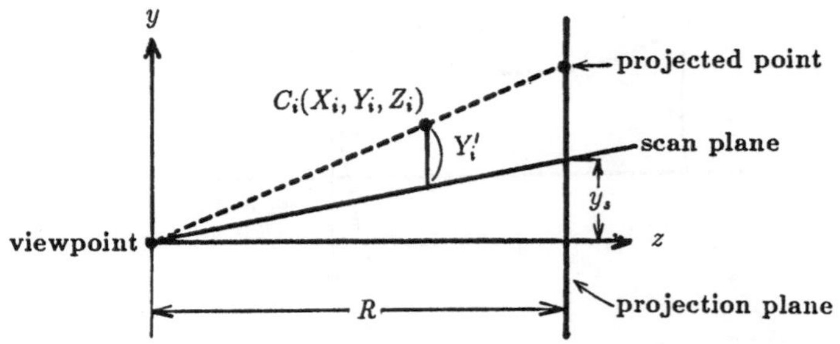

Figure 2: Relationship between control points of a curved surface and a scan plane.

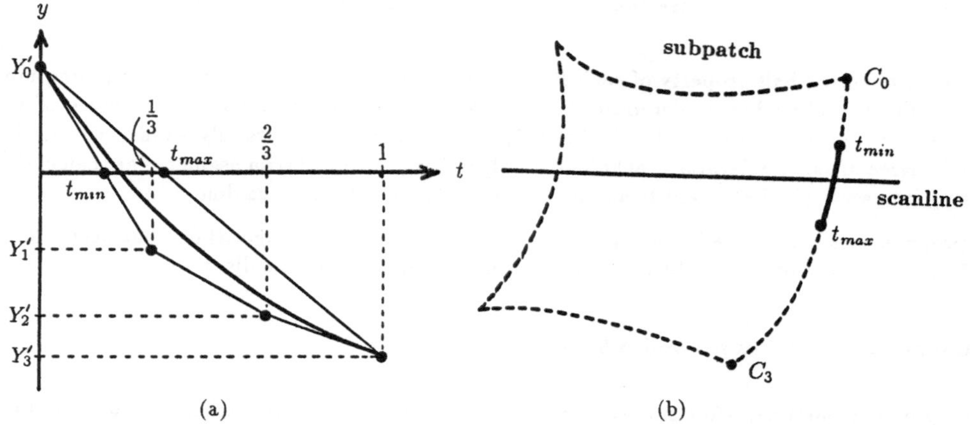

Figure 3: Calculation of intersections in parametric space and clipping a boundary curve.

where $z(t)$ is the depth defined as $z = 1$ at every point on the projection plane. As the line equation of the scan line is expressed by $y - y_s = 0$, the following equation is derived by substituting this into Eq. 2.

$$\sum_{i=0}^{n} Y_i' B_i^n(t) = 0, \tag{3}$$

where $\quad Y_i' = Y_i - (y_s/R)Z_i.$

Y_i' corresponds to the distance in the y direction between the scan plane and a control point C_i as shown in Fig. 2. If a parameter, t, which satisfies Eq. 3 is calculated, then the depth, z, and x coordinates of the intersection on the projection plane can be derived.

The parameter t in Eq. 3 can be solved by using the Newton-Raphson method, because the equation is a polynomial of degree n, however, the calculation is not always robust. To overcome the problem, the authors propose the following method. When the curve intersects with the scanline, the root of Eq. 3 always exists between the intersections of the convex hull determined by the vertexes, $(i/n, Y_i')$ $(i = 0, 1, \cdots, n)$, and the t-axis, because the curve defined by Eq. 3 is non-parametric function (see Fig. 3 (a)), while the curve does not intersect with the scanline when Y_i' $(i = 0, 1, \cdots, n)$ are positive for all i or negative for all i. Only when Y_i' has both positive and negative value (in this condition the roots exist), the outside of the interval $[t_{min}, t_{max}]$ of the curve is clipped away as shown in Fig. 3 (a). As the intersections of the convex hull formed by the control points of the clipped curve (as shown in Fig. 3 (b)) and the t-axis are recursively

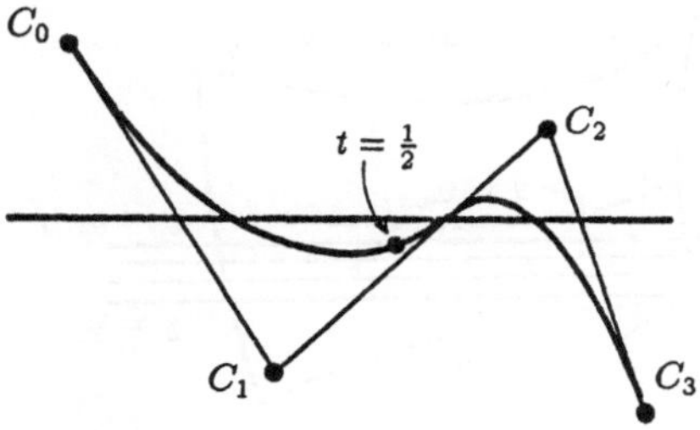

Figure 4: More than two intersections of a curve and a line.

calculated, the interval where the roots exist becomes narrow. The root of t converges with the advance of the clipping process. If Eq. 3 has more than two roots, the ratio of the convergency of the interval becomes small. In this case the curve is divided into two curves (divided at the point $t = 1/2$ in Fig. 4), and the same process as mentioned above is continued for each divided curve; from then, all of the roots can be calculated. This clipping method consists of two processes, that is, calculation of the interval of t and clipping a curve. Generally speaking, the latter process needs extensive calculation time because curves in a space have three components, x, y, and z, while in our method, calculation time can be saved because only one component, Y', is used to clip a curve; de Casteljau's subdivision algorithm is employed for the clipping.

4 Clipping a Curved Surface

The method generating for subpatches intersecting with the scanline is described here. In Lane and Carpenter's method, a curved surface is subdivided into four subpatches. The subpatches on the scanline are extracted, and the subdivision is recursively continued until surface flatness is satisfied. In this method, not only the subdivision process but also the extracting of the subpatches existing on the scanline are necessary. Authors propose a more efficient method of generating subpatches on the scanline. An area of a curved surface is recursively subdivided by clipping away where the surface does not intersect with the scanline. In many cases a subpatch intersects with several scanlines. In this paper, subpatches intersecting with every few scanlines (e. g., every three or four scanlines) are generated, and the intersections of the boundary curves of subpatches and the scanline are calculated.

Assumed that the coordinates of a control point are (X_{ij}, Y_{ij}, Z_{ij}) in the eye coordinate systems, Bezier surfaces of degree n are defined as follows:

$$\begin{aligned} x(u,v) &= \textstyle\sum_{i=0}^{n}\sum_{j=0}^{n} X_{ij} B_i^n(u) B_j^n(v) \\ y(u,v) &= \textstyle\sum_{i=0}^{n}\sum_{j=0}^{n} Y_{ij} B_i^n(u) B_j^n(v) \\ z(u,v) &= \textstyle\sum_{i=0}^{n}\sum_{i=0}^{n} Z_{ij} B_i^n(u) B_i^n(v). \end{aligned} \tag{4}$$

When the range for generating for subpatches is a band between the two scanlines, y_1 and y_2 ($y_1 > y_2$) as shown in Fig. 5, equations of the scan planes determined by each scanline and the viewpoint are as follows:

$$\begin{aligned} y - (y_1/R)z = 0 \\ y - (y_2/R)z = 0. \end{aligned} \tag{5}$$

If the functions, f_1 and f_2, are expressed as following:

$$\begin{aligned} f_1(y,z) = y - (y_1/R)z \\ f_2(y,z) = y - (y_2/R)z, \end{aligned}$$

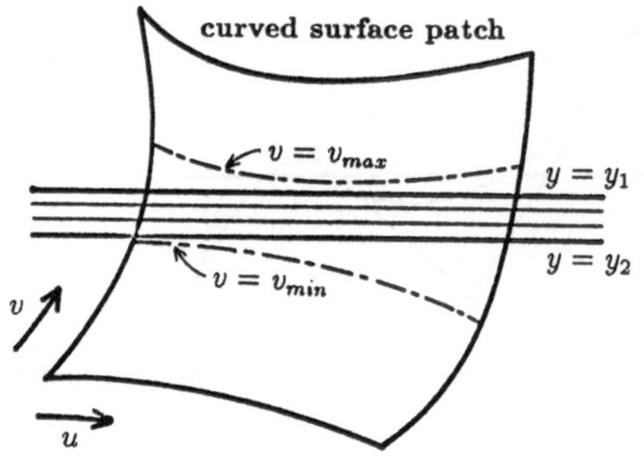

Figure 5: Intersection of a group of scanlines and a surface patch.

the region formed by these two scanlines satisfies the condition, $f_1 \leq 0$ and $f_2 \geq 0$. From this, the interval of u and v intersecting with the scan planes defined by Eq. 5 satisfies the following conditions:

$$\begin{aligned} f_1 &= \sum_{i=0}^{n}\sum_{j=0}^{n}(Y_{ij} - (y_1/R)Z_{ij})B_i^n(u)B_j^n(v) \leq 0 \\ f_2 &= \sum_{i=0}^{n}\sum_{j=0}^{n}(Y_{ij} - (y_2/R)Z_{ij})B_i^n(u)B_j^n(v) \geq 0. \end{aligned} \tag{6}$$

That is,

$$\begin{aligned} &\sum_{i=0}^{n}\sum_{j=0}^{n} f_1(Y_{ij}, Z_{ij})B_i^n(u)B_j^n(v) \leq 0 \\ &\sum_{i=0}^{n}\sum_{j=0}^{n} f_2(Y_{ij}, Z_{ij})B_i^n(u)B_j^n(v) \geq 0. \end{aligned} \tag{7}$$

The clipping described in the previous section is also available to calculate the interval of u and v in Eq. 7.

A curved surface is clipped taking into account the obtained interval of u and v. If flatness of the clipped surface, a subpatch, is not enough, the subpatch is divided into two subpatches and this process is continued until every subpatch satisfies the flatness tolerance given in advance. Finally, several subpatches intersecting with the scanline are generated as shown in Fig. 6. Surface flatness is measured by the maximum distance between the curved surface and the plane determined by three corner control points [Whitted 78] [Lane 80].

5 Hidden Surface Removal and Shading

After generating subpatches, a line segment between intersections of a subpatch and each scanline located between $y = y_1$ and $y = y_2$ is calculated by using the method described in the previous section. This line segment is called a scan segment. Scan segments can be reckoned as straight lines because subdivided subpatches are flat enough. Except for the original boundaries, boundary curves consisting of subpatches are classified into two types. One is a boundary caused by clipping away the outside of the region determined by the interval of u or v obtained by Eq. 7, and the other is a boundary caused by dividing a subpatch into two subpatches. In the calculation of intersections of subpatches and the scanline, it is enough to examine only the latter's boundaries (usually, two edges as shown in bold lines in Fig. 6) because the former never intersect with the scanline.

After the calculation of scan segments, visible parts of each scan segment are determined by using a traditional scanline algorithm, and Phong's shading algorithm is employed to display curved surfaces. In this paper penetrations of each curved surface are allowed; hidden surfaces are removed by taking account of the intersection of scan segments in the depth direction.

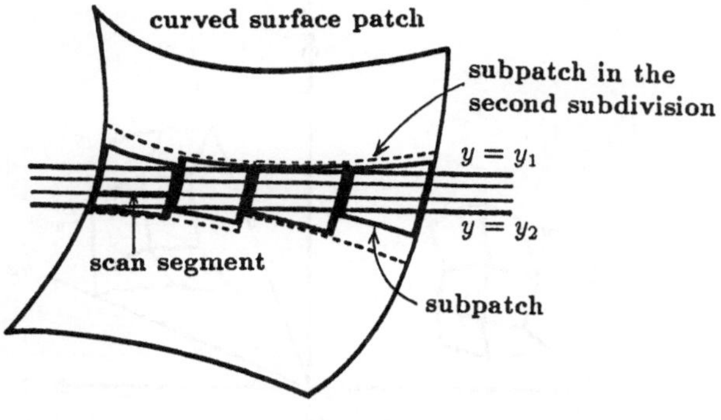

Figure 6: Subpatches on a scanline.

For the visibility test and smooth shading mentioned above, a depth, z, and a normal vector at both endpoints of a scan segment are required. Normal vectors at both endpoints of a scan segment are only slightly different because of flatness of the subpatch. When the difference between the normal vectors at both endpoints is greater than a threshold, the subpatch is divided again. Therefore, accurate intensities can be obtained, even if a linear interpolation is employed to calculate the normal vectors on the scan segment.

To discuss accuracy of shading proposed here, some previous methods are referred here. In Schweitzer's method [Schweitzer 82], a cubic interpolation is employed to calculate normal vectors on a scan segment. However, the accuracy of the normal vectors is not enough to faithfully display an original curved surface, because the normal vectors on the scan segment are interpolated by using only the normal vectors at the intersections of the scanline and a fairly large subpatch (and/or a silhouette.) In Pueyo's method [Pueyo 87], a curved surface is decomposed (equidistantly in parametric space) into grid cells, and linear interpolation is employed to the normal vectors on the grid cells. As the difference between the normal vectors at the adjacent grid points depends upon the size of grid cells, the size of grid cells should be small enough in order to obtain accurate normal vectors. In order to get more precise coordinates and normals at pixels within the scan segments, marching technique, such as Satterfield and Rogers' method[Satter 85], may be effective, even though their method is developed for generating contour lines from a B-spline after triangular mesh approximation.

6 Silhouettes of a Curved Surface

The detection of accurate silhouettes of a curved surface is one of the important elements for displaying realistic curved surfaces. As described in the introduction, traditional calculation methods are not always robust nor so accurate for silhouette edges [Blinn 78] [Whitted 78] [Schweitzer 82]. Even some methods addressing these problems still have some disadvantages, such as very complicated process and missing silhouettes formed by relatively small loops. In the subdivision methods taking into account surface flatness [Lane 80] [Clark 79], only when the tolerance of surface flatness is within one pixel, the silhouettes become smooth; in this case every curved surface needs to be excessively subdivided even though it dose not always have silhouettes. To solve these problems, the authors propose the following efficient subdivision method.

It is useful to classify all curved surfaces into two types – those which probably have silhouettes, and those which never have them before scan-conversion because all the curved surfaces do not necessarily have silhouettes. After subdividing curved surfaces into subpatches on the scanline, only the subpatches probably having the silhouettes are examined as to whether they really have

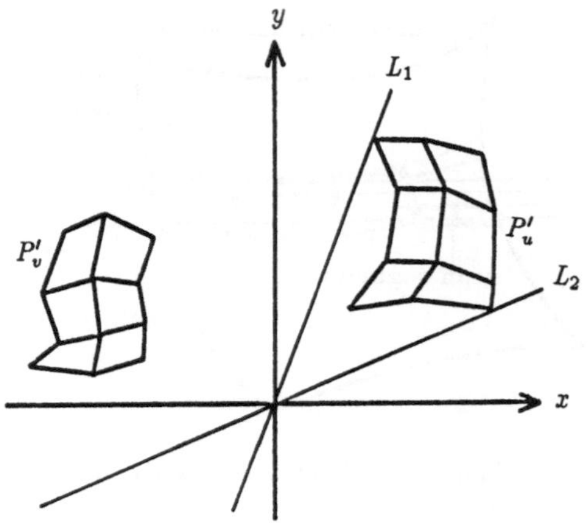

Figure 7: Hodograph for calculating directions of normals.

silhouettes or not. If they have, the subdivision process is applied until the flatness is satisfied. (The lower tolerance of flatness should be set to the subpatches with silhouette.) This method never leaves any silhouette undetected. In the following, how to examine whether or not a curved surface probably has a silhouette is discussed.

First, the classification into a front face, a back face, or the other (i. e., surfaces probably having silhouettes), is necessary. A front face has a normal vector toward the viewpoint throughout the surface (an inner product of the viewing vector and the normal vector is positive), while a back face has a normal vector away from the viewpoint.

The normal vector at a point (u, v) is defined by a vector product of $P_u(u, v)$ and $P_v(u, v)$ derived from the derivative of $P(u, v)$ with regard to u and v, respectively. Let's assume that the normal vector, $P_u \times P_v$, is defined as the direction toward the outside of the surface. If the condition, $P(u, v) \cdot P_u(u, v) \times P_v(u, v) < 0$, is satisfied for all u $(0 \leq u \leq 1)$ and v $(0 \leq v \leq 1)$ in the eye coordinate systems, then the curved surface is a front surface toward the viewpoint. To find out the curved surfaces having silhouettes this condition may be used; however, the calculation cost is probably very high. To address this problem, in this paper the projected control points of curved surfaces (so called 'wedge test') is used.

After perspective transformation the direction of a surface can be tested by using only the signs of the z-component of the normal vectors. That is, only the x and y components of P'_u and P'_v are used for the test where P' is a projected curved surface. Derivatives of Bezier surfaces can be obtained from the control points geometrically. For example, the control points $P'_{ui,j}$ of P'_u is expressed by $n(P'_{i+1,j} - P'_{i,j})$ $(i = 0, 1, \cdots, n-1,\ j = 0, 1, \cdots, n)$. The range of P'_u and P'_v can be obtained by hodograph [Sederberg 88] as shown in Fig. 7. The direction of the tangent with respect to the parameter u exists in the wedge area intercepted by the lines L_1 and L_2 which holds P'_u as shown in Fig. 7. The equations of the lines L_1 and L_2 are defined by

$$\begin{aligned} f_1(x, y) &= a_1 x + b_1 y = 0 \\ f_2(x, y) &= a_2 x + b_2 y = 0. \end{aligned} \tag{8}$$

Every control point P'_{uij} belonging to P'_u locates in the positive side of the line L_1 while P'_{uij} in the negative side of the line L_2. That is, the straight lines satisfy the following conditions.

$$\begin{aligned} \forall P_{uij} &: f_1(x_{uij}, y_{uij}) \geq 0 \\ \forall P_{uij} &: f_2(x_{uij}, y_{uij}) \leq 0. \end{aligned} \tag{9}$$

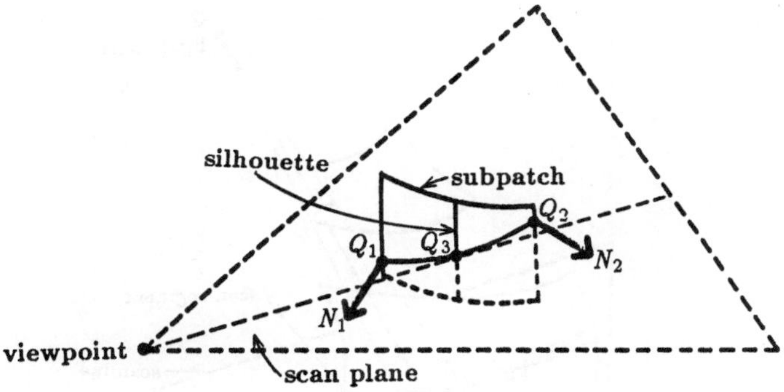

Figure 8: Subpatch with a silhouette.

Therefore,

$$\begin{array}{ll}\text{(a) If } \forall P_{vij} : f_1(x_{vij}, y_{vij}) \geq 0 \text{ and } f_2(x_{vij}, y_{vij}) \geq 0 \text{ then a front face.} & \\ \text{(b) If } \forall P_{vij} : f_1(x_{vij}, y_{vij}) \leq 0 \text{ and } f_2(x_{vij}, y_{vij}) \leq 0 \text{ then a back face.} & (10) \\ \text{(c) Other than the above, a twisted face.} & \end{array}$$

In other words, if any P_v overlaps with the wedge intercepted by L_1 and L_2, then the curved surface is a twisted surface. Note that the curved surface classified into a twisted surface does not always have a silhouette. For a more detailed test the curved surface must be further subdivided, but, it is enough to find out only the probability of having silhouettes. In this process of face classification, if L_1 and L_2 cannot be obtained, the surface probably has silhouettes.

Curved surfaces requiring scan-conversion can be reduced in number by culling back faces in the step of the wedge test, because of the invisibility of back faces. (15 percent of the total CPU time was cut down by culling back faces in our experiment.)

A bisectional method is employed to calculate the intersection of silhouettes and each scanline, because the interval between the parameters at the endpoints of a scan segment is very small. That is, if normal vectors N_1 and N_2 at the endpoints (Q_1 and Q_2 in Fig. 8) of a segment have an opposite direction with respect to the direction of the viewpoint, subdivision of the subpatch is executed, because the scanline intersects with the silhouette (at Q_3 in Fig. 8.) The subdivision process is continued until the viewpoint direction component of both normal vectors at the endpoints becomes smaller than a specified tolerance.

7 Shadowing

Even though the papers referred to here use scanline algorithms ([Blinn 78] [Whitted 78] [Lane 80] [Clark 79] [Schweitzer 82] [Griffiths 84] [Pueyo 87]) none of them mention shadowing. Shadows are one of the important elements for displaying realistic images. Calculation method for shadowed sections on each scan segment is discussed here. Shadows are invisible sections when a light source is reckoned as a viewpoint. Therefore, a shadow cast by a curved surface can be calculated as follows. If a triangle formed by both endpoints of a scan segment and the viewpoint (see Fig. 9) intersects with a curved surface, the shadows due to the curved surface are cast on at least a part of the scan segment. By reckoning the light source as a viewpoint, the triangle formed by the scan segment and the light source is treated as a scan plane; the scanline algorithm mentioned before can be employed. That is, the shadow sections on the scan segment can be determined by using the intersection test between the scanline and curved surfaces when viewed from the light source.

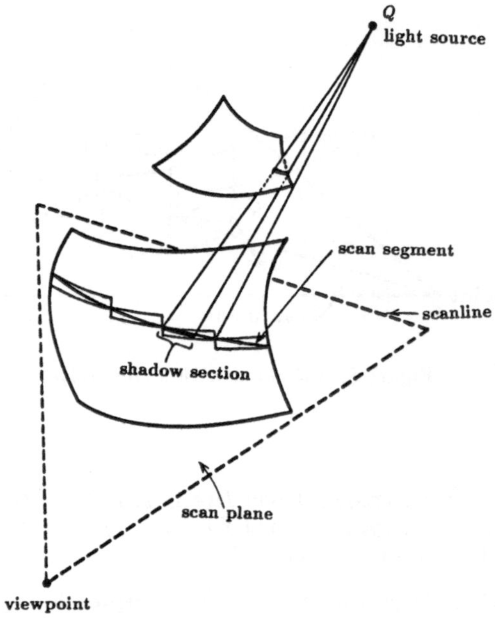

Figure 9: Shadow area on a scan segment.

Table 1: Relationship between the tolerance, the average iterations, and the CPU time (in the case of (a)).

tolerance	average iterations	CPU time (sec.)
10^{-3}	1.6	27.3
10^{-5}	2.1	28.9
10^{-7}	2.4	29.1

8 Examples

Four examples are shown in Fig. 10. Fig. (a) shows a tea pot as an example of standard data. It consists of 32 patches and the CPU time was 27.3 sec. (144.6 sec. in case with shadows) by using IRIS-4D/120GTX and the size of screen is 500 × 500.

Tab. 1 shows relationships among the tolerance of the parameter t regarding the calculation of intersections of a scanline and subpatches, the average number of iterations, and the CPU time. It is evident that iterations are fairly few, because of quick convergence due to the fact that the shapes of boundaries of every subdivided subpatch are close to straight segments. When the tolerance is set at 10^{-3}, even one patch covering all of the screen size, 1000 × 1000, is displayed with the accuracy within one pixel. Therefore, it is set at 10^{-3} in the examples. Even when the resolution of the screen becomes higher and the tolerance is set at 10^{-7}, the average number of iterations increases by only 0.8, and the CPU time increases by less than 1 percent. Calculation time for generating subpatches takes 60 percent of all calculation time, and for calculating intersections of

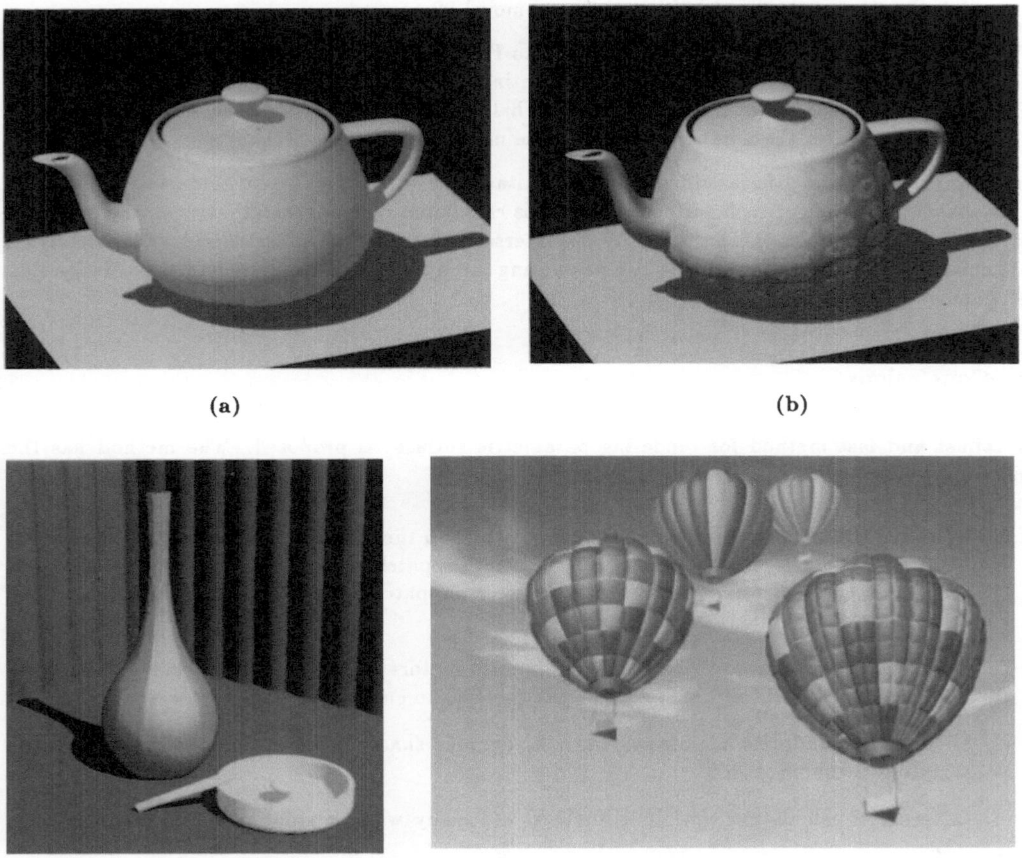

(a) (b)

(c) (d)

Figure 10: Examples.

subpatches and a scanline and hidden surface removal 22 percent.

Fig. (b) shows an example of texture mapping to Fig. (a). Fig. (c) shows a base and an ash tray consisting of 133 patches. In case Fig. (d) depicting hot air balloons considered foggy effect, the CPU time is only 228.8 sec., although all of the balloons consist of 1064 patches. These examples show that the greater the number of patches, the more effective the method is.

In these examples a multi-scanning method [Nishita 84] developed by the authors was employed for anti-aliasing; the area of each surface in a pixel is calculated by trapezoidal integral; the precision of the area depends on the accuracy of the intersections between sub-scanlines and boundaries of surfaces. That is, the accuracy of anti-aliasing is improved. Anti-aliased image composition [Nakamae 86] were used for Fig. (d).

9 Conclusions

A robust and fast method for rendering parametric surfaces is proposed. The method has the following advantages:

1. Boundaries of displayed objects are quite faithful to the defined curved surfaces, and therefore extremely smooth, because intersections of subpatches and each scanline are calculated accurately and robustly. No gap arises between subpatches. Intersections can be calculated by few iterations (about 2 iterations.)
2. Even in the area where the changing of normal vectors is drastic, the intensity is accurate, because curved surfaces are sampled in proportion to curvature of the surfaces.
3. Shadowed boundaries are always smooth, because shadows faithful to the defined curved surfaces can be displayed.
4. In terms of calculation time it is low cost especially when a number of patches exist in a scene.
5. The accuracy of anti-aliasing is improved because of calculating the accurate intersections.

The method proposed here is applied for Bezier surfaces. Developing the scanning method for rendering directly from the other types of surfaces, such as B-spline, is expected, even though almost all surfaces can be converted into Bezier surfaces.

Acknowledgment

We would like to thank Dr. Thomas W. Sederberg for his discussion about the method for calculating intersections by surface clipping when the first author stayed at Brigham Young University. We are also grateful to Mr. Mikio Munetomo for his coding anti-aliasing and texture mapping.

REFERENCES

[Blinn 78] Blinn JF (1978) "Simulation of Wrinkled Surfaces," Computer Graphics 12(3):286-292

[Clark 79] Clark JH (1979) "A First Scan-Line Algorithm for Rendering Parametric Surfaces," Computer Graphics 13(2):174

[Griffiths 84] Griffiths JG (1984) "A Depth-Coherence Scanline Algorithm for Displaying Curved Surfaces," CAD 16(2):91-101

[Lane 80] Lane JM, Carpenter LC, Whitted T, and Blinn JF (1980) "Scan Line Methods for Displaying Parametrically Defined Surfaces," Comm. ACM 23(1):23-34

[Nakamae 86] Nakamae E, Harada K, Ishizaki T, and Nishita T (1986) "A Montage: The Overlaying of the Computer Generated Images onto a Background Photograph," Computer Graphics 20(4):207-214

[Nishita 84] Nishita T and Nakamae E (1984) "Half-Tone Representation of 3-D Objects with Smooth Edges by Using a Multi-Scanning Method," Trans. IPSJ 25(5):703-711

[Pueyo 87] Pueyo X and Brunet P (1987) "A Parametric-Space-Based Scan-Line Algorithm for Rendering Bicubic Surfaces," IEEE CG & A 7(8):17-24

[Satter 85] Satterfield SG and Rogers DF (1985) "A Procedure for Generating Contour Lines From a B-Spline Surface," IEEE CG & A 5(4):71-75

[Schweitzer 82] Schweitzer D and Cobb ES (1982) "Scanline Rendering of Parametric Surfaces," Computer Graphics 16(3):265-271

[Sederberg 88] Sederberg TW and Meyers RJ (1988) "Loop Detection in Surface Patch Intersections," CAGD 5(2):161-171

[Watkins 70] Watkins GS (1970) "A Real-Time Visible Surface Algorithm," University of Utah Compt. Sc. Dept. UTEC-CSC-70-101, NTIS AD-762 004

[Whitted 78] Whitted T (1978) "A Scan Line Algorithm for Computer Display of Curved Surfaces," Computer Graphics 12(3):26

Tomoyuki Nishita is an associate professor in the department of Electronic and Electrical Engineering at Fukuyama University, Japan. He was on the research staff at Mazda from 1973 to 1979 and worked on design and development of computer-controlled vehicle system. He joined Fukuyama University in 1979. He was an associate researcher in the Engineering Computer Graphics Laboratory at Brigham Young University from 1988 to the end of March, 1989. His research interests involve computer graphics including lighting model, hidden-surface removal, and antialiasing.
Nishita received his BE, ME and Ph. D in Engineering in 1971, 1973, and 1985, respectively, from Hiroshima University. He is a member of ACM, IPS of Japan and IEE of Japan.
Address: Faculty of Engineering, Fukuyama University, Sanzo, Higashimura-cho, Fukuyama, 729-02 Japan.

Kazufumi Kaneda is a research associate in Faculty of Engineering at Hiroshima University. He worked at the Chugoku Electric Power Company Ltd., Japan from 1984 to 1986. He joined Hiroshima University in 1986. His research interests include computer graphics and image processing.
Kaneda received the BE and ME in 1982 and 1984, respectively, from Hiroshima University. He is a member of IEE of Japan, IPS of Japan and IEICE of Japan.
Address: Faculty of Engineering, Hiroshima University, Saijo-cho, Higashi-hiroshima, 724 Japan.
E-mail: kin@eml.hiroshima-u.ac.jp

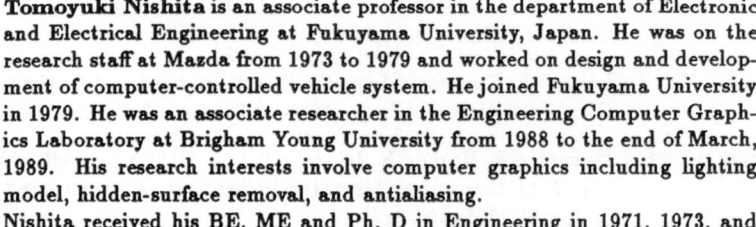

Eihachiro Nakamae is a professor at Hiroshima University where he was appointed as research associate in 1956 and a professor in 1968. He was an associate researcher at Clarkson College of Technology, Potsdam, N. Y., from 1973 to 1974. His research interests include computer graphics and electric machinery.
Nakamae received the BE, ME, and DE degrees in 1954, 1956, and 1967 from Waseda University. He is a member of IEEE, IEE of Japan, IPS of Japan and IEICE of Japan.
Address: Faculty of Engineering, Hiroshima University, Saijo-cho, Higashi-hiroshima, 724 Japan.
E-mail: naka@eml.hiroshima-u.ac.jp

Design and Display of an Analytical Surface Composed of Super- and Para-Ellipses

Tao Hong and Hua Cao

ABSTRACT

In this paper the authors present a theory to construct an analytical surface composed of super- and/or para-ellipses blended with other splines. This new type of surface quite fits the needs of the preliminary contour design of complex industrial products such as aircraft and automobile bodies and ship hulls. Based on this idea, two geometric modeling systems have been created for a minicomputer and for a PC. Input data to design and control the shape of the new product are less than that of other methods. It is very easy to modify and adjust the local contour of the product with smoothing features.

Keywords: Computer Graphics, CAGD, Geometric Modeling, Analytical Composite Surface, Super- and Para-Ellipse Surface, Preliminary Contour Design.

* - The project supported by Science Foundation of Aeronautics.

1. INTRODUCTION

Many graphics systems allow users to describe 3-dimensional objects with surface patches. However, it is unnecessary to define regular contours of an industrial product with complicated surface patches. The major disadvantage of this representation is that one may need a very large amount of input data to produce a smooth surface. The shapes of most industrial products are non-sculptured surfaces. One important feature or demand on the contours for these industrial products is smoothness and fairness. The other characteristics for most of its cross-sections are closed curve and symmetry at least about one coordinate axis. So it is essential to find a new representation to fit the shapes of these products. An analytical surface representation may meet the needs of this contoured surface design.

The authors proposed a new idea to construct a contoured surface consisted of super-ellipses, para-ellipses or hypocycloids blended with other splines such as cubic parametric splines, piecewise generalized ellipse curves, B-splines and revised generalized conic splines and so forth. This new type of surface will well suit to the demands on preliminary contour design of the complex industrial products.

2. ANALYTICAL REPRESENTATION OF THE COMPOSITE SURFACE

For simplicity, suppose that the cross-sections of the object are parallel to the X-Y plane of the coordinate system and the major axis of its cross-section will coincide with Z-axis. Then the general representation of the composite surface can be written as following vector form:

$$F(x,y,z) = \left[\frac{x - fx(z)}{fa(z)}\right]^{2/fn(z)} + \left[\frac{y - fy(z)}{fb(z)}\right]^{2/fm(z)} = 0 \qquad (1)$$

where fa(z), fb(z) are functions of semiaxes of the cross-sections for the composite surface, fx(z), fy(z) are the functions of the center coordinates on the cross-sections, and fn(z), fm(z) are the functions of the shape factors of the cross-sections.

If F(x,y,z) value is less than or equal to 0, and in the field $z \in (z_0, z_n)$, we can define the solid and its boundary surface.

The equation of the composite surface also can be rewritten as following parametric form:

$$x = fx(t) + fa(t) * (\cos\theta)^{fn(t)}$$

$$y = fy(t) + fb(t) * (\sin\theta)^{fm(t)} \qquad (2)$$

$$z = t$$

The exponent values of the shape factor function fn(t) and fm(t) must always be positive. When the values of the fn(t) and fm(t) are less than 1, the cross-section of the surface presents a super-ellipse curve, and fn(t) = fm(t) = 1 is an ordinary ellipse. If the values of fn(t) and fm(t) are greater than 1 and less than 2, the cross-section curve of the surface was called para-ellipse by the authors. And if fn(t) = fm(t) =2 , the cross-section curve is degenerated into a straight line. When the exponent values of the functions fn(t) and fm(t) are greater than 2 , the cross-section curve is called hypocycloid. If the values of the shape factor functions fn(t) and fm(t) are different, a special kind of cross-section curve can be obtained. The photo of Figure 1 shows the contour curves of the cross-sections for the composite surfaces. The shape factor function fn(t) is the same as fm(t) on the left-hand cross-sections and on the upper-right part of the cross-sections. The fn(t) and fm(t) are different on the lower-right part of the cross-section in the photo.

According to the mathematical analysis of the derivatives of these cross-section curves or from direct observation through the curve in the photo, the tangent vectors of super-ellipse and para-ellipse or hypocycloid at the point on major and minor axes will be perpendicular or tangent to each axis, except where the curve has degenerated into a straight line.

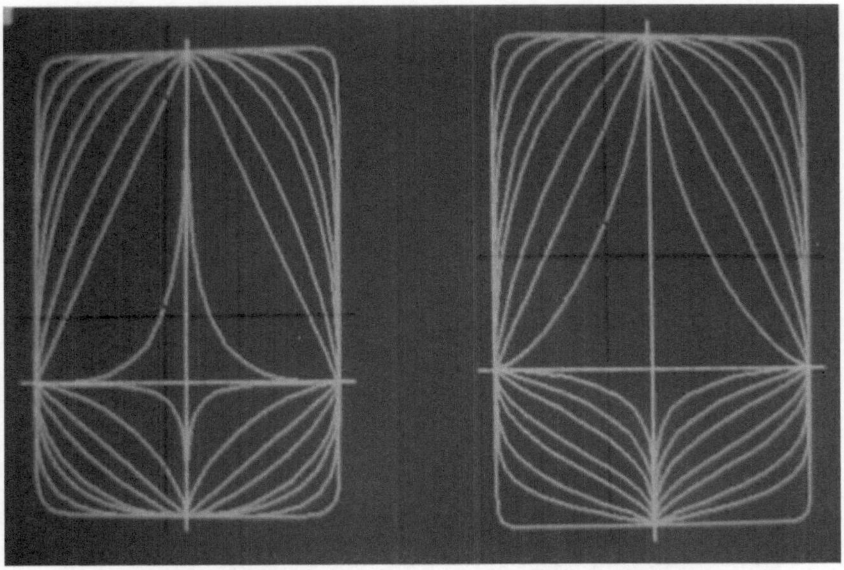

Fig. 1: Generalized ellipse section curves

3. LONGITUDINAL CONTROL CURVES

Almost any spline function can serve as the longitudinal section curve and shape factor curve of the analytical surface. But the lengthwise control splines must meet following demands:

(a) The spline methods are easy to adjust and control its shape especially for local modification.
(b) The constructed splines are smooth and fair except for necessary straight line sections and some sharp points.
(c) Selected spline method should minimize the input data to control the whole surface.

The longitudinal section curves fx(t), fy(t), fa(t), fb(t) and the shape factor functions fn(t), fm(t) in the representation (2) of the composite surface can be defined independently by the users according to the demands on the longitudinal splines. Because there is not any functional relation among these lengthwise control functions, the parametric form of the longitudinal curves is simple and suitable for calculating the interpolation points of the analytical surface. In the simplest situation we need only three longitudinal control curves as shown in Figure 2. The lower part in the photo of Fig 2 is a half of the maximum width curve of the car shown in Fig 8, the middle curve displayed in the photo is the utmost top curve of the car and the upper part in Fig 2 is the shape factor curve magnified by 100 times in Y-direction.

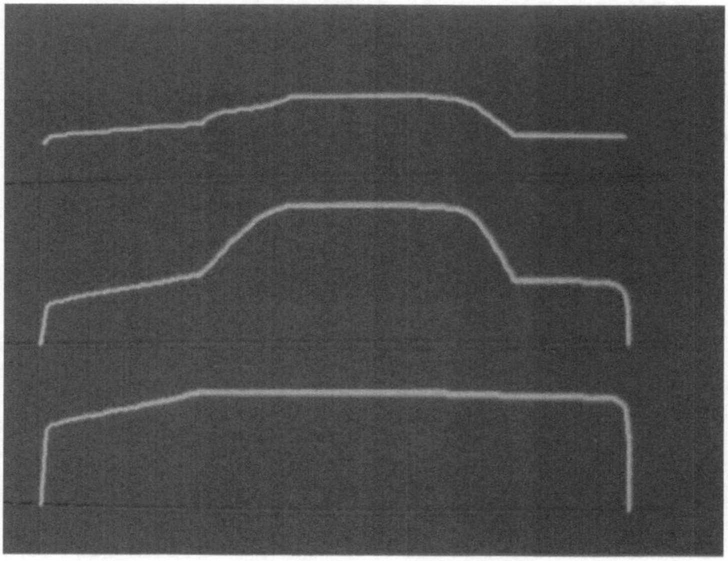

Fig. 2: The longitudinal control curves for the car

The parametric cubic equations for curves can act as the longitudinal section functions fx(t), fy(t), fa(t), fb(t) and the shape factor representation fn(t), fm(t). The segments of parametric cubic curves are described by following equation:

$$r(t) = [\; t^3 \;\; t^2 \;\; t \;\; 1 \;] \begin{bmatrix} 2 & -2 & 1 & 1 \\ -3 & 3 & -2 & -1 \\ 0 & 0 & 1 & 0 \\ 1 & 0 & 0 & 0 \end{bmatrix} \begin{bmatrix} Pi-1 \\ Pi \\ P'i-1 \\ P'i \end{bmatrix}$$

The good point of this spline as the longitudinal control curves is that all input points are on the curves, and a limited number of control points define the curve and, therefore, the whole surface. In Fig 5 three lengthwise control curves describe the shape of the flower vase, and each curve only includes six points and two tangent vectors. The weakness of parametric cubic spline method is that it is difficult to fit a curve with multiple straight line segments and to give the appropriate magnitudes of the tangent vectors T0 and Tn at starting and ending points for a designer unfamiliar with computational geometry theory.

Cubic B-spline curves as the longitudinal control curves of the composite surface are very flexible. Their representation can be written in the following vector form:

$$Pi(u) = [\; 1 \;\; u \;\; u^2 \;\; u^3 \;] \frac{1}{6} \begin{bmatrix} 1 & 4 & 1 & 0 \\ -3 & 0 & 3 & 0 \\ 3 & 6 & 3 & 0 \\ -1 & -3 & -3 & 1 \end{bmatrix} \begin{bmatrix} Vi \\ Vi+1 \\ Vi+2 \\ Vi+3 \end{bmatrix}$$

Cubic B-spline curve can include straight line segments and sharp points as shown in Fig 2. But the input data of B-spline method to control a longitudinal curve will be a little more than that of parametric cubic spline.

Piecewise super- and para-ellipses also can serve as the longitudinal control curves. In this situation it is desirable to cut the curve on the points which tangent slopes equal zero or infinity (Fig 3). When there are straight line segments or sharp points on the curve, the ending points of the curve or the sharp point can used as the piecewise points. First or higher order continuity can be reached with this kind of piecewise curve except at sharp points, if fn(t) and fm(t) are chosen appropriately.

A disadvantage of the piecewise generalized ellipses as the longitudinal control curves is that segmentation and calculation will be troublesome.

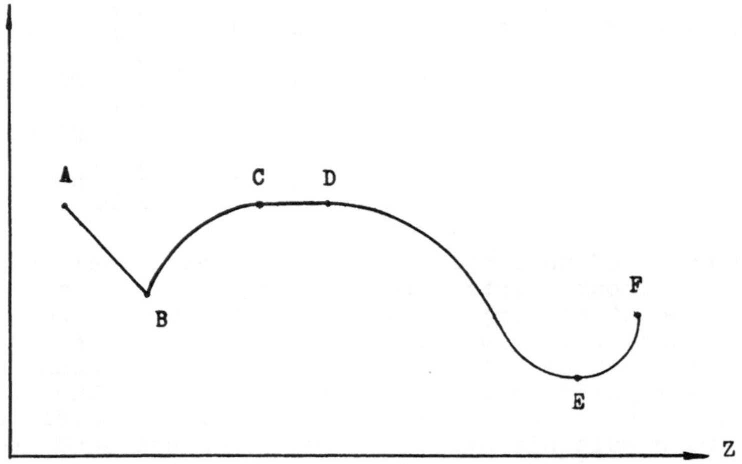

Fig. 3: Segmentation of the piecewise generalized ellipses

Revised generalized conic curve can also serve as the longitudinal control curve. The representation of the planar control curve can be written as follows:

$$ri(u) = [\ 1 \quad u \quad u^2 \quad u^3\ ]\ Mrg \begin{bmatrix} (1-f)\ Vi \\ f\ V'i+1 \\ f\ V'i+2 \\ (1-f)\ Vi+3 \end{bmatrix} \Big/ \ H(u)$$

where $$Mrg = \begin{bmatrix} 1 & 0 & 0 & 0 \\ -2 & 2 & 0 & 0 \\ 1 & -4 & 2 & 1 \\ 0 & 2 & -2 & 0 \end{bmatrix}$$

and $$H(u) = [\ 1 \quad u \quad u^2 \quad u^3\ ]\ Mrg\ [\ 1-f \quad f \quad f \quad 1-f\ ]$$

The value $f = BD/SD \in [0,1]$, which denotes the shape factor of the curve , and vertex V'i+1, V'i+2 can adjust its characteristic polygon. The shape factor f will affect the fullness and the curvature of the curve in the characteristic polygon (Fig 4). If the value of f approaches 1, the fullness of the curve is greater than that of others. Otherwise, for f approaches to zero the curve will change into a straight line. Unlike planar generalized conic spline, V'i+1 do not coincide with V'i+2 in one point for the revised generalized conic curve.

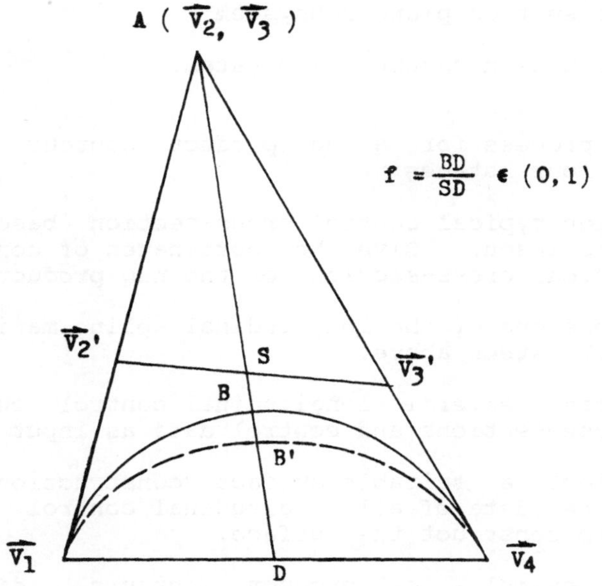

Fig. 4: Characteristic polygon of revised generalized conic curve

4. DESIGN PROCESS OF A PRODUCT CONTOUR

We have created two geometric modeling systems on the PRIME 550-11 minicomputer and the SUPER- 286 AT personal computer. The functions of these systems mainly are as follows:

(a) Aircraft preliminary design subsystem;

(b) Automobile preliminary design subsystem;

(c) Ruled surface design subsystem;

(d) Closed surface design subsystem;

(e) Unclosed surface design subsystem;

(f) Piecewise generalized ellipse control curve subsystem;

(g) Parametric cubic spline subsystem;

(h) B-spline control curve subsystem;

(i) Revised generalized conic spline subsystem;

(j) Intersection plane subsystem;

(k) Data base management subsystem.

The design process for a new product contour generally takes place in four stages:

(a) Design typical control cross-section based on the demands on shape and space. Give the coordinates of control points for several typical cross-sections of the new product.

(b) Choose one of the longitudinal spline manipulation methods from the subsystems above.

(c) Design several longitudinal control curves using the typical cross-sections and control data as input (Fig 2).

(d) Select a suitable surface construction subsystem and transmit the data of all longitudinal control data into this subsystem to construct the surface.

Here some examples of product contours, displayed on the screens, are shown in following photos. Fig 5 is a special flower vase composed of parametric cubic splines blended with super-ellipses. The left part of the photo is a front view and the right part is the axonometric view of the flower vase.

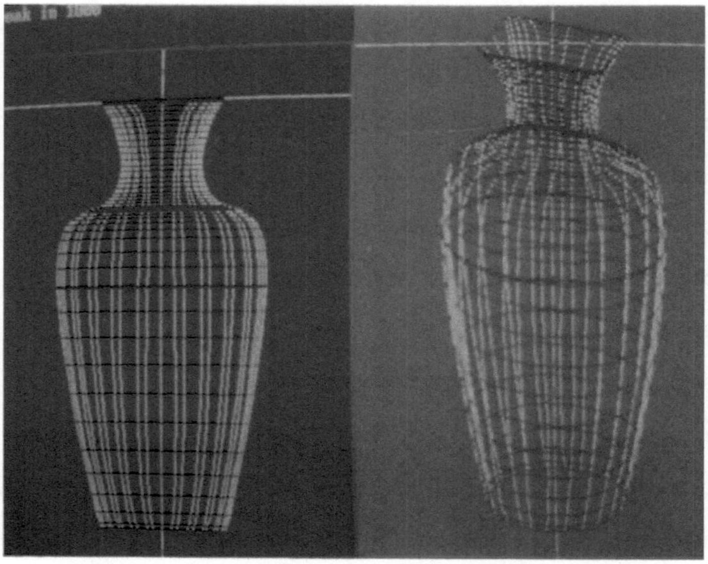

Figure 5: Flower vase with non-revolution cross-sections

Another flower vase constructed by B-splines and super-ellipses is shown in Fig 6. The cross-sections of the vase mouth are super-ellipses, and the body of the flower vase is a revolution surface with a square base.

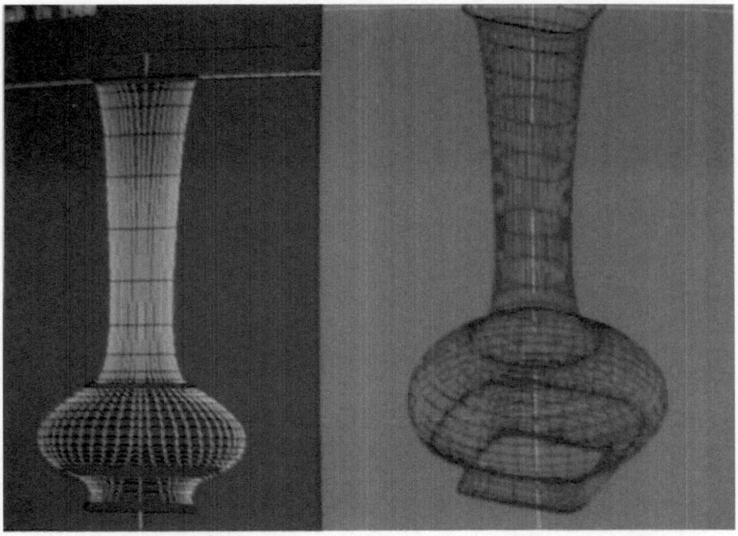

Fig. 6: Vase constructed by B-splines and super-ellipses

Fig 7 is a CRT shell composed of B-splines and generalized ellipses.

The automobile contours designed on the PC screen are as Fig 8. Using this method the car contours are easy to modify. We did four variants of the car contour in about one day.

Also a transportation aircraft model was designed on the PRIME 550 -11 computer and its shaded picture was calculated by ray tracing algorithm and displayed on the APOLLO workstation (Fig 9 and Fig 10). Its wings and the horizontal and the vertical stabilizers consisted of ruled surfaces. Models of the foils were constructed using the revised generalized conic splines. If the cross-sections (Fig 11) of the airliner fuselage are composed of arcs of super-ellipses, the useful space of the fuselage will obviously greater than that of the circles and ellipses, and layout of seats can be more comfortable for the passengers, because there are curved contours at the inner wall of fuselage consisted of circular and elliptical arcs. Super-ellipses as cross-sections are much easier to adjust and modify than the other curves . The twisting and bending strength and the rigidity of the aircraft fuselage are obviously stronger than that of circular or elliptical sections.

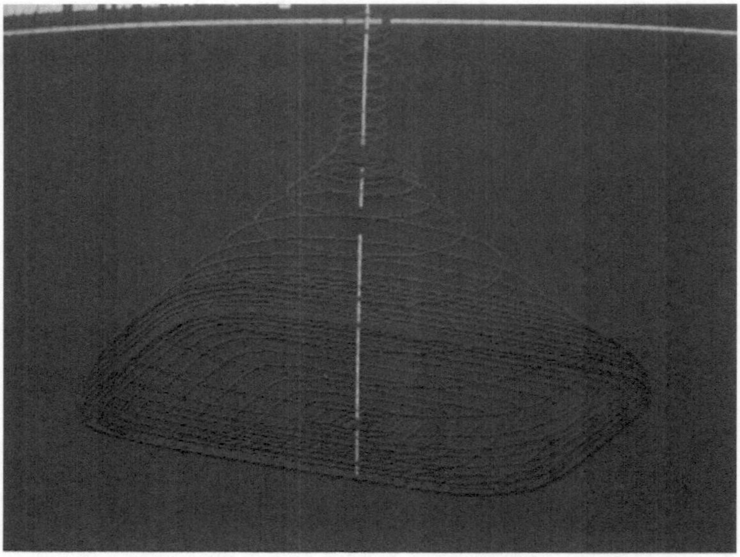

Fig. 7: The cross-sections of the CRT shell

Figure 8: The contours of an automobile

Figure 9: A model of a transportation aircraft

Figure 10: A shaded picture of the transportation aircraft

These composite surfaces also can construct several kinds of objects with special shapes. As an example an unordinary torus with variable cross-sections was shown in Fig 12.

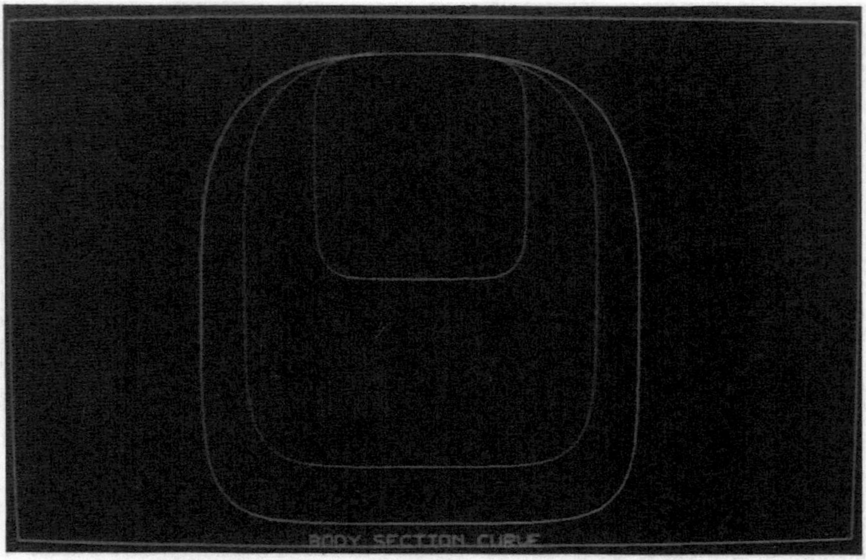

Figure 11: Cross-sections of the fuselage

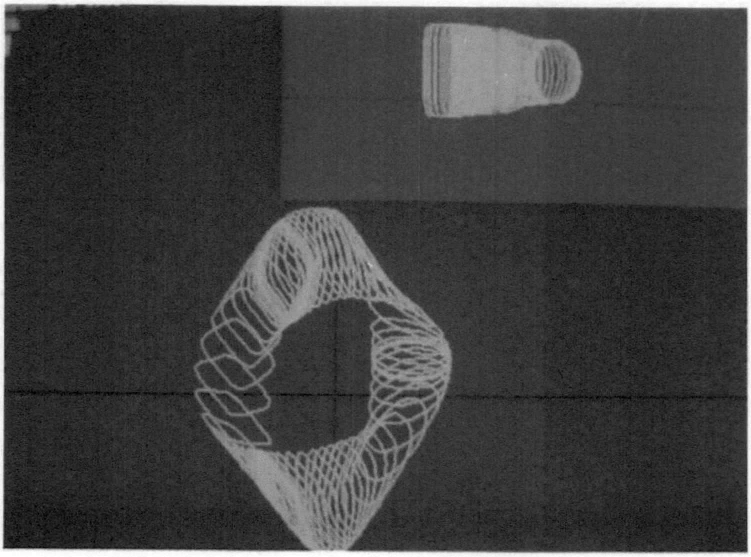

Figure 12: A torus with variable cross-sections

5. CONCLUSIONS

Super-ellipses as the cross-sections of any product have a good looking and symmetrical configuration. So they are well suited to design in industrial arts and various applications, for examples: flower vases, CRT shells and other utensils.

This kind of analytical surface, composed of generalized ellipses blended with other splines, can be programmed quickly and easily. The surface modeling package is smlll enough to fit on a personal computer.

It is much easier to master the design process of the geometric modeling system for a designer especially for a beginer.

It is convenient in real time by interaction means to control and modify the shape of the composite surface.

The only disadvantage of the geometric surface modeling method is that it is difficult to describe a complex sculptured surface.

ACKNOWLEDGEMENT

We wish to thank our graduate students, particularly Wen-Zhong Xie for their contribution to this research.

REFERENCES

Ball, A. A. (1974) CONSURF. Part 1: Introduction of the Conic Lofting Tile, CAD, 6, 4, 243-249.
Ball, A. A. (1975) CONSURF. Part 2: Description of the Algorithms. CAD, 7, 4, 237-242.
Ball, A. A. (1977) CONSURF. How the Program is used, CAD, 9, 1, 9-12.
Cao, H. and Hong, T. (1987) The Recurrence Algorithm for Super-Ellipse and Para-Ellipse Generation, Engineering Graphics Journal (in chinese) 2, 41-48.
De Groot, D. J. (1977) Designing Curved Surfaces with Analytical Functions, CAD, 9, 1, 3-8.
Faux, I. D. and Pratt, M. J. (1979) Computational Geometry for Design and Manufacture, Ellis Horwood Limited, England pp 230 -231.

Flanagan, D. L. and Hefner, O. V. (1967) Surface Modeling-New Tool for the Beginner, Astronautics and Aeronautics, 58-62.
Gordon, W. J. and Riesenfeld, R. F. (1974) B-Spline Curves and Surfaces in Computer Aided Geometric Design, Proc. of Utah Conference, Academic Press, New York.
Sylvan H. Chasen (1978) Geometric Principles and Procedures for Computer Graphics Applications, Prentice - Hall, Inc., Englewood Cliffs, NJ 07632 pp 104 - 108

BIOGRAPHY

Hong,Tao (T. Hong) is currently a professor of Aircraft Manufacturing Engineering Department at Northwestern Polytechnical University in Xi'an, China. He interested in aircraft, helicopter and hovercraft design and manufacture. In recent year he turned his interest in computer graphics and its applications.
Hong is a Council Member of China Higher Education Society and a Member of China Society of Aeronautics. He was elected to a Member of Editorial Board of the Chinese Journal "Precision Manufacturing Technology of Aeronautics". In 1954 he graduated from the Aircraft Engineering Department of Beijing University of Aeronautics and Astronautics.
Address: South 15-4-8, Northwestern Polytechnical University, Xi'an 710072, People's Republic of China.

Cao, Hua (H. Cao) is professor of Aircraft Manufacturing Engineering Department at Northwestern Polytechnical University in Xi'an, China. She started her teaching and research work in Theory and Application to Metal Forming Processes. Recently her research interest includes Simulation of Sheet Metal Forming and Airworthness.
Cao is a Member of China Society of Aeronautics and a Member of Mechanical Engineering Society of China. In 1954 she graduated from the Aircraft Engineering Department of Beijing University of Aeronautics and Astronautics.
Address: South 15-4-8, NPU, 710072 Xi'an, People's Rep. of China

Basis Functions for Rational Continuity

Dinesh Manocha[1] and Brian A. Barsky[2]

Abstract: The parametric or geometric continuity of a rational polynomial curve has often been obtained by requiring the homogeneous polynomial curve associated with the rational curve to possess parametric or geometric continuity, respectively. Recently this approach has been shown overly restrictive. We make use of the necessary and sufficient conditions of rational parametric continuity for defining basis functions for the homogeneous representation of a rational curve.

These functions are represented in terms of shape parameters of rational continuity, which are introduced due to these exact conditions. The shape parameters may be varied globally, affecting the entire curve, or modified locally thereby affecting only a few segments. Moreover, the local parameters can be represented as continuous or discrete functions. Based on these properties, we introduce three classes of basis functions which can be used for the homogeneous representation of rational parametric curves.

Keywords: Rational Curves, Parametric Continuity, Geometric Continuity, Shape Parameters, Splines

---

[1]Supported in part by Alfred and Chella D. Moore Fellowship.

[2]Supported in part by a National Science Foundation Presidential Young Investigator Award (number CCR-8451997)

1 Introduction

The rational formulation of polynomials and splines has received considerable interest in the areas of computer graphics and geometric modeling. The main advantage of the rational form is its ability to represent conic curves and quadric surfaces, as well as free-form curves and surfaces (Piegl 1985; Piegl 1986a; Piegl 1986b; Piegl 1986c; Piegl and Tiller 1987; Salmon 1879; Tiller 1983; Versprille 1975). Moreover, it is invariant under affine as well as projective transformations, though the latter is possible with changed weights (Lee 1987).

A single rational polynomial usually does not have enough freedom to represent a given curve; several rational polynomial segments are used instead. To obtain a curve of satisfactory smoothness, the segments must connect with some amount of continuity. Thus, the use of rational curves, independent of the particular variety, creates the problem of connecting rational polynomial segments to form piecewise rational curves that are smooth.

To obtain rational curves with either parametric or geometric continuity, the parametric continuity constraints or geometric continuity constraints, respectively, have been applied to the components of the curve in homogeneous coordinates, but not to the components of the rational curve (Barsky 1988a; Boehm 1987; Farin 1983; Goldman and Barsky 1989a; Goldman and Barsky 1989b; Joe 1989; Tiller 1983). If the homogeneous curve satisfies the relevant continuity constraints then the rational curve will have the corresponding continuity.

There are two kinds of continuity for parametric curves: *parametric* continuity and *geometric* (or *visual*) continuity. A curve is said to possess parametric continuity (denoted C^n) if each segment of the curve is C^n and the adjacent segments are connected with C^n continuity at the joints. There are two notions of geometric continuity. The first is based on parametric continuity after a suitable reparametrization. That is, a curve is said to be geometrically continuous (denoted G^n) if there exists some *reparametrization* of its segments such that the resulting curve is C^n. The reparametrization criterion on its segments leads to the derivation of *Beta-constraints* (Barsky 1988b; Barsky and DeRose 1989; Barsky and DeRose 1990; DeRose 1985). The second notion of geometric continuity of parametric curves is based on the continuity of *Frenet Frame* and higher order curvatures (Boehm 1985; Boehm 1987; Dyn and Micchelli 1985; Hagen 1985). A curve possesses geometric continuity G^n if each of its components satisfies the corresponding constraints at the joints.

However, these constraints are sufficient but not necessary for the continuity of rational curves (Hohmeyer and Barsky 1989). The necessary and sufficient constraints for rational continuity (parametric or geometric continuity), as applied to the homogeneous curve, give rise to *shape parameters.* These shape parameters are different from and in addition to those obtained from the geometric continuity of polynomial or rational curves and surfaces (dubbed as *Betas*). They are used for modifying the curve independent of the control vertices. Experience has shown us that shape parameters provide a designer with intuitive control of shape. Some of the properties of these parameters are very useful for the development of modern geometric modeling system.

In this paper, we introduce three categories of *basis functions*[1] for the homogeneous representation of rational curves. These basis functions are based upon the necessary and sufficient conditions

[1] Any homogeneous representation of a fixed degree will be a linear combination of these functions. However, they do not form any basis spanning a vector space, since the rational curves of a fixed degree do not constitute a vector space.

for *rational parametric continuity.* The different categories are obtained by varying the shape parameters globally, which affects the entire curve, or locally, which affects only a few segments only. For the local variation, the shape parameters may be either continuously varying functions or be discretely specified at the knot values. The resulting basis functions differ in the amount of local control (with respect to shape parameters) and evaluation cost.

The rest of the paper is organized in the following manner: In Section 2, we give a brief overview of rational curves and specify the notation. The necessary and sufficient conditions for the parametric continuity of rational curves are mentioned in Section 3. They are used in Section 4 for defining the basis functions for the homogeneous representation of rational curves with uniform shape parameters. In Section 5, the uniform shape parameters are generalized into continuously varying shape parameters by quintic Hermite interpolation. Section 6 specifies a discretely-shaped homogeneous basis. Finally, in Section 7 we present the formulation which can be used for constructing rational curves satisfying the necessary and sufficient conditions for geometric continuity.

2 Rational Curves

A *rational polynomial function* is a scalar function, $r : \mathcal{R} \rightarrow \mathcal{R}$ that can be expressed as

$$r(u) = \frac{f(u)}{g(u)}$$

where *f(u)* and *g(u)* are polynomials in *u*. We will restrict our use of the word polynomial in the following manner: a rational function is not a polynomial function unless its denominator divides its numerator. Such a function is at times referred to as an *integral* function to distinguish it from a rational function. A *curve* is simply a vector-valued function $\mathbf{q} : \mathcal{R} \rightarrow \mathcal{R}^d$. A *rational curve* is a vector-valued function, each component of which is a rational function. There are at least two ways to represent a rational curve (Hohmeyer and Barsky 1989). First, the curve $\mathbf{q}(\mathrm{u})$ can be thought of as a vector-valued function, each component of which is a rational function. Alternatively, $\mathbf{q}(\mathrm{u})$ can be thought of as a vector-valued function $\mathbf{Q} : \mathcal{R} \rightarrow \mathcal{R}^{d+1}$ with a projection function that projects $(x_1, \ldots, x_d, x_{d+1})$ to $(x_1/x_{d+1}, \ldots, x_d/x_{d+1})$. That is, the function is originally in $(d+1)$-dimensional space but is then projected down to a d-dimensional space.

In the first representation, we write:

$$\mathbf{q}(u) = (r_1(u), r_2(u), \ldots, r_d(u))$$

where each component function, $r_i(u)$, is a rational function of the form $\frac{f_i(u)}{g(u)}$. In the second representation, one might consider the same curve as a polynomial curve whose range is the homogeneous coordinate system of dimension $d+1$. The rational curve $\mathbf{q}(u)$, discussed above, would be represented in this scheme by the polynomial curve $\mathbf{Q}(u)$, where

$$\mathbf{Q}(u) = (f_1(u), \ldots, f_d(u), g(u))$$

which is in $(d+1)$-dimensional space.

We refer to $\mathbf{Q}(u)$ as the *homogeneous curve* associated with $\mathbf{q}(u)$, the *rational curve* or the *projected curve*, and $\mathbf{q}(u)$ as the *projection* of $\mathbf{Q}(u)$. The homogeneous curve is not unique, whereas the projection is. Moreover, we use italics to indicate scalar-valued functions, such as $f(u)$ or $g(u)$, boldface lower case to indicate vector-valued rational curves, such as $\mathbf{q}(u)$, whose range is $\mathcal{R}^d$, and bold face upper case to indicate the associated homogeneous polynomial curve, such as $\mathbf{Q}(u)$, whose range is $\mathcal{R}^{d+1}$. The *degree* of a rational curve is the degree of its homogeneous representation.

To illustrate more concretely, consider a curve formulation such as the rational Bézier curve, the rational B-spline curve, or the rational Beta-spline curve of a fixed degree. Each is a function $\mathbf{q} : \mathcal{R} \rightarrow \mathcal{R}^{\mathbf{d}}$ that can be expressed as

$$\mathbf{q}(u) \quad = \quad \sum_{i=0}^{m} \mathbf{V}_i [\frac{w_i B_i(u)}{\sum_{j=0}^{m} w_j B_j(u)}] \tag{1}$$

where $\mathbf{V}_i \in \mathcal{R}^d$ are the control vertices, $B_i(u)$ are the basis functions for the homogeneous curve, defined as a polynomial curve, and w_i are the weights, for $i = 0, \ldots, m$, which are independent of the control vertices and the basis functions. One can also consider such a curve as a polynomial Bézier curve, B-spline curve, or Beta-spline curve in the homogeneous space:

$$\mathbf{Q}(u) = \sum_{i=0}^{m} \mathbf{W}_i B_i(u)$$

where $\mathbf{W}_i$ are control vertices in $\mathcal{R}^{d+1}$, whose coordinates are expressed as $\mathbf{W}_i = (w_i \mathbf{V}_i, w_i)$ for $i = 0, \ldots, m$. Whenever the $\mathcal{R}^d$ coordinates of $\mathbf{q}$(u) are required, the division must be performed. For example, the circle in Fig. I is a rational curve in $\mathcal{R}^2$, which is a projection of a polynomial curve in $\mathcal{R}^{2+1}$. The points on the $\mathcal{R}^2$ curve are obtained by projecting the $\mathcal{R}^{2+1}$ curve onto the $w = 1$ plane.

The advantage of this perspective is that the algorithms to manipulate rational curves (i.e. evaluation, subdivision, degree elevation etc.) can be obtained by using the corresponding algorithm for polynomial curves. This method of reducing a problem associated with a rational curve to the analogous problem for its homogeneous counterpart has also been used for the problem of continuity, parametric or geometric, between rational segments. It is true that if the homogeneous curve satisfies the relevant continuity constraints then the rational curve will have the corresponding continuity. However, there are cases when the projected curve satisfies the required continuity constraints, whereas the corresponding homogeneous curve does not (Hohmeyer and Barsky 1989). Thus, the above approach is overly restrictive. One such case is shown in Fig. I. A circle is being generated with C^0 rational curves. In the figure, the circle has been shown as a projection of a homogeneous curve, $\mathbf{Q}$(u) $\in \mathcal{R}^{2+1}$, onto the $w = 1$ plane. The axis of the cone (whose base is also shown) lies along the w-axis. The tip is at the origin and the homogeneous curve $\mathbf{Q}$(u) consists of four segments, lying on the surface (including the base) of the cone and it is C^0 continuous. $\mathbf{Q}$(u) is neither C^1 nor even G^1, whereas $\mathbf{q}$(u) is trivially C^2.

The necessary and sufficient constraints on the homogeneous curve engenders shape parameters (Hohmeyer and Barsky 1989). The basis functions for the homogeneous representation, $B_i(u)$, as specified in (1), become functions of these shape parameters. Changing the shape parameters changes the projected curve, while still satisfying the necessary continuity constraints.

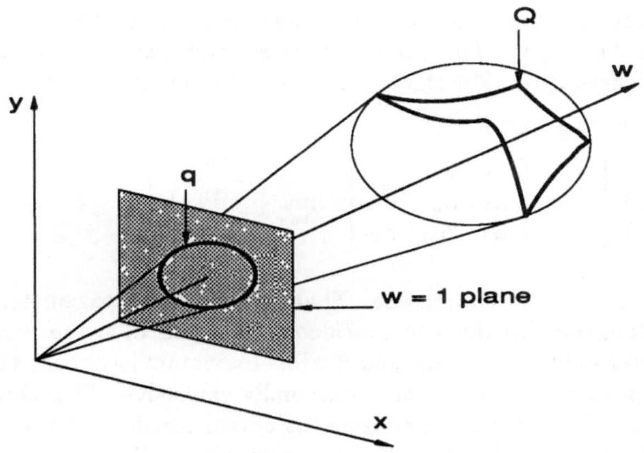

Fig. I
A circle q(u) represented by a piecewise rational **Q**(u).
There are *kinks* in **Q**(u), but **q**(u) is C^2 continuous.

3 Continuity Constraints

In our case the ***smoothness*** of a curve has been measured by testing the parametric continuity of the functions defining the curve. If we have a homogeneous curve **Q**(u) that is C^n, then the projection q(u) of **Q**(u) will also be C^n. However, the converse is not true. As mentioned earlier, there are homogeneous curves **Q**(u) that are not C^n even though their projections **q**(u) are C^n. The curve $q(u)$ is C^n, say at $u = u_0$, if and only if each component of **q**(u), which is of the form $f_i(u)/g(u)$, is C^n at $u = u_0$. Consider a generic quotient function of the type $f(u)/g(u)$. The necessary and sufficient conditions so that such a quotient function would be C^n at a point $u = u_0$ are that there exist α_i's such that

$$\lim_{u \to u_0 +} \begin{bmatrix} f^{(0)}(u) \\ f^{(1)}(u) \\ f^{(2)}(u) \\ \vdots \\ f^{(n)}(u) \end{bmatrix} = \begin{bmatrix} \alpha_0 & 0 & 0 & \cdots & 0 & 0 \\ \alpha_1 & \alpha_0 & 0 & \cdots & 0 & 0 \\ \alpha_2 & 2\alpha_1 & \alpha_0 & \cdots & 0 & 0 \\ \vdots & \vdots & \vdots & \cdots & \vdots & \vdots \\ \alpha_n & \binom{n}{1}\alpha_{n-1} & \binom{n}{2}\alpha_{n-2} & \cdots & \binom{n}{n-1}\alpha_1 & \alpha_0 \end{bmatrix} \lim_{u \to u_0 -} \begin{bmatrix} f^{(0)}(u) \\ f^{(1)}(u) \\ f^{(2)}(u) \\ \vdots \\ f^{(n)}(u) \end{bmatrix} \quad (2)$$

and similarly for the function *g(u)* (with the same set of α_i's). At any point $u = u_0$, all the functions $f_i(u)$ and $g(u)$ need to satisfy the above relation for any set of α's where $\alpha_0 \neq 0$ (Hohmeyer and Barsky 1989). In other words, each component of **Q**(u) is related by the above constraint at each knot value and the set of α's must be the same for all components.

We use the α's defined above as shape parameters. Changing the values of the α's gives a different projected curve **q**(u), which maintains the desired continuity. In most computer graphics applications, cubic curves are used because they provide a balance between computational cost and the desired smoothness and flexibility. The desired smoothness is frequently ensured by requiring the curve to be C^2 continuous in the desired interval. So we formulate a cubic basis for the homogeneous curve and generate a C^2 projected curve $\mathbf{q}(\mathrm{u})$. Thus, there are *three shape parameters*, α_0, α_1, and α_2, that determine our projected curve $\mathbf{q}(\mathrm{u})$. For this case, (2) can be rewritten in the following manner (n=2):

$$\lim_{u \to u_0+} \begin{bmatrix} f^{(0)}(u) \\ f^{(1)}(u) \\ f^{(2)}(u) \end{bmatrix} = \begin{bmatrix} \alpha_0 & 0 & 0 \\ \alpha_1 & \alpha_0 & 0 \\ \alpha_2 & 2\alpha_1 & \alpha_0 \end{bmatrix} \lim_{u \to u_0-} \begin{bmatrix} f^{(0)}(u) \\ f^{(1)}(u) \\ f^{(2)}(u) \end{bmatrix} \tag{3}$$

We will initially use α's as *uniform* shape parameters. That is, each shape parameter has the same value at the knots. We later generalize them to *continuous* functions of shape parameters, where the user is not constrained to use the same value and it offers maximum local control of these parameters. The latter formulation turns out to be computationally expensive. Therefore, at the end we introduce a discretely-shaped basis for the homogeneous curve, which provides a balance between evaluation cost and the degree of local control of shape parameters. For each case, we will define a basis function and use (1) to determine the projected curve $\mathbf{q}(\mathrm{u})$.

4 Uniform Shape Parameters

In this section, we define the basis functions for the homogeneous curve. Our terminology is similar to that described in (Bartels et. al. 1987, Chapter 2). The rational curve is obtained by projecting the linear combinations of the basis functions. The scalar multiples used for the linear combinations are determined by the control vertices and weights. The representation of a rational curve $\mathbf{q}(u)$, as defined in (1), leads to the formation of the following functions:

$$R_i(u) = \frac{w_i B_i(u)}{\sum_{j=0}^{m} w_j B_j(u)}, \quad i = 0, \ldots, m \tag{4}$$

where the $B_j(u)$ are the basis functions for the homogeneous curve. The resulting curve $\mathbf{q}(u)$ must be C^2 continuous in the specified interval. The desired continuity could be achieved if $R_i(u)$ were themselves C^2 functions, since the rational curve is a linear combination of these functions. This happens if each $B_j(u)$ and its first two derivatives are related by (3) at u_i. To simplify, we work over a *uniform knot* sequence and derive the canonical basis function in a manner similar to that described in (Bartels et. al. 1987).

4.1 The Basis Functions

Each $B_i(u)$ consists of four basis segments. We denote these segments by $b_i(u)$, $i = 0, 1, 2, 3$. Each segment is a cubic polynomial of the form

$$b_i(u) = p_i + q_i u + r_i u^2 + s_i u^3, \qquad u \in [0, 1) \quad i = 0, 1, 2, 3$$

At the knot values, the $B_j(u)$ are related by (3). This engenders the following fifteen relations among the $b_i(u)$:

$$
\begin{array}{rclrclrcl}
0 &=& b_0(0), & 0 &=& b_0^1(0), & 0 &=& b_0^2(0)\\
\alpha_0 b_0(1) &=& b_1(0), & \alpha_1 b_0(1)+\alpha_0 b_0^1(1) &=& b_1^1(0), & \alpha_2 b_0(1)+2\alpha_1 b_0^1(1)+\alpha_0 b_0^2(1) &=& b_1^2(0)\\
\alpha_0 b_1(1) &=& b_2(0), & \alpha_1 b_1(1)+\alpha_0 b_1^1(1) &=& b_2^1(0), & \alpha_2 b_1(1)+2\alpha_1 b_1^1(1)+\alpha_0 b_1^2(1) &=& b_2^2(0)\\
\alpha_0 b_2(1) &=& b_3(0), & \alpha_1 b_2(1)+\alpha_0 b_2^1(1) &=& b_3^1(0), & \alpha_2 b_2(1)+2\alpha_1 b_2^1(1)+\alpha_0 b_2^2(1) &=& b_3^2(0)\\
\alpha_0 b_3(1) &=& 0, & \alpha_1 b_3(1)+\alpha_0 b_3^1(1) &=& 0, & \alpha_2 b_3(1)+2\alpha_1 b_3^1(1)+\alpha_0 b_3^2(1) &=& 0
\end{array}
$$

There are four cubic functions, $b_0(u), b_1(u), b_2(u)$ and $b_3(u)$, which constitute $B_j(u)$. Each has four unknowns (equal to the order of each polynomial). Thus, there are sixteen variables in all. Any sixteen independent variables, each being defined over the real field $\mathcal{R}$, belong to the 16-dimensional *vector space* $\mathcal{R}^{16}$. In our case, the variables are not independent. On applying the fifteen constraints we obtain a 1-dimensional *subspace* of the 16-dimensional vector space. Geometrically, the fifteen constraints given above determine a line in the 16-dimensional space. Moreover, that line passes through the origin (as it is a vector subspace). Any point lying on that line, except the origin, would determine a solution set to the sixteen variables. That solution set is of the following form:

$$[s_1 g, s_2 g, \ldots, s_{15} g, s_{16} g]^T$$

where each s_i is a function of α_0, α_1, and α_2.

The variable g acts as a *normalizing factor.* If $g = 0$ then the basis function $B_j(u)$ becomes equal to a zero function (it is zero throughout). We let $b_i(u)$ be defined in terms of g. The rational basis functions $R_i(u)$ are independent of g, as it cancels out in the numerator and denominator terms of (4), since $g \neq 0$.

In the case of polynomial B-splines and Beta-splines, formed from C^2 and G^2 continuity constraints, respectively, the fact that the basis functions should form a *partition of unity* gives rise to the sixteenth constraint and the system of equations used for determining the coefficients of basis functions has a unique solution (Bartels et. al. 1987). The fact that $R_i(u)$, $i = 0, \ldots, m$, should form a partition of unity is embedded in their formulation and no such constraint is required on $B_i(u)$. That property engenders another shape parameter, expressed above as g. If we use a different value of g for each $B_i(u)$, then it has a local effect on the curve. The effect is similar to that of the weights for rational curves expressed as (1). However, the weights are present due to the homogeneous representation of the vertices; i.e., $\mathbf{W}_i = (w_i \mathbf{V}_i, w_i)$. If we want to use these basis functions for homogeneous representations of tensor product surfaces, the g's will affect the surface in a different manner as compared to the weights.

Using Macsyma (Fateman 1982), we obtain the following basis functions[2] for the homogeneous representation of the rational curve:

$$
\begin{aligned}
b_0(u) &= g u^3\\
b_1(u) &= g\,(\alpha_0 + [\alpha_1 + 3\alpha_0]u + [\frac{\alpha_2 + 6\alpha_1 + 6\alpha_0}{2}]u^2 - [\frac{\alpha_2 + 6\alpha_1 + 6\alpha_0}{2}]u^3)\\
b_2(u) &= g\,([\alpha_0\alpha_1 + 4\alpha_0^2] + [\frac{\alpha_0(4\alpha_1 - \alpha_2) + 2\alpha_1^2}{2}]u + \qquad (5)
\end{aligned}
$$

[2]This is one of the many of formulations of the basis functions. We can let g be a function of the α's. We tried many combinations and this is the simplest we could achieve in terms of the size of the coefficients.

$$[\alpha_0(\alpha_2 - 6\alpha_1) - 2\alpha_1^2 - 6\alpha_0^2]u^2 + [\frac{\alpha_0(6\alpha_1 - \alpha_2) + 2\alpha_1^2 + 6\alpha_0^2}{2}u^3])$$
$$b_3(u) = g\alpha_0^3(1 - 3u + 3u^2 - u^3)$$

If we set

$$\alpha_0 = 1, \quad \alpha_1 = 0, \quad \alpha_2 = 0$$

then the above basis reduces to a basis for the uniform cubic B-spline (Bartels et. al. 1987). These are the default values of the shape parameters and the resulting function is a basis for the homogeneous representation of a cubic rational B-spline with uniform knot spacing. To determine a curve, we select a set of control vertices $\mathbf{V}_i$ and use (1) to define the curve. The $B_i(u)$ used in the definition of $R_i(u)$ in (4) are defined in terms of the segments $b_i(u)$ (5). Each $B_i(u)$ is nonzero over four successive intervals only, say from u_i to u_{i+4}. Thus, over the knot interval $[u_{i+3}, u_{i+4})$, the portion of the curve defining $\mathbf{q}(u)$ can be represented as

$$\mathbf{S}_i(u) = \frac{\mathbf{V}_i w_i b_3(u) + \mathbf{V}_{i+1} w_{i+1} b_2(u) + \mathbf{V}_{i+2} w_{i+2} b_1(u) + \mathbf{V}_{i+3} w_{i+3} b_0(u)}{w_i b_3(u) + w_{i+1} b_2(u) + w_{i+2} b_1(u) + w_{i+3} b_0(u)} \tag{6}$$

The whole curve $\mathbf{q}(u)$ is composed of $m-2$ segments, $\mathbf{S}_i(u)$, $i = 0, \ldots, m-3$.

It is also desirable for the resulting curve $\mathbf{q}(u)$ obtained from (1) to lie in the convex hull of the control vertices $\mathbf{V}_i$. Using (4), $\mathbf{q}(u)$ can be expressed as

$$\mathbf{q}(u) = \sum_{i=0}^{m} \mathbf{V}_i R_i(u). \tag{7}$$

Since we are considering a uniform knot sequence, all these relations are defined for $u \in [0,1)$. From the definition of $R_i(u)$ in (4), we know that:

$$\sum_{i=0}^{m} R_i(u) = 1$$

The only other condition that needs to be satisfied for the convex hull property is

$$R_i(u) \geq 0, \quad u \in [0,1), \quad i = 0, \ldots, m \tag{8}$$

A sufficient condition for the above inequality may be obtained by non-negative values of α_0, α_1, and α_2. Large positive values of α_2 result in the loss of convex hull property. Each segment of $\mathbf{q}(u)$ lies in the convex hull of the four vertices used for defining it (6).

4.2 Varying the α's

Varying the α's changes the rational curve. A detailed analysis and explanation of their behavior can be found in (Manocha and Barsky 1990). The shape parameters α_0 and α_1 are found to behave very similar to the *bias* and *tension* parameters, β_1 and β_2, respectively, of the polynomial and rational Beta-spline curves (Barsky 1988b; Barsky and Beatty 1983; Barsky and DeRose 1989; Barsky and DeRose 1990; DeRose 1985). The planar rational curves resulting from different values of α_0 and α_1 have been shown in Fig. II and Fig. III respectively. Some negative values lead to the occurrence of loops or self-intersections. The positions where adjacent segments meet, called *joints*, of the rational curve are invariant with respect to altering α_2 (as shown in Fig. IV).

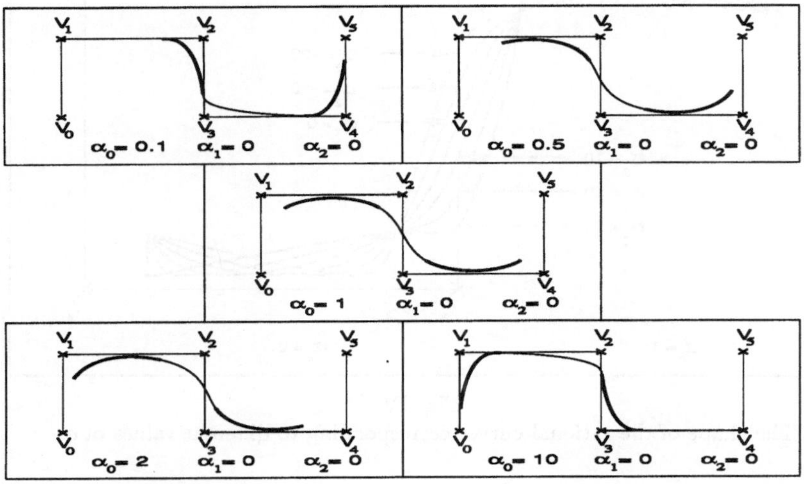

Fig. II
The shape of the rational curves corresponding to different values of α_0.

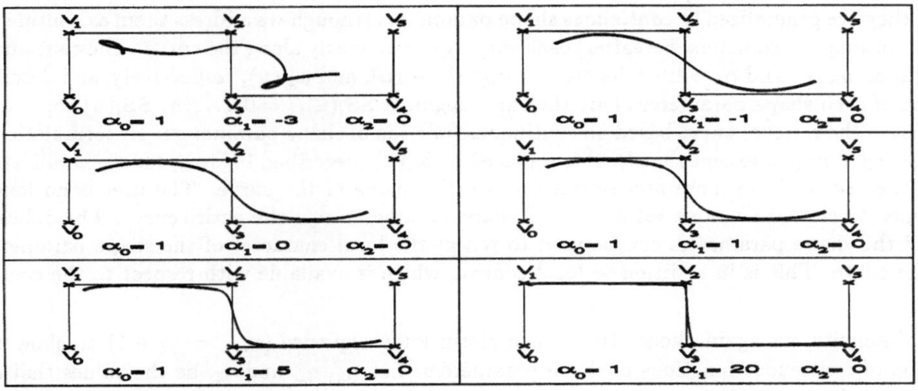

Fig. III
Different rational curves corresponding to different values of α_1.

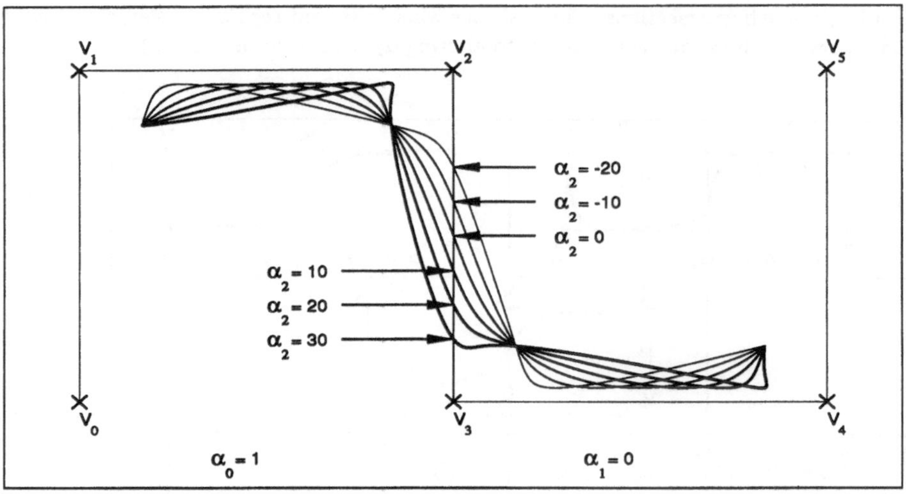

Fig. IV
The shape of the rational curves corresponding to different values of α_2.

5 Continuous Shape Parameters

In the previous sections the formation and usage of *basis functions*, have been based on the fact that the α's are *uniform* shape parameters; i.e., each parameter assumes a unique value. In this section, they are generalized to *continuous* shape parameters (though we address them as continuous functions of shape parameters, hereafter) each varying continuously along the curve. The continuous analogues of α_0, α_1, and α_2 will be denoted by $\alpha_{0_i}(u)$, $\alpha_{1_i}(u)$, and $\alpha_{2_i}(u)$, respectively, and describe the value of each shape parameter along the curve segment $\mathbf{SS}_i(u), i = 0, \ldots, m$. $\mathbf{SS}_i(u)$ represents a segment of the rational curve based on continuous function of shape parameters. Its formulation is similar to $\mathbf{S}_i(u)$ in (6), except that $b_i(u)$ is replaced by $bb_i(u)$ (described below). This generalization enables the user to have more precise control over the shape of the curve. The user is no longer constrained to choose a unique value for each shape parameter over the entire curve. The different values of the shape parameters can be used to reflect the local character of the shape parameters along the curve. This is in addition to local control, which is available with respect to the control vertices.

For simplicity, we again choose to use a uniform knot sequence ($u_{i+1} = u_i + 1$) to show the derivation of continuous functions of shape parameters. Let γ_{0_i}, γ_{1_i} and γ_{2_i} be the values that are associated with the continuous functions of shape parameters corresponding to the knot value u_i (as shown in fig. V). They are specified by the user and used for changing the curve. We will refer to these values as the *user_specified* values for the continuous functions of shape parameters. Now each component of the homogeneous curve, $\mathbf{Q}(\mathrm{u})$, is modified so that in the neighborhood of the knot u_i, it is related in the following manner:

$$\lim_{u\to u_i+}\begin{bmatrix} f^{(0)}(u) \\ f^{(1)}(u) \\ f^{(2)}(u) \end{bmatrix} = \begin{bmatrix} \gamma_{0_i} & 0 & 0 \\ \gamma_{1_i} & \gamma_{0_i} & 0 \\ \gamma_{2_i} & 2\gamma_{1_i} & \gamma_{0_i} \end{bmatrix} \lim_{u\to u_i-}\begin{bmatrix} f^{(0)}(u) \\ f^{(1)}(u) \\ f^{(2)}(u) \end{bmatrix} \tag{9}$$

The above relation is satisfied by each component of $\mathbf{Q}(u)$, so that the projected curve, $\mathbf{q}(u)$, is C^2 continuous. We choose the basis functions for the $f_i(u)$'s and g(u) (components of $\mathbf{Q}(u)$) by replacing the uniform parameters by their continuous analogues in (5)

$$\begin{aligned}
bb_0(u) &= gu^3 \\
bb_1(u) &= g(\alpha_{0_i}(u) + [\alpha_{1_i}(u) + 3\alpha_{0_i}(u)]u + \frac{[\alpha_{2_i}(u) + 6\alpha_{1_i}(u) + 6\alpha_{0_i}(u)]}{2}u^2 - \\
&\quad \frac{[\alpha_{2_i}(u) + 6\alpha_{1_i}(u) + 6\alpha_{0_i}(u)]}{2}u^3) \\
bb_2(u) &= g([\alpha_{0_i}(u)\alpha_{1_i}(u) + 4(\alpha_{0_i}(u))^2] + \frac{[\alpha_{0_i}(u)(4\alpha_{1_i}(u) - \alpha_{2_i}(u)) + 2(\alpha_{1_i}(u))^2]}{2}u + \\
&\quad [\alpha_{0_i}(u)(\alpha_{2_i}(u) - 6\alpha_{1_i}(u)) - 2\alpha_{1_i}(u)^2 - 6(\alpha_{0_i}(u))^2]u^2 + \\
&\quad \frac{[\alpha_{0_i}(u)(6\alpha_{1_i}(u) - \alpha_{2_i}(u)) + 2(\alpha_{1_i}(u))^2 + 6(\alpha_{0_i}(u))^2]}{2}u^3) \\
bb_3(u) &= g(\alpha_{0_i}(u))^3(1 - 3u + 3u^2 - u^3)
\end{aligned} \tag{10}$$

The basis functions of $\mathbf{Q}(u)$ can be represented by many formulations. It is certainly of interest to know about the class of functions which can be used for the continuously varying shape parameters so that (9) holds. Many factors play an important role in the generation of the family of functions. Frequently (i.e., for the choice of *user_specified* values and continuous functions for the shape parameters), the convex hull property would not be retained and at times visually undesirable effects like cusps or loops are introduced in the curve. We think that using functions, which represent $\alpha_{j_i}(u)$ as piecewise and local in nature, as compared to global functions, would be of great use since they represent the local behavior of these rational curves in the best possible manner, thereby providing us a lot of flexibility for our applications.

Each of the $\alpha_{j_i}(u)$, $(j \in \{0,1,2\})$, is a piecewise function that must interpolate the *user_specified* values at the knot value. The fact that the resulting function must satisfy the constraints mentioned in (9) limits the class of functions that can be used for $\alpha_{j_i}(u)$. Currently, our aim is to choose one of minimal degree, in terms of u, since it will be more efficient to evaluate. We determine the continuous functions of shape parameters as polynomials of degree five. These functions are obtained by a special case of quintic interpolation. This is derived in detail in (Manocha and Barsky 1990) yielding:

$$\alpha_{j_i}(u) = \gamma_{j_{i-1}} + (\gamma_{j_i} - \gamma_{j_{i-1}})u^3[10 - 15u + 6u^2]$$

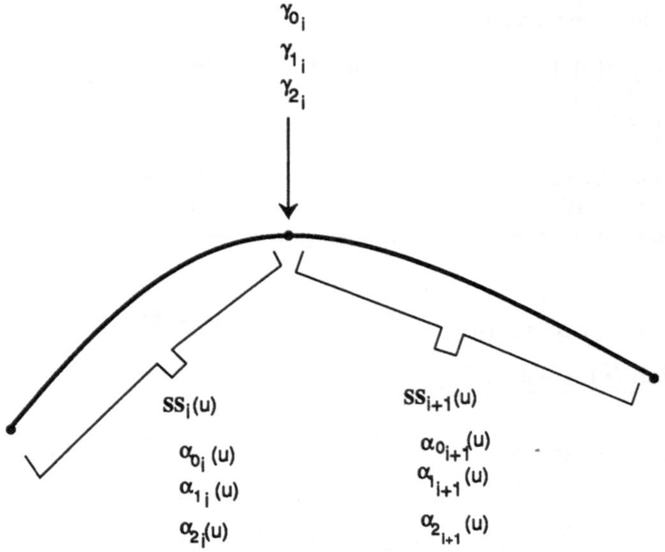

Fig. V
Continuous and discrete shape parameters for curves

5.1 Locality

We have derived the basis functions for the homogeneous curve by using continuous functions of shape parameters. This representation gives the user more precise control over the shape of the curve. Moreover, a change in any γ_{j_i} affects only two adjacent segments $\mathbf{SS}_i(u)$ and $\mathbf{SS}_{i+1}(u)$ as their shape parameter functions are affected by it. However, we pay a price for this extra control in terms of cost of evaluation. Our basis functions are now polynomials of degree eighteen. But they can be decomposed into products of polynomials of degree five and three.

Any movement of a control vertex affects only four segments. This choice is independent of the choice of shape parameters (whether uniform or continuous). This occurs because any basis function will be nonzero only over four intervals.

5.2 Varying the γ's

Different values of γ_{j_i} affect the adjacent segments. A detailed analysis of the behavior of the rational curves in terms of these parameters is given in (Manocha and Barsky 1990). The parameters γ_0 and γ_1 behave very similarly to the *bias* and *tension* parameters of the polynomial and rational Beta-spline curves (Bartels et. al. 1987; Barsky 1988). In Fig. VI, the planar rational curves resulting from different values of γ_0's are shown. A large ratio in the values of γ_0 at two adjacent joints results in *cusps*. Methods to analyze an arbitrary degree rational curve for cusps are given in (Manocha and Canny 1990). A modest reduction in the ratios of adjacent γ_0's ameliorates this effect (as shown in Fig. VI). This behavior seems to be independent of the control vertices and the weights associated with the knots. The choice of the functions $\alpha_{0_i}(u)$ is responsible for this behavior. γ_1 behaves like the *tension* parameter, and the effect is local, as shown in Fig. VII. Changes in the values of the γ_2's do not affect the position of the joints of the resulting curve (as has been shown in Fig. VIII). However, large values of the γ_2's introduce loops in a curve segment and intersections among different segments.

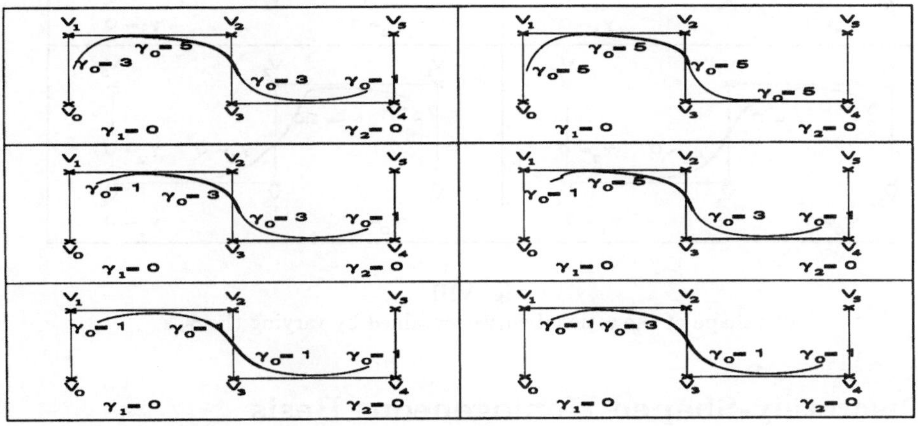

Fig. VI
The shape of the rational curves obtained by varying the γ_0's.

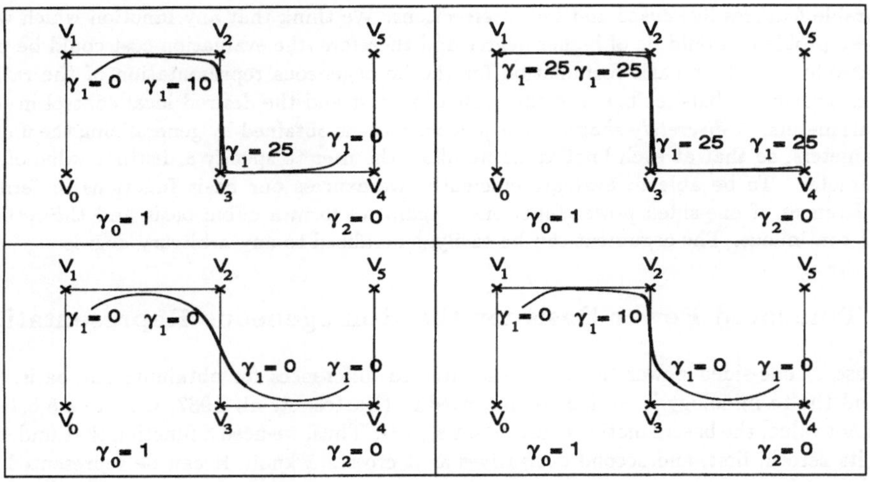

Fig. VII
Different rational curves obtained by varying the γ_1's.

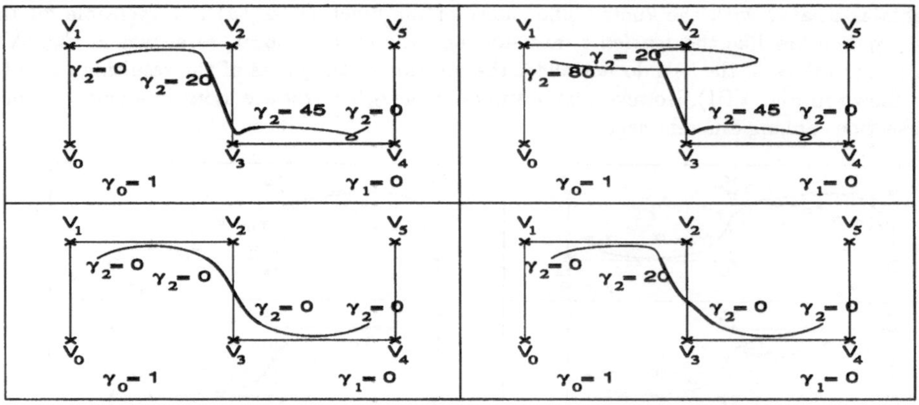

Fig. VIII
The shape of the rational curves obtained by varying the γ_2's.

6 Discretely-Shaped Homogeneous Basis

In the previous section, we specified a *basis* for the homogeneous representation, based on the continuous variation of shape parameters. Although, it provides us with a great amount of local control, in terms of shape parameters, the evaluation cost is high. Moreover, our current formulation has undesirable features like cusps and self-intersections. We think that any function which would address these problems would be of higher degree and therefore, the evaluation cost could be more. We now introduce another basis formulation for the homogeneous representation of the rational curve, which provides a balance between the evaluation cost and the desired local control in terms of shape parameters. A *discretely-shaped* homogeneous basis is obtained by generalizing the uniform shape parameters, so that at each knot value we allow the user to specify a distinct value of each shape parameter. To be able to evaluate efficiently, we express our basis functions in terms of divided differences of one-sided power functions. Again we form a cubic basis and the resulting curve is C^2 continuous. The argument can be easily generalized to any arbitrary degree.

6.1 A Truncated Power Basis for the Homogeneous Representation

We make use of one-sided power functions and divided differences for obtaining our basis. The notation and the terminology is similar to that used in (Bartels et. al. 1987, Chapters 5,6,7). At any given knot value, the basis functions need to satisfy (3). Thus, we need a function that undergoes a jump in its zeroth, first, and second derivatives as it crosses a knot. It can be represented by a function of the type:

$$p(\overline{u}) + a_{i,i+1}(\overline{u} - \overline{u}_{i+1})^0_+ + b_{i,i+1}(\overline{u} - \overline{u}_{i+1})^1_+ + c_{i,i+1}(\overline{u} - \overline{u}_{i+1})^2_+ \qquad (11)$$

The zeroth, first, and second derivatives from the left at $\overline{u} = \overline{u}_{i+1}$ are $p(\overline{u}_{i+1})$, $p^{(1)}(\overline{u}_{i+1})$, and $p^{(2)}(\overline{u}_{i+1})$, respectively. The corresponding derivatives from the right are $p(\overline{u}_{i+1}) + a_{i,i+1}$, $p^{(1)}(\overline{u}_{i+1}) + b_{i,i+1}$, and $p^{(2)}(\overline{u}_{i+1}) + 2c_{i,i+1}$, respectively. Thus, there is a jump of $a_{i,i+1}$, $b_{i,i+1}$, and $2c_{i,i+1}$ in the zeroth, first, and second derivatives, respectively, at $\overline{u} = \overline{u}_{i+1}$. Let $\alpha_{0,j}$, $\alpha_{1,j}$, and $\alpha_{2,j}$ be the values of shape parameters at the knot $\overline{u}_j$. Since the function must satisfy the constraints mentioned in (3), we have

$$\begin{aligned} p(\overline{u}_{i+1}) + a_{i,i+1} &= \alpha_{0,i+1} p(\overline{u}_{i+1}) \\ p^{(1)}(\overline{u}_{i+1}) + b_{i,i+1} &= \alpha_{1,i+1} p(\overline{u}_{i+1}) + \alpha_{0,i+1} p^{(1)}(\overline{u}_{i+1}) \\ p^{(2)}(\overline{u}_{i+1}) + 2c_{i,i+1} &= \alpha_{2,i+1} p(\overline{u}_{i+1}) + 2\alpha_{1,i+1} p^{(1)}(\overline{u}_{i+1}) + \alpha_{0,i+1} p^{(2)}(\overline{u}_{i+1}) \end{aligned} \tag{12}$$

From equations (12), the coefficients $a_{i,i+1}$, $b_{i,i+1}$, and $c_{i,i+1}$ in equation (11) can be determined. These equations show how to modify the coefficients of the functions used for representing the homogeneous basis of the *discretely-shaped* rational curve, so that they satisfy the necessary and sufficient conditions for rational parametric C^2 continuity. To construct a one-sided basis function for the homogeneous representation, we start with $(\overline{u} - \overline{u}_i)_+^3$ since it introduces the third derivative discontinuity at $\overline{u} = \overline{u}_i$, and the resulting rational curve can be at most C^2 continuous. We modify it as we cross a knot value. Consider the following function:

$$\begin{aligned} h_i(\overline{u}) = {} & (\overline{u} - \overline{u}_i)_+^3 + a_{i,i+1}(\overline{u} - \overline{u}_{i+1})_+^0 + \ldots + a_{i,m+3}(\overline{u} - \overline{u}_{m+3})_+^0 + \\ & b_{i,i+1}(\overline{u} - \overline{u}_{i+1})_+^1 + \ldots + b_{i,m+3}(\overline{u} - \overline{u}_{m+3})_+^1 + \\ & c_{i,i+1}(\overline{u} - \overline{u}_{i+1})_+^2 + \ldots + c_{i,m+3}(\overline{u} - \overline{u}_{m+3})_+^2 \end{aligned} \tag{13}$$

We want the coefficients of $h_i(\overline{u})$ to satisfy (3). In (Manocha and Barsky 1990), we impose the constraints in the following algorithm to compute the coefficients:

for i $\leftarrow$ 0 **step** 1 **until** m+2 **do**
  Sa $\leftarrow$ 0
  Sb $\leftarrow$ 0
  Sc $\leftarrow$ 0
  for j $\leftarrow$ i+1 **step** 1 **until** min(i+4,m+3) **do**
    $p_{left}^{(0)} \leftarrow (\overline{u}_j - \overline{u}_i)^3 + Sa + \sum_{k=i+1}^{j}(b_{i,k}(\overline{u}_j - \overline{u}_k) + c_{i,k}(\overline{u}_j - \overline{u}_k)^2)$
    $p_{left}^{(1)} \leftarrow 3(\overline{u}_j - \overline{u}_i)^2 + Sb + 2\sum_{k=i+1}^{j}(c_{i,k}(\overline{u}_j - \overline{u}_k))$
    $p_{left}^{(2)} \leftarrow 6(\overline{u}_j - \overline{u}_i) + 2Sc$
    $a_{i,j} \leftarrow (\alpha_{0,j} - 1)p_{left}^{(0)}$
    $b_{i,j} \leftarrow \alpha_{1,j} p_{left}^{(0)} + (\alpha_{0,j} - 1)p_{left}^{(1)}$
    $c_{i,j} \leftarrow \frac{1}{2}[\alpha_{2,j} p_{left}^{(0)} + 2\alpha_{1,j} p_{left}^{(1)} + (\alpha_{0,j} - 1)p_{left}^{(2)}]$
    $Sa \leftarrow Sa + a_{i,j}$
    $Sb \leftarrow Sb + b_{i,j}$
    $Sc \leftarrow Sc + c_{i,j}$
  endfor
endfor

Thus, given a knot sequence and the shape parameters at the knot values, the functions $h_i(\overline{u})$ form a basis for the homogeneous representation of C^2 rational parametric curves. We plan to use this procedure for computing the a_i's, b_i's and c_i's for the local basis defined in the next section.

The *min* operator in line 5 has been specified for that purpose. The argument is analogous to that given in (Bartels et. al. 1987) for C^2 and G^2 polynomial splines.

6.2 A Local Basis for the Homogeneous Representation

We can construct any homogeneous representation for a C^2 rational curve as a linear combination of one-sided power functions. We are not allowed to choose any arbitrary linear combination. The coefficients used are determined by the shape parameters at the knot values as shown in (12) and the resulting functions are of the type $h_i(\overline{u})$. However, these functions are computationally unsatisfying. They are only useful for their simplicity and ease of understanding. For constructing splines, they suffer from two severe shortcomings: *numerical instability* and *lack of local control* (Bartels et. al. 1987; Barsky 1988b). Therefore, we need to apply differencing operations so as to obtain a local basis and to be able to compute them quickly.

Let $\overline{u}_j \leq \overline{u} < \overline{u}_{j+1}$. Equation (13) can be expressed as

$$\begin{aligned} h_i(\overline{u}) &= \overline{u}^3 + [\sum_{k=i+1}^{j} c_{i,k} - 3\overline{u}_i]\overline{u}^2 + [\sum_{k=i+1}^{j} b_{i,k} - 2\sum_{k=i+1}^{j} c_{i,k}\overline{u}_k + 3\overline{u}_i^2]\overline{u} + \\ & [\sum_{k=i+1}^{j} (a_{i,k} - b_{i,k}\overline{u}_k + c_{i,k}\overline{u}_k^2) - \overline{u}_i^3] \end{aligned} \tag{14}$$

Our aim is to apply some form of differencing operator to $h_i(u)$ so as to obtain a local basis. We do so by successively eliminating the higher powers of $\overline{u}$ and normalizing each time, as explained in (Manocha and Barsky 1990).

We now define the constants, which are used for normalization. Let

$$\begin{aligned} A_{i,j} &= \sum_{k=j+1}^{i+4} c_{j,k} - 3\overline{u}_j \\ B_{i,j} &= \sum_{k=j+1}^{i+4} [b_{j,k} - 2c_{j,k}\overline{u}_k] + 3\overline{u}_j^2 \\ C_{i,j} &= \sum_{k=j+1}^{i+4} [a_{j,k} - b_{j,k}\overline{u}_k + c_{j,k}\overline{u}_k^2] - \overline{u}_j^3 \end{aligned} \tag{15}$$

for $j = i,\ i+1,\ i+2,\ i+3$ and

$$\begin{aligned} A_{i,i+4} &= -3\overline{u}_{i+4} \\ B_{i,i+4} &= 3\overline{u}_{i+4}^2 \\ C_{i,i+4} &= -\overline{u}_{i+4}^3 \\ D_{i,j} &= \frac{B_{i,j+1} - B_{i,j}}{A_{i,j+1} - A_{i,j}} \\ E_{i,j} &= \frac{C_{i,j+1} - C_{i,j}}{A_{i,j+1} - A_{i,j}} \\ F_{i,j} &= \frac{E_{i,j+1} - E_{i,j}}{D_{i,j+1} - D_{i,j}} \end{aligned}$$

Furthermore, we define

$$\begin{aligned}
h_j(\overline{u}) &= \overline{u}^3 + A_{i,j}\overline{u}^2 + B_{i,j}\overline{u} + C_{i,j} \quad for \quad \overline{u}_{i+4} \le \overline{u} < \overline{u}_{i+5}, \\
\Delta_i^1 h_j(\overline{u}) &= \frac{h_{j+1}(\overline{u}) - h_j(\overline{u})}{A_{i,j+1} - A_{i,j}} \quad for\ \overline{u}_{i+4} \le \overline{u} < \overline{u}_{i+5}, \\
\Delta_i^2 h_j(\overline{u}) &= \frac{\Delta_i^1 h_{j+1}(\overline{u}) - \Delta_i^1 h_j(\overline{u})}{D_{i,j+1} - D_{i,j}} \quad for\ \overline{u}_{i+4} \le \overline{u} < \overline{u}_{i+5}, \\
\Delta_i^3 h_j(\overline{u}) &= \frac{\Delta_i^2 h_{j+1}(\overline{u}) - \Delta_i^2 h_j(\overline{u})}{F_{i,j+1} - F_{i,j}} \quad for\ \overline{u}_{i+4} \le \overline{u} < \overline{u}_{i+5}, \\
\Delta_i^4 h_j(\overline{u}) &= -[\Delta_i^3 h_{j+1}(\overline{u}) - \Delta_i^3 h_j(\overline{u})] \quad for\ \overline{u}_{i+4} \le \overline{u} < \overline{u}_{i+5}.
\end{aligned}$$

The function $\Delta_i^4 h_i(\overline{u})$ is defined for any value of $\overline{u}$, but we ensured that it would be zero whenever $\overline{u} \in [\overline{u}_{i+4}, \overline{u}_{i+5})$ or $\overline{u} < \overline{u}_i$. To arrange for locality, we define our homogeneous basis function $H_i(\overline{u})$ as

$$H_i(\overline{u}) = \begin{cases} 0 & \overline{u} < \overline{u}_i \ or\ \overline{u} \ge \overline{u}_{i+4} \\ \Delta_i^4 h_i(\overline{u}) & \overline{u}_i \le \overline{u} < \overline{u}_{i+4} \end{cases}$$

Given a knot sequence comprising $m+5$ knots $\overline{u}_0, \ldots, \overline{u}_{m+4}$ and shape parameters $\alpha_{0,i}, \alpha_{1,i}$ and $\alpha_{2,i}$ associated with each knot value, we construct the $m+1$ basis functions $H_i(\overline{u})$ in the manner defined above. Given $m+1$ control vertices $\mathbf{V}_0, \ldots, \mathbf{V}_m$, a C^2 discretely-shaped rational curve is defined as

$$\mathbf{Q}(\overline{u}) = \sum_{i=0}^{m} \mathbf{W}_i H_i(\overline{u}) \quad \overline{u}_3 \le \overline{u} < \overline{u}_{m+1}$$

in the homogeneous space or as

$$\mathbf{q}(\overline{u}) = \sum_{i=0}^{m} \mathbf{V}_i \frac{w_i H_i(\overline{u})}{\sum_{j=0}^{m} w_j H_j(\overline{u})} \quad \overline{u}_3 \le \overline{u} < \overline{u}_{m+1}$$

in the projected space, where $\mathbf{W}_i = (w_i \mathbf{V}_i, w_i)$.

7 Rational Geometric Continuity

All our analysis thus far has been for *parametric continuity* of rational curves. For each notion of geometric continuity of parametric curves, the necessary and sufficient conditions for the corresponding geometric continuity of rational curves are derived in (Hohmeyer and Barsky 1989). Let us consider the notion corresponding to reparametrization. The necessary and sufficient conditions can be expressed as replacing the matrix consisting of α*'s* in (2) by a matrix that is expressed as the product of an α matrix (the same as the one defined in (2)) and a β matrix as defined in (Barsky and DeRose 1989; Barsky and DeRose 1990; DeRose 1985). Thus, for second order rational geometric continuity, we will have five shape parameters α_0, α_1, α_2, β_1, and β_2. A rational curve $\mathbf{q}$(u) is said to possess second order rational geometric continuity at a knot value $u = u_0$ if and only if each component of its homogeneous representation, $\mathbf{Q}$(u), say *f(u)*, satisfies the following relation:

$$\lim_{u \to u_0+} \begin{bmatrix} f^{(0)}(u) \\ f^{(1)}(u) \\ f^{(2)}(u) \end{bmatrix} = \begin{bmatrix} \alpha_0 & 0 & 0 \\ \alpha_1 & \alpha_0 & 0 \\ \alpha_2 & 2\alpha_1 & \alpha_0 \end{bmatrix} \begin{bmatrix} 1 & 0 & 0 \\ 0 & \beta_1 & 0 \\ 0 & \beta_2 & {\beta_1}^2 \end{bmatrix} \lim_{u \to u_0-} \begin{bmatrix} f^{(0)}(u) \\ f^{(1)}(u) \\ f^{(2)}(u) \end{bmatrix}$$

This relation can be used for developing basis functions for second order rational geometric continuous curves, whose homogeneous representation is cubic. We can use this relation to develop all the three types of basis functions; i.e., we can develop basis functions for homogeneous representation of uniformly-shaped, continuously-shaped, and discretely-shaped curves. A similar relationship has been defined for Frenet frame continuity of rational curves (Hohmeyer and Barsky 1989)

8 Conclusion

The rational curve is more versatile than its polynomial counterpart. The connection with constructions in a higher dimensional space offers extra degrees of freedom. These degrees of freedom were exploited in (Hohmeyer and Barsky 1989) to determine the necessary and sufficient conditions for parametric and geometric continuity of rational curves. We used the exact conditions for defining the basis functions for the homogeneous representation of C^2 cubic rational curves. Although our analysis has been for parametric continuity of rational curves, we have shown how to obtain rational curves with geometric continuity as well.

We have highlighted three different formulations for constructing basis functions of C^2 continuous rational curves. Each form has its relative advantages and disadvantages in terms of evaluation cost and the degree of local control relative to the shape parameters. The shape parameters have been shown to provide us with an intuitive way of changing the curve independent of the control vertices (Manocha and Barsky 1990). In particular, we observed that two of the three uniform shape parameters, α_0 and α_1, behave like the *bias* and *tension* parameters, β_1 and β_2, respectively, of the G^2 cubic polynomial and rational Beta-splines. The third shape parameter, α_2, acts like a *joint-invariant* parameter.

The formulation of $R_i(u)$ in (4) possesses the *partition of unity* property irrespective of the $B_i(u)$'s and no normalization constraint is required on the $B_i(u)$'s. Therefore, while determining the basis functions for homogeneous representation, there are sixteen unknowns and fifteen continuity constraints (for parametric or geometric continuity). We have not exploited this property in determining basis functions for continuously-shaped or discretely-shaped curves. Moreover, this can be used as a shape parameter whenever these basis functions are used for tensor product surfaces. The use of these basis functions and shape parameters for applications involving surfaces needs further investigation.

9 Acknowledgements

We are grateful to John Canny and Michael Hohmeyer for productive discussions and also to Ray Sarraga who read an earlier draft of this paper and gave useful suggestions.

10 References

Barsky, Brian A. (1988a) "Introducing the Rational Beta-spline," *Proceedings of the Third International Conference on Engineering Graphics and Descriptive Geometry,* vol. **1**, pp. 16-27, Vienna.

Barsky, Brian A. (1988b) *Computer Graphics and Geometric Modeling Using Beta-splines,* Springer-Verlag, Heidelberg.

Barsky, Brian A. and Beatty, John C. (1983) "Local Control of Bias and Tension in Beta-splines," *ACM Transactions on Graphics,* vol. **2**, no. **2**, pp. 109-134, April, 1983. Also published in *SIGGRAPH '83 Conference Proceedings*, vol. **17**, no. **3**, pp. 193-218, ACM, Detroit, July 1983.

Bartels, Richard H.; Beatty, John C.; and Barsky, Brian A. (1987) *An Introduction to Splines for Use in Computer Graphics and Geometric Modeling,* Morgan Kaufmann Publishers, Inc., San Mateo, California.

Barsky, Brian A. and DeRose, Tony D. (November 1989) "Geometric Continuity of Parametric Curves: Three Equivalent Characterizations," *IEEE Computer Graphics and Applications* vol. **9**, no. **6**, pp. 60-68.

Barsky, Brian A. and DeRose, Tony D. (January 1990) "Geometric Continuity of Parametric Curves: Constructions of Geometrically Continuous Splines," to appear in *IEEE Computer Graphics and Applications* vol. **10**, no. **1**, pp. 60-68.

Boehm, Wolfgang (December 1985) "Curvature Continuous Curves and Surfaces," *Computer Aided Geometric Design,* vol. **2**, no. **4**, pp. 313-325.

Boehm, Wolfgang (July 1987) "Rational Geometric Splines," *Computer Aided Geometric Design,* vol. **4**, no. **12**, pp. 67-77.

Cohen, Danny and Lee, T.M.P. (1969) "Fast Drawing of Curves for Computer Display," *Proceedings of the Spring Joint Computer Conference,* vol. **34**, pp. 297-307, AFIPS Press, Montvale, N.J..

DeRose, Tony D. (August 1985) *Geometric Continuity: A Parametrization Independent Measure of Continuity for Computer Aided Geometric Design,* Ph.D. thesis, Computer Science Division, Electrical Engineering and Computer Sciences Department, University of California, Berkeley, California.

DeRose, Tony D. and Barsky, Brian A. (January 1988) "Geometric Continuity, Shape Parameters, and Geometric Constructions for Catmull-Rom Splines," *ACM Transactions on Graphics,* vol. **7**, no. **1**, pp. 1-41.

Dyn, Nira and Micchelli, Charles A. (September 1985) *Piecewise Polynomial Spaces and Geometric Continuity of Curves,* IBM Thomas J. Watson Research Center, Yorktown Heights, New York.

Farin, Gerald (May 1982) "Visually C2 Cubic Splines," *Computer Aided Design,* vol. **14**, no. **3**, pp. 137-139.

Farin, Gerald (March 1983) "Algorithms for Rational Bézier Curves," *Computer Aided Design,* vol. **15**, no. **2**, pp. 73-77.

Fateman, Richard (1982) *Addendum to the MACSYMA Reference Manual,* University of California, Berkeley.

Goldman, Ronald N. and Barsky, Brian A. (1989a) "On Beta-continuous Functions and Their Applications to the Construction of Geometrically Continuous Curves and Surfaces," in *Mathematical Methods in Computer Aided Geometric Design,* ed. Lyche, Tom and Schumaker, Larry L., pp. 299-311, Academic Press, Boston.

Goldman, Ronald N. and Barsky, Brian A. (1989b) "Beta-continuity and Its Applications to Rational Beta-splines," *Proceedings of the Computer Graphics'89 Conference, Smolenice, Czechoslovakia,* pp. 5-11.

Hagen, Hans (September 1985) "Geometric Spline Curves," *Computer Aided Geometric Design,* vol. **2**, no. **1-3**, pp. 223-227.

Hohmeyer, Michael E. and Barsky, Brian A. (October 1989) "Rational Continuity: Parametric, Geometric, and Frenet Frame Continuity of Rational Curves," *ACM Transactions on Graphics,* Special Issue on Computer-Aided Geometric Design and Geometric Modeling, vol. **8**, no. **2**, pp. 335-359.

Joe, Barry (April 1989) "Multiple-Knot and Rational Cubic Beta-Splines," *ACM Transactions on Graphics,* vol. **8**, no. **2**, pp. 100-120.

Lee, Eugene T.Y. (1987) "The Rational Quadratic Bézier Representations for Conics," *in Geometric Modeling: Algorithms and New Trends,* ed. Farin, Gerald, SIAM.

Manocha, Dinesh and Barsky, Brian A. (1990) "Varying the Shape Parameters of Rational Continuity," in preparation.

Manocha, Dinesh and Canny, John F. (January 1990) "Detecting Cusps and Inflection Points in Parametric Curves," Technical Report no. UCB/CSD 90/549, Computer Science Division, University of California, Berkeley.

Piegl, Leslie (September 1985) "Representation of Quadric Primitives by Rational Polynomials," *Computer Aided Geometric Design,* vol. **2**, no. 1-3, pp. 151-155.

Piegl, Leslie (May 1986) "The Sphere as a Rational Bézier Surface," *Computer Aided Geometric Design,* vol. **3**, no. **1**, pp 45-52.

Piegl, Leslie (September 1986) "Representation of Rational Bézier Curves and Surfaces by Recursive Algorithms," *Computer Aided Design,* vol. **18**, no. **7**, pp. 361-366.

Piegl, Leslie (October 1986) "A Geometric Investigation of the Rational Bézier Scheme of Computer Aided Design," *Computers in Industry,* vol. **7**, no. **5**, pp. 401-410.

Piegl, Leslie and Tiller, Wayne (November 1987) "Curve and Surface Constructions for Computer Aided Design Using Rational B-splines", *Computer Aided Design,* vol. **19**, no. **9**, pp. 485-498.

Salmon, George (1879) *A Treatise on Conic Sections,* Longmans, Green, & Co., London 1879. Sixth edition. Reprinted by Dover Publications Inc., New York.

Tiller, Wayne (September 1983) "Rational B-Splines for Curve and Surface Representation," *IEEE Computer Graphics and Applications,* vol. **3**, no. **6**, pp. 61-69.

Versprille, Kenneth J. (February 1975) *Computer Aided Design Applications of the Rational B-spline Approximation Form,* Syracuse University, Syracuse, N.Y..

Dinesh Manocha is currently a doctoral student and research assistant in the computer science division at the University of California, Berkeley. His research interests include computer graphics, geometric modeling and symbolic computation. In 1987 he received his Bachelor of Technology degree in computer science at the Indian Institute of Technology, Delhi.

Brian A. Barsky is Associate Professor of Computer Science at the University of California at Berkeley, and Adjunct Associate Professor of Computer Science at the University of Waterloo. He was an Attache de Recherche Invite at the Laboratoire Image of Ecole Nationale Superieure des.Telecommunications in Paris and a visiting researcher with the Computer Aided Design and Manufacturing Group at the Sentralinsitutt for Industriell Forskning (Central Institute for Industrial Research) in Oslo.

His research interests include computer aided geometric design and modeling, interactive three-dimensional computer graphics, and visualization in scientific computing.

He attended McGill University where he received a D.C.S. in engineering and a B.Sc in mathematics and computer science. He studied computer graphics and computer science at Cornell University where he earned an M.S. degree. His Ph.D. degree is in computer science from the University of Utah.

Professor Barsky is the author of Computer Graphics and Geometric Modeling Using Beta-splines (Springer-Verlag, Heidelberg, Germany) and co-author of An Introduction to Splines for Use in Computer Graphics and Geometric Modeling (Morgan Kaufmann Publishers, Inc., San Mateo, California). He was the Technical Program Committee Chair for the Association for Computing Machinery/SIGGRAPH'85 conference.

Address: Computer Science Division, Department of Electrical Engineering and Computer Science, University of California, Berkeley, CA 947220, USA.

A Method to Convert a Gregory Patch and a Rational Boundary Gregory Patch to a Rational Bézier Patch and Its Applications

Teiji Takamura, Masataka Ohta, Hiroshi Toriya, and Hiroaki Chiyokura

ABSTRACT

A Gregory patch and a rational boundary Gregory patch have characteristics such that any n-sided loop is interpolated smoothly and that many patches can be generated to connect smoothly with each other. However, since the mathematical form of these patches is different from conventional surface patches such as the Bézier patch, no algorithm was known to subdivide them. The subdivision algorithm that could be applied to other surface patches could not be applied to them.

This paper proves that the bicubic Gregory patch can be converted to a bi-7th degree rational Bézier patch and moreover, that the bicubic rational boundary Gregory patch can be converted to a bi-11th degree rational Bézier patch. Because these rational Bézier patches can be subdivided, by using this conversion algorithm, we have developed a method to get the intersection curves between a Gregory patch or a rational boundary Gregory patch and a plane. The rational Bézier patch is also a good medium for transferring Gregory patch data to other systems.

Keywords: Gregory patch, rational boundary Gregory patch (RBG patch), rational Bézier patch, intersection calculations

1 Introduction

In the design process of three dimensional shapes using a solid modeler, the free-form surface has an important role. However various kinds of surface patches such as the Coons patch, Bézier patch or B-spline patch all have the problem that n-sided loops cannot be interpolated and that it is difficult to connect patches smoothly in arbitrary curve meshes.

Chiyokura and Kimura (1983) proposed the Gregory patch, which can smoothly interpolate irregular polygonal curve meshes. Recently Chiyokura et al. (1990) proposed a new surface patch called the rational boundary Gregory patch (RBG patch) which can connect arbitrary rational curve meshes smoothly. The advantages of these two patches are that any n-sided loop is interpolated smoothly and that many patches can be generated to connect to each other with G^1 continuity.

One constraint of these patches is that they cannot be subdivided in their present form. The problem is that the inner cross-section curves become higher-order rational curves, but a Gregory patch has all Bézier curves as its boundary and an RBG patch has rational Bézier curves. This means that the form of the subdivided patches cannot be the same as the original (Beeker 1986; Tan 1986). Therefore the Gregory patch and the RBG patch should be converted into a more general representation method of a surface patch that is applicable for subdivision.

In this paper, we demonstrate that a bicubic Gregory patch can be converted to a bi-7th degree rational Bézier patch. We also show that a bicubic RBG patch can be converted to a bi-11th degree rational Bézier patch. By subdividing these rational Bézier patches, we will show that many conventional algorithms can be applied to the Gregory patch and the RBG patch.

Since it is easy to convert a rational Bézier patch to a non-uniform rational B-spline (NURBS) patch, by using the converted patch data, the Gregory patch and the RBG patch data can also be passed by IGES (Smith 1988) to other systems.

2 Gregory patch

If $B_{n,i}(t)$ is a Bernstein basis function given by

$$B_{n,i}(t) = \binom{n}{i} t^i (1-t)^{n-i}, \tag{1}$$

the bicubic Gregory patch $\mathbf{G}(u,v)$ is then given by

$$\mathbf{G}(u,v) = \sum_{i=0}^{3}\sum_{j=0}^{3} B_{3,i}(u)B_{3,j}(v)\mathbf{P}_{ij}(u,v), \tag{2}$$

where

$$\begin{aligned}
\mathbf{P}_{ij}(u,v) &= \mathbf{P}_{ij} \qquad (ij \neq 11, 21, 12, 22)\\
\mathbf{P}_{11}(u,v) &= \frac{u\mathbf{P}_{110} + v\mathbf{P}_{111}}{u+v}\\
\mathbf{P}_{21}(u,v) &= \frac{(1-u)\mathbf{P}_{210} + v\mathbf{P}_{211}}{(1-u)+v}\\
\mathbf{P}_{12}(u,v) &= \frac{u\mathbf{P}_{120} + (1-v)\mathbf{P}_{121}}{u+(1-v)}\\
\mathbf{P}_{22}(u,v) &= \frac{(1-u)\mathbf{P}_{220} + (1-v)\mathbf{P}_{221}}{(1-u)+(1-v)}
\end{aligned}$$

and where u and v are the surface parameters and $\mathbf{P}_{00}, \cdots, \mathbf{P}_{33}$ are the control points of the Gregory patch (Figure 1).

3 Rational boundary Gregory patch

An RBG patch, which is proposed to interpolate irregular rational curve meshes smoothly, can be converted to the rational Bézier patch using a similar method to the one above.

The bicubic RBG patch is defined by 32 control points $\mathbf{P}_{ijk}(i = 0, \cdots, 3, j = 0, \cdots, 3, k = 0, 1)$ and their weights w_{ijk} as shown in Figure 2.

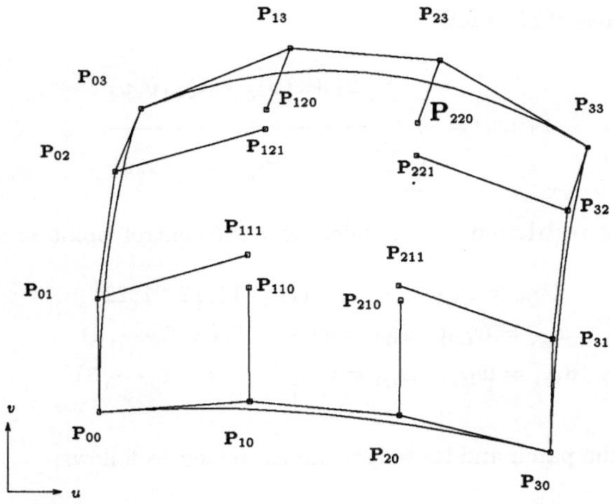

Figure 1: A Gregory patch

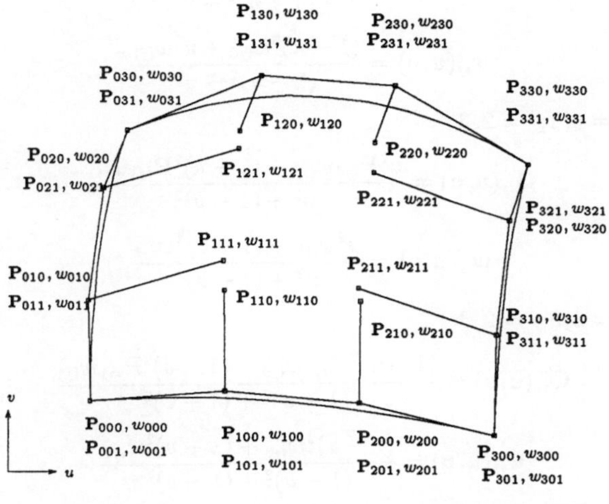

Figure 2: A rational boundary Gregory patch

The RBG patch is represented as follows:

$$\mathbf{S}(u,v) = \frac{\sum_{i=0}^{3}\sum_{j=0}^{3} B_{3,i}(u)B_{3,j}(v)\mathbf{Q}_{ij}(u,v)}{\sum_{i=0}^{3}\sum_{j=0}^{3} B_{3,i}(u)B_{3,j}(v)w_{ij}(u,v)}. \tag{3}$$

However, the following restrictions are applied to each control point and its corresponding weight:

$$\begin{aligned} &\mathbf{P}_{ij0} = \mathbf{P}_{ij1} && (ij \neq 11, 12, 21, 22) \\ &w_{i00} = w_{i10}, \quad w_{i20} = w_{i30} && (i = 0, \cdots, 3) \\ &w_{0j1} = w_{1j1}, \quad w_{2j1} = w_{3j1} && (j = 0, \cdots, 3) \end{aligned}$$

Each control point of the patch and its weight are expressed as follows:

In the case of $i = 0, 1; j = 0, 1$

$$\mathbf{Q}_{ij}(u,v) = \frac{u^2\mathbf{P}_{ij0}w_{ij0} + v^2\mathbf{P}_{ij1}w_{ij1}}{u^2 + v^2}$$

$$w_{ij}(u,v) = \frac{u^2 w_{ij0} + v^2 w_{ij1}}{u^2 + v^2}$$

In the case of $i = 2, 3; j = 0, 1$

$$\mathbf{Q}_{ij}(u,v) = \frac{(1-u)^2\mathbf{P}_{ij0}w_{ij0} + v^2\mathbf{P}_{ij1}w_{ij1}}{(1-u)^2 + v^2}$$

$$w_{ij}(u,v) = \frac{(1-u)^2 w_{ij0} + v^2 w_{ij1}}{(1-u)^2 + v^2}$$

In the case of $i = 0, 1; j = 2, 3$

$$\mathbf{Q}_{ij}(u,v) = \frac{u^2\mathbf{P}_{ij0}w_{ij0} + (1-v)^2\mathbf{P}_{ij1}w_{ij1}}{u^2 + (1-v)^2}$$

$$w_{ij}(u,v) = \frac{u^2 w_{ij0} + (1-v)^2 w_{ij1}}{u^2 + (1-v)^2}$$

In the case of $i = 2, 3; j = 2, 3$

$$\mathbf{Q}_{ij}(u,v) = \frac{(1-u)^2\mathbf{P}_{ij0}w_{ij0} + (1-v)^2\mathbf{P}_{ij1}w_{ij1}}{(1-u)^2 + (1-v)^2}$$

$$w_{ij}(u,v) = \frac{(1-u)^2 w_{ij0} + (1-v)^2 w_{ij1}}{(1-u)^2 + (1-v)^2}$$

Note that $0 \leq u, v \leq 1$.

This patch equation has the following features:

1. When the weight is greater than 0, the patch has a convex hull property as is the case with a Gregory patch. This means that any point on the surface has the characteristic that it resides within an area formed by the control points of the surface. Therefore a quick rough check of surface intersections can be made.

2. A special case of a bicubic RBG patch is the bicubic rational Bézier patch. If $\mathbf{P}_{110} = \mathbf{P}_{111}, \mathbf{P}_{210} = \mathbf{P}_{211}, \mathbf{P}_{120} = \mathbf{P}_{121}$ and $\mathbf{P}_{220} = \mathbf{P}_{221}$ and also if $w_{ij0} = w_{ij1}$, then the RBG patch becomes equal to the rational Bézier patch. The RBG patch can represent quadric surfaces as accurately as the rational Bézier patch.
3. The form of the derivative vector along the boundary curve is simple. Due to this characteristic, patches that are next to each other can be easily connected.
4. The corner of the patch is the terminating point of two boundary curves. Since each corner has two weights from each boundary curve, the shape of one boundary curve can be controlled by changing its weights without affecting the shape of the other boundary curve.

4 Conversion from a Gregory patch and an RBG patch to a rational Bézier patch

As is clear from (2), the boundary curve of a Gregory patch is a Bézier curve. However, as the internal cross-section curve is not a Bézier curve, what is obtained by dividing a Gregory patch cannot become a Gregory patch. Since a Gregory patch cannot be divided in its present form, it must first be converted into a more general patch representation.

In what follows, it is shown that a Gregory patch can be converted to a rational Bézier patch. To accomplish this, the multiplication of the denominators is expressed by $W(u,v)$ as follows:

$$W(u,v) = (u+v)(1-u+v)(u+1-v)(1-u+1-v). \tag{4}$$

If both the side members of (2) are multiplied by (4), the term of the denominator of the right side member of (2) will disappear. Now we define $\mathbf{Q}(u,v)$ as

$$\mathbf{Q}(u,v) = W(u,v)\mathbf{G}(u,v). \tag{5}$$

Since (5) is a 7th degree polynomial in u and v, it can be expressed as

$$\mathbf{Q}(u,v) = \sum_{i=0}^{7}\sum_{j=0}^{7} F_i(u)F_j(v)\mathbf{P}'_{ij}, \tag{6}$$

where $F_i(u)$ is an i-th degree polynomial of u, $F_j(v)$ is a j-th degree polynomial in v, and $\mathbf{P}'_{ij}$ is a vector determined by a control point in the Gregory patch and the form of $F_i(u)$ and $F_j(v)$.

From (5) and (6), $\mathbf{G}(u,v)$ becomes

$$\mathbf{G}(u,v) = \sum_{i=0}^{7}\sum_{j=0}^{7} F_i(u)F_j(v)\mathbf{P}'_{ij}/W(u,v). \tag{7}$$

The numerator of (7) is a 7th degree equation of u and v and the denominator of (7) is a quartic equation. The denominator and numerator of (7) are rearranged into a 7th degree homogeneous equation of $u, (1-u), v$, and $(1-v)$ using the following equation:

$$1 = u + (1-u) = v + (1-v). \tag{8}$$

For example, by using equations (4) and (8), $W(u,v)$ becomes

$$\begin{aligned} W(u,v) \;=\; & (u(v+(1-v)) + v(u+(1-u))) \times \\ & ((1-u)(v+(1-v)) + v(u+(1-u))) \times \\ & (u(v+(1-v)) + (1-v)(u+(1-u))) \times \\ & ((1-u)(v+(1-v)) + (1-v)(u+(1-u))). \end{aligned} \tag{9}$$

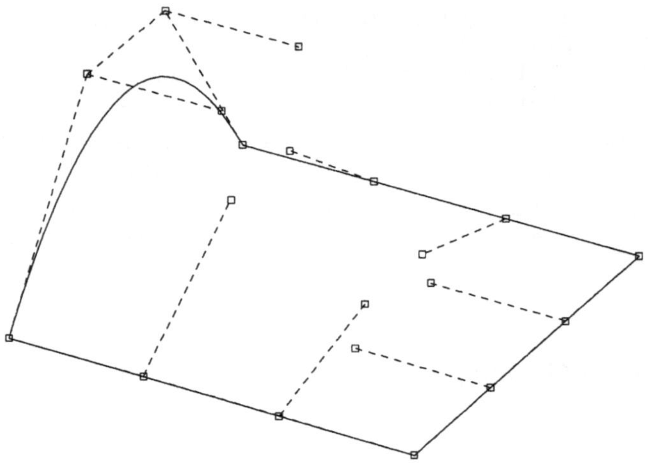

Figure 3: A bicubic Gregory patch and its control points

As this is a homogeneous equation of $u, (1-u), v$ and $(1-v)$, it can be rewritten as

$$W(u,v) = \sum_{i=0}^{4}\sum_{j=0}^{4} B_{4,i}(u)B_{4,j}(v)\mu_{ij}. \tag{10}$$

By comparing coefficients of $u^i(1-u)^{4-i}v^j(1-v)^{4-j}$ of equations (9) and (10), we can calculate values of μ_{ij} $(i,j = 0,\ldots,4)$. Equation (10) is easily elevated to the 7th degree. Therefore, equation (7) can be modified so as to have Bernstein basis functions $B_{7,i}(u)$ and $B_{7,j}(v)$. By this modification, $\mathbf{G}(u,v)$ can be rewritten as

$$\mathbf{G}(u,v) = \frac{\sum_{i=0}^{7}\sum_{j=0}^{7} B_{7,i}(u)B_{7,j}(v)w_{ij}\mathbf{Q}_{ij}}{\sum_{i=0}^{7}\sum_{j=0}^{7} B_{7,i}(u)B_{7,j}(v)w_{ij}}. \tag{11}$$

Equation (11) represents a bi-7th degree rational Bézier patch, where $\mathbf{Q}_{ij}$ is a control point of the rational Bézier patch and w_{ij} is the weight acting on respective control points. This proves that a cubic Gregory patch can be transformed to a bi-7th degree rational Bézier patch.

Figure 3 shows a bicubic Gregory patch and its control points, Figure 4 shows a bi-7th degree rational Bézier patch and its control points obtained by the transformation of a bicubic Gregory patch. Appendix A shows the conversion expressions from the control points of a Gregory patch to the control points of a rational Bézier patch.

The conversion procedure from an RBG patch to a rational Bézier patch is basically the same as from a Gregory patch, however $W(u,v)$ must be expressed as follows:

$$W(u,v) = (u^2+v^2)((1-u)^2+v^2)(u^2+(1-v)^2)((1-u)^2+(1-v)^2). \tag{12}$$

Therefore, (3) becomes

$$\mathbf{S}(u,v) = \frac{\sum_{i=0}^{11}\sum_{j=0}^{11} B_{11,i}(u)B_{11,j}(v)w_{ij}\mathbf{Q}_{ij}}{\sum_{i=0}^{11}\sum_{j=0}^{11} B_{11,i}(u)B_{11,j}(v)w_{ij}}. \tag{13}$$

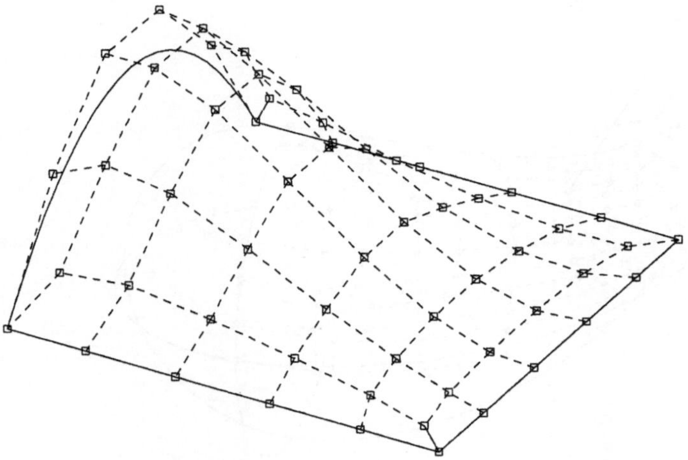

Figure 4: A bi-7th degree rational Bézier patch and its control points

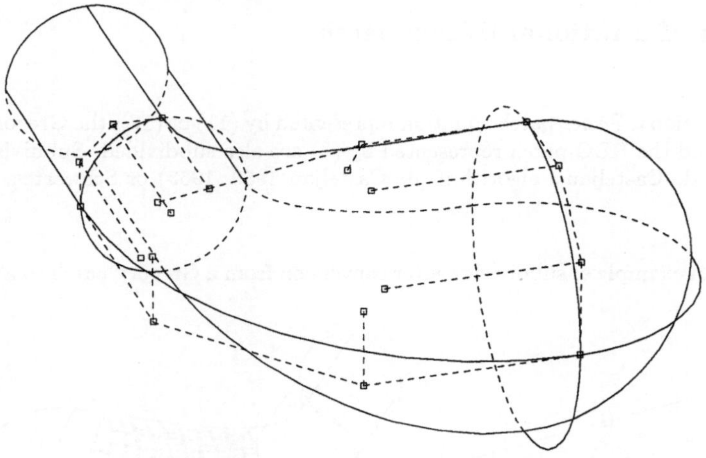

Figure 5: A bicubic RBG patch and its control points

This shows that an RBG patch can be converted to the bi-11th degree rational Bézier patch. Figure 5 shows a bicubic RBG patch and its control points. A bi-11th degree rational Bézier patch and its control points obtained by the transformation of an RBG patch are drawn in figure 6.

According to Appendix A, the value of the weight of each corner point is equal to 0 and some control points are degenerated; this is shown in Figures 4 and 6.

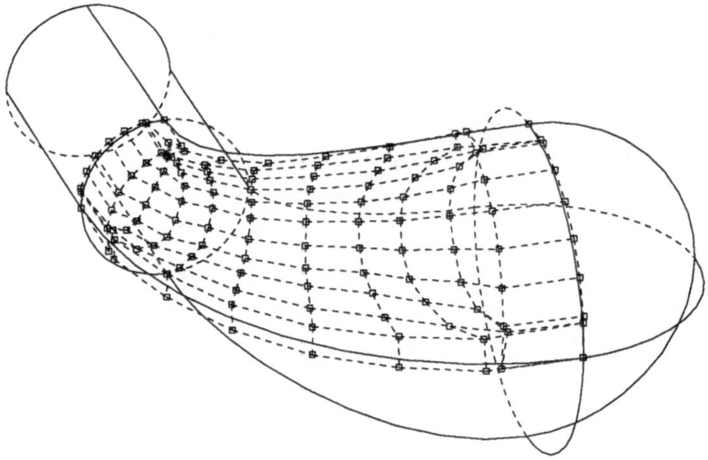

Figure 6: A bi-11th degree rational Bézier patch and its control points

5 Subdivision of a rational Bézier patch

By subdividing the rational Bézier patch equation represented by (11) or (13), the Gregory patch represented by (2) and the RBG patch represented by (3) are also subdivided. Subdivision can be applied by using de Casteljau's algorithm (de Casteljau 1959, 1963) or Schwartz's method (Schwartz 1987).

Figure 7 illustrates an example of subdivision after conversion from a Gregory patch to a rational Bézier patch.

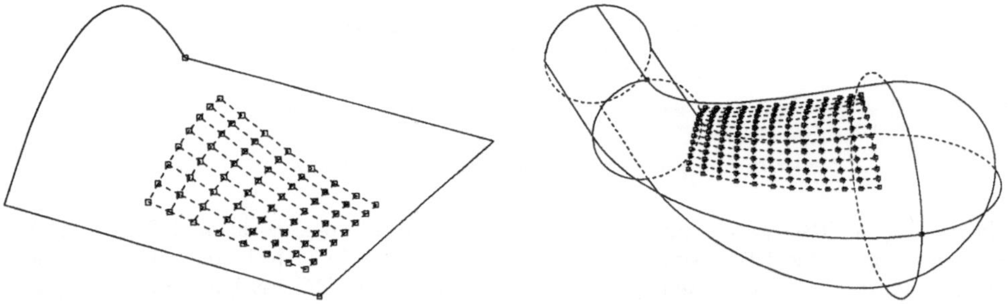

Figure 7: An example of a rational Bézier patch subdivision

6 Intersection calculations between a plane and a Gregory patch or an RBG patch

By using the method which was described previously, subdivision can be achieved by converting a Gregory patch or an RBG patch to a rational Bézier patch, and various subdivision algorithms can be applied to the converted rational Bézier patch. An example of applying the subdivision method (Cohen 1980; Peng 1984; Houghton 1985; Dokken 1985; Koparkar 1986) to obtain the intersection curve between a plane and a Gregory patch or an RBG patch is described next. A marching method (Barnhill 1987; Chen 1988; Bajaj 1988) can also be used to compute the intersection calculations, and in that case the conversion to a rational Bézier patch is unnecessary. However a marching method needs a starting point for the intersection calculations, which is sometimes difficult to find, and also some intersection curves may be missed.

6.1 Generation of a subdivision tree

First the patch is converted to a rational Bézier patch, then parts of the patch that may intersect with the plane are subdivided.

Step 1

The bounding box of the Gregory patch or the RBG patch is calculated and is verified to check whether it intersects the plane or not. If they intersect (Figure 8), the patch and the plane may intersect, so Step 2 is processed. If they do not intersect (Figure 9), there is no intersection line, so the process is terminated.

Step 2

Conversion to a rational Bézier patch from a Gregory patch or from an RBG patch is performed. Since the bounding box of the rational Bézier patch is smaller than that of the original patch, a rough check of the bounding box is made again at this stage.

Step 3

The rational Bézier patch is subdivided, the bounding box of each of the resulting subpatches is calculated, and the intersection with the plane is checked; if the bounding box does not intersect with the plane, then the subpatch does not intersect with the plane, thus this process is terminated. If it intersects, then the subpatch and the plane may intersect. In that case, if the subpatch is flat within the limits of error and if the boundary curves of the subpatch are straight lines within the limits, then the process described in the next section is performed. In other cases, Step 3 is repeated recursively.

A tree structure which has been subdivided to sufficiently flatten all parts which may intersect with the plane is built as the result of performing Steps 1 to 3. Actually, in this implementation, the subpatch data is kept in the form of a quad tree by subdividing the patch data into four parts (Figure 10).

6.2 Intersection line between a subdivided patch and a plane

In the procedure described in the previous section, a patch which may intersect with a plane was subdivided until it became sufficiently flat. These subpatches can be approximated by two triangles, and when they intersect a plane, the intersecting line can be easily obtained.

By using this procedure, the subdivided patch cell which actually intersects with the plane will keep the intersection data.

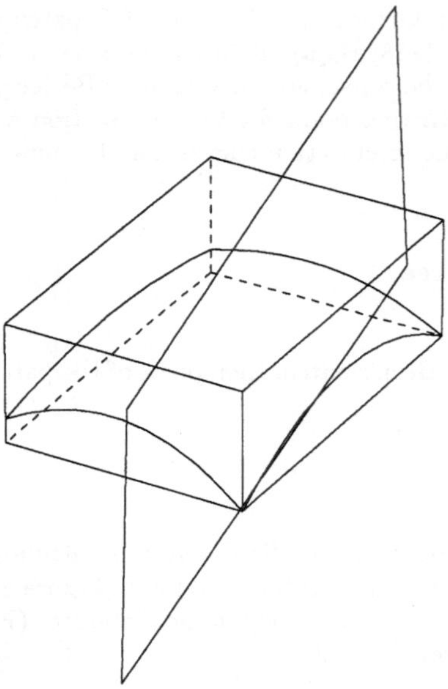

Figure 8: Rough intersection check (may intersect)

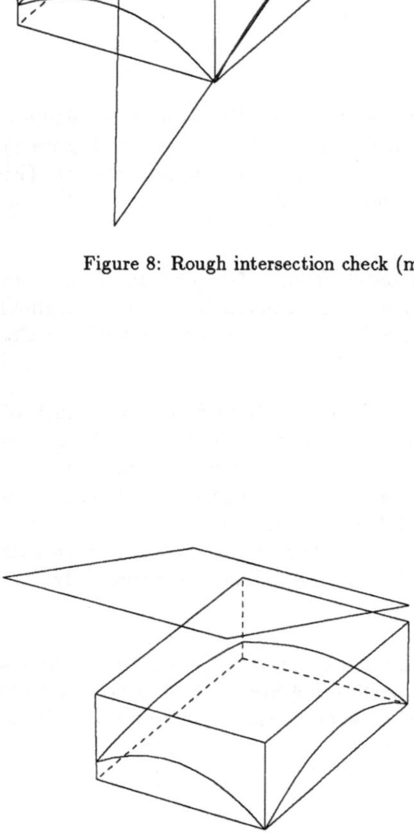

Figure 9: Rough intersection check (not intersect)

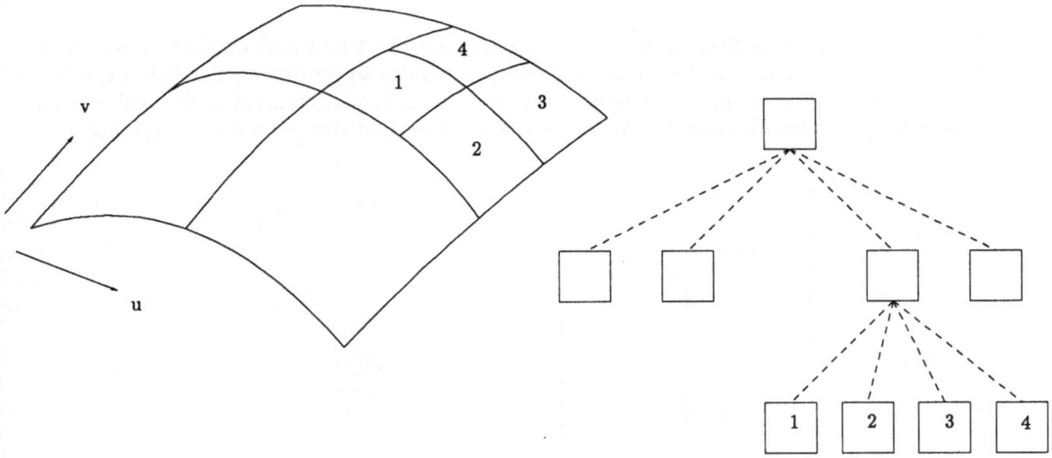

Figure 10: The quad tree structure representing the subpatch data

As a result, a line segment which approximates the intersection curve between each subdivided patch and the plane is obtained.

6.3 Connecting line segments

In the procedures described previously, every line segment existed independently of each other, thus intersection points could not be obtained in a continuous form. In the following procedure, the line segments are connected to obtain an array of intersection points. All cells in the quad tree are initialized to not-marked.

To connect line segments, follow the steps below:

Step 1

If there is a cell in the terminating nodes of the quad tree which has intersection line information, and if that cell is not marked, then mark that cell and get the information.

Step 2

The terminating points of the line segment that the cell obtained in Step 1 are located on a rational Bézier patch. From the parameter values of the patch, a line segment which may connect to that line segment is found from a nearby cell.

For example, consider a patch within the uv parameter space, then a subpatch should exist within a segment shown by Figure 11. When a line segment AB exists within an area such as illustrated by Figure 12, to find the line segment which is connected to AB, the cell which is above A, and the cell which is on the right side of B should be checked.

If a terminating point of a line segment is the corner of a cell, the cells which share that corner should be checked. For example, when subpatches P1, P2, P3 and P4 are located as in Figure 13, the subpatches P2, P3, P4 should be all checked to find the line segment which connects to the line segment in P1.

Step 3

By using Step 2, cells that connect to a line segment are found and marked, and lists of line segments are made. If there is no line segment which can connect to the end of the list, check whether there is any unmarked cell which has a line segment; if such a cell exists, repeat Step 1, otherwise the line segments are returned and this procedure terminates.

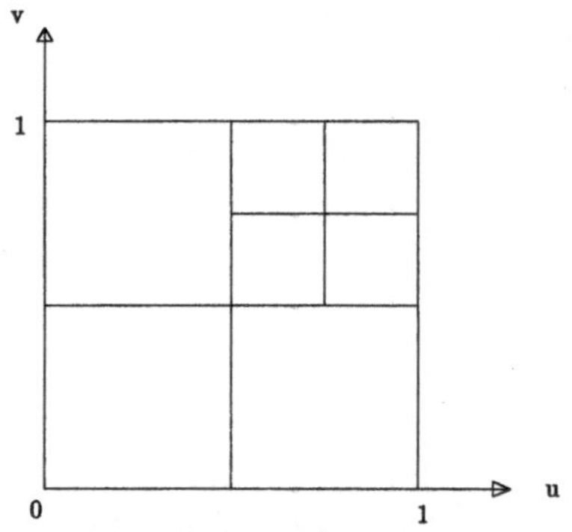

Figure 11: A subpatch segment in a parameter space

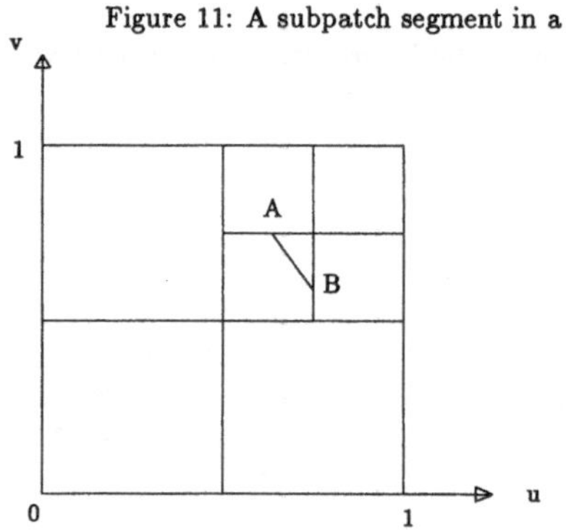

Figure 12: A subpatch and a line segment in a parameter space

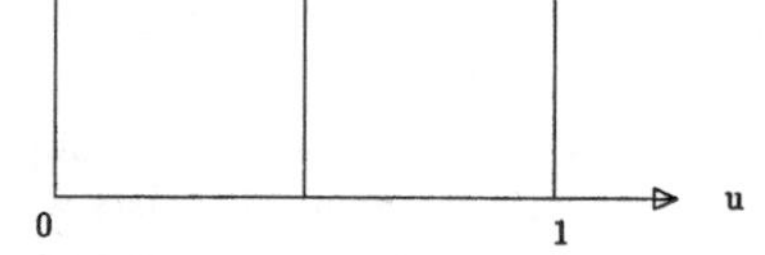

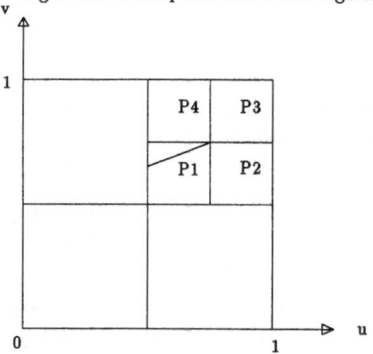

Figure 13: A line segment terminating points are on the corner of a cell

6.4 Refining arrays of intersection points

With the procedures described so far, lists of intersection points are obtained. But since they have been approximated, if a more accurate curve is needed, error resulting from the approximation of the subpatch to a plane must be minimized. However, with the polygonal approximation of a patch, to increase the precision, the number of times the patch is subdivided obviously increases, and a greater amount of time becomes necessary for subdivision, computation of the intersection line with each cell and connection of line segments. The level of precision does not greatly increase with a higher division number.

Thus, in order to raise the precision of the array of intersection points, each intersection point which was obtained with the procedures described previously is considered as the starting point of the Newton-Raphson method, and the value of each intersection point is corrected (McCalla 1967). Let the patch and plane equations be

$$\mathbf{S}(u,v) \equiv (X(u,v), Y(u,v), Z(u,v))$$

$$\begin{aligned}\mathbf{P}(s,t) &= \mathbf{P}_0 + s\mathbf{v}_1 + t\mathbf{v}_2 \\ &\equiv (x(s,t), y(s,t), z(s,t))\end{aligned}$$

where $\mathbf{S}$ represents a patch and $\mathbf{P}$ a plane, $\mathbf{P}_0$ is a point on the plane and $\mathbf{v}_1$ and $\mathbf{v}_2$ are orthogonal vectors on the plane. Let F, G and H be defined as follows:

$$\begin{aligned}F(u,v,s,t) &= X(u,v) - x(s,t) \\ G(u,v,s,t) &= Y(u,v) - y(s,t) \\ H(u,v,s,t) &= Z(u,v) - z(s,t).\end{aligned}$$

Now we will try to solve the equations:

$$F(u,v,s,t) = 0, \quad G(u,v,s,t) = 0, \quad H(u,v,s,t) = 0$$

To solve these equations, we use the Newton-Raphson method, with starting points u_0, v_0, s_0, t_0, to give values to F_0, G_0 and H_0. Let $\delta F, \delta G, \delta H$ be delta values of F, G, H and $\delta u, \delta v, \delta s, \delta t$ be delta values of u, v, s, t, then

$$\begin{aligned}\delta F &= \frac{d}{du}F_0\delta u + \frac{d}{dv}F_0\delta v + \frac{d}{ds}F_0\delta s + \frac{d}{dt}F_0\delta t \\ \delta G &= \frac{d}{du}G_0\delta u + \frac{d}{dv}G_0\delta v + \frac{d}{ds}G_0\delta s + \frac{d}{dt}G_0\delta t \\ \delta H &= \frac{d}{du}H_0\delta u + \frac{d}{dv}H_0\delta v + \frac{d}{ds}H_0\delta s + \frac{d}{dt}H_0\delta t.\end{aligned}$$

Also, by $\delta F = -F_0, \delta G = -G_0, \delta H = -H_0$,

$$\begin{aligned}-F_0 &= \frac{d}{du}F_0\delta u + \frac{d}{dv}F_0\delta v + \frac{d}{ds}F_0\delta s + \frac{d}{dt}F_0\delta t \\ -G_0 &= \frac{d}{du}G_0\delta u + \frac{d}{dv}G_0\delta v + \frac{d}{ds}G_0\delta s + \frac{d}{dt}G_0\delta t \\ -H_0 &= \frac{d}{du}H_0\delta u + \frac{d}{dv}H_0\delta v + \frac{d}{ds}H_0\delta s + \frac{d}{dt}H_0\delta t.\end{aligned}$$

From these equations, the values of $\delta u, \delta v, \delta s, \delta t$ cannot be determined uniquely. This means that the intersection of the patch and the plane is not a point but a line. For example, by

$$\delta u = 0$$

then, when $u = u_0$, a better approximation of v, s, t can be obtained by:

$$\begin{aligned} v_0 &+ \delta v \\ s_0 &+ \delta s \\ t_0 &+ \delta t. \end{aligned}$$

Each intersection point that has an error is corrected to a precise value by applying the Newton-Raphson method described above. If the intersection line is to be precisely complemented with more points, then some points on the line formed by two intersection points are calculated and they are refined by using the Newton-Raphson method so that they lie on both the surface and the plane (Figure 14).

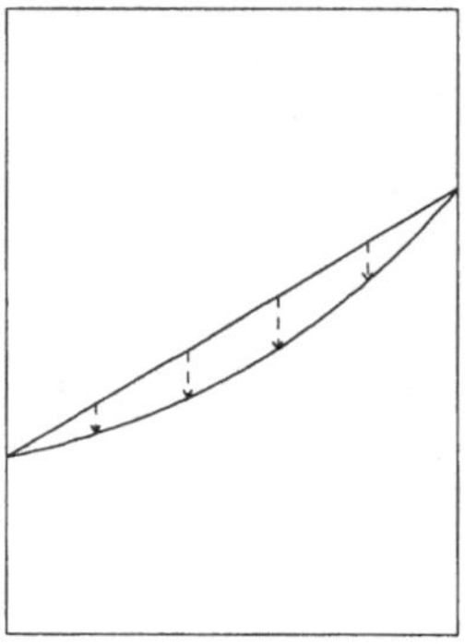

Figure 14: The precise calculation for intersection points

Figure 15 and Figure 16 show examples of cutting a solid. Figure 17 and Figure 18 show examples of contour line drawing. This method can be easily extended to obtain arrays of intersection points between Gregory or RBG patches.

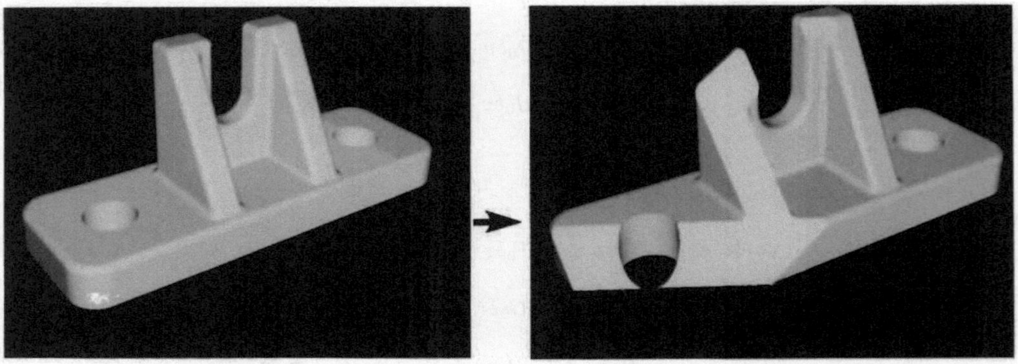

Figure 15: An example of a cutting operation (1)

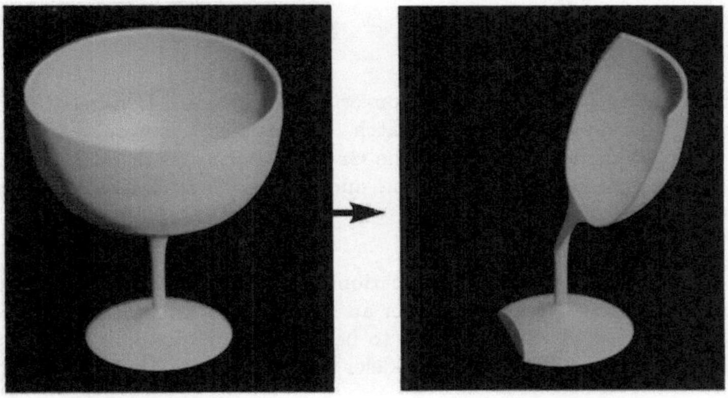

Figure 16: An example of a cutting operation (2)

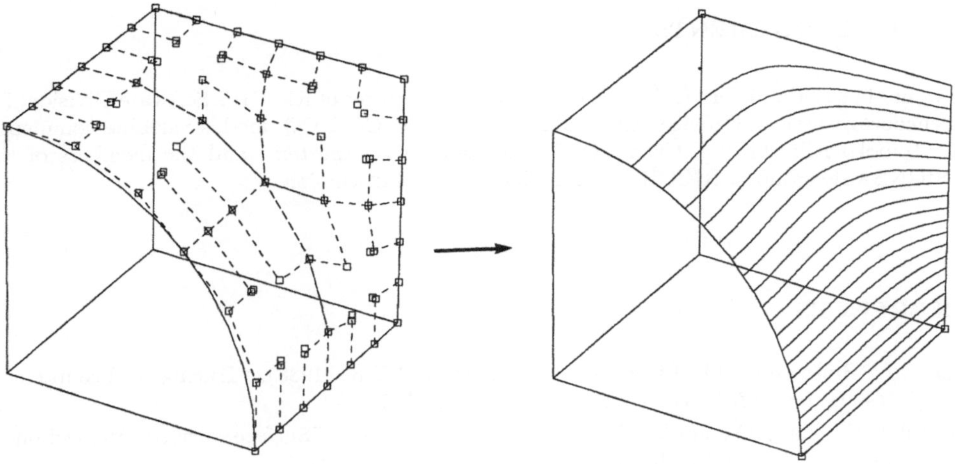

Figure 17: An example of contour lines (1)

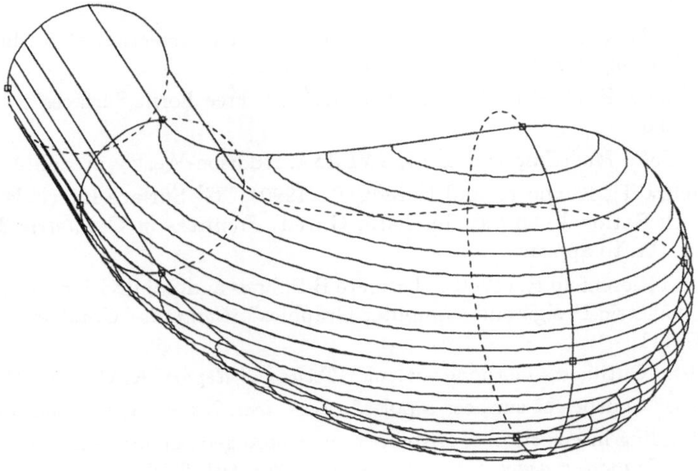

Figure 18: An example of contour lines (2)

7 Conclusion

A Gregory patch and an RBG patch were converted to a rational Bézier patch, and a method was developed to subdivide the converted patch. Operations that were used with the rational Bézier patch were also made available for the Gregory patch and the RBG patch. A method to obtain the intersection line between a plane and a Gregory patch or an RBG patch was also described as an example of an application.

By using the present method in other applications, various algorithms that require patch subdivision can be applied to a Gregory patch or an RBG patch. This method is also of great use when Gregory patch, or RBG patch data is to be output in a standard format such as IGES. This method is implemented in the solid modeler DESIGNBASE (Chiyokura 1988).

ACKNOWLEDGEMENTS

We would like to thank Dr. Hideko S. Kunii, general manager of RICOH's Software Division, for her encouragement and advice; Mr. Aidan O'Neill of RICOH CO. for his valuable comments; Ms. Tomoko Kikuchi of RICOH CO. for assistance with the text; and the members of the DESIGNBASE group of RICOH CO. for their help and discussion.

REFERENCES

Bajaj C.L., Hoffmann C.M., Lynch R.E. and Hopcroft J.E.H. (1988), "Tracing surface intersections", *Computer Aided Geometric Design*, 5(4):285-307

Barnhill R.E., Farin G., Jordan M. and Piper B.R. (1987), "Surface/surface intersection ", *Computer Aided Geometric Design*, 4(1-2):3-16

Beeker E. (1986), "Smoothing of shapes designed with free-form surfaces" *Computer-Aided Design*, 18(4):224-232

Chen J.J. and Ozsoy T.M. (1988), "Predictor-corrector type of intersection algorithm for C^2 parametric surfaces", *Computer-Aided Design*, 20(6):347-352

Chiyokura H. and Kimura F. (1983), "Design of Solids with Free Form Surfaces", *Computer Graphics*, 17(3):289-298

Chiyokura H. (1988), *Solid Modelling with DESIGNBASE*, Addison-Wesley, Reading, MA

Chiyokura H., Takamura T., Konno K. and Harada T. (1990), "G^1 Surface Interpolation over Irregular Meshes with Rational Curves", In: Farin G. (ed) *Frontiers in Geometric Modeling*, SIAM, Philadelphia, PA, to appear

Cohen E., Lyche T. and Riesenfeld R. (1980), "Discrete B-Splines and Subdivision Techniques in Computer-Aided Geometric Design and Computer Graphics", *Computer Graphics and Image Processing*, 14(2):87-111

de Casteljau P. (1959), "Outillages méthodes calcul", *Technical Report*, A. Citroen, Paris

de Casteljau P. (1963), "Courbes et surfaces à poles", *Technical Report*, A. Citroen, Paris

Dokken T. (1985), "Finding intersection of B-spline represented geometries using recursive subdivision techniques", *Computer Aided Geometric Design*, 2(1-3):189-195

Hearn A.C. (1987), *REDUCE USER'S MANUAL Version 3.3*, RAND, Santa Monica, CA

Houghton E.G., Emnett R.F., Factor J.D. and Sabharwal C.L. (1985), "Implementation of a divide-and-conquer method for intersection of parametric surfaces", *Computer Aided Geometric Design*, 2(1-3):173-183

Koparkar P.A. and Mudur S.P. (1986), "Generation of continuous smooth curves resulting from operations on parametric surface patches", *Computer-Aided Design*, 18(4):193-206

McCalla T.R. (1967), *Introduction to Numerical Methods and FORTRAN Programming*, John Wiley & Sons, New York, NY

Peng Q.S. (1984), "An Algorithm for finding the intersection Line between two B-spline Surfaces", *Computer-Aided Design*, 16(4):191-196

Schwartz A.J. (1987), "Subdividing Bézier Curves and Surfaces", In: Farin G. (ed) *Geometric Modeling: Algorithm and New Trends*, SIAM, Philadelphia, PA, pp.55-66

Smith B., Rinaudot G.R., Reed K.A. and Wright T. (1988), *Initial Graphics Exchange Specification (IGES) Version 4.0*, National Bureau of Standaards, U.S. Department of Commerce, Gaithersburg, MD

Tan S.T. and Chan K.C. (1986), "Generation of high order surfaces over arbitrary polyhedral meshs" *Computer-Aided Design*, 18(8):411-423

Appendix A: Converted control points from a Gregory patch to a rational Bézier patch

$\mathbf{Q}_{ij}$ and w_{ij} of equation (11) are represented as follows where $\mathbf{Q}_{ij}$ are the control points of the converted rational Bézier patch and w_{ij} $(i,j = 0,\ldots,7)$ are their weights and $\mathbf{P}_{klm}$ $(k,l = 0,\ldots,3; m = 1,2)$ are the control points of the original Gregory patch. REDUCE (Hearn 1987) was used for the calculations.

$$
\begin{aligned}
\mathbf{Q}_{00} &= \mathbf{P}_{00} \\
\mathbf{Q}_{01} &= \mathbf{P}_{00} \\
\mathbf{Q}_{02} &= (5\mathbf{P}_{00} + 6\mathbf{P}_{01})/11 \\
\mathbf{Q}_{03} &= (2\mathbf{P}_{00} + 15\mathbf{P}_{01} + 6\mathbf{P}_{02})/23 \\
\mathbf{Q}_{04} &= (6\mathbf{P}_{01} + 15\mathbf{P}_{02} + 2\mathbf{P}_{03})/23 \\
\mathbf{Q}_{05} &= (6\mathbf{P}_{02} + 5\mathbf{P}_{03})/11 \\
\mathbf{Q}_{06} &= \mathbf{P}_{03} \\
\mathbf{Q}_{07} &= \mathbf{P}_{03} \\
\mathbf{Q}_{10} &= \mathbf{P}_{00} \\
\mathbf{Q}_{11} &= (7\mathbf{P}_{00} + 3\mathbf{P}_{01} + 3\mathbf{P}_{10})/13 \\
\mathbf{Q}_{12} &= (18\mathbf{P}_{111} + 28\mathbf{P}_{00} + 42\mathbf{P}_{01} + 6\mathbf{P}_{02} + 15\mathbf{P}_{10})/109 \\
\mathbf{Q}_{13} &= (45\mathbf{P}_{111} + 18\mathbf{P}_{121} + 14\mathbf{P}_{00} + 84\mathbf{P}_{01} + 42\mathbf{P}_{02} + 2\mathbf{P}_{03} + 6\mathbf{P}_{10})/211 \\
\mathbf{Q}_{14} &= (18\mathbf{P}_{111} + 45\mathbf{P}_{121} + 2\mathbf{P}_{00} + 42\mathbf{P}_{01} + 84\mathbf{P}_{02} + 14\mathbf{P}_{03} + 6\mathbf{P}_{13})/211 \\
\mathbf{Q}_{15} &= (18\mathbf{P}_{121} + 6\mathbf{P}_{01} + 42\mathbf{P}_{02} + 28\mathbf{P}_{03} + 15\mathbf{P}_{13})/109 \\
\mathbf{Q}_{16} &= (3\mathbf{P}_{02} + 7\mathbf{P}_{03} + 3\mathbf{P}_{13})/13 \\
\mathbf{Q}_{17} &= \mathbf{P}_{03} \\
\mathbf{Q}_{20} &= (5\mathbf{P}_{00} + 6\mathbf{P}_{10})/11 \\
\mathbf{Q}_{21} &= (18\mathbf{P}_{110} + 28\mathbf{P}_{00} + 15\mathbf{P}_{01} + 42\mathbf{P}_{10} + 6\mathbf{P}_{20})/109 \\
\mathbf{Q}_{22} &= (63\mathbf{P}_{110} + 63\mathbf{P}_{111} + 18\mathbf{P}_{121} + 18\mathbf{P}_{210} + 52\mathbf{P}_{00} + 84\mathbf{P}_{01} + 15\mathbf{P}_{02} + 84\mathbf{P}_{10} + 15\mathbf{P}_{20})/412 \\
\mathbf{Q}_{23} &= (63\mathbf{P}_{110} + 189\mathbf{P}_{111} + 18\mathbf{P}_{120} + 108\mathbf{P}_{121} + 27\mathbf{P}_{210} + 18\mathbf{P}_{211} + 9\mathbf{P}_{220} + 9\mathbf{P}_{221} + 28\mathbf{P}_{00} + 156\mathbf{P}_{01} \\
&\quad +84\mathbf{P}_{02} + 5\mathbf{P}_{03} + 42\mathbf{P}_{10} + 6\mathbf{P}_{13} + 6\mathbf{P}_{20})/703 \\
\mathbf{Q}_{24} &= (18\mathbf{P}_{110} + 108\mathbf{P}_{111} + 63\mathbf{P}_{120} + 189\mathbf{P}_{121} + 9\mathbf{P}_{210} + 9\mathbf{P}_{211} + 27\mathbf{P}_{220} + 18\mathbf{P}_{221} + 5\mathbf{P}_{00} + 84\mathbf{P}_{01} \\
&\quad +156\mathbf{P}_{02} + 28\mathbf{P}_{03} + 6\mathbf{P}_{10} + 42\mathbf{P}_{13} + 6\mathbf{P}_{23})/703 \\
\mathbf{Q}_{25} &= (18\mathbf{P}_{111} + 63\mathbf{P}_{120} + 63\mathbf{P}_{121} + 18\mathbf{P}_{220} + 15\mathbf{P}_{01} + 84\mathbf{P}_{02} + 52\mathbf{P}_{03} + 84\mathbf{P}_{13} + 15\mathbf{P}_{23})/412 \\
\mathbf{Q}_{26} &= (18\mathbf{P}_{120} + 15\mathbf{P}_{02} + 28\mathbf{P}_{03} + 42\mathbf{P}_{13} + 6\mathbf{P}_{23})/109
\end{aligned}
$$

$$\mathbf{Q}_{27} = (5\mathbf{P}_{03} + 6\mathbf{P}_{13})/11$$

$$\mathbf{Q}_{30} = (2\mathbf{P}_{00} + 15\mathbf{P}_{10} + 6\mathbf{P}_{20})/23$$

$$\mathbf{Q}_{31} = (45\mathbf{P}_{110} + 18\mathbf{P}_{210} + 14\mathbf{P}_{00} + 6\mathbf{P}_{01} + 84\mathbf{P}_{10} + 42\mathbf{P}_{20} + 2\mathbf{P}_{30})/211$$

$$\mathbf{Q}_{32} = (189\mathbf{P}_{110} + 63\mathbf{P}_{111} + 18\mathbf{P}_{120} + 27\mathbf{P}_{121} + 108\mathbf{P}_{210} + 18\mathbf{P}_{211} + 9\mathbf{P}_{220} + 9\mathbf{P}_{221} + 28\mathbf{P}_{00} + 42\mathbf{P}_{01} + 6\mathbf{P}_{02} + 156\mathbf{P}_{10} + 84\mathbf{P}_{20} + 5\mathbf{P}_{30} + 6\mathbf{P}_{31})/703$$

$$\mathbf{Q}_{33} = (234\mathbf{P}_{110} + 234\mathbf{P}_{111} + 108\mathbf{P}_{120} + 144\mathbf{P}_{121} + 144\mathbf{P}_{210} + 108\mathbf{P}_{211} + 63\mathbf{P}_{220} + 63\mathbf{P}_{221} + 14\mathbf{P}_{00} + 84\mathbf{P}_{01} + 42\mathbf{P}_{02} + 2\mathbf{P}_{03} + 84\mathbf{P}_{10} + 15\mathbf{P}_{13} + 42\mathbf{P}_{20} + 6\mathbf{P}_{23} + 2\mathbf{P}_{30} + 15\mathbf{P}_{31} + 6\mathbf{P}_{32})/1064$$

$$\mathbf{Q}_{34} = (108\mathbf{P}_{110} + 144\mathbf{P}_{111} + 234\mathbf{P}_{120} + 234\mathbf{P}_{121} + 63\mathbf{P}_{210} + 63\mathbf{P}_{211} + 144\mathbf{P}_{220} + 108\mathbf{P}_{221} + 2\mathbf{P}_{00} + 42\mathbf{P}_{01} + 84\mathbf{P}_{02} + 14\mathbf{P}_{03} + 15\mathbf{P}_{10} + 84\mathbf{P}_{13} + 6\mathbf{P}_{20} + 42\mathbf{P}_{23} + 6\mathbf{P}_{31} + 15\mathbf{P}_{32} + 2\mathbf{P}_{33})/1064$$

$$\mathbf{Q}_{35} = (18\mathbf{P}_{110} + 27\mathbf{P}_{111} + 189\mathbf{P}_{120} + 63\mathbf{P}_{121} + 9\mathbf{P}_{210} + 9\mathbf{P}_{211} + 108\mathbf{P}_{220} + 18\mathbf{P}_{221} + 6\mathbf{P}_{01} + 42\mathbf{P}_{02} + 28\mathbf{P}_{03} + 156\mathbf{P}_{13} + 84\mathbf{P}_{23} + 6\mathbf{P}_{32} + 5\mathbf{P}_{33})/703$$

$$\mathbf{Q}_{36} = (45\mathbf{P}_{120} + 18\mathbf{P}_{220} + 6\mathbf{P}_{02} + 14\mathbf{P}_{03} + 84\mathbf{P}_{13} + 42\mathbf{P}_{23} + 2\mathbf{P}_{33})/256$$

$$\mathbf{Q}_{37} = (2\mathbf{P}_{03} + 15\mathbf{P}_{13} + 6\mathbf{P}_{23})/23$$

$$\mathbf{Q}_{40} = (6\mathbf{P}_{10} + 15\mathbf{P}_{20} + 2\mathbf{P}_{30})/23$$

$$\mathbf{Q}_{41} = (18\mathbf{P}_{110} + 45\mathbf{P}_{210} + 2\mathbf{P}_{00} + 42\mathbf{P}_{10} + 84\mathbf{P}_{20} + 14\mathbf{P}_{30} + 6\mathbf{P}_{31})/256$$

$$\mathbf{Q}_{42} = (108\mathbf{P}_{110} + 18\mathbf{P}_{111} + 9\mathbf{P}_{120} + 9\mathbf{P}_{121} + 189\mathbf{P}_{210} + 63\mathbf{P}_{211} + 18\mathbf{P}_{220} + 27\mathbf{P}_{221} + 5\mathbf{P}_{00} + 6\mathbf{P}_{01} + 84\mathbf{P}_{10} + 156\mathbf{P}_{20} + 28\mathbf{P}_{30} + 42\mathbf{P}_{31} + 6\mathbf{P}_{32})/703$$

$$\mathbf{Q}_{43} = (144\mathbf{P}_{110} + 108\mathbf{P}_{111} + 63\mathbf{P}_{120} + 63\mathbf{P}_{121} + 234\mathbf{P}_{210} + 234\mathbf{P}_{211} + 108\mathbf{P}_{220} + 144\mathbf{P}_{221} + 2\mathbf{P}_{00} + 15\mathbf{P}_{01} + 6\mathbf{P}_{02} + 42\mathbf{P}_{10} + 6\mathbf{P}_{13} + 84\mathbf{P}_{20} + 15\mathbf{P}_{23} + 14\mathbf{P}_{30} + 84\mathbf{P}_{31} + 42\mathbf{P}_{32} + 2\mathbf{P}_{33})/1064$$

$$\mathbf{Q}_{44} = (63\mathbf{P}_{110} + 63\mathbf{P}_{111} + 144\mathbf{P}_{120} + 108\mathbf{P}_{121} + 108\mathbf{P}_{210} + 144\mathbf{P}_{211} + 234\mathbf{P}_{220} + 234\mathbf{P}_{221} + 6\mathbf{P}_{01} + 15\mathbf{P}_{02} + 2\mathbf{P}_{03} + 6\mathbf{P}_{10} + 42\mathbf{P}_{13} + 15\mathbf{P}_{20} + 84\mathbf{P}_{23} + 2\mathbf{P}_{30} + 42\mathbf{P}_{31} + 84\mathbf{P}_{32} + 14\mathbf{P}_{33})/1064$$

$$\mathbf{Q}_{45} = (9\mathbf{P}_{110} + 9\mathbf{P}_{111} + 108\mathbf{P}_{120} + 18\mathbf{P}_{121} + 18\mathbf{P}_{210} + 27\mathbf{P}_{211} + 189\mathbf{P}_{220} + 63\mathbf{P}_{221} + 6\mathbf{P}_{02} + 5\mathbf{P}_{03} + 84\mathbf{P}_{13} + 156\mathbf{P}_{23} + 6\mathbf{P}_{31} + 42\mathbf{P}_{32} + 28\mathbf{P}_{33})/703$$

$$\mathbf{Q}_{46} = (18\mathbf{P}_{120} + 45\mathbf{P}_{220} + 2\mathbf{P}_{03} + 42\mathbf{P}_{13} + 84\mathbf{P}_{23} + 6\mathbf{P}_{32} + 14\mathbf{P}_{33})/256$$

$$\mathbf{Q}_{47} = (6\mathbf{P}_{13} + 15\mathbf{P}_{23} + 2\mathbf{P}_{33})/23$$

$$\mathbf{Q}_{50} = (6\mathbf{P}_{20} + 5\mathbf{P}_{30})/11$$

$$\mathbf{Q}_{51} = (18\mathbf{P}_{210} + 6\mathbf{P}_{10} + 42\mathbf{P}_{20} + 28\mathbf{P}_{30} + 15\mathbf{P}_{31})/109$$

$$\mathbf{Q}_{52} = (18\mathbf{P}_{110} + 63\mathbf{P}_{210} + 63\mathbf{P}_{211} + 18\mathbf{P}_{221} + 15\mathbf{P}_{10} + 84\mathbf{P}_{20} + 52\mathbf{P}_{30} + 84\mathbf{P}_{31} + 15\mathbf{P}_{32})/412$$

$$\mathbf{Q}_{53} = (27\mathbf{P}_{110} + 18\mathbf{P}_{111} + 9\mathbf{P}_{120} + 9\mathbf{P}_{121} + 63\mathbf{P}_{210} + 189\mathbf{P}_{211} + 18\mathbf{P}_{220} + 108\mathbf{P}_{221} + 6\mathbf{P}_{10} + 42\mathbf{P}_{20} + 6\mathbf{P}_{23} + 28\mathbf{P}_{30} + 156\mathbf{P}_{31} + 84\mathbf{P}_{32} + 5\mathbf{P}_{33})/703$$

$$\mathbf{Q}_{54} = (9\mathbf{P}_{110} + 9\mathbf{P}_{111} + 27\mathbf{P}_{120} + 18\mathbf{P}_{121} + 18\mathbf{P}_{210} + 108\mathbf{P}_{211} + 63\mathbf{P}_{220} + 189\mathbf{P}_{221} + 6\mathbf{P}_{13} + 6\mathbf{P}_{20} + 42\mathbf{P}_{23} + 5\mathbf{P}_{30} + 84\mathbf{P}_{31} + 156\mathbf{P}_{32} + 28\mathbf{P}_{33})/703$$

$$\mathbf{Q}_{55} = (18\mathbf{P}_{120} + 18\mathbf{P}_{211} + 63\mathbf{P}_{220} + 63\mathbf{P}_{221} + 15\mathbf{P}_{13} + 84\mathbf{P}_{23} + 15\mathbf{P}_{31} + 84\mathbf{P}_{32} + 52\mathbf{P}_{33})/412$$

$$\mathbf{Q}_{56} = (18\mathbf{P}_{220} + 6\mathbf{P}_{13} + 42\mathbf{P}_{23} + 15\mathbf{P}_{32} + 28\mathbf{P}_{33})/109$$

$$\mathbf{Q}_{57} = (6\mathbf{P}_{23} + 5\mathbf{P}_{33})/11$$

$$\mathbf{Q}_{60} = \mathbf{P}_{30}$$

$$\mathbf{Q}_{61} = (3\mathbf{P}_{20} + 7\mathbf{P}_{30} + 3\mathbf{P}_{31})/13$$

$$\mathbf{Q}_{62} = (18\mathbf{P}_{211} + 15\mathbf{P}_{20} + 28\mathbf{P}_{30} + 42\mathbf{P}_{31} + 6\mathbf{P}_{32})/109$$

$$\mathbf{Q}_{63} = (45\mathbf{P}_{211} + 18\mathbf{P}_{221} + 6\mathbf{P}_{20} + 14\mathbf{P}_{30} + 84\mathbf{P}_{31} + 42\mathbf{P}_{32} + 2\mathbf{P}_{33})/256$$

$$\mathbf{Q}_{64} = (18\mathbf{P}_{211} + 45\mathbf{P}_{221} + 6\mathbf{P}_{23} + 2\mathbf{P}_{30} + 42\mathbf{P}_{31} + 84\mathbf{P}_{32} + 14\mathbf{P}_{33})/256$$

$$\mathbf{Q}_{65} = (18\mathbf{P}_{221} + 15\mathbf{P}_{23} + 6\mathbf{P}_{31} + 42\mathbf{P}_{32} + 28\mathbf{P}_{33})/147$$

$$\mathbf{Q}_{66} = (3\mathbf{P}_{23} + 3\mathbf{P}_{32} + 7\mathbf{P}_{33})/13$$

$$\mathbf{Q}_{67} = \mathbf{P}_{33}$$

$$\mathbf{Q}_{70} = \mathbf{P}_{30}$$

$$\mathbf{Q}_{71} = \mathbf{P}_{30}$$

$$\mathbf{Q}_{72} = (5\mathbf{P}_{30} + 6\mathbf{P}_{31})/11$$

$$\mathbf{Q}_{73} = (2\mathbf{P}_{30} + 15\mathbf{P}_{31} + 6\mathbf{P}_{32})/23$$

$$\mathbf{Q}_{74} = (6\mathbf{P}_{31} + 15\mathbf{P}_{32} + 2\mathbf{P}_{33})/23$$

$$\mathbf{Q}_{75} = (6\mathbf{P}_{32} + 5\mathbf{P}_{33})/11$$

$$\mathbf{Q}_{76} = \mathbf{P}_{33}$$

$$\mathbf{Q}_{77} = \mathbf{P}_{33}$$

$$
\begin{aligned}
&w_{00} = w_{70} = w_{07} = w_{77} = 0 \\
&w_{01} = w_{71} = w_{06} = w_{76} = w_{10} = w_{60} = w_{17} = w_{67} = 2/7 \\
&w_{02} = w_{72} = w_{05} = w_{75} = w_{20} = w_{50} = w_{27} = w_{57} = 11/21 \\
&w_{03} = w_{73} = w_{04} = w_{74} = w_{30} = w_{40} = w_{37} = w_{47} = 23/35 \\
&w_{11} = w_{61} = w_{16} = w_{66} = 26/49 \\
&w_{12} = w_{62} = w_{15} = w_{65} = w_{21} = w_{51} = w_{26} = w_{56} = 109/147 \\
&w_{13} = w_{63} = w_{14} = w_{64} = w_{31} = w_{41} = w_{36} = w_{46} = 211/245 \\
&w_{22} = w_{52} = w_{25} = w_{55} = 412/441 \\
&w_{23} = w_{53} = w_{24} = w_{54} = w_{32} = w_{42} = w_{35} = w_{45} = 256/245 \\
&w_{33} = w_{43} = w_{34} = w_{44} = 282/245
\end{aligned}
$$

BIOGRAPHY

Teiji Takamura, a member of the 3D CAD project at RICOH's Software Division, is interested in solid modeling, free-form surface interpolation and computer graphics. His current research includes general free-form surface intersections and rational parametric surface interpolations by using rational boundary Gregory patches. He received a BS in information science in 1982 from the University of Tokyo. He entered the solid modeling project at RICOH in 1984, which has now developed into the product DESIGNBASE. He is a member of ACM SIGGRAPH and the IEEE Computer Society. Several of his papers have been selected by NICOGRAPH.
Address: RICOH Co., Ltd. Software Division, 1-17, Koishikawa-cho 1-Chome Bunkyo-ku, Tokyo, 112, Japan
E-mail: takamura@src.ricoh.co.jp

Masataka Ohta received a BS in computer science 1982 and then MS in 1984 from the University of Tokyo. At the same time, he engaged in creating computer graphics systems and computer generated images at Life Structure Institute, Seibu Digital Communications and FROGS. He is now working at the Computer Center of Tokyo Institute of Technology as a research associate. He is a member of ACM and the Information Processing Society of Japan.
Address: Tokyo Institute of Technology, 12-1, Ohokayama 2-Chome Meguro-ku, Tokyo, 152, Japan
E-mail: mohta@cc.titech.ac.jp

Hiroshi Toriya is a member of the 3D CAD project at RICOH's Software Division. His research interests include solid modeling, geometric modeling, computer graphics, and their applications. He received a BS in information science in 1983 from the University of Tokyo where his research included octree data structures and their manipulations. He earned his Dr.Sc. in information science from the University of Tokyo in 1989. He is a member of the Information Processing Society of Japan.
Address: RICOH Co., Ltd. Software Division, 1-17, Koishikawa-cho 1-Chome Bunkyo-ku, Tokyo, 112, Japan
E-mail: toriya@src.ricoh.co.jp

Hiroaki Chiyokura is a manager of the 3D CAD project at RICOH's Software Division. His research interests are solid modeling, computer graphics, and their applications to computer-aided design and manufacturing. He received his BS and MS in mathematics from Keio University in 1979 and 1980, respectively. He earned his Dr.Eng. in precision machinery engineering from the University of Tokyo in 1984. He has written a book "Solid Modelling with DESIGNBASE: Theory and Implementation", published by Addison-Wesley. He is a member of ACM SIGGRAPH.
Address: RICOH Co., Ltd. Software Division, 1-17, Koishikawa-cho 1-Chome Bunkyo-ku, Tokyo, 112, Japan
E-mail: chiyo@src.ricoh.co.jp

An Enhanced Rounding Operation Between Curved Surfaces in Solid Modeling

T. Harada, H. Toriya, and H. Chiyokura

Abstract

This paper introduces a method using the rolling ball technique to generate geometrical and topological information to blend two surfaces in B-reps-based solid modeling systems. At first, a ball is positioned so that it touches both surfaces to be blended, and the trajectories of the tangent points of the ball and the surfaces are computed. Edges are generated on the surfaces along the trajectories, and are then joined by arcs to create the blending surfaces. The created surface depends on the shape of the surrounding edges, and is interpolated using rational boundary Gregory(RBG) patches. By using this method, blending surfaces can be connected smoothly, even at the corner of a solid. This method can also be applied to surface blends other than those using the rolling ball technique. Variable-radius blends which are essential in free-form surface design can also be generated using this method.

Keywords: *blending surface, rounding operation, RBG patch, rolling ball, variable-radius blending*

1 Introduction

The role of CAD systems in the design process has become more and more important, and designers' interests are now moving towards systems which not only can handle 2D and 3D shape data, but can also represent complicated surfaces. Solid modeling is basically a method in 3D CAD systems to represent the 3D shapes of solids in computers. Systems which handle such models are called solid modelers. Existing solid modelers widely use either the constructive solid geometry (CSG) proposed by [Okino 73], or the boundary representations (B-reps) proposed by [Braid 73]. Solids with complicated free-form surfaces can be easily represented in B-reps-based solid modelers, because B-reps can have both topological data of solids and geometrical data of surfaces.

Solids which are actually used in the design process are often composed of complex curved surfaces. When designing shapes of mechanical parts, blending surfaces often appear. A blending surface is a surface which appears where the corner of a solid has been smoothly rounded. This blending surface is widely used to enhance the strength of mechanical parts, as well as to increase ease of processing at the production stage, and to create aesthetic shapes. Therefore, solid modelers that are used as the basis of 3D CAD systems must easily generate the blending surface.

2 Background

The mathematical definition of blending surfaces is necessary to realize blending surface generation on solid modelers. Woodwark has described several methods to define blending surfaces [Woodwark 87], but the most general one is the rolling ball blending method. This method defines the blending surface as the trajectory drawn by a ball which rolls between two surfaces of a solid. It is appropriate for 3D CAD systems, since designers usually specify the cross-section radius of the blending surface.

Many research projects on blending surfaces related to the rolling ball method have been conducted. Most of the projects are concerned with the mathematical calculation and representation of such surfaces' shapes. It is extremely complicated to make an accurate mathematical representation of such surfaces. Holmström, Martin and Pratt succeeded by imposing restrictions on shapes that can generate blending surfaces [Holmström 88] [Martin 82] [Pratt 88]. They used only sweep surfaces based on cylindrical, toroid or cyclide ones. In methods proposed by Rossignac and Rockwood, blending surfaces are approximated by subdividing or by using high degree implicit functions [Rossignac 84] [Rockwood 87]. Choi and Varady calculated the trajectories drawn by the tangent points of a rolling ball and two curved surfaces, and used them for representing blending surfaces [Choi 89] [Varady 89]. The research described here concerns only geometrical shapes of blending surfaces.

In the process of blending surface generation on solid modelers, the mathematical calculation of the blending surface's shape is important. Creation of vertices and edges during blending surface generation is also an important topic, especially in B-reps-based solid modelers. Surface blending in B-reps-based solid modelers requires the following:

- A method to calculate the shape of the blending surface, that is, a method to calculate geometrical information.
- A generation method for the vertices and edges forming the blending surface, that is, a method to generate topological information.

A method to generate geometrical and topological information of the blending surface for polyhedrons is already shown in [Chiyokura 87]. However, on a solid represented by B-reps, especially with many complicated free-form surfaces, there still remain many unsolved problems such as the generation of topological information. Also, no method has yet been proposed to connect blending surfaces smoothly at the corner vertex of a solid where more than two blending surfaces intersect.

This paper describes a method to generate blending surfaces on a solid model containing various kinds of surfaces. A method to generate topological information that is necessary in B-reps-based solid modelers is also explained. We define the operation that creates blending surfaces, the rounding operation. The new implementation method of the rounding operation is an extension of our method for polyhedrons. The major characteristic is that even where more than two blending surfaces intersect, they can be smoothly connected. We also propose two methods other than the rolling ball blends, and demonstrate that they can be used to generate any type of blending surface easily. We also show how variable-radius blending surfaces, whose cross-section radii vary little by little, can be generated. The methods described here have been successfully implemented on the B-reps-based solid modeler DESIGNBASE [Chiyokura 88].

3 Rounding Operations in Solid Modeling

3.1 Problems of rounding operations in solid modeling

Solid modeling is the basis of 3D CAD systems, and it covers various types of design; for example, some design types, such as mechanial parts design, are concerned solely with function, whereas others focus on appearance such as the body of a car. No matter what the field, blending surfaces, the rounding of an edge or a corner of a solid, are used. Therefore, ease of generation of the blending surface needed by the user is a subject of great importance in solid modeling. To implement a rounding operation, the following problems must be overcome.

- In solid modeling, there is no method to generate the edges and vertices that are needed to create the blending surface. In other words, there is no established method to generate topological information.
- It is too complicated to represent the blending surface by existing free-form surfaces; there is no appropriate free-form surface to represent complex shapes such as blending surfaces.
- It is still not known what type of blending surface designers need.
- It is difficult to generate variable-radius blending surfaces whose cross-section radii vary little by little.

We have solved all the problems mentioned above, and established a rounding operation method for solid models. The features of our rounding operation are described in Section 3 and the implementation method is described in detail in Section 4, 5 and 6.

3.2 Features of our rounding operation

We have implemented the rounding operation on a solid modeler called DESIGNBASE. The main features are as follows:

- Blending surface generation has been implemented not only on a polyhedron, but also on a solid model that has various curved surfaces.
- Blending surfaces can be smoothly connected due to the adoption of the rational boundary Gregory patch (RBG patch)[Chiyokura 90] as the representation method of blending surfaces.
- Three types of blending surface generation method including the rolling ball technique have been proposed and implemented on our system.
- Variable-radius blending surfaces can be generated.

These features are described in Sections 3.3, 3.4, 3.5 and 3.6.

3.3 Rounding operation between curved surfaces

We have already proposed a method concerning rounding operations on solid models. This method creates blending surfaces at the intersection of two flat surfaces, so only the rounding operation on polyhedrons has been implemented. This paper has extended this operation to solids which have curved surfaces. By using our method, the rounding operation can be performed even when the surfaces around edges to be rounded are natural quadric surfaces or free-form surfaces. In our system, a general surface which represents any quadric surface or free-form surface is supported, and the rounding operation does not depend on any representation method of surfaces. Thus, when a new free-form surface representation is introduced, the rounding operation can be extended easily. The structure of a general surface is shown in Figure 1.

```
struct general_surface {
        int     type;
        union {
                struct plane                        plane;
                struct sphere                       sphere;
                struct cylinder                     cylinder;
                struct cone                         cone;
                struct Bezier                       bezier;
                struct rational_Bezier              r_bezier;
                struct Gregory                      gregory;
                struct rational_boundary_Gregory    r_gregory;
                                          :
        }       *data;
};
```

Figure 1: The structure of a general surface

3.4 Representing blending surfaces by RBG patches

Since our system supports a method to interpolate a surface, the geometric information of the surface is determined by the created vertices and edges that surround the blending surface. The RBG patch is adopted to interpolate the surface. This patch is an extension of the Gregory patch[Chiyokura 83] which we have already proposed, and has the following three characteristics:

- Rational curves (including arcs) can be used as boundary curves.
- Two RBG patches can be connected smoothly.
- Irregular meshes other than rectangular meshes can be interpolated.

These characteristics are necessary for blending surface representation, especially to smoothly connect blending surfaces where they intersect (Figure 2).

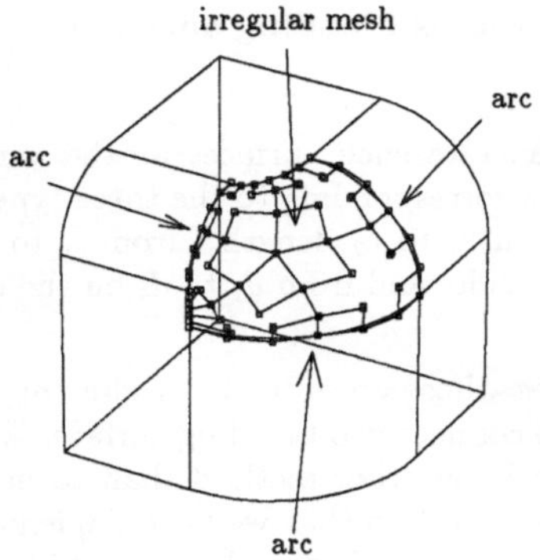

Figure 2: Features of RBG patch

3.5 Different types of blending surface

It is necessary to define the type of blending surface which is to be generated in order to create blending surfaces with the rounding operation. We explained in Section 1 that the rolling ball blending method is the most general one for blending surfaces. When designing mechanical part shapes, the cross-section of the blending surface to be generated often has a constant radius. Therefore, the blending surface created by the rolling ball blending method fits the designer's need for a constant radius. However, there are times when the width of the blending surface must be constant even if the cross-section radius varies. To satisfy such a requirement, three types of blending surface including the one created by the rolling ball method are defined. They are described below.

- A ball of constant radius is positioned so that it touches the two surfaces where the blending surface is to be generated. In this method, the trajectory drawn by the ball is defined as the blending surface (Figure 3 (a)). In this rolling ball blending method, the cross-section radius of the blending surface is constant.
- A stick of constant length is slid so that its two ends touch the two surfaces where the blending surface is to be generated. Distances between the original edge and the two ends of the stick should be the same. In this method, the two curves drawn by the two ends are joined by arcs to define the blending surface (Figure 3 (b)). By using this method, the width of the blending surface becomes constant.
- Two curves are created on two surfaces where the blending surface is to be generated so that the distance from the original edge is constant. In this method, those two curves are joined by free-form curves to define the blending surface (Figure 3 (c)). By using this method, a non-symmetrical blending surface can be generated.

To generate a solid model containing many blending surfaces, designers can freely combine surfaces of the three types on our system.

3.6 Generation of variable-radius blending surfaces

The rounding operation can generate such surfaces as the variable-radius blending surface. Variable-radius blending surfaces corresponding to the three types in Section 3.5 are illustrated in Figure 4. Radius r varies from r_1 to r_2, length l from l_1 to l_2, and distance d continually changes from d_1 to d_3 on the left side, and from d_2 to d_4 on the right side.

Variable-radius blending surfaces whose cross-section radius or width vary are widely used in the design field. For example, to connect two blending surfaces with different cross-section radii into one blending surface, there is no other method than to use the variable-radius blending surface. Therefore, the rounding operation that we have implemented is necessary for 3D CAD systems. Figure 5 illustrates an example of variable-radius blending surface generation. Edges with thick lines in Figure 5 (a) are rounded, and constant-radius blending surfaces are generated in Figure 5 (b). Figure 5 (c) shows variable-radius blends.

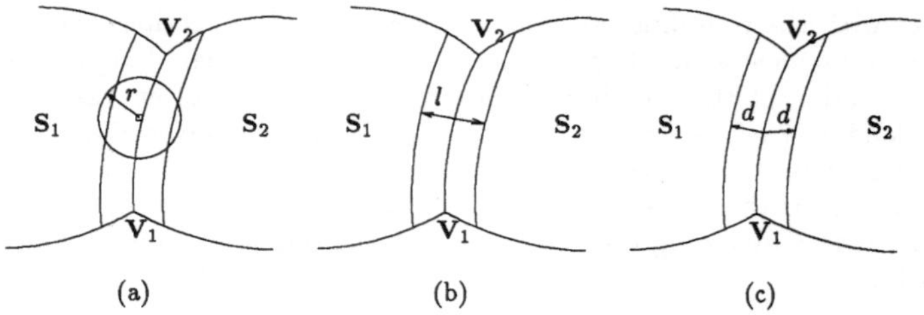

Figure 3: Types of blending surface

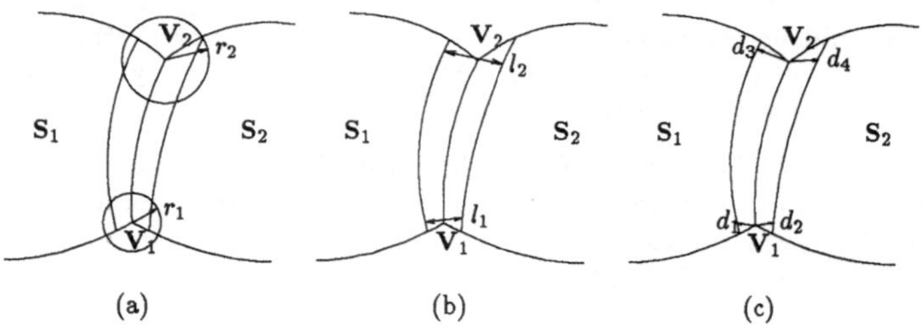

Figure 4: Three types of variable-radius blending surface

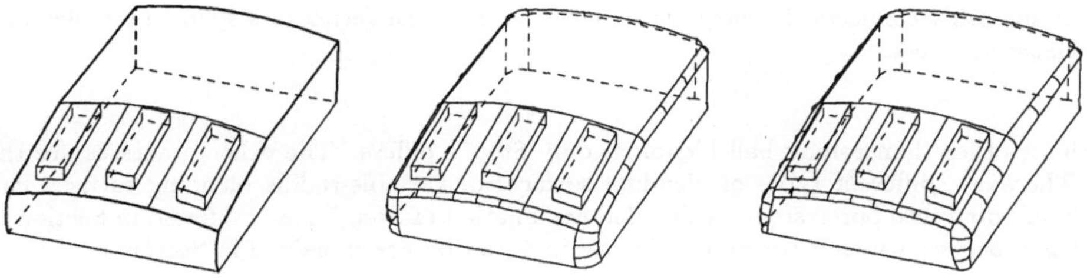

(a) (b) (c)

Figure 5: An example of variable-radius blending surface generation

4 Outline of the Rounding Operation

In our rounding operation, the three types of blending surface described in Section 3.5 can be created by specifying the blending type for the edge to be rounded on the original solid. For the sake of simplicity, only the rolling ball method will be explained as follows. The other methods are implemented in a similar manner. Here, blending surfaces are generated along edges with thick lines as shown in Figure 6 (a).

1. A ball is positioned so that it touches the curved surfaces on both sides of all edges which are to be rounded, and trajectories of the tangent points between the ball and the curved surfaces are calculated (Figure 6 (b)). All tangent points are calculated, then curves that interpolate the points are generated. Thus the trajectory is composed of approximated curves.

2. New vertices are generated where the curves representing the trajectories of the tangent points intersect with the edges of the original solid. The original edges are subdivided by creating new vertices. (Figure 6 (c)).

3. Edges are generated along the trajectories, and the vertices generated in Step 2 are connected with each other by the edges. As a result, new edges are generated on the surfaces located on both sides of all edges to be rounded (Figure 6 (d)). In this paper, the edge which is generated in this step will be called the R-edge. At a concave or a flat corner on the surface, another new edge is generated so that it connects the end points of the R-edges with each other.

4. The original edges to be rounded are deleted, and many arc edges are generated so that the end points of the R-edges on both side surfaces are connected by them (Figure 6 (e)). After this process, blending surfaces are generated, and most of the processing concerning the rounding operation is complete.

5. The vertices which are connected to two R-edges are deleted, and the two R-edges are transformed to one smooth edge (Figure 6 (f)). This process generates a free-form surface

that smoothly connects the blending surfaces, even at the vertex of a solid where blending surfaces intersect.

In methods other than rolling ball blending, only Step 1 differs. The other processes are the same. Therefore, different types of blending surfaces or variable-radius blending surfaces can be easily adopted into our system. A detailed explanation of Step 1 may be found in Section 5. The other processes which generate topological information are explained in Section 6.

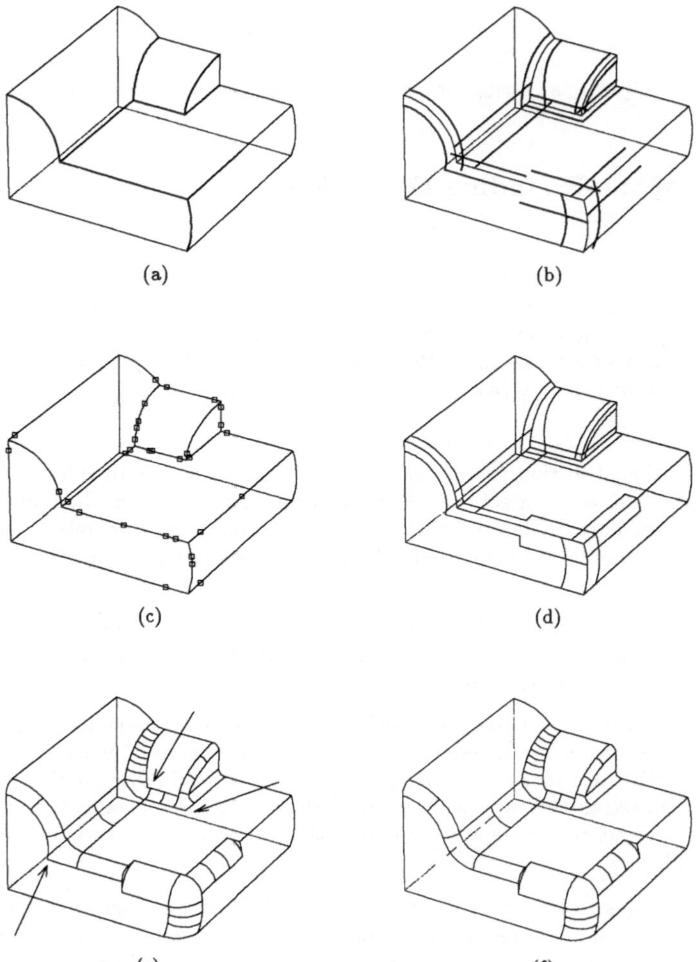

Figure 6: Outline of the implementation of the rounding operation

5 Calculation of the Geometry of Blending Surfaces

5.1 Outline of the geometrical information calculation

The method to calculate the trajectories drawn by the tangent points will now be explained. These trajectories represent the shapes of curves around blending surfaces.

First, the classification procedure of the tangent points will be described. Next, the calculation method of their positions will be explained. We will also explain the method to calculate the direction vectors which represent the movements of the tangent points. Lastly, the method to approximate the trajectories from a few calculated tangent points and their direction vectors will be described.

5.2 Classification of tangent points

In our rounding operation, the tangent points of the ball and the curved surfaces are classified as follows (Figure 7). This classification will play an important role in creating vertices and edges to generate blending surfaces.

- E-point

  A tangent point on the winged edge of the edge which is to be rounded. This is the tangent point when we place a ball so that it touches the winged edge and the other side surface. It appears only when the edge to be rounded forms a convex angle with its winged edge.

- C-point

  A tangent point corresponding to a corner with a concave angle. This is where the edge to be rounded and the connecting winged edge form a concave angle (or 180 degrees); the tangent point is positioned on a plane which is determined by the connecting point and the tangent vectors of the two edges.

- I-point

  A tangent point on an intersection of two trajectories. Such a tangent point can be found on the surface when two continuous edges are rounded simultaneously.

- M-point

  Any tangent point that does not correspond to any of the classifications above. This is a tangent point which is usually calculated between E, C, and I-points. It is used to obtain the trajectories of the tangent points when a ball is positioned, during curve interpolation.

When a ball is positioned so that it touches two curved surfaces, a tangent point exists on each curved surface. If the tangent point on one side surface is either an E, C or I-point, then the other point is usually an M-point.

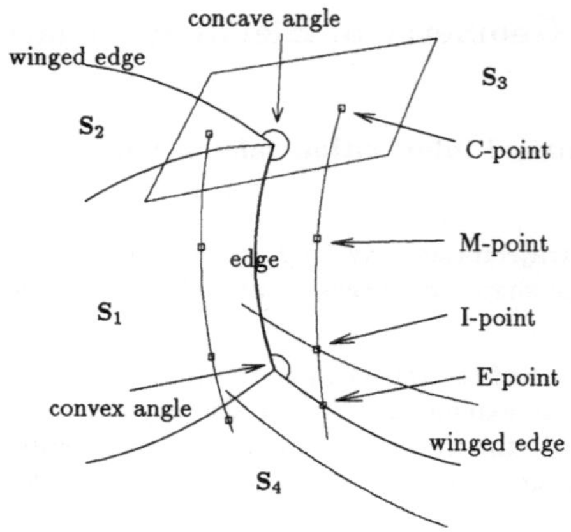

Figure 7: Classification of tangent points between a ball and two surfaces

5.3 Calculation of the positions of the tangent points

The positions of the four types of tangent points are all calculated using the geometric Newton method. For the sake of simplicity, we will describe here the calculation method when the tangent points of both sides are M-points and they are on free-form surfaces. The method is basically the same for E, C, and I-points and for flat or quadric surfaces.

When two tangent points on both side surfaces are classified as M-points, a point $\mathbf{P}_0$ on the original edge is first selected. Then, by using it as the basis, the positions of the two M-points $\mathbf{P}_1$ and $\mathbf{P}_2$ are calculated. The basis point $\mathbf{P}_0$ positioned on the edge is a function of parameter t. The position of the starting point of the edge corresponds to $t = 0.0$ and the terminal point to $t = 1.0$. Since the radius of the ball r is defined as a function of t in our rounding operation, the method explained here can also be applied to variable-radius blending surfaces. The geometric Newton method which is used to calculate M-points $\mathbf{P}_1$ and $\mathbf{P}_2$ is now described in detail (Figure 8).

1. Initial points $\mathbf{P}_1$, $\mathbf{P}_2$ lie on the free-form surfaces $\mathbf{S}_1$ and $\mathbf{S}_2$. Here, the points $\mathbf{P}_1$, $\mathbf{P}_2$ are positioned at the point $\mathbf{P}_0$. Let (u_1, v_1) be a parameter on surface $\mathbf{S}_1$ corresponding to point $\mathbf{P}_1$, and (u_2, v_2) be on $\mathbf{S}_2$ corresponding to $\mathbf{P}_2$.
2. Tangent planes $\mathbf{F}_1$, $\mathbf{F}_2$ at the two starting points $\mathbf{P}_1$, $\mathbf{P}_2$ are calculated. The normal vector $\mathbf{n}$ of the tangent plane on the free-form surface $\mathbf{S}$ can be calculated with the next equation, if parameter (u, v) is given.

$$\mathbf{n}'(u,v) = \frac{\partial \mathbf{S}(u,v)}{\partial u} \times \frac{\partial \mathbf{S}(u,v)}{\partial v}, \quad \mathbf{n}(u,v) = \frac{\mathbf{n}'}{|\mathbf{n}'|}$$

3. The plane $\mathbf{F}_0$ which is defined by the point $\mathbf{P}_0$ and is perpendicular to the two planes $\mathbf{F}_1, \mathbf{F}_2$

is calculated. Its normal vector can be obtained by calculating the outer product of the normal vectors $\mathbf{n}_1$, $\mathbf{n}_2$ of the two planes $\mathbf{F}_1$, $\mathbf{F}_2$.

4. The ball with radius r is placed so that it touches both planes $\mathbf{F}_1$ and $\mathbf{F}_2$. The center of the ball should be positioned on plane $\mathbf{F}_0$. If the tangent points of the ball and the two planes are given as $\mathbf{P}_1'$ and $\mathbf{P}_2'$, then they are obviously positioned on the plane $\mathbf{F}_0$.

5. If points $\mathbf{P}_1$ and $\mathbf{P}_1'$ are determined as being the same point, and $\mathbf{P}_2$ and $\mathbf{P}_2'$ the same point, then they both become M-points when the ball is placed on both free-form surfaces. The geometric Newton method thus terminates here.

6. Points $\mathbf{P}_1'$, $\mathbf{P}_2'$ are used to obtain the following starting points (u_1', v_1') and (u_2', v_2') on the two free-form surfaces $\mathbf{S}_1$ and $\mathbf{S}_2$. To calculate the starting point (u_1', v_1'), the following equation is used
$$\mathbf{P}_1' - \mathbf{P}_1 = \Delta u_1 \frac{\partial \mathbf{S}_1(u_1, v_1)}{\partial u} + \Delta v_1 \frac{\partial \mathbf{S}_1(u_1, v_1)}{\partial v}$$
In order to calculate Δu_1 and Δv_1, the inner products of this equation and the two vectors $\partial \mathbf{S}_1(u_1, v_1)/\partial u$, $\partial \mathbf{S}_1(u_1, v_1)/\partial u$ are calculated, and linear equations with two unknowns are obtained. A new starting point $u_1' = u_1 + \Delta u_1$, $v_1' = v_1 + \Delta v_1$ is obtained by solving this equation for Δu_1, Δv_1. The other starting point (u_2', v_2') is calculated in the same way.

7. The new starting points (u_1', v_1') and (u_2', v_2') are assigned to (u_1, v_1) and (u_2, v_2). Points $\mathbf{P}_1$, $\mathbf{P}_2$ on the free-form surface are newly computed from these parameters, and we return to Step 2.

Sometimes, the geometric Newton method fails, when the radius of curvature of the free-form surface is smaller than the radius r of the ball to be placed. In this case, the rounding operation cannot be continued.

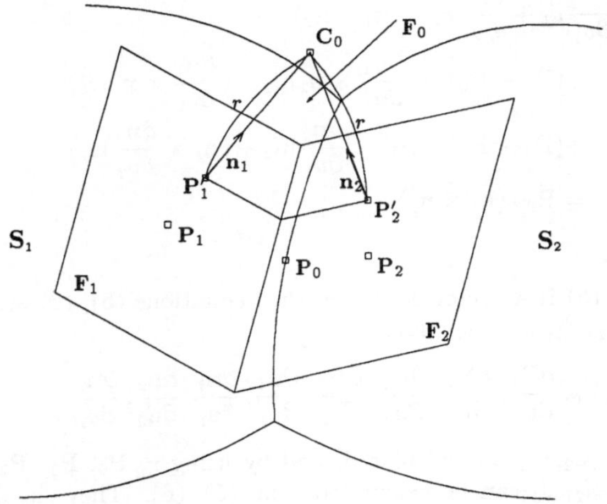

Figure 8: Calculation method of the positions of the tangent points

5.4 Calculation of the direction vectors of the tangent points

The vectors indicating the movement of M-points $\mathbf{P}_1$ and $\mathbf{P}_2$ when a ball rolls are calculated, that is, the following equations representing $\mathbf{P}_1$ and $\mathbf{P}_2$ derived at parameter t are calculated. (Note that $df/dt = \dot{f}$)

$$\dot{\mathbf{P}}_1 = \frac{\partial \mathbf{P}_1}{\partial u_1}\dot{u}_1 + \frac{\partial \mathbf{P}_1}{\partial v_1}\dot{v}_1 \tag{1}$$

$$\dot{\mathbf{P}}_2 = \frac{\partial \mathbf{P}_2}{\partial u_2}\dot{u}_2 + \frac{\partial \mathbf{P}_2}{\partial v_2}\dot{v}_2 \tag{2}$$

To calculate these formulas, we will describe the following two equations which represent the relationships of the point $\mathbf{P}_0$ and the two tangent points $\mathbf{P}_1$, $\mathbf{P}_2$. Note that r is the radius of the ball and $\mathbf{n}_1$, $\mathbf{n}_2$ are the normal vectors of the tangent planes at $\mathbf{P}_1$, $\mathbf{P}_2$. These equations are illustrated in Figure 8.

$$\mathbf{P}_1 + r\mathbf{n}_1 = \mathbf{P}_2 + r\mathbf{n}_2 \tag{3}$$

$$(\mathbf{P}_1 - \mathbf{P}_0) \cdot (\mathbf{n}_1 \times \mathbf{n}_2) = 0 \tag{4}$$

Equations (3), (4) are derived at parameter t, and become as follows.

$$\begin{aligned}
&(\frac{\partial \mathbf{P}_1}{\partial u_1} + r\frac{\partial \mathbf{n}_1}{\partial u_1})\dot{u}_1 + (\frac{\partial \mathbf{P}_1}{\partial v_1} + r\frac{\partial \mathbf{n}_1}{\partial v_1})\dot{v}_1 \\
&\quad -(\frac{\partial \mathbf{P}_2}{\partial u_2} + r\frac{\partial \mathbf{n}_2}{\partial u_2})\dot{u}_2 - (\frac{\partial \mathbf{P}_2}{\partial v_2} + r\frac{\partial \mathbf{n}_2}{\partial v_2})\dot{v}_2 \\
&\quad = \dot{r}(\mathbf{n}_2 - \mathbf{n}_1)
\end{aligned} \tag{5}$$

$$\begin{aligned}
&(\frac{\partial \mathbf{P}_1}{\partial u_1}\dot{u}_1 + \frac{\partial \mathbf{P}_1}{\partial v_1}\dot{v}_1) \cdot (\mathbf{n}_1 \times \mathbf{n}_2) \\
&\quad +(\mathbf{P}_1 - \mathbf{P}_0) \cdot ((\frac{\partial \mathbf{n}_1}{\partial u_1} \times \mathbf{n}_2)\dot{u}_1 + (\frac{\partial \mathbf{n}_1}{\partial v_1} \times \mathbf{n}_2)\dot{v}_1) \\
&\quad +(\mathbf{P}_1 - \mathbf{P}_0) \cdot ((\mathbf{n}_1 \times \frac{\partial \mathbf{n}_2}{\partial u_2})\dot{u}_2 + (\mathbf{n}_1 \times \frac{\partial \mathbf{n}_2}{\partial v_2})\dot{v}_2) \\
&\quad = \dot{\mathbf{P}}_0 \cdot (\mathbf{n}_1 \times \mathbf{n}_2)
\end{aligned} \tag{6}$$

The differential equation (5) is a vector equation, thus equations (5), (6) are linear equations with four unknowns $\dot{u}_1$, $\dot{v}_1$, $\dot{u}_2$, $\dot{v}_2$. Therefore,

$$\dot{r}, \dot{\mathbf{P}}_0, \frac{\partial \mathbf{P}_1}{\partial u_1}, \frac{\partial \mathbf{P}_1}{\partial v_1}, \frac{\partial \mathbf{P}_2}{\partial u_2}, \frac{\partial \mathbf{P}_2}{\partial v_2}, \frac{\partial \mathbf{n}_1}{\partial u_1}, \frac{\partial \mathbf{n}_1}{\partial v_1}, \frac{\partial \mathbf{n}_2}{\partial u_2}, \frac{\partial \mathbf{n}_2}{\partial v_2}$$

at parameters t, (u_1, v_1), (u_2, v_2) are calculated, and by using r, $\mathbf{P}_0$, $\mathbf{P}_1$, $\mathbf{P}_2$, $\mathbf{n}_1$, $\mathbf{n}_2$ that are already obtained, $\dot{u}_1$, $\dot{v}_1$, $\dot{u}_2$, $\dot{v}_2$ can be calculated from (5), (6). They should be assigned to equations (1), (2) to calculate the two direction vectors $\dot{\mathbf{P}}_1$, $\dot{\mathbf{P}}_2$. The method described here can also be applied to the case where one of the tangent points is an E, C or I-point.

5.5 Generation of curves representing trajectories

A method to approximate two trajectories drawn by the tangent points is described here. One edge to be rounded is selected. At first, we put many balls on both side surfaces of the edge. E, C and I-points at four corners formed by the edge and its winged edges, and M-points between them are calculated. If one ball is placed on the two surfaces, information of the tangent points is obtained as follows.

Parameter on edge (t)		
Type of tangent point(L)	Position of tangent point(L)	Direction vector(L)
Type of tangent point(R)	Position of tangent point(R)	Direction vector(R)

L: Left Side Surface, R: Right Side Surface

Information of tangent points is stored in an array, which we call the tangent point information table. Because all tangent point information has a corresponding parameter t on the edge, the table is sorted in the order of increasing t.

Next, the tangent point information table is searched in increasing t. If either the left or right tangent point is not an M-point, then that location is marked. Thus, marked locations correspond to cases where one of the tangent points is either an E, C or I-point.

Lastly, the table is searched again from the smallest t. Tangent point information from one marked location to the next is retrieved, and the positions and vectors that were included therein are used for interpolation by the curves on both left and right sides (Figure 9). Each curve is generated by combining the tangent point information of three parameters, so several curves are usually generated. Our method generates a rational quadric Bézier curve when the positions and vectors found in the tangent point information of three parameters are all on one flat surface. In other cases, it generates a cubic Bézier curve. The trajectories of the tangent points on the left side and right side are approximated with the same number of curves, by repeating this process until the last item of tangent point information is retrieved. The curves representing the trajectories are the results of smoothly connecting marked E, C and I-points.

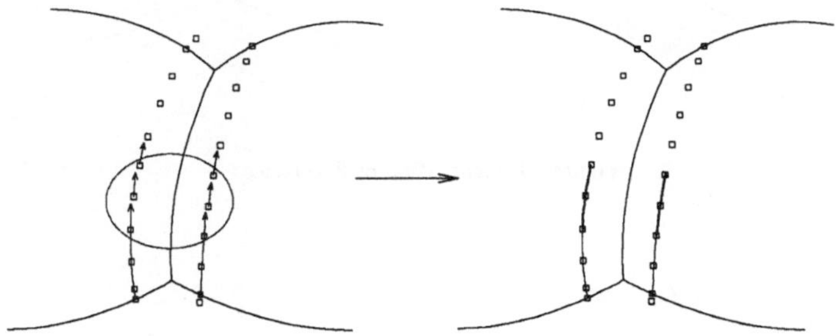

Figure 9: Calculation method of the trajectories of the tangent points

6 Generation of the Topology of Blending Surfaces

6.1 Outline of the topological information generation

The generation of vertices and edges around blending surfaces is described in this section. At first, new vertices are created at the positions of E-points, and the edges on the original solid are subdivided. After generating the new vertices on all edges, new edges are created on all faces by following the trajectories calculated in Section 5. As described in Section 4, such edges are called R-edges. Next, all original edges to be rounded are deleted and many arc edges are generated to connect end points of R-edges on both sides of the edges to be rounded. Lastly, vertices which connect only two R-edges are deleted, and one smooth edge is created from the two R-edges.

6.2 Generation of E-vertices

The process of the generation of E-vertices is as follows. One edge on the solid is selected. In B-reps-based solid models, an edge is connected to four winged edges. If an edge to be rounded is found among the four winged edges, the E-point in Section 5.2 may be positioned on the selected edge. When the E-point exists(the selected edge and the winged edge form a convex angle), a new vertex is generated at that position, and the selected edge is subdivided (Figure 10). The generated vertex is called an E-vertex. Because there are four winged edges connecting to one edge, a maximum of four E-vertices may be generated on the edge.

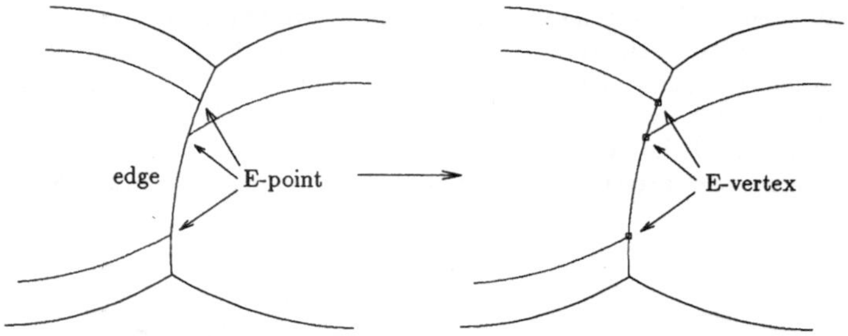

Figure 10: Generation of E-vertices

6.3 R-edge generation along the trajectories

To generate R-edges along the trajectories, one face on the solid is selected. When there are edges to be rounded around the face, the trajectories of the tangent points have already been calculated as described in Section 5.5. We generate R-edges on the face along the calculated trajectories, to connect the E-vertices explained in Section 6.2 with each other. The process to generate new R-edges inside a face is illustrated in Figure 11. As we described in Section 5.5, the trajectory of the tangent point is approximated by several curves. Each curve corresponds to one R-edge, and a continuous R-edge sequence is formed by several R-edges on one trajectory.

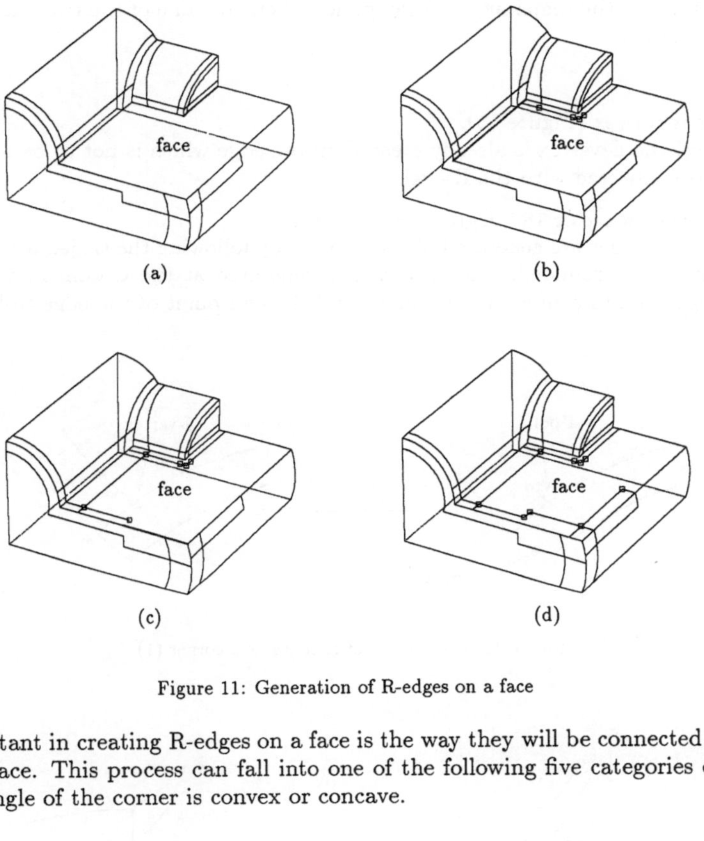

Figure 11: Generation of R-edges on a face

What is important in creating R-edges on a face is the way they will be connected at the corner points of the face. This process can fall into one of the following five categories depending on whether the angle of the corner is convex or concave.

We will now explain the first three categories where both edges forming the angle are to be rounded. The last two categories are when only one of the two edges forming the angle is to be rounded. These will be explained later.

- The angle is convex (Figure 12).
  In this case, the trajectories corresponding to both edges intersect on the face, and an I-point exists at that position. An E-vertex is also generated on each edge. Therefore, a new vertex should be created at the I-point, and it should be connected to both E-vertices by R-edges. The vertex which is generated here is called an I-vertex.

- The angle is 180 degrees (Figure 13).
In this case, the trajectories do not intersect on the face, but a C-point described in Section 5.2 exists at the end point of every trajectory. Therefore, R-edges are first generated along every trajectory to the C-point. Next, a new edge is created to connect the two C-points. If they are positioned at the same place, then R-edges are simply connected there; a new edge is not needed. The vertex generated at the C-point is called a C-vertex.

- The angle is concave (Figure 14).
In this case, the trajectories corresponding to both edges to be rounded intersect on the face. An I-point exists at that position. Therefore, an I-vertex is generated where the two R-edges are to be connected.

Next, we will describe the remaining two categories when only one of the two edges forming the angle is to be rounded.

- The angle is convex (Figure 15).
In this case, the E-vertex is already created on the edge which is not to be rounded, so the E-vertex is connected with the R-edge.

- The angle is concave or 180 degrees (Figure 16).
In this case, R-edges are generated to the C-point by following the trajectory corresponding to the edge to be rounded. The C-vertex is generated at the C-point, and another new edge is generated to connect the C-vertex and the end point of the edge to be rounded.

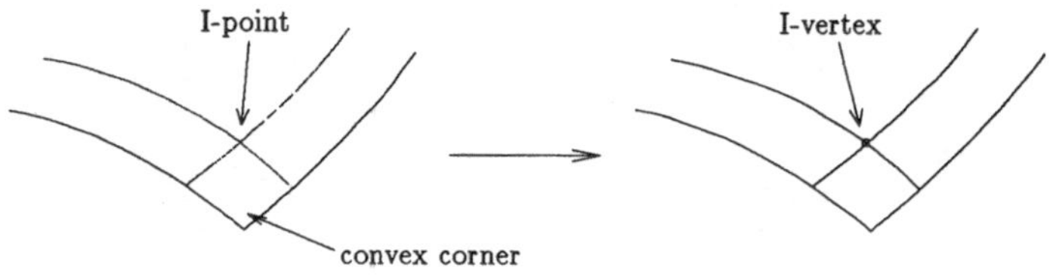

Figure 12: Connection of R-edges at a corner (1)

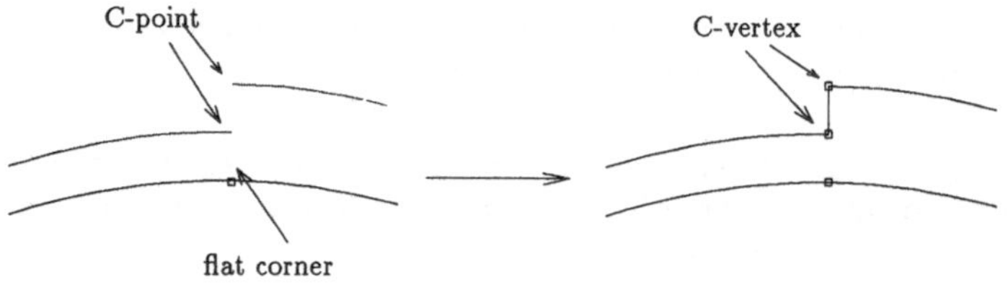

Figure 13: Connection of R-edges at a corner (2)

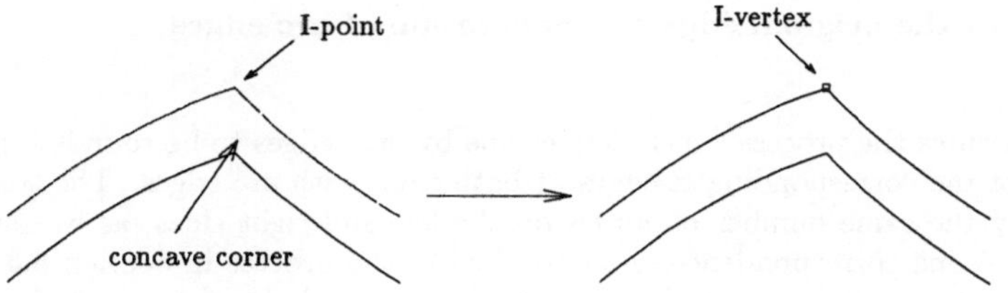

Figure 14: Connection of R-edges at a corner (3)

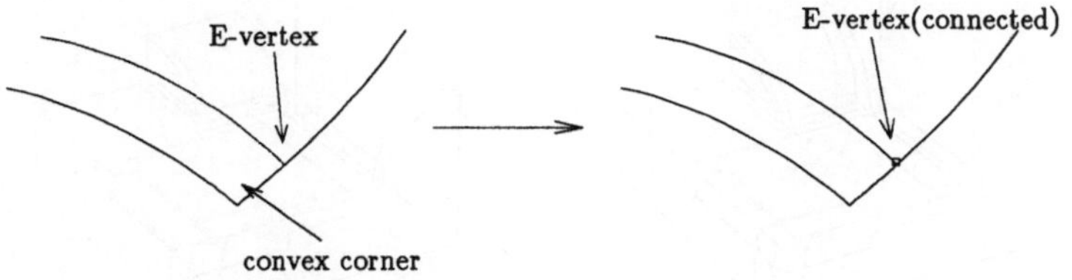

Figure 15: Connection of R-edges at a corner (4)

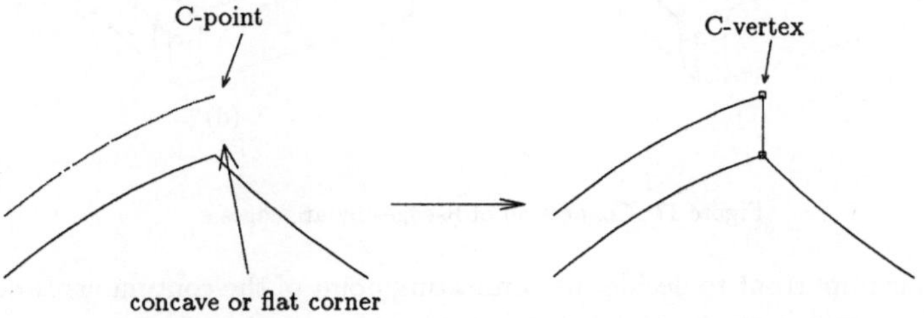

Figure 16: Connection of R-edges at a corner (5)

6.4 Deletion of the original edge and generation of arc edges

This section describes the process which deletes one by one, edges to be rounded, and connects the end points of the corresponding R-edges at both sides with arc edges. The trajectories are approximated by the same number of curves on the left and right sides, as we saw in Section 5.5, with a one-to-one correspondence. As described in the process in Section 6.3, one R-edge sequence is generated on the surface for every trajectory, and there are always corresponding R-edges on both sides of the edge to be rounded.

The original edge to be rounded is first deleted, and the corresponding R-edges for the left and right side are searched. Then the end points of the two R-edges that were found are connected by arc edges whose radius is the same as that of the ball. Unnecessary edges on the original solid are deleted at this stage. Figure 17 shows this process.

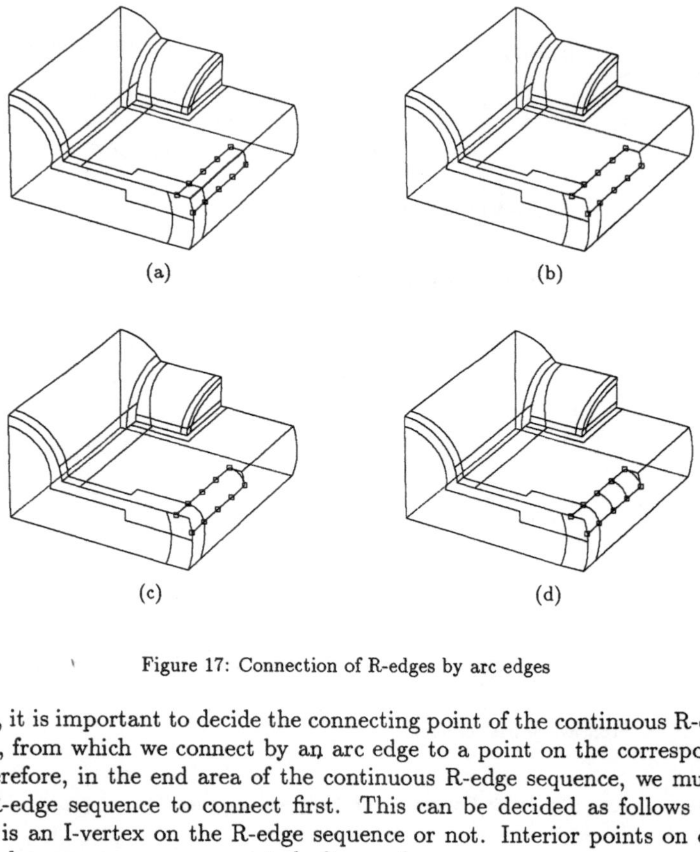

Figure 17: Connection of R-edges by arc edges

In this process, it is important to decide the connecting point of the continuous R-edge sequence on one surface, from which we connect by an arc edge to a point on the corresponding R-edge sequence. Therefore, in the end area of the continuous R-edge sequence, we must find which point of the R-edge sequence to connect first. This can be decided as follows depending on whether there is an I-vertex on the R-edge sequence or not. Interior points on corresponding continuous R-edge sequences are connected afterward.

- There is an I-vertex on the continuous R-edge sequence of each side (Figure 18).
  In this case, the arc edges are generated from the I-vertex that is the closest to the inside.
- There is an I-vertex on the continuous R-edge sequence of one side (Figure 19).

In this case, the arc edges are generated from the I-vertex.

- There are no I-vertices on the continuous R-edge sequences of both sides (Figure 20).
  In this case, the vertices at the end of the continuous R-edge sequences are connected by a free-form curve edge so that the curve is tangent to both curved surfaces. Next, all the vertices on the R-edge sequence are connected to their corresponding vertices by arc edges. Some vertices in the end area of the R-edge sequence may not be connected here (marked "not connected" in Figure 20).

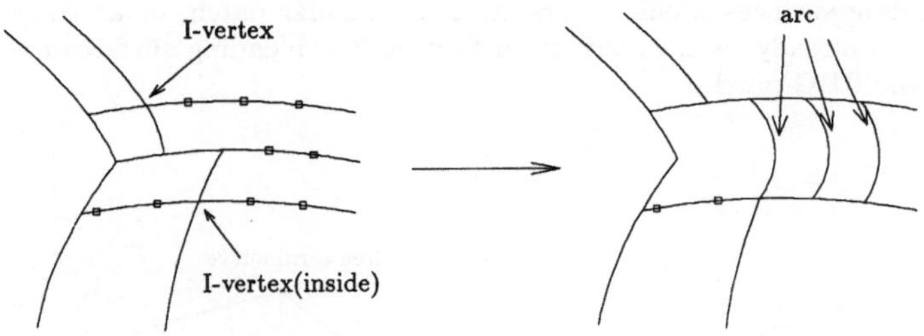

Figure 18: Arc edge generation at the end point (1)

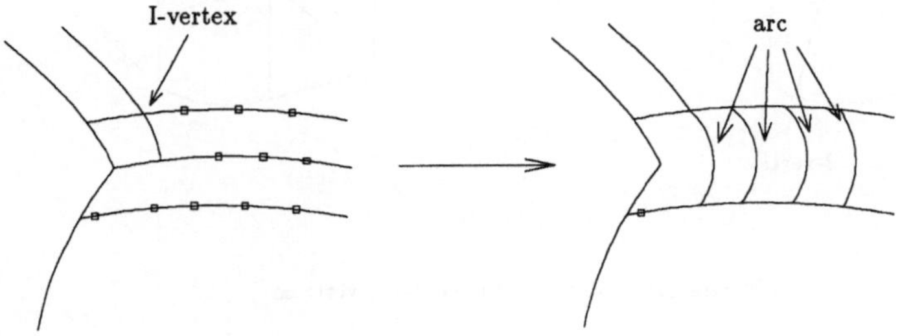

Figure 19: Arc edge generation at the end point (2)

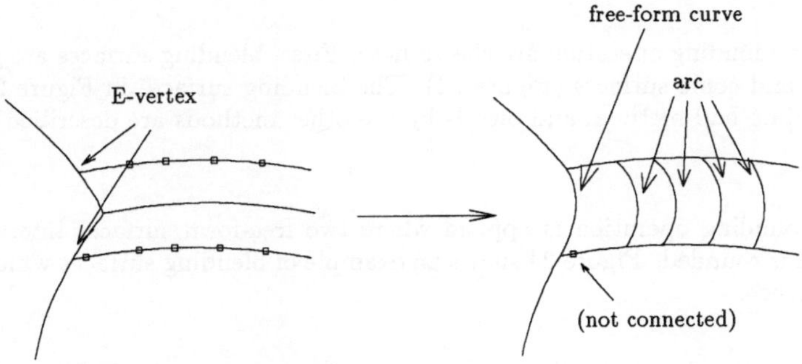

Figure 20: Arc edge generation at the end point (3)

6.5 Deletion of unnecessary vertices

After the edge to be rounded on the original solid is deleted and the end points of the corresponding R-edges are connected by arc edges, I-vertices on the R-edge still remain as corners. In this case, such I-vertices are deleted, and smooth edges are generated from the two R-edges that were connected to that vertex (Figure 21). There are also cases where vertices that were not used in the process described in Section 6.4 remain. In such cases, the two original R-edges are substituted by one edge of similar shape. By performing this process, most of the blending surfaces become a rectangular patch where two sides are arc edges. Also, at the vertex of the solid where blending surfaces should intersect, a rectangular patch, or an irregular patch is generated. As it has already been described in Section 3.4, blending surfaces are smoothly connected by using the RBG patch.

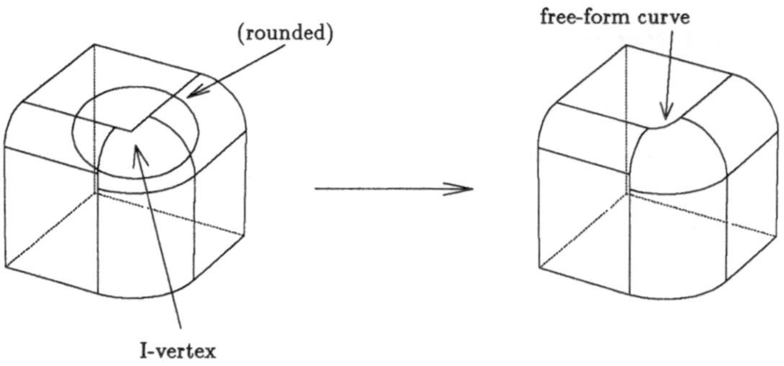

Figure 21: Deletion of unnecessary vertices

7 Examples of the Rounding Operation

Five examples of our rounding operation are shown here. First, blending surfaces are generated between cylindrical and conic surfaces (Figure 22). The blending surfaces in Figure 22 (b) are generated by the rolling ball method, and blends by the other methods are described in Figure 22 (c), (d).

In Figure 23, our rounding operation is applied where two free-form surfaces intersect. The shape of a television is rounded. Figure 24 shows an example of blending surfaces which contain non-rectangular patches.

A mechanical part is rounded and blending surfaces are generated at corners in Figure 25. There are many blending surfaces between natural quadric surfaces in this example. In Figure 26, The shape of a car is created on our solid modeler. There are many blending surfaces between free-form ones.

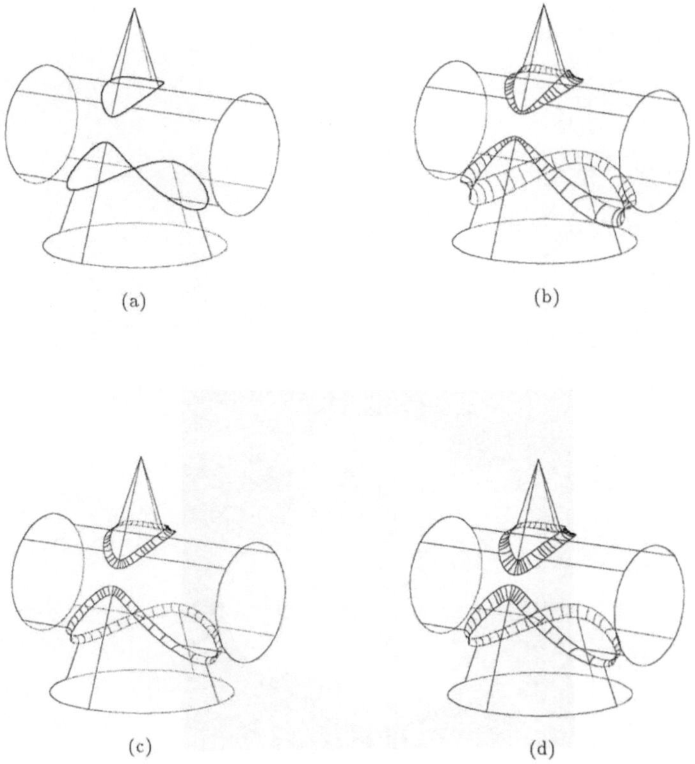

Figure 22: Blending surface generation between two quadric surfaces

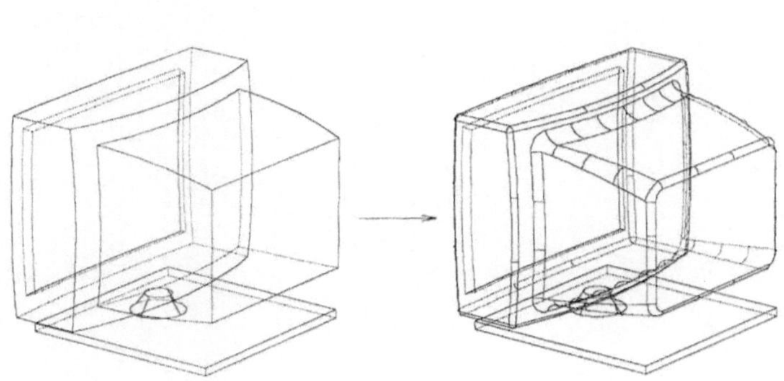

Figure 23: Blending surface generation between two free-form surfaces

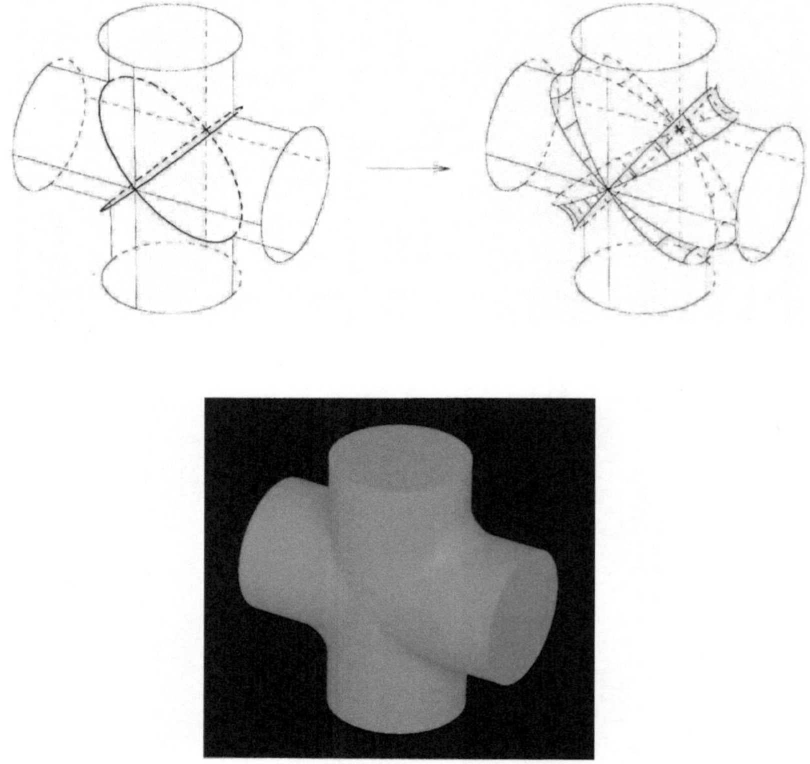

Figure 24: Blending surface generation between two cylindrical surfaces

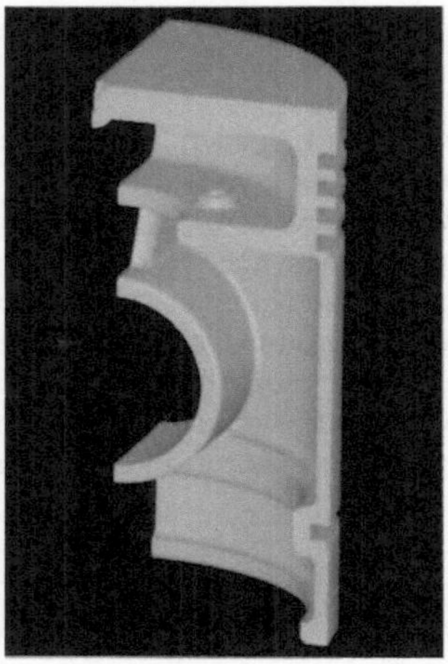

Figure 25: Blending surface generation for a mechanical part

Figure 26: Blending surface generation for a car

8 Conclusion

This paper shows the effectiveness of creating blending surfaces in solid modeling, and presents the implementation method of the rounding operation between two curved surfaces. In rounding operations on B-reps-based solid modelers, not only is the calculation and representation of blending surface shapes important, so is the generation of vertices and edges. In our method of the rounding operation, we emphasized the generation of topological information. It is easy to create various kinds of surface blends including rolling ball blends and variable-radius blending surfaces. Solids in 3D CAD systems have many blending surfaces between curved surfaces, and their cross-section radii vary. Therefore, the rounding operation that we have presented in this paper is the basic technique for practical use in a solid modeler.

9 Acknowledgements

We would like to thank Fumihiko Kimura, a professor of the University of Tokyo, for his valuable suggestion; Hideko S. Kunii, general manager of RICOH's Software Division and Teiji Takamura of RICOH CO. for their valuable comments and discussion; and Aidan O'Neill and Tomoko Kikuchi of RICOH Co. for assistance with the text.

References

[Braid 73] Braid,I.C. and Lang,C.A., "Computer-aided design of mechanical components with volume building bricks", *Computer Languages for Numerical Control*, J.Hatvany Ed., North-Holland, Amsterdam, pp.173-184 (1973).

[Chiyokura 83] Chiyokura,H., "Design of solids with free-form surfaces", *Computer Graphics (SIGGRAPH '83 Proc.)*, Vol 17, pp.289-298 (1983).

[Chiyokura 87] Chiyokura,H., "An extended rounding operation for modeling solids with free-form surfaces", *IEEE Computer Graphics and Applications*, Vol 7, No 6, pp.27-36 (1987).

[Chiyokura 88] Chiyokura,H., *Solid Modelling with DESIGNBASE*, Addison-Wesley, Reading, MA (1988).

[Chiyokura 90] Chiyokura,H., Takamura,T., Konno,K. and Harada,T., "The interpolation of a rational curved mesh by a rational boundary Gregory patch", *Frontiers in Geometric Modeling*, G.Farin Ed., SIAM, Philadelphia, PA, to be published.

[Choi 89] Choi,B.K. and Ju,S.Y., "Constant-radius blending in surface modelling", *Computer Aided Design*, Vol 21, No 4, pp.213-220 (1989).

[Holmström 88] Holmström,L. and Laakko, T., "Rounding facility for solid modelling of mechanical parts", *Computer Aided Design*, Vol 20, No 10, pp.605-614 (1988).

[Martin 82] Martin,R.R., *Principal Patches for Computational Geometry*, Ph.D. Thesis, Cambridge University, Engineering Department (1982).

[Okino 73] Okino,N., Kakazu,Y. and Kubo,H., "TIPS-1; technical information processing system for computer-aided design, drawing and manufacturing", *Computer Languages for Numerical Control*, J.Hatvany Ed., North-Holland, Amsterdam, pp.141-150 (1973).

[Pratt 88] Pratt,M.J., "Blending with Cyclide Patches", 3rd IMA Conference on the Mathematics of Surfaces, Oxford (1988).

[Rockwood 87] Rockwood,A.P. and Owen,J.C., "Blending Surfaces in Solid Modelling", *Geometric Modeling SIAM*, G.Farin Ed., Philadelphia, PA, USA, pp.367-383 (1987).

[Rossignac 84] Rossignac,A.R. and Requicha,A.A.G., "Constant Radius Blending in Solid Modelling", *Computers in Mechanical Engineering*, pp.65-73 (1984).

[Varady 89] Varady,T., "Rolling Ball Blends in Solid Modelling", *Computer Applications in Production and Engineering*, F.Kimura and A.Rolstadas Ed., Elsevier Science Publishers B.V., North-Holland, pp.295-308 (1989).

[Woodwark 87] Woodwark,J.R., "Blends in Geometric Modelling", *The Mathematics of Surfaces II*, R.R.Martin Ed., Oxford University Press, pp.255-297 (1987).

Tsuyoshi HARADA a member of the 3D CAD project at RICOH's Software Division, is interested in solid modeling, geometric modeling and their applications. His current research includes the continuity of rational free-form surfaces for rounding operations. He received a BS and an MS in precision machinery engineering from the University of Tokyo in 1986 and 1988 respectively. He entered the solid modeling project at RICOH in 1988, which has now developed into the product DESIGNBASE.
Address: RICOH Co., Ltd. Software Division, 1-17, Koishikawa-cho 1-Chome Bunkyo-ku, Tokyo, 112, Japan
E-mail: harada@src.ricoh.co.jp

Hiroshi TORIYA is a member of the 3D CAD project at RICOH's Software Division. His research interests include solid modeling, geometric modeling, computer graphics, and their applications. He received a BS in information science in 1983 from the University of Tokyo where his research included octree data structures and their manipulations. He earned his Dr.Sc. in information science from the University of Tokyo in 1989. He is a member of the Information Processing Society of Japan.
Address: RICOH Co., Ltd. Software Division, 1-17, Koishikawa-cho 1-Chome Bunkyo-ku, Tokyo, 112, Japan
E-mail: toriya@src.ricoh.co.jp

Hiroaki CHIYOKURA is a manager of the 3D CAD project at Software Research Center at RICOH CORPORATION. His research interests are solid modeling, computer graphics, and their applications to computer-aided design and manufacturing. He received his BS and MS in mathematics from Keio University in 1979 and 1980, respectively. He earned his Dr.Eng. in precision machinery engineering from the University of Tokyo in 1984. He has written a book "Solid Modelling with DESIGNBASE: Theory and Implementation", published by Addison-Wesley. He is a member of ACM SIGGRAPH.
Address: RICOH Co., Ltd. Software Division, 1-17, Koishikawa-cho 1-Chome Bunkyo-ku, Tokyo, 112, Japan
E-mail: chiyo@src.ricoh.co.jp

Conference Organization Committee

General Chair:
J. Motiwalla (Institute of Systems Science, Singapore)

International Program Committee Co-chairs:
T.S. Chua (Institute of Systems Science, Singapore)
T.L. Kunii (The University of Tokyo, Japan)

International Advisor:
R.A. Earnshaw (University of Leeds, UK)

Finance Chair:
W.S. Teh (Institute of Systems Science, Singapore)

Publicity Chair:
J. McCallum (National University of Singapore , Singapore)

Registration Chair:
J. Waterworth (Institute of Systems Science, Singapore)

Tutorial Chair:
Y.H. Ang (Institute of Systems Science, Singapore)

Panel and Demonstrations Chair:
G. Singh (Institute of Systems Science, Singapore)

Audio Visual Chair:
L. Serra (Institute of Systems Science, Singapore)

Local Arrangements Chair:
T.H. Tng (Institute of Systems Science, Singapore)

Exhibition Chair:
Y.S. Tao (Information Technology Institute, Singapore)

List of Sponsors

Organized by:

Institute of Systems Science, Singapore
Computer Graphics Society

Sponsored by:

Institute of Systems Science, Singapore

In Cooperation with:

Association of Computing Machinery
British Computer Society
IEEE Computer Society

Supported by:

AV&T Pte Ltd
Graphica Computer Corporation
Hewlett Packard Pte Ltd
Hitachi Ltd
IBM Singapore Pte Ltd
Japan Systems Company Ltd
Silicon Graphics Computer Systems
Sun Microsystems, Inc

List of Technical Reviewers

Aono, M. (IBM Tokyo Research Lab, Japan)
Asami, S. (University of Tokyo, Japan)
Breen, D. (Rensselaer Polytechnic Institute, USA)
Chua, T.S. (ISS, Singapore)
Dong, X. (Rensselaer Polytechnic Institute, USA)
Earnshaw, R.A. (University of Leeds, UK)
Enomoto, H. (University of Tokyo, Japan)
Farin, G. (Arizona State University, USA)
Fuchs, H. (University of North Carolina, USA)
Fujishiro, I. (University of Tsukuba, Japan)
Gay, R. (Nanyang Technology Institute, Singapore)
Georges, M. (Rensselaer Polytechnic Institute, USA)
Getto, P. (Rensselaer Polytechnic Institute, USA)
Goldman, R. (Control Data Corporation, USA)
Gotoda, H. (University of Tokyo, Japan)
Green, M. (University of Alberta, Canada)
Guo, Q.L. (University of Tokyo, Japan)
Haber, R. (National Center for Supercomputer Applications, Illinois, USA)
Herr, C. (University of Calgary, Canada)
Hill, D. (University of Calgary, Canada)
Ichikawa, Y. (University of Tokyo, Japan)
Imai, H. (Kyushu University, Japan)
Jevans, D. (University of Calgary, Canada)
Kacic-Alesic, Z. (University of Calgary, Canada)
Kaneda, K. (Hiroshima University, Japan)
Kawai, S. (University of Tokyo, Japan)
Kergosien, Y.L. (Universite Paris Sub, France)
Kin, N. (University of Tokyo, Japan)
Krishnan, D. (University of Tokyo, Japan)
Kuhn, V. (Rensselaer Polytechnic Institute, USA)
Kunii, T.L. (University of Tokyo, Japan)
Lee, K.J. (University of Tokyo, Japan)
Lee, M.W. (University of Tokyo, Japan)
Maeda, J. (University of Tokyo, Japan)
Maeda, K. (University of Tokyo, Japan)
Magnenat-Thalmann, N. (University of Geneva, Switzerland)
Maulsby, D. (University of Calgary, Canada)
McCallum, J.C. (National University of Singapore, Singapore)
Meagher, D. (Octree Corporation, USA)
Nakamae, E. (Hiroshima University, Japan)
Nakamura, T. (Tohoku University, Japan)
Nishimura, S. (University of Tokyo, Japan)
Nishita, T. (Fukuyama University, Japan)
O'bara, R. (Rensselaer Polytechnic Institute, USA)
Patrikalakis, N.M. (MIT, USA)
Piper, B. (Rensselaer Polytechnic Institute, USA)
Porter, G.J. (University of Bradford, UK)
Rheingans, P. (University of North Carolina, USA)

Rogers, D.F. (US Naval Academy, USA)
Rokne, J. (University of Calgary, Canada)
Saji, H. (University of Tokyo, Japan)
Selbie, S. (University of Calgary, Canada)
Serra, L. (ISS, Singapore)
Shirai, Y. (University of Tokyo, Japan)
Shirota, Y. (University of Tokyo, Japan)
Shu, R.B. (ISS, Singapore)
Singh, G. (ISS, Singapore)
Sun, L. (University of Tokyo, Japan)
Tan, D. (Nanyang Technological Institute, Singapore)
Thalmann, D. (Swiss Federal Institute of Technology, Switzerland)
Toh, G.N. (Nanyang Technological Institute, Singapore)
Toussaint, G.T. (McGill University, Canada)
Waterworth, J. (ISS, Singapore)
Woo, T.C. (University of Michigan, USA)
Wozny, M.J. (Rensselaer Polytechnic Institute, USA)
Wyvill, B. (University of Calgary, Canada)
Wyvill, G. (University of Otago, New Zealand)
Yamashita, H. (Hiroshima University, Japan)
Yap, K.T. (Nanyang Technological Institute, Singapore)

List of Contributors

Author Index

Keyword Index